Lecture Notes in Computer Science 2626

Edited by G. Goos, J. Hartmanis, and J. van Leeuwen

Springer
Berlin
Heidelberg
New York
Hong Kong
London
Milan
Paris
Tokyo

James L. Crowley   Justus H. Piater
Markus Vincze   Lucas Paletta (Eds.)

Computer Vision Systems

Third International Conference, ICVS 2003
Graz, Austria, April 1-3, 2003
Proceedings

Springer

Series Editors

Gerhard Goos, Karlsruhe University, Germany
Juris Hartmanis, Cornell University, NY, USA
Jan van Leeuwen, Utrecht University, The Netherlands

Volume Editors

James L. Crowley
INRIA Rhône-Alpes
655 Ave de l'Europe, 38330 Montbonnot, France
E-mail: Crowley@imag.fr

Justus H. Piater
University of Liège, Montefiore Institute
4000 Liège Sart-Tilman, Belgium
E-mail: Justus.Piater@ULg.ac.be

Markus Vincze
Vienna University of Technology, Automation and Control Institute
Gusshausstraße 27/376, 1040 Vienna, Austria
E-mail: vincze@acin.tuwien.ac.at

Lucas Paletta
Joanneum Research, Institute of Digital Image Processing
Wastiangasse 6, 8010 Graz, Austria
E-mail: vincze@acin.tuwien.ac.at

Cataloging-in-Publication Data applied for
A catalog record for this book is available from the Library of Congress.

Bibliographic information published by Die Deutsche Bibliothek.
Die Deutsche Bibliothek lists this publication in the Deutsche Nationalbibliografie;
detailed bibliographic data is available in the Internet at <http://dnb.ddb.de>.

CR Subject Classification (1998): I.4, I.2.9-10, I.5.4-5, I.3.1-2, D.2

ISSN 0302-9743
ISBN 3-540-00921-3 Springer-Verlag Berlin Heidelberg New York

Springer-Verlag Berlin Heidelberg New York
a member of BertelsmannSpringer Science+Business Media GmbH

http://www.springer.de

© Springer-Verlag Berlin Heidelberg 2003
Printed in Germany

Typesetting: Camera-ready by author, data conversion by PTP-Berlin GmbH
Printed on acid-free paper   SPIN: 10873023   06/3142   5 4 3 2 1 0

Preface

Over the past decade, great progress has been made in the geometrical foundations of computer vision. This progress has provided a solid mathematical foundation for the use of images to reconstruct and model the environment. The next step is to advance computer vision from a science of machines that reconstruct to a science of machines that see. Such a theory will require the emergence and recognition of verifiable theories and methods for performance evaluation, systems architectures, learning and control of perception.

The goal of the International Conference on Vision Systems is to document the emergence of an engineering science of Computer Vision. The first ICVS was organized in January 1999 in Las Palmas in the Canary Islands (Spain). ICVS'99 provided a forum for early work in systems architecture and performance evaluation. ICVS 2001 was organized as a two-day workshop associated with the International Conference on Computer Vision held in Vancouver in July 2001. ICVS 2001 helped complete ICCV 2001 by providing a forum for recent progress in computer vision system architectures and performance evaluation.

The ICVS 2003 was organized in April 2003 in the city of Graz, Austria. Graz was declared the "Cultural Capital of Europe" for 2003. The participants of ICVS 2003 were invited to breathe in the charming atmosphere in the alleys of the Old City.

The special theme for the third ICVS was methods for "Cognitive Vision Systems." Cognitive Computer Vision is concerned with integration and control of vision systems using explicit models of context, situation and goal-directed behavior. Cognitive vision implies functionalities for knowledge representation, learning, reasoning about events and about structures, recognition and categorization, and goal specification.

ICVS 2003 solicited original unpublished high-quality scientific papers on the design, control and evaluation of vision systems and on theories and methods of cognitive vision. The conference organizers were particularly interested in papers providing methods for the following problems:

- Architectural models for computer vision systems.
- Design methods for vision systems.
- Cognitive models for interpretation, integration and control.
- Methods and metrics for performance evaluation.

The program committee was composed of 70 internationally recognized researchers. A total of 109 unique papers were submitted for evaluation by the program committee. Program committee members were asked to evaluate papers based on pertinence, scientific quality, impact, generality and innovation. We wish to thank all of the reviewers for their serious and insightful reviews. The quality of their comments greatly aided the paper selection process. From these reviews we were able to compose a high-quality single-track program including 22 podium presentations and 29 posters.

We especially wish to thank the authors for the many serious and high-quality papers that were submitted. We received many excellent papers. Selection of the program was based on the dual criteria of scientific excellence and relevance to the conference topic. Many excellent papers were not selected for presentation because they did not fit in with the themes of the conference. We encourage the publication of these papers in other scientific forums.

The third ICVS was made possible by the support and participation of the European Network of Excellence on Cognitive Vision Systems (ECVision). We wish to thank David Vernon (Coordinator of ECVision), and Colette Maloney of the European Commission's IST Program on Cognitive Vision for their financial and moral support. We also wish to thank Daniela Hall, the conference webmaster, for doing the difficult task of assembling these proceedings.

We hope that you enjoy and profit from the scientific papers published in this volume.

January 2003

James L. Crowley, Justus H. Piater,
Markus Vincze, Lucas Paletta

Executive Committee

Conference Chair:	Markus Vincze (TU Vienna)
Program Chair:	James L. Crowley (INP Grenoble)
Program Co-chair:	Justus H. Piater (University Liège)
Local Arrangements Chair:	Lucas Paletta (Joanneum Research)
Workshops and Tutorial Chair:	Hilary Buxton (University of Sussex)
Exhibition Chair:	Georg Thallinger (Joanneum Research)
Steering Committee:	Henrik Christensen (KTH)
	David Vernon (CAPTEC Ltd.)
Manuscript Preparation:	Daniela Hall (INP Grenoble)

Program Committee

Helder Araujo	Henrik Christensen	Cornelia Fermüller
Dana Ballard	Carlo Colombo	Robert Fisher
Csaba Beleznai	Peter Corke	Wolfgang Förstner
Ross Beveridge	Patrick Courtney	Uwe Franke
Horst Bischof	James L. Crowley	Martin Fritzsche
Paolo Bottoni	Alberto Del Bimbo	Catherine Garbay
Kevin Bowyer	Ernst Dickmanns	Luc van Gool
Alberto Broggi	Rüdiger Dillmann	Roderic A. Grupen
Chris Brown	Bruce Draper	Allen Hansen
Heinrich Bülthoff	Christof Eberst	Martial Hebert
Hilary Buxton	Toshiakii Ejima	Vaclav Hlavac
Jorge Cabrera Gamez	Jan-Olof Eklundh	David Hogg

Table of Contents

IV Computer Vision Architectures

V Performance Evaluation

VI Implementation Methods

VIII Video Annotation

Implementing the Expert Object Recognition Pathway

Bruce A. Draper, Kyungim Baek, and Jeff Boody

Colorado State University, USA

Abstract. Brain imaging studies suggest that expert object recognition is a distinct visual skill, implemented by a dedicated anatomic pathway. Like all visual pathways, the expert recognition pathway begins with the early visual system (retina, LGN/SC, striate cortex). It is defined, however, by subsequent diffuse activation in the lateral occipital cortex (LOC), and sharp foci of activation in the fusiform gyrus and right inferior frontal gyrus. This pathway recognizes familiar objects from familiar viewpoints under familiar illumination. Significantly, it identifies objects at both the categorical and instance (subcategorical) levels, and these processes cannot be disassociated. This paper presents a four-stage functional model of the expert object recognition pathway, where each stage models one area of anatomic activation. It implements this model in an end-to-end computer vision system, and tests it on real images to provide feedback for the cognitive science and computer vision communities.

1 Introduction

In the introduction to his book, David Marr argued that complex systems are more than just the easily extrapolated properties of their primitive components, and need to be modeled at many levels of abstraction [22]. As an example, Marr sited gases in physics, which can be modeled either at the molecular level or at the level of the ideal gas law. The ideal gas law describes gases in terms of collective properties such as temperature and pressure that are not easily extracted from the molecular model. By analogy, Marr proposed three levels for modeling information processing systems: the functional level, an algorithm and representation level, and the implementation level.

Marr proposed these three levels while studying human vision in the 1970's. His argument is even stronger today, with the advent of brain imaging technologies such as fMRI, PET, and rTMS. These sensors measure responses not of individual neurons, but of large collections of neurons. This is more like measuring the pressure of a gas than the properties of individual molecules. We therefore model the human visual system at the functional level based on data from brain imaging studies.

The human visual system, however, is not one pathway but a collection of related subsystems. The best known division is the ventral/dorsal split [34], but brain imaging studies suggest that the ventral and dorsal streams are themselves divided into many subsystems. One of the ventral subsystems is the expert object recognition pathway, which recognizes familiar objects such as human faces, pets and chairs, when seen from familiar viewpoints. The expert recognition pathway begins with the early vision system. It is anatomically defined in brain imaging studies by additional

J.L. Crowley et al. (Eds.): ICVS 2003, LNCS 2626, pp. 1–11, 2003.

centers of activation in the fusiform gyrus and right inferior frontal gyrus, and diffuse activation in the lateral occipital complex (LOC).

The goal of this paper is to present an implementation of a functional model of the expert object recognition pathway. The model is divided into four stages: Gabor-based edge detection in the early visual system, non-accidental feature transformations in the LOC, unsupervised clustering in the fusiform gyrus and PCA-based subspace matching in the right inferior frontal gyrus. Sections 2-4 of this paper provide background on expert object recognition and appearance-based models of human object recognition. Section 5 describes the four processing stages. Section 6 applies the system to real-world data, and Section 7 draws conclusions.

2   Expert Object Recognition

The expert object recognition pathway was first identified in fMRI studies of human face recognition [6, 14, 29]. In these studies, patients were shown images of faces while in a scanner. The resulting fMRI images revealed activation not only in the primary visual cortex, but also in the fusiform gyrus. Subsequent PET studies (which imaged a larger portion of the brain) confirmed the activation in the fusiform gyrus, while also noting activation in the right inferior frontal gyrus, an area previously associated through lesion studies with visual memory [20] (see also [23]).

More recent evidence suggests that this pathway is used for more than recognizing faces. Tong, et al. report that the fusiform gyrus is activated by animal faces and cartoon faces [33]. Chao, et al. report that the fusiform gyrus is activated by images of full-bodied animals with obscured faces [5]. Ishai et al. find that the fusiform gyrus responds to chairs [11]. Tarr and Gauthier considered the past experience of their subjects, and found fusiform gyrus activation in dog show judges when they view dogs, and in bird experts when they view birds [31]. Most important of all, Tarr and Gauthier show that the expert recognition pathway is trainable. They created a class of cartoon characters called greebles, which are grouped by gender and family. When novice subjects view greebles, fMRIs show no activity in the fusiform gyrus. The subjects are then trained to be experts who can identify a greeble's identity, gender or family in equal time. When the experts view greebles, their fusiform gyrus is active [31]. Gauthier and Logothetis provide evidence that training produces similar results in monkeys [8]. We conclude that expert object recognition is a general mechanism that can be trained to recognize any class of familiar objects.

3   Properties of Expert Object Recognition

People become expert at recognizing familiar objects, such as faces, animals and chairs. As experts, they can recognize these objects at both the instance and category level. Kosslyn uses pencils as an example [15]: we can all recognize pencils, but if we have one long enough we also recognize *our* pencil, from its dents and imperfections. This multiple-level categorization is used to define expert recognition in the greeble studies sited above.

Expert object recognition is also viewpoint dependent. In fMRI studies, the response of the fusiform gyrus to images of upside down faces is minimal [10]. When upright and inverted greebles are presented to experts, only the upright greebles activate the fusiform gyrus [9]. Expert recognition is also illumination dependent; our accuracy at face recognition, for example, drops if the faces are presented upside down or illuminated from below [2].

Expert object recognition is fast. In ERP studies, face recognition can be detected through a negative N170 signal that occurs 140-188 ms post stimulus [30]. Since the fusiform gyrus and right inferior frontal gyrus are the unique structures in expert recognition, we assume that one or both become active at this time, leaving only about 140ms for processing in the early vision system and LOC.

Finally, expert object recognition is probably appearance based. We know that expert recognition activates the right inferior frontal gyrus, an area associated with visual memories. We also know from PET and rTMS data that visual memories can reconstruct image-like representations in the primary visual cortex [16]. These memories can therefore be viewed as a form of compressed image [15], implying that expert recognition is a form of image matching.

4 Modeling the Expert Object Recognition Pathway

We interpret the activation data from fMRI and PET studies of expert object recognition as a four-stage pipeline. Processing begins in the early visual system, and then proceeds through the LOC to the fusiform gyrus and the right inferior frontal gyrus, as shown in Figure 1. This model is similar to Kosslyn's model of the ventral visual stream, which also featured an early visual system, feature-based "pre-processing", and interacting categorization and exemplar matching subsystems [15]. This section describes each stage; the next section applies the model to real data.

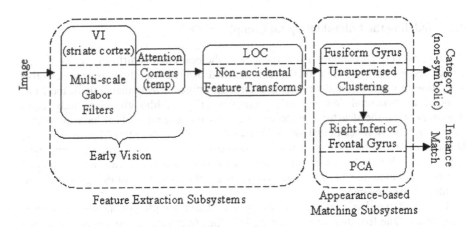

Fig. 1. The major components of the human expert object recognition pathway.

4.1 Early Vision

Computational models of the early visual system have a long history [26]. Of particular interest are functional models of simple and complex cells in V1. Through single cell recordings, Pollen and others have shown that the outputs of cells in V1 can be directly modeled in terms of visual stimuli, combining the effects of retinal, LGN and V1 processing. Simple cell responses in V1 can be modeled as Gabor filters of the stimulus, parameterized by location, orientation, scale and phase. Complex cell responses combine the energy of Gabor filters across phases [28]. Following Pollen, this work models early vision as a bank of multi-scale Gabor filters. Our system computes an image pyramid from the input, convolves it with non-symmetric even and odd Gabor filters at every 15° of orientation, and computes the resulting energy.

It should be noted that the responses of V1 cells can be modulated by portions of the stimulus outside their classically defined receptive fields [18, 35]. This conflicts with the model of complex cells as Gabor filters, but the first modulation effects do not occur until 80-120ms post stimulus. From ERP studies, it seems unlikely that contextual modulation effects appear soon enough to influence expert recognition.

Although the early vision system processes the whole retinal image through a bank of Gabor filters, not all of this information is passed downstream to the ventral and dorsal systems. Instead, a portion of this data is selected by position (and possibly scale or frequency [24]) for further processing. Parkhurst, et al are able to show a positive correlation between human eye tracking and a bottom-up model of attention selection based on color, intensity and orientation. [27]. Maki et al present a model based on image flow, motion and stereo [21]. Unfortunately, the system described in this paper does not yet use a biological model of attention selection. Instead, it runs a corner detector over the image, and successively selects image patches around each corner. In the future, we hope to replace this with the attentional model in the Neuormorphic Vision Toolkit [12] (this is the system evaluated by Parkhurst, et al).

4.2 Modeling the Lateral Occipital Complex (LOC)

The lateral occipital complex is a large area of the brain that is diffusely active during object recognition. Using fMRI, Kourtzi and Kanwisher show object selective activation in the LOC, and demonstrate through fatigue effects that cells in the LOC respond to structural (edge-based) properties [17]. Although their study can't determine what the structural properties are, Kosslyn and others [15] have suggested they could be non-accidental properties of the type proposed by Lowe [19] and Biederman [1]. Examples include edge collinearity, parallelism, symmetry and anti-symmetry. Psychological studies show that line drawings with non-accidental features obscured are harder to recognize than obscured line drawings with non-accidental features intact [1].

This work models the LOC as computing fixed length non-accidental feature transforms. The first and simplest example is the Hough transform – it projects edge responses into the space of geometric lines, thereby making collinearity explicit. As long as the temptation to threshold the Hough space and produce symbolic lines is avoided, the Hough space is an appropriate feature representation for appearance-based recognition. We are currently developing new transforms to capture other non-accidental features, such as parallelism, symmetry and anti-symmetry. The preliminary results in this paper, however, show the surprisingly powerful results of modeling the LOC as a Hough transform.

4.3 Categorization: Modeling the Fusiform Gyrus

Together, the early vision system and the LOC form a feature extraction subsystem, with the early vision system computing Gabor features and the LOC transforming them into non-accidental feature vectors, as shown in Figure 1. Similarly, the fusiform gyrus and right inferior frontal gyrus combine to form a feature-based appearance matching subsystem.

The appearance-based matching system is divided into two components: an unsupervised clustering system and a subspace projection system. This is motivated by the psychological observation that categorical and instance level recognition cannot be disassociated, and the mathematical observation that subspace projection methods exploit the commonality among images to compress data. If the images are too diverse, for example pictures of faces, pets, and chairs, then there is no commonality for the subspaces to exploit.

To avoid this, we model the fusiform gyrus as an unsupervised clustering system, and the right inferior frontal gyrus as a subspace matching system. This anatomical mapping is partly for simplicity; the exact functional division between these structures is not clear. Lesion studies associate the right inferior frontal lobe with visual memory [20], and rTMS and PET data suggest that these memories are compressed images [16]. Since compressed memories are stored in the frontal gyrus, it is easy to imagine that they are matched there as well, perhaps using an associative network. At the same time, clustering is the first step that is unique to expert recognition and the fusiform gyrus is the first anatomically unique structure on the expert pathway, so it makes sense to associate clustering with the fusiform gyrus. Where images are projected into cluster-specific subspaces is not clear however; it could be in either location, or both.

It is important to note that the categories learned by the clustering mechanism in the fusiform gyrus are non-linguistic. The images in a cluster do not need to be of the same object type or viewpoint, nor do all images of one object need to appear in one cluster. Clustering simply divides the training data into small groups of similar samples, so that PCA can fit a unique subspace to each group. This is similar to the localized subspace projection models in [7, 13]. We have implemented K-Means and an EM algorithm for mixtures of PCA analyzers similar to [32]. Surprisingly, so far we get the best results by using K-Means and overestimating the number of clusters K, possibly because non-symmetric Gaussians can be estimated by collections of symmetric ones.

4.4 Appearance Matching in the Right Inferior Frontal Gyrus

The last stage applies subspace projection to every cluster of feature vectors, and stores the training sample in the compressed subspaces. Currently, PCA is used as the subspace projection mechanism. New images are assigned to a cluster and projected into that cluster's PCA subspace, where nearest neighbor retrieval selects the best available instance match.

PCA is not a new model of human object recognition. Bülthoff and Edelman first used PCA to model of human object recognition [3], and O'Toole showed that human memories for individual faces correlate to the quality of their PCA reconstruction [25]. Bülthoff in particular has focused on view interpolation for viewpoint invariant appearance-based object recognition [4].

The computational model presented in this paper is more modest than Bülthoff's proposal, in the sense that it only models expert object recognition, not human object recognition in general. As a result, PCA is not used for view interpolation, since expert recognition is not viewpoint invariant. Moreover, our system first transforms the source image with non-accidental features of the Gabor responses, and then groups these features into localized subspaces prior to matching, where Bülthoff's model uses a single PCA space to match images.

5   Performance

We implemented the system described in Section 4 and tested it on two domains: aerial images of Fort Hood, TX, and facial images of cats and dogs. For the cat and dog data (shown in Figure 2), the images were already small (64x64 pixels) and hand registered, so the selective attention mechanism was disabled. For the Fort Hood data, each source image is 1000x1000 pixels and contains approximately 10,000 corners (i.e. possible attention points). We randomly selected 100 points on each of four object types for further processing. Similarly, we randomly selected 400 attention points on another, non-overlapping image for testing. Figure 3 shows example attention windows for each type of object (two building styles, paved parking lots, and unpaved parking areas).

Fig. 2. Examples of images from the cat and dog data base.

Our model of expert object recognition uses only unsupervised learning, so no object labels were provided during training. During testing, the system retrieves a cluster and stored image for every attention window. Since clusters do not correspond to semantic labels, the cluster response is not evaluated. A trial is a success if the retrieved instance match is of the same object type as the test window.

| Building Style 1 | Building Style 2 | Paved Parking Lot | Unpaved Parking Lot |

Fig. 3. Examples of Building Styles 1 & 2 and paved and unpaved parking lots in aerial images of Fort Hood, TX.

In Figure 4, we compare the performance of the biomimetic system to a baseline system that applies PCA to the pixels in an image pyramid. The horizontal axis is the number of PCA dimensions retained; and the vertical axis is the instance-level recognition rate. The biomimetic model clearly outperforms PCA, which is reassuring, since it uses PCA as its final step. It would have been disappointing if all the additional mechanisms failed to improve performance!

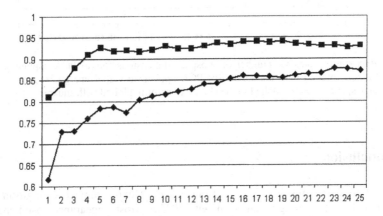

Fig. 4. Recognition rates for the proposed biomimetic system (plotted with squares) versus a baseline PCA system (plotted with diamonds) on the cat and dog data. The horizontal axis is the number of PCA dimension retained.

The more interesting question is why the system performs better. Figure 5 shows the results from a credit assignment experiment on the cat and dog data where system components isolated. In the baseline system, an image pyramid is computed for each image, and a single PCA is computed for pixels in the pyramid. In other words, the Gabor filters, non-accidental transforms and clustering have been disabled. (This is also the baseline for Figure 4.) We then reintroduced the Gabor filters, applying PCA to the energy values produced by the complex cell models. Performance does not improve, in fact it degrades, as shown in Figure 5. Next we reintroduced the Hough transform, so that PCA is applied to the Hough space. Performance improves markedly, approaching the best recognition rates for the system as a whole. This suggests that the LOC model is critical to overall system performance. It also calls into question the need for clustering, since recognition performance is essentially the same with or without it (see Figures 4 & 5).

Further experiments confirm that clustering only marginally improves recognition rates when the number of subspace dimensions is large (see Figure 6). What clustering does is force the images stored in a subspace to be similar, allowing for more compression. As a result, peak recognition performance is reached with fewer subspace dimensions, as shown iconically at the bottom of Figure 6. Clustering therefore improves the system's ability to compress visual memories.

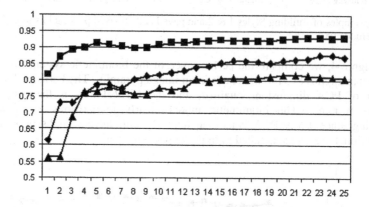

Fig. 5. Recognition rates vs. number of subspace dimensions for (a) PCA applied to image pyramid pixels, plotted with diamonds; (b) PCA applied to Gabor energy responses, plotted with triangles; and (c) PCA applied to the Hough transform, plotted with squares.

6   Conclusion

The most surprising result so far from our model of expert object recognition is the performance of the Hough transform with PCA. Most appearance-based methods apply PCA to raw images or to the results of simple image operations (e.g. image differences). We observe a significant benefit, however, from applying PCA to the output of a Hough transform in two domains, even though cat and dog faces have few straight lines. We do not observe the same benefit when PCA is applied to the outputs of the Gabor filters. We hypothesize that the recognition rate increases because the Hough transform makes collinearity (a non-accidental property) explicit.

We also observe that clustering to create localized PCA projections improves compression more than recognition. This may only be true for instance matching tasks; in classification tasks the PCA subspace represent an underlying class probability distribution, and Mahalanobis distances are meaningful. Localized PCA subspaces may therefore improve the recognition rate. In instance matching, however, clustering improves compression but not recognition.

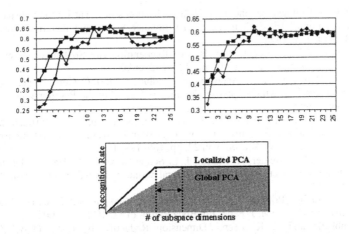

Fig. 6. The number of subspace dimensions (horizontal) vs. recognition rate (vertical) with and without localized clustering for the Fort Hood data. The plot on the left is for localized PCA applied to the Hough transform; the plot on the right is for localized PCA applied to complex cell responses. The bottom figure summarizes these and other plots, showing how clustering improves compression by achieving the maximum recognition rate with fewer subspace dimensions.

Finally, our work suggests that the LOC needs to be studied more closely. The LOC determines the overall recognition rate for our computational model, yet we have less information about it than any other anatomical component of the system. We cannot even be sure that the results reported by Kourtzi and Kanwisher [17] and Biederman [1] apply in the special case of expert recognition. More studies are needed.

References

[1.]   I. Biederman, "Recognition-by-Components: A Theory of Human Image Understanding," *Psychological Review*, vol. 94, pp. 115–147, 1987.

[2.]   V. Bruce and A. Young, *In the Eye of the Beholder: The Science of Face Perception.* New York: Oxford University Press, 1998.

[3.]   H. H. Bülthoff and S. Edelman, "Psychophysical Support for a 2-D View Interpolation Theory of Object Recognition," *Proceedings of the National Academy of Science*, vol. 89, pp. 60–64, 1992.

[4.]   H. H. Bülthoff, C. Wallraven, and A. Graf, "View-based Dynamic Object Recognition based on Human Perception," International Conference on Pattern Recognition, Quebec City, 2002.

[5.]   L. L. Chao, A. Martin, and J. V. Haxby, "Are face-responsive regions selective only for faces?," *NeuroReport*, vol. 10, pp. 2945–2950, 1999.

[6.]   V. P. Clark, K. Keil, J. M. Maisog, S. Courtney, L. G. Ungeleider, and J. V. Haxby, "Functional Magnetic Resonance Imaging of Human Visual Cortex during Face Matching: A Comparison with Positron Emission Tomography," *NeuroImage*, vol. 4, pp. 1–15, 1996.

[7.]   B. J. Frey, A. Colmenarez, and T. S. Huang, "Mixtures of Local Linear Subspaces for Face Recognition," IEEE Conference on Computer Vision and Pattern Recognition, Santa Barbara, CA, 1998.

[8.]   I. Gauthier and N. K. Logothetis, "Is Face Recognition Not So Unique After All?," Cognitive Neuropsychology, vol. 17, pp. 125–142, 2000.

[9.]   I. Gauthier, M. J. Tarr, A. W. Anderson, P. Skudlarski, and J. C. Gore, "Behavioral and Neural Changes Following Expertise Training," Meeting of the Psychonomic Society, Philadelphia, 1997.

[10.] J. V. Haxby, L. G. Ungerleider, V. P. Clark, J. L. Schouten, E. A. Hoffman, and A. Martin, "The Effect of Face Inversion on Activity in Human Neural Systems for Face and Object Recognition," Neuron, vol. 22, pp. 189–199, 199.

[11.] A. Ishai, L. G. Ungerleider, A. Martin, J. L. Schouten, and J. V. Haxby, "Distributed representation of objects in the human ventral visual pathway," Science, vol. 96, pp. 9379–9384, 1999.

[12.] L. Itti, "Modeling Primate Visual Attention," in Computational Neuroscience: A Comprehensive Approach, J. Feng, Ed. Boca Raton, FL: CRC Press, 2002.

[13.] N. Kambhatla and T. K. Leen, "Dimension Reduction by Local PCA," Neural Computation, vol. 9, pp. 1493–1516, 1997.

[14.] N. Kanwisher, M. Chun, J. McDermott, and P. Ledden, "Functional Imaging of Human Visual Recognition," Cognitive Brain Research, vol. 5, pp. 55–67, 1996.

[15.] S. M. Kosslyn, Image and Brain. Cambridge, MA: MIT Press, 1994.

[16.] S. M. Kosslyn, A. Pascual-Leone, O. Felician, S. Camposano, J. P. Keenan, W. L. Thompson, G. Ganis, K. E. Sukel, and N. M. Alpert, "The Role of Area 17 in Visual Imagery: Convergent Evidence from PET and rTMS," Science, vol. 284, pp. 167–170, 1999.

[17.] Z. Kourtzi and N. Kanwisher, "Cortical Regions Involved in Perceiving Object Shape," The Journal of Neuroscience, vol. 20, pp. 3310–3318, 2000.

[18.] T. S. Lee, D. Mumford, R. Romero, and V. A. F. Lamme, "The role of the primary visual cortex in higher level vision," Vision Research, vol. 38, pp. 2429–2454, 1998.

[19.] D. G. Lowe, Perceptual Organization And Visual Recognition. Boston: Kluwer, 1985.

[20.] E. Maguire, C. D. Frith, and L. Cipolotti, "Distinct Neural Systems for the Encoding and Recognition of Topography and Faces," NeuroImage, vol. 13, pp. 743–750, 2001.

[21.] A. Maki, P. Nordlund, and J.-O. Eklundh, "Attentional Scene Segmentation: Integrating Depth and Motion from Phase," Computer Vision and Image Understanding, vol. 78, pp. 351–373, 2000.

[22.] D. Marr, Vision. Cambridge, MA: Freeman, 1982.

[23.] K. Nakamura, R. Kawashima, N. Sata, A. Nakamura, M. Sugiura, T. Kato, K. Hatano, K. Ito, H. Fukuda, T. Schormann, and K. Zilles, "Functional delineation of the human occipito-temporal areas related to face and scene processing: a PET study," Brain, vol. 123, pp. 1903–1912, 2000.

[24.] A. Oliva and P. G. Schyns, "Coarse Blobs or Fine Edges? Evidence That Information Diagnoticity Changes the Perception of Complex Visual Stimuli," Cognitive Psychology, vol. 34, pp. 72–107, 1997.

[25.] A. J. O'Toole, K. A. Deffenbacher, D. Valentin, and H. Abdi, "Structural Aspects of Face Recognition and the Other Race Effect," Memory and Cognition, vol. 22, pp. 208–224, 1994.

[26.] S. E. Palmer, Vision Science: Photons to Phenomenology. Cambridge, MA: MIT Press, 1999.

[27.] D. Parkhurst, K. Law, and E. Neibur, "Modeling the role of salience in the allocation of overt visual attention," Vision Research, vol. 42, pp. 107–123, 2002.

[28.] D. A. Pollen, J. P. Gaska, and L. D. Jacobson, "Physiological Constraints on Models of Visual Cortical Function," in Models of Brain Functions, M. Rodney and J. Cotterill, Eds. New York: Cambridge University Press, 1989, pp. 115–135.

[29.]   A. Puce, T. Allison, J. C. Gore, and G. McCarthy, "Face-sensitive regions in human extrastriate cortex studied by functional MRI," *Journal of Neurophysiology*, vol. 74, pp. 1192–1199, 1995.

[30.]   J. W. Tanaka and T. Curran, "A Neural Basis for Expert Object Recognition," *Psychological Science*, vol. 12, pp. 43–47, 2001.

[31.]   M. J. Tarr and I. Gauthier, "FFA: a flexible fusiform area for subordinate-level visual processing automatized by expertise," *Neuroscience*, vol. 3, pp. 764–769, 2000.

[32.]   M. E. Tipping and C. M. Bishop, "Mixtures of Probabilistic Principal Component Analysers," *Neural Computation*, vol. 11, pp. 443–482, 1999.

[33.]   F. Tong, K. Nakayama, M. Moscovitch, O. Weinrib, and N. Kanwisher, "Response Properties of the Human Fusiform Face Area," *Cognitive Neuropsychology*, vol. 17, pp. 257–279, 2000.

[34.]   L. G. Ungeleider and M. Mishkin, "Two cortical visual systems," in *Analysis of visual behavior*, D. J. Ingle, M. A. Goodale, and R. J. W. Mansfield, Eds. Cambridge, MA: MIT Press, 1982, pp. 549–586.

[35.]   K. Zipser, V. A. F. Lamme, and P. H. Schiller, "Contextual Modulation in Primary Visual Cortex," *Neuroscience*, vol. 16, pp. 7376–7389, 1996.

Efficient Pose Estimation Using View-Based Object Representations

Gabriele Peters

Universität Dortmund, Informatik VII,
Otto-Hahn-Str. 16, D-44227 Dortmund, Germany,
peters@ls7.cs.uni-dortmund.de,
http://ls7-www.cs.uni-dortmund.de/~peters/

Abstract. We present an efficient method for estimating the pose of
a three-dimensional object. Its implementation is embedded in a computer vision system which is motivated by and based on cognitive principles concerning the visual perception of three-dimensional objects. View-
point-invariant object recognition has been subject to controversial discussions for a long time. An important point of discussion is the nature of
internal object representations. Behavioral studies with primates, which
are summarized in this article, support the model of *view-based* object
representations. We designed our computer vision system according to
these findings and demonstrate that very precise estimations of the poses
of real-world objects are possible even if only a few number of sample
views of an object is available. The system can be used for a variety of
applications.

1   Implications from Cognition

Each object in our environment can cause considerably different patterns of
excitation in our retinae depending on the observed viewpoint of the object.
Despite this we are able to perceive that the changing signals are produced by
the same object. It is a function of our brain to provide this constant recognition
from such inconstant input signals by establishing an internal representation of
the object.

There are uncountable behavioral studies with primates that support the
model of a view-based description of three-dimensional objects by our visual
system. If a set of unfamiliar object views is presented to humans their response
time and error rates during recognition increase with increasing angular distance
between the learned (i.e., stored) and the unfamiliar view [1]. This angle effect
declines if intermediate views are experienced and stored [2]. The performance
is not linearly dependent on the shortest angular distance in three dimensions
to the best-recognized view, but it correlates with an "image-plane feature-by-
feature deformation distance" between the test view and the best-recognized
view [3]. Thus, measurement of image-plane similarity to a few feature patterns
seems to be an appropriate model for human three-dimensional object recognition.

J.L. Crowley et al. (Eds.): ICVS 2003, LNCS 2626, pp. 12–21, 2003.

Experiments with monkeys show that familiarization with a "limited number" of views of a novel object can provide viewpoint-independent recognition [4].

In a psychophysical experiment subjects were instructed to perform mental rotation, but they switched spontaneously to "landmark-based strategies", which turned out to be more efficient [5] .

Numerous physiological studies also give evidence for a view-based processing of the brain during object recognition. Results of recordings of single neurons in the inferior temporal cortex (IT) of monkeys, which is known to be concerned with object recognition, resemble those obtained by the behavioral studies. Populations of IT neurons have been found which respond selectively to only some views of an object and their response declines as the object is rotated away from the preferred view [6].

The capabilities of technical solutions for three-dimensional object recognition still stay far behind the efficiency of biological systems. Summarizing, one can say that for biological systems object representations in form of single, but connected views seem to be sufficient for a huge variety of situations and perception tasks.

2   Description of the Vision System

In this section we introduce our approach of learning an object representation which takes these results about primate brain functions into account.

We automatically generate sparse representations for real-world objects, which satisfy the following conditions:

a1. They are constituted from *two-dimensional* views.

a2. They are *sparse*, i.e., they consist of *as few views as possible*.

a3. They are capable of *performing perception tasks*, especially pose estimation.

Our system consists of a *view representation builder* and an *object representation builder*. They are shown, together with their input and output data, in the diagram in figure 1, which depicts a one-directional flow of information.

Of course, feedback from higher levels of processing to lower ones would allow for, e.g., unsupervised system tuning or an improved segmentation, but this is not subject of this contribution. We start with the recording of a densely sampled set of views of the upper half of the viewing sphere of a test object. In the following we aim at choosing only such views for a representation which are representative for an area of viewpoints as large as possible.

2.1   View Representation Builder

Each of the recorded views is preprocessed by a *Gabor wavelet transform*, which is biologically inspired because Gabor wavelets approximate response patterns of neurons in the visual cortex of mammals [7,8]. A *segmentation* based on gray level values [9] follows. It separates the object from the background. This results

learning object representations

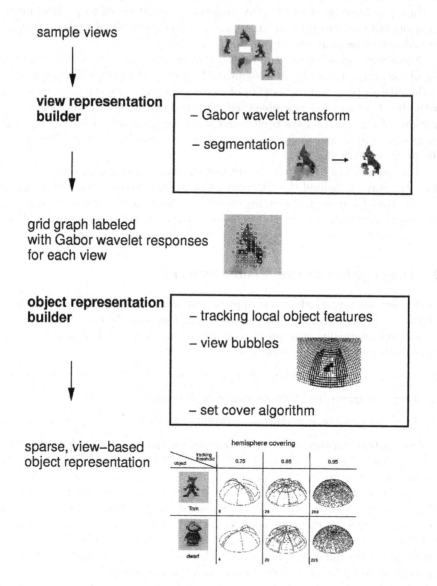

sample views

view representation
builder
– Gabor wavelet transform
– segmentation

grid graph labeled
with Gabor wavelet responses
for each view

object representation
builder
– tracking local object features
– view bubbles
– set cover algorithm

sparse, view–based
object representation

Fig. 1. The system for learning sparse object representations consists of a view and an object representation builder. The resulting object representation consists of single but connected views. The numbers next to the resulting partitionings of the viewing hemisphere are the numbers of view bubbles which constitute the representation

in a representation of each view in form of a *grid graph labeled with Gabor wavelet responses*. The graph covers the object segment. Each vertex of such a graph is labeled with the responses of a set of Gabor wavelets, which describe the local surroundings of the vertex. Such a feature vector is called *jet*.

2.2   Object Representation Builder

To facilitate an advantageous selection of views for the object representation a surrounding area of similar views is determined for each view. This area is called *view bubble*. For a selected view it is defined as the largest possible surrounding area on the viewing hemisphere for which two conditions hold:

b1. The views constituting the view bubble are *similar* to the view in question.

b2. *Corresponding object points* are known or can be inferred for each view of the view bubble.

The similarity mentioned in **b1** is specified below. Condition **b2** is important for a reconstruction of novel views as, e.g., needed by our pose estimation algorithm. A view bubble may have an irregular shape. To simplify its determination we approximate it by a rectangle with the selected view in its center, which is determined in the following way.

The object representation builder starts by *tracking local object features*. Jets can be tracked from a selected view to neighboring views [10]. A similarity function $S(\mathcal{G}, \mathcal{G}')$ is defined between a selected view and a neighboring view, where $\mathcal{G}$ is the graph which represents the selected view and $\mathcal{G}'$ is a tracked graph which represents the neighboring view. Utilizing this similarity function we determine a *view bubble* for a selected view by tracking its graph $\mathcal{G}$ from view to view in both directions on the line of latitude until the similarity between the selected view and either the tested view to the west or to the east drops below a threshold τ, i.e., until either $S(\mathcal{G}, \mathcal{G}^w) < \tau$ or $S(\mathcal{G}, \mathcal{G}^e) < \tau$. The same procedure is performed for the neighboring views on the line of longitude, resulting in a rectangular area with the selected view in its center. The representation of a view bubble consists of the graphs of the center and four border views

$$\mathcal{B} := \langle \mathcal{G}, \mathcal{G}^w, \mathcal{G}^e, \mathcal{G}^s, \mathcal{G}^n \rangle, \tag{1}$$

with w, e, s, and n standing for *west, east, south,* and *north*. As this procedure is performed for each of the recorded views, it results in view bubbles overlapping on a large scale on the viewing hemisphere (see figures 1 and 2).

To meet the first condition **a1** of a sparse object representation we aim at choosing single views (in the form of labeled graphs) to constitute it. To meet the second condition **a2** the idea is to reduce the large number of overlapping view bubbles and to choose as few of them as possible which nevertheless cover the whole hemisphere. For the selection of the view bubbles we use the *greedy set cover algorithm* [11]. It provides a set of view bubbles which covers the whole viewing hemisphere. We define the *sparse, view-based object representation* by

$$\mathcal{R} := \{\langle \mathcal{G}_i, \mathcal{G}_i^w, \mathcal{G}_i^e, \mathcal{G}_i^s, \mathcal{G}_i^n \rangle\}_{i \in R} \tag{2}$$

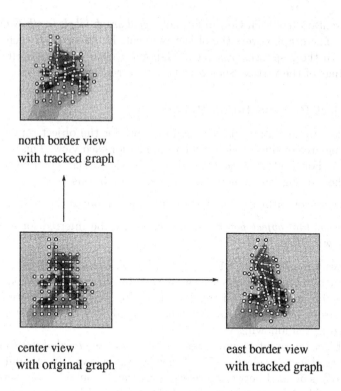

north border view
with tracked graph

center view
with original graph

east border view
with tracked graph

Fig. 2. This figure shows a graph of the center view of a view bubble tracked to its east and north border views

where R is a cover of the hemisphere. Neighboring views of the representation are "connected" by known corresponding object points (the correspondences between center and border views), which have been provided by the tracking procedure. Figure 1 shows different covers of the hemisphere for two test objects.

3   Pose Estimation

Given the sparse representation of the object in question and given a test view of the object, the aim is the determination of the object's pose displayed in the test view, i.e., the assignment of the test view to its correct position on the viewing hemisphere. In this section a solution to this problem is proposed (subsection 3.1) and the results of simulations with a series of test views are reported (subsection 3.2) and discussed (subsection 3.3).

Many approaches to pose estimation have been proposed, starting from closed form solutions for not more than four noncollinear points [12,13,14] up to iterative non-linear optimization algorithms, which have to rely on a good initial guess to converge to a reasonable solution [15,16]. We propose a model based pose estimation algorithm. In a first step it determines the rough position of the given pose on the viewing hemisphere as initial guess. Then this estimate is re-fined in a second step. It requires the generation of *virtual views*, i.e., artificially generated images of unfamiliar views, which are not represented in the object representation. For this purpose we

(1) calculate linear combinations of corresponding vertex positions in the center and border graphs of view bubbles and

(2) interpolate the corresponding jets attached to these vertices.

The new positions and jets define a representing graph of the virtual view. From this graph the virtual view can be generated by reconstructing the information contained in Gabor wavelet responses [17]. To interpolate between jets we calcu-late the weighted sum of corresponding jets in the sample views. The weights are chosen according to the relative position of the unfamiliar view with respect to the sample views. Our method of deriving vertex positions in unfamiliar views follows Ullman and Basri's [18] purely two-dimensional approach of generating unfamiliar views by linear combination of sample views. Detailed formula are given in [19].

3.1   Methods

Let T be the test view, the pose of which should be estimated, and $\mathcal{G}_T$ be its representing graph, which is extracted from the original image of view T after the test view has been divided into object and background segments as described in section 2.1. This means that no a priori knowledge about the object is provided. A view is determined by its position on the viewing hemisphere.

Let $I_i, i \in R$, be the center images of the view bubbles the graphs $\mathcal{G}_i$ of the object representation $\mathcal{R}$ are extracted from. The *pose estimation algorithm* for estimating the pose of a single test view T proceeds in two steps:

1. Match $\mathcal{G}_T$ to each image $I_i, i \in R$, using a graph maching algorithm [20]. As a *rough estimate* of the object's pose choose that view bubble $\widehat{B}$ the center image I_i of which provides the largest similarity to $\mathcal{G}_T$.

2. Generate the representation $\widehat{\mathcal{G}}$ for each unfamiliar view which is included inside the area defined by $\widehat{B}$ by (1) a linear combination of corresponding vertex positions in the center and one border graph of $\widehat{B}$ and (2) an inter-polation of the corresponding jets as described in section 3. (We choose the graph of that border view which lies closest to the unfamiliar view.) From each of the calculated graphs $\widehat{\mathcal{G}}$ reconstruct a corresponding virtual view $\widehat{V}$ using an algorithm which reconstructs the information contained in Gabor wavelet responses [17]. Accordingly, reconstruct a virtual test view $\widehat{V}_T$ from $\mathcal{G}_T$ (figure 3). Compare each of the virtual views $\widehat{V}$ with the virtual view $\widehat{V}_T$ using an error function $\epsilon(\widehat{V}, \widehat{V}_T)$ which performs a pixelwise comparison between $\widehat{V}_T$ and each $\widehat{V}$. The estimated pose $\widehat{T}$ of the test view T is the position on the viewing hemisphere of that virtual view $\widehat{V}$ which provides the smallest error ϵ.

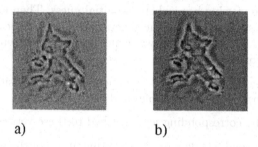

a)   b)

Fig. 3. a) Virtual view $\widehat{V}$ reconstructed from interpolated graph $\widehat{\mathcal{G}}$. b) Virtual test view $\widehat{V}_T$ reconstructed from its original graph $\mathcal{G}_T$

The *estimation error* between T and $\widehat{T}$ can be determined by the Euclidean distance: $\epsilon_{esti}(T, \widehat{T}) = d(T, \widehat{T})$.

3.2   Results

For the evaluation of the algorithm 30 test views have been chosen. The positions of them on the viewing hemisphere are displayed in figure 4. For two different toy objects and for three different partitionings of the viewing hemisphere, which have been derived by applying different tracking thresholds τ, the poses of these 30 test views have been estimated. The light gray squares indicate the views which are represented in the object representation $\mathcal{R}$, black dots mark the positions of the test images and the estimated positions are tagged by dark gray circles. The arrow points at the test images and their estimations which are displayed in figure 5.

The illustrations in figure 4 indicate that pose estimation becomes more precise with an increasing number of sample views in the object representation. This result has been expected and is confirmed by an inspection of the mean estimation errors taken over the 30 test views for each object and each partitioning of the hemisphere separately. They are summarized in table 1. With one exception for the "object" Tom the mean errors are decreasing with an increasing value of τ, i.e., with an increasing number of views in $\mathcal{R}$.

3.3   Discussion

The results of the pose estimation experiments are amazingly good. This is particularly obvious for the example displayed in figure 5, taking into account that the sparse representation of the object "Tom" contains only the representations of 30 views. This have been the test images for which the best result for $\tau = 0.75$ was obtained, but also for a reasonable partitioning of the viewing hemisphere ($\tau = 0.85$) the mean estimation errors are smaller than 5° for both objects, which can be regarded as a remarkable result, taking into account that humans are hardly able to recognize a difference of 5° between two object poses.

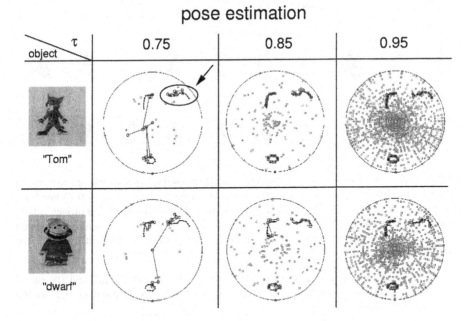

Fig. 4. Results of pose estimations for three different partitionings of the viewing hemisphere and two different objects are depicted. The tracking threshold τ influences the resulting number of views in the final representations. As for each view bubble of the final representation the graphs of the center and four border views are stored, the border views of neighboring view bubbles lie close together. This is obvious especially for $\tau = 0.75$

As experiments reported in [21] have shown, the method proposed in section 3.1 cannot be improved very much by a more elaborate determination of the initial guess, e.g., by testing more neighboring candidates.

4   Conclusion

We proposed a computer vision system based on cognitive principles which is able to estimate the pose of a three-dimensional object from an unobstructed view in an efficient manner. The pose estimation results support a good quality of our sparse object representation and allow the conclusion that a view-based approach to object perception with object representations that consist of only single views, which are connected, is suitable for performing perception tasks as it is advocated by brain researchers. Besides the biological relevance of our approach, there are a variety of possible applications, such as object recognition, view morphing, or data compression.

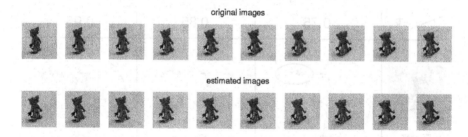

pose estimation, object "Tom", $\tau = 0.75$

original images

estimated images

Fig. 5. This figure shows the test images and their estimations which are marked in figure 4. For this example the representation of the object "Tom" for $\tau = 0.75$ has been chosen. It consists of only 30 views. In the first row the true poses of the object, which should be estimated, are displayed. The second row shows the poses which have been estimated by treating each view of the sequence independently. The estimation error for this sequence averages $5.78°$

Table 1. Mean pose estimation errors. For example, for object "Tom" and the partitioning of $\tau = 0.75$ the average estimation deviation of the estimated pose $\hat{T}$ to the true pose T is $36.51°$

mean pose estimation errors					
τ	0.75	0.8	0.85	0.9	0.95
object "Tom"	36.51°	3.63°	0.77°	3.35°	0.36°
object "dwarf"	20.54°	19.47°	4.2°	2.65°	1.71°

References

1. S. Edelman and H. H. Bülthoff. Orientation Dependence in the Recognition of Familiar and Novel Views of Three-Dimensional Objects. *Vision Research*, 32(12):2385–2400, 1992.
2. M. J. Tarr. *Orientation Dependence in Three-Dimensional Object Recognition.* Ph.D. Thesis, MIT, 1989.
3. F. Cutzu and S. Edelman. Canonical Views in Object Representation and Recognition. *Vision Research*, 34:3037–3056, 1994.
4. N. K. Logothetis, J. Pauls, H. H. Bülthoff, and Poggio T. View-Dependent Object Recognition by Monkeys. *Current Biology*, 4:401–414, 1994.
5. M. Wexler, S. M. Kosslyn, and A. Berthoz. Motor processes in mental rotation. *Cognition*, 68:77–94, 1998.
6. N. K. Logothetis, J. Pauls, and Poggio T. Shape Representation in the Inferior Temporal Cortex of Monkeys. *Current Biology*, 5(5):552–563, 1995.
7. D. C. Burr, M. C. Morrone, and D. Spinelli. Evidence for Edge and Bar Detectors in Human Vision. *Vision Research*, 29(4):419–431, 1989.

8. J. P. Jones and L. A. Palmer. An evaluation of the two-dimensional gabor filter model of simple receptive fields in cat striate cortex. *Journal of Neurophysiology*, 58(6):1233–1258, 1987.

9. C. Eckes and J. C. Vorbrüggen. Combining Data-Driven and Model-Based Cues for Segmentation of Video Sequences. In *Proc. WCNN96*, pages 868–875, 1996.

10. T. Maurer and C. von der Malsburg. Tracking and Learning Graphs and Pose on Image Sequences of Faces. In *Proc. Int. Conf. on Automatic Face- and Gesture-Recognition*, pages 176–181, 1996.

11. V. Chvatal. A Greedy Heuristic for the Set-Covering Problem. *Mathematics of Operations Research*, 4(3):233–235, 1979.

12. R. Horaud, B. Conio, O. Leboulleux, and B. Lacolle. An Analytic Solution for the Perspective 4-Point Problem. *Computer Vision, Graphics and Image Processing*, 47:33–44, 1989.

13. M. Dhome, M. Richetin, J. Lapreste, and G. Rives. Determination of the Attitude of 3-D Objects from a Single Perspective View. *IEEE Transactions on Pattern Analysis and Machine Intelligence*, 11(12):1265–1278, 1989.

14. R. M. Haralick, C. Lee, K. Ottenberg, and M. Nölle. Analysis and Solutions of the Three Point Perspective Pose Estimation Problem. In *Proc. of the IEEE Comp. Society Conf. on Computer Vision and Pattern Recognition*, pages 592–598, 1991.

15. D. G. Lowe. Three-Dimensional Object Recognition from Single Two-Dimensional Images. *Artificial Intelligence*, 31:355–395, 1987.

16. J. Yuan. A General Photogrammetric Method for Determining Object Position and Orientation. *IEEE Journal of Robotics and Automation*, 5(2):129–142, 1989.

17. M. Pötzsch. Die Behandlung der Wavelet-Transformation von Bildern in der Nähe von Objektkanten. Technical Report IRINI 94-04, Institut für Neuroinformatik, Ruhr-Universität Bochum, Germany, 1994.

18. S. Ullman and R. Basri. Recognition by Linear Combinations of Models. *IEEE Transactions on Pattern Analysis and Machine Intelligence*, 13(10):992–1006, 1991.

19. G. Peters and C. von der Malsburg. View Reconstruction by Linear Combination of Sample Views. In *Proc. BMVC 2001*, pages 223–232, 2001.

20. M. Lades, J. C. Vorbrüggen, J. Buhmann, J. Lange, C. von der Malsburg, R. P. Würtz, and W. Konen. Distortion Invariant Object Recognition in the Dynamic Link Architecture. *IEEE Trans. Comp.*, 42:300–311, 1993.

21. G. Peters. *A View-Based Approach to Three-Dimensional Object Perception*. Ph.D. Thesis, Shaker Verlag, Aachen, Germany, 2002.

Integrating Context-Free and Context-Dependent Attentional Mechanisms for Gestural Object Reference

Gunther Heidemann[1], Robert Rae[2], Holger Bekel[1],
Ingo Bax[1], and Helge Ritter[1]

[1] Neuroinformatics Group, Faculty of Technology, Bielefeld University,
Postfach 10 01 31, D-33501 Bielefeld, Germany
{gheidema,hbekel,ibax,helge}@techfak.uni-bielefeld.de
http://www.TechFak.Uni-Bielefeld.DE/ags/ni/index_d.html
[2] Now at *PerFact Innovation*, Lampingstr. 8,
D-33615 Bielefeld, Germany
{robrae}@techfak.uni-bielefeld.de

Abstract. We present a vision system for human-machine interaction that relies on a small wearable camera which can be mounted to common glasses. The camera views the area in front of the user, especially the hands. To evaluate hand movements for pointing gestures to objects and to recognise object reference, an approach relying on the integration of bottom-up generated feature maps and top-down propagated recognition results is introduced. In this vision system, modules for context free focus of attention work in parallel to a recognition system for hand gestures. In contrast to other approaches, the fusion of the two branches is not on the symbolic but on the sub-symbolic level by use of attention maps. This method is plausible from a cognitive point of view and facilitates the integration of entirely different modalities.

1 Introduction

One of the major problems in human-machine interaction is to establish a common focus of attention. In current computer systems the mouse is used as an input device to select the windows to which keystrokes refer, which can be looked upon as a simple means to establish a common focus of attention. However, when human-machine interaction refers to real world objects or does not take place in front of a terminal, computer vision will be needed. In this case, *hand gestures* are most natural to guide attention of the machine.

The problem with hand gestures is that they are not precise according to the requirements of a machine. Humans do not point with high angular accuracy, instead, they rely (*i*) on the understanding of the dialog partner and (*ii*) on supplementing modalities like speech. Hence, it is not sufficient for visual evaluation of pointing gestures to calculate direction angles as accurately as possible.

In this contribution, we present a system which uses an *attention map* as a representation of focus of attention. The attention map allows integration of

J.L. Crowley et al. (Eds.): ICVS 2003, LNCS 2626, pp. 22–33, 2003.

entirely different modalities and thus facilitates solution of the above mentioned problems: (*i*) The machine needs a basic understanding of the scene. Only by this means the "continuous valued problem" of evaluating pointing directions (which might point everywhere) with possibly high accuracy can be transformed into a "discrete valued problem". In the latter case, the machine analyses the scene for salient points or regions and thus restricts the possible pointing directions to a small subset of the whole angular range. In the system proposed here, several context-free attentional mechanisms (entropy, symmetry and edge-corner detection) are adopted to activate certain areas of the attention map and thus establish an "anticipation" of the system where the user might point to. (*ii*) The attention map allows the future integration of symbolic information from speech recognition systems. Hints like "right" or "above" can easily be expressed in terms of the manipulator maps outlined in sections 3 and 4.2.

An earlier version of the approach was successfully applied in human machine interaction [5]. It is related to the data driven component of the attention system introduced by Backer et al. [1], which combines several feature maps for gaze control of an active vision system. Similarly motivated architectures for focus of attention were proposed by Itti et al. [10] and Walther et al. [23]. A system for hand tracking and object reference that also allows the integration of modalities other than vision was proposed by Theis et al. [21] for the Cora robot system.

First we will describe the experimental setup and the image processing architecture, then the single context-free attentional features and their adaptive weighting, and finally the integration of the pointing direction recognition.

2   System Description

2.1   Scenario: Gestural Reference

The experimental setup is part of the VAMPIRE project (Visual Active Memory Processes and Interactive REtrieval) of the IST programme. The project aims at the development of an active memory and retrieval system in the context of

Fig. 1. Left: Miniature camera mounted to glasses. Middle: User points at an object (a button of the power supply unit on the table). Right: Setup used for evaluation, see section 5.

an Augmented Reality scenario. The user wears a head-mounted camera like in Fig. 1 and a display such that the system is able to build up a hierarchically structured memory of what the user sees. In future work, query results will be re-visualised in a virtual world or projected into the real world using the head-mounted display.

In the VAMPIRE scenario user-machine interaction is possible only using vision and speech, so recognition of gestural reference to memorised as well as *unknown* objects is a key ability. Therefore goal-oriented segmentation techniques are not feasible, instead context-free algorithms have to be used.

In this paper we present part of the attentional subsystem of the VAMPIRE project by which objects or other visual entities can be referenced using hand gestures. As a sample task, we chose the setup of Fig. 1, right, where the user points to different objects on a table. As long as the user changes pointing directions quickly, the system assumes that large object entities are indicated. When movements become slow, the attentional focus established by the detected pointing direction is narrowed down to facilitate reference to details ("virtual laser pointer"), so e.g. a button on a technical device can be selected.

2.2   Processing Architecture

Figure 2 shows a system overview. From the image captured by the camera first three feature maps are calculated by different modules: Entropy, symmetry and edge-corner detection (section 3.1). In these maps, different image features stand out, for an example see Fig. 5. The attention map module (ATM) calculates a weighted sum of the basic feature maps using an adaptive weighting as described in section 3.2. Maxima of the attention map correspond to areas considered as "interesting" by the system and serve as a preselection of possible pointing targets.

Pointing directions are classified by the neural VPL classification module described in section 4.1 (left branch in Fig. 2). The classifier works on image patches found by a previous skin colour segmentation module and yields as a

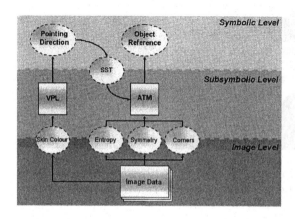

Fig. 2. System architecture. In contrast to approaches which integrate pointing gesture information and object locations on the symbolic level [2], the pointing angle is down-propagated to the sub-symbolic level using a "symbol-signal-transformer" (SST) and integrated as a spatial weighting of the feature maps.

result (i) a classification whether the patch is an irrelevant object or a pointing hand and in the latter case (ii) an estimate of the 2D pointing angle.

To figure out which image part the user is actually pointing to, knowledge based approaches would process both the pointing angle and the positions of the maxima of the attention map on the symbolic level. A good survey of knowledge based image processing is given in [4].

In contrast, in our approach the pointing direction is transformed back to the sub-symbolic level using a so called "manipulator map". The manipulator map serves as a multiplicative spatial weighting of the attention map to intensify attention maxima in the pointing direction while inhibiting others. Therefore, the manipulator map shows a cone of high values in the pointing direction, starting at the hand centre (Fig. 3, right). The cone is widened or narrowed depending on the context as described in section 4.2 and can be viewed as a "spotlight of attention".

3 Integrating Attention Maps

3.1 Generation of Context-Free Feature Maps

We use three different context-free methods to determine focus of attention: Local entropy, local symmetry and an edge-corner detector. These methods use entirely different principles to judge saliency and are best suited for different scales. We describe the algorithms ordered by scale "from coarse to fine".

Entropy map: Judging saliency from local entropy relies on the assumption that semantically meaningful areas have also a high information content in the sense of information theory. This method was proposed by Kalinke and von Seelen [13] and has been integrated in a larger vision architecture in [12]. Calculation of an entropy map M_E is based on a grey value image, usually at low resolution:

$$M_E(x,y) = - \sum_q \tilde{H}(x,y,q) \cdot \log \tilde{H}(x,y,q), \qquad \tilde{H}(x,y,q) = \frac{H(x,y,q)}{\sum_{q'} H(x,y,q')}, \quad (1)$$

where H denotes the histogram within a $n_E \times n_E$-window ($n_E \geq 3$ and odd) around the pixel (x,y):

$$H(x,y,q) = \sum_{y'=y-\tilde{n}}^{y+\tilde{n}} \sum_{x'=x-\tilde{n}}^{x+\tilde{n}} \delta_{I(x',y'),q}, \qquad (2)$$

with $\tilde{n} = (n_E - 1)/2$, δ the Kronecker symbol, $I(x,y)$ the grey values, and $q = 0 \ldots 2^{Q_E} - 1$. Q_E denotes the quantisation of the histogram which should be about $2^{Q_E}/n_E^2 \approx 10 - 20$. The crucial parameter in entropy calculation is the window size n_E in combination with the resolution of the intensity image. It determines the scale on which structures are evaluated. A window which is too small to capture object structure is mainly working as an edge detector. Here, we use windows large enough to direct attention to large objects (Fig. 5).

Symmetry map: The second saliency feature is local grey value symmetry as proposed by Reisfeld et al. [17]. While entropy serves for a primary detection of large objects regardless of structure, the symmetry map M_{Sym} yields a stronger focus to object details which are locally symmetric. The use of symmetry is cognitively motivated by psychophysical findings, see e.g. [3,15]. For the calculation of M_{Sym} we use a more efficient version of the original algorithm [17], which can be outlined here only in short. M_{Sym} relies on the grey value derivatives $I_x(p), I_y(p)$, from which the gradient magnitude $G_I(p) = \sqrt{I_x(p)^2 + I_y(p)^2}$ and direction $\theta_I(p) = \arctan(I_y(p)/I_x(p))$ are calculated. The symmetry value M_{Sym} of a pixel p is a sum over all pixel pairs (p_i, p_j) within a circular surroundings around p of radius R:

$$M_{Sym}(p) = \sum_{(i,j) \in \Gamma(p)} PWF(i,j) \cdot GWF(i,j) \quad \text{with} \tag{3}$$

$$\Gamma(p) = \{(i,j) \mid (p_i + p_j)/2 = p \ \wedge \ \|p_i - p_j\| \le R\}. \tag{4}$$

Gradient directions γ_i, γ_j at p_i and p_j are judged for the probability to be part of the contours of a symmetric object by the *Phase Weight Function PWF*

$$PWF(i,j) = [1 - \cos(\gamma_i + \gamma_j)] \cdot [1 - \cos(\gamma_i - \gamma_j)], \tag{5}$$

where γ_i, γ_j denote the angles between the line $\overline{p_i p_j}$ connecting p_i and p_j and the gradients at p_i and p_j, respectively. The *Gradient Weight Function GWF* weights contributions of pixels (p_i, p_j) higher if they are both on edges because they might relate to object borders:

$$GWF(i,j) = \log(1 + G_I(p_i)) \cdot \log(1 + G_I(p_j)), \tag{6}$$

The logarithm attenuates the influence of very strong edges. Figure 5 shows an example of M_{Sym}, in which the symmetric buttons can be clearly detected.

Edge and corner detection: The third feature map is aimed to yield small, salient details of objects. Since small-scale saliency can hardly be detected from complex image structures, the local grey value gradients I_x, I_y have to be evaluated for corners and edges. As a detector we chose the method proposed by Harris and Stephens [6], which could be shown to be superior to others in [20]. It is based on an approximation of the auto-correlation function of the signal

$$A(p) = \begin{pmatrix} <I_x^2>_{W(p)} & <I_x I_y>_{W(p)} \\ <I_x I_y>_{W(p)} & <I_y^2>_{W(p)} \end{pmatrix}, \tag{7}$$

where $< \cdot >_{W(p)}$ denotes a weighted averaging over a window $W(p)$ centred at p. The weight function inside the window is a Gaussian. Saliency of a point is high if both eigenvalues of A are large, however, to reduce the computational effort, the feature map is calculated from

$$M_{Harris}(p) = \det(A) - \alpha \cdot (\text{Trace}(A))^2. \tag{8}$$

Derivatives I_x, I_y are computed by 5×5-Sobel operators. The Gaussian weighting function for the components of A inside W has width $\sigma = 2$. As suggested in [20], a value of 0.06 is used for the constant α.

3.2   Adaptive Integration Algorithm

The adaptive integration of the various maps, in this case consisting of three feature maps $M_i(x,y)$, $i = 1,2,3$, and one manipulator map $M_m(x,y)$, takes place in the "ATM" module as illustrated in Fig. 3.

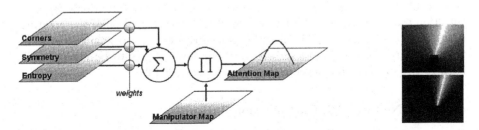

Fig. 3. Left: Processing flow of the ATM-module (central box in Fig. 2). The attention map is generated from an (adaptively) weighted superposition of the feature maps. The manipulator map, which allows the coupling of information from other modules like the pointing direction recognition, is multiplied to the attention map. Right: Examples of manipulator maps ("spotlight of attention"). A wide cone is used as long as the user wants to indicate large objects, a narrow one for precise pointing to details.

The output $C(x,y)$ is calculated by a weighted summation over the input feature maps and a product of contributing manipulator maps:

$$C(x,y) = \sum_{i=1}^{N} \theta(w_i * M_i(x,y)) * \prod_{m=1}^{l} M_m(x,y), \qquad (9)$$

with $\theta(\cdot)$ as a threshold function. The maximum of the output attention map $C(\cdot,\cdot)$ determines the *point of common attention* of man and machine, which can be used for further processing.

To equalise contributions of all saliency features to the attention map, we calculate the contributions S_i as a sum over all pixels of each map M_i. To reach approximate equalisation of the S_i, the map weights w_i are adapted by iterating

$$w_i(t+1) = w_i(t) + \epsilon(w_i^s(t) - w_i(t)), \quad 0 < \epsilon \leq 1, \qquad (10)$$

with the following target weights w_i^s:

$$w_i^s = \frac{1}{n^2} \cdot \frac{\sum_{k=1}^{n} S_k}{S_i} \qquad \text{with} \qquad S_i = \frac{\sum_{(x,y)}(M_i(x,y) + \gamma)}{\xi_i}. \qquad (11)$$

γ enforces a limit for weight growing. The parameters ξ_i can be used if certain saliency features should a priori be weighted higher. In section 4.2 we make use of this possibility to give entropy higher weight for large-scale selection of objects and low weight when object details are pointed at.

4   Pointing Gesture Evaluation

In section 3.1 the contributing context-free feature maps to the attention map $C(x, y)$ were described. To guide attention to objects or object substructures selected by the user, the pointing direction of the hand has to be evaluated. In a first step, a skin colour segmentation yields a candidate region for the hand. This ROI is subsequently classified by a neural system for two informations: (*i*) classification into *pointing hand* and *other object* and (*ii*) recognition of the pointing direction if applicable. We will describe this subsystem first (section 4.1). Since the output of the classifier is on the symbolic level, it has to be "translated" back to the sub-symbolic level as described in section 4.2.

4.1   The Neural VPL Classification System

The classifier is a trainable system based on neural networks which performs a mapping $x \to y, x \in \mathbb{R}^D, y \in \mathbb{R}^N$. In this case, the input dimension D is the number of pixels of the skin-segmented windows. The window vector x is mapped to a three-dimensional output $y \in \mathbb{R}^3$: Two of the output channels denote the class, one the pointing angle. The class is coded in the first two components in the form $(1, 0)$ for "pointing hand" and $(0, 1)$ for "other object", the third component is the continuous valued pointing angle. Classification of unknown windows x is carried out by taking the class k of the channel with maximal output: $k = \arg\max_{i=1,2}(y_i(x))$. Only in case of a "pointing hand" the angle y_3 is relevant.

Training is performed with hand labelled sample windows of the cropped pointing hand plus objects assigned to a rejection class. The rejection class contains other objects which are part of the scenario, e.g. the objects the user points at or parts of the background. In addition, hand postures other than pointing gestures are part of the rejection class, e.g. a fist. So the rejection class is not "universal" but reflects the scenario — a totally unknown object might be mistaken for a pointing hand.

The VPL classifier combines visual feature extraction and classification. It consists of three processing stages which perform a local principal component analysis (PCA) for dimension reduction followed by a classification by neural networks, see Fig. 4. Local PCA [22] can be viewed as a nonlinear extension of simple, global PCA [11]. "VPL" stands for the three stages: **V**ector quantisation, **P**CA and **L**LM-network. The vector quantisation is carried out on the raw

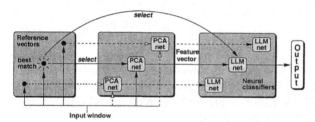

Fig. 4. The VPL classifier performs a local PCA for feature extraction and a subsequent neural classification.

image windows to provide a first data partitioning with N_V reference vectors $r_i \in \mathbb{R}^M, i = 1 \dots N_V$. For vector quantisation we use the Activity Equalisation Algorithm proposed in [8].

To each reference vector r_i a single layer feed forward network for the successive calculation of the principal components (PCs) as proposed by Sanger [19] is attached which projects the input x to the $N_P < D$ PCs with the largest eigenvalues: $x \to p_l(x) \in \mathbb{R}^{N_P}, l = 1 \dots N_V$. To each of the N_V different PCA-nets one "expert" neural classifier is attached which is of the Local Linear Map – type (LLM network), see e.g. [18] for details. It performs the final mapping $p_l(x) \to y \in \mathbb{R}^N$. The LLM network is related to the self-organising map [14] and the GRBF-approach [16]. It can be trained to approximate a nonlinear function by a set of locally valid linear mappings.

The three processing stages are trained successively, first vector quantisation and PCA-nets (unsupervised), finally the LLM nets (supervised). For classification of an input x first the best match reference vector $r_{n(x)}$ is found, then x is mapped to $p_{n(x)}(x)$ by the attached PCA-net and finally $p_{n(x)}(x)$ is mapped to y: $p_{n(x)}(x) \to y$.

The major advantage of the VPL classifier is its ability to form many highly specific feature detectors (the $N_V \cdot N_P$ local PCs), but needing to apply only $N_V + N_P - 1$ filter operations per classification. It has been successfully applied to several vision tasks (e.g. [7]), for an application in robotics see [9]. Especially, it could be shown that classification performance and generalisation properties are well-behaved when the main parameters are changed, which are N_V, N_P and the number of nodes in the LLM nets N_L.

4.2   Translation from Symbolic to Sub-symbolic Level

Skin colour segmentation and the VPL classifier yield the position of the hand (x_H, y_H) and the pointing direction α, respectively. Both these (symbolic) informations are translated to a manipulator map M_m and thus back to the sub-symbolic level. The manipulator map shows a "Gaussian cone" of width σ_c which determines the effective angle of beam spread

$$M_m(x,y) = \frac{1}{\sqrt{2\pi}\sigma_c} \exp\left(-\frac{(\arctan(\frac{y-y_H}{x-x_H}) - \alpha)^2}{\sigma_c^2}\right), \tag{12}$$

here in the form for the first quadrant for simplicity, see Fig. 3. The cone gives higher weight in the attention map to image regions in the pointing direction and thus "strengthens" salient points in this area.

To facilitate selection of objects on differing scales, σ_c is adjusted online according to the user behaviour. The pointing angles α and hand positions (x_H, y_H) are recorded over the last six frames. If they show large variance, it is assumed that the user moves the hand on large scale to select a big object, so also a large σ_c is chosen. In contrast, σ_c is reduced for small variance to establish a "virtual laser pointer" since it is assumed that the user tries to select a detail.

As an additional assistance for coarse / fine selection, the a priori weights ξ_i of (11) are changed such that the large scale entropy map M_E dominates for large pointing variance whereas the symmetry map M_{Sym} and the corner saliency M_{Harris} are weighted higher for detail selection.

5   Results

Figure 5 shows a typical result together with intermediate processing stages. The user has just slowed down the pointing movement, so the manipulator map shows a cone of medium width in the pointing direction, starting at the approximate position of the hand centre. Still, weighting of the entropy map is considerable, so the entire object (the power supply unit) stands out in the feature map, but as the user now holds still the smaller-scale features begin to shine through, especially the symmetry of the referenced button.

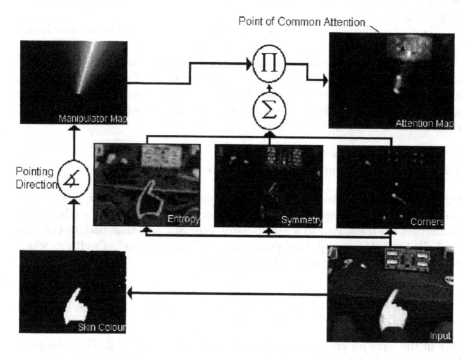

Fig. 5. Processing results for a pointing gesture towards an object. From the input image (bottom right) skin colour is segmented (bottom left), the VPL classifier calculates the angle which is transformed to a manipulator map (top left). The manipulator cone "illuminates" the object, the maxima of the feature maps stand out.

To evaluate the system performance we choose a setup which is based on a "generic" pointing task that can be easily reproduced: A proband has to point on a row of six white circles on a black board (Fig. 1, right). The diameter of each circle is 12 mm for distances between the circles from 3 to 20 cm (measured from the centre of the circles). To test performance for pointing to details, in an additional experiment circles of diameter 6 mm with a distance of 1.5 cm were used. The distance between the hand and the board is approximately 40 cm, so angular resolutions from 2° to 28° could be tested for targets of about 0.9° or 1.7° angular range, respectively. A supervisor gives the command to point at one of the circles by telling a randomly chosen circle number. We use only the inner four circles to avoid border effects. A match is counted if the system outputs a focus point on the correct circle within three seconds. The results of the experiment under two conditions are shown in Fig. 6. The left and right bars show the result of the condition *without feedback* and *full visual feedback* respectively. Under the condition *full visual feedback* the proband sees the calculated focus points on a screen while pointing. Here the match percentage is quite high even for small target distances, whereas the values decrease substantially under the *without feedback* condition at small distances. Surprisingly the number of matches with a target distance of 3 cm is higher than at 5 and 10 cm. The reason for this behaviour is that the probands tend to carry out more translatory movements of the hand and less changes of the pointing angle for smaller target distances, which leads in some cases for yet unknown reasons to more stable results.

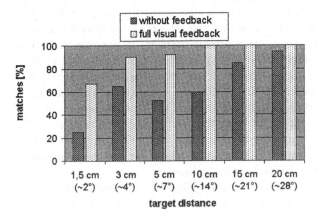

Fig. 6. The chart shows the results of the evaluation experiment. The values are averaged for three probands with 20 items each. On the x-axis the distances between the centres of the targets and the corresponding angles for a pointing distance of about 40 cm are shown.

The major result achieved in this test scenario is that system performance can be significantly increased by giving feedback because (*i*) the user is enabled to adjust single pointing gestures to a target and (*ii*) the user can adapt himself or herself to the system behaviour. This way the achievable *effective resolution* can be improved, because it does not solely rely on the accuracy of the pointing gesture recognition any more. Since the *full visual feedback* as used in the test scenario is rather unrealistic in natural settings, future work will focus on developing other feedback methods like auditory feedback or visual feedback using a head mounted display.

Still, the system has several limitations: The hand has to be completely visible, otherwise the centre of the skin-segmented blob shifts position so that the VPL classifier gets an unknown input. A "beep" is used as auditory feedback to the user if the hand is too close to the border. Another restriction is that the saliency operators do not yield maxima on all of the objects or not on the desired locations, in particular, edges of strong contrast indicating object boundaries are sometimes weighted higher than object centres.

6   Conclusion and Acknowledgement

We have presented a system for visual detection of object reference by hand gestures as a component of a mobile human-machine interface. Feature maps based on different context-free attentional mechanisms were integrated as adaptively weighted components of an attention map. Areas of high "interestingness" in the attention map serve to establish anticipations what the user might be pointing at. A neural classifier gives an estimate of the pointing direction which is integrated using a "manipulator cone" into the attention map.

The functionality of the presented system is not limited to the current scenario. Since arbitrary other saliency features like colour or movement can be integrated, the bottom-up focus of attention can be directed to a wide variety of objects. Even more important is the possibility to transform cues from other modules top-down to the sub-symbolic level. One of the first steps will be the integration of speech-driven cues to generate spatial large scale anticipations.

Still, precision and user independence are big problems in the area of gesture recognition. A major advantage of the new approach is that it does not require high recognition accuracy. This is achieved by the systems anticipation that only salient image points will be selected. In addition, the system offers the possibility to integrate feedback to the user, so in future work we hope to compensate for shortcomings of gesture recognition by using the flexibility of humans to adapt to the machine. In a further advanced version also the user will be enabled to give feedback ("I mean more to the left") in order to adapt the gesture recognition module to the individual user characteristics online.

This work was supported within the project VAMPIRE (Visual Active Memory Processes and Interactive REtrieval) which is part of the IST programme (IST-2001-34401).

References

1. G. Backer, B. Mertsching, and M. Bollmann. Data- and Model-Driven Gaze Control for an Active-Vision System. *IEEE Trans. on Pattern Analysis and Machine Intelligence*, 23(12):1415–1429, 2001.
2. C. Bauckhage, G. A. Fink, J. Fritsch, F. Kummert, F. Lömker, G. Sagerer, and S. Wachsmuth. An Integrated System for Cooperative Man-Machine Interaction. In *IEEE Int.'l Symp. on Comp. Intelligence in Robotics and Automation*, Banff, Canada, 2001.

3. V. Bruce and M. Morgan. Violations of Symmetry and Repetition in Visual Patterns. *Psychological Review*, 61:183–193, 1954.
4. D. Crevier and R. Lepage. Knowledge-based image understanding systems: A survey. *Computer Vision and Image Understanding*, 67(2):161–185, 1997.
5. M. Fislage, R. Rae, and H. Ritter. Using visual attention to recognize human pointing gestures in assembly tasks. In *7th IEEE Int'l Conf. Comp. Vision*, 1999.
6. C. Harris and M. Stephens. A Combined Corner and Edge Detector. In *Proc. 4th Alvey Vision Conf.*, pages 147–151, 1988.
7. G. Heidemann, D. Lücke, and H. Ritter. A System for Various Visual Classification Tasks Based on Neural Networks. In A. Sanfeliu et al., editor, *Proc. 15th Int'l Conf. on Pattern Recognition ICPR 2000, Barcelona*, volume I, pages 9–12, 2000.
8. G. Heidemann and H. Ritter. Efficient Vector Quantization Using the WTA-rule with Activity Equalization. *Neural Processing Letters*, 13(1):17–30, 2001.
9. G. Heidemann and H. Ritter. Visual Checking of Grasping Positions of a Three-Fingered Robot Hand. In G. Dorffner, H. Bischof, and K. Hornik, editors, *Proc. ICANN 2001*, pages 891–898. Springer-Verlag, 2001.
10. L. Itti, C. Koch, and E. Niebur. A Model of Saliency-Based Visual Attention for Rapid Scene Analysis. *IEEE Trans. on Pattern Analysis and Machine Intelligence*, 20(11):1254–1259, 1998.
11. I. Jolliffe. *Principal Component Analysis*. Springer Verlag, New York, 1986.
12. T. Kalinke and U. Handmann. Fusion of Texture and Contour Based Methods for Object Recognition. In *IEEE Conf. on Intelligent Transportation Systems 1997*, Stuttgart, 1997.
13. T. Kalinke and W. v. Seelen. Entropie als Maß des lokalen Informationsgehalts in Bildern zur Realisierung einer Aufmerksamkeitssteuerung. In B. Jähne et al., editor, *Mustererkennung 1996*. Springer, Heidelberg, 1996.
14. T. Kohonen. Self-organization and associative memory. In *Springer Series in Information Sciences 8*. Springer-Verlag Heidelberg, 1984.
15. P. J. Locher and C. F. Nodine. Symmetry Catches the Eye. In A. Levy-Schoen and J. K. O'Reagan, editors, *Eye Movements: From Physiology to Cognition*, pages 353–361. Elsevier Science Publishers B. V. (North Holland), 1987.
16. J. Moody and C. Darken. Learning with localized receptive fields. In *Proc. of the 1988 Connectionist Models Summer School*, pages 133–143. Morgan Kaufman Publishers, San Mateo, CA, 1988.
17. D. Reisfeld, H. Wolfson, and Y. Yeshurun. Context-Free Attentional Operators: The Generalized Symmetry Transform. *Int'l J. of Computer Vision*, 14:119–130, 1995.
18. H. J. Ritter, T. M. Martinetz, and K. J. Schulten. *Neuronale Netze*. Addison-Wesley, München, 1992.
19. T. D. Sanger. Optimal Unsupervised Learning in a Single-Layer Linear Feedforward Neural Network. *Neural Networks*, 2:459–473, 1989.
20. C. Schmid, R. Mohr, and C. Bauckhage. Evaluation of Interest Point Detectors. *Int'l J. of Computer Vision*, 37(2):151–172, 2000.
21. C. Theis, I. Iossifidis, and A. Steinhage. Image processing methods for interactive robot control. In *Proc. IEEE Roman International Workshop on Robot-Human Interactive Communication*, Bordeaux and Paris, France, 2001.
22. M. E. Tipping and C. M. Bishop. Mixtures of probabilistic principal component analyzers. *Neural Computation*, 11(2):443–482, 1999.
23. D. Walther, L. Itti, M. Riesenhuber, T. Poggio, and C. Koch. Attentional Selection for Object Recognition – a Gentle Way. In *Proc. 2nd Workshop on Biologically Motivated Computer Vision (BMCV'02)*, Tübingen, Germany, 2002.

Reflections on Cognitive Vision Systems

Hans-Hellmut Nagel

Institut für Algorithmen und Kognitive Systeme
Universität Karlsruhe (TH), 76128 Karlsruhe, Germany
nagel@IAKS.uni-karlsruhe.de

Abstract. A long list of buzzwords which percolated through the computer vision community during the past thirty years leads to the question: does 'Cognitive Vision Systems' just denote another such 'fleeting fad'? Upon closer inspection, many apparent 'buzzwords' refer to aspects of computer vision systems which became a legitimate target of widespread research interest due to methodological advances or improvements of computer technology. Following a period during which particular topics had been investigated intensively, associated results merged into the general pool of commonly accepted methods and tools, their preponderance faded and time appeared 'ripe again for the next buzzword'. Such a non-pejorative use of buzzword in the sense of 'focus of research attention' appears appropriate, too, for cognitive vision.

It will be argued that cognitive vision could be characterized by a systematic attempt to conceive and implement computer vision systems based on *multiple variably-connected, multi-scale consistency requirements* extending beyond the domain of signal and geometric processing into the domain of conceptual representations. This in turn necessitates that methods of formal logic will have to be incorporated into computer vision systems. As a consequence, knowledge has to be explicated in order to facilitate its exploitation in many different contexts.

Keywords: System aspects, consistency requirements, conceptual system levels, integration of geometric and conceptual aspects, integration of inference engines into vision

1 Introduction

Computer Vision (CV) as a field of scientific research has accumulated already a history of over fourty years. It should not come as a surprise, therefore, that during this period single topics dominated the discussion for a while to the extent that one could consider them to take on aspects of a 'fad', a slogan or a buzzword, for example: (i) blocksworld scenes, (ii) stereo vision, (iii) color, (iv) knowledge-based vision, (v) motion, (vi) shape-from-shading, (vii) active vision, (viii) 'parallel vision' (relying, e. g., on 'Thinking Machines' or other special purpose computers), (ix) trinocular camera set-ups, (x) real-time vision, (xi) self-calibration, (xii) mosaicking, (xiii) projective geometry for CV, (xiv) cue integration, (xv) CAD-based vision, (xvi) appearance-based vision, (xvii)

J.L. Crowley et al. (Eds.): ICVS 2003, LNCS 2626, pp. 34–43, 2003.

omnidirectional cameras. In addition to these, efforts devoted to CV based on Neural Networks or to 'CV and Machine Learning' had almost acquired 'cult status' for a while. It will be left to the reader to decide on suitable references regarding the examples enumerated above.

One may thus ask oneself whether 'Cognitive Vision' is just another such fleeting 'nouvel vogue' or not. At this point, it will pay to stop and ponder the ever reccurring attraction of slogans and buzzwords: they are used by (serious) politicians in order to gain sufficiently many supporters who enable them to realize their idea(s) about how things should be done in the future. In a democracy, politicians need a majority. They are forced to come up, therefore, with 'formulas' which are both 'new' to raise interest and are simultaneously 'immediately accepted' by sufficiently many people. The more vague a new slogan is, the more probable it is that a majority of people interpret it the way they like it – and thus initially support the new movement. After a while, most people associate particular politicians and experiences with a slogan which then begins to loose its 'drawing power'.

Some slogans thus serve a serious purpose, namely to help 'engineer a majority consensus' without which nothing of lasting impact or value is going to happen in a democracy. A successful slogan is likely, therefore, to comprise at least a 'grain of truth'.

2   The Many Facets of Cognitive Vision (CogV)

Rather than expanding on an endeavor to ridicule the parade of buzzwords related to CV, one may look at the above-mentioned list as cues to what CV 'really is' or to what people considered important at a certain period during the development of CV as a field. Most of these items refer to some aspect of CV research which had become technically and methodologically feasible at about the time the corresponding 'fad' gained support. Against such a background, the question is raised what in particular is characteristical for 'Cognitive Vision (CogV)'. In an attempt to circumscribe CogV, five subareas may be distinguished:

1. The *'interdisciplinary'* one, relating CogV to neurophysiology (see, e. g., [2]) or to psychology (see, e. g., [17]). If the lively discussion regarding 'Cognitive Sciences' is taken into account – see [16] – it is by no means evident that CogV can be defined simply as the 'vision part' of Cognitive Sciences.
2. The *'exploratory'* one, which selects a prominent vision-related capability and aims at realizing an artefact which performs at least as well as a human expert. Playing world-champion-class chess provides an illustrative example from AI: originally considered to be an impossibility in the eyes of some and a dream in those of others, this 'useless' goal has been achieved after more than a quarter of a century of intensive research [1]. Significant scientific progress has been realized as a by-product [13], for example regarding search methods – see [10] or [12].
3. The *'task-oriented'* one: this variant emphasizes the development of methods in order to solve a particular application task (rather than choosing some

application in order to develop a method, as in the preceding case). The development of advanced driver assistance systems (see, e. g., [18]) provides a good example.

4. The *'hybrid'* one, which combines different – already (partially) explored – approaches in order to realize improvements in handling potential applications in a more or less well circumscribed area. In this case, the tendency prevails to *define* CogV by a particular combination of 'methodological features', for example the requirement that it involves machine learning.

5. The *'method-oriented'* one, which emphasizes the development of precisely defined methodological steps, a detailed investigation of their interactions, and a discussion of comparative (dis-)advantages with respect to well-defined evaluation criteria.

Each one among these approaches can be justified – to a degree of satisfaction which rests in the eye of the beholder. Once the differences in emphasis are clearly understood, it does not make sense to 'canonize' one of the above-mentioned approaches – or an additional one – and to reject alternatives as 'not being Cognitive Vision'.

It appears attractive, though, to discuss current goals, achievements, shortcomings, and explicitly enumerable alternatives for *method-oriented* approaches towards CogV: the reason is simply that the better defined the challenge, the more precisely it is possible to arrive at a judgement whether or not the postulated goals have been achieved and which property of an approach may be responsible for a deficiency.

3 Text Generation from Video: A Sample CogV Approach

Subsequent discussions are based on the following hypothesis: a system *which transforms a video input stream into a textual description of the temporal developments in the recorded scene* constitutes an example for a cognitive vision system (for example, [11], [7], [6], [9], [3]). Most likely, such a system can be divided into at least four components, namely

1. a *signal-related* subsystem for camera control, video recording, and signal-processing operations;

2. a *geometry-oriented* subsystem for the estimation and update of a system-internal representation for 3D-scene geometry;

3. a *conceptual* subsystem which characterizes the scene, its components, their relation with respect to each other and to whatever is treated as 'background', and the temporal variation of properties and relations at a qualitative, conceptual – as opposed to a quantitative (geometrical) – level of representation;

4. a *linguistic* subsystem which converts a conceptual representation into a natural language text.

Provided the signal-related and geometry-oriented subsystems can be designed and implemented in sufficiently general versions – an expectation assumed to constitute an aim of CV – they could equally well serve as subsystems in a re-active vision-based robot. In case a robot should be endowed with greater autonomy, a planning component will become necessary. It is postulated that such planning constitutes a necessary component of any more broadly applicable conceptual subsystem: with other words, the first three subsystems enumerated above should be discernible, too, in vision-based (semi-)autonomous robot systems. Given the wide range of environmental conditions with which a truly (semi-)autonomous robot system should be able to cope, the mere problem to debug such a system efficiently will immediately recommend to endow it with some kind of natural-language-like (user) interface.

The above-mentioned example appears as a perfectly legitimate 'guinea pig' system to study the interaction between computer vision processes at a signal-, a geometry and a conceptual level of representation. As will be shown in subsequent sections, the explication of knowledge – introduced originally for a particular purpose – starts a development towards a *multiply-interconnected time-varying network of relations* whose exploitation brings along both challenging inference options and simultaneously considerable risks.

4   Consistency at a Geometric Representation Level

The developments hinted at in the preceding section will be illustrated with examples from the literature. These will first address geometric reasoning and later extend to conceptual reasoning.

4.1   Geometric Consistency in Single Vehicle Tracking

A simple case treats model-based tracking of a single vehicle – see, e. g., [15, 5]. Exploitation of explicit knowledge about the vehicle shape (represented internally by a polyhedron) and about the camera (pinhole, with internal and external calibration parameters known) allows already to remove self-occluded line segments at the intersection of two neighboring polyhedral facets. Adding the assumption that the vehicle moves along the road plane allows initially to restrict admissible changes from frame to frame, thereby increasing the success rate of model-based tracking. This simple starting case comprises consistency relations among a *triple* of 3D-scene objects, namely the camera, the vehicle, and the road plane.

4.2   Taking a *Given* Illumination Direction into Account

Experience has shown that shadows cast by a vehicle onto the road plane can lead to edges which frequently enough are stronger than data edges within the vehicle itself, resulting in mismatches where model edge segments are related to shadow edge segments. The obvious solution consists in modeling the shadow-casting process, too: this just requires two additional parameters, namely the direction of the incoming light. Such an extension of model-based tracking exploits already relations between a *quadruple* of 3D-entities: in addition to camera, vehicle, and road plane, a light source is included – albeit in the very simplified form of incoming parallel light.

Once this extension has been realized, one is likely to encounter situations where a large building casts a strong shadow onto the road. Since this shadow is assumed to remain more or less stationary while a vehicle passes, one may be tempted to treat such a configuration as irrelevant for tracking. The problem is, however, that the building may shadow the vehicle so that the vehicle no longer casts a shadow onto the road plane. If this condition remains undetected, the system may attempt to match synthetic shadow edge segments of the vehicle not to real shadow edge elements, but to other edge elements which happen to be around, for example from tram rails or lane markings. In order to exclude such a dangerous mismatch, the quadruple of camera, vehicle, road plane and source of illumination has to be extended into a *quintuple* by inclusion of the shadow-casting building. In addition, the road model may be extended by including the geometry of lane markings and tram rails, quickly catapulting the number of entities to be considered into the two-digit range.

4.3   Tracking *Multiple* Vehicles

As long as the system is restricted to track a single vehicle, one can concentrate on tuning the numerous parameters involved in such a 3D-model-based tracking process. If two vehicles have to be tracked simultaneously, additional complications arise: (i) one vehicle may occlude the other, and (ii) the shadow of a vehicle may be cast onto another vehicle and not onto the road plane, in which case the correct correspondence between edge elements extracted from an image frame and the image projection of the current 3D estimate of the vehicle configuration becomes much more complicated. Although treating such a quintuple of 3D enti-ties seems not to introduce additional methodological difficulties (computing the model projection into the image plane is a standard computer graphics problem under these conditions), a new problem pops up once the tracking of one vehicle begins to derail: it appears to be an open problem *how to decide algorithmically* which of the two vehicles is tracked incorrectly – possibly even both are.

4.4   Estimation of Current Illumination *Type*

The simple case of model-based tracking we started with may be pursued one twist further. As long as the image sequence to be evaluated is not too long and well known beforehand, one can determine prior to the start of the tracking pro-cess whether the recorded scene is illuminated diffusely (overcast sky) or directly (bright sunshine). If the system has to perform 'continuously', it will no longer be feasible to provide the required parameters (including the direction of the incoming light) interactively. In addition, the prevailing mode of scene illumina-tion may change within 5-10 frames, for example on a windy day with a partially clouded sky. The illumination mode thus has to be determined automatically in order to compute appropriate synthetic shadow edge segments (see, e. g., [8]).

One possibility to do this exploits the assumption that the road scene comprises a tall mast, perpendicular to the road plane, which casts a shadow onto the road plane. If one assumes that the camera parameters include its geographical latitude and longitude (nowadays feasible due to Global Positioning Systems), additional knowledge about the time when each frame was recorded enables the system to compute the expected shadow edge segments due to such a mast and to estimate their coverage by edge elements: if the synthetic shadow edge segments are well covered by edge elements extracted from the current image frame, the system concludes that the scene is currently illuminated by the sun and takes shadow edges due to sunlight into account for tracking vehicles. At this point, another selection of five entities are related to each other in a complex, non-local manner: camera, vehicle, road plane, illumination source, and a mast extending perpendicular from the road plane. Note that such a continuous estimation of the current illumination condition can be considered to constitute a 'learning process', although one might speak more appropriately about an adaptation process. 'Learning' may be appropriate, however, if the position of the mast in the scene is not given a-priori, but has to be estimated from an extended image sequence by looking for the characteristic 'sundial-like' shadow pattern wandering with time around the mast's base on the groundplane.

Again, like in the case of two vehicles being tracked simultaneously, the continuous automatic estimation of illumination conditions can have rather adverse effects. Consider a vehicle – for example a large truck or bus – which happens to drive across that part of the road where a shadow cast by the (now assumed to be known) mast is expected. Even if the sky is overcast, edge elements of such a large vehicle may accidentally match the expected shadow segments of the mast to a degree where the system decides in favor of 'directed illumination'. As a consequence, the system will attempt to match synthetic shadow segments due to vehicles to be tracked with edge elements extracted from the current image frame. Similarly to the case of a building shadowing a vehicle, non-existing vehicle shadow segments may be matched accidentally to other edge segments not related to the current vehicle pose – with potentially desastrous long-time consequences for the tracking process. During a *short* period of several frames, tracking will usually not be upset by an inappropriate illumination estimate. Such an effect can have more serious consequences, however, during critical phases like initialisation, partial occlusion, or insufficient contrast between vehicle and background image areas.

Note that a purely local test might not be able to detect the root cause for such trouble since the mast may be positioned within the field of view of the recording camera at the opposite corner to where the vehicle has to be tracked. One may now argue that the coverage of a hypothetical shadow boundary of a *single* mast by edge elements extracted from the current image frame will naturally result in a brittle decision procedure. A more robust approach should evaluate the edge element coverage of *several* potential shadow images. Incorrect accidental short-time illumination cues – for example caused by a long moving vehicle – could then be counteracted by evidence from the majority of other shadow sources.

Upon a moment's thought, one will realize two more basic weak points in this line of argumentation. First, masts are mostly positioned along roads and thus their shadows will fall onto the road plane where testing the coverage of shadow boundaries normally is straightforward. In case of congestions, however, the aforementioned erroneous coverage of mast shadows by edge elements is likely to affect possibly the shadows of the majority of masts taken into consideration. Another problem addresses the question how conflicting evidence from different illumination cues will have to be treated.

4.5   Transition from Numerical to Conceptual Consistency Tests

At this point, the – implicit – thrust of the preceding argumentation hopefully becomes plausible. Rather than attempting to combine ever more cues from different sources of evidence by numerical weighting or case-based branching for further processing, a more fundamental approach appears appropriate. It is suggested to convert the various pieces of evidence from a numerical into a conceptual representation and to *continue their evaluation on the basis of fuzzy or probabilistic reasoning*. Such an extension has to include *feedback* from the conceptual level of representation back to the geometrical one (see, e. g., [4])

This change in the manner how evidence is treated can be pushed even a step further in the case of taking the illumination into account. The coverage of hypothetical shadow boundaries should be evaluated separately for *all* bodies explicitly modelled in the scene in order to combine this evidence by reasoning processes into a decision about the currently prevailing type of illumination. Such an inference process offers two advantages. First, more sources of evidence can be evaluated, in the example of innercity road traffic used above evidence from (mast-like) *stationary* structures in the scene *and* evidence from *moving* vehicles to be tracked. In addition, it should become possible to incorporate more detailed reasoning steps in those cases which appear to contradict the principally supported hypothesis: could it be that conflicting evidence can be traced back to any one from a number of possible explanations such as a temporary occlusion of the normal background by another vehicle or the gradual coverage of a scene area by large area shadows cast, e. g., by trees or high-rise buildings? Once the decision has been made to incorporate a fuzzy or probabilistic inference engine into a computer vision system, many problems – nowadays buried in the code and treated by various ad-hoc approaches – should become amenable to a more transparent and principled treatment which should be open to logical tests regarding correctness and completeness.

5   Consistency at a Conceptual Representation Level

There is an additional reason to incorporate a logical inference engine and the associated conceptual representation of knowledge into a CogV-system. It is argued in the sequel that, quite apart from its necessity for the transformation of video data into a natural language text, *behaviour-related* evidence can be handled more easily at the conceptual than only at a geometrical level of representation.

Imagine a double-carriage road crossing another road at an innercity intersection. During rush-hours, both lanes are assumed to be occupied and traffic will proceed in Stop-and-Go manner. Many countries enforce a traffic regulation that a vehicle must not enter the intersection area proper unless the driver is sure to have space enough at the other side for leaving the intersection area immediately after having crossed it.

Suppose that a sport car A waits at such an intersection in front of 'Red' traffic lights on the right lane and a heavier vehicle B comes to a stop next to A on the left lane. The drivers of both these vehicles realize that the 'leaving arms' of the double-carriage road at the other side of the intersection are occupied by vehicles although there seems to be a bit more space on the left outgoing lane than on the right one. When the traffic lights switch to 'Green', the driver of car A accelerates strongly, switches lanes while crossing the intersection, and squeezes his small vehicle onto the barely sufficient space of the left outgoing lane. The driver of the heavier and thus slower vehicle B recognizes this maneuver in time to avoid entering the intersection and waits for his next chance.

From a geometrical point of view, the trajectory of vehicle A will be almost indistinguishable from the initial phases of a maneuver where vehicle A intends to *overtake* the vehicle in front of him *on the same lane at the other side* of the intersection. A simple behavioural modeling would likely predict such an overtaking maneuver and thus would not anticipate the sharp acceleration and immediately following deceleration phases described above. It is now assumed that a (semi-)advanced tracking system conditions tracking parameters according to the anticipated maneuver, with other words, the short-term frame-to-frame tracking process operating at the signal and geometric level of representation may depend on parameters chosen on the basis of 'longer term' behavioural predictions.

Regarding both aspects, the selection of appropriate tracking parameters and of an appropriate schema for the maneuver representation as a precondition for the formulation of adequate textual descriptions, it will be advantageous to categorize the initial phases of the behaviour observable in this example by taking more evidence into account than merely the initial part of the vehicle trajectory. Such a postulate, however, is likely to entail the evaluation of numerous potential maneuvers – which in turn is more easily performed at a conceptual than at a geometrical representation level. The reason is simply that a number of details have already been *abstracted away* during the transition from a geometrical towards a conceptual level of representation. In addition, experience supports the conclusion that the required inferences can be formulated more perspicuously at the conceptual representation level. In case one accepts the desirability to let a CogV-system communicate with its user predominantly on the basis of conceptual terms, such a representation has to be provided in any case and should be exploited, therefore, whenever it offers additional advantages.

Very preliminary experimental investigations in a similar direction can be found, e. g., in attempts to describe the accumulation and dissolution of traffic queues at intersections on the basis of video sequence evaluations [3].

6   Conclusions

In order to achieve a level of performance comparable to that of humans regarding scope and robustness, future CogV-systems will have to take more considerations into account than usually done so far. The resulting increase in system complexity practically enforces that more emphasis has to be devoted to structuring CogV-systems. To some extent, this may be achievable within a Bayesian framework at a signal and geometric level of representation – see, e. g., [14].

The preceding discussions follow a somewhat different road and argue in favor of the following postulate: robustness will be bought – at least partially – by incorporating numerous consistency checks. Their evaluation, in turn, will be eased considerably if knowledge can be represented, too, at a *conceptual level of representation* such that logic inference engines can access and exploit it. This should apply to both a-priori knowledge in the form of some schemata and to a-posteriori knowledge accumulated during the interpretation of such schematic a-priori knowledge on the basis of signal level and spatio-temporal geometric evidence extracted from video sequences.

This contribution thus *extends* the definition of a CogV-system by the *inclusion of logical inferences as a constitutive part of CogV*.

Referring back to the examples presented above, one may realize that two different types of consistency requirement have been used. The discussion of illumination estimation emphasized a rather large spatial scale, comprising potentially the entire field of view, whereas the temporal scale of the postulated spatial consistency has been restricted to a few frames. On the other hand, discussion of behaviour places more emphasis on a larger temporal scale, extending potentially throughout major parts of the entire sequence to be evaluated. It thus appears natural to generalize that, in the future, consistency will have to be established simultaneously across many spatio-temporal scales. This in turn will be facilitated by incorporating the required knowledge in a manner most appropriate for the particular consistency check. In case some of this knowledge has to be exploited in consistency checks related to different scales, a CogV-system should be able to *automatically* convert a given knowledge representation into the currently required one – as opposed to the alternative that the same knowledge is provided (implicitly) in several different forms which might be partially incomplete and possibly even partially contradictory.

Incorporation of an inference engine into a CogV-system could offer the additional advantage that the completeness and internal consistency of the current knowledge representation could be checked automatically by the CogV-system itself. At this point, another fundamental facet of such investigations will have to be taken into account: experimental systems with a scope comparable to that outlined above will necessarily be complicated and thus require a continuous effort of many people with diverse specializations. Automatic checks on the internal consistency of explicated knowledge thus is likely to further the cooperation of scientists in attempts to expand the scope of a CogV-system. Apart from this consideration, progress is likely to be realized incrementally because even a seemingly small improvement may have repercussions throughout the entire system which in many cases can not be implemented and checked out in a single attack by an isolated researcher.

References

1. M. Campbell, A.J. Hoane Jr., F.-H. Hsu: *Deep Blue*. AIJ **134** (2002) 57–83.
2. M. Gazzaniga (Ed.): *The Cognitive Neurosciences*. MIT Press: Cambridge 1995.
3. R. Gerber, H.–H. Nagel, and H. Schreiber: *Deriving Textual Descriptions of Road Traffic Queues from Video Sequences*. In: F. van Harmelen (Ed.): Proc. ECAI–2002, 21–26 July 2002, Lyon, France. IOS Press: Amsterdam 2002, pp. 736–740.
4. M. Haag und H.-H. Nagel: *'Begriffliche Rückkopplung' zur Behandlung von Verdeckungssituationen in der Bildfolgenauswertung von Straßenverkehrsszenen*. In J. Dassow, R. Kruse (Hrsg.), Informatik '98 – Informatik zwischen Bild und Sprache, Springer-Verlag Berlin·Heidelberg 1998, pp. 13–22 (in German).
5. M. Haag and H.-H. Nagel: *Combination of Edge Element and Optical Flow Estimates for 3D-Model-Based Vehicle Tracking in Traffic Image Sequences*. International Journal of Computer Vision **35**:3 (1999) 295–319.
6. R.J. Howarth and H. Buxton: *Conceptual Descriptions from Monitoring and Watching Image Sequences*. Image and Vision Computing **18**:2 (2000) 105–135.
7. St. Intille and A. Bobick: *Visual Recognition of Multi-Agent Action Using Binary Temporal Relations*. In Proc. IEEE Conf. Computer Vision and Pattern Recognition (CVPR'99), 23–25 June 1999, Fort Collins, Colorado, Vol. 1, pp. 56–62.
8. H. Leuck and H.-H. Nagel: *Model-Based Initialisation of Vehicle Tracking: Dependency on Illumination*. Proc. 8th Intern. Conf. Computer Vision, 9–12 July 2001, Vancouver/BC, Canada, Vol. I, pp. 309–314. IEEE CS: Los Alamitos/CA.
9. Z.-Q. Liu, L.T. Bruton, J.C. Bezdek, J.M. Keller, S. Dance, N.R. Bartley, and C. Zhang: *Dynamic Image Sequence Analysis Using Fuzzy Measures*. IEEE Trans. Systems, Man, and Cybernetics–Part B **31**:4 (2001) 557–572.
10. J. Pearl: *Heuristics: Intelligent Search Strategies for Computer Problem Solving*. Addison-Wesley Publ. Co.: Reading, MA 1984.
11. P. Remagnino, T. Tan, and K. Baker: *Agent Oriented Annotation in Model Based Visual Surveillance*. Sixth ICCV, 4–7 January 1998, Bombay, India, pp. 857–862.
12. S. Russell and P. Norvig: *Artificial Intelligence – A Modern Approach*. Prentice-Hall, Inc.: Upper Saddle River, NJ 1995.
13. J. Schaeffer and H. Jaap van den Herik: *Games, Computers, and Artificial Intelligence*. Artificial Intelligence Journal (AIJ) **134** (2002) 1–7.
14. M. Spengler and B. Schiele: *Multi-Object Tracking: Explicit Knowledge Representation and Implementation for Complexity Reduction*. Proc. Workshop on Cognitive Vision, 19–20 September 2002, Zurich, CH, pp. 9–16.
15. T.N. Tan, G.D. Sullivan, and K.D. Baker: *Model-Based Localisation and Recognition of Road Vehicles*. Intern. Journal of Computer Vision **27**:1 (1998) 5–25.
16. R.A. Wilson: *The Cognitive Sciences: A Comment on 6 Reviews of 'The MIT Encyclopedia of the Cognitive Sciences'*. Artif. Intelligence **130**:2 (2001) 223–229.
17. R.A. Wilson and F.C. Keil (Eds.): *The MIT Encyclopedia of the Cognitive Sciences*. The MIT Press: Cambridge, MA 1999.
18. *Proc. IEEE Intelligent Vehicles Symposium*, 18–20 June 2002, Versailles/France

Towards Ontology Based Cognitive Vision

Nicolas Maillot, Monique Thonnat, and Alain Boucher

INRIA Sophia Antipolis - Orion Team
2004 Route des lucioles - B.P. 93
06902 Sophia Antipolis, France
{nicolas.maillot, monique.thonnat, alain.boucher}@sophia.inria.fr
http://www.inria.fr/orion

Abstract. Building knowledge bases for knowledge-based vision systems is a difficult task. This paper aims at showing how an ontology composed of visual concepts can be used as a guide for describing objects from a specific domain of interest. One of the most important benefits of our approach is that the knowledge acquisition process guided by the ontology leads to a knowledge base closer to low-level vision. A visual concept ontology and a dedicated knowledge acquisition tool have been developed and are also presented. We propose a generic methodology that is not linked to any application domain. Nevertheless, an example shows how the knowledge acquisition model can be applied to the description of pollen grain images. The use of an ontology for image description is the first step towards a complete cognitive vision system that will involve a learning layer.

Keywords: cognitive vision, ontological engineering, knowledge-based vision systems.

1 Introduction

Many knowledge-based vision systems have been suggested in the past (SCHEMA [1], SIGMA [2], SYGAL and PROGAL [3]). They all need knowledge bases specifically designed for the application domain. As explained in [1], designing such bases is very time consuming. This task also needs multidisciplinary skills. Indeed, both domain knowledge and image processing techniques are involved in this process. Our goal is to acquire domain knowledge without requiring image processing skills. We propose to use a visual concept ontology to hide the low-level vision layer complexity and to guide the expert in the description of the objects of his/her domain.

We are planning to build a complete classification system that will use the resulting knowledge base. Please note that our approach is different from certain kinds of ontology-based image retrieval techniques [4] where a domain-dependent ontology is used to annotate images : retrieval is based on attached annotations and not on image analysis techniques.

This paper first details our proposed approach in section 2. Section 3 introduces the reader to ontological engineering. Section 4 is dedicated to the

J.L. Crowley et al. (Eds.): ICVS 2003, LNCS 2626, pp. 44–53, 2003.
© Springer-Verlag Berlin Heidelberg 2003

knowledge acquisition process we propose. Section 5 presents an ontology composed of three different types of visual concepts : spatio-temporal, texture and colour related concepts. Section 6 shows how the proposed ontology can be used for describing objects from a specific domain. Finally, section 7 details the features of the specific knowledge acquisition tool we have developed and used for the description of several pollen grains types.

2   Proposed Approach

As described in [2], several types of knowledge can be identified in knowledge-based vision systems (Fig. 1) : (1) domain knowledge, (2) knowledge about the mapping between the scene and the image, (3) image processing knowledge.

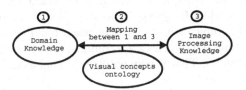

Fig. 1. Knowledge Overview

Our work is focused on the mapping betwen domain knowledge and image processing knowledge. Extracting domain knowledge means producing a hierarchical structure of domain concepts associated with their subparts (Fig. 2). This knowledge belongs to the domain of interest and is shared by the specialists of the domain. It is important to note that domain knowledge is independant of any vision layer and can be reused for other purposes. In our approach, the mapping between the scene and the image is done during a separate step and leans on a visual concept ontology. This ontology is used as a guide which provides a simple vocabulary used to give the visual description of domain concepts.

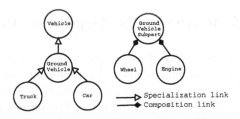

Fig. 2. Domain Knowledge Structure

3   Ontological Engineering

Tom Gruber gives a **definition** of the notion of ontology in [5] : "An ontology is an explicit specification of a conceptualization".

As explained by B. Bachimont (see [6]), the aim of ontologies is to define which primitives, provided with their associated semantics, are necessary for knowledge representation in a given context.

An ontology is composed of the set of objects that can be represented and also of relations between objects. It is important to notice that a semantic must be given to the ontology. This can be achieved by specifying axioms. An exhaustive list of axioms is given in [6]. They can be related to reflexivity, symmetry or transitivity of relations.

To be efficient, communication between people and software systems must rely on a shared understanding. As explained in [6], lack of shared understanding leads to difficulties in identifying requirements and to limited inter-operability or reusability. These problems are often met when building or interacting with computer vision systems. Ontologies are a common base to build on and a shared reference to align with [6]. That is why ontological engineering can be useful for our community.

A relevant example of ambiguity was given by Gómez-Pérez during a talk at ECAI98 [6]. What should be answered to the question "What is a pipe?". There are several possible answers: a short narrow tube with a small container at one end, used for smoking tobacco; a long tube made of plastic or metal that is used to carry water or oil or gas; a temporary section of computer memory that can link two different computer processes.

Ontological engineering is based on a consensus that avoids ambiguous situations. As explained in [7], ontology development process has to be done in four distinct phases. The first one is called specification and states why the ontology is built and who are the end-users. The next phase is conceptualization and leads to a structured domain knowledge. Then comes the formalization phase that transforms the conceptual model into a formal model. Finally, implementation transforms the formal model into a computational model. This methodology has been used to obtain the visual concept ontology presented in section 5.

4   Overview of the Knowledge Acquisition Process

As described in Fig. 3, the proposed knowledge acquisition process leans on the visual concept ontology. The expert starts by producing domain knowledge[1]. Then comes the visual concept ontology-driven description phase. This means that the expert uses the vocabulary provided by the ontology to describe the objects of the domain. This task is performed in a user-friendly way with a graphical user interface. The result of the description phase is a knowledge base composed of the visual concepts provided by the ontology associated with domain

---

[1] Structured as a hierarchy of domain concepts with their subparts

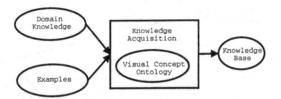

Fig. 3. Knowledge Acquisition Process

concepts. For example, the visual concept "Circular surface" provided by the ontology can be used to describe the shape of a domain object.

Our final goal is to build a classification system that will make a relevant use of examples associated with domain concepts. That is why domain objects examples are also provided. Once again, a user interface is used to provide these examples.

5   An Ontology for Computer Vision

5.1   Motivations

We believe that the creation of a standardized ontology for computer vision would be a great step forward and would ease interoperability between vision systems. In this section, we propose a prototype of an ontology for computer vision. We did not intend to build an exhaustive ontology. Our goal is to give an overview of a methodology based on a visual concept ontology. Due to the limited number of pages of this paper, some parts of the ontology are not presented. It is important to note that this ontology is not application-dependent.

We have structured this ontology in three main parts. The first one contains spatio-temporal related concepts, the second one contains texture related concepts and the last one is made of colorimetric concepts. Each part of this ontology is going to be detailed in the next sections.

5.2   Spatio-Temporal Concepts

This part of the ontology is used for describing domain objects from a spatio-temporal point of view. For example, a part of the hierarchy is composed of geometric concepts that can be used to describe the shape of domain objects (Fig. 4). A justification of an approach based on geometric shapes can be found in [8]. The size of an object can also be described and quantified with a set of quantifiers. Note that quantification can be done in an absolute way or relatively to another concept. This means that size of object A can be described as being important relatively to object B. The notion of elongation is also present and can be quantified. We have also added a set of spatial relations based on the RCC-8 model [9] that can be used to define relations between objects and their subparts. Temporal relations have not yet been introduced in the ontology.

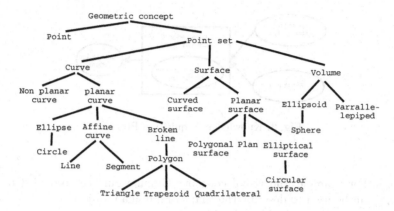

Fig. 4. Geometric Concepts

5.3 Texture Concepts

This part of the ontology has been inspired by [10] which is the result of two experiments. The first one is on the categorization of texture words in order to identify the underlying dimensions used to categorize texture words. The second part of the experiment measures the strength of association between words and texture images. The resulting hierarchy is given in Fig. 5. A very interesting aspect of this study is that hundreds of synonyms have been gathered in association with texture notions. This rich terminology gives expressivness to the knowledge acquisition system we propose. Once again, several texture concepts can be quantified : the quantifier "important" can be used in association with the "granulated texture" concept.

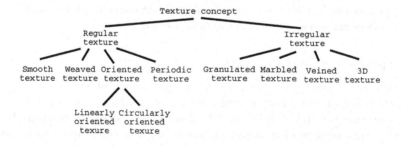

Fig. 5. Texture Concepts

5.4   Colour Concepts

This part of the ontology allows the description of objects from the following points of view : luminosity, hue, transparency. These concepts can be quantified to allow a more precise description. For example, the quantifier "important" can be used to quantify colorimetric concept "dark".

5.5   Link with the Low-Level Vision Layer

The previous subsections have quickly introduced the reader to the structure of a proposed visual concept ontology. The knowledge base resulting from our knowledge acquisition process is for classification purposes. During the classification of a given object, numerical descriptors are computed. To be interpreted as visual concepts, a link must be established between computed numerical descriptors and symbolic visual concepts. Currently the link between symbolic visual concepts and numerical descriptors is statically defined. For example, the ratio *length/height* computed for a region is used to characterize the "elongation" visual concept.

There is not a unique way to associate a visual concept with a set of numerical descriptors. That is why we are planning to introduce a descriptor selection layer that chooses the most discriminative descriptors for a given application domain. Examples of numerical descriptors for texture discrimination are statistical moments or descriptors obtained with gabor filtering. Colour characterization can be done with numerical entities like histograms, colour coherence vectors or auto-correlograms.

5.6   Context Description

Experts often observe the objects of their domain in precise observation conditions. For example, when using a microscope, magnification or lighting conditions are controled. This kind of information must be given because it is linked to the way objects are described. Context knowledge is necessary to build coherent sets of examples. Context depends on the application domain. That is why context hierarchy given in Fig. 6 can be extended for a particular domain.

6   Knowledge Representation

In the previous section, we have made a conceptualization of a specific domain knowledge. The result of the conceptualization process is an abstract object. Before obtaining an operational entity, a formalism has to be chosen. This is called the formalization process which implies the choice of a representation formalism. Different kinds of representation formalisms are enumerated in [11]. Commonly used techniques are formal logics, fuzzy logics, frames or semantic nets. We wanted an expressive and powerful formalism. Several reasons exposed

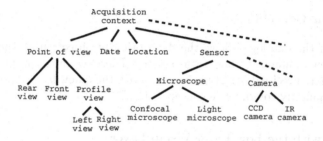

Fig. 6. Context Concepts

in [12] lead us to description logics (DL). DL is the family name of object-based knowledge representation formalisms which provide formal semantics for semantic nets and the logical fundations for inferences.

A concept of the domain is described through four relations : *hasForSpatioTemporalDescription, hasForTexturalDecription, hasForColorimetricDescription* and *hasForDescriptionContext*.

Description logics are used to structure the description information:

$$C_i \equiv C_j \sqcap (\exists \, "hasForSpatioTemporalDesc" . C_{SpatioTemporal_i})$$

$$\sqcap (\exists \, "hasForTextureDesc" . C_{Texture_i})$$

$$\sqcap (\exists \, "hasForColorimetricDesc" . C_{Colour_i})$$

$$\sqcap (\exists \, "hasForDescContext" . C_{Context_i}) \sqcap (\exists \, "isASubpartOf" . C_k)$$

This means that C_i is a subconcept of C_j and a subpart of C_k. Relations *hasForSpatioTemporalDescription, hasForTexturalDescription, hasForColorimetricDescription, hasForDescriptionContext* are respectively restricted to concepts $C_{SpatioTemporal_i}$, $C_{Texture_i}$, C_{Colour_i}, $C_{Context_i}$. The powerful expressivness of description logics allows to define $C_{SpatioTemporal_i}$, $C_{Texture_i}$, C_{Colour_i}, $C_{Context_i}$ as unions or intersections of concepts provided by the visual concept ontology.

7   A Knowledge Acquisition Tool for Image Description

7.1   Overview

Section 5 contains details about the structure of a visual concept ontology. To be used as a guide for the description of domain concepts, a dedicated graphical tool has been developed. This tool is currently able to carry out three distinct tasks : domain knowledge definition; visual concept ontology-driven symbolic description of concepts and their subparts; examples management.

The output result of the acquisition process is a knowledge base composed of domain concepts described by some visual concepts provided by the ontology.

The formalism used to structure the resulting knowledge is based on description logics. The Java platform has been used to create this tool. The knowledge layer leans on DAML+OIL[2], an ontology language based on the formal rigor of description logics.

7.2   Tool Characteristics

Our tool allows domain knowledge creation. As can be seen in Fig. 7, domain knowledge is organized as a taxonomy of domain concepts in a specialization tree. This approach is natural for people who are familiar with a taxonomic approach (Ex.: biologists). Whenever a concept is added to the tree, the visual concept ontology is displayed on the screen. The user is then able to describe a new concept with the terminology contained in the ontology. As it was previously explained, a concept can be composed of subparts (*isASubpartOf* relation).

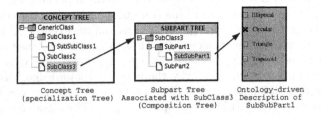

Concept Tree   Subpart Tree   Ontology-driven
(specialization Tree) Associated with SubClass3 Description of
                          (Composition Tree)   SubSubPart1

Fig. 7. Description of subpart "SubSubPart1" of Concept "SubClass3"

Subparts description is performed in the same way as the description of domain concepts. Note that the subpart tree is a composition tree and not a specialization tree. Every domain concept has an associated subpart tree.

Another important characteristic of our tool is the example management module which allows to provide examples of the visual concepts used during the description phase. First of all, a set of examples has to be chosen. Then, a region of interest is selected (with a drawing tool) and used to compute the required numerical descriptors. Fig. 8 describes how an example of the subpart Pori[3] is provided. Since the Pori subpart is described as being circular, the computation of a form factor on this particular image gives an example of what is the notion of circularity in this particular application domain.

7.3   Results

Automatic pollen grains classification is useful for clinicians so as to provide near real time accurate information on aeroallergens and air quality to the sensitive

---

[2] DAML+OIL belongs to the family of XML languages
[3] A subpart of certain pollen grains

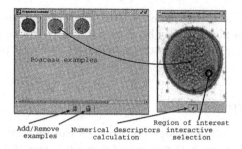

Fig. 8. An example of Poaceae's Subpart "Pori" Provided by Interactive Selection of a Region of Interest

users. Our tool is currently used as a help for communicating with experts in palynology. This tool is useful to guide the description of pollen grains in a user-friendly and efficient manner. The visual concepts contained in the ontology can be seen as a communication language between us and the experts. Although sets of numerical descriptors are associated with visual concepts, they are hidden to the expert : when choosing a visual concept, the expert implicitly chooses a set of numerical descriptors. This why the generated knowledge base is closer to low-level vision. 350 images of 30 different types of pollen grains have been acquired during the A.S.T.H.M.A[4] european project. This database is useful to give examples of the visual concepts used to describe these pollen grains.

A possible example could be the symbolic description of the specific pollen grain type *Poaceae*[5] (Fig. 8). This concept can be described as a subconcept of *Pollen with apertures*. It is described as an **elliptical or circular surface**[6]. The **size** of this pollen type is quantified with the following quantifiers : **small**, **average** or **important**. Palynogists use the concept **granulated texture** to describe Poaceae's texture. The colorimetric concept **dark** is used to describe the subpart *Pori*. Finally comes acquisition context : In this case, a **light microscope** is used to acquire pollen images.

8   Conclusion and Future Work

We have proposed an original approach to the creation of knowledge-based vision systems. The notion of visual concept ontology has been introduced. Its structure is based on three distinct notions : spatio-temporal, texture, colour concepts. The description is contextualized by a set of context concepts. This ontology can be used as a guide for describing the objects from a specific domain. We are planning to extend the ontology : our efforts are now focused on creating an ontology that will allow the definition of improved spatio-temporal relations. We aim at applying this future ontology to the description of video content.

---

[4] http://www-sop.inria.fr/orion/ASTHMA/
[5] Italic terms are provided by the expert
[6] Bold terms are provided by the ontology

Another important aspect of the model we propose is the examples database. In the future, this database will feed a supervised learning process of the symbolic visual concepts. Different kinds of texture in the provided examples will allow to learn the difference between a granulated texture and a smooth texture. The remaining step is the generation of a complete classification system which should make heavy use of the resulting learned concepts.

A difficult remaining problem is the segmentation process. Indeed, in order to be classified, images have to be segmented to allow descriptor computation. The symbolic description made by the expert may help finding the image processing tasks required for extracting the pertinent information from the provided images. As an example, an object described with the "granulated texture" concept may be segmented with a texture based segmentation algorithm. The regions of interest selected by the expert (see Fig. 8) should be used to validate the resulting segmentation.

References

1. Draper, B., Hanson, A., Riseman, E.: Knowledge-directed vision: control, learning and integration. In: Proc. of IEEE. Volume 84. (1996) 1625–1681
2. Matsuyama, T., Hwang, V.S.: SIGMA - A Knowledge-Based Aerial Image Understanding System. Plenum Press New York USA (1990)
3. Thonnat, M., Bijaoui., A.: Knowledge-based galaxy classification systems. Knowledge-based systems in astronomy, Lecture Notes in Physics. **329** (1989)
4. Soo, V.W., Lee, C.Y., Yeh, J.J., chih Chen, C.: Using sharable ontology to retrieve historical images. In: Proceeding of the second ACM/IEEE-CS joint conference on Digital libraries, ACM Press (2002) 197–198
5. Gruber, T.R.: Towards Principles for the Design of Ontologies Used for Knowledge Sharing. In Guarino, N., Poli, R., eds.: Formal Ontology in Conceptual Analysis and Knowledge Representation, Deventer, The Netherlands, Kluwer Academic Publishers (1993)
6. Gandon, F.: Ontology engineering: A survey and a return on experience. Technical Report 4396, INRIA (2002) `http://www.inria.fr/rrrt/rr-4396.html`.
7. Blazquez, M., Fernandez, M., Garcia-Pinar, J., Gómez-Pérez, A.: Building ontologies at the knowledge level using the ontology design environment. In: KAW98. (1998)
8. Sciascio, E., M.Donini, F., Mongiello., M.: Structured knowledge representation for image retrieval. Journal of Artificial Intelligence Research **16** (2002) 209–257
9. Cohn, A.G., Hazarika, S.M.: Qualitative spatial representation and reasoning: An overview. Fundamenta Informaticae **46** (2001) 1–29
10. Bhushan, N., Rao, A., Lohse, G.: The texture lexicon: Understanding the categorization of visual texture terms and their relationship to texture images. Cognitive Science **21** (1997) 219–246
11. Crevier, D., R.Lepage: Knowledge-based image understanding systems: A survey. Computer Vision and Image Understanding **67** (1997) 161–185
12. Moller, R., Neumann, B., Wessel, M.: Towards computer vision with description logics: some recent progress. In: Proc. Integration of Speech and Image Understanding. (1999)

A Self-Referential Perceptual Inference Framework for Video Interpretation

Christopher Town[1] and David Sinclair[2]

[1] University of Cambridge Computer Laboratory, 15 JJ Thomson Avenue,
Cambridge CB3 0FD, UK cpt23@cam.ac.uk
[2] Waimara Ltd, 115 Ditton Walk, Cambridge UK das@waiamara.com

Abstract. This paper presents an extensible architectural model for general content-based analysis and indexing of video data which can be customised for a given problem domain. Video interpretation is approached as a joint inference problems which can be solved through the use of modern machine learning and probabilistic inference techniques. An important aspect of the work concerns the use of a novel active knowledge representation methodology based on an ontological query language. This representation allows one to pose the problem of video analysis in terms of queries expressed in a visual language incorporating prior hierarchical knowledge of the syntactic and semantic structure of entities, relationships, and events of interest occurring in a video sequence. Perceptual inference then takes place within an ontological domain defined by the structure of the problem and the current goal set.

1 Introduction

The content-based analysis of digital video footage requires methods which will automatically segment video sequences and key frames into image areas corresponding to salient objects (e.g. people, vehicles, background objects, etc.), track these objects in time, and provide a flexible framework for further analysis of their relative motion and interactions.

We argue that these goals are achievable by following the trend in Computer Vision research to depart from strict "bottom-up" or "top-down" hierarchical paradigms and instead place greater emphasis on the mutual interaction between different levels of representation. Moreover, it is argued that an extensible framework for general robust video object segmentation and tracking is best attained by pursuing an inherently flexible "self-referential" approach. Such a system embodies an explicit representation of its own internal state (different sources of knowledge about a video scene) and goals (finding the object-level interpretation which is most likely given this knowledge and the demands of a particular application). The resulting framework can be customised to a particular problem (e.g. tracking human beings from CCTV footage) by integrating the most appropriate low-level (e.g. facial feature extraction) and high-level (e.g. models of human motion) sources of domain-specific knowledge. The system can then be regarded as combining this information at a meta-level to arrive at the most

J.L. Crowley et al. (Eds.): ICVS 2003, LNCS 2626, pp. 54–67, 2003.

likely interpretation (e.g. labelling a block of moving image regions as representing a human body) of the video data given the available information, possibly undergoing several cycles of analysis-integration-conclusion in the process.

In order to make meaningful inferences during this iterative fusion of different sources of knowledge and levels of feature extraction/representation, it is necessary to place such a methodology within the sound theoretical framework afforded by modern probabilistic inference techniques such as the adaptive Bayesian graphical methods known as Dynamic Belief networks. Dynamic Belief networks are particularly suitable because they model the evolution and integration of stochastic state information over time and can be viewed as generalisations of a broad family of probabilistic models.

A key part of the proposed approach concerns the notion that many tasks in computer vision are closely related to, and may be addressed in terms of, operations in language processing. In both cases one ultimately seeks to find symbolic representations which can serve as meaningful interpretations of underlying signal data. Such an analysis needs to incorporate a notion of the syntax and semantics which are seen as governing the domain of interest so that the most likely explanation of the observed data can be found. Whereas speech and language processing techniques are concerned with the analysis of sound patterns, phonemes, words, sentences, and dialogues, video analysis is confronted with pixels, video frames, primitive features, regions, objects, motions, and events. An important difference [32] between the two arises from the fact that visual information is inherently more ambiguous and semantically impoverished. There consequently exists a wide semantic gap between human interpretations of image information and that currently derivable by means of a computer.

We argue that this gap can be narrowed for a particular application domain by means of an ontological language which encompasses a hierarchical representation of task-specific attributes, objects, relations, temporal events, etc., and relates these to the processing modules available for their detection and recognition from the underlying medium. Words in the language therefore carry meaning directly related to the appearance of real world objects. Visual inference tasks can then be carried out by processing sentence structures in an appropriate ontological language. Such sentences are not purely symbolic since they retain a linkage between the symbol and signal levels. They can therefore serve as a computational vehicle for active knowledge representation which permits incremental refinement of alternate hypotheses through the fusion of multiple sources of information and goal-directed feedback to facilitate disambiguation in a context specified by the current set of ontological statements. Particular parts of the ontological language model may be implemented as Dynamic Belief networks, stochastic grammar parsers, or neural networks, but the overall frameworks need not be tied to a particular formalism such as the propagation of conditional probability densities. Later sections will discuss these issues further in light of related work and ongoing research efforts.

2   Related Work

2.1   Visual Recognition as Perceptual Inference

An increasing number of research efforts in medium and high level video analysis
can be viewed as following the emerging trend that object recognition and the
recognition of temporal events are best approached in terms of generalised language processing which attempts a machine translation [14] from information in
the visual domain to symbols and strings composed of predicates, objects, and
relations. The general idea is that recognising an object or event requires one to
relate ill-defined symbolic representations of concepts to concrete instances of the
referenced object or behaviour pattern. This is best approached in a hierarchical
manner by associating individual parts at each level of the hierarchy according
to rules governing which configurations of the underlying primitives give rise to
meaningful patterns at the higher semantic level. Many state-of-the-art recognition systems therefore explicitly or implicitly employ a probabilistic grammar
which defines the syntactic rules which can be used to recognise compound objects or events based on the detection of individual components corresponding
to detected features in time and space. Recognition then amounts to parsing a
stream of basic symbols according to prior probabilities to find the most likely
interpretation of the observed data in light of the top-level starting symbols in
order to establish correspondence between numerical and symbolic descriptions
of information. This idea has a relatively long heritage in syntactic approaches
to pattern recognition [39,4] but interest has been revived recently in the video
analysis community following the popularity and success of probabilistic methods such as Hidden Markov models (HMM) and related approaches adopted
from the speech and language processing community.

While this approach has shown great promise for applications ranging from
image retrieval to face detection to visual surveillance, a number of problems
remain to be solved. The nature of visual information poses hard challenges
which hinder the extent to which mechanisms such as Hidden Markov models
and stochastic parsing techniques popular in the speech and language processing community can be applied to information extraction from images and video.
Consequently there remains some lack of understanding as to which mechanisms
are most suitable for representing and utilising the syntactic and semantic structure of visual information and how such frameworks can best be instantiated.
The role of machine learning in computer vision continues to grow and recently
there has been a very strong trend towards using Bayesian techniques for learning and inference, especially factorised graphical probabilistic models [23] such as
Dynamic Belief networks (DBN). While finding the right structural assumptions
and prior probability distributions needed to instantiate such models requires
some domain specific insights, Bayesian graphs generally offer greater conceptual transparency than e.g. neural network models since the underlying causal
links and prior beliefs are made more explicit. The recent development of various approximation schemes based on iterative parameter variation or stochastic
sampling for inference and learning have allowed researchers to construct proba-

bilistic models of sufficient size to integrate multiple sources of information and model complex multi-modal state distributions. Recognition can then be posed as a joint inference problem relying on the integration of multiple (weak) clues to disambiguate and combine evidence in the most suitable context as defined by the top level model structure.

One of the earlier examples of using Dynamic Belief networks (DBN) for visual surveillance appears in [5]. DBNs offer many advantages for tracking tasks such as incorporation of prior knowledge and good modelling ability to represent the dynamic dependencies between parameters involved in a visual interpretation. Their application to multi-modal and data fusion [38] can utilise fusion strategies of e.g. Kalman [10] and particle filtering [20] methods. As illustrated by [11] and [33], concurrent probabilistic integration of multiple complementary and redundant cues can greatly increase the robustness of multi-hypothesis tracking.

In [29] tracking of a person's head and hands is performed using a Bayesian Belief network which deduces the body part positions by fusing colour, motion and coarse intensity measurements with context dependent semantics. Later work by the same authors [30] again shows how multiple sources of evidence (split into necessary and contingent modalities) for object position and identity can be fused in a continuous Bayesian framework together with an observation exclusion mechanism. An approach to visual tracking based on co-inference of multiple modalities is also presented in [41] which describes an sequential Monte Carlo approach to co-infer target object colour, shape, and position. In [7] a joint probability data association filter (JPDAF) is used to compute the HMM's transition probabilities by taking into account correlations between temporally and spatially related measurements.

2.2 Recognition of Actions and Structured Events

Over the last 15 years there has been growing interest within the computer vision and machine learning communities in the problem of analysing human behaviour in video. Such systems typically consist of a low or mid level computer vision system to detect and segment a human being or object of interest, and a higher level interpretation module that classifies motions into atomic behaviours such as hand gestures or vehicle manoeuvres. Higher-level visual analysis of compound events has in recent years been performed on the basis of parsing techniques using a probabilistic grammar formalism. Such methods are capable of recognising fairly complicated behavioural patterns although they remain limited to fairly circumscribed scenarios such as sport events [18,19], small area surveillance [36, 26], and game playing [25]. Earlier work on video recognition such as [40] and [15] already illustrated the power of using a context dependent semantic hierarchy to guide focus of attention and combination of plausible hypothesis, but lacked a robust way of integrating multiple sources of information in a probabilistically sound way.

The role of attentional control for video analysis was also pointed out in [6]. The system described there performs selective processing in response to user queries for two cellular imaging applications. This gives the system a goal directed attentional control mechanism since the most appropriate visual analysis routines are performed in order to process the user query. Selective visual processing on the basis of Bayes nets and decision theory has also been demonstrated in control tasks for active vision systems [28]. Knowledge representation using Bayesian networks and sequential decision making on the basis of expected cost and utility allow selective vision systems to take advantage of prior knowledge of a domain's cognitive and geometrical structure and the expected performance and cost of visual operators. An interesting two-level approach to parsing actions and events in video is described in [21]. HMMs are used to detect candidate low-level temporal features which are then parsed using a SCFG parsing scheme which adds disambiguation and robustness to the stream of detected atomic symbols. A similar approach is taken by [25] which uses the Earley-Stolcke parsing algorithm for stochastic context-free grammars to determine the most likely semantic derivation for recognition of complex multi-tasked activities from a given video scenario. A method for recognising complex multi-agent action is presented in [19]. Belief networks are again used to probabilistically represent and infer the goals of individual agents and integrate these in time from visual evidence. Bayesian techniques for integrating bottom-up information with top-down feedback have also been applied to challenging tasks involving the recognition of interactions between people in surveillance footage [26]. [24] presents an ontology of actions represented as states and state transitions hierarchically organised from most general to most specific (atomic).

3 Proposed Approach and Methodology

3.1 Overview

We propose a cognitive architectural model for video interpretation. It is based on a self-referential (the system maintains an internal representation of its goals and current hypotheses) probabilistic model for multi-modal integration of evidence (e.g. motion estimators, edge trackers, region classifiers, face detectors, shape models, perceptual grouping operators) and context-dependent inference given a set of representational or derivational goals (e.g. recording movements of people in a surveillance application). The system is capable of maintaining multiple hypotheses at different levels of semantic granularity and can generate an consistent interpretation by evaluating a query expressed in an ontological language. This language gives a probabilistic hierarchical representation incorporating domain specific syntactic and semantic constraints to enable robust analysis of video sequences from a visual language specification tailored to a particular application and for the set of available component modules.

From an Artificial Intelligence point of view this might be regarded as an approach to the *symbol grounding problem* [16] (sentences in the ontological language have an explicit foundation of evidence in the feature domain, so there is a way of bridging the semantic gap between the signal and symbol level) and *frame problem* [12] (there is no need to exhaustively label everything that is going on, one only needs to consider the subset of the state space required to make a decision given a query which implicitly narrows down the focus of attention).

The nature of such queries will be task specific. They may either be explicitly stated by the user (e.g. in a video retrieval task) or implicitly derived from some notion of the system's goals. For example, a surveillance task may require the system to register the presence of people who enter a scene, track their movements, and trigger an event if they are seen to behave in a manner deemed "suspicious" such as lingering within the camera's field of view or repeatedly returning to the scene over a short time scale. Internally the system could perform these functions by generating and processing queries of the kind "does the observed region movement correspond to a person entering the scene?", "has a person of similar appearance been observed recently?", or "is the person emerging from behind the occluding background object the same person who could no longer be tracked a short while ago?". These queries would be phrased in a language which relates them to the corresponding feature extraction modules (e.g. a Dynamic Belief network for fusing various cues to track people-shaped objects) and internal descriptions (e.g. a log of events relating to people entering or leaving the scene at certain locations and times, along with parameterised models of their visual appearance). Formulating and refining interpretations then amounts to selectively parsing such queries.

3.2 Recognition and Classification

The notion of image and video interpretation relative to the goal of satisfying a structured user query (which may be explicit or implicitly derived from a more general specification of system objectives) follows the trend in recent approaches to robust object recognition on the basis of a "union of weak classifiers". Such an approach hierarchically integrates trained parts-based relationships between lower level feature classifiers to recognise composite objects. Salient perceptual groupings of image features are detected as *non-accidental* image structure identified by means of a particular set of predicates over lower-level image properties (e.g. texture, shape, colour). Making such methods robust, scalable, and generally applicable has proven a major problem.

We argue that in order to come closer to capturing the semantic "essence" of an image or sequence, tasks such as feature grouping and object identification need to be approached in an adaptive goal oriented manner. This takes into account that criteria for what constitutes non-accidental and perceptually significant visual properties necessarily depend on the objectives and prior knowledge of the observer. Such criteria can be ranked in a hierarchy and further divided into those which are *necessary* for the object or action to be recognised and those which are merely *contingent*. Such a ranking makes it possible to quickly eliminate highly improbable or irrelevant configurations and narrow down the search window. The combination of individually weak and ambiguous clues to determine object presence and estimate overall probability of relevance builds on recent approaches to robust object recognition and can be seen as an attempt at extending the success of indicative methods for content representation in the field of information retrieval. Devising a strategy for recognising objects by applying the most appropriate combination of visual routines such as segmentation and classification modules can also be learned from data [13].

3.3   The Role of Language in Vision

As mentioned above, many problems in vision such as object recognition ([14]), video analysis ([18,27,24]), gesture recognition ([3,21,25]), and multimedia retrieval ([22,2,37]) can be viewed as relating symbolic terms to visual information by utilising syntactic and semantic structure in a manner related to approaches in speech and language processing [34]. A visual language can also serve as an important mechanism for attentional control by constraining the range of plausible feature configurations which need to be considered when performing a visual tasks such as recognition. Processing may then be performed selectively in response to queries formulated in terms of the structure of the domain, i.e. relating high-level symbolic representations to extracted features in the signal (image and temporal feature) domain. By basing such a language on an ontology one can capture both concrete and abstract relationships between salient visual properties. Ontologies encode the relational structure of concepts which one can use to describe and reason about aspects of the world.

Since the language is used to express queries and candidate hypotheses rather than exhaustively label image content, such relationships can be represented explicitly without prior commitments to a particular interpretation or having to incur the combinatorial explosion of a full annotation of all the relations that may hold in a given image or video. Instead, only those image aspects which are of value given a particular query are evaluated and evaluation may stop as soon as the appropriate top level symbol sequence has been generated.

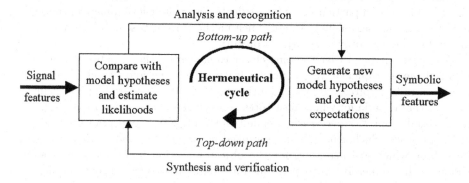

Fig. 1. The Hermeneutical cycle for iterative interpretation in a generative (hypothesise and test) framework.

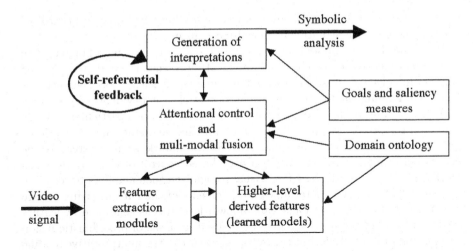

Fig. 2. Sketch of the proposed approach to goal-directed fusion of content extraction modules and inference guided by an attentional control mechanism. The fusion process and selective visual processing are carried out in response to a task and domain definition expressed in terms of an ontological language. Interpretations are generated and refined by deriving queries from the goals and current internal state.

3.4   Self-Referential Perceptual Inference Framework

In spite of the benefits of DBNs and related formalisms outlined above, probabilistic graphical models also have limitations in terms of their ability to represent structured data at a more symbolic level and the requirement for normalisations to enable probabilistic interpretations of information. Devising a probabilistic model is in itself not enough since one requires a framework which determines which inferences are actually made and how probabilistic outputs are to be interpreted.

Interpreting visual information in a dynamic context is best approached as an iterative process where low-level detections are compared (induction) with high-level models to derive new hypotheses (deduction). These can in turn guide the search for evidence to confirm or reject the hypotheses on the basis of expectations defined over the lower level features. Such a process is well suited to a generative method where new candidate interpretations are tested and refined over time. Figure 1 illustrates this approach.

However, there is a need to improve on this methodology when the complexity of the desired analysis increases, particularly as one considers hierarchical and interacting object and behavioural descriptions best defined in terms of a syntax at the symbolic level. The sheer number of possible candidate interpretations and potential derivations soon requires a means of greatly limiting the system's focus of attention. A useful analogy is selective processing in response to queries [6]. Visual search guided by a query posed in a language embodying an ontological representation of a domain allows adaptive processing strategies to be utilised and gives an effective attentional control mechanism.

We argue that an ontological content representation and query language can be used as an effective vehicle for hierarchical representation and goal-directed inference in video analysis tasks. As sketched in figure 2, such a language serves as a means of guiding the fusion of multiple sources of visual evidence and refining symbolic interpretations of dynamic scenes in the context of a particular task. By maintaining representations of both the current internal state and derivational goals expressed in terms of the same language framework, such a system can be seen as performing self-referential feedback based control of the way in which information is processed over time. Visual recognition then amounts to selecting a parsing strategy which determines how elements of the current string set are to be processed further given a stream of lower level tokens generated by feature detectors. Parts of the language may be realised in terms of probabilistic fusion mechanisms such as DBNs, but the overall structure of the interpretative module is not limited to a particular probabilistic framework and allow context-sensitive parsing strategies to be employed where appropriate.

4   Applications

4.1   Image and Video Indexing

In [37] we proposed an ontological query language called OQUEL as a novel query specification interface and retrieval tool for content based image retrieval and presented results using the ICON system. The language features an extensible language framework based on a formally specified grammar and vocabulary which are derived from a general ontology of image content in terms of categories, objects, attributes, and relations. Words in the language represent predicates on image features and target content at different semantic levels. Sentences are prescriptions of desired characteristics which are to hold for relevant retrieved images. Images are retrieved by deriving an abstract syntax tree from a textual or forms-based user query and probabilistically evaluating it by analysing the composition and perceptual properties of salient image regions in light of the query. The matching process utilises automatically extracted image segmentation and classification information and can incorporate any other feature extraction mechanisms or contextual knowledge available at processing time to satisfy a given user request. Perceptual inference takes the form of identifying those images as relevant for which one can find sufficient support for the candidate hypotheses derived from the query relative to other images in the collection. Examples of queries are *"some sky which is close to buildings in upper corner, size at least 20%"* and *"(some green or vividly coloured vegetation in the centre) which is of similar size as (clouds or blue sky at the top)"*.

The OQUEL language is currently being extended to the video domain for indexing purposes. This work employs the region based motion segmentation method described in [31] which uses a Bayesian framework to determined the most likely labelling of regions according to motion layers and their depth ordering. The inference framework described above is then utilised to integrate information form the neural network region classifiers to modify the prior probabilities for foreground/background layer assignments of image regions. A face detector and simple human shape model have recently been used to identify and track people. An ontological language is under development which extends the static scene content descriptions with motion verbs ("moves", "gestures"), spatial and temporal prepositions ("on top of", "beside", "before"), and adverbs ("quickly", "soon") for indexing and retrieval of video fragments.

4.2 Multi-modal Fusion for Sentient Computing

Interesting avenues for refinement, testing and deployment of the proposed cognitive inference framework arise from the "sentient computing" ([17,1]) project developed at AT&T Laboratories Cambridge and the Cambridge University Laboratory for Communications Engineering (LCE). This system uses mobile ultrasonic sensor devices known as "bats" and a receiver infrastructure to gather high-resolution location information for tagged objects such as people and machines in order to maintain a sophisticated software model of an office environment. Applications can register with the system to receive notifications of relevant events to provide them with an awareness of the spatial context in which users interact with the system. As indicated in figures 3 and 4, the system's internal dynamic representation is based on an ontology in terms of locations and spatial regions, objects (people, computers, phones, devices, cameras, furniture etc.), and event states (motions, spatial overlap, proximity, button events etc.).

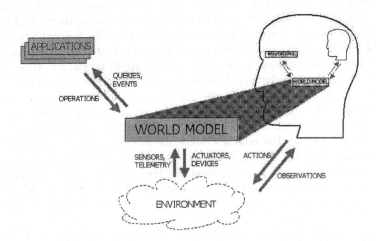

Fig. 3. Diagrammatic overview of the world model maintained by the sentient computing system.

Combining vision with other sensory modalities is a very promising research avenue in ubiquitous perceiving systems [8,35,9]. Computer vision methods can

Fig. 4. The world as perceived by (a) users and (b) the sentient computing system.

provide multi-modal human-computer interfaces with transparent detection, recognition, and tracking capabilities, but on their own suffer from a lack of robustness and autonomy in real world interaction scenarios. The sentient computing system provides a variable granularity spatial model of the environment and a reliable device tracking facility which can be used to automatically (re)initialise and re-focus vision modules whenever an event or scene context of interest is observed by a camera. Location events from the sentient computing architecture are being used to provide ground truth information about objects and object movements occurring within the known field of view of a calibrated camera to yield training and test data for individual video analysis components. A number of applications of the sentient computing technology can in turn benefit from our proposed video interpretation framework through the fusion of the ultrasonic and visual modalities. One such application currently under development concerns user authentication for security critical applications, e.g. those which allow users to automatically unlock office doors or automatically login to a computer in their vicinity. In this case the system uses the bat sensor information to detect that a person is present and select one or more camera views to verify their identity as indicated by the identity tag of their bat. The location of the bat is used to constrain the search window for a head and face detector which forwards an image of the detected face to a face recogniser. Rather than solving the extremely difficult problem of general face recognition, visual authentication is approached as a verification problem and greatly constrained by fusing other kinds of information about assumed identity, face location, lighting conditions, and local office geometry.

Having visual information as an additional sensory modality is also useful when the system has trouble detecting a person (e.g. they are not wearing a bat or it is temporarily concealed) or when an application requires additional information about a person's posture, direction of gaze, gestures, interactions with devices and other people, or facial expression to enhance visually mediated human computer interaction and provide a richer model of the context in which such interactions take place. At a more mundane level, vision technology makes the installation, maintenance and operation of a sentient computing system easier by providing additional means of calibrating sensory infrastructure and adapting a model of the static environment (such as furniture and partition walls).

By ensuring that the symbolic inferences drawn by the system remain grounded in the signal domain, the system can support a range of possible queries as inferences and adapt its hypotheses in light of new evidence. To ensure sufficient performance to enable real-time processing, the fusion of individual perceptual modalities is set up as a hierarchy where inexpensive detectors (e.g. finding the rough outline of a person) narrow down the search space to which more specific modules (e.g. a face spotter or gesture recogniser) are applied. The system thereby remains robust to error rates by integrating information vertically (applying detectors with high false acceptance rates to guide those with potentially high false rejection rates) and horizontally (fusing different kinds of information at the same level to offset different error characteristics for disambiguation). In our cognitive framework, vision is therefore used to enhance the perceptual inference capabilities of the sentient computing infrastructure by adding further sources of information to update, query, and extend the system's internal ontology and external event model. By maintaining a notion of its own internal state and goals the system can restrict its focus of attention to perform only those inferences which are required for the current task (e.g. verifying the identity of a person who just entered the visual field). Real-time requirements and other resource limitations can be used as additional constraints for the fusion process.

5   Conclusion

This paper presents an extensible video analysis framework which can be customised for a given task domain by employing appropriate data sources and application-specific constraints. Recent advances in graph-based probabilistic inference techniques allow the system to propagate a stochastic model over time and combine different types of syntactic and semantic information. The process of generating high-level interpretations subject to system goals is performed by parsing sentence forms in an ontological language for visual content at different levels of analysis.

Acknowledgements. The authors would like to acknowledge directional guidance and support from AT&T Laboratories and the Cambridge University Laboratory for Communications Engineering. The principal author received financial support from the Royal Commission for the Exhibition of 1851.

References

1. M. Addlesee, R. Curwen, S. Hodges, J. Newman, P. Steggles, A. Ward, and A. Hopper. Implementing a sentient computing system. *IEEE Computer*, 34(8):50–56, 2001.
2. K. Barnard and D. Forsyth. Learning the semantics of words and pictures. In *Proc. International Conference on Computer Vision*, 2001.

3. A. Bobick and Y. Ivanov. Action recognition using probabilistic parsing. In *Proc. Conference on Computer Vision and Pattern Recognition*, 1998.
4. H. Bunke and D. Pasche. *Structural Pattern Analysis*, chapter Parsing multivalued strings and its application to image and waveform recognition. World Scientific Publishing, 1990.
5. H. Buxton and S. Gong. Advanced visual surveillance using bayesian networks. In *Proc. International Conference on Computer Vision*, 1995.
6. H. Buxton and N. Walker. Query based visual analysis: Spatio-temporal reasoning in computer vision. *Vision Computing*, 6(4):247–254, 1988.
7. Y. Chen, Y. Rui, and T. Huang. JPDAF based HMM for real-time contour tracking. In *Proc. Conference on Computer Vision and Pattern Recognition*, 2001.
8. J. Crowley, J. Coutaz, and F. Berard. Things that see: Machine perception for human computer interaction. *Communications of the ACM*, 43(3):54–64, 2000.
9. J. Crowley, J. Coutaz, G. Rey, and P. Reignier. Perceptual components for context aware computing. In *Proc. Ubicomp 2002*, 2002.
10. J. Crowley and Y. Demazeau. Principles and techniques for sensor data fusion. *Signal Processing*, 32(1–2):5–27, 1993.
11. T. Darrell, G. Gordon, M. Harville, and J. Woodfill. Integrated person tracking using stereo, color, and pattern detection. In *Proc. Conference on Computer Vision and Pattern Recognition*, 1998.
12. D. C. Dennett. *Minds, machines, and evolution*, chapter Cognitive Wheels: The Frame Problem of AI, pages 129–151. Cambridge University Press, 1984.
13. B. Draper, U. Ahlrichs, and D. Paulus. Adapting object recognition across domains: A demonstration. *Lecture Notes in Computer Science*, 2095:256–270, 2001.
14. P. Duygulu, K. Barnard, J.F.H. De Freitas, and D.A. Forsyth. Object recognition as machine translation: Learning a lexicon for a fixed image vocabulary. In *Proc. European Conference on Computer Vision*, 2002.
15. J. Glicksman. A cooperative scheme for image understanding using multiple sources of information. Technical Report TR-82-13, University of British Columbia, Department of Computer Science, 1982.
16. S. Harnad. The symbol grounding problem. *Physica D*, 42:335–346, 1990.
17. A. Harter, A. Hopper, P. Steggles, A. Ward, and P. Webster. The anatomy of a context-aware application. In *Mobile Computing and Networking*, pages 59–68, 1999.
18. G. Herzog and K. Rohr. Integrating vision and language: Towards automatic description of human movements. In I. Wachsmuth, C.-R. Rollinger, and W. Brauer, editors, *KI-95: Advances in Artificial Intelligence. 19th Annual German Conference on Artificial Intelligence*, pages 257–268. Springer, 1995.
19. S. Intille and A. Bobick. Representation and visual recognition of complex, multi-agent actions using belief networks. In *IEEE Workshop on the Interpretation of Visual Motion*, 1998.
20. M. Isard and A. Blake. ICONDENSATION: Unifying low-level and high-level tracking in a stochastic framework. *Lecture Notes in Computer Science*, 1406, 1998.
21. Y. Ivanov and A. Bobick. Recognition of visual activities and interactions by stochastic parsing. *IEEE Trans. on Pattern Analysis and Machine Intell.*, 22(8), 2000.
22. A. Jaimes and S. Chang. A conceptual framework for indexing visual information at multiple levels. In *IS&T SPIE Internet Imaging*, 2000.
23. F.V. Jensen. *An Introduction to Bayesian Networks*. Springer Verlag, 1996.

24. A. Kojima, T. Tamura, and K. Fukunaga. Natural language description of human activities from video images based on concept hierarchy of actions. Int. Journal of Computer Vision (to appear), 2002.
25. D. Moore and I. Essa. Recognizing multitasked activities using stochastic context-free grammar. In *Proc. Workshop on Models vs Exemplars in Computer Vision*, 2001.
26. N. Oliver, B. Rosario, and A. Pentland. A bayesian computer vision system for modeling human interactions. *IEEE Trans. on Pattern Analysis and Machine Intell.*, 22(8):831–843, 2000.
27. C. Pinhanez and A. Bobick. Approximate world models: Incorporating qualitative and linguistic information into vision systems. In *AAAI'96*, 1996.
28. R. Rimey. *Control of Selective Perception using Bayes Nets and Decision Theory*. PhD thesis, University of Rochester Computer Science Department, 1993.
29. J. Sherrah and S. Gong. Tracking discontinuous motion using bayesian inference. In *Proc. European Conference on Computer Vision*, pages 150–166, 2000.
30. J. Sherrah and S. Gong. Continuous global evidence-based bayesian modality fusion for simultaneous tracking of multiple objects. In *Proc. International Conference on Computer Vision*, 2001.
31. P. Smith. *Edge-based Motion Segmentation*. PhD thesis, Cambridge University Engineering Department, 2001.
32. K. Sparck Jones. Information retrieval and artificial intelligence. *Artificial Intelligence*, 114:257–281, 1999.
33. M. Spengler and B. Schiele. Towards robust multi-cue integration for visual tracking. *Lecture Notes in Computer Science*, 2095:93–106, 2001.
34. R. Srihari. Computational models for integrating linguistic and visual information: A survey. *Artificial Intelligence Review, special issue on Integrating Language and Vision*, 8:349–369, 1995.
35. S. Stillman and I. Essa. Towards reliable multimodal sensing in aware environments. In *Proc. Perceptual User Interfaces Workshop, ACM UIST 2001*, 2001.
36. M. Thonnat and N. Rota. Image understanding for visual surveillance applications. In *Proc. of 3rd Int. Workshop on Cooperative Distributed Vision*, 1999.
37. C.P. Town and D.A. Sinclair. Ontological query language for content based image retrieval. In *Proc. IEEE Workshop on Content-based Access of Image and Video Libraries*, pages 75–81, 2001.
38. K. Toyama and E. Horvitz. Bayesian modality fusion: Probabilistic integration of multiple vision algorithms for head tracking. In *Proc. Asian Conference on Computer Vision*, 2000.
39. W. Tsai and K. Fu. Attributed grammars - a tool for combining syntactic and statistical approaches to pattern recognition. *IEEE Transactions on Systems, Man and Cybernetics*, SMC-10(12), 1980.
40. J. Tsotsos, J. Mylopoulos, H. Covvey, and S. Zucker. A framework for visual motion understanding. *IEEE Trans. on Pattern Analysis and Machine Intell.*, Special Issue on Computer Analysis of Time-Varying Imagery:563–573, 1980.
41. Y. Wu and T. Huang. A co-inference approach to robust visual tracking. In *Proc. International Conference on Computer Vision*, 2001.

Recurrent Bayesian Network for the Recognition of Human Behaviors from Video

Nicolas Moënne-Loccoz, François Brémond, and Monique Thonnat

INRIA Sophia Antipolis 2004, route des Lucioles, BP93 - 06902 Sophia Antipolis
Cedex, France
{Nicolas.Moenne-Loccoz, Francois.Bremond,
Monique.Thonnat}@sophia.inria.fr,
http://www-sop.inria.fr/orion/index.html

Abstract. We propose an original bayesian approach to recognize human behaviors from video streams. Mobile objects and their visual features are computed by a vision module. Then, using a Recurrent Bayesian Network, behaviors of the mobile objects are recognized through the temporal evolution of their visual features.

1 Introduction

Many works have used learning methods to recognize human activities from video streams in a cluttered, noisy and uncertain environment. None has solved the problem due to the temporal nature of human activities. We propose a learning method to recognize human behaviors from video streams in the context of metro station monitoring. Our approach is a particular form of a Dynamic Bayesian Network : a Recurrent Bayesian Network. A RBN models the temporal evolution of the visual features characterizing a human behavior and infers its occurence whatever its time-scale. In the second section we present the related work and show the need for a better temporal learning method. In the third section, we present the video interpretation system that computes the visual features used as input by the RBN, in the fourth section we formally present the RBN and in the fifth section we describe the results of our experiments.

2 Related Works

Learning methods have been used for the interpretation of video streams for the past ten years. There are two main approaches : probabilistic graph models and neural networks.

2.1 Probabilistic Graph Models

The probabilistic graph models allow to handle the uncertainty of the video processing task and to represent the prior knowledge of the application domain.

J.L. Crowley et al. (Eds.): ICVS 2003, LNCS 2626, pp. 68–77, 2003.

Bayesian Network. BN are directed acyclic graphs. Each node represents a random variable and the links between the nodes represent a causality between random variables (e.g. A imply B) ; the links are associated to the conditional probabilities of that dependency. A BN is able to model the causalities between variables of a particular domain. Conditional probabilities are in general learned from a set of examples of the domain.

In [3], the team of H. Buxton uses BNs for the interpretation of video streams in a traffic monitoring system to recognize situation such as a traffic jam. BNs are used at two different levels : for the computation of simple but uncertain features of the scene and for the recognition of more complex behaviors. For example, a BN is used to infer the position of an object in the scene, using its orientation and its size. The orientation and the size of the object are inferred, in the same fashion, from visual features of the objects computed during the segmentation and the tracking process (object speed, object width ...).

The team of R. Nevatia [6] uses a naive bayesian classifier to recognize complex behaviors in the context of parking lot monitoring. For example the behavior *slowing down toward object of reference* is inferred from the events *moving toward object of reference, slowing down* and *distance from the object of reference is decreasing* by using prior probabilities computed during a learning phase.

BNs have the main advantage to use prior knowledge modeling the causalities between visual features as dependencies between random variables and to handle the uncertainty inherent to the video processing task.

Hidden Markov Models. HMMs are a statistical tool for the processing of sequential data mainly used for the detection of pattern inside temporal sequences. They have been used successfully for speech recognition and recently for video interpretation. An HMM is a kind of finite state probabilistic automaton which transitions between states represent temporal causalities characterized by a probability distribution, generally learned from a set of examples of the domain. An HMM models a markovian temporal process, i.e. follows the Markov's hypothesis which states that a state depends only on the previous one.

The team of R. Nevatia [7] presents an approach using an HMM for the recognition of complex behaviors. A complex behavior is a behavior that can be represented by a sequence of simple behaviors. For example, the behavior *contact with an object of reference* can be represented by the sequence of behaviors *slowing down toward object of reference, contact with the object of reference* and *turn around and leave object of reference*. For that model, an HMM is constructed, which conditional probabilities are learned from a training set.

A.F. Bobick and Y.A. Ivanov [1] use a set of HMMs with a stochastic context free grammar to recognize simple gestures such as the movement of a hand drawing a square. Some HMMs are used to recognize elementary hand movements (*moving from bottom to top, moving from left to right...*) which sequence is syntactically analyzed by the grammar to recognize complex movements.

Team of A. Pentland [2] uses a particular form of HMM (*coupled HMM*) to recognize gestures of an asian gymnastic (*Tai'Chi*). Coupled HMMs are able to model interactions between processes such as the movements of the different hands of a subject. Hands gestures are independent but interact to form a *Tai'Chi* movement. But, coupling HMMs increases the learning complexity.

A. Galata, N. Johnson and D.Hogg [4] propose HMMs with variable length to model simple body exercises (*raise the left arm, flex the right arm...*) from the shape of the subject. The length of the HMM is chosen during the learning phase. The idea is, from a single state HMM, to evaluate the information gained by the use of a new state (increasing the length). Then, iterating the process, the best length is found, according to the evaluation of the information gain. Moreover, in order to recognize exercises of different level of abstraction, i.e. in different temporal scale, authors use a hierarchy of variable length HMMs.

Finally, an approach that uses hierarchical and unsupervised HMMs is presented by J. Hoey in [5]. The task of the presented system is to recognize facial expressions characterizing user emotions in order to interact with him. The originality of the approach is the unsupervise learning technique, that is learning from non-annotated examples.

HMMs model temporal dependencies of the phenomena. It is the learning method the most used for video interpretation, but HMMs are limited because of the Markovian hypothesis (most of human behaviors aren't markovian processes).

2.2   Neural Networks

Artificial neural networks are a set of simple information processing units (*artificial neurons*) that are organized in several layers and strongly interconnected. Each connection is characterized by a weight. Learning a processing task in a neural network is the task to find for a given network, the weights of the connections that model the best the processing task using a set of examples of that processing task.

H. Buxton [8] uses a Time Delay Radial Basis Functions Network. A TDRBF is a kind of neural network with an input layer, a hidden layer and an output layer. Neurons of the hidden layer are Gaussian radial functions. To provide a time delay, the network has as input a temporal window of the data which slides at each time. The TDRBF is used to recognize head movements from its rotation. The approach is interesting because it allows to learn a simple behavior on a time interval without knowing the model of that behavior. But the time interval is fixed and as the network structure, is chosen arbitrary. Moreover, the learning phase needs many examples : the experiments have used between 1000 and 5000 examples.

Only few works have used the possibilities of the neural networks for video interpretation. It seems to be an interesting solution because neural networks don't need prior knowledge but they need lots of examples.

3   Overview of a Video Interpretation System

We use a video interpretation system which is composed of two modules. The first module processes video streams : segmentation, classification and tracking of the mobile objects of the scene (essentially individuals or groups of individuals). The second module interprets the scene : it recognizes behaviors related to the mobile objects. Figure 1 presents an overview of the video interpretation system.

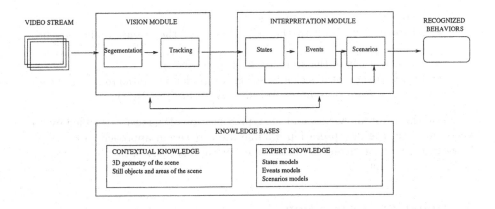

Fig. 1. Overview of the video interpretation system.

3.1 Vision

Processing of a video stream by the vision module provides a representation of the scene in terms of the mobile objects detected with a set of visual features characterizing these objects. More precisely, the task of this module is to :

- detect mobile objects of the scene,
- classify detected mobile objects (noise, individuals, groups of individuals),
- compute visual features of the detected mobile objects (size, direction, speed ...),
- track detected mobile objects as isolated individuals or globally as groups of individuals.

3.2 Interpretation

The task of the interpretation module is to recognize a set of behaviors that can occur inside the scene such as fighting or vandalism. As suggested by M. Thonnat and N. Rota [9], to ease the interpretation task, we introduce three entities which describe behaviors :

- State : a state is a mobile object property computed on a given time interval (*seating/standing, still/walking/running...*).
- Event : an event characterizes a change of state (*to sit down/to stand up, to stop/to begin running*). For example the event *to sit down* is the change of the state *standing* into the state *seating*.

- Scenario : a scenario is a combination of states, events and/or sub-scenarios (*graffiti on the wall, following someone, running toward the train...*).

In order to interpret the content of the scene, prior knowledge is provided to the interpretation system :

- Knowledge on the scene environment :
  - nature and position of the still objects of the scene (walls, benches, doors...),
  - semantic areas of the scene (platform, tracks...).
- Expert knowledge : states,events, scenarios models (*running toward the train = running + train present + trajectory is toward the train*).

From this prior knowledge and the representation of the scene provided by the vision module, the interpretation module use a bayesian approach to recognize hierarchically all occurrences of states, events and scenarios, i.e. all occurences of human behaviors.

4   Behavior Recognition

4.1   Motivations

To recognize human behaviors from a set of visual features, we use a bayesian approach because of its ability to solve uncertainty, lack of knowledge and dependence on the scene environment. However, as seen in the section 2, the learning approaches for video interpretation are limited due to their inability to solve the problem of the temporal dimension. Effectively, there is no solution that handles the dependency on the time-scale of what has to be recognized. For example, it is necessary to be able to recognize a behavior lasting 10 seconds even if it usually lasts 20 seconds.

To overcome that limitation we propose an original form of a Dynamic Bayesian Network that is able to capture behavior whatever its time-scale.

4.2   Bayesian Inference

A Recurrent Bayesian Network is a particular form of a Dynamic Bayesian Network dedicated to the recognition of behaviors. The behavior is inferred by the values of some visual features of the considered mobile object. The structure of a RBN takes as input the values of visual features during a fixed period of time and propagates the information of the previous periods of time through a recurrent dependency (previous occurrence of the behavior). Figure 2 shows the general structure of a RBN.

The inference process in a RBN is the same as for a Bayesian Classifier. Formally, we have a behavior to recognize, B, and a set of dependencies $O=\{R, F1_t, F1_{t-1}, ... , F1_{t-n}, F2_t, F2_{t-1}, ... , F2_{t-n}, ..., Fk_t, Fk_{t-1}, ... , Fk_{t-n}\}$ where R is the recurrent dependency and Fi_t is dependency to the visual features i at time t. To simplify the formalism, we denote the dependencies by $O=\{O_1, O_2, ...,$

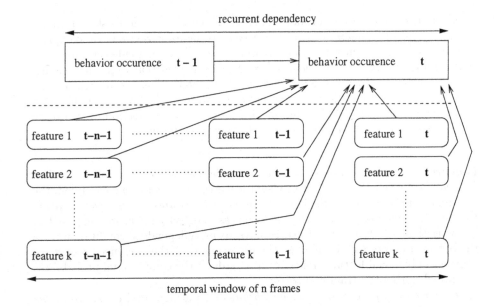

Fig. 2. Structure of a Recurrent Bayesian Network.

O_{nk+1}} where n is the size of the temporal window and k the number of visual features used to infer the occurrence of the behavior. The idea is to compare the conditional probabilities $P(B|O)$ and $P(\bar{B}|O)$, and according to the maximum, decide weither B or $\bar{B}$ occures. From the Bayes theorem and if the O_i are independent conditionnaly to B (Bayes hypothesis) we obtain :

$$P(B \mid O) = \frac{P(O_1, O_2, ..., O_{nk+1} \mid B) * P(B)}{P(O_1, O_2, ..., O_{nk+1})} = \frac{\prod_i P(O_i \mid B) * P(B)}{P(O_1, O_2, ..., O_{nk+1})}$$

As we just need to compare $P(B|O)$ with$P(\bar{B}|O)$, the probability P(O_1, O_2, ... , O_{nk+1}) is constant and has no influence on the comparison. And finally, in order to recognize B and $\bar{B}$ with the same probablility, we make the assumption that $P(B)=P(\bar{B})$. Finally we have :

$$\frac{P(B \mid O)}{P(\bar{B} \mid O)} = \frac{\prod_i P(O_i \mid B)}{\prod_i P(O_i \mid \bar{B})}$$

Probabilities $P(O_i|B)$ are computed during a training process, from a learning set $\{(b,o)_1, (b,o)_2, ..., (b,o)_m\}$ where each couple (b, o) represents a manually annotated example, i.e. a frame characterized by the value of the behavior B and the value of all the dependencies O_i.

4.3 Network Conception

Behavior reduction. To model the network, the behavior as to be expressed as concrete as possible. For example, we are interessted to recognize a *violent*

behavior involving a group of individuals in the context of metro station monitoring. A *violent behavior* is too abstract to be recognized. So we have to express
it in term of a more concrete behavior. In our case, observing video streams that
show groups involved in a *violent behavior*, we conclued that a group is saying
having a *violent behavior* when it is globally agitated. Then we recognize a *violent behavior* as a high level of the *global agitation* of the group. Furthermore
we observed that the *global agitation* of a group is the expression of two more
simple behaviors : *internal agitation* and *external agitation*.

Features selection. In order to recognize a human behavior such as a *violent
behavior* we have to select a set of visual features from which one can infers the
occurence of the behavior. Such a relation (*visual features → behavior*) appears
to be not so obvious and a method is to use as many visual features as possible,
knowing that selected visual features have to be independent conditionnaly to
the behavior of interest. To increase the performance of the inference process, we
consider only visual features relevant in regards to the conditionnal probabilites
computed during the training process.

In our case, to recognize a *violent behavior* as a high level of *agitation*, we
obtained the *recurrent bayesian network* of the figure 3.

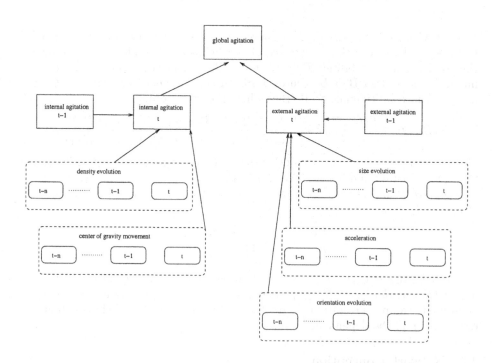

Fig. 3. Recurrent Bayesian Network for the recognition of the levels of the *global agitation* of a group.

The visual features used to infer the level of *global agitation* are :

- *Internal agitation* : the internal agitation is the visual agitation inside the group. From our experiments, we observed that internal agitation can be inferred by two visual features of the group :
  - *Evolution of the density* : the evolution of the ratio of the number of pixels that compose the group and the size of the group. It captures the agitation of the pixels inside the group.
  - *Movment of the center of gravity* : the movment of the center of gravity of all the blobs (set of pixels) of the group. It captures the agitation of the blobs relatively to each others.
- *External agitation* : the agitation of the individual relatively to the scene. External agitation is inferred by visual features that capture its movment in the scene :
  - *Evolution of the size (3d height * 3d width) of the group*
  - *Acceleration of the group*
  - *Evolution of the trajectory (orientation) of the group*

The *internal agitation* and the *external agitation* are inferred using a RBN because they are time dependent behaviors. The *global agitation* is infered using a simple bayesian classifier because the time is already captured by the subsequent behaviors : *internal & external agitation*.

4.4   Learning

Annotation. The process of annotating the video stream to compute the conditionnal probabilities presents some difficulties. The process is to decide for each frame if, given the information of the previous period of time, the behavior of interest is happening or not. A human operator has to take the decision on the basis of the observed period of time. Such an annotation is particularly subjective and repeating the process frequently gives different results, i.e. annotations.

Training. Learning methods are limitated due to the lack of examples. To overcome this problem, we train the RBN with a set of nine video streams (a set of about 800 frames) and get the result for the tenth one (a set of 50-100 frames), iterating the process for each video stream.

5   Results

We validate the proposed formalism by analysing a set of video streams that show groups (of individuals) having either a *violent behavior* or not. These video streams are taken from the european ADVISOR project, in the context of monitoring a metro station.

As seen in section 4, a *violent behavior* is recognize as a high level of *global agitation* which is modeled by the RBN shown by the figure 3.

To train the network, we dispose of 10 video streams from the same site. 80% of the streams shows people fighting and the 20% others shows people not violent. The training set contains about 600 examples, i.e. frames that are annotated by a human operator according to the levels of *global, internal and external agitation* of the group present in the scene. Figure 4 shows the result for one of the stream with a group having a *violent behavior*, i.e. a high level of *global agitation*.

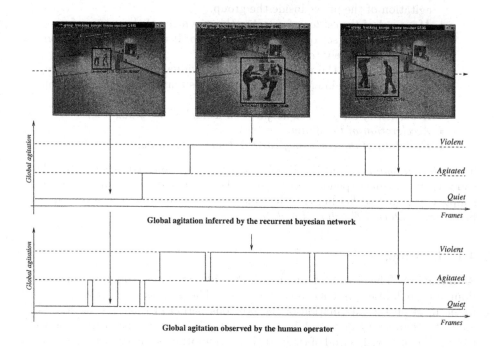

Fig. 4. Result for a sequence containing a *"violent behavior"*.

5.1 Performance

The temporal evolution of the *global agitation* of the group is correctly recognized. We observe two phenomena :

- a time delay : the recognition is done after a time delay, this is due to the time period in which we consider the visual features values.
- a time smoothing : ponctual changes are not recognized due to the recurrent dependency. This allows the recognition of the behavior to be made on the entire time period instead of for each frame.

Results are very encouraging : a *violent behavior* is recognized for each positive example and no *violent behavior* is detected for the two false examples.

5.2   Knowledge Acquisition

Conditionnal probabilities computed during the training process give some knowledge about the domain of application. For example, we learned that the *external agitation* of a group is mainly inferred by the evolution of its size during the last 3 frames while its acceleration has only few influence and the evolution of its trajectory has a medium influence uniformly distributed on the temporal window.

6   Conclusion

We have proposed a Recurrent Bayesian Network to recognize human behaviors from video streams independently to their time-scale. We have validated the approach in the context of monitoring a metro station, for the recognition of *"Violent behaviors"*. Future works will validate the approach on several other behaviors in different contexts. Futhermore, as the learning process is tedious, we plan to use the RBN in an unsupervised mode.

References

1. A. F. Bobick and Y. A. Ivanov. Action recognition using probabilistic parsing. In *Computer Vision and Pattern Recognition*, 1998.
2. M. Brand, N. Oliver, and A. Pentland. Coupled hidden markov models for complex action recognition. In *Computer Vision and Pattern Recognition*, 1997.
3. H. Buxton and S. Gong. Advanced Visual Surveillance using Bayesian Networks. In *International Conference on Computer Vision*, 1995.
4. A. Galata, N. Johnson, and D. Hogg. Learning behavior models of human activities. In *British Machine Vision Conference*, 1999.
5. J. Hoey. Hierarchical unsupervised learning of facial expression categories. In *IEEE Workshop on Detection and Recognition of Events in Video*, 2001.
6. S. Hongeng, F. Brémond, and R. Nevatia. Bayesian framework for video surveillance application. In *International Conference on Pattern Recognition*, 2000.
7. S. Hongeng, F. Brémond, and R. Nevatia. Representation and optimal recognition of human activities. 2000.
8. A. J. Howell and H. Buxton. Recognizing simple behaviors using time-delay rbf network. 1997.
9. M. Thonnat and N. Rota. Image understanding for visual surveillance application. In *Workshop on Cooperative Distributed Vision*, 1999.

Implementation of Traffic Flow Measuring Algorithm Using Real-Time Dynamic Image Processing

Tae-Seung Lee, Eung-Min Lee, Hyeong-Taek Park, Young-Kil Kwag,
Sang-Seok Lim, Joong-Hwan Baek, and Byong-Won Hwang

Hankuk Aviation University, School of Electronics, Telecommunication and Computer
Engineering, 200-1, Hwajon-dong, Deokyang-gu, Koyang-city, Kyonggi-do, 412-791, Seoul,
The Republic of Korea
thestaff@hitel.net, {emlee, htpark, ykwang, sslim, jhbaek,
bwhwang}@mail.hangkong.ac.kr

Abstract. In this paper, an automatic traffic flow measuring system and a real-time image processing algorithm have been developed. The picture of moving vehicles taken by an industrial television (ITV) camera are digitized into sample points in odd ITV frames and the points are processed in even ITV frames by a personal computer. We detect the presence of vehicles by comparing the brightness of the sample points of vehicle with that of the road. After eliminating noises contained in the digitized sample points by appropriate smoothing techniques, we obtain a contour of each vehicle. Using the contour, the number of passing vehicles is effectively measured by counting the number of sample points of each vehicle. Also the type of a vehicle is easily figured out by counting the number of sample points corresponding to the width of vehicle's contour. The performance of the proposed algorithm is demonstrated by actual implementation. From the experimental results $1 \sim 2\%$ measurement error was observed.

1 Introduction

Recent development on road traffic surveillance and control system using computers gives rise to the necessity of gathering large quantity of traffic information in real time basis. Information on special traffic parameters such as the length of queue and the grade of congestion and also information on unusual traffic incident are requested in particular.

Real time processing of moving pictures of traffic flow is considered to be useful for obtaining various types of special traffic parameters. It is also expected to reduce time and work required in traffic investigation.

So far, vehicle detection and tracking systems [1], [2], [3], [4], road surveillance system [5], [6], [7], [8] and traffic analysis for control [9], [10], [11] have been developed. However, most of those systems are difficult to implement for the real-time processing in the field.

The previous works in this field can be broadly divided into two groups [15]. One group utilizes vision sensors to take the traffic image. The video image is processed by image processing algorithm to extract traffic data. The other group's approaches

J.L. Crowley et al. (Eds.): ICVS 2003, LNCS 2626, pp. 78–87, 2003.
© Springer-Verlag Berlin Heidelberg 2003

are based on the magnetic loop, infrared or ultrasonic sensors. These are weather-independent, applicable in the night or under poor visibility conditions, costly, limited to single lane coverage, hard to maintain, and difficult to relocate. The vision sensor based methods are cost effective, easy to maintain, easy to relocate, low detection error rated, but fails to use in poor visibility condition. Microwave radar based system [16] is also recently employed and is capable of multi-lane, weather-independent, roadside mountable, but its performance is limited by blockage of small size vehicles by neighboring larger ones. Both approaches have widely used in traffic control systems yet their performances were somewhat limited.

A traffic flow measuring system using industrial television (ITV) camera [12], [13] and charge coupled device (CCD) camera [14] was developed by Hwang et al. In [14], they designed and made a special device called Video Information Sampler and Converter(VISC) for real time image processing. In this system, real time measurement was made possible by dealing with only the information on brightness at the relatively few number of sample points on the picture instead of dealing with all of the picture elements. Although the VISC achieved a notable improvement in the real-time processing of the traffic image, the performance was not quite satisfactory.

Recently a new system using ITV or CCD camera and an efficient real-time processing algorithm have been developed by the authors. The new system is more flexible compared with the previous VISC system. The conventional video image processing methods is based on the average intensity of the road image and resulted in large detection errors. However, the proposed algorithm in this paper is based on the pixel's intensity of actual (not averaged) background and hence the detection errors are small. Consequently the performance is further improved while the algorithm is simple enough to be implemented in *real-time* in the filed.

The paper is organized as follows. Section 2 describes the new traffic image processing system using ITV or CCD camera. The traffic-flow measuring algorithm based on real-time image processing is presented in section 3. The results obtained from experimental implementation are analyzed in section 4.

2 The Image Processing System

The configuration of the traffic image processing system is displayed in Fig. 1. Pictures taken by the ITV or CCD camera in the field are recorded and played back in our laboratory to be processed by the proposed automatic image processing algorithm. After the algorithm is developed, the ITV or CCD camera is connected directly to the image processing system that is capable of processing in real time.

In this system, to obtain the digital image of picture taken by camera, we use the Frame Grabber instead of VISC mentioned above. VISC samples a video signal at maximum 64 points from 256*256 points in the picture. In VISC the brightness of a sample point is digitized into 16 discrete levels ($0 \sim 15$) using 4-bits.

The Frame Grabber can sample a video signal into 640x480 pixels (maximum). The brightness or intensity of each pixel (*sample point*) is digitized into 256 discrete levels using 8-bits. In our experiment, we choose only 160 sample points (equally separated) by selecting one pixel every four pixels out of 640 sample points per scan line. Then each brightness of 160 sample points is individually quantized into 16 discrete levels ($0 \sim 15$) using 4-bits by the image processing algorithm. Although 640 pixels have to be employed for best resolution of the picture, it was found from our experiments that 160 pixels are good enough for the traffic flow measurement without losing any integrity of the essential information of the image. Concerning the quantization level, usage of 8-bits is preferable than 4-bits to obtain better distinction from the road. However, the quantization using 8-bits needs more processing time and memory in practical implementation. Hence in our experiments we selected 160 samples and 4-bits quantization for fast processing and cost-effective system. The experimental results presented in section 4 indicate excellent performance of the proposed algorithm for measuring the traffic flow data.

Basically the operation of the system carried out in two cycles alternatively running. The first cycles are performed in the odd ITV frames and the second cycles are done in the even ITV frames. The first cycle is a process of taking pictures of the traffic scene and digitizing the picture image. The second cycle is a process of extracting the traffic data from the digitized image.

3 The Traffic Flow Measuring Algorithm

3.1 The Objective and Method

In this section, an automatic measuring system and real-time image processing algorithm for measuring traffic-flow are presented. In the sequel, "traffic-flow data" inclusively means the number of passing vehicles per lane, the total number of passing vehicles and the types of vehicles. The sample points are set across the lanes at the 15m from the footprint of the camera. Sample points of moving pictures taken by an ITV or CCD camera are digitized in odd ITV frames and the points are processed in even ITV frames by a personal computer. We can detect presence of vehicles by comparing the brightness of the sample points of vehicle image with that of the road (background).

Let *reference line* denote the line of reference to measure the traffic data along the spatial axis perpendicular to the time axis. The reference line, parallel to the spatial axis, is an arbitrary line pre-set across the lanes of the road. The relationship between the position of the camera and the reference line is illustrated in Fig. 2. The sample points on the reference line are established equally at 8cm interval and perpendicularly to the moving direction of vehicles.

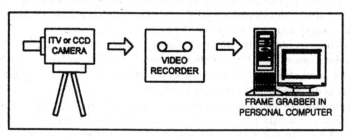

Fig. 1. The configuration of the traffic image processing system

By eliminating optical and electrical noises contained in the digitized image of a vehicle by smoothing techniques in STEP 4 of section 3.2, we obtain the pure digital image of the vehicle. We define *contour* of a vehicle as the outline of the sample points sequence of the digitized image. Then the number of vehicles passing through the reference line is obtained by counting the number of passing center-points of the contours. The size of a vehicle is also measured by counting the number of sample points belonging to the contour of a vehicle.

3.2 The Algorithm

Fig. 3 shows the flow chart of the algorithm for measuring the number of the passing vehicles per lane, the total number of passing vehicles and the sizes of vehicles. The algorithm consists of five units. Each part of the units is described in detail.

3.2.1 Initial Processing Unit

(1) Selection of the Initial Value of the Road Brightness
For setting the initial value of the road, the value of brightness of the first frame is stored. If the value of brightness of the next frame is different from that of the first frame, the stored value is renewed. When the same brightness continues R times, the value is selected to be the value of road brightness at that time. The above processing is repeated for each sample point. When the values of the road brightness at all sample points are determined, the initial setting is completed. R is experimentally determined to reduce the time for setting the initial value and to use them for measurement more effectively. For initial trial, the parameter R is set to 5 empirically. Once the values of all sample points are set, this processing for image data is skipped and then updating of road brightness is carried out automatically as follows.

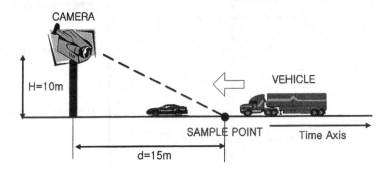

Fig. 2. The relationship between the position of the camera and the sample point

(2) Automatic Adjustment of Road Brightness
The brightness of background (road) changes not only by sudden variations of weather condition but also with the passage of time. Hence, we must develop an

algorithm such that the background brightness is adjusted automatically in response to the variations of the brightness of the road due to environmental change. In our proposed algorithm this is handled as follows.

Initially the background brightness of the road $X(I)$ is set to a trial parameter. Let T1, T2 and T3 are the pre-selected threshold parameters for effective adjustments of background brightness. When $A = X(I) - 1$ or $B = X(I) + 1$ continues T1 times, the background brightness $X(I)$ is replaced by A or B. For larger changes like sudden appearance of clouds, $C = X(I) - 2$, $D = X(I) + 2$, $E = X(I) - 3$ and $F = X(I) + 3$ are computed. When C or D continues T2 times, or when E or F continues T3 times, the background brightness $X(I)$ is replaced by C, D, E or F, respectively. This adjustment must be done for all sample points of the background. The brightness of the background can be adjusted successfully by means of correctly selecting the parameters T1, T2 and T3 by taking into account the road conditions and environmental factors.

3.2.2 Pre-processing Unit (STEP 1)

Pre-Processing unit is to detect the region where the brightness of sample point of a vehicle is different from that of road surface as a background. Let $I(n,t)$ denote the brightness at the time t of n-th sample point of the image and t the interval of 1/15 sec. Then the $I(n,t)$ is compared with the upper limit of background brightness $L_U(n,t)$ and the lower limit $L_L(n,t)$.

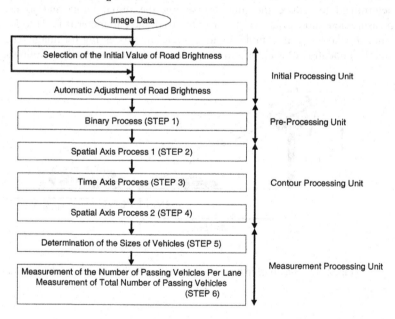

Fig. 3. Flow chart of the measuring algorithm.

The index $p(n,t)$ is obtained by binary process as follows.

$$p(n,t) = \begin{cases} 1, & if \ I(n,t) < L_L \ or \ I(n,t) > L_U \\ 0, & otherwise \end{cases}. \tag{1}$$

where, $L_U = X(I) + 1$ and $L_L = X(I) - 1$.

3.2.3 Contour Processing Unit

In the p pattern "1" is assigned to the sample point of a vehicle, and "0" to the background sample point. The background samples are extracted from the background image by the binary processing of the pre-processing unit. In the process following problems can be arisen owing to electrical and optical noise.

① There can exists noise assigned to "0" inside vehicle region
② There can exists noise assigned to "1" inside background region
③ If the brightness of middle part between front part and rear part of a large vehicle like cargo truck or trailer is similar to that of the background, then in this case one vehicle could be recognized as two vehicles.

The contour processing unit solves these problems and produce contours. To obtain the contour, the unit carries out the spatial- and time- axis processing as follows.

(1) Spatial Axis Processing 1 (**STEP 2**)
This step eliminates the noise assigned to "0" inside the contour of each vehicle:

If $p(n,t)$ is "0" successively not less than 2 times, then we set $P(n,t) = 0$.
Otherwise $P(n,t) = 1$.

(2) Time Axis Processing1 (**STEP 3**)
This step prevents any part of a vehicle from recognizing as a separate vehicle. That is, from time sequence $P(n,t)$, the index of presence of a vehicle $P^{\check{}}(n,t)$ is obtained as follows.

If $P(n,t-1) = 0$ and $P(n,t)$ is successively "1" Δ_1 times since $P(n,t-\Delta_1+1)$, then we set $P^*(n,t) = 1$.
If $P(n,t-1) = 1$ and $P(n,t)$ is successively "0" Δ_2 times from $P(n,t-\Delta_2+1)$, then we set $P^*(n,t) = 0$.
where, Δ_1 and Δ_2 are set to 3 and 5 respectively chosen from experiments.

(3) Spatial Axis Processing 2 (**STEP 4**)
In this step we eliminate the noises assigned to "1" in the background (road) region:

If $P^*(n,t)$ is "1" successively not less than 3 times in the spatial axis, then we set
$P^{**}(n,t)=1$. Otherwise $P^{**}(n,t)=0$.

3.2.4 Measurement Processing Unit

Based on the previous steps, we obtain the contours of vehicles. From the contours we measure the number of passing vehicles in each lane, the total number of passing vehicles and the size of each vehicle.

(1) Determination of the Size of Vehicles (**STEP 5**)
The size of a vehicle is determined by counting the number of sample points corresponding to the width and length of the contour of a vehicle. Though we can identify the size of a vehicle more precisely by utilizing both the width and length of a vehicle, in this paper, our analysis was focused on measuring only the width of each vehicle. We define small-size car as a vehicle with its width less than 1.7m. Similarly middle-size and large-size cars are defined as vehicles having the widths between 1.8m and 2.3m, and larger than 2.4m, respectively. This is further discussed in section 4.

(2) Measurement of the Number of Passing Vehicles (**STEP 6**)
In this step, the centerline of a contour is detected as follows. To measure the number of passing vehicles in a lane, first we determine the lane to which the contour belongs. This is done by simply checking the ordinal number of the sample points along the reference line in a contour, since the sample points on the line are equally spaced. Once the lane is known, we can measure the number of passing vehicles per lane by counting the number of the first sample points on the centerline of the contour belonging to the lane of interest. Also we can measure the total number of passing vehicles by adding up the number of vehicles for entire lanes. This step is described below.

Let τ and τ_1 denote the time of the first frame of the vehicle image and that of the last frame respectively. P_{LC} stands for the value of a pixel in the left of the centerline and similarly P_{RC} that in the right. It is assumed that from $t=\tau_1$ the pattern $P^{**}(n,t)$ begins to be "1".

i) If $\sum_{t=\tau_1}^{\tau} P^{**}(n,t) \geq \sum_{t=\tau_1}^{\tau} P^{**}(n-1,\tau)$, then we set $P_{RC}(n,\tau)=1$.

Otherwise $P_{RC}(n,\tau)=0$.

ii) If $\sum_{t=\tau_1}^{\tau} P^{**}(n,t) \geq \sum_{t=\tau_1}^{\tau} P^{**}(n+1,\tau)$, then we set $P_{LC}(n,\tau)=1$.

Otherwise $P_{LC}(n,\tau)=0$.

iii) When $P^{**}(n,t)$ is successively "1" from $t=\tau-\Delta_3$ to $t=\tau$, then we set $P_{RC}(n,\tau)=0$ and $P_{LC}(n,\tau)=0$.

iv) $P_C(n,t)$ is set by the logical AND of $P_{RC}(n,\tau)$ and $P_{LC}(n,\tau)$.

4 Experimental Results

For illustration of the performance of the proposed algorithm, we carried out experiments. In the experiment, the total width of the three lanes was 1050cm and the number of sample points for three lanes was 120. Hence the interval between any two neighboring sample points is 8cm. We can determine the size of each vehicle by counting the number of sample points corresponding to the width of the contour of the vehicle. The maximum error might be 16cm and can be reduced by increasing the number of the sample points on the reference line. Similarly we can measure the length of a vehicle by counting the number of sample points within the contour in the direction of vehicle's movement if the speed of a vehicle is known. The speed of a vehicle can be calculated by measuring the elapsed time passing through two reference lines. However, the speed measurement is not considered here and the results will be reported in a forthcoming paper.

In our experiment we measured the number of passing vehicles per lane and total number of passing vehicles for three lanes. For the case of a single lane, we tested the traffic data of 7 blocks. Each block contains 750 frames (50 seconds). For the three lanes, we measured 10 blocks, each block containing 450 frames (30 seconds). The results are summarized in Table 1 and Table 2. The computer display of the traffic flow measuring system using real-time dynamic image processing is shown in Fig. 4. In the display screen, we selected the 350-th scan line from the top as the reference line of sample points.

The error rate is 2% for a single lane and 1.4% for three lanes. In both cases, the results indicate excellent performance of the proposed algorithm. The errors are mainly attributed to the fact that the vehicle contours with similar brightness to that of the road are eliminated by the contour processing unit (STEP 2).

The algorithm was implemented using Turbo C++ 3.0 with "speed optimize option". In the simulation discussed above, no attention was paid to optimize the

Table 1. The result of experiments for one lane

Blocks	1	2	3	4	5	6	7	Total
Observed number	11	13	13	23	17	12	12	101
Measured number	11	13	13	22	17	12	11	99
Error				-1			-1	-2

Table 2. The result of experiments for 3 lanes

Blocks	1	2	3	4	5	6	7	8	9	10	Total
Observed number	28	25	25	30	26	26	26	22	29	39	276
Measured number	26	25	26	30	26	26	26	21	29	39	274
Error	-2		1					-1			-2(4)

computational time for the traffic image processing algorithm, yet the time was found to be reasonably small. The processing time for 1528 frames (except for A/D conversion time by the Frame Grabber) was 12,985 msec (8.45 msec for each frame) on a Pentium III -700MHz personal computer at Hankuk Aviation University. This clearly indicates that the algorithm can be implemented in real-time. It is expected that the computational time could be further decreased by exploiting more efficient programming techniques.

5 Conclusion

In this paper, we have developed an automatic measuring system and its real-time image processing algorithm for traffic flow measurement. In the algorithm, the image of vehicles is quantized to obtain sample points and the brightness of each point. By comparing the brightness of the sample points of vehicle with that of the road, we detect the presence of vehicles. After eliminating noises by using smoothing techniques we obtain the contours of vehicles from the sampled image. The size of a vehicle is identified by counting the number of sample points corresponding to the width of the contour. We obtain the number of passing vehicles by counting the number of the sample points on the centerline of the contour. The measurement error was within of $1 \sim 2\%$ in our experiment. This clearly indicates excellent performance of the proposed algorithm. Speed of each vehicle can be measured by computing the time difference between a pair of sample points on two reference lines.

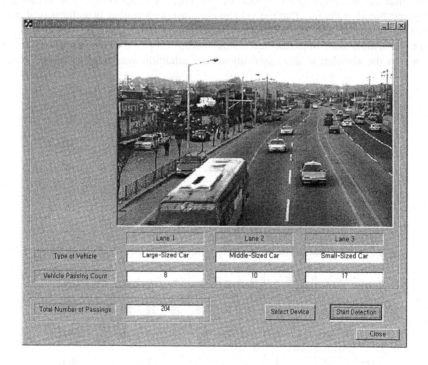

Fig. 4. Computer display of the traffic flow measuring system

References

1. Gloyer, B., Aghajan, H. K., Siu, K. Y., Kailath, T.: Vehicle Detection and Tracking for Freeway Traffic Monitoring. IEE Record of the Twenty-Eighth Asilomar Conference on Signals, Systems and Computers. **2** (1994) 970–974
2. Cucchiara, R. and Piccardi, M.: Vehicle Detection under Day and Night Illumination. ISCSIIA99, (1999)
3. Fathy, M., Siyal, M. Y.: An Image Detection Technique Based on Morphological Edge Detection and Background Differencing for Real-Time Traffic Analysis. Pattern Recognition Letters. **16** (1995) 1321–1330
4. Ali, A. T., Dagless, E. L.: Computer Vision for Automatic Road Traffic Analysis. International Conference on Automation, Robotics and Computer Vision. (1990) 875–879
5. Malik, J.: A Machine Vision Based Surveillance System for California Roads. PATH Project MOU-83 Final Report. University of California Berkeley (1994)
6. Jung, Y. K., Ho, Y. S.: Robust Vehicle Detection and Tracking for Traffic Surveillance. Picture Coding Symposium'99. (1999) 227–230
7. Rao, B. S. Y., Durrant-Whyte, H. F. and Sheen, J. A.: A Fully Decentralized Multi-Sensor System for Tracking and Surveillance. The International Journal of Robotics Research. **12** (1993) 20–24
8. Dickinson, K. W., Waterfall, R. C.: Video Image Processing for Monitoring Road Traffic. IEE International Conference on Road Traffic Data Collection. (1984) 105–109
9. Koller, D., Weber, J., Huang, T., Malik, J., Ogasawara, G., Rao, B. and Russell, S.: Towards robust automatic traffic scene analysis in real-time. 12th IAPR International Conference on Pattern Recognition. **1** (1994) 126–131
10. Fathy, M., Siyal, M. Y.: Real-Time Measurement of Traffic Queue Parameters by Using Image Processing Techniques. Fifth International Conference on Image Processing and Its Applications. (1995) 450–453
11. Soh, J., Chun B. T., Wang, M.: Analysis of Road Sequences for Vehicle Counting. IEEE International Conference on Systems, Man and Cybernetics. **1** (1995) 22–25
12. Hwang, Byong-Won, et al.: Measurement of Traffic Flow Using Real Time Processing of Moving Pictures. IEEE International Conference on Vehicular Technology (1982) 488–494
13. Hwang, Byong-Won, et al.: A Study on the Real Time Measurement of Vehicle Speed Using Dynamic Image Processing. 5th World Congress on Intelligent Transport Systems. (1998)
14. Hwang, Byong-Won, et al.: A Traffic Flow Measuring System Using a Solid-State Image Sensor. IEE International Conference on Road Traffic Data Collection. (1984)
15. Klein, L.A. and Kelly, M.R.: Detection Technology For IVHS, Vol. I, Final report No. FHWA-RD-95-100, FHA, DOT, McLean, Virginia. (1996)
16. EIS Inc.: RTMS User Manual, Issue 3.0, EIS Electronic Integrated Systems Inc., Toronto, Canada. (2002)

Efficient Fingertip Tracking and Mouse Pointer Control for a Human Mouse

Jiyoung Park and Juneho Yi

School of Information and Communication Engineering
Sungkyunkwan University
Suwon 440-746, Korea
{jiyp, jhyi}@ece.skku.ac.kr

Abstract. This paper discusses the design of a working system that visually recognizes hand gestures for the control of a window based user interface. We present a method for tracking the fingertip of the index finger using a single camera. Our method is based on CAMSHIFT algorithm and it tracks well particular hand poses used in the system in complex backgrounds. We describe how the location of the fingertip is mapped to a location on the monitor, and how it is both necessary and possible to smooth the path of the fingertip location using a physical model of a mouse pointer. Our method is able to track in real time, yet does not absorb a major share of computational resources. The performance of our system shows a great promise that we will be able to use this methodology to control computers in near future.

1 Introduction

Computer vision has a significant role to play in the human-computer interaction devices of the future. There have been reported many research results [1-5, 7, 8] in the literature that try to substitute the currently used devices such as mouse and keyboard with a vision based natural interface. Rehg and Kanade described "DigitEyes"[4], a model-based hand tracking system that uses two cameras to recover the state of a hand. Kjeldsen and Kender suggested a simple visual gesture system to manipulate graphic user interface of a computer [5]. Andrew et al. presented a method for tracking the 3D position of a finger, using a single camera placed several meters away from the user [7]. DigitEyes is based on a 3D model of a human hand and is computationally very expensive. The performance of the other two approaches is not robust to complex background.

This research presents a system that efficiently tracks the fingertip of the index finger for the purpose of application to a human mouse. The main features of the proposed system are as follows. First, adaptive online training of skin color distribution is employed to reliably detect human hand regions. Segmentation of hand regions is robust to noise, and is very accurate because a user-specific lookup table is used. Second, we have proposed a tracking method based on CAMSHIFT algorithm [1] where the method is particularly tuned for tracking hand regions. As can be seen in the experimental results, the tracking performance is robust to cluttered background having colors similar to those of skin regions. Third, a novel method to display the

J.L. Crowley et al. (Eds.): ICVS 2003, LNCS 2626, pp. 88–97, 2003.

mouse pointer gives users a natural feeling of controlling a mouse by physically modeling the mouse pointer. As a result, the motion of the mouse pointer on the monitor is very smooth even though actual tracking rate is as low as 5-6 Hz. The problem due to the difference of resolution between the input image from the camera and the monitor has also been resolved. The experimental results show a great promise that the proposed system can be applied to control computers in near feature.

This paper is organized as follows. The following section briefly reviews an overview of our system. Section 3 and 4 present the proposed methods for fingertip detection and the display of the mouse pointer on the monitor, respectively. Experimental results are reported in section 5.

2 System Overview

Let us briefly overview the entire system. Fig. 1 shows a block diagram of the computation in the system. Details of each computation will be presented in later sections.

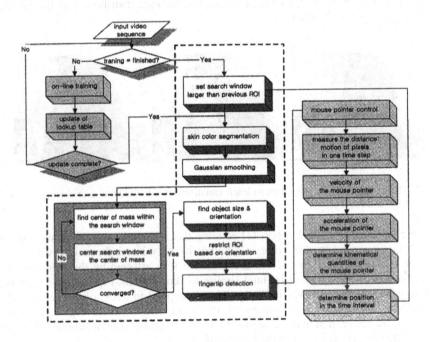

Fig. 1. System overview

The system is divided into three parts: adaptive on-line training of skin colors for hand region segmentation, fingertip tracking, and mouse pointer display. The first part is on-line training of skin colors robust to changes of illumination and hand poses, and complex backgrounds. The system learns the probability distribution of skin colors of the current user. The second part is fingertip tracking (dashed region in Fig. 1). Hand regions are segmented in the input image sequence using the learned skin color lookup table computed in the first part. After segmentation of the hand regions, we compute the location of the fingertip. To rapidly detect the fingertip location, we have employed a region of interest (ROI) using the information about the size and the orientation of a hand region. The last part is for the control of the mouse pointer. The mapping between camera coordinates and monitor coordinates of the fingertip location is computed. In addition, smoothing of the mouse pointer path is performed so that the user can have natural feeling as if he or she were using a real mouse.

3 Fingertip Detection

3.1 Adaptive Online Training of Skin Colors

We use an on-line training method as can be seen in Fig. 2. The user is asked to place his or her hand so that the rectangular box can stay in the hand. The method gets the system to learn variations of skin colors due to changes of local illumination and hand poses. The advantage of this method is that the accurate distribution of the current user's skin colors is obtained.

Fig. 2. The on-line training procedure to learn variations of skin colors due to changes of local illumination and hand poses.

There has been a research report [1] claming that, "Humans are all the same color (hue)". However, when skin color is detected by only hue information, we find it difficult to find skin regions of the user because it is affected by the colors of the environment having values of H (hue) similar to skin regions. Fig. 3 shows a couple of examples when the CAMSHIFT algorithm is applied to track a hand region. The intersection of the two lines represents the center of the hand region detected. However, the result of skin color segmentation is wrong because of (a) the red sleeve of the jacket and (b) the color of the bookshelf.

We have employed H (hue) and S (saturation) values of HSV color space for learning the probability distribution of skin colors. A 2D look up table is computed using H and S as the result of on-line training of skin colors. The entries of this table are the probability density of hue and saturation values.

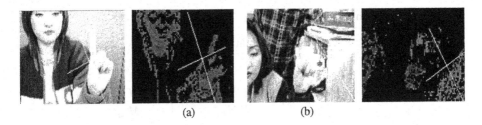

(a)   (b)

Fig. 3. Examples of wrong segmentation results of CAMSHIFT algorithm when only hue (H) value is used. (a) the effect of the red sleeve of the jacket, (b) the effect of the color of the bookshelf

3. 2 Detection and Tracking of Hand Regions

Determining the location and size of an ROI. The computation time is saved a lot by confining necessary computation to ROI. The hand region is tracked in the current frame within the ROI that was computed in the previous frame. In the ROI of the current frame, the hand region is detected but the centers of the ROI and the hand region detected do not accord because of the hand motion. The center of the hand region within the current ROI becomes the center of ROI to be used in the next frame.

Noise around the hand region may cause the propagation of errors in detection of the hand region. When there is noise around the hand region, the location (i.e. center) of ROI to be used in the next frame is not computed correctly and this has an effect on detection of the hand region. We can reduce the effect due to noise by not considering pixels in the skin region of which probability density is less than some threshold value. After thresholding, we obtain a binary image, $B(x,y)$, in ROI. $B(x,y)=1$ for pixels belonging to hand region. However, in some cases, part of the hand region is not detected due to this thresholding operation. The size of an ROI is determined by considering the size and the orientation of the hand region. The center coordinates (x_c, y_c) of the hand region can be simply computed using the 0th, 1st order moments [6] as follows.

$$x_c = \frac{M_{10}}{M_{00}}, \quad y_c = \frac{M_{01}}{M_{00}} \tag{1}$$

$$M_{00} = \sum_x \sum_y B(x, y), \quad M_{10} = \sum_x \sum_y xB(x, y), \quad M_{01} = \sum_x \sum_y yB(x, y)$$

The 2D orientation of the detected hand region is also easy to obtain by using the 2nd order moments. The 2nd order moments are computed as follows.

$$M_{20} = \sum_x \sum_y x^2 B(x, y), \quad M_{02} = \sum_x \sum_y y^2 B(x, y) \tag{2}$$

Then the object orientation (major axis) is;

$$\theta = \frac{\arctan\left(b, (a-c)\right)}{2} \tag{3}$$

where $a = \dfrac{M_{20}}{M_{00}} - x_c^2$, $b = 2\left(\dfrac{M_{11}}{M_{00}} - x_c y_c\right)$, $c = \dfrac{M_{02}}{M_{00}} - y_c^2$.

The size of an ROI can be determined by the orientation, θ, of the hand region by using the moments computed and by scaling the horizontal and vertical lengths of the ROI as in equation (4). The horizontal and vertical lengths for the ROI are denoted by R_x and R_y, respectively.

$$R_x = s_x \sqrt{M_{00}}, \ R_y = s_y \sqrt{M_{00}}, \tag{4}$$
$$\text{where } s_x = \cos|\theta| + 1, \ s_y = \sin|\theta| + 1, \ \max(s_x, s_y) + 0.1$$

The scaling factors, s_x and s_y, are determined from the statistical knowledge that the length ratio of the elongated axis vs. its perpendicular axis of a human hand does not exceed 2.1:1.

Hand tracking. The algorithm for tracking a hand region is based on the CAMSHIFT algorithm. The main difference between the CAMSHIFT algorithm and our algorithm is the way to determine the ROI. Fig. 4 shows an example of three successive updates of the search window when the CAMSHIFT algorithm is applied to track a hand region. The search window tends to include noise regions next to the previous search window that have the colors similar to skin regions. We can see that the size of the search window has grown and that the center of the detected hand region is not correctly computed.

Fig. 4. Growing the search window in the CAMSHIFT algorithm

In contrast to CAMSHIFT, computes the ROI in a particular way that is tuned for a human hand while the CAMSHIFT is not. Therefore, the tracking performance of our algorithm is tweaked, especially when there are colors in the background similar to those of skin region. A block diagram of the algorithm is shown in Fig. 5.

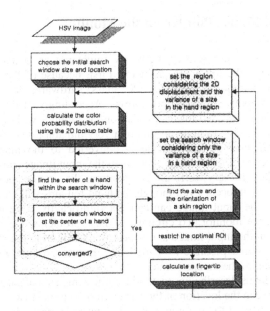

Fig. 5. A block diagram of hand tracking

3. 3 Computation of the Fingertip Location

If there is no noise, skin regions are detected perfectly. In this case, to compute the location of the fingertip, we can simply use the coordinates of boundary pixels [7] or can compute the center coordinates of the first knuckle of the index finger. However, detection of skin region cannot be perfect due to noise. We have used a way robust to noise for the detection of the fingertip location. We assume that the fingertip location lies in the first knuckle of the index finger. The length of the elongated axis of the hand region can be simply computed using equation (5) [8]. The end point of l is determined as the location of the fingertip. Refer to Fig. 6.

$$l = \sqrt{\frac{(a+c)+\sqrt{b^2+(a-c)^2}}{2}} \tag{5}$$

where a, b and c are the same as in equation (3).

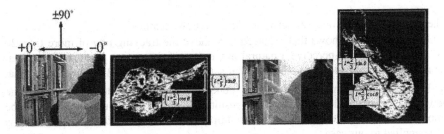

Fig. 6. Computation of the fingertip location in the cases of $\theta < 0$ (left) and $\theta > 0$ (right)

4 Display of a Mouse Pointer on the Monitor

Even if the fingertip is detected correctly, we might not get a natural motion of a mouse pointer due to the following problems. First, because of the limitation on the tracking rate on commonly available PC class hardware, we can merely get discontinuous coordinates of fingertip locations. Accordingly, if these coordinates of the fingertip locations are used for the display on the monitor without any smoothing, the mouse pointer is going to jump around in a very unnatural fashion. Second, if the location of the fingertip in each frame is converted to the monitor coordinates directly, the difference of the resolution between the input image from the camera and the monitor makes it very difficult to position the mouse pointer accurately. Moreover, the jitter can occur even though the hand remains still. A small movement of the fingertip in the input image can cause a significantly large movement of the mouse pointer on the monitor. To circumvent these problems, we describe how the fingertip location in the input image is mapped to a location on the monitor, and how it is both necessary and possible to smooth the trajectory of the mouse pointer by physically modeling of the mouse pointer.

For simplicity, let us describe our method for one-dimensional case. In the ith frame, the difference between the location of the current mouse pointer (X_{i-1}) and the fingertip location (H_i) is converted to an amount of force that accelerates the mouse pointer in an appropriate direction as in equation (6).

$$D_i = H_i - X_{i-1} , \quad F_i = f(D_i) \tag{6}$$

If the displacement of the fingertip location in the input image is smaller than a predetermined threshold, the minimum force, F_{min}, will be set to zero because the mouse pointer should remain still on the monitor. The threshold is set to 1% of the resolution of each axis on the monitor. The mouse pointer is treated as an object having mass and velocity as well as position. Its motion can be described using the second-order differential equation for the position $x(t)$ based on the Newton's law.

$$\frac{d^2 x(t)}{dt^2} = \frac{F}{m} \tag{7}$$

where F and m denote the amount of force and the mass of an object, respectively. For the solution of equation (7), we use Euler-Cromer algorithm [9] as follows.

$$x_{n+1} = x_n + v_n \Delta t \tag{8}$$

where Δt is the time interval between successive two frames.

Our observations shows that we need to achieve the tracking rate of more than 20 fps so that a user can perceive a natural movement of the mouse pointer. If a system cannot support this rate, the value of k that satisfies $\Delta t / k = 0.03(s)$ is chosen. That is, locations of the mouse pointer are generated on the monitor during the time between two image frames so that the resulting path of the mouse pointer may be smooth. This one-dimensional method is simply extended to two dimensions, x and y, to be applied to our case.

5 Experimental Results

Fig. 7 shows examples of the tracking results for three lighting conditions: (a) natural and artificial lighting, (b) natural lighting and (c) artificial lighting. The rectangular boxes represent ROI depending on the size and the orientation of the hand region. The location of the fingertip is reliably computed in spite of the background having colors similar to those of skin regions.

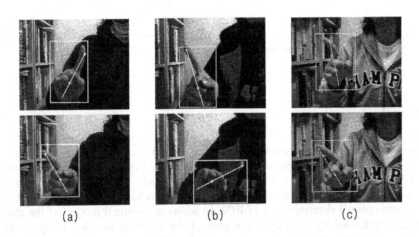

(a)   (b)   (c)

Fig. 7. Tracking results of the fingertip location. (a) natural and artificial lighting, (b) natural lighting, (C) artificial lighting

Table 1 summarizes the experimental results. The accuracy measures the frequency of correct detection of fingertip location.

Table 1. The accuracy of detecting a fingertip location

	# total frames	# detected frames	accuracy (%)
natural and artificial lighting	400	373	93.25
natural lighting	400	368	92
artificial lighting	400	387	96.75
total	1200	1128	94

We can see that the tracking performance is quite robust to lighting conditions. Fig. 8 shows the smoothing result of the mouse pointer path when the tracking rate is 6Hz. With raw tracking results, the monitor coordinates of the mouse pointer are quite discontinuous and not smooth as can be seen in Fig. 8 (a). The path of the mouse pointer is smoothed using the proposed method that physically models the mouse pointer.

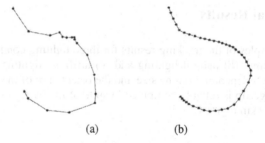

(a)   (b)

Fig. 8. An example trajectory of the mouse pointer. (a) raw tracking results (6Hz), (b) a smoothed version of the raw tracking results

6 Conclusion

In this paper we have proposed a method to detect and track the fingertip of the index finger for the purpose of application to a human mouse system. The proposed method for fingertip tracking shows a good performance under cluttered background and variations of local illumination due to hand poses by virtue of online training of skin colors and optimal determination of ROI. In addition, a natural motion of the mouse pointer is achieved by smoothing the path of the fingertip location using physical model of the mouse pointer. The experimental results show a great promise that the proposed method can be applied to manipulate computers in near future.

Acknowledgements. This work was supported by grant number R01-1999-000-00339-0 from the Basic Research program of the Korean Science and Engineering Foundation.

References

1. Gary R. Bradski, "Computer Vision Face Tracking For Use in a Perceptual User Interface", *Intel Technology Journal Q2*, 1998.
2. R. Kjeldsen and J. Kender "Interaction with On-Screen Objects using Visual Gesture Recognition" *IEEE Conference on Computer Vision and Pattern Recognition*, pp. 788–793, 1997.
3. C. Jennings, "Robust finger tracking with multiple cameras", *International Workshop on Recognition, Analysis, and Tracking of Faces and Gestures in Real-Time Systems*, pp. 152–160, 1999.
4. J. Rehg and T. Kanade, "Visual Analysis of High DOF Articulated Object with Application to Hand Tracking", *CMU Tech. Report CMU-CS-95-138*, Carnegie Mellon University, April, 1993.

5. R. Kjeldsen and J. Kender, "Towards the use of Gesture in Traditional User Interfaces", *International Conference on Automatic Face and Gesture Recognition,* pp. 151–156, 1996.

6. B. K. P. Horn, "Robot vision", MIT Press, 1986.

7. Andrew Wu, Mubarak Shah and N. da Vitoria Lobo, " A Virtual 3D Blackboard: 3D Finger Tracking using a Single Camera" *Proceedings of the Fourth International Conference on Atomatic Face and Gesture Reconition,* pp. 536–543, 2000.

8. W. T. Freeman, K. Tanaka, J. Ohta and K. Kyuma, "Computer vision for computer games" *Proceedings of the Second International Conference on Automatic Face and Gesture Recognition,* pp. 100–105, 1996.

9. Harvey Gould and Jan Tobochnik, "An Introduction to Computer Simulation Methods", Addison Wesley Publishing Company, 1996.

Real-Time Camera Pose in a Room

Manmohan Krishna Chandraker, Christoph Stock, and Axel Pinz

Institute of Electrical Measurement and Measurement Signal Processing
Graz University of Technology, Austria
{manu, stock}@emt.tugraz.at, axel.pinz@tugraz.at
http://www.emt.tugraz.at/~tracking

Abstract. Many applications of computer vision require camera pose in real-time. We present a new, fully mobile, purely vision-based tracking system that works indoors in a prepared room, using artificial landmarks. The main contributions of the paper are: improved pose accuracy by subpixel corner localization, high frame rates by CMOS image aquisition of small subwindows, and a novel sparse 3D model of the room for a spatial target representation and selection scheme which gains robustness.

Keywords: Tracking, camera pose, CMOS camera, sparse 3D modeling

1 Introduction

Many applications of computer vision require camera pose in real-time. This is a hard problem which is known as 'real-time pose computation' in computer vision, or as 'vision-based inside-out tracking' in virtual and augmented reality. Existing vision-based systems suffer from several major deficiencies:

- motion blur, rapid change of field of view,
- occlusion, blocked line-of-sight,
- complexity of matching in a cluttered scene,
- multiple motion (ego-, target-, other objects),
- processing speed of the vision-based system in general.

Potential remedies are:

- hybrid systems (vision+inertial, GPS, magnetic, compass,...),
- active vision (laser pointing, control of mobile platform,...),
- *improved concepts for a computer vision system.*

We present a new, fully mobile, purely vision-based tracking system for indoor tracking applications in a prepared room with artificial landmarks. Only points are tracked (corner features). The main contributions of this paper are:

- accuracy (subpixel corner localisation),
- speed (CMOS camera, direct access of small subwindows), and
- representation of the scene in terms of landmarks (target selector).

J.L. Crowley et al. (Eds.): ICVS 2003, LNCS 2626, pp. 98–110, 2003.

1.1   Related Work

The problem of recovering camera pose from perspective n points (the PnP-problem) has been discussed as early as 1981 by Fischler and Bolles [6], but linear and real-time PnP algorithms are still an active research topic (e.g. [11, 1]). Vision-based ([9,2,5]), and hybrid sensor pose ([18,12,14,16]) are required in many application areas of virtual and augmented reality [13,4].

2   Tracking Methods

Figure 1 presents a schematic overview of our complete tracking system, which has been designed to work under varying conditions, indoors and outdoors, and with several kinds of sensors like CCD- and CMOS-cameras, and inertial trackers, which motivates the term 'hybrid tracker'. The modular system splits into five distinct blocks.

The tracker continuously delivers pose information (i.e. the sensor's pose w.r.t. the world coordinate system) to the pose client. To cut down the complexity of the correspondence problem a target selector module pre-selects features from the model database in a context-dependent way. Thus, only subsets of the model database are used during the tracking process once the initialization has been finished. As the pose client, the target selector requires the actual pose information to maintain the *active* set of model features. However, compared to the tracking loop, target selector runs take place at a considerably lower rate (about 1 Hz).

The hybrid tracker module has direct access to the sensor pool module which holds the array of sensors and their corresponding calibration data. Additionally, the operator can perform a number of maintenance and control tasks using the operator interface. Though the interfaces between adjacent modules in this design are not restricted to be of any distinct type, we prefer to use TCP/IP connections for data communication, which allows to easily split up the tracker to run on different CPUs. We subsequently describe all components of this system which are involved in the scenario (real-time camera pose in a room) and the experiments of this paper. Several other features of the hybrid tracker, like sensor fusion, are not discussed here.

2.1   Target Design

We want to use corners as our trackable features, so that the target design has to satisfy the following three requirements: High accuracy of the feature position; Uniqueness of targets; Fast correspondence verification. This leads us to the following considerations in target design:

Target Size: We found that for the dimensions of our laboratory (approx. $5 \times 6m$), a target should fit in roughly a $20cm \times 20cm$ area. Too large a target would mean that there are increased chances that fewer than the minimum number of targets (i.e. 2) are within the field of view for a certain camera pose. Equivalently,

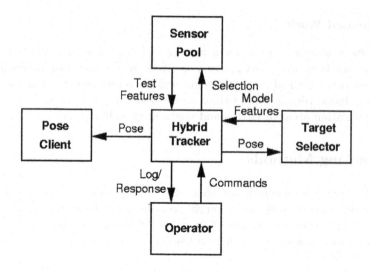

Fig. 1. Schematic outline of our hybrid tracking system.

it means that the minimum distance that we must set between wall and camera would be too large. On the other hand, too small a target would lead to corners on the same edge being too close, so that the corner detector would not be able to distinguish between them.

Target Shape: The basic shape of the target is as drawn in fig. 2. The idea is to have exactly 4 corners along each straight edge of the target which define a cross-ratio which is invariant under perspective projection. For the above mentioned target size constraints, not many unique cross-ratios (about 10) can be generated for accurate identification within limits of experimental error. In our target design, two cross-ratios are constrained to include a common corner, so even 10 cross-ratios can generate (10 choose 2) = 45 unique targets, which is sufficient for a representation of the room. In a recent paper, Naimark and Foxlin present an alternative approach based on circular landmarks with interior patterns for unique landmark identification [12].

2.2   Corner Detection and Subpixel Localisation

The basic procedure for extraction of corners is derived from the morphological scheme detailed in [10]. This approach satisfies our demands on fast corner extraction and high detection performance. A series of dilations and erosions by kernels of four different shapes - square, cross, plus, lozenge - results in a corner strength image.

The problem with such an approach is that a number of false corners are detected around, very close to, the true corner position. A heuristic procedure chooses only one corner out of this cluster, which is either used for pose calcu-

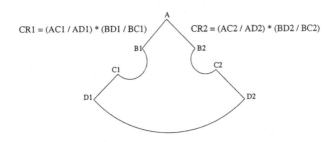

Fig. 2. The target design combines two different cross-ratios to identify three corners (A, D1 and D2).

lation or as the initial point for the sub-pixel accurate corner detector described in [17].

Random variations in light intensity, uneven cuts along the target edges and even faulty regions within the sensor array lead to detection of several corners besides the ones which are part of the targets. Complexity and error of the correspondence search algorithm increase drastically with increase in the number of detected corners. The way out is to simply count the ratio of black and white pixels on a pre-defined contour around each corner and to eliminate those corners which do not correspond to a ratio approximately between 60 and 120 degrees (the assumption is that only moderate projective distortions occur).

Sets of four corners on a straight line (referred to as quadruples) are formed and the cross-ratio is defined for each such quadruple. There might be quadruples which are formed due to corners from different targets and still have the same cross-ratio as a desired quadruple on the edge of a single target. Such quadruples are eliminated by utilizing certain orientational relationships between corners of the same edge as shown in fig. 3.

2.3 Corner Tracking with a CMOS Camera

Due to the fact that corners are local features of an image, only small subsets of the whole image are necessary to compute the corner position. After an initialization process over the whole image, only small sub-images suffice to track the corner position from one frame to another.

True random access of pixels, in any image, at any time, requires full asynchronous reading of the sensor. In this case, fixed integration time concepts cannot be maintained. The pixels should therefore not be of the classic charge integrating type. Unlike CCD (Charge-Coupled Device) sensors, CMOS sensors use an active pixel structure type that yields an instantaneous signal that is proportional to the instantaneous light intensity and can be used to access small sub-regions of an image.

Active pixel structures allow random access, which provides high-speed imaging of a new dimension in combination with fast self-setting bandwidth control.

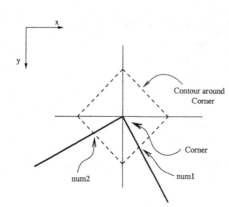

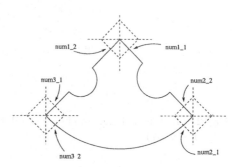

(a) A square contour of 10×10 pixels is drawn around the corner. It intersects the target at num1 and num2. The corner is classified according to the ratio $int((num2 - num1)/9)$ having the value 0, 1, 2 or 3.

(b) Depending upon the values of num1 and num2 for the first and fourth corner of a quadruple, we can straightaway eliminate those quadruples that are formed with corners from more than one target.

Fig. 3. Rejection scheme for (a) false corners, (b) false quadruples.

This means that the region of interest can be individually set by the user. Reducing the image field to marked subsets speeds up the image acquisition drastically. Frame rates of several hundred frames per second (fps) can be easily obtained, which is a big advantage over the currently established video frame rates of 30 to 60 fps.

2.4   Spatial Representation and Selection of Landmarks

The complexity of the tracking process can be reduced greatly by just concentrating on the targets that are within the field of view. The target selector (see fig.1) fulfills this function precisely. Moreover, it enables the isolation of the tracking process from the learning-based methods that could be employed in future context-dependent scenarios.

The target selector receives the current pose estimate from the tracker. Using this pose estimate, it tries to determine which of the targets in the target database is likely to be in the field of view (FoV), by determining whether the pre-specified center of gravity (CoG) of the target is within the FoV. If a target is visible, it proceeds to update the feature list for that target, that is, it sets the visibility flags for each of the features of that target according to whether that feature is within the FoV or not. This updated list of targets is then sent to the tracker.

The target selector computes the 2D-position (in pixels) of the *visible* features using the built-in camera model. Then small images are grabbed around these pixel values, the corner is extracted and the updated value is stored for grabbing in the next frame. If a prediction module is present, the update should also incorporate the motion estimate from the predictor. As of now, there is no prediction. All the extracted corners are used for a robust estimation of the camera pose, as described in the following section.

2.5   Pose Computation

Consistent with our objective of achieving real-time or greater tracking rates, we place greater emphasis on the speed of the pose estimation algorithm. An algorithm that combines concepts from projective geometry and an SVD solution to the absolute orientation problem in a RANSAC paradigm is employed to optimize between speed and robustness, as described below.

If ϵ be the proportion of outliers among a large data set of size S and N samples of size s chosen randomly, the probability p that at least one of the samples is free from outliers is given by

$$p = 1 - (1 - (1 - \epsilon)^s)^N \tag{1}$$

The algorithm begins with a worst case assumption for the proportion of outliers and this assumption is updated when a larger consensus set is found. A sample is deemed belonging to the consensus set if its distance from the proposed model, K, is less than a threshold, t. Instead of following the more theoretically correct approach of using the probability distribution of the distance of an inlier point (x, y) from the proposed model we use an empirical measure :

$$t = \sqrt{\frac{(x - K(x))^2 + (y - K(y))^2}{(x + K(x))^2 + (y + K(y))^2}}$$

Note that N is also updated to correspond to the best consensus set found so far. If the number of trials exceeds N or a pre-defined limit, the algorithm terminates. The pose corrsponding to the maximal consensus set is declared the correct pose. A sample size of 4 is sufficient to determine the camera pose from a data set of coplanar points. Next, we describe the actual pose computation algorithm.

Let $\{P\}$ be the set of image points and $\{Q\}$ be the set of corresponding object points. A purely geometric method described in [6] computes the translation vector from the origin, **t**. As formulated in [11], the absolute orientation problem deals with estimation of the rotation matrix, **R** and the translation vector, **t** from a set of 3D-camera space co-ordinates, $\{q\}$ and the corresponding scene coordinates, $\{p\}$, where each such observation satisfies

$$\mathbf{q}_i = \mathbf{R}\mathbf{p}_i + \mathbf{t} \tag{2}$$

But we have already estimated **t** by an independent method. We use this known **t** to determine geometrically the camera space coordinates $\{q\}$. The scene geometry is depicted in figure 4. Let **O** be the origin of the camera space coordinates.

Let the point **a** be the image of point **A**. Since magnitude of **t** is known and position of **A** is also known (both in scene coordinates), the magnitude of the vector $\overline{OA}$ can be computed. Its direction is determined by the known x and y coordinates ($z = 1$ in normalized camera space) of pixel **a** once the corner has been extracted and the pixel size is known. Then the vector $\overline{OA}$ is precisely the vector **q** corresponding to point **A**.

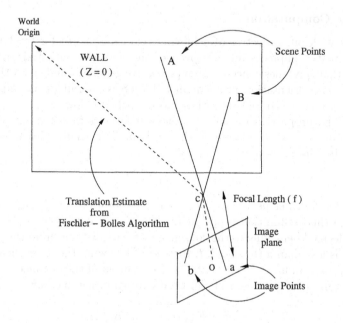

Fig. 4. Computation of **q** from known pixel values and camera translation.

Next, the centroids are computed :

$$\overline{\mathbf{p}} = \frac{1}{n}\sum_{i=1}^{n}\mathbf{p}_i \quad , \quad \overline{\mathbf{q}} = \frac{1}{n}\sum_{i=1}^{n}\mathbf{q}_i$$

Define

$$\mathbf{p}'_i = \mathbf{p}_i - \overline{\mathbf{p}} \quad , \quad \mathbf{q}'_i = \mathbf{q}_i - \overline{\mathbf{q}}$$

and

$$\mathbf{M} = \sum_{i=1}^{n}\mathbf{q}'_i\mathbf{p}'^{T}_i \tag{3}$$

Now, all the four points that we use are on the same plane $Z = 0$ in scene coordinates. Consequently, the last column of **M** is $[0, 0, 0]^T$ and **M** has a rank 2.

So we cannot use the simple SVD scheme and must use the approach outlined in [8]. This method would fail for $\mathbf{M}$ having rank 1, but such a situation arises only when the measurements are all collinear, in which case the absolute orientation problem can anyway be not solved. Any square matrix $\mathbf{M}$ can be decomposed into the product of an orthonormal matrix $\mathbf{U}$ and a positive semi-definite matrix $\mathbf{S}$. It is well-known that for a non-singular $\mathbf{M}$ having positive eigenvalues

$$\mathbf{S} = \left(\mathbf{M}^T\mathbf{M}\right)^{1/2} = \left(\frac{1}{\sqrt{\lambda_1}}\hat{\mathbf{u}}_1\hat{\mathbf{u}}_1^T + \frac{1}{\sqrt{\lambda_2}}\hat{\mathbf{u}}_2\hat{\mathbf{u}}_2^T + \frac{1}{\sqrt{\lambda_3}}\hat{\mathbf{u}}_3\hat{\mathbf{u}}_3^T\right)^{-1} \tag{4}$$

Here λ_1, λ_2, λ_3 are the eigenvalues of $\mathbf{M}$ and $\hat{\mathbf{u}}_1$, $\hat{\mathbf{u}}_2$, $\hat{\mathbf{u}}_3$ are the corresponding eigenvectors. $\mathbf{U}$ is easily determined as

$$\mathbf{U} = \mathbf{M}\mathbf{S}^{-1}$$

When $\mathbf{M}$ has a rank of only 2, we must use the pseudo-inverse, rather than the inverse, of $\mathbf{S}$. Thus,

$$\mathbf{S}^+ = \left(\frac{1}{\sqrt{\lambda_1}}\hat{\mathbf{u}}_1\hat{\mathbf{u}}_1^T + \frac{1}{\sqrt{\lambda_2}}\hat{\mathbf{u}}_2\hat{\mathbf{u}}_2^T\right)$$

If the Singular Value Decomposition of $\mathbf{M}\mathbf{S}^+$ be given by $\mathbf{M}\mathbf{S}^+ = U_0\Sigma_0V_0$ and $\hat{\mathbf{u}}_{03}$, $\hat{\mathbf{v}}_{03}$ be the third columns of U_0 and V_0, respectively, then we have

$$\mathbf{U} = \mathbf{M}\mathbf{S}^+ \pm \hat{\mathbf{u}}_{03}\hat{\mathbf{v}}_{03}^T \tag{5}$$

The rotation matrix $\mathbf{R}$ is given by choosing the sign in the above expression which makes the determinant of $\mathbf{U}$ positive.

2.6   Reinitialization

The tracker reinitializes itself under two distinct conditions:

1. When there are not enough corners to compute the pose. This can happen if the camera is too close to the wall, so that the minimum number of targets (2, in our case) are not visible. It can also be the case that 2 or more targets are visible, but due to some lighting variations, all corners are not detected. Severe projective distortions can lead to quadruples being rejected as incorrect when the corner is extracted a little away from the true position and the resulting cross-ratio is beyond the tolerance limits.
2. When the difference between successive pose estimates is too large.

The reinitialization conditions must be judiciously set since too many reinitializations slow down the tracking process substantially.

3   Experiments and Results

3.1   Experimental Setup

Figure 5.a shows a simple experimental setup, which we have used for the experiments described below. One can see three of our targets. We use a Fuga 15d 512×512 monochrome CMOS Camera with a common PCI interface, mounted on a tripod. The camera is mounted on top of a pan-tilt unit that can be used for rotation experiments with 'ground truth'. Figure 5.b sketches a fully mobile application scenario - real-time camera pose is used for head-pose estimation in an augmented reality application. All necessary hardware is carried on a backpack (see [15] for more details).

(a)   (b)

Fig. 5. Experimental setup: Stationary experiments with a CMOS camera, mounted on a pan-tilt head and our special target design (a). Real-time head-pose is required in mobile augmented reality applications (b).

3.2   Spatial Accuracy

The reliability of the pose computation is demonstrated by evaluating the pose error for a stationary camera. Table 1 shows three different poses w.r.t. planar targets, which were mounted on a wall (see Figure 5.a). Only four corners were needed to compute the pose of the camera. On the one hand the corners were extracted with the Standard-Plessey operator [7] and on the other hand with a new model-based subpixel corner-detector [17]. Due to the fact that the maximal pose error occurs in depth, Table 1 shows only accuracy-results in $z-$direction (depth). View-Point 1 (VP1) indicates a viewing direction perpendicular to the

Table 1. Pose Accuracy for a stationary camera, for three different view points.

		Absolute Pose-Error in m	Standard Deviation	Max. Jitter
VP1	Plessey	0.07	0.0029	0.0715
	Sub-Pixel	0.01	0.008	0.0427
VP2	Plessey	0.44	0.0274	0.2428
	Sub-Pixel	0.034	0.019	0.0919
VP3	Plessey	0.0935	0.0258	0.1258
	Sub-Pixel	0.0177	0.0119	0.0655

Table 2. Run-time Behavior depending on Window-size,
Total Time = Time for Initialization (0.88 sec) + 100 Tracker Runs.

Window Size	Total time (sec)	Time for 1 tracker run (msec)	Tracking Rate
31 × 31	2.96 sec	(2.96 − 0.88) /100 = 20.8 msec	48.0 Hz
11 × 11	1.43 sec	(1.43 − 0.88) /100 = 5.5 msec	181.8 Hz

Table 3. Tracking Rates depending on Window-size and Number of tracked corners.

Number of corners	Tracking Rate(in fps) for Window Size		
	11 × 11	21 × 21	31 × 31
1	1111	526	294
2	417	244	145
3	286	164	97
4	200	120	71
10	79	48	28

wall, the other two entries (VP2 and VP3) depict positions with arbitrarily chosen angles.

Although in the absence of motion prediction it is not possible to quantify the speed of camera motion without making a gross underestimation, we moved the camera along different trajectories and each time noted that the pose error was within acceptable limits. These experiments also give a glimpse of the reinitialization process within the target selector.

3.3 Tracking Speed

The obtained experimental data justifies that grabbing small windows with a CMOS sensor only around the points of interest (which is not possible with a traditional CCD sensor) can dramatically speed up the tracking process. The improvement in frame rates over contemporary trackers' 30-50 Hz is substantial.

Table 2 shows the time-behavior of our algorithm for the initialization process, followed by 100 tracker runs. The time needed for the initialization process is 0.88 sec.

The utility of the Target Selector lies, among others, in the fact that it allows us to get reliable pose estimates without needing to keep track of *all* the corners. It was found that grabbing and corner extraction were the slowest components of the entire algorithm. So, we demonstrate the time behavior of this component of the algorithm across different number of corners and different window-sizes (cf. table 3).

The improvement in frame rate with decrease in window-size is obvious and remarkably high. But a smaller window-size means greater chances of the corner getting lost due to abrupt motion. A good prediction module can overcome this problem.

3.4   Target Selector Functionality

Experiments were conducted that showed the independence of the target selector and the tracker processes. Projective distortions or poor lighting can lead to inaccurate cross-ratio computation at the initialization step. Our target selector is robust to such inaccuracies, as long as the minimum number of 4 corners are identifiable for pose computation. Based on the current pose, the targets within the field of view are reported to be visible after the target selector is invoked and these targets are then tracked.

4   Discussion and Outlook

We have presented a new system for vision-based pose determination. We achieve real-time performance and reasonable pose accuracy by subpixel corner detection and CMOS camera handling combined with a specific target design and target selector.

Our experiences with real-time tracking systems indicate clearly that the overall performance of a complex tracking system depends on many individual system components and their smooth interaction, so that it makes sense to design specific experimental setups and to study *isolated* problems in detail (e.g. the subpixel corner detector [17], or the complexity of correspondence search [3]).

Several future improvements of our system are on the way. We are developing a motion prediction module to allow fast camera motions, especially rotations. Although we have demonstrated the feasibility of a purely vision-based approach, robustness will be improved by using complementary sensors, as was shown for our hybrid outdoor system [15]. Whenever the system loses track, a rather time-consuming bootstrap (re-initialization) of the tracker is required. Dynamic interpretation tree as presented in [3] will be used to cut down complexity. Several other tracking systems use prepared environments and track artificial blob-like features (e.g. [12]). We hope that for our approach (tracking of corners), it will be easier to adapt to unprepared 'natural' scenes.

Acknowledgements. This research was supported by the following projects: VAMPIRE - Visual Active Memory Processes and Interactive REtrieval (EU-IST Programme - IST-2001-34401), and MCAR — Mobile Collaborative Augmented Reality (Austrian 'Fonds zur Förderung der wissenschaftlichen Forschung' project number P14470-INF).

References

1. Adnan Ansar and Kostas Daniilidis. Linear pose estimation from points or lines. In A. Heyden et al., editor, *Proc. ECCV*, volume 4, pages 282–296, Copenhagen, Denmark, May 2002. Springer LNCS 2353.
2. Mark Billinghurst, Hirokazu Kato, and Ivan Poupyrev. The MagicBook: a transitional AR interface. *Computers and Graphics*, 25:745–753, 2001.
3. M. Brandner and A. Pinz. Real-time tracking of complex objects using dynamic interpretation tree. In Luc Van Gool, editor, *Pattern Recognition, Proc. 24th DAGM Symposium, Zurich*, volume LNCS 2449 of *Schriftenreihe*, pages 9–16. Springer, 2002.
4. S.K. Feiner. Augmented reality: A new way of seeing. *Scientific American*, 4, 2002.
5. Vittorio Ferrari, Tinne Tuytelaars, and Luc Van Gool. Real-time affine region tracking and coplanar grouping. In *Proc. CVPR*, volume 2, pages 226–233, Kauai, Hawaii, USA, December 2001.
6. M. A. Fischler and R. C. Bolles. Random sample consensus: A paradigm for model fitting with applications to image analysis and automated cartography. *Communications of the ACM*, 24(6):381–395, June 1981.
7. C. Harris and M. Stephens. A combined corner and edge detector. In *Proc. of the 4th Alvey Vision Conference*, pages 189–192, Manchester, 1988.
8. B.K.P. Horn, H.M. Hilden, and S. Negahdaripour. Closed-form solution of absolute orientation using orthonormal matrices. *J.Opt.Soc.Am.A*, 5:1127–1135, 1988.
9. Dieter Koller, Gudrun Klinker, Eric Rose, David Breen, Ross Whitaker, and Mihran Tuceryan. Real-time vision-based camera tracking for augmented reality applications. In *Proc. CVPR*, 1997.
10. R. Laganière. Morphological corner detection. In *Proc. ICCV*, pages 280–285, Bombay, 1998.
11. C.P. Lu, G.D. Hager, and E. Mjolsness. Fast and globally convergent pose estimation from video images. *IEEE Trans. PAMI*, 22(6):610–622, June 2000.
12. L. Naimark and E. Foxlin. Circular data matrix fiducial system and robust image processing for a wearable vision-inertial self-tracker. In *Proceedings ISMAR 2002, Darmstadt*, pages 27–36. IEEE Comp Soc, 2002.
13. U. Neumann. STAR: Tracking for object-centric augmented reality. In W. Barfield and T. Caudell, editors, *Fundamentals of Wearable Computers and Augmented Reality*, chapter 10. Lawrence Erlbaum Associates, 2001.
14. U. Neumann, S. You, Y. Cho, J. Lee, and J. Park. Augmented reality tracking in natural environment. In *International Symposium on Mixed Realities*, Tokyo, Japan, 1999.
15. M. Ribo, H. Ganster, M. Brandner, P. Lang, Ch. Stock, and A. Pinz. Hybrid tracking for outdoor AR applications. *IEEE Computer Graphics and Applications Magazine*, 22(6):54–63, 2002.
16. Kiyohide Satoh, Mahoro Anabuki, Hiroyuki Yamamoto, and Hideyuki Tamura. A hybrid registration method for outdoor augmented reality. In *Proc. ISAR*, pages 67–76, 2001.

17. C. Stock, U. Mühlmann, M. Chandraker, and A. Pinz. Subpixel corner detection for tracking applications using cmos camera technology. In *26th Workshop of the AAPR/ÖAGM*, volume 160, pages 191–199, Graz, 2002. OCG Schriftenreihe.
18. S. You, U. Neumann, and R.T. Azuma. Hybrid inertial and vision traking for augmented reality registration. In *IEEE Conference on Virtual Reality*, pages 260–267, Houston, USA, March 1999.

Recognition of Obstacles on Structured 3D Background

Reinhold Huber, Jürgen Biber, Christoph Nowak, and Bernhard Spatzek*

Advanced Computer Vision GmbH - ACV
Tech Gate Vienna, Donau–City–Straße 1
A–1220 Vienna, Austria
Tel.: +43 (0)1 269 62 55 - 137, Fax: +43 (0)1 269 62 55 - 200
reinhold.huber@acv.ac.at

Abstract. A stereo vision system for recognition of 3D–objects is presented. The method uses a stereo camera pair and is able to detect objects located on a structured background constituting a repetitive 3D pattern, e.g. a staircase. Recognition is based on differencing stereo pair images, where a perspective warping transform is used to overlay the left onto the right image, or vice versa. The 3D camera positions are obtained during a learning phase where a 3D background model is employed. Correspondence between images and stereo disparity are derived based on the estimated pose of the background model. Disparity provides the necessary information for a perspective warping transform used in the recognition phase. The demonstrated application is staircase surveillance. Recognition itself is based on a pyramidal representation and segmentation of image intensity differences.

1 Introduction

This paper describes a stereo vision system for recognition of obstacles placed in front of a structured 3D background, e.g. a staircase. In particular, the task is to recognize objects on an escalator, which can be considered as a moving background, under real–world illumination conditions. Therefore, this task involves a learning phase, where the structured background is reconstructed, and a recognition phase, where obstacles are recognized using the acquired information about the background. The suggested solution consists of model based background reconstruction, perspective warping of one image to the other in a stereo setup, and the final detection of intensity differences based on an image pyramid representation. An earlier version of this paper, containing preliminary results, appeared in [9], more details and results can be found in [6] and [7].

Detection of anomalies on a floor plane using stereo techniques for navigation, vehicle guidance and obstacle avoidance was presented by several authors [10],

---

* This work was carried out within the K plus Competence Center ADVANCED COMPUTER VISION and was funded from the K plus program. We thank Professor Walter Kropatsch (Pattern Recognition and Image Processing Group, Technical University of Vienna) for critical comments, which helped to improve the paper.

J.L. Crowley et al. (Eds.): ICVS 2003, LNCS 2626, pp. 111–120, 2003.

[1], [12], [16]. The detection of staircases as an aid for the partially sighted was discussed in [13]. We describe a combination and extension of ideas presented in those papers with respect to detection of staircases as well as objects on staircases. Specifically, we employ a model based staircase pose estimator based on grouping of line features by the use of geometric invariants. The detection is based on measuring absolute pixel differences between unwarped and warped images. Image differences are represented in an image pyramid [2] and segmented into background (staircase) and foreground (obstacles) employing the algorithm suggested in [15]. The area of application is surveillance of staircases for security reasons, i.e. detection of occupancy or disposed items. Furthermore, our approach might be useful for applications involving staircase traversal, e.g. [3].

The main components of the presented system are the acquisition part, the offline (or learning) part and the online (or recognition) part. The most interesting subparts, i.e. geometric matching in the offline part and detection in the online part, will be discussed in some detail in the following.

2   Establishing Correspondences between 2D–Data and 3D–Model

In model–based pose estimation parameters describing relative orientation and position, i.e. the extrinsic camera parameters, are found using correspondence between data and model. In our case, the data are 2D lines extracted from single images and the model is a 3D wireframe object. Nearly horizontal lines are derived from the image data using standard edge detection algorithms based on directional image gradient and Hough transform techniques. On the top of Figure 1 an empty staircase image and corresponding vertical edges (derived from negative gradients along the vertical direction) are shown. The extracted lines are shown on the bottom left, on the bottom right the matched wireframe model is projected to the image plane. To establish correspondence between data and model lines (for each image in the stereo pair), and furthermore, between the two stereo pairs, the following matching procedure is applied.

2.1   Grouping Based on the Cross Ratio

The first step in matching is to identify possible correspondences between data and model lines. Under perspective projection, ratios of ratios of lines and ratios of ratios of angles, the so called cross ratios, are invariant [14]. We employ cross ratios to identify groups of four lines out of a larger set of possible lines. Such a group of four lines, which in our case is characterized by the cross ratio obtained for the intersection points with an approximately orthogonal line, serves as a matching candidate to the staircase pattern. The definition for the cross ratio for four points $p_1, \ldots, p_4$ on a line is given as:

$$Cr(p_1, \ldots, p_4) = [(x_3 - x_1)(x_4 - x_2)]/[(x_3 - x_2)(x_4 - x_1)],$$

where the $x_1, \ldots, x_4$ are the corresponding positions of each point on the line.

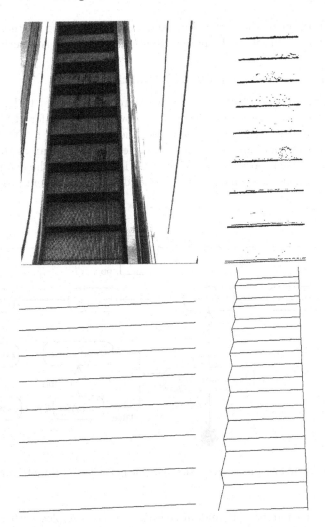

Fig. 1. Empty staircase image, extracted frontal edges, fitted frontal lines, estimated model lines projected to the image plane

The following strategy for selecting data lines, which are good candidates for correspondence to model lines, was employed:

1. Calculate the theoretical cross ratio, e.g. for four equally spaced points on a line this is $Cr_t = 4/3$.
2. Detect a reasonable set L (of size N) of close to horizontal lines from the data.
3. Calculate intersection points of those lines with a close to vertical line.
4. Calculate all $M = \binom{N}{4}$ four–element subsets of lines $l_i \subset L, i = 1, \ldots, M$.
5. Calculate all cross ratios c_i corresponding to sets l_i.
6. Sort the l_i with respect to $|c_i - Cr_t|$ (in ascending order).

Only a portion of the sorted line groups, corresponding to those of lower distance to Cr_t, is input to the pose estimation step, which is described below.

2.2 Estimation of Position and Orientation

Corresponding groups of lines are input to a procedure similar to RANSAC [4]. Grouping based on cross ratio delivers improved sampling for RANSAC and reduces the number of necessary iterations. The basic idea in RANSAC is, that RANSAC uses as small an initial data set as feasible and enlarges this set with consistent data when possible, see Figure 2. Figure 2 shows the enlargement of the set of lines in cases when a group of 4 lines delivers a sufficient pose estimate.

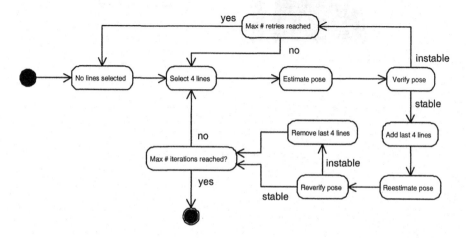

Fig. 2. Finite state machine showing the dynamic behavior of the matching procedure

The required number of random selections n_s of samples with a size of s features is given by Fischler and Bolles as [4]:

$$n_s = log(1 - p_c)/log(1 - p_i^s),$$

where p_c is the probability, that at least one sample of $s = 4$ lines (in our case) is free from outliers. The probability that any selected sample is an inlier is denoted by p_i. In our case, due to the improved sampling based on cross ratio, we can safely assume a high p_i, e.g. $p_i = 0.8$, and choosing $p_c = 0.99$, we obtain a number of necessary RANSAC iterations as low as $n_s = 9$.

Verification of the pose is based on the procedure devised by Lowe [11]. Lowe approaches the problem of derivation of object pose from a given set of known correspondences between 3D–model lines and 2D image lines by liberalization of projection parameters and application of Newton's method. The result of the pose estimation step are two transformations from world to camera coordinate system, i.e. three translational and three rotational parameters for each camera.

3   Recognition from Stereo Images

Recognition uses the information of a prior learning step, i.e. derivation of disparity and the two–dimensional warping transform. The recognition itself consists of the following steps. The first step is warping of one image to the other (e.g. the left image to the right one, see Figure 3). The next step is differencing of warped and unwarped images (see Figure 3 on the bottom left, where white means no difference and black corresponds to high difference). Finally, segmentation of the difference image is performed (see Figure 3 on the bottom right) in order to obtain a decision.

Fig. 3. Images and results for a person on a staircase: left and right images, absolute differences of left image warped to right image, and pyramid–based segmentation result

3.1 Image Warping

The warping transform is found from the staircase model, the world to camera coordinate system transforms for the left and right image, which are obtained by the pose estimation procedure mentioned above, and the projective transforms determined by camera properties. A perspective warping transform provides us with two warping tables which contain the coordinate mapping for both coordinate directions in the image plane. The warping tables are calculated from disparity, which is accurately given due to correspondence via the model. In particular, the perspective warping is controlled by quadrilaterals, i.e. the four points of a staircase face. Those four points determine the eight degrees of freedom of the following perspective mapping equations for a pixel coordinate (x', y') mapped to (x, y) [5]:

$$x = \frac{c_{00}x' + c_{01}y' + c_{02}}{c_{20}x' + c_{21}y' + c_{22}}, \quad y = \frac{c_{10}x' + c_{11}y' + c_{12}}{c_{20}x' + c_{21}y' + c_{22}},$$

where we can chose $c_{22} = 1$, arbitrarily. Given the disparity $d = (d_x, d_y) = (x' - x, y' - y)$ in four points, we are able to solve the mapping equation for the remaining c_{ij}. As the resulting pixel positions are usually not integer values, resampling is required, which in turn requires interpolation of resulting pixel values. We used bilinear interpolation of pixel values.

3.2 Recognition of Obstacles

The main idea in detection is to warp one image, e.g. the left image to the right one, and perform some comparison. The objects on the staircase, which should be recognized, have the property of being closer to the camera than the staircase on which they are placed. Therefore, objects in the image being warped appear at different positions than they appear in the unwarped image. On the other hand, disturbances like dirt, shadows or inscriptions on the staircase, appear on the same position in warped and unwarped image. Figure 3 showed initial images and some intermediate steps, i.e. the difference image generated by absolute pixel–wise differencing and the segmentation results applied to a difference image pyramid. Figure 4 shows image difference and segmentation pyramids. Details of the pyramid representation and segmentation algorithm can be found in [15].

4 Application and Results

We demonstrate our approach for the application of staircase surveillance, e.g. recognition of persons and disposed items on a staircase of known geometry. Figure 5 shows snapshots of the staircase with and without obstacles together with the recognition result, where **r/r** means correct recognition of obstacle, **r/e** no recognition of an obstacle, **e/e** means correct recognition of an empty staircase, and **e/r** recognition of an obstacle on an empty staircase.

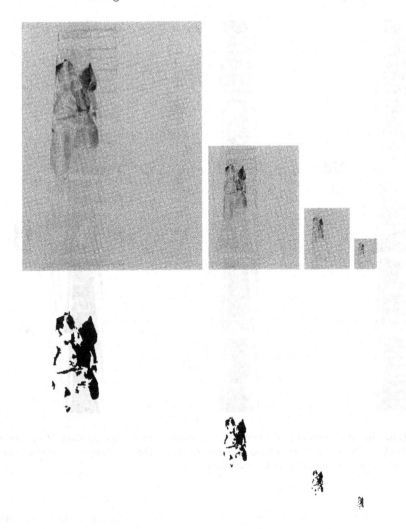

Fig. 4. Absolute intensity difference between warped and unwarped images and segmentation pyramids

Table 1 gives observed values for four different groups of image contents: empty staircases, persons standing or walking on a staircase, persons sitting on a staircase and a small cylindrical object, with a height of 30 centimeters, placed on a staircase. Each group contains 1000 different images. For the group of empty staircase images, a false alarm rate, i.e. an obstacle was recognized in absence of an obstacle, of 8.2 percent was observed. False recognition occurred during adaptation to sudden brightness changes as the test system was placed outdoors. In the test setting, environmental conditions included foggy, cloudy, rainy and sunlight weather with illumination ranging from 400 to 20000 lux.

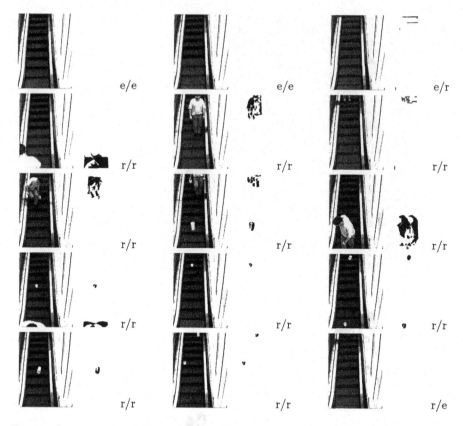

Fig. 5. Images segmentation results: r/r means correct recognition of one or more obstacles, r/e missing recognition, e/e means correct recognition of an empty staircase, and e/r recognition on an empty staircase

For the two groups showing images of single persons on a staircase rates of omission, i.e. a person was not recognized, in the order of 0.6 percent for standing or walking persons and 0.4 percent for sitting persons was observed. Here, the omissions occurred in cases where only a very small portion of the person was seen in the image, e.g. one leg only. In practice, this problem becomes irrelevant, as a typical escalator is covered by repeated placement of camera pairs. This means, a person whose legs are seen in one camera pair becomes nearly fully visible a subsequent camera pair.

Fully visible and bright cylindrical objects down to a size of 30 centimeters in height were recognized reliably with a rate of omission of 0 percent.

For all experiments the camera image acquisition was limited to a region of interest, which is the staircase area in our case. Adaption to changing illuminations was achieved by controlling the camera aperture with respect to image contents in the region of interest. Details of the camera adaptation procedure can be found in [8].

Table 1. Obstacle recognition performance observed for: an empty staircase, a single person standing on a staircase, a single person sitting on a staircase, and for a small cylindrical object on a staircase (1000 images were taken for each group)

Image	Recognition Result	
Group	Obstacle	Empty
Empty Staircase	82	918
Person Standing	994	6
Person Sitting	996	4
Cylindrical Object	1000	0

From the performance point of view, it takes 37.1 milliseconds to decide whether there is an obstacle present or not on a 2 GHz Intel Pentium P4. Including the grabbing of the image, which is left to a specific hardware, it takes 39.3 milliseconds. This means we are able to observe the escalator at a frame rate of $1/0.04 = 25$ fps. To achieve this high frame rate, we use a collection of prestored warping tables corresponding to different states of the staircase, i.e. different positions of the steps, which puts some demand on the memory consumption. In our case we require a total of 95 megabytes for grabbing and recognition data and program working memory. Apart from the recognition part, the learning part is much more demanding, i.e. in the order of seconds depending on parameter seconds. However, this is not problem as this step is usually performed offline, i.e. at escalator installation time.

5   Conclusion

An extension of stereo based obstacle detection procedures to regularly structured and non–flat background was presented. The reconstruction of the background is considered to be a learning task where a model–based approach for grouping and pose estimation was chosen. Learning can be extended to any background model described by a CAD model and some recurrent properties of a line pattern, e.g. zebra crossings, railway tracks. Grouping based on a cross ratio constraint improved RANSAC sampling. Pose estimation provides externally calibrated cameras, which simplify and accelerate stereo processing. The object recognition task itself is performed using a pyramid based segmentation procedure. A high reliability of the approach was found experimentally, i.e. a rate of omission of an obstacle of less than 1 percent, and a rate of false recognition of an obstacle in the order of magnitude of 8 percents was observed. Further research might include reduction of the false alarm rate through reasoning over time, as false alarms were observed to be isolated events in most cases.

References

1. Peter Burt, Lambert Wixson, and Garbis Salgian. Electronically Directed 'Focal' Stereo. In *Proceedings of International Conference on Computer Vision*, pages 94–101, Cambridge, MA, USA, June 1995.

2. Peter J. Burt, Tsai-Hong Hong, and Azriel Rosenfeld. Segmentation and Estimation of Image Region Properties Through Cooperative Hierarchical Computation. *IEEE Transactions on Systems, Man and Cybernetics*, 11(12):802–809, December 1981.

3. M. Fair and D.P. Miller. Automated Staircase Detection, Alignment & Traversal. In *Proceedings of International Conference on Robotics and Manufacturing*, pages 218–222, Cancun, Mexico, May 2001.

4. M.A. Fischler and R.C. Bolles. Random Sample Concensus: A Paradigm for Model Fitting with Applications to Image Analysis and Automated Cartography. *Communications of the ACM*, 24(6):381–395, 1981.

5. Paul S. Heckbert. Fundamentals of Texture Mapping and Image Warping. Technical Report CSD–89–516, Department of Electrical Engineering and Computer Science, University of Berkeley, CA, USA, June 1989.

6. Reinhold Huber. 3D Object Detection in Stereo Geometry. Technical Report ACV_TR_61, Advanced Computer Vision GmbH - ACV, Kplus Competence Center, Vienna, Austria, 2002.

7. Reinhold Huber. Matching and Pose Estimation for Regular Rigid 3D Objects. Technical Report ACV_TR_60, Advanced Computer Vision GmbH - ACV, Kplus Competence Center, Vienna, Austria, 2002.

8. Reinhold Huber, Christoph Nowak, Bernhard Spatzek, and David Schreiber. Adaptive Aperture Control for Video Acquisition. In *Proceedings of IEEE Workshop on Applications of Computer Vision*, pages 320–324, Orlando, FL, USA, December 2002.

9. Reinhold Huber, Christoph Nowak, Bernhard Spatzek, and David Schreiber. Reliable Detection of Obstacles on Staircases. In *Proceedings of IAPR Workshop on Machine Vision Applications*, pages 467–479, Nara, Japan, December 2002.

10. M. Jenkin and A. Jepson. Detecting Floor Anomalies. In E. Hancock, editor, *Proceedings of British Machine Vision Conference*, pages 731–740, York, UK, 1994.

11. David G. Lowe. Fitting Parameterized 3–D Models to Images. *IEEE Transactions on Pattern Analysis and Machine Intelligence*, 13(5):441–450, May 1991.

12. Q.-T. Luong, J. Weber, D. Koller, and J. Malik. An Integrated Stereo–based Approach to Automatic Vehicle Guidance. In *Proceedings of the International Conference on Computer Vision*, pages 52–57, Cambridge, MA, USA, June 1995.

13. N. Molton, S. Se, M. Brady, D. Lee, and P. Probert. Robotic Sensing for the Partially Sighted. *Robotics and Autonomous Systems*, 26(3):185–201, 1999.

14. J. Mundy and A. Zisserman. Appendix: Projective Geometry for Machine Vision. In J. L. Mundy and A. Zisserman, editors, *Geometric Invariance in Computer Vision*, pages 463–519. MIT Press, 1992.

15. M. Spann and R. Wilson. A Quad–Tree Approach to Image Segmentation which Combines Statistical and Spatial Information. *Pattern Recognition*, 18(3/4):257–269, 1985.

16. Todd Williamson and Charles Thorpe. Detection of Small Obstacles at Long Range using Multibaseline Stereo. In *Proceedings of International Conference on Intelligent Vehicles*, 1998.

Virtual Post-its: Visual Label Extraction, Attachment, and Tracking for Teleconferencing

Indra Geys[1] and Luc Van Gool[1,2]

[1] Katholieke Universiteit Leuven, ESAT/VISICS,
Kasteelpark Arenberg 10, 3001 Leuven, Belgium
{indra.geys, luc.vangool}@esat.kuleuven.ac.be
http://www.esat.kuleuven.ac.be/psi/visics/
[2] Swiss Federal Institute of Technology, ETH/BIWI,
Gloriastrasse 35, 8092 Zurich, Switzerland
vangool@vision.ee.ethz.ch
http://www.vision.ee.ethz.ch

Abstract. We present a novel functionality for tele-conferencing and tele-teaching, coined 'virtual post-IT'. A virtual label can be cut out of a scene or can have been determined beforehand. This label can then be virtually attached to either a part of the screen or to an object in the scene. When made part of the screen, it remains there as a reminder, e.g. to a complicated formula. When glued to an object, the label automatically follows it when the speaker moves the object around. This real-time tracking includes out-of-plane rotation and does not require any special markers. The selection of the pattern to be used as a label can be carried out on-line by the speaker, by simply encircling it with a laser pointer. S/he can also determine on which object it has to be glued and where. Also these commands are given through simple, intuitive motions with a laser pointer. As the encircling motion to cut out the label will be rather sloppy, the system autonomously determines a rectangle that encloses the data and that has edges which are aligned with the dominant directions of the environment (typically horizontal and vertical).

Keywords: virtual and augmented reality, visual annotation, laser point detection, real-time and markerless tracking, affine invariant features

1 Introduction

With the appearance of the Internet and relatively cheap cameras, tele-teaching [2] and video-conferencing have the potential of becoming really widespread. In a couple of years, it will e.g. be possible to point a couple of mobile phones with cameras at a scene and generate video streams that can be broadcasted via the Internet. Whereas video-conferencing and tele-teaching now still tend to take place in special designed rooms with a lot of staff and expensive infras-tructure [3,4], the tele-X landscape may look drastically different within a few years. Of course, the other extreme of the single PC-user with her web-cam is

J.L. Crowley et al. (Eds.): ICVS 2003, LNCS 2626, pp. 121–130, 2003.

already popular among chatters. Nevertheless, when it comes to it, for now the production of high quality, enticing video programmes still requires a human editor and this keeps costs high.

It is interesting to consider what kind of functionalities the increased role of computers can bring to this area. These novel functionalities can help to render video stream less dull and better intelligible. They will also be available when the human editor is no longer in the loop and can help to reduce the dependency on human intervention. This paper proposes one such functionality, namely that of adding visual labels or 'virtual post-its' to the video stream. A presenter is able to cut out part of the scene and virtually glue it to the screen or to an object. If s/he moves the object around, the label seems to be fixed to it. This functionality makes it e.g. possible to keep a complicated, but crucial formula on the screen after it has been introduced on a slide so that it can be referred at throughout the talk, or to attach labels with the names of parts to an object that is the subject of a talk. The operation of cutting out the pattern to be used as a label from the scene (e.g. from a slide being projected on a wall) and that of specifying its target position on the screen or on an object are intuitive and only require a normal laser pointer.

The organisation of the paper is as follows. In Section 2 a general description of the system is given. Section 3 explains how a label is extracted. Tracking of the label is described in Section 4. Some experimental results are shown in Section 5, followed by conclusion in Section 6.

2   Description & System Setup

Fig. 1. *Typical setup: a user 'cuts out' a part of the black-board*

The virtual post-IT system creates an enhanced reality environment, for the moment still with one camera. A live scene and virtual labels are integrated. The contents of the labels can be part of a previous camera-view of the scene, an off-line recorded image or some text info. The most fancy possibility is indeed to cut out part of the scene at a certain point during the presentation – e.g. part of a slide that is being projected – and to use this as a label pattern. The selection of this part can be made by the speaker, without the need of an external editor. A certain area of the scene is used to activate the functionality. By simply moving a laser spot through that region, the computer will interpret subsequent laser movements as a cutout operation. Also the cutout operation is driven by the detection and tracking of the laser spot. If the speaker draws a closed contour in the scene with the laser pointer, as shown in fig. 1, the encircled area can be cut out of the camera view. In fact, a parallelogram with sides parallel to the dominant orientations in the scene – which are supposed to be almost horizontal and vertical – is fitted around this area. This works especially well if a label is cut out of a presentation projected onto a vertical screen.

After we have selected a label, it can be attached to the scene. One possibility is to attach the label to a fixed position in every frame of the camera output, e.g. the top left corner. The audience will see a label as a fixed part of the screen. No further image processing has to be done in that case.

More interesting from a computer vision point of view is when the virtual label is attached to an object. Again, the target region is selected by moving the laser pointer first through a (small) region of the scene that activates the attach operation. Then, the presenter encircles the region on an object where the virtual label should be glued to (see fig. 2). After being virtually attached to the object, the label seems to be part of the scene. To accomplish this, it is necessary to track the exact movement of the object, to be able to adjust the label in a way that it follows all the movements, including out of plane rotations.

Fig. 2. *Label attached to object*

3   Label Extraction

The label extraction from the scene is completely controlled by the speaker, with the help of a laser pointer. When the speaker outlines an area in the scene, this area is cut out of the camera image and saved to disk. A robust way to detect the laser spot is a prerequisite to accomplish this. Also a way to determine when a closed region has been outlined with the spot, is provided. This is the sign for the computer that the label selection has been completed.

The manually selected outlines of the label (the laser point trajectory) will be too irregular and jerky to yield a pleasing impression. Therefore the computer will attempt to 'clean up' the label region by fitting a parallelogram around it, such that the encircled region is included completely and that the sides are parallel to the dominant (horizontal/vertical) directions found in the scene.

3.1   Laser-Point Detection

The user-guided segmentation used for extracting the contents for the label works as follows. The system searches in the camera images for a laser spot. Based on colour and intensity constraints, relatively few candidate pixels can be singled out. The algorithm is described in Table 1, under the assumption that a red laser light is used. After applying this thresholds, we group the retrieved pixels according to their position in the image, and store those groups in memory. One group represents one hypothesised position of the spot. Groups that contain more than 60 pixels are considered to be too big for a laser spot and are removed. From all the remaining groups we calculate the median position, as indication of the centre of the possible laser spot. Initially we have no idea about the position of the laser point in the image, so no definite further selection can be carried out.

Table 1.

for (whole image $I_{R,(i,j)}$)[1] {

  − calculate mean μ_R and std σ_R:

$$\mu_R = mean\ red\ value(I) = \frac{\sum_i \sum_j I_{R,(i,j)}}{width * height}, \quad \sigma_R = \sqrt{\frac{\sum_i \sum_j (\mu_R - I_{R,(i,j)})^2}{width * height}}$$

  − determine threshold: $T_R = $ min { $\mu_R + 2.5 * \sigma_R$, 255-0.5*σ_R }
  − select pixels if: pix.R > T_R && pix.R-pix.G > 10 && pix.R-pix.B > 10 }

Nevertheless, an ordering based on average intensity ranks the candidates, with the highest intensities on top. The situation becomes clearer after a few frames, as the true laser point is supposed to move. Even when keeping the laser point still in one's hand, the point will move at least a little bit. Median positions that remain fixed are no longer considered. Hence, the brightest, moving spot is our favourite candidate. But first we have to check the temporal trajectories of the different candidate spots to find out which ones do move and which ones stand still. A number of trajectories are built up by looking at the subsequent positions of possible spots, where each spot is assigned to the one closest in the previous image. Only points that more or less form a curve through the different frames are kept (see fig. 3 [left]). The complete first part of the algorithm (the general detection phase) is outlined in Table 2.

Table 2.

  − determine pixels with laser spot characteristics, with algorithm in table 1 and store them into memory S
  − cluster S into groups G, according to position in the image:
    $S=\{I_{(i1,j1)}, I_{(i2,j2)},...\}$ => $S=\{G_1, G_2, ...\}$
    with $G_1=\{I_{(i1,j1)}, I_{(i3,j3)},...\}$, $G_2=\{I_{(i2,j2)}, I_{(i4,j4)}, I_{(i5,j5)}, ...\}$, ...
  − remove too big clusters: if(size(G_i) > 60) {S = S \ G_i}
  − determine median position MD_i, and the mean intensity MI_i of the remaining groups G_i
  − store in memory buffer B the values MD_i for which:
    - or $MI_i ==$ max {all MI_i's}
    - or distance(MD_i, MD_i' stored in buffer B from previous frame) is smallest

After the first phase, i.e. after a few frames during which moving points were separated from static ones, the brightest moving spot is selected. The detection then switches to the tracking of this point. The search region is reduced to an area close to the previous position and in keeping with the motion just observed (see fig. 3 [middle]).

The size and location of this search area is determined based on a prediction from the points in the previous frames. The candidate laser point found in this area stands a very high chance of corresponding to the true laser point. If no

---

[1] in case of a red laser pointer (the subscripts are used to describe the colour)

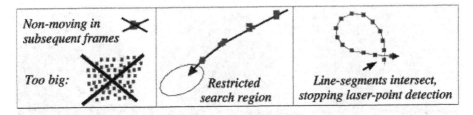

Fig. 3. [left] *To big groups and non-moving spots are removed from the buffer.*, [middle] *During the second phase, the search area can be restricted*, [right] *Laser-points form a closed region -> detection stops*

spot is found in this area, it is made bigger for the following frame. When more than one possible spot is found, the one with the highest possibility to be on the same path as the previous points is regarded as the correct one.

The detection of laser spots continues until the user manually stops the search by moving the laser through a small region of the scene designated with an 'abort' role, or until the laser point has described a closed contour (see fig. 3 [right]), which is the normal way to end the operation. A line between the last point found and the one in the previous frame is every time considered. If this line crosses another line between two previous points along the laser trajectory, part of this trajectory forms a closed contour. The laser point search is stopped and the closed area so specified can then be used as a label, or as the region to attach a label on.

The total outline of the algorithm is given in Table 3.

Table 3.

1. 'clean out' the buffer B => N points left in buffer
2. if(N < 10) { load image, restart the algorithm of table 2 and go back to step 1. }
else { while (!stop-condition) {
• load image and do laser-point search in restricted area
• check stop-condition } }
— *note*: stop-condition is *or* a command of the user, *or* the curve connecting the points is a closed loop.

Normally the area specified with the laser does not have a nice shape. This is why we draw a parallelogram around the appointed area, and cut this parallelogram out of the image and save it to disk, to be used as a label afterwards. A segmentation step inside this label can optionally follow. The sides of the parallelogram are determined by the scene, in order to align them with 'natural directions' like horizontal and vertical, and to allow the system to create a head-on view of the label, enclosed by a rectangle. This step is referred to as 'rectification' of the label and is described in more detail next.

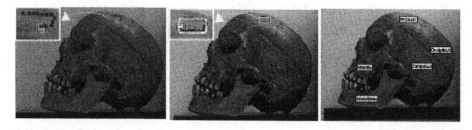

Fig. 4. [left] *Already some laser-points are detected.* [middle] *Laser-points form a closed region, label position is outlined in white.* [right] *Several labels attached on positions outlined with laser pointer.*

3.2   Rectification

The camera image is a perspective image of the scene, it is subjected to a projective transformation. We will calculate this transformation, and will rectify the label.

To determine the transformation, we use the directions of the main 'horizontal' and 'vertical' lines in the image. First the image is pre-processed to make the lines more salient (grey-value image, Sobel filtered, line thinning). Then a Hough transform is applied to the image for the horizontal and for the vertical direction. The peaks corresponding to straight lines are assumed to point at the dominant horizontal and vertical directions. The result of this line detection step is shown in fig. 5.

Fig. 5. *Image and detection of vertical and horizontal lines*

The actual calculation of the transformation is done in two stages. First a rectification from projective to affine deformation is performed. In the second stage the affine deformation is rectified to the Euclidean, head-on viewing conditions (see also [8]).

Affine rectification: The 'horizontal' and 'vertical' lines are not parallel lines because of the projective transformation. So it is possible to determine the crosspoint of all the 'horizontal' lines, and also that of all the 'vertical' lines. The line formed by those two points, $1 = (l_1, l_2, l_3)^T$, is the 'line at infinity'. It doesn't lie at infinity here because of the transformation. By calculating the transformation necessary to transform this line back to infinity $1_\infty = (0, 0, 1)^T$, we obtain the affine rectification. This projective point transformation matrix is given by:

$$H = \begin{bmatrix} 1 & 0 & 0 \\ 0 & 1 & 0 \\ l_1 & l_2 & l_3 \end{bmatrix} * H_A$$

with H_A any affine transformation. This rectification is applied to the 'horizontal' and 'vertical' lines, and to the buffer of laser-points.

Metric rectification: After the affine rectification, the main lines are now parallel to each other, but they are still not exactly horizontal or vertical. By determining the direction of these lines, we can calculate the transformation that's necessary to make them all perfectly horizontal or vertical. Also this transformation is applied to the buffer of laser points.

4   Label Tracking

When a label is attached to an object in the scene, it is necessary to track the movement of that object, in order to be able to keep the label 'visually' fixed to the object. For the purpose of tracking we use affine invariant regions. These are regions that select the corresponding parts of objects, irrespective of affine deformations due to difference in viewing directions, and irrespective of simple linear changes in the three colour bands. That is, their construction is invariant under affine and photometric changes. The regions undergo affine deformations as the object is moved around. These deformations are determined by a tracker specialised on following such invariant regions. Fixing a virtual label or a post-it on an object, amounts to applying to the label the transformations of the invariant region closest to it (ideally an invariant region covered by the target region where the label should be attached).

4.1   Region Extraction

The selection of the part of an object to which a label has to be attached, can be done by the speaker by encircling that part with a laser pointer. The detection of the spot is the same as the one used for label extraction, as described above. But instead of cutting the outlined area out of the camera image, the area determines the invariant region to which the virtual label will be attached and that has to be tracked (see fig. 7).

The construction of invariant regions is explained in detail elsewhere [5,6]. Here the process is only sketched to make the paper more self-contained. The first step is the selection of 'anchor points' in the selected area, around which the regions will be constructed. Harris corners are detected in the image, together with the edges in their neighbourhood, which are found with Canny's edge detector. Two relative affine invariant parameters l_1 and l_2 are defined for the two edges. The ratio l_1/l_2 is then absolutely invariant and the association of a point on one edge with a point on the other edge is also affine invariant. We can simply use l referring to $l_1=l_2$. On that way two points, one on both edges, define a parallelogram together with the anchor point. The finding of an affine invariant region then boils down to selecting a value for l on a photometrically and geometrically invariant way.

To accomplish this, a function is evaluated over the regions (1) that reaches its extrema in an invariant way for both geometric and photometric changes. Then the regions for which the function reaches a local extreme are selected. This results mostly in multiple regions of different sizes that coexist around the same corner.

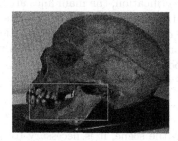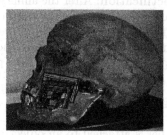

Fig. 6. *Area outlined by laser-points. All detected regions in this area.*

A good region detection requires that the object has some texture, so that corners and edges can be easily detected. In that case region extraction results in a lot of regions. Since we only want to add one label to the object, we only need one region. If several regions are close to the target area where the label is to be attached, the biggest ones are selected. With these regions the tracking process is started to find them in the next frame. Out of this first tracking step we can derive the region that is the easiest and most robust for tracking. For every region the cross correlation between the two frames is calculated. The region with the highest correlation is selected as the best one, and will be used to attach the label to. This region will be tracked in the next frames, with the label always attached to it.

4.2   Region Tracking

We want to track a region R from frame F_i to the next frame of the image sequence, frame F_{i+1}. To that end, a tracker dedicated to tracking the invariant regions is applied [7]. The tracker first computes an estimate of the region in frame F_{i+1}, by applying the affine transformation between the previous two frames. Also an estimate for the region's anchor point is computed. Around this anchor point, a search area is defined. In this area we will search for Harris corners, that are possible anchor points for region R_{i+1}. With a canny edge detector, also edges are detected in the same search region. The size of the search region is a critical issue. It has to be big enough to tolerate large image displacements, but as small as possible to limit the search time.

The corner closest to the predicted anchor point (ap_{i+1}) has the biggest chance to be the correct anchor point for the region, so the corners are investigated from the closest to the one farthest from ap_{i+1}. When edges are lying in the neighbourhood of a corner, a region can be formed with them. The direction of two sides of the parallelogram are then fixed already. But we still need to determine the size of these edges and so the position of the fourth corner (q) of the parallelogram. As an initial estimate we use the estimate of region R_{i+1}. We adjust this in a way to maximise the similarity between this resulting region R_{i+1} and the region in the previous frame. As similarity measure we use the normalised cross-correlation between the region in frame F_i and the new region $R_{i+1}(q)$, after aligning them with A(q), the affine transformation mapping R_i to $R_{i+1}(q)$. So we maximise:

$$f(q) = CrossCorr(A(q)R_i, R_{i+1}(q))$$

The tracking is relatively robust against changing lighting conditions, since this function is not only invariant under geometric affine transformations, but also under linear transformations of the pixel intensities.

Sometimes it is possible that no region can be found. This can be due to occlusions of the region, sudden acceleration or failure of the corner detector. In that case the anchor point is set to the prediction ap_{i+1} and the search region is made larger in the next frame. In most cases this is enough to recover the region in one of the next frames.

As initialisation of the tracker, region extraction is used. In the very first frame, regions are extracted, as explained above. Their affine transformation matrix is set to the identity matrix. So in the next frame, the predicted region falls on the same place as the extracted one in the frame before. In that neighbourhood the new region is then searched for. Because of this, the initial movement is not allowed to be too big, or the search area in the beginning should be large enough.

During the tracking of the region(s), also the visualisation of the label is needed. To visualise the label in the first frame, we align the rectified rectangles of the label and the target area. For the following updates to the next frames, we use the calculated transformation for the underlying, affine invariant region. This way, the label always moves exactly the same as the region, and so also as the object.

5   Results

The system works in real-time and performs well in most circumstances. The real-time laser detection works with an input video stream of 640x480 pixels at 20fps. The time needed for rectification can almost be neglected. Afterwards the tracking works at 5fps (Intel Pent-III @1GHz). The laser point detection is almost insensitive to the light condition of the environment, as long as the illumination of the scene is more or less uniform. If there are small and very bright spots, the system can be fooled and will start to classify them as possible laser spots.

The rectification of the label is based on the detection of straight lines in the image. In a situation of tele-teaching or video-conferencing, sufficient structures like the walls and corners of the room, the borders of the blackboard and tables, etc... indicate the dominant horizontal and vertical directions. Invariant region extraction needs sufficient texture on the object's surface where the labels have

Fig. 7. *Label tracked during several frames.*

to attached. The tracking works real-time for the tracking of only a couple of regions, with their labels superimposed, if the object is not moved about too fast.

6   Conclusion

The paper proposes virtual post-ITs as an additional functionality, offered through the digital editing of video-conferencing streams. Labels can be added to any object in the scene, or fixed to the screen. A real-time implementation (on a Intel Pent-III @1GHz) has been realised. In a setup with one fixed camera and one speaker the system works reliably already. In the near future, this will be extended to a multi-camera setup

Acknowledgements. This work has been carried out with support of the European IST project 'STAR' (Services and Training through Augmented Reality) and the K.U.Leuven GOA project VHS+. The authors also gratefully acknowledge support by dr. Tinne Tuytelaars and Vittorio Ferrari, for making available initial versions of the affine regions extraction and tracking software.

References

1. IST-project STAR (Services and Training through Augmented Reality), http://www.realviz.com/STAR/
2. Pentalfa project of the medical faculty of the K.U.Leuven, http://www.med.kuleuven.ac.be/pentalfa/
3. M.Chen, Design of a Virtual Auditorium, Proceedings of ACM Multimedia 2001
4. R.Herpers, K.Derpanis, W.J.MacLean, G.Verghese, M.Jenkin, E.Millios, A.Jepson, J.K.Tsotos, SAVI: an actively controlled teleconferencing system, Elsevier: Image and Vision Computing 19 (2001), pp. 793–804
5. L.Van Gool, T.Tuytelaars, A.Turina, Local features for image retrieval, State-of-the-Art in Content-Based Image and Video Retrieval, Kluwer Academic Publishers 2001, pp. 21–41
6. T.Tuytelaars, L.Van Gool, Content-based Image Retrieval based on Local Affinely Invariant Regions, International Conference on Visual Information Systems, VISUAL'99, pp. 493–500, Amsterdam, June 2-4, 1999
7. V.Ferrari, T.Tuytelaars, L.Van Gool, Markerless Augmented Reality with Real-time Affine Region Tracker, Proc. Int'l Symposium on Augmented Reality, pp. 87–96, New York, october 2001.
8. Richard Hartley, Andrew Zisserman, book: Multiple view geometry in computer vision, Cambridge University Press 2001

Architecture for Image Labelling in Real Conditions*

Juan Manuel García Chamizo, Andrés Fuster Guilló, Jorge Azorín López, and
Francisco Maciá Pérez

U.S.I. Informática Industrial y Redes de Computadores. Dpto Tecnología Informática y
Computación. Universidad de Alicante. Apdo. Correos 99. E-03080. Alicante. España
{juanma, fuster, jazorin, pmacia}@dtic.ua.es
http://www.ua.es/i2rc

Abstract. A general model for the segmentation and labelling of acquired
images in real conditions is proposed. These images could be obtained in
adverse environmental conditions, such as faulty illumination, non-
homogeneous scale, etc. The system is based on surface identification of the
objects in the scene using a database. This database stores features from series
of each surface perceived with successive optical parameter values: the
collection of each surface perceived at successive distances, and at successive
illumination intensities, etc. We propose the use of non-specific descriptors,
such as brightness histograms, which could be systematically used in a wide
range of real situations and the simplification of database queries by obtaining
context information. Self-organizing maps have been used as a basis for the
architecture, in several phases of the process. Finally, we show an application of
the architecture for labelling scenes obtained in different illumination
conditions and an example of a deficiently illuminated outdoor scene.

1 Introduction

One of the obstacles for a wider acceptance of artificial vision systems is the
consideration of the realism in the acquired images. The studies dealing with
situations in real environments taking the realism of scenes into account must
consider situations where natural light is changeable and non homogeneous; the
different planes of scene become unfocused; the scale of perception of an object can
change according to its distance; etc. [1], [2], [3], [4], [5].

Typically, the problem of realistic vision has been approached to at low level, with
specific pre-processing methods such as enhancement or restoration [6], [7], [8]. In
these methods the input and the improved output are intensity images. The problem
can also be solved at intermediate level of vision systems, where one of the main
objectives is the segmentation of the objects in a real scene. The task of interpreting a
real scene can be made easier if the configuration at surface texture level is known [9]
[10]. Many techniques highlight the classification capacity of the descriptors extracted
from images, searching for invariant features regardless of the variation of optical
parameters [11], [12], [13]. Some of these techniques use these features to carry out
unsupervised segmentation of the scene [14], [15]. Other works approach the

---

* This work was supported by the CICYT TAP1998-0333-C03-03

J.L. Crowley et al. (Eds.): ICVS 2003, LNCS 2626, pp. 131–140, 2003.

complete segmentation of the image by labelling the regions using databases made up of descriptors or texture properties [1] [10].

We are interested in region labelling as a complete segmentation of the objects in real scenes, using techniques that query databases with non-specific features from the images obtained in different calibration conditions [16] [17]. The objective of practical implantation forces the harmony between viability and innovation. Aware that the use of data bases is not new, our principal contribution is the use of knowledge based vision systems, obtaining context information [18], and non-specific descriptors. These descriptors provide general and efficient solutions that could be systematically used in a wide range of real conditions (illumination, scale, non-uniform focus...). The simplicity of the descriptors used in the system will result in low computing costs and in the possibility of formulating iterative algorithms aimed at solving real time problems. The proposed model is independent of the descriptors used. The use of non-specific descriptors and the consideration of several calibration variables complicate the database queries. We propose the use of context information to simplify these queries by partial viewing of these databases.

Region classification in real scenarios is carried out by querying databases that store brightness histograms [19] of each surface captured with successive optical parameter values: the collection of each surface perceived at successive distances, and at different illumination intensities, etc. Self-organizing maps [20], [21] have been used to organize these databases enabling their discrimination capacity to be exploited and spatiotemporal costs to be reduced.

2   Problem Formulation

The problem of realistic vision is related to the influence of variables that represent the calibration of the vision device on image formation. Consequently, the problem can be formulated in terms of the influence of certain calibration conditions on the sensitivity of the camera. A given vision device, with a given calibration and in environmental conditions, has a sensitivity around the value of the variable on which it operates. That value is the so-called calibration point. The function that describes the behaviour of the device acquires values at an interval around the calibration point. Generally speaking, we can assume that the calibration function is different for another calibration point. There will be a calibration point that generates an optimum calibration chart for each vision device.

Let Ψ be the value of the input to a vision system (characteristic magnitude of the scene that is being interpreted), and let $\Lambda^{\alpha} = \Lambda(^{\alpha}z_j)$ be the function that represents the calibration to the values $^{\alpha}z_j$ of the n variables that characterize the vision device (environmental conditions or characteristics of the vision device).

Then the vision device output could be expressed as a function of the input Ψ and the calibration of the device Λ^{α}.

$$^{\alpha,\Psi}f = f\left(\Psi, \Lambda\left(^{\alpha}z_j\right)\right) \quad \forall\, ^{\inf}z_j \leq z_j \leq {}^{\sup}z_j \quad j = 1 \cdots n \,. \tag{1}$$

For the same input Ψ and another calibration Λ^β, the vision device output will be:

$$^{\beta,\Psi}f = f\left(\Psi, \Lambda^\beta\right). \tag{2}$$

The input Ψ (for example the surface distribution in the scene or the interpretation at object level) and calibration variables $\Lambda(^\alpha z_j)$ (for example illumination or scale levels, ...) in vision systems have spatial distribution in the scene and, consequently, in the projected image. Therefore, we will be able to express $\Psi(x,y)$ and $z_j(x,y)$ as functions of the coordinates of the image.

In order to deal with real acquired scenes, we propose the transformations expressed in (3) (4) y (5). The use of these transformations at the intermediate level of vision systems improves the interpretation processes at high levels.

The interpretation of an input $\mathbf{T}^\Psi$. This transformation model provides the region labelling function at surface level of the image $^{\beta,\Psi}f$, acquired with different values of the calibration function Λ^β.

$$\Psi = T^\Psi\left(^{\beta,\Psi}f\right). \tag{3}$$

The estimation of the calibration function $\mathbf{T}^\Lambda$. This transformation model obtains the calibration function value Λ^β that generates the image $^{\beta,\Psi}f$ for a given input Ψ.

$$\Lambda^\beta = T^\Lambda\left(^{\beta,\Psi}f\right). \tag{4}$$

The synthesis of an image. The output $^{\beta,\Psi}f$ for another calibration could be synthesized from an input Ψ and the system output $^{\alpha,\Psi}f$ for one of the calibrations.

$$^{\beta,\Psi}f = T^s\left(\Lambda^\beta, ^{\alpha,\Psi}f\right). \tag{5}$$

The interest of this research is that it proposes a general method for carrying out these transformations, independently of the studied variables z_j of the calibration function $\Lambda(^\alpha z_j)$. This approach enables us to achieve our aim of proposing a general architecture for realistic vision. The calibration variables could reflect, for example, illumination conditions of the acquisition: the method will allow us to interpret the input Ψ, to estimate the calibration function Λ^α, or to synthesize a new image $^{\beta,\Psi}f$ with improved illumination levels Λ^β, from an image $^{\alpha,\Psi}f$ captured in deficient illumination $\Lambda^\alpha = \Lambda(^\alpha z_{illumination})$. The same can be said for other variables, such as scale, angle, etc.

The complexity of the problem of obtaining the transformation T, is related to the possibility of obtaining identical or very similar results at the output of the vision device $^{\alpha,\Psi}f$, as a consequence of different combinations from the input. For example, the image of two different surfaces can be very similar in different illumination conditions, even in identical but deficient illumination conditions (clear or dark).

$$f(\Psi^1, \Lambda^\alpha) = f(\Psi^2, \Lambda^\beta). \tag{6}$$

In this paper, we will focus on the use of the transformations expressed in (3) and (4) to deal with the segmentation and labelling of a scene from an image.

3   Solution Proposal

The formulation of the problem in the previous section is open and different methods could be proposed for transformation functions T (3) (4) and (5). In this paper the proposed general model of transformation T uses knowledge bases to infer the region labelling function Ψ (3) or provide the calibration function values Λ^{α} (4). In any case, the inference from image $^{\beta,\Psi}f$, with the image $^{\alpha,\Psi}f$ for different calibration values Λ^{α} being known, is suggested. We will call these database $DB(^{\alpha,\Psi}f,\Lambda^{\alpha},\Psi)$. Consequently, we could formulate the expressions:

$$\Psi = T_{DB}^{\Psi}\left(^{\beta,\Psi}f, DB\left(^{\alpha,\Psi}f,\Lambda^{\alpha},\Psi\right)\right). \tag{7}$$

$$\Lambda^{\beta} = T_{DB}^{\Lambda}\left(^{\beta,\Psi}f, DB\left(^{\alpha,\Psi}f,\Lambda^{\alpha},\Psi\right)\right). \tag{8}$$

The complexity of the database queries in (7) and (8) expressed in (6), could be simplified by obtaining context information, we can then assume that the range of a variable in a region of the space is limited. Consequently, if we can estimate the average value of the variable in any one region, the probability of exceeding the expressed range of the variable in the region is low. In other words, the probability of obtaining values out of the context is low. The database queries in (7) and (8) can be simplified by obtaining context information, estimating the values Λ^{α} or Ψ and querying the partial view of the databases for the known values of Λ^{α} or Ψ. We will call these partial views $DB_{\Lambda\alpha}(^{\alpha,\Psi}f,\Lambda^{\alpha},\Psi)$ or $DB_{\Psi}(^{\alpha,\Psi}f,\Lambda^{\alpha},\Psi)$.

For the input of the system Ψ, heuristics can be designed to detect the simultaneous presence of certain groups of materials in the scene (contexts). Given the heuristic nature of this problem, this study is focused on obtaining context information for the calibration variables. If we can affirm that the range of the calibration variables, which we expressed as $^{inf}z_j < ^{\alpha}z_j < ^{sup}z_j$ (1), in a certain region of the image ($x_a < x < x_b$; $y_c < y < y_d$), is limited to $^iz_j < ^{\alpha}z_j < ^sz_j$, with $^{inf}z_j < ^iz_j < ^{\alpha}z_j < ^sz_j < ^{sup}z_j$, we can affirm that in this region we only need to query the part of the database corresponding to this range $DB_{\Lambda\alpha}(^{\alpha,\Psi}f,\Lambda^{\alpha},\Psi)$ with $\Lambda^{\alpha}(^iz_1 < ^{\alpha}z_1 < ^sz_1,\ldots,^iz_n < ^{\alpha}z_n < ^sz_n)$

In this proposal, the calibration function Λ^{α} will be previously estimated by means of (8). That will enable us to obtain the region labelling function Ψ more precisely by querying the partial view of the database $DB_{\Lambda\alpha}(^{\alpha,\Psi}f,\Lambda^{\alpha},\Psi)$ (9).

$$\Psi = T_{DB,\Lambda}^{\Psi}(^{\beta,\Psi}f,\Lambda^{\beta},DB_{\Lambda^{\alpha}}(^{\alpha,\Psi}f,\Lambda^{\alpha},\Psi)). \tag{9}$$

1. Pre-processing. Obtaining context information. Calibration estimation (8)
  - Scan the image using a window and classify each of the elements according to the best match found in the database. Label the region with the calibration value.
  - Estimate the image calibration as a statistical parameter of the elemental calibrations obtained for each position of the scan window.
2. Processing. Region labelling (9)
  - Scan the image again using a window and classify each image element according to the best match found in the partial view of the database for that calibration.

4   Architecture Based on SOM

In order to tackle the classification task of the scan windows of the unknown image by comparing them with different images stored in databases, self-organizing maps have been used because of their discriminating capacity and high degree of parallelism inherent to connectionist methodologies. These self-organizing maps enable the discriminating capacity of different features extracted from the images to be evaluated, that is, their suitability for grouping the unknown images together in accordance with different classification criteria, such as region labelling or the calibration value. The architecture will be general and will enable the problems of realism introduced by the different calibration variables to be dealt with by means of reconfigurations of the self-organizing maps neurons. Although, self-organizing maps are only one of the options for the model, in this study we use them with supervised training to illustrate the implementation of the databases.

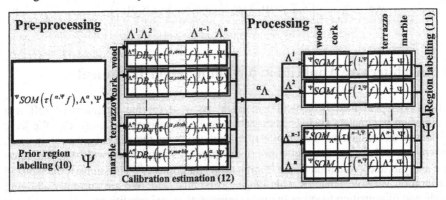

Fig. 1. Whole architecture for image labelling in real conditions based on SOMs

The SOMs (10) (11) have been constructed from features extracted from the images $\tau(^{\alpha,\Psi}f)$ belonging to the database $DB(^{\alpha,\Psi}f,\Lambda^{\alpha},\Psi)$ (different materials Ψ with different calibration function values Λ^{α}) and classified according to material $^{\Psi}SOM(\tau(^{\alpha,\Psi}f),\Lambda^{\alpha},\Psi)$. The labelling of self-organizing maps per surface may provide success levels that indicate the suitability, in certain cases, of using the whole database to carry out region labelling Ψ (10).

$$\Psi = T_{SOM}^{\Psi}\left(^{\beta,\Psi}f, {}^{\Psi}SOM\left(\tau\left(^{\alpha,\Psi}f\right),\Lambda^{\alpha},\Psi\right)\right). \tag{10}$$

Database queries can be simplified by prior estimation of the calibration values Λ^{α} and the subsequent query of the partial view of the databases $DB_{\Lambda\alpha}(^{\alpha,\Psi}f,\Lambda^{\alpha},\Psi)$. These database partial views will be classified per material $^{\Psi}SOM_{\Lambda\alpha}(\tau(^{\alpha,\Psi}f),\Lambda^{\alpha},\Psi)$. Once the calibration value Λ^{β} has been estimated, the map corresponding to this value is activated, as expressed in (11). These partial maps separated by calibration levels Λ^{β} ovoid the overlapping of some patterns (6) and thus offer better results.

$$\Psi = T_{SOM,\Lambda}^{\Psi}\left(^{\beta,\Psi}f,\Lambda^{\beta}, {}^{\Psi}SOM_{\Lambda^{\alpha}}\left(\tau\left(^{\alpha,\Psi}f\right),\Lambda^{\alpha},\Psi\right)\right). \tag{11}$$

In the pre-processing step, the calibration Λ^{β}, could also be estimated by means of database queries. Obtaining features of the images that allow the calibration to be estimated without knowing the superficial configuration, is a complex task. In addition, not all materials are as suitable for calibration estimation. We have previously established the interest in considering calibration to enhance region labelling. Now, we have observed the interest in knowing the region configuration to estimate calibration. In order to solve this paradox (Fig.1), first, the complete database is used to carry out prior region labelling (10). Next, the surfaces suitable for estimating Λ^{β} will be selected, and a database query of the partial view of the database for the known values of Ψ DB$_{\Psi}$($^{\alpha,\Psi}f$,Λ^{α},Ψ) is carried out (12). The use of SOMs in (12) depends on the complexity of the features for calibration estimation. In the last stage, once the calibration function value of a region is known as a statistical parameter of the elemental calibrations, the final enhanced region labelling is carried out by querying the partial views of the database for the calibration known (11).

$$\Lambda^{\beta} = T^{\Lambda}_{DB,\psi}\left(\ ^{\beta,\Psi}f, \Psi, DB_{\Psi}\left(\tau\left(\ ^{\alpha,\Psi}f\right), \Lambda^{\alpha}, \Psi\right)\right). \tag{12}$$

5   Architecture Application for Illumination Treatment

The model presented is general and could be used for the treatment of different calibration parameters such as illumination, scale, focusing conditions, etc. We have reflected the results of the architecture application in the scale treatment in [17], where we deal with scale estimation. In this paper, its application will be specified on the analysis and estimation of the illumination conditions Λ^{β}. The study of the isolated calibration variables enables wide ranges to be analyzed. We are currently studying scale and illumination together in ranges representing real conditions.

An extensive collection of images capturing 16 materials (7 fabrics, 3 woods, marble, cork, 2 earthenware, terrazzo, wall) with 90 illumination levels has been created (1,440 images). The variations in illumination conditions have been obtained by automatically changing the iris aperture. The number of pixels of the images containing the materials is 110x110 in order to obtaining a real world area of 30,5 cm^2. After the initial cutting of the material surfaces, they were cut into smaller samples of 80x80 pixels each, in order to ensure the coherence with the scan window size of the labelling algorithms. The number of samples in the database is 70,560.

Table 1. Some of the samples of the database. Different materials and different illuminations

	Illu. 0	Illu. 1	Illu. 2	Illu. 3	Illu. 4	Illu. 5	Illu. 6	Illu. 7	Illu. 8
fabric 1									
Terrazzo									

5.1   Experimental Results of the Self-Organizing Maps

Below, we will describe the properties of each of the maps used in the process (descriptors used, number of neurons, success rates ...). We have previously mentioned that one of the advantages of the system is the use of simple descriptors. For surface labelling of the functions (10) and (11), a generic descriptor such as the brightness histogram was used. With regard to illumination value estimation (12), an interpolation function method has been used. These functions store the average tone of the images of the different materials in different illumination conditions.

a) Classification rate of the self-organizing map to classify the complete database according to materials (10): The normalized brightness histogram was used for these databases (the average of the histogram is shifted to central tone, to avoid the illumination effect). The global SOM for the illumination, containing all the patterns for all the calibration levels, has a low success rate, due to the presence of many patterns with similar black or white tones. Consequently, we are going to show the success rates of the SOM to classify the database according to materials, with the patterns at illumination levels from 2 to 5. A classification rate of over 84% was obtained, that is, 84% of the 31,360 patterns of the database were correctly classified, the remaining 16% activated neurons linked to several materials. This enables us to approach region labelling in applications with relaxed requirements using this part of the process exclusively. The number of neurons was 60 x 60.

b) Classification rates of the SOM for partial views of the database per illumination values and labelling per surface (11). The normalized brightness histogram was used again for these databases. We observed improved results using partial views of database. The 90 illumination levels are grouped into 9. We found that the black (0,1) and white (6,7,8) illumination levels, offer succes rates of below 80%, as a result of reflecting images very near to black and white. The central levels (2,3,4,5) offer rates of over 80%, in cases (3,4) of nearly 100%.

Table 2. Classification rates of self-organizing maps for the expression (11)

Illumination	C. rate	Illumination	C. rate	Illumination	C. rate
0	23,18%	3	96,10%	6	43,78%
1	71,77 %	4	96,23%	7	28,91%
2	91,10%	5	83,23%	8	16,10%

c) In order to estimate the average value of the calibration (12) in a region of the scene, with regard to illumination, a simple interpolation of the functions that relate the average tone of the image for each surface to the different illumination levels is all that is required. Following the proposed general model, a prior surface estimation is carried out for each scan window of the input image. We then obtain the average tone in the window and interpolate the illumination level with the function corresponding to the estimated surface. This method has a high success rate, depending on the success of the prior surface estimation.

5.2 Scene Labelling

Once the classification capacities of the SOMs had been reviewed, a series of tests involving scenes were designed. We have constructed two types of scene. The first type are mosaic scenes, based on the composition of real images not included in the database. In this type of scene, our aim is to evaluate the architecture application results accurately over a wide range of illumination levels, avoiding the influence of particular surface spatial distributions or variations out of range of calibration values on the results. Each of these scenes contains the different surfaces in the same proportions, corresponding to one of the illumination values (Fig.2).

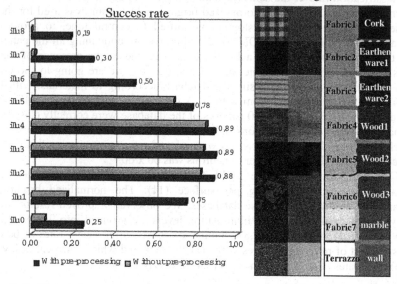

Fig. 2. In this graph we can see the success rates of the use of the complete architecture as opposed to the architecture without pre-processing. The central levels (2,3,4) offer rates of nearly 90%. An example of a mosaic scene with its labelling results (90%) using the complete model with pre-processing is shown

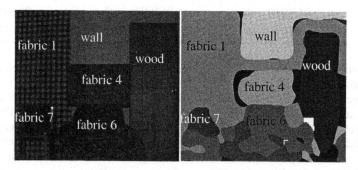

Fig. 3. We can see the results (71,03 %) of the application of the architecture in a real scene of the third illumination level. The fault in the labelling process is centred on the border of the surfaces of the scene. This fault could be improved by decreasing the scan window size (80x80)

Fig. 4. We can observe the labelling results (92,82 %) of the architecture application in a natural scene. For this scene we have constructed a different database that contains the surfaces of the scene perceived in different illumination conditions. We note the accurate labelling of the sky and ground surfaces and the difficulty in labelling the trees and grass

In the second type of scene our aim is to evaluate the architecture application in real conditions with non-homogeneous illumination. We can observe the results in indoor scenes (Fig.3) corresponding to the database in (Table.1), where the scale is constant and illumination remains on the third of nine levels, except in the lower part of the image. In (Fig.4) we can observe the application in outdoor scenes where the scale influence is low due to surface homogeneity. The influence of other variables such as perspective is not relevant in these particular scenes. We are interested in the application of the model with other variables to deal with different real conditions.

6 Conclusions

This study offers a model for the segmentation and labelling of images acquired in realistic environmental conditions that has been conceived to systematically deal with the different causes that make vision difficult and may be applied in a wide range of real situations: changes in illumination, changes in scale, faulty focusing, etc. The proposal is based on surface classification using self-organizing maps for the organization of databases that store series of each surface perceived with successive optical parameter values. More specifically, the results of the architecture applications in the labelling and segmentation of real scenes, perceived with different illumination values, are reflected. The results show high success rates in the labelling of real scenes captured in different illumination conditions, using non-specific features, such as brightness histograms. The main contribution of this study is the use of non-specific descriptors that could be systematically used in a wide range of real situations and will result in low computing costs. In addition, the proposed model is independent of the descriptors used. Our interest is directed towards jointly considering the influence of other variables and tackling the implantation of the classifier module in order to deal with the different causes by reconfiguration of the same hardware.

References

1. Campbell, N.W., Mackeown, W.P.J., Thomas B.T., and Troscianko T.: Interpreting Image Databases by Region Classification. Pattern Recognition (Special Edition on Image Databases), 30(4):555–563, April 1997.
2. Dana, K.J., Ginneken, B., Nayar S., and Koenderink J.J.: Reflectance and Texture of Real-World Surfaces. ACM Transactions on Graphics, Vol. 18, No. 1, Pages 1–34. January 1999.
3. Flusser J., and Suk T.: Degraded Image Analysis: An Invariant Approach. IEEE Transactions on Pattern Analysis and Machine Intelligence, Vol. 20, No. 6. June 1998.
4. Biemond, J., Lagendijk R.L., and Mersereau R.M.: Iterative Methods for Image Deblurring. Proc. IEEE. Vol. 78, pp. 856–883, 1990.
5. Moik J.G.: Digital Processing of remotely sensed images. NASA SP-431, Washington DC 1980.
6. Rosenfeld, A., and Kak, A.C.: Digital picture processing. Academic Press. New York, 2nd Ed.
7. González, R.C., and Woods, R.E.: Digital Image Processing. Addison-Wesley Publishing Company Inc. 1992.
8. Sonka, M., Hlavac, V., and Boyle, R.: Image Processing, Analysis, and Machine Vision (2nd edition). Brooks/Cole Publishing Company, 1998.
9. Shanahan, J.G., Baldwin, J.F., Thomas, B.T., Martin, T.P., Campbell, N.W., and Mirmehdi., M.: Transitioning from Recognition to Understanding in Vision using Cartesian Granule Feature Models. Additive Proceedings of the Intn'l conference of the North American Fuzzy Information Processing Society, New York, pp 710–714. NAFIPS 1999.
10. Malik J., Belongie S., Leung T., and Shi J.: Contour and Texture Analysis for Image Segmentation. International Journal of Computer Vision 43(1), 7–27, 2001.
11. Tamura, H., Mori S., and Yamawaki, T.: Textural features corresponding to visual perception. IEEE Transactions on SMC. 8(6): 460 473, 1978.
12. Leow, W.K., and Lai, S.Y.: Scale and orientation-invariant texture matching for image retrieval. Texture Analysis in Machine Vision. World Scientific 2000.
13. Haralick, R.M.: Statistical and structural approaches to texture. Proceedings of IEEE. Vol 67. Pag 786–804. 1979.
14. Won, C.S.: Block-based unsupervised natural image segmentation. Optical Engineering. Vol. 39(12). December 2000.
15. Bhalerao, A., and Wilson, R.: Unsupervised Image Segmentation Combining Region and Boundary Estimation. Image and Vision Computing, volume 19, N° 6, pp. 353–368. 2001.
16. Pujol, F., García, J.M., Fuster, A., Pujol, M., and Rizo, R.: Use of Mathematical Morphology in Real-Time Path Planning. Kybernetes (The International Journal of Systems & Cybernetics). Editorial: MCB University Press. Vol. 31 No. 1 pp. 115–124. 2001.
17. García, J.M., Fuster, A., and Azorín, J.: Image Labelling in Real Conditions. Application in Scale Treatment. Advances in Systems Engineering, Signal Processing and Communications. WSEAS Press. Oct 2002.
18. Strat, T., and Fischler, M.: The Role of Context in Computer Vision. In Proceedings of the International Conference on Computer Vision, Workshop on Context-Based Vision.1995.
19. Hadjidemetriou, E., Grossberg, M.D., Nayar, S.K.: Histogram Preserving Image Transformations. International Journal of Computer Vision 45(1), 5–23. October 2001.
20. Fritzke, B.: Some Competitive Learning Methods. Draft Paper, System Biophysics, Institute for Neural Computation, Rurh-Universität Bochum, 1997.
21. Kohonen, T.: Self-Organizing Maps. Springer-Verlag, Berlin Heidelberg, 1995.

Alignment of Sewerage Inspection Videos for Their Easier Indexing

Karel Hanton, Vladimír Smutný, Vojtěch Franc, and Václav Hlaváč

Czech Technical University, Faculty of Electrical Engineering
Department of Cybernetics, Center for Machine Perception
121 35 Prague 2, Karlovo náměstí 13, Czech Republic
{hanton,smutny,xfrancv,hlavac}@cmp.felk.cvut.cz
http://cmp.felk.cvut.cz

Abstract. The paper describes a new module of the developed robotic sewerage inspection system. The sewerage pipe is inspected by a remotely controlled inspection tractor equipped by a camera head able to rotate and zoom. This contribution describes a method and a software solution which allows to align the new inspection video and the archived video of the same pipe section (typically captured ten years ago). The aim of the analysis is to see how the pipe defects develop in time.

The alignment of videos based on correspondences sought in images is overambitious. We have chosen the pragmatic approach. The text information from odometer which is superimposed in the video is automatically located and recognized using Optical Character Recognition (OCR) technique. The recognized distance from man-hole of the pipe allows to align both videos easily. The sewerage rehabilitation expert can then use only one remote control of the VCR for video positioning.

This contribution describes the proposed solution, briefly mentions its implementation and demonstrate its function on practical sewerage inspection videos. However, our indexing approach can be used with any videos with superimposed text.

1 Introduction and Problem Formulation

This paper reports about the subproblem[1] studied within the EU Take-up project ISAAC (Inspecting Sewerage Systems and Image Analysis by Computer), IST-2001-33266, running from January till December 2002. The aim of the ISAAC project is to transfer several computer vision technologies to an established robotics area – sewerage inspection by the remotely operated inspection tractor equipped with a TV camera. The sewerage bylaws in some countries require that each sewerage section is inspected every ten years at least.

---

[1] Acknowledgement: This research was supported by the EU project ISAAC, IST-2001-33266, Czech Ministry of Education, project LN00B096. The part related to the development of multiclass SVM classifier was supported by the EU project ActIPret, IST-IST-2001-32184 and CTU grant 0208313.

J.L. Crowley et al. (Eds.): ICVS 2003, LNCS 2626, pp. 141–150, 2003.

The tractor operator captures a VHS video of the examined sewerage section. He/she seeks for defects, e.g. cracks in the sewerage walls. There is an important step which compares the newly captured inspection video with the video from the same sewerage section captured several years ago. This is performed off-line in the laboratory. The most important result of the analysis is the assessment how sewerage defects develop in years. This information is essential to managers who prepare the plan of sewerage repairs.

Our end-user in the ISAAC project, the Prague Water and Sewerage Company, also has to compare new and old videos. Their inspection tractor augments text information to the video stream. One of it is the position of the robot in the pipe obtained from the inspection tractor. There is an odometer which measures the distance information from the cable which is pulled by the tractor. The distance from odometer is displayed as a text in the video.

When the operator wants to compare old and new video about the same sewerage section he would use two VCRs. It is likely that the two videos were taken by two different equipments and several years apart. The were likely taken with different zoom and direction of view. The result is that it is almost impossible to use only the image content for video alignment. The operator aligns videos by operating two remote controllers simultaneously. The operator visually compares two images and evaluates defects and their development in time. This work is tedious and error-prone as operators spend most of their time and efforts by watching uninteresting parts of videos.

This paper describes a simple but powerful trick. The text information from the odometer, which is superimposed in the video, is automatically located in image frames and recognized using OCR techniques. The recognized distance from man-hole of the pipe allows easily to align both videos. The operator can then use only one remote control for video positioning.

The paper is organized as follows. Section 2 informs about the state-of-the-art. Section 3 describes the proposed method. Section 4 reports about implementation and experimental results. Section 5 draws conclusions.

2   State-of-the-Art

To our knowledge the visual comparison of old and new sewerage inspection analog videos is performed manually as described above in most of the waste water treatment organizations.

Digital videos have been becoming popular in recent years. The digital video can store additional information including distance information from the odometer. It is likely that in the future the distance information will be recorded and will allow an easy indexing. However, due to the need to compare with old analog videos it is foreseen that the proposed method will be needed in the future too.

3   Proposed Solution

Our problem of comparing two video sequences (tapes) can be transformed to a more general problem of locating desired frame in the video sequence. This desired image frame is specified by some indexing parameters.

This case embodies our 'comparison' problem because the parameters can be acquired from the second (archive) video sequence. There are several such indexing parameters as, e.g., the frame number, the time mark, auxiliary information placed in the frame image, etc.

In our case of comparing two sequences of sewerage inspections, the natural parameter indexing the video sequence is the position of the inspecting tractor in the pipe. The position is meant as an absolute distance along the pipe from the man-hole (coordinate origin) through which the robot was inserted to the pipe. Having such location of the inspection tractor, the practical issues can be addressed, e.g.: What is the distance to the lateral pipe from the man-hole? Move the tractor to the location X.

The problem was transformed from comparing two video sequences to determining the distance (a single parameter) between the actual robot location in which the corresponding image frame was captured and a beginning of the inspection tractor trajectory (most often in the man-hole). The distance can be neither derived from the frame number nor from the time mark because the two videos were likely acquired in different speed or unknown pauses were inserted. Thus the distance has to be determined directly from the content of image frames. The first natural idea is to try to 'understand' the seen pipe surface via, e.g., some markers on it as the pipe joints, laterals, defects. The use of pipe invariants (e.g., its diameter, length of segments) could be used to overcome the problem that the images could be taken by different inspection tractors, cameras could look to different direction, have different zoom, etc. This was an overambitious idea for the ISAAC project.

The second idea was rather pragmatic. Most inspection tractors count the distance from the beginning of inspection path by odometer on the cable. This is also the case with several different tractors manufactured by the German company Rausch which have been used by the Prague Water and Sewerage Company. The distance along the inspection path is also measured and displayed by tractors manufactured by the the the ISAAC project partner – the Pearpoint Ltd from the U.K. The only place where the tractor position information has been stored on analog video tapes is its superposition as the text to video frames, see Fig. 1.

The robot localization problem was converted to reading the odometry information from image frames. The good news is that for a particular inspection system the odometry information is written in the fixed position of the frame, in a priori known format, using a nonproportional font. The bad news are that quality and resolution of images on VHS-tapes is low and different systems have different form of overlaid text. However, the latter problem can be overcome by training the system for a new device.

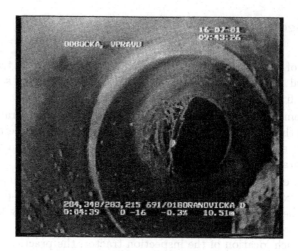

Fig. 1. Example of the image frame from the inspection video with the text information superimposed.

The proposed text recognition consists of four steps: (1) localization of odometry information in the image frame by circumscribing it by rectangular region of interest, (2) splitting the text in the region of interest into individual characters, (3) recognition of each character, and (4) interpretation of recognized characters.

For a video from a particular inspection tractor the odometry text is on the same position. The localization is given by a rectangular window (region of interest) which is slightly bigger than the odometry information on the screen. The position and size of the window was either stored before for a particular video sequence or the user performs additional learning step, i.e. the user draws manually a rectangle encompassing the text information on her/his computer screen and specifies the format in the text. The described procedure constitutes the step (1).

In the step (2), the text in the region of interest is separated into individual characters. The characters do not overlap, are written in the nonproportional font in the fixed raster. The problem is undersampling as the width of the raster cell for one character has been typically from 10 to 14 pixels in our experiments. The quality of the image digitized from the analog video tape is low too. The method used to segment individual characters is described in Section 3.1.

Step (3) recognizes individual characters into twelve classes using Support Vector Machine classifier. This is performed by the SVM classifier, which classifies each character to one of twelve classes: numerals 0-9, full stop, and character m (for meters). The classification is explained in Section 3.2.

Step (4) interprets the recognized text. This allows to perform the consistency check. The text has a fixed syntax. For example for the German sewerage inspection system Rausch we expect number in followed format [*?.??m] (in regular expression notation). There are additional constraints stemming from the context given by neighboring video frames. For instance, due to certain maximal speed of the inspection tractor the difference between two consequent image can be a few centimeters at most.

Let us describe steps (2) and (3) in more detail in the following two sections.

3.1   Segmenting Text of Interest into Individual Characters

Step (1) provided the rectangular region of interest encompassing the text. Step (2), which is being described now, has to segment individual characters. The character separation method depends on the way the odometry information is superimposed to the video. The all different inspection tractors we have seen so far superimpose white characters on the mostly darker video background.

The rectangle encompassing text is resized to fit most tightly around the text. The thresholding with automatically set threshold from the histogram was used to separate the text from the background. The minimal bounding box is calculated. The obtained rectangle is enlarged in horizontal direction both to the left and to the right by 2 pixels to be sure that the text does not start, resp. finishes in the first, resp. last, column of the rectangle. This extended rectangle constitutes the new region of interest. The underlying grey scale image G constitutes the input information for the OCR procedure. As the inspection tractors use color cameras the intensity has to be calculated from RGB values, $G = 0.29I_R + 0.58I_G + 0.11I_B$.

The intensity profile obtained by summing up (squared) intensities along the columns is used to uncover the regular grid underlying the text. The periodicity of the profile can be unveiled.

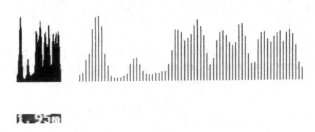

Fig. 2. Example of analyzed text and intensity profile. The original image G with the text is bottom left. Above it (top left) is the profile H. The same profile stretched so that the periodicity is visible better is top right..

The following intensity profile H, see Fig. 2, is calculated for the image $G(i, j)$ with characters, where i is the row index and j is the column index of an individual pixel. For each column j, the value of the profile is given by the sum of squared intensities,

$$H_j = \sum_k G^2(k,j) \,.$$

The intensity values were squared when contributing to the profile because it better indicates which column is occupied by the character (higher intensity value) and which column corresponds to the inter-character space (lower intensity value). For example, if there are two neighboring zeros in the image then the space between these zeros is lighter than the background in general. This is caused by the influence of neighboring pixels. If just intensities were summed along the column it could easily happen that the sum for the space was the same as the sum over the central column of the number zero because there might be only two white pixel there. Squaring the intensity value solves the problem in our experience.

The profile H shows the amount of white pixels in each column. It can be treated as a probability distribution of the event that the column belongs to the character. The desire is to unveil the width w of the character grid and the start column ϕ of the grid with respect to the region of interest given by image G. The base frequency unveiled by the one-dimensional Fourier transformation provides the width w (length of the period corresponding to the base frequency) and start column ϕ (phase).

The static component of the profile H is suppressed by subtracting the mean value μ of the profile H. The resulting new profile h is given by the vector

$$h = H - \mu(H) \,.$$

The best periodic signal fitting to the profile h is found by varying the width of the characters w in the range expected in the image, i.e. from 9 to 15 pixels in our experiments. The periodicity of character grid is found by maximizing

$$\max_w \left\{ \left(\sum_i h_i \sin\left(\frac{2\pi i}{w}\right) \right)^2 + \left(\sum_i h_i \cos\left(\frac{2\pi i}{w}\right) \right)^2 \right\} \,.$$

The value of w maximizing the above expression corresponds to the width of one cell in the character raster. Let us denote it r. The angle between the sin and cos components of the first harmonic gives the phase ϕ,

$$\phi = \arctan\left(\frac{\sum_i h_i \sin\left(\frac{2\pi i}{r}\right)}{\sum_i h_i \cos\left(\frac{2\pi i}{r}\right)} \right) \,.$$

The phase ϕ corresponds to the shift of the beginning of the character grid with respect to the left column of the image G, which is constitutes the region of interest. The profile h was calculated from it. The phase ϕ is proportional to the shift of the character grid from the left column of G in pixels s,

$$s = \phi \frac{r}{2\pi} \,.$$

Having this information, the image G is segmented into individual characters.

Next, the intention is to represent characters in the form which is invariant to slight geometric and radiometric changes. Such a representation decreases complexity of involved classifier learning. Individual letters are geometrically transformed into the 10×10 pixel grid using the nearest neighbor interpolation method. The underlying grey scale image is radiometrically normalized by histogram equalization.

3.2   Recognition of Individual Characters by the Support Vector Machine

We selected the Support Vector Machines (SVM) [6] approach for recognition task. The SVM have been shown to perform well on variety of problems such as handwritten character recognition [4]. The standard SVM are designed for dichotomic classification problem.

We used our method [2] based on the transformation of a slightly modified multi-class criterion to the single-class SVM problem, see 3(a). The single-class SVM problem is simple to optimize and a variety of sophisticated optimization algorithms can be employed. We used a modification of the Sequential Minimal Optimizer (SMO) [5] which is simple and fast. The characters to be classified are

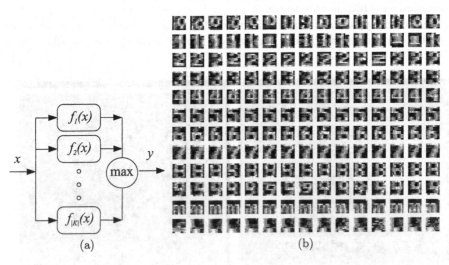

(a)   (b)

Fig. 3. (a) Classification strategy. (b) A sample of gray-scale 10×10 images of digits captured from video records.

digits $1, 2, \ldots, 9$ and characters "." and "m" presented as a 10×10 gray-scale images obtained by the procedure described above. A sample of images can be seen in Figure 3(b). The training set used contained 4331 examples of characters. The pixel gray-scale values from the interval $[0, 255]$ were mapped to the interval $[0, 1]$. Each image is represented as a $10 \times 10 = 100$-dimensional feature vector containing intensities of corresponding pixel.

We selected Radial Basis Function (RBF) kernel $k(x, x') = e^{-0.5||x-x'||^2/\sigma^2}$ for which the training data are separable. This implies that the regularization constant can be set to infinity $C = \infty$. The only free parameter to be determined is the width σ of the RBF kernel. We computed five-fold cross-validation error rate for parameters $\sigma = [0.2, 0.5, 1, 2, 3, \ldots, 10]$. The best cross-validation 0.74% (percentage of missclassifications) was obtained for the kernel width $\sigma = 2$. The number of unique support vectors is 757 (17%). The classifier is able to process about 550 characters per second on K7/1800MHz computer. Further speed up can be achieved using approximated classification rule with less number of Support Vectors [1,7].

4   Implementation and Experiments

We implemented an experimental version of the methods that demonstrate feasibility of the approach. We currently negotiate with the customer – Prague Water and Sewerage Company about the final implementation.

The main part of the code is in the Visual C++ 6.0 under the Microsoft Windows. Video for Windows functions (AVIFile) included in Visual C++ 6.0 libraries were used to process videos. The experimental implementation has an user interface which is easy to use.

The learning part of classifier is implemented in Matlab. This implementation is part of our Statistical Pattern Recognition Toolbox which is freely available [3].

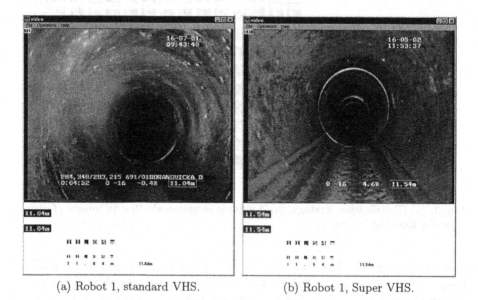

(a) Robot 1, standard VHS.   (b) Robot 1, Super VHS.

Fig. 4. (a) Screen shots showing the quality of input images and demonstrating processing.

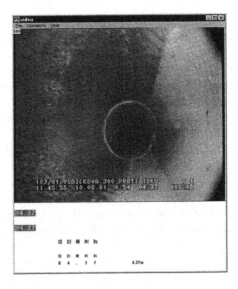

Fig. 5. Screen shot. Robot 2, 'satellite' camera on a string able to inspect lateral pipes, standard VHS showing the quality of input images and demonstrating processing.

The SVM classifier parameters calculated by the Matlab code are stored to a parameter file. The main program sets up the classifier from this parameter file which defines a specific classifier tuned for a particular type of characters (font). If there is a need to classify another type of characters originating in different sewerage inspection tractor then the parameter file is replaced only.

In the error correcting part, we have only checked the specific format in "*?.??m".

We performed tests on several videos from the Prague Water and Sewerage Company. Videos were captured by two two types of robots, see Fig. 4 and Fig. 5. The first robot superimposes white text on the sewerage image. The second robot uses grey rectangular area underlying the text. We have tested bad quality video from a VHS tape and the best available quality captured as a direct copy on the Super-VHS tape.

The recognition success rate even for the VHS quality was over 99%. This quality could be further improved if the error correction based on the context were implemented.

5   Conclusions and Outlook

This contribution described the method which allows to align two analog videos stored on the tape provided the textual information is superimposed in image frames. The text information is localized in the image and recognized. The recognized data serve as indexes to a video.

In our particular case, we experimented with videos captured by a camera placed in a special robotic vehicle for sewerage surveys. Such equipment is manufactured by several producers worldwide.

We described our prototype implementation which proved that the approach is feasible. The accuracy, speed and ease of handling are sufficient. The actual fully operational implementation is under negotiations.

The proposed method has more applications. The approach can be also used for converting older analog video records (e.g., VHS) to a new digital records with the indexing and content information written to additional tracks of the video record.

The approach can be used to generate automatically the interpretation database of the video provided the relevant information was superimposed as text on the video. In our particular sewerage domain it can be declination/inclination, position of lateral pipes, man-holes, images for a particular location (e.g., with the defect), etc.

References

1. C.J.C. Burges and B. Schölkopf. Improving the accuracy and speed of support vector machines. In Michael C. Mozer, Michael I. Jordan, and Thomas Petsche, editors, *Advances in Neural Information Processing Systems*, volume 9, page 375. The MIT Press, 1997.
2. V. Franc and V. Hlaváč. Multi-class Support Vector Machine. In R. Kasturi, D. Laurendeau, and Suen C., editors, *16th International Conference on Pattern Recognition*, volume 2, pages 236–239, Los Alamitos, CA 90720-1314, August 2002. IEEE Computer Society.
3. V. Franc and V. Hlaváč. Statistical pattern recognition toolbox for Matlab, 2000–2002. http://cmp.felk.cvut.cz.
4. Y. LeCun, L. Botou, L. Jackel, H. Drucker, C. Cortes, J. Denker, I. Guyon, U. Muller, E. Sackinger, P. Simard, and V. Vapnik. Learning algorithms for classification: A comparison on handwritten digit recognition. *Neural Networks: The Statistical Mechanics Perspective*, pages 261–276, 1995.
5. J.C. Platt. Fast training of support vectors machines using sequential minimal optimization. In B. Scholkopf, C.J.C. Burges, and A.J. Smola, editors, *Advances in Kernel Methods*. MIT Press, Cambridge, MA., USA, 1998.
6. V. Vapnik. *Statistical Learning Theory*. John Wiley & Sons, 1998.
7. X. Xiao, H. Ai., and G. Xu. Pair-wise Sequential Reduced Set for Optimization of Support Vector Machines. In *16th International Conference on Pattern Recognition*, 2002.

Information Selection and Probabilistic 2D – 3D Integration in Mobile Mapping

Lucas Paletta and Gerhard Paar

Joanneum Research
Institute of Digital Image Processing
Wastiangasse 6, 8010 Graz, Austria
{lucas.paletta,gerhard.paar}@joanneum.at

Abstract. Visual object recognition using single cue information has been successfully applied in various tasks, in particular for near range. While robust classification and probabilistic representation enhance 2D pattern recognition performance, they are 'per se' restricted due to the limited information content of single cues. The contribution of this work is to demonstrate performance improvement using *multi-cue* information integrated within a probabilistic framework. 2D and 3D visual information naturally complement one another, each information source providing evidence for the occurrence of the object of interest. We demonstrate preliminary work describing Bayesian decision fusion for object detection and illustrate the method by robust recognition of traffic infrastructure.

1 Introduction

Object recognition and detection based on visual information has been successfully applied in various tasks [9,8,26,25], in particular for near range recognition [25,12,10,20,18]. Specific tasks impose additional challenges on the robustness of such a system, such as outdoor imaging (e.g., illumination variations) or automatic object recognition from preprocessed regions of interest (ROIs) in real-world images. To overcome these problems, robust recognition [10], illumination tolerant classification [2] and probabilistic detection [12,20,18] have been introduced to enhance the performance of 2D pattern recognition methods. However, performance gains from these methods remain restricted as long as they rely on the limited information content of single information cues.

The original contribution of this work is to demonstrate that the *integration of multi-cue* visual *information* improves regognition performance within a *probabilistic framework*. The essential role of information fusion in image understanding [23] and pattern recognition has already been sufficiently outlined. Though, most work on fusion focuses either on the integration of multi-source data [6] or on the dynamic accumulation of evidence from single-cue information [3,19]. The utility of multi-cue evidence has been stressed for tracking issues [5] and visual servoing tasks [24]. The presented work outlines integration within the mathematical framework of Bayesian decision fusion and with respect to the context of visual object detection. Detection is here triggered by the fusion of 2D

J.L. Crowley et al. (Eds.): ICVS 2003, LNCS 2626, pp. 151–161, 2003.
© Springer-Verlag Berlin Heidelberg 2003

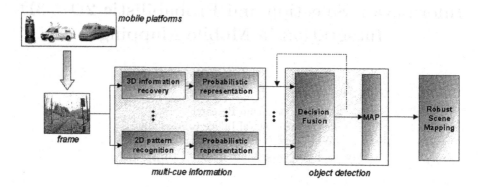

Fig. 1. Concept of the object detection system using multi-cue information fusion.

and 3D information which naturally complement one another, each information source providing evidence for the occurrence of the object of interest.

Multi-cue object detection is evaluated within experiments of a characteristic Mobile Mapping application. Mobile Mapping of environment information from a moving platform plays an important role in the automatic acquisition of GIS (Geographic Information Systems). The extraction of traffic infrastructure from video frames captured on a moving vehicle requires a robust visual object recognition system that provides both high localization accuracy and the capability to cope with uncertain information [18]. The efficient extraction of vertical object 3D structure [14] and the robust detection of traffic signs using 2D appearance based object recognition [17] are now combined to give an improved estimate on the object identity and location within the video frame.

The method on probabilistic multi-cue information fusion is sketched as follows (Figure 1),

1. Object specific 3D reconstruction and range segmentation.
2. Probabilistic modeling of object relevant 3D information.
3. View based object detection using a probabilistic neural network.
4. Bayesian decision fusion of 2D and 3D multi-cue confidence support maps.
5. Maximum-A-Posteriori (MAP) classification with respect to the object confidence maps.

The paper gives an outline of the probabilistic multi-cue object detection and recognition methodology and demonstrates preliminary results.

2   Probabilistic Object Localization from 3D Information

In order to achieve a probabilistic representation of object location, the 3D information is first recovered from a video frame sequence. In Mobile Mapping applications, object location refers in many cases to a ground plane (road, railroad embankment, etc.). Redundant data on object height is therefore used for aggregation of object evidence which is here formulated within a probabilistic framework to enable segmentation and multi-cue fusion in the sequel.

2.1   Recovery of 3D Information

3D reconstruction of the environment is here accomplished by structure from motion. Corresponding points in successive images are obtained by a stereo matching tool (*Hierarchical Feature Vector Matching, HFVM,* [15]) which has been adopted for the case of motion stereo [16]. It generates a dense disparity map (correspondences on almost each pixel). For 3D reconstruction, the orientation of the camera with respect to the moving vehicle [27] is determined in a calibration step. We assume odometry and velocity information to be available for each image. This enables, together with the system calibration, the exact orientation of each camera position with respect to the route and to determine both the distance to a matched point and the exact position within 3D space. Any uncertainties in relative orientation between successive frames can be corrected by photogrammetric methods utilizing the disparity map and the travelled distance measured by odometry.

The idea of 3D object specific segmentation is based on the fact that - for many cases in Mobile Mapping - objects of interest are mounted vertically (Figure 2a,b). As a consequence, the projection of all measured object points accumulates a point scatter on the horizontal plane (Figure 2c). Stored in a digital elevation model (DEM), these aggregations can be easily segmented into connected components, e.g., by lowpass filtering and thresholding. Since the geometric relation between local DEM and input frames is known, a backprojection of the identified segments is possible. Bounding boxes around the connected components define ROI's in the input frame (Figure 2d). As a byproduct, for each pixel on these segments the distance as well as the global coordinates give important scaling information for the following object recognition steps. Additional

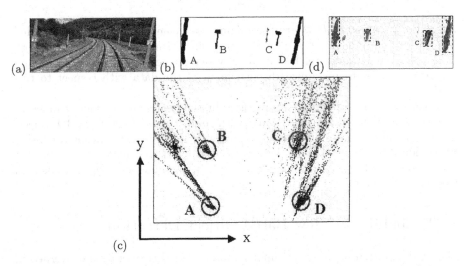

Fig. 2. Object specific segmentation of 3D information. (a) Video frame of reference, (b) vertically accentuated 3D structure (A-D, schematic), (c) 3D point aggregations from motion stereo, (d) associated 2D regions of interest.

valuable information such as a prediction for the track angles in the image, a prediction for the sky region, or the region around the Focus of Expansion (FOE, where no 3d information can be obtained) can be extracted directly from the orientation data.

2.2   Probabilistic Representation of Object Location

Each single object location - which has been derived from a point aggregation (Section 2.1) - impicitly represents uncertain information. We propose to model this local uncertainty by a multivariate unimodal Gaussian $\varphi_j(\mathbf{y})$,

$$\varphi_j(\mathbf{y}) =$$
$$\frac{1}{(2\pi)^{d/2}|\Sigma|^{1/2}} exp\left\{-\frac{1}{2}(\mathbf{y} - \mu)^T \Sigma^{-1}(\mathbf{y} - \mu)\right\},$$

with mean μ_j and covariance matrix Σ_j and with respect to a sample $\mathbf{y}$ within the ground plane. $\varphi_j(\mathbf{y})$ represents thus the probability density function given an object o_j by $p(\mathbf{y}|o_j)$ (Figure 3(a)).

For each video frame and its mapping of 3D locations onto the ground plane, one can automatically find the appropriate locations of means, μ_j, by applying a clustering scheme. A statistically efficientuseful cluster algorithm which naturally makes sense out of these local Gaussian distributions, is the *expectation-maximization* (EM) algorithm [7]. It approximates an entire distribution of samples by a mixture density model, i.e.,

$$p(\mathbf{y}) = \sum_{j=1}^{M} P(j)\varphi_j(\mathbf{y}) \tag{1}$$

where the parameters $P(j)$ are the mixing coefficients. $P(j)$ can be regarded as prior probabilities for the data points to have been generated from the jth component of the mixture. EM iteratively determines appropriate means and covariances so as to maximize the likelihood of the data with respect to this model.

Each single cluster kernel - represented by the Gaussian - is then assumed to represent the localization uncertainty with respect to a single local 3D object. These confidence values are then backprojected into the input frame according to Section 2.1 (Figure 3, 7(b). Backprojected points are members of cluster j (up to some confidence threshold) and result in a confidence support map with respect to object specific 3D information.

3   Probabilistic View Based Object Detection

Object recognition based on 2D information is a further operation concerned in a multi-cue detection scheme. The classification is based on a model database of image templates which were, e.g., manually segmented from real imagery. Efficient object localization and detection is correspondingly outlined in [12,17]. The

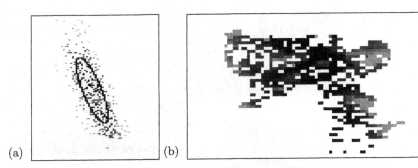

Fig. 3. (a) Single-class Gaussian with ellipsoid of uniform Mahalanobis distance to mean μ_j superimposed, (b) projected confidences into 3D object related ROIs (zoomed out from Figure 7(b)).

presented work outlines appearance based pattern matching in a probabilistic framework [12,21,19] to quantify the level of uncertainty in the classification and hence further enable reasoning on the dynamics of visual information.

Appearance based representation. The detection process is based on a recognition module operating on local image patterns which are successively extracted from the image (Figure 4). Appearance based object representations [13] consist of a collection of raw sensor footprints combining effects of shape and reflectance [12, 21,19]. In contrast, geometric models suffer from matching complexity and fail to work for complex shapes [8]. Instead of storing high-dimensional pixel patterns $\mathbf{x}$, the sensor vector can be transformed by principal component analysis (PCA) to a low-dimensional representation $\mathbf{y}$ in feature space, called *eigenspace* [13]. It captures the maximum variations in the presented data set whereas distances are a measure of image correlation [13,12]. Recognition is supported by the property that close points in subspace correspond to similar object appearances.

Probabilistic matching.   Object representations with models of uncertainty in eigenspace require estimates of the data density [12]. The present system uses this concept under definition of a *rejection class* with respect to background for a closed world interpretation [21]. A posterior neural classifier maps then the PCA description to a distribution over predefined object classes [21,18]. Radial basis functions (RBF) networks [4,21] apply a Bayesian framework with density estimations provided by unsupervised clustering, where the confidence estimates are refined by supervised learning. The feature vector $\mathbf{y}$ is fed to the network and mapped to the output z_κ, $\kappa = 1..\Omega$, Ω is the number of objects, for a posterior estimate, $\hat{P}(o_\kappa|\mathbf{y}) = \alpha z_\kappa(\mathbf{y})$, α is a normalizing constant. A decision on object recognition is applied using a Maximum A Posteriori (MAP) decision on z_κ.

4   Multi-cue Decision Fusion for Object Detection

Fusion with respect to 2D and 3D information on object specific evidence is here applied to the corresponding posterior estimation, i.e., the belief distributions

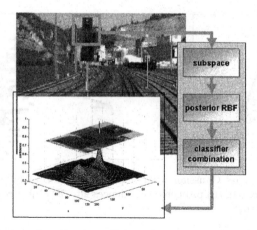

Fig. 4. Object detection of traffic signs. Subwindows from the image are projected to eigenspace (PCA) and mapped by RBF networks for a probabilistic interpretation. The indicated ROI is a rectangular bounding box around the detected maximum.

related to 2D and 3D information. In particular, Bayesian decision fusion [1,6] is operated on the 2D and 3D multi-cue confidence support maps: A naive Bayes classifier [17] represents then the simplified Bayesian update of the probability distribution on object hypotheses (results in Figure 7(d)).

The fusion method is outlined as follows. In a set of $\gamma = 1..\Gamma$ different confidence support maps, global confidence in the classification is updated by *fusion* of a 'current' cue specific belief $\hat{p}(o_\kappa|\mathbf{g}_\Gamma)$ with the integrated hypotheses $\hat{p}(o_\kappa|\mathbf{y}_1,\ldots,\mathbf{y}_{\Gamma-1})$. The overall belief in hypothesis o_κ is calculated by Bayesian inversion [22], $\hat{p}(o_\kappa|\mathbf{y}_1,\ldots,\mathbf{y}_\Gamma) = \alpha\hat{p}(\mathbf{y}_1,\ldots,\mathbf{y}_\Gamma|o_\kappa)\hat{p}(o_\kappa)$, where α is a normalizing constant. Recursive updating is simplified assuming conditional independence of the measurements [22] which implies

$$\hat{p}(o_\kappa|\mathbf{y}_1,\ldots,\mathbf{y}_\Gamma) = \alpha\hat{p}(o_\kappa) \prod_{\gamma=1}^{\Gamma} \hat{p}(\mathbf{y}_\gamma|o_\kappa). \tag{2}$$

A local decision on object identity is then performed via Maximum-A-Posteriori (MAP) [11] classification with respect to a location represented in the Γ confidence maps.

5   Experimental Results

The presented multi-cue detection system is a general purpose system to automatically localize objects such as traffic signs [17], subway or railway objects [18], etc. The images used for the experiment were captured from top of the *measurement waggon* of the Austrian Federal Railways, during a regular train trip from Vienna to Graz.

For the 2D detection classifier, the posterior belief function was estimated by a radial basis functions (RBF) neural network classifier which was trained

Fig. 5. Data involved in 3D segmentation (left upper to right lower): Successive frames 1 and 2, column component of disparity map, DEM, scattered points of DEM connected components projected back into Frame 1, bounding boxes of segments overlaid to Frame1.

using 724 sample templates from 7 highly relevant sign classes. The evidence contributed by different R,G,B channels was fused according to a classifier combination [17] to receive increased detection performance, i.e., $\approx$ 89% recognition accuracy on the complete test set, including severe illumination changes and noise in the image extraction [18]. A detailed description of the 2D recognition experiments is found in [17].

Table 1. Object classes for traffic light/sign recognition (object terminology according to Austrian Federal Railways).

class	symbol	sample
Hauptsignal-HS		
Hauptsignal (back)-HSb		
Vorsignal-VS		
Vorsignal (back) -VSb		
Fahrleitungssignal-FS		
Geschwindigkeitstafel-GT		
Signalnachahmer-SNA		

The performance of the 3D segmentation method was monitored on extended video frame sequences, mostly demonstrating robust performance [16,18]. Figure 5 shows an example for a data set acquired within a station as well as the individual stages of the 3D segmentation process and its result. However, in rare cases the 3D information was not recovered, possibly due to the large extent of visual motion which is encountered when the observer is in the process of passing by. Since a detection system must minimize its resulting *negative false* classifications and should not overlook any objects along the route, these cases require even more robust methods as the presented multi-cue information fusion.

Figure 7(a) depicts a typical video frame from a railway route including a near range object (traffic light). Here, the resulting scatter image of the ground plane (Figure 6(a)) will not enable an accurate localization. Therefore, the scatter image is processed by the EM clustering algorithm (Section 2.2, Figure 6(b)) to provide a probabilistic representation of object location. Due to the axial geometry the localization accuracy is only in the range of 1m in viewing direction (object distance 40 m), perpendicular to the viewing direction an accuracy of 10 cm can be obtained. The cluster points are then backprojected into 2D (Figure 7(b)) to enable information fusion (section 4). Figure 7(c) illustrates the confidence support map as result of the 2D classifier. The final confidence map according to pixel-wise multi-cue decision fusion is presented in Figure 7(d). It is clearly seen that the fusion operation is capable to 'wash out' multiple erroneous and ambiguous confidence values from 3D and 2D processing.

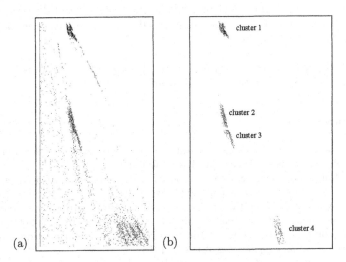

Fig. 6. (a) Scatter image with origin of observer to object distance (x,y) at the top left corner, (b) location specific probability distributions extracted by EM clustering algorithm (Section 2.2).

6   Discussion

The presented work provides a system prototype that successfully demonstrates the concept of multi-cue - i.e., 2D and 3D - information fusion within a probabilistic framework, with the aim to render object detection more robust. The method represents a starting point for more complex Mobile Mapping systems that would be capable to perform reasoning for the efficient use of uncertain multi-cue visual information.

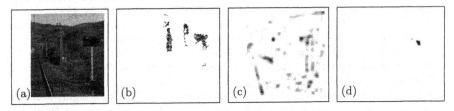

Fig. 7. (a) Original image, (b) confidence ROIs from original image - high confidences in black, (c) confidence results from scanned 2D information object interpretation, (d) confidence map fused from 2D and 3D information. The power pole in the middle is rejected due to bad confidence with respect to the used training traffic signs.

This paper demonstrates preliminary work which we account as a promising basis to profoundly investigate multi-cue fusion with respect to various informatio sources. Future work will focus on extended statistical evaluations of the presented system, the effect on multi-frame tracking and decision fusion on spatio-temporal cues, and on attention based mechanisms that enable efficient use of the given visual information.

Acknowledgments. This work has been supported by the K plus Competence Center ADVANCED COMPUTER VISION.

References

1. M. A. Abidi and R. C. Gonzalez, editors. *Data Fusion in Robotics and Machine Intelligence.* Academic Press, San Diego, CA, 1992.
2. H. Bischof, H. Wildenauer, and A. Leonardis. Illumination insensitive eigenspaces. In *Proc. ICCV01,* volume 1, pages 233–238. IEEE Computer Society, 2001.
3. H. Borotschnig, L. Paletta, M. Prantl, and A. Pinz. Appearance-based active object recognition. *Image and Vision Computing,* 18(9):715–727, 2000.
4. D. S. Broomhead and D. Lowe. Multivariable functional interpolation and adaptive networks. *Complex Systems,* 2:321–355, 1988.
5. J. L. Crowley and F. Berard. Multi-modal tracking of faces for video communications. In *Proc. Conference on Computer Vision and Pattern Recognition,* 1997.
6. B. Dasarathy. *Decision Fusion.* IEEE Computer Society Press, Los Alamitos, CA, 1994.
7. A. P. Dempster, N. M. Laird, and D. B. Rubin. Maximum likelihood from incomplete data via the EM algorithm. *Journal of the Royal Statistical Society, B,* 39(1):1–38, 1977.
8. S. Edelman. Computational theories of object recognition. *Trends in Cognitive Sciences,* 1:296–304, 1997.
9. S. Grossberg, H. Hawkins, and A. Waxman. Special Issue - Automatic Target Recognition. *Neural Networks,* 8:1003–1360, 1995.
10. A. Leonardis and H. Bischof. Robust recognition using eigenimages. *Computer Vision and Image Understanding,* 78(1):99–118, 2000.
11. T. M. Mitchell. *Machine Learning.* McGraw-Hill, New York, NY, 1997.
12. B. Moghaddam and A. Pentland. Probabilistic visual learning for object representation. *IEEE Transactions on Pattern Analysis and Machine Intelligence,* 19(7):696–710, 1997.
13. H. Murase and S. K. Nayar. Visual learning and recognition of 3-D objects from appearance. *International Journal of Computer Vision,* 14(1):5–24, 1995.
14. G. Paar. Segmentation of vertical objects using motion-based stereo. In *Proc. Workshop of the AAPR,* pages 49–54. Berchtesgaden, Germany, 2001.
15. G. Paar and W. Pölzleitner. Robust disparity estimation in terrain modeling for spacecraft navigation. In *Proc. International Conference on Pattern Recognition,* The Hague, Netherlands, 1992.
16. G. Paar, O. Sidla, and W. Pölzleitner. Genetic feature selection for highly-accurate stereo reconstruction of natural surfaces. In *Proc. SPIE Conference on Intelligent Robots and Computer Vision XVII, Paper 3522-50,* 1998.
17. L. Paletta. Detection of railway signs using posterior classifier combination. In *Proc. International Conference on Pattern Recognition,* Quebec City, Canada, 2002, *in print.*

18. L. Paletta, G. Paar, and A. Wimmer. Mobile visual detection of traffic infrastructure. In *Proc. IEEE International Conference on Intelligent Transportation Systems*, pages 616–621, Oakland, CA, 2001.
19. L. Paletta, M. Prantl, and A. Pinz. Learning temporal context in active object recognition using Bayesian analysis. In *Proc. International Conference on Pattern Recognition*, pages 695–699, 2000.
20. L. Paletta and E. Rome. Learning fusion strategies for active object detection. In *Proc. International Conference on Intelligent Robots and Systems*, pages 1446–1452. Takamatsu, Japan, 2000.
21. L. Paletta, E. Rome, and A. Pinz. Visual object detection for autonomous sewer robots. In *Proc. International Conference on Intelligent Robots and Systems, IROS'99*, pages 1087–1093. Kyongju, South Korea, 1999.
22. J. Pearl. *Probabilistic Reasoning in Intelligent Systems.* Morgan Kaufmann, San Francisco, CA, 1988.
23. A. Pinz and R. Bartl. Information fusion in image understanding. In *Proc. International Conference on Pattern Recognition*, pages 366–370. Silver Springs, MD, 1992.
24. P. Pirjanian, J.A. Fayman, and H. I. Christensen. Improving task reliability by fusion of redundant homogeneous modules using voting schemes. In *Proc. IEEE International Conference on Robotics and Automation*, pages 425–430, 1997.
25. T. Poggio and S. Edelman. A network that learns to recognize three-dimensional objects. *Nature*, 317:314–319, 1990.
26. F. Sadjadi. *Automatic Target Recognition XII.* Proc. of SPIE Vol. 4726, Aerosense 2002, Orlando, FL, 2002.
27. R. Y. Tsai. A versatile camera calibration technique for high-accuracy 3d machine vision metrology using off-the-shelf tv cameras and lenses. *IEEE Transactions on Robotics and Automation*, 3(4):323–344, 1987.

Tree Supported Road Extraction from Arial Images Using Global and Local Context Knowledge

Matthias Butenuth, Bernd-M. Straub, Christian Heipke, and Felicitas Willrich

Institute of Photogrammetry and GeoInformation (IPI)
University of Hannover, Nienburger Str. 1, 30167 Hannover
{butenuth, straub, heipke, willrich}@ipi.uni-hannover.de

Abstract. The quality control and update of geo-data, in this case especially of road-data, is the primary aim of the system, which is presented in the paper. One important task of the system is the automatic extraction of roads from aerial images. Structural knowledge about the scene, provided by existing information from a GIS database, is subdivided into global and local context knowledge. The "classical" global context approach was enhanced in such a way that additional context regions and relations were defined, mainly based on the different appearance of roads in these regions. Additionally, trees were added to the context model on the local level. After the extraction of rows of trees the road network is generated using this information as candidates for road segments. The rows of trees obtain evidence from the functional part of the road network model. Both extensions make the approach for road extraction more robust and more general, as is shown in various examples using 1:12500 panchromatic orthoimages.

1 Introduction

In this paper we describe our work on automated quality control and update of road data (i.e. freeways, main and side roads, paths) given in the German ATKIS DLMBasis. The ATKIS DLMBasis which is a part of the German Authoritative Topographic-Cartographic Information System (ATKIS), which is an object based digital landscape model of the whole country [4].

Germany has approximately 1.1 Mio. km of roads, and it is estimated that there are 10 - 15% changes per year. At the same time roads are probably the most important topographic object class of the country and it is of paramount interest to have very short updating cycles for roads, which can only be realized on terrestrial methods. Nevertheless, a periodic quality control, with the help of aerial imagery is an important safeguard against the deterioration of the database.

In a common project between the Bundesamt für Kartographie und Geodäsie (BKG, Federal Agency for Cartography and Geodesy) and the University of Hannover (IPI, Institut für Photogrammetrie und GeoInformation and TNT, Institut für Theoretische Nachrichtentechnik und Informationsverarbeitung) we develop a system for deriving quality description and update information from aerial imagery for geo-data, in this special case for road data. Our developments exploit the ATKIS scene description while extracting the roads from panchromatic orthoimages and comparing the extraction results to the ATKIS information [3]. The system has been

J.L. Crowley et al. (Eds.): ICVS 2003, LNCS 2626, pp. 162–171, 2003.

tested with 30 panchromatic orthoimages covering an area of 10 x 12 km^2 near Frankfurt/Main, Germany. The used orthoimages are available as standard products from the State Survey Authorities and have a ground resolution of 0.4 m. A similar project , called ATOMI, was accomplished at the ETH Zürich in cooperation with the Swiss Federal Office of Topography [16, 17].

In published work the use of additional knowledge for feature extraction from imagery is applied in several approaches: The use of global context for the extraction of roads was introduced in [1]. The focus in [6] is on the extraction of roads based on generic knowledge of road design rules and existing road data. The problem of the extraction of road intersections is addressed in [2] and [13]. Different models of intersections are used, for example simple intersections, roundabouts, complex and highway intersections. In [12] context information is used for additional knowledge for linear feature extraction. Different methods for extraction are categorized based on functionality, which enables the automatic process to choose the best one for a given application. Most of the approaches are designed to run in open, rural areas. There, the roads are often not occluded by buildings or trees and are relatively easy to detect, compared with European urban areas. In urban areas cars can be used as a reason for gaps in the road network, see investigations in [8, 9].

We use the approach developed at TU Munich by Wiedemann [13, 14] for the extraction of roads. The algorithm is optimized for open, rural terrain and images having a relatively low spatial resolution of about 1,5 – 2 m[1]. The adaption of the algorithm for our specific tasks is carried out by incorporating prior GIS knowledge, for example the road direction in the verification step and more specialized context information based on the ATKIS DLMBasis data during the change acquisition.

This paper deals with the strategy for automated quality control and update of road data by implementing global and local context knowledge: In addition to the road extraction we also extract rows of trees and combine both extraction results to generate the road network.

2 System Components

The quality control and update system of geo-data is designed to combine a commercial GIS as backend with fully automatic image analysis, it consists of three major parts (see Fig. 1).

1. A *GIS Component*, which basically selects and exports the object data from a database, and supports the manual post-editing of the results.
2. A *Process Control Component*, which selects the strategy for image analysis routines from the GIS data.
3. An *Image Analysis Component*, which automatically checks the existing geo-data (verification) and examines the imagery for additional data (change acquisition).

---

[1] We usually subsample the available orthoimages from 0.4 m to 1.6 m.

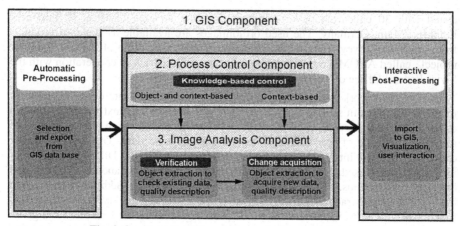

Fig. 1. Components of the quality control and update system

Here, we focus mainly on the implementation of the *Image Analysis Component*. We distinguish the *verification* and the *change acquisition* (Fig. 1): The verification means that existing roads of the database are investigated and a quality description is derived. Details and results of the investigations of the 30 black and white orthoimages of the test area are shown in [15]. Change acquisition means the extraction of new roads, which have not yet been stored in the database. Investigations in this subject-matter are the content of the paper, and some representive results of the test area will be shown.

3   Context-Based Strategy for Road Extraction

In this chapter we describe our work about the enhancement of the *Image Analysis Component* (see Fig. 1) of the quality control and update system in order to overcome two problems: The first problem we want to solve is the different appearance of the roads in the images depending on the global context. We enhance the strategy of using *global context knowledge* by means of additional priorknowledge about the landscape. The global context defines a frame for the extraction of individual objects, and makes the automatic analysis of imagery more feasible. An early implementation of this strategy is the multi scale road extraction approach of [1], in which three global context regions (open landscape, settlement and forest) were introduced. Here, we define additional global context regions: The *OpenLandscape* context region is subdivided into *AgriculturalArea* and *Grassland*, the *Settlement* is divided into *SmallStructures* and *BuildingArea* (Fig. 2). *SmallStructures* contains regions with narrow roads, e.g. allotments or golf courses. The main reason for this classification is, that a road looks different in these different context regions (cf. next chapter). In all cases the *Process Control Component* initiates an optimized knowledge-based parameter control for the algorithm, which extracts the roads inside these *global context* regions. The second problem, which we deal with, is that roads are occluded by trees leading to missing road segments. Therefore we have included a *Tree* in the scene model (Fig. 2). The whole graph representing the scene description can be decomposed into different sub-graphs. These sub-graphs are the *Landscape* (1) sub-graph, the *OpenLandscape* (2) sub-graph and the *Settlement* (3) sub-graph (cf. Fig. 2). The sub-graphs represent different parts of the landscape, but overlap where an object can appear in more than one sub-graph. In this case, however, the object "knows" from the context into which sub-graph it belongs. Therefore, models and methods which are relevant in this sub-graph can be chosen for the extraction. In previous work we have shown, that the regions of the landscape sub-graph can be automatically extracted from orthoimages [7], and how the settlement sub-graph can be used to simultaneously extract buildings and trees in settlement areas [5]. Here the landscape sub-graph is known a priori from the ATKIS DLMBasis, the decomposition of the scene into *AgriculturalArea*, *Grassland* and *SmallStructures*, is performed by using this knowledge.

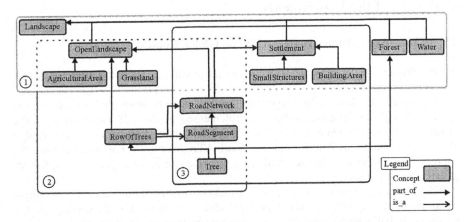

Fig. 2. Overview of the used global context regions and their relations to the extracted objects

An overview of the global context regions and their interrelations based on local context is given in Fig. 2. A *RoadSegment* is modeled as a line, having a higher or lower reflectance than the surroundings. Geometry is explicitly introduced into the model of the road by the assumption that roads are composed of long and straight segments. Roads are also described in terms of topology: the road segments form a network, in which all segments are topologically linked to each other. The extraction strategy is derived from the model and is composed of different steps. After line extraction according to [10] postprocessing of the lines is performed with several tasks in mind: (1) to increase the probability that lines either completely correspond to roads or to linear structures not being roads, (2) to evaluate the extracted line segments, (3) to fuse lines, e.g. from different data sets, (4) to prepare lines for the generation of junctions and (5) to construct a weighted graph from the lines and the gaps between them. The weights for the road segments are derived from radiometric and geometric criteria. From the weighted graph the road network is extracted by selecting the best paths between various pairs of points which are assumed to lie on the road network with high probability [13, 14].

In this project we have restricted ourselves using panchromatic images of a relative small resolution. Therefore, the hypotheses for *RowOfTrees* objects are created based only on greyvalues, the local greyvalue variance, and on the shape of the extracted regions. The skeletons of these regions are introduced as possible *RoadSegments* into a weighted graph, with a low weight, from which the road network is extracted. A hypothesis is accepted only if it gives evidence to the road network, otherwise it is rejected. On the one hand this means, that only the evidence from the road network characteristic preserves the system from accepting wrong hypotheses. On the other hand the results show that this strategy helps closing gaps in the road network. The alternative would be closing these gaps without any evidence from the imagery.

Further information, which would make the extraction of the trees more reliable, would be for example a red and near infrared channel (used in [11]) and other textural descriptors [15].

4   Results of the Experiments

4.1   Control of Parameters Depending on Global Context

In this chapter we describe the advantages and possibilities in exploiting the *global* and *local context knowledge*.

We derive the knowledge about the *global context* from the objects in the ATKIS DLMBasis database, which is implemented in the *GIS Component* of the quality control and update system. We derive the object geometry and knowledge about the thematic attributes from the areal ATKIS objects. For this purpose the appropriate areal objects are selected from the database and merged to the different global context regions.

The knowledge-based control of the algorithm is embedded in the *Process Control Component* of the system, where an individual parameter set, depending on the different global context regions, is chosen automatically based on prior empirical investigations. With this additional information it is easier to accomplish the extraction of roads.

The applied road extraction algorithm [13, 14] is known to work reliably in the open landscape. In this context region the roads are normally not completely occluded as in forest, and only few buildings occur compared with settlement regions. The buildings make the extraction more complicated because – this is valid mainly for panchromatic imagery – they have a quite similar appearance as roads, and lead also to shadows, if they are located close to roads. We have investigated how the performance of the road extraction algorithm can be enhanced by means of subdividing the context region *OpenLandscape* in *AgricultureArea* and *Grassland* (see Fig. 2). Decisive for the definition of the context regions is the different appearance of the roads in different environments, e.g. high or low contrast between the road and the environment, or occlusions and shadows caused by trees or buildings. Another possible criterion is the varying road width and distance of crossings, e.g. in open landscape the distance is larger than in urban areas. Based on these characteristics, a refined control of the road extraction algorithm is necessary in order to reach a high degree of completeness under the boundary condition, that the correctness is as high as possible. In the approach of Wiedemann [13, 14] there are several possibilities to affect the underlying road model to optimize it to the appearance of the roads in each global context region. The best control sets were acquired through empirical studies by means of 30 orthoimages of the test area, representative results will be shown in this chapter.

Table 1. Part of the parameter sets for the context regions *AgriculturalArea*, *Grassland* and *SmallStructures*

Parameter	AgriculturalArea	Grassland	SmallStructures
contrast_high	40	15	40
contrast_low	20	15	20
line_width [m]	5.0	5.0	4.0
fuzzy_length [m]	5 50	5 50	2 40

The most important parameters of the road extraction module, which are influenced by the context regions *AgriculturalArea*, *Grassland* and *SmallStructures*, are shown in Table 1. The parameter *contrast_high* defines the upper border for the grey value difference between a candidate for a road pixel and the neighborhoods, *contrast_low* is the border with respect to other road pixels. The parameter *line_width* defines the width of a road, and the parameters *fuzzy_length* evaluates the length of a line segment with the help of the smallest possible value for a road segment, and the value which defines a membership of 1.

Fig. 3. Extraction result of the *AgriculturalArea*, shown is a quarter of a typical 2 x 2 km² orthoimage on the left side and the results of the evaluation superimposed to the reference data on the right side. White lines in the right figure correspond to correctly extracted roads, black lines to non-extracted roads, and dashed lines to incorrectly extracted roads

In Fig. 3 an example of the context region *AgriculturalArea* is shown: White lines depict reference roads, which were extracted by the system from the orthoimages, black lines depict the part of reference roads, which were not located by the system. The completeness of the extraction result in this typical orthoimage is 81% and the correctness is 72%, using the measures defined in [13].

False positives are often caused by borderlines between light and dark fields, because there are linear structures resulting from the borderline on the one side together with machine tracks on the other side. This fact leads to the relatively poor values for the correctness in this example.

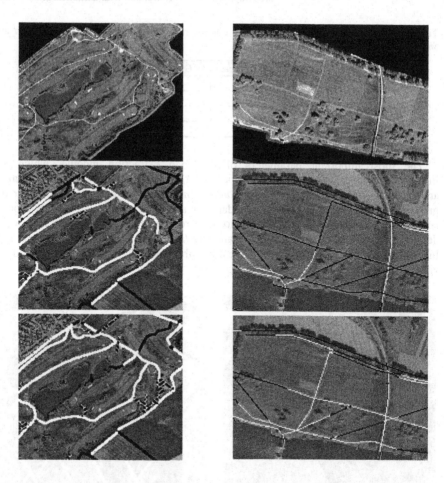

Fig. 4. Extraction results of the region *SmallStructures*: Original orthoimage (top) and evaluation with reference data with unsuitable (center) and suitable parameter set (bottom); White lines correspond to correctly extracted roads, black lines to non-extracted roads, dashed lines to incorrectly extracted roads.

Fig. 5. Extraction results of the region *Grassland*: Original orthoimage (top) and evaluation with reference data with unsuitable (center) and suitable parameter set (bottom). White lines correspond to correctly extracted roads, black lines to non-extracted roads.

The influence of the refined parameter sets is demonstrated in Fig. 4 and 5: The extraction results of the orthoimage in the context region *SmallStructures* (Fig. 4) show a significant difference between the parameters used for the whole *OpenLandscape* and the refined parameter set. In this example the completeness of the road network increases from 36% to 55% and the correctness from 70% to 78%. Also for the context region *Grassland*, the quality of the results increases when refined parameters are used (see Fig. 5): the completeness increases from 49% to 64% and the correctness from 78% to 82%. However, the quality of the results in

Grassland and *SmallStructures* remains worse than in *AgriculturalArea*, because the contrast between the roads and the neighbouring areas is much lower, and there are significant occlusions by single trees and buildings.

4.2   Supporting the Road Extraction with Rows of Trees

In this section the combined extraction of roads and trees is described. There is one obvious local context relation between roads and trees, namely *"trees may occlude roads"*. This leads to the demand that trees and roads should be extracted in two independent steps. The knowledge of *Forest* area (see Fig. 2) from the global context extraction gives us the possibility to learn the actual appearance of trees in the image data, assuming that the greyvalues and the texture of trees is independent of the context region.

In the *OpenLandscape* trees are often arranged in rows close to roads, these rows of trees are explicitly modeled in the ATKIS data model. In the feature catalogue one finds the following constraints for the object *RowOfTrees*. The data capture criteria according to ATKIS is: *"A row of trees has to be captured if it is longer than 200 m and lies along roads or is formative for the landscape"*. The extraction of instances of the object *RowOfTrees* in image space is executed as follows: First, elongated regions with similar greyvalue and textural appearance as *Forest* areas are searched inside the context regions of *OpenLandscape*. The skeletons of the resulting elongated tree/bush regions are selected according to their length as possible road candidates.

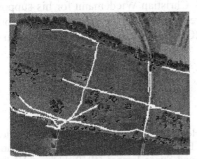 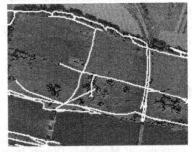

Fig. 6. Results of the road extraction without the support of trees depicted in the left image, the image on the right side shows the results of the road extraction algorithm together with rows of trees.

These skeletons are introduced into a graph as possible roads segments with relatively low weights, before the road network is generated. Then all the road segments were investigated in a fusion step, if they are close to each other than they are merged to one object. In this case the best hypothesis is chosen, and its weight increases.

The results of this process are for the context region *Grassland* depicted in Fig. 6. The road in the upper part of the image was not extracted due to the occlusions by trees (left image). Many connections in the road network could be closed (right image), as one can see near to the road junction in the upper-right part of the image. The short black lines depict extracted line segments, which were not accepted as road segments. The number of false positives is relatively low, and the improvement of the completeness is relatively high, which is obvious by a visual inspection of the two images in Fig. 6. The completeness of the road extraction supported by trees increases from 64% to 80%. The correctness decreases from 82% to 74%, because there were some false roads generated due to rows of trees.

5 Conclusions

We have shortly introduced our system for quality control and update of roads. The work described in this paper was focused on developments concerning the refinement of global context knowledge and the support of road extraction with rows of trees. Global context regions were refined by means of additional knowledge from a GIS database with the focus on the appearance of roads in these context regions. The global context region open landscape was subdivided into agricultural and grassland, the context region settlement in small structures and building area. The investigation has shown, that this strategy leads to better results in completeness and correctness. Furthermore, we have shown how the explicit modelling of disturbances can improve the performance of the system. Rows of trees were introduced as possible candidates for road segments with a lower weight in the road network generation step, in this way gaps could be closed.

Acknowledgement. The authors want to thank Christian Wiedemann for his support in the test phase of the road extraction software. The tree extraction part of the work was partly funded within the IST project CROSSES, the system development and testing was funded by the BKG.

References

1. Baumgartner, A., Eckstein, W., Mayer, H., Heipke, C., Ebner, H.: Context-Supported Road Extraction. In: Gruen, A., Baltsavias, E. P., Henricsson, O. (eds.): Automatic Extraction of Man-Made Objects from Aerial and Space Images (II) Birkhäuser Verlag Basel Boston Berlin (1997) 299–308
2. Boichis, N., Viglino, J.-M., Cocquerez, J.-P.: Knowledge Based System for the Automatic Extraction of Road Intersections from Aerial Images. In: International Archives of Photogrammetry and Remote Sensing, Vol. XXXIII, B3 (2000) 27–34
3. Busch, A., Willrich, F.: System Design for Automated Quality Control of Geodata by Integration of GIS and Imagery. In: International Archieves of Photogrammetry, Remote Sensing and Spatial Information Sciences, Vol. XXXIV, Part 2, Commission II (2002) 53–58
4. Endrullis, M.: Bundesweite Geodatenbereitstellung durch das Bundesamt für Kartographie und Geodäsie (BKG). In: R.Bill and F. Schmidt (eds.): ATKIS – Stand und Fortführung. Beiträge zum 51. DVW-Seminar am 25. und 26.9.2000 an der Universität Rostock, Schriftenreihe des DVW, Band 39, Verlag Konrad Wittwer, Stuttgart (2000) 39–52
5. Gerke, M., Heipke, C., Straub, B.-M.: Building Extraction From Aerial Imagery Using a Generic Scene Model and Invariant Geometric Moments. In: Proceedings of the IEEE/ISPRS Joint Workshop on Remote Sensing and Data Fusion over Urban Areas, IEEE Piscataway (2001) 85–89

6.   de Gunst, M., Vosselmann, G.: A Semantic Road Model for Arial Image Interpretation. In: Förstner, W., Plümer, L. (eds.): Semantic Modeling for the Acquisition of Topographic Information from Images and Maps, Birkhäuser Publishers Basel (1997) 107–122

7.   Heipke C., Straub, B.-M.: Towards the Automatic GIS Update of Vegetation Areas from Satellite Imagery Using Digital Landscape Model as Prior Information. In: International Archieves of Photogrammetry and Remote Sensing, Vol. XXXII, Part 3-2W5 (1999) 167–174

8.   Hinz, S., Baumgartner, A., Mayer, H., Wiedemann, C., Ebner, H.: Road Extraction Focussing on Urban Areas. In: Baltsavias, E., Gruen, L., van Gool, L. (eds.): Automatic Extraction of Man-Made Objects from Arial and Space Images (III), A.A. Balkema Publishers Lisse Abington Exton (PA) Tokio (2001) 255–265

9.   Hinz, S., Baumgartner, A.: Urban Road Net Extraction Integrating Internal Evaluation Models. In: International Archives of Photogrammetry, Remote Sensing and Spatial Information Sciences, Vol. XXXIV, Part 3A, Commission III (2002) 163–168

10.   Steger, C.: An Unbiased Detector of Curvilinear Structures. In: IEEE Transaction on Pattern Analysis and Machine Intelligence, Vol. 20 No. 2 (1998) 113–125

11.   Straub, B.-M., Wiedemann, C., Heipke, C.: Towards the Automatic Interpretation of Images for GIS Update. In: International Archives of Photogrammetry and Remote Sensing, Vol. XXXIII, Part B2, Commission II (2000) 525–532

12.   Wallace, S. J., Hatcher, M. J., Priestnall, G., Morton, R. D.: Research into a Framework for Automatic Linear Feature Identification and Extraction. In: Baltsavias, E., Gruen, L., van Gool, L. (eds.): Automatic Extraction of Man-Made Objects from Arial and Space Images (III), A.A. Balkema Publishers Lisse Abington Exton (PA) Tokio (2001) 381–390

13.   Wiedemann, C.: Extraktion von Straßennetzen aus optischen Satellitenbildern. DGK Reihe C, No. 551 (2002)

14.   Wiedemann, C., Ebner, H.: Automatic Completetion and Evaluating of Road Networks. In: International Archives of Photogrammetry and Remote Sensing, Vol. XXXIII, Part B3/2, Commission III (2000) 979–986

15.   Willrich, F.: Quality Control and Updating of Road Data by GIS-Driven Road Extraction from Imagery. In: International Archives of Photogrammetry, Remote Sensing and Spatial Information Sciences, Vol. XXXIV, Part 4, Commission IV (2002) 761–767

16.   Zhang, C., Baltsavias, E.: Improving Cartographic Road Databases by Image Analysis. In: International Achieves of Photogrammetry and Remote Sensing, Vol. XXXIV, Part 3A, Commission III (2002) 400–405

17.   Zhang, C.: Updating of Cartographic Road Databases by Image Analysis. Ph. D. Dissertation, Report No. 79, Institute of Geodesy and Photogrammetry, ETH Zurich, Switzerland (2003)

Automatic Bridge Detection in High-Resolution Satellite Images

Roger Trias-Sanz* and Nicolas Loménie

Université de Paris 5, laboratoire SIP-CRIP5.
45, rue des Saints-Pères; 75006 Paris; France
Roger.Trias.Sanz@gmx.net

Abstract. A set of methodologies and techniques for automatic detection of bridges in pan-chromatic, high-resolution satellite images is presented. These methods rely on (a) radiometric features and neural networks to classify each pixel into several terrain types, and (b) fixed rules to find bridges in this classification. They can be easily extended to other kinds of geographical objects, and integrated with existing techniques using geometric features. The proposed method has been tested in a number of experiments.

1 Introduction

Automatically detecting geographical objects such as bridges, roundabouts or road crossings on high-resolution satellite images is useful for keeping up to date geographical databases, automatically locating the imaging satellite at low cost and easily and quickly assessing the extent of damages in case of natural disasters such as flooding or earthquakes. In addition, it may help in content-based indexing of such satellite images.

A very limited number of articles exist in this particular direction. However, a lot of work has been done on sub-problems, such as terrain classification, that could be part of a geographical object detection system.

A system capable of detecting objects —such as chairs, cars, tables— which are large with respect to the image they appear in is described in [12]. It uses multiple cooperating, negotiating agents. No learning mechanism is used.

In [8], a system capable of extracting objects and regions such as roads, lakes and fields from aerial images is presented. It uses a few agents or specialists which are trained using a corpus-based learning mechanism.

Neural networks are used in [4] to classify pixels in LANDSAT images. [5] uses spatial regularities to do an unsupervised terrain classification. This kind of systems tend to give visually imperfect results: [2] proposes a rule-based system to improve the results of these classifications, but uses data which is not available to our system, such as terrain elevation.

---

* This author is also with Institut Géographique National; 2-4 av. Pasteur; 94165 Saint-Mandé cedex; France.

J.L. Crowley et al. (Eds.): ICVS 2003, LNCS 2626, pp. 172–181, 2003.
© Springer-Verlag Berlin Heidelberg 2003

A previous approach [6] was developed at the SIP-CRIP5 center using only geometric models of bridges and roundabouts. It turned out not to be totally satisfying.

In contrast to [6], we wanted to incorporate radiometry —and in particular texture— into the detection process, and to use learning methods so that the system would be more adaptable.

2   System Overview

We present a set of techniques and methodologies to automatically detect bridges on small high-resolution pan-chromatic satellite images. These are real images, provided by the French space agency (CNES), which feature bridges in different positions, orientations and sizes, and of different kinds (road over water, road over road, walkway over road, rail over water, ...). Modeling the "bridge" concept turns out to be a very difficult task.

Bridges appear together with other complex objects in these images, such as roundabouts, buildings, and road crossings. In addition, we not only want to decide the presence or absence of a bridge in an image, but also to determine its position, size and orientation.

These detection techniques rely on radiometric features and neural networks to classify each pixel into several terrain types, and fixed rules to find bridges in this classification.

We produced a hybrid system: a bottom-up part uses (mainly) texture analysis, neural networks and a voting mechanism to classify each image pixel into terrain classes: water, road, green, ... A top-down part uses fixed rules to detect bridges given that classification. To detect the bridges in an image (see figure 1):

1. a certain number of textural and geometric parameters are calculated for each pixel in the image (Sect. 3);
2. for each pixel, the set of parameters corresponding to it are fed into a neural network. This network tries to determine the kind of terrain the pixel belongs to (Sect. 4). The response is noisy and imperfect; a post-processing phase tries to improve it (Sect. 4.3);
3. a set of subroutines look for regions of a certain type and dimensions, according to some manually-produced detection rules (Sect. 5).

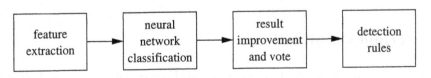

Fig. 1. Processing steps

This article is structured as follows: first Sect. 3 describes the extraction of radiometric and geometric features , terrain type analysis is presented on Sect. 4, and detection rules on Sect. 5. Evaluation of the system's performances can be found on Sect. 6. In Sect. 7 we give some directions for future research. Some conclusions close the main part of this article.

3   Low-Level Feature Extraction

In the first step of the detection process, we calculate a feature vector field for the source image. Each feature vector describes the neighborhood of one pixel using textural, radiometric and geometric attributes.

The original image, the original image with histogram equalization, and a denoised version are included into the feature vector field. The feature vector contains, in addition, the following parameters:

1. Intensity gradient (module and argument) calculated using Deriche's method for several values of α. Using different values of α gives us an edge detection at different levels of detail.
2. Entropic structure: This parameter [1] gives the level of structuration on the neighborhood of a pixel. It allows us to distinguish among homogeneous areas, areas structured by man-made constructions, and unstructured areas (see appendix A).
3. Shadow predicate: This parameter (adapted from [1]) indicates which pixels belong to "shadow" areas. This is done by finding a "shadow threshold" from the position of the first local minimum in the intensity histogram.
4. First-order texture parameters: The mean μ, entropy, energy, variance σ^2, skewness and kurtosis of that histogram, and a variation coefficient $c_v = |\sigma|/\mu$, of the first-order intensity histograms.
5. Texture signal activity.
6. Local histograms.
7. Fourier transform texture parameters: The maximum, mean, root-mean-square and variance, of the amplitude of the complex Fourier transform on a square neighborhood of each pixel.
8. Gray-level difference texture parameters (see appendix A).
9. Region size and compactness. For four different sets of parameters, each giving different levels of detail, we segment the original image into regions. We use, as image parameters, the area and compactness of the region each pixel belongs to.

4   Terrain Classification

After the feature vector field for an image has been calculated, we use a neural network to try to determine which type of terrain each pixel belongs to. For this particular application, we chose the following terrain types: water, vegetation, building, railroad, road, bridge and roundabout.[1] Of course we do not expect to detect bridges at this step, we just want to detect pixels that locally, look like belonging to a bridge. Each feature vector for an image is fed to a neural network in succession. This neural network has 8 outputs, one for each terrain type (there are two classes for roundabout terrain). The network sets each output to a real value in $[0, 1]$, higher values meaning higher "confidence" that the pixel belongs to that terrain type.

The Stuttgart Neural Network Simulator (SNNS) has been used to train and run a 4-layer feed-forward neural network with 107 input neurons, 39 hidden neurons on the first hidden layer, 20 on the second, and 8 output neurons, fully connected. The parameters of the RPROP learning algorithm (resilient back-propagation) have been set to $\Delta_0 = 0.2$, $\Delta_{max} = 50$ and no weight decay. Neurons had logistic activation functions; weights and biases were randomly initialized with a $\mathcal{U}(-1, 1)$ uniform distribution, and training patterns were randomly permuted. These parameters were determined empirically.

4.1   Training the Neural Network

A set of images containing bridges, roundabouts and counterexamples, provided by CNES (the French space agency) has been manually labeled. For cross-validation, we divided our images into three homogeneous groups, a, b and c.

Then training on three networks has been performed using two groups as training sets and the remaining group as validation set (on one network we used a and b for training, on another we used a and c, and on the last one we used b and c as training data). After 200 training iterations, we obtained validation error rates of 0.222, 0.212 and 0.223. Error rates are given in root-mean-square error (RMSE) per output neuron (see appendix A). For the rest of this project, we selected one of the three networks.

These error rates look large, but are acceptable because we do not need to obtain a perfect detection at this step and because errors are distributed in a way that makes the results satisfactory. See some examples in Fig. 2.

4.2   Multiple Resolutions

This system is able to work with images taken at different resolutions, if all of them are present in the training set: The neural network module should be capable of learning characteristic features for different resolutions without modification. We then scale the results of the neural network so that the following phases operate on images all at the same resolution. Scaling must be done at this point and not before, because images at different resolutions have different texture characteristics.

---

[1] In the first stages of this project we also wanted to automatically detect roundabouts. However, we were not supplied with enough training images for that.

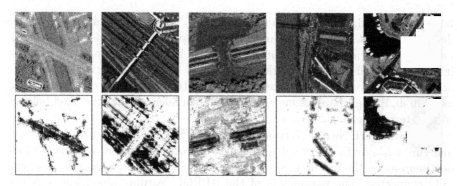

Fig. 2. Sample neural network output; top: source images, bottom: network output (darker pixels represent stronger responses); from left to right, example of *bridge*, *railroad*, *road*, *building* and *water* output channels

4.3   Results Improvement and Voting Phase

The results of the neural network are noisy, fuzzy and full of holes and other artifacts. To improve them,

1. each channel (corresponding to one terrain type) is smoothed by convolution with a Gaussian mask, and then thresholded;
2. in a neighborhood of each pixel, we calculate a weighted histogram of terrain types. We weight each pixel in the neighborhood based on its distance from the base pixel and its terrain type. For each pixel, the terrain type with higher histogram count wins the "voting"; finally
3. we further regularize the resulting regions by mathematical morphology opening and closing operations, and by removing small regions.

5   Rule-Based Detection

The final step towards bridge detection, once we have a good classification of pixels into terrain types as given by the neural network and the vote procedure, is to apply a certain number of "detection rules" to that terrain classification.

These manually-produced rules match particular combinations of regions of a certain type and geometry, returning a possible bridge location, dimensions and orientation. We give here an informal description of some of them. Expressions such as "large" or "near" are in fact translated into hard thresholds, but this would be a good place to put fuzzy logic in. See [10] for the formal definition of these rules and for the specific threshold values.

1. Two large regions of water or rail terrain (same type for both regions) are separated by a narrow and long strip. This strip is a bridge.
2. One large and narrow region of bridge terrain is a bridge.

3. There is a narrow and long region of bridge or road terrain separating two large regions of water or rail terrain (same type for both regions). This strip is a bridge.

4. Two regions of road terrain, long and narrow, are separated by less than a certain distance. Additionally, they are *aligned*. There is a bridge at the middle of the separation between the two regions.

5. We apply rule (4) not to road terrain, but to the terrain channel resulting of taking all road and bridge terrain and removing any water, vegetation or rail intersecting it.

6. One long and narrow region of road or bridge terrain intersects a very narrow strip of road or bridge terrain —both regions of *different* type. Both regions are roughly orthogonal. Then there is a bridge at the intersection.

See Fig. 3 for some examples.

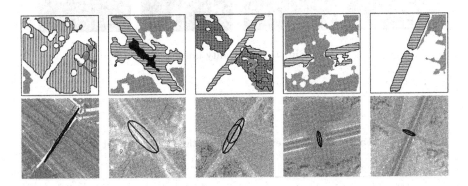

Fig. 3. Detection rules; top: input to the detection rules (black=bridge, gray=green, vertical=railroad, horizontal=road, crosses=water), bottom: corresponding source images and detected bridges; these bridges are detected by (from left to right) rule 1, rule 2, rules 1 and 3, rule 4, rules 4 and 5

6 Evaluation

Evaluation is performed on a set of small (100×100 and 200×200 pixels), gray-level, high-resolution satellite images (Ikonos-2 images at $1\,\mathrm{m}^2$ or $16\,\mathrm{m}^2$ per pixel) containing bridges, roundabouts and counterexamples (objects that look like bridges or roundabouts, but are not). The complete system using these techniques processes input images at one to two minutes per image on a 900 MHz Pentium III computer.

Performance of the whole system has been evaluated by running the detection process for each image in our database.

Table 1 gives the number of images with scores of correct detections (real bridges that the system detects) and false alarms for a typical set of parameters.

A large part (43%) of our images were of low quality (fuzzy images, images where not even a human observer could decide on the presence of a bridge, bad lightning or sensor saturation) or of significantly lower resolution than the others (see Fig. 4). Bad classification by the neural network module caused 29% of the errors. Low image quality caused 41% of the errors. Because of the strong effect of abnormally low image quality on the system's performances, we also give results taking into account only good-quality images.

Fig. 4. Low quality images

Table 1. System evaluation with the final image set

	whole set	good quality
total images	254	146
images with bridges	99	41
correct bridge detection (over img. with bridges)	21%	41.5%
false bridge detection (over all images)	7.1%	5.5%

The system correctly processes 70.5% of all images. It correctly processes 21% of images containing bridges, and 85% of images containing false bridges (objects resembling bridges). This performance is satisfactory given the experimental nature of this system and the difficulty to model such a complex concept as bridge. Besides, all validation test have been made on real images, often of very poor quality.

The system is clearly biased towards under-detection. If this is not the desired behavior, we can change that by modifying the weights in the vote process and the thresholds in the detection rules.

7   Suggestions for Future Research

We present in this section some suggestions for future research on the area of this project.

7.1   Automatic Rule Construction

A technically more interesting approach to the top-down detection part would be to use, there too, learning methods instead of fixed, human-programmed rules.

We tried to use mobile, situated agents endowed with a learning mechanism. This novel approach (we could not find references on similar work; but see [3] for a system using non-mobile, non-situated multi-agent systems) is inspired by reinforcement learning methods used in the Animat Approach to robotics [7, and others]. Robots move and act in their environment, of which they have a partial knowledge given by their sensors. Their actions have an effect on the environment, which in turn produces *reward* or *punishment* stimuli for the robots.

We programmed software agents that could move on an artificial environment which was in fact the feature vector field described in Sect. 3. Agents are "located" on pixels on the image. Their "sensors" perceive the feature vector at that position only. Agents may move or classify the current pixel. During learning, the environment reacts to a classification decision by rewarding or punishing the agent, depending on its correctness and other criteria, such as coverage or speed.

As a proof-of-concept experiment, we gave these agents the task of improving the results of the neural networks, given these results and the feature vector field for an image. However, the experiments were a failure. Analysis of the system's output suggests that there may be problems in the fitness function used in the genetic programming-based learning mechanism.

We believe there is still plenty of room for further research into this direction. Automatic rule construction using data mining techniques, such as decision trees, should also be explored.

7.2   Integration with Geometry-Based System

Related work at the SIP-CRIP5 laboratory [6] was made about using geometric features and models to detect bridges and roundabouts in satellite images, with some success. Both systems can be combined by using the output of [6] could be used as an additional channel to the feature vector field of this system. In that way, our terrain classification would be based not only on radiometry attributes, but also on higher-level geometric properties.

7.3   Larger-Scale Descriptors

This system relies on image descriptors calculated on small neighborhoods of each pixel. We found that it was difficult, even for a human, to detect bridges and roundabouts using local information only, as our system was requested to do. Combining the system with larger-scale detectors such as detectors for road networks [9] may help. The output of such detectors can be used as an additional component of the feature vector field.

8   Conclusion

Our initial goal was to develop a set of techniques and methods to automatically detect bridges in high-resolution satellite images. We have presented several such techniques: terrain classification by neural networks operating on textural parameters, learning mobile agents, and static detection rules. We have implemented and integrated them in a running system which can easily cooperate with other approaches such as a geometry-based approach [6]. We have evaluated its performance, with satisfactory results. We believe that our techniques are easily generalizable to other kinds of objects; however we have not conducted experiments to show it.

We have shown that using texture information to classify terrain areas, and combining the resulting regions using geometrical properties, is enough to detect some kinds of bridges. We have experimented, unsuccessfully, with learning mobile agents as a tool for object detection and image enhancement, and we have pointed to future experiments to be done on that area.

Acknowledgments. This work was partly supported by the French National Center for Space Studies (CNES). We would like to thank the reviewers for their constructive remarks.

References

[1] C. Baillard. *Analyse d'images aériennes stéréo pour la restitution des milieux urbains.* PhD thesis, Institut Géographique National, 2-4 Av. Pasteur, 94165 Saint-Mandé, France, 1997.

[2] J. Desachy. A knowledge-based system for satellite image interpretation. In *Proc. 11th IAPR Intl. Conf. on Pattern Recognition (ICPR '92)*, volume 1, pages 198–201, The Hague, The Netherlands, August 1992. IAPR, IEEE.

[3] R. J. Gallimore et al. 3D scientific data interpretation using cooperating agents. In *Proc. 3rd Intl. Conf. on the Practical Applications of Agents and Multi-Agent Systems (PAAM-98)*, pages 47–65, London, UK, 1998.

[4] S. Kamata et al. A neural network classifier for LANDSAT image data. In *Proc. 11th IAPR Intl. Conf. on Pattern Recognition (ICPR '92)*, volume 2, pages 573–576, The Hague, The Netherlands, August 1992. IAPR, IEEE.

[5] A. Ketterlin, D. Blamont, and J. J. Korczak. Unsupervised learning of spatial regularities. http://citeseer.nj.nec.com/1418.html.

[6] N. Loménie, J. Barbeau, and F. Cloppet-Oliva. Détection de carrefours routiers et de ponts dans les images satellitales à haute résolution. Technical report, CRIP5-SIP, Université de Paris 5, Paris, France, November 2001.

[7] J.-A. Meyer and S. W. Wilson, editors. *From Animals to Animats: Proc. 1st Intl. Conf. on Simulation of Adaptive Behavior.* MIT Press, February 1991.

[8] P. Robertson. Grava – a corpus based approach to the interpretation of aerial images. http://citeseer.nj.nec.com/25230.html.

[9] R. Stoica, X. Descombes, and J. Zerubia. A Markov point process for road extraction in remote sensed images. Technical Report RR-3923, INRIA, Sophia-Antipolis, France, April 2000.

[10] R. Trias-Sanz. Automatically detecting geographical objects in high-resolution satellite images. Master's thesis, Laboratoire SIP, CRIP5, Université René Descartes-Paris 5, 45 rue des Saints-Pères; F-75006 Paris; France, September 2002.

[11] J. S. Weszka, C. R. Dyer, and A. Rosenfeld. A comparative study of texture measures for terrain classification. *IEEE Transactions on Systems, Man and Cybernetics*, 6:269–285, 1976.

[12] K. Yanai and K. Deguchi. An architecture of object recognition system for various images based on multi-agent. In *Proc. 14th Intl. Conf. on Pattern Recognition (ICPR '98)*, volume 1, pages 278–281, Brisbane, Australia, August 1998. IEEE.

A Some Definitions

Entropic Structure. Let G be the gradient vector field of the image, in our case calculated using Deriche's method with $\alpha = 0.65$, r a neighborhood radius and t_1, t_2 two thresholds. Let D be the domain of G. For a pixel p, we find $N_p := \{z : z \in D, \|z - p\| \leq r, \|G(z)\| > t_1\}$. If card $N_p < t_2$, p is deemed to belong to a homogeneous area. Otherwise, its entropic structuration is the entropy of the histogram $h_p(i)$ (see [1]). We used $r = 8$, $t_1 = 4000$ and $t_2 = 25$.

Gray-Level Difference Texture Parameters. For each pixel p we take a square neighborhood N (of size 15×15 in our case) centered on p. For each one of the eight offset vectors $\{v_{ij} = (i, j) : i, j \in \{0, 1, 2\}, i + j > 0\}$, we select the pairs of pixels in N separated by v_{ij}, $S_{ij} = \{(a, b) : a \in N, b \in N, a + v_{ij} = b\}$, and calculate, for each such set of pairs of pixels, the histogram h_{ij} of the differences between the intensity value at a and at b. For each h_{ij} we compute the mean, energy (also called second angular moment in this context), entropy, variance, skewness, kurtosis, contrast, and inverse differential moment (see [11]).

RMSE for Neural Networks. This error metric is computed as follows: for a validation set of N samples, and a network of K output neurons, let $R(n, k)$ be the output of the k-th output neuron on the n-th input pattern, and let $D(n, k)$ be the desired output in the same conditions. Then,

$$RMSE^2 := \frac{1}{N}\frac{1}{K} \sum_{n=1}^{N} \sum_{k=1}^{K} \|R(n, k) - D(n, k)\|^2 \ . \tag{1}$$

Since neurons have an output in $[0, 1]$, the minimum RMSE is 0 (perfect learning), and the theoretically worst RMSE is 1.

Computer Platform for Transformation of Visual Information into Sound Sensations for Vision Impaired Persons

Bogusław Cyganek and Jan Borgosz

University of Mining and Metallurgy
Department of Electronics
Al. Mickiewicza 30, 30-059 Kraków, Poland
{cyganek,borgosz}@uci.agh.edu.pl

Abstract. The paper presents concepts and the practical implementation of the vision processing system for transformation of visual information, as seen by a computer, into specific sound sensations. Such a system can be used to help partially sighted and vision impaired persons to navigate and move safely, avoiding collisions with surrounding objects. In the paper we discuss also advantages and limitations of the proposed system. The special attention was also devoted to a choice of the stereo processing algorithm. Finally, software structure and experimental results are presented.

1   Introduction

The purpose of this work is to address a generic application of machine vision processing to transformation of vision information into other signal representations. Specifically, the presented system transforms depth information recovered from $n\times2D$ images into sound sensations. The system was built and tested to prove its usefulness in helping with daily navigation for vision impaired or partially sighted persons.

There are few reported attempts to construct such an aid for this group of persons. For an overview see work by Molton [9]. The system that utilizes stereo processing for detection of obstacles presented Molton et.al. [8]. Their method relies on comparison of the disparity with the expected position of the ground. Similar idea, proposed by Se and Brady, is also a key issue of the system intended for partially sighted people [11]. Another interesting propositions for zebra-crossings detection and stair-cases navigation are presented in [13][12], respectively.

The problem of recognition of objects in a 3D environment belongs to a class of very challenging tasks in machine vision [5][6][3]. It can be attacked in many different ways, none of them present an ultimate solution, however. The situation can be mitigated somehow if it is possible to restrict requirements of a final solution. In the system described in this paper the problem of 3D recognition is restricted by limitations of the sound channel, which is in an obvious way quite limited in comparison with the vision channels.

The next challenge is to built a proper sound code that can be learned by a blind person and then used for transfer of information on recognized objects. This problem

J.L. Crowley et al. (Eds.): ICVS 2003, LNCS 2626, pp. 182–191, 2003.
© Springer-Verlag Berlin Heidelberg 2003

touches upon psychophysiology at least in two ways, that can be stated as follows: what are the limits of a human perception to a potentially chaotic sound mixtures (cacophony) that can arise from a transformation of vision information, and second – can we propose any *code* or *alphabet* to describe kinds of object-building-blocks and what, if any, are those blocks.

The third issue concerns computational complexity, since the system to be useful have to be designed as to perform in a real-time.

In this paper we report our approach to the solution of the navigation problem by visually impaired persons, having in mind that this is only one of the simplest possible realizations. However, because of its simplicity it is computationally efficient and can pose a starting point for more sophisticated implementations.

2 Foundations of the System

As alluded to previously, the presented system has a twofold construction: It consists of a depth recovery block at the one side, and a sound coding and generation unit at the other. However, these two blocks have been additionally augmented by some data conversion adapters, necessary due to significant imbalance in amount of available data at both ends of the system (Fig. 1).

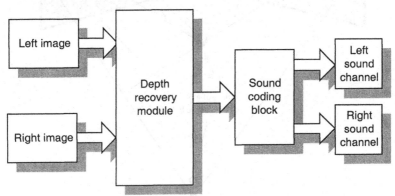

Fig. 1. Basic building blocks of the *2×2D* image to sound transformation system. Although an input is built based on left and right video signals, whereas an output consists of left and right sound channels, the depth information from the Depth Recovery Module is changed and encoded by the Sound Coding Block

Both images of a stereo-pair are acquired by separate cameras and passed to the depth recovery module. In some cases, however, depending on a stereo algorithm, the input images are filtered or transformed (e.g. a *Census* transformation, see Sect. 3.1). Output of the depth recovery module consists always of a disparity (or a relative depth) which is then led to the sound coding block (Sect. 4) and – in a form of coded stereophonic sound sensations – output to an user.

3 Depth Recovery for Visual Aid

The 3D image processing block retrieves depth information in a system of two cameras, simultaneously supplying two images, denoted further on as a left and right image. Although other camera setups are certainly possible to be considered, such as catadioptric ones [3], the two camera system has been chosen due to planned hardware realization, where the two pen-like cameras are to be mounted in a glasses wore by a person [4].

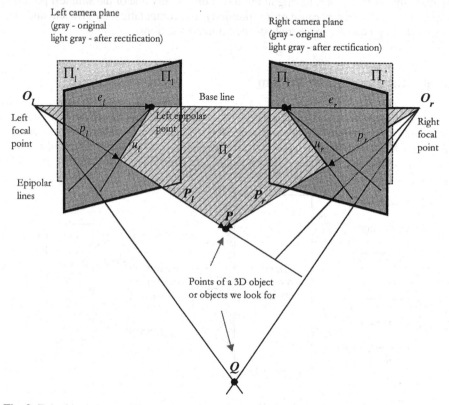

Fig. 2. Epipolar geometry of a stereo camera setup. All images of 3D points of opaque objects can lie only on corresponding epipolar lines. Camera planes Π_l and Π_r are from the original camera setup (gray), whereas Π_l' and Π_r' represent rectified setup (light-gray) in which epipolar lines are parallel and collinear with image scan lines

Depth recovery is done in a stereo setup, which model is shown in Fig. 2. It is assumed that the cameras can be represented by a pinhole models. For each non occluded 3D point, belonging to an opaque object, we obtain two image points, each on a different camera plane, Π_l or Π_r. The aforementioned three points are related by the following formula:

$$\mathbf{p}_r^T \mathbf{E} \mathbf{p}_l = 0 \,, \tag{1}$$

where p_r and p_l are image points expressed in the camera coordinate system, E is so called essential matrix [5][6].

For machine computations it is much easier to express image points not in the camera coordinate system but to use the coordinate systems associated with image planes. Under the assumption given by (1) we have the following formula:

$$\overline{\mathbf{p}_r^T}\mathbf{F}\overline{\mathbf{p}_l} = 0 \ , \tag{2}$$

where F is called a fundamental matrix which determines epipolar geometry associated with a given camera setup.

Thus, knowledge of the matrix F allows us to find epipolar lines and, as a consequence, limits the stereoscopic search to only one dimension. However, the problem still exists, since generally this matrix is not know beforehand. It can be determined by a choice of well matched points and solved linearly if at least eight such points are found or nonlinearly in a case of at least six matched points [6]. Alternatively, one can restrict the camera setup to a standard (or canonical) setup where epipolar lines are collinear with image scan lines. This was assumed in the system described in this paper, what was motivated also by the planned camera mounting on the cap or glasses worn by a person.

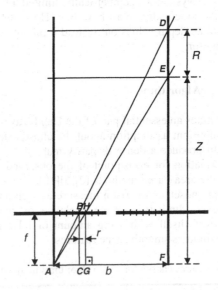

Fig. 3. A geometrical limitation of depth accuracy computation in a canonical stereo setup because of camera resolution (f denotes focus length, b base line, r camera resolution, Z scene depth, R depth resolution at Z)

For real applications it is essential do discuss allowable depth range that can be conceived by a system with canonical stereo setup – Fig. 3.

It can be shown [3] that the depth resolution at a given absolute depth is related by the following approximate formula:

$$R \approx \frac{rZ^2}{fb}, \qquad Z \gg R . \tag{3}$$

where R is depth resolution at a absolute depth Z, f denotes a camera focus length, b stands for length of a base line, and r is a camera resolution. Some practical values of R for two camera setups presents Table 1.

Table 1. Exemplary depth resolution values R for a setup with cameras 1024×1024 pixels, viewing angle 60°, base line b equal to six (human eyes average distance, although eyes are not in a canonical position but have much better resolution) and twenty two centimeters (distance of cameras in our system)

Z[m] / b[m]	0.1	0.5	1.0	5	10
0.06	0.000188	0.0047	0.019	0.518	2.314
0.22	0.000051	0.00128	0.0051	0.132	0.54

Thus, in practice our system is geometrically limited in an accuracy of depth recovery because of the practically small base line. However, the presented system does not compute absolute depth values but instead it outputs relative depths that can be easily adjusted by a user.

3.1 Choice of a Stereo Algorithm

A stereo method constitutes an essential part of the Depth Recovery Module, depicted in Fig. 1. The most important assumption about the chosen stereo algorithm for this system is that it should produce a dense disparity map, since we want to be able to generate a sound information for each point of the observed scene. This limits our domain essentially to the area-based methods [2][3][10]. However, their performance is greatly dependent on chosen comparison measure as well as on matching window size. This poses a severe limitations since a choice of small window preserves features but can manifests itself with a big amount of false matches. At the other hand, large matching windows smooth scene features.

Table 2. Comparison measures chosen for stereo algorithms in the Depth Recovery Module

SAD	$\displaystyle\sum_{(i,j)\in U} \left| I_1(x+i,y+j) - I_2(x+d_x+i,y+d_y+j) \right|$
CoVar	$\displaystyle\frac{\sum_{(i,j)\in U}\left(I_1(x+i,y+j)-\overline{I_1(x,y)}\right)\cdot\left(I_2(x+d_x+i,y+d_y+j)-\overline{I_2(x+d_x,y+d_y)}\right)}{\sqrt{\sum_{(i,j)\in U}\left(I_1(x+i,y+j)-\overline{I_1(x,y)}\right)^2 \cdot \sum_{(i,j)\in U}\left(I_2(x+d_x+i,y+d_y+j)-\overline{I_2(x+d_x,y+d_y)}\right)^2}}$
CENSUS	$\displaystyle\sum_{(i,j)\in U} IC_1(x+i,y+j)\otimes IC_2(x+d_x+i,y+d_y+j)$

Taking into an account this and other comparative studies on the subject [2][14], we chose three area-based algorithms for this project that use the following measures (see Table 2): *SAD* – Sum of Absolute Differences, *CoVar* – Covariance-Variance. In the Table 2 we used the following notation: $I_k(x,y)$, $\overline{I_k(x,y)}$, $IC_k(x,y)$ are intensity, mean intensity, and *Census* [16] values for a k-*th* image at a point *(x,y)* in image coordinates, *i* and *j* are integer indices, d_x and d_y disparity values for *x* and *y* direction, respectively, *U* defines a set of points of a local neighborhood of a point at *(x,y)*, i.e. $U=\{(i,j):p(x+i,y+j)\in I_k\}$, finally, $\otimes$ denotes a Hamming operator.

The fourth stereo algorithm that was employed in the presented system, and gave the best results, is an area-based version of the stereo method based on a tensor representation of local structures [3][1]. In this method the structural vector is computed for each image point, according to the following formula:

$$\mathbf{w}' = \begin{bmatrix} \mathrm{Tr}(\mathbf{T}) \\ \mathbf{w} \end{bmatrix} = \begin{bmatrix} T_{xx} + T_{yy} \\ T_{xx} - T_{yy} \\ 2T_{xy} \end{bmatrix}. \tag{4}$$

T is a symmetric tensor defined as follows:

$$\mathbf{T} = \begin{bmatrix} T_{xx} & T_{xy} \\ T_{yx} & T_{yy} \end{bmatrix}, \quad T_{ij} = \int_U q_i(\vec{x})q_j(\vec{x})d\vec{x}, \tag{5}$$

where $q(x)$ stands for an intensity gradient tensor, whereas *U* is a local neighborhood of pixels around a certain point x_0.

It can be shown [3][1] that the first component in (4), describing a trace of **T**, allows us to distinguish the case of constant intensity in an image from the case of ideal isotropy (Fig. 4).

The formulas (4) and (5) constitute a background to the computation of a disparity map between two images. Essentially, there are two phases of computations:

1. Elimination of non-structural places, i.e. those that the texture does not allow for reliable application of the second stage which is area-based comparison. This is done by cropping those image blobs for which computed trace of **T** is below a certain threshold.

2. Disparity computation by comparison of potentially corresponding regions in both sub-images of the original images. This is done in accordance with the following assumptions:

- Regions are compared by means of the *SAD* measure given in Table 2 but now for structural tensor components (4) *and* image intensity values.
- For stereo correspondance considered are only those regions that have not been eliminated in the step (1).
- The whole depth recovery is computed exclusively in a window that constitutes only a portion of the original image, since only this part of information is necessary at a time to be further transformed into a sound sensation – which in this system is a uniform noise modulated in amplitude by disparity values (see Sec. 4).
- A comparison window is collinear with epipolar lines of the stereo setup.

Fig. 4. Structural tensor operator abilities to eliminate non structural places in real images (a,b,c). Results constitute binary image masks (d,e,f) in which white areas denote places with insufficient texture for matching that should be eliminated from further processing

4 Depth Information Conveyed by Sound

As alluded to previously, depth information acquired in an acquisition window is encoded into a uniform noise modulated in amplitude by disparity values, as given by the following discrete time formula:

$$s[n,k] = d[k]\sigma[n] , \tag{6}$$

where $d[k]$ denotes disparity at a point k of a scanning profile, $\sigma[n]$ is a synthesized noise at a discrete time point n.

The acquisition window is chosen at the virtual center of the two input images, what can be conceived also as a kind of a cyclopean eye. The whole process is depicted in Fig. 5.

Disparity is searched only in a virtual center of the two input images, thus the computation time is significantly reduced to the processing of the depth acquisition window. The virtual center is found as a geometrical center extended in horizontal direction by an expected disparity range and in the vertical direction by some threshold value. Obtained in such a way window disparity is further divided into vertical stripes that are median filtered to eliminate outstanding values – only the median value is taken for further computations.

The acquisition window is also divided into *two equal horizontal panes* that are processed in the same way, but fed to different ears, thus enabling perception of the stereo-sound effect. The two depth profiles are encoded according to (6) in the Sound Coding Block (Fig. 1). In practice, the acquisition window size was chosen to be 5-45 pixels vertically by 25-150 pixels horizontally, depending on scene type.

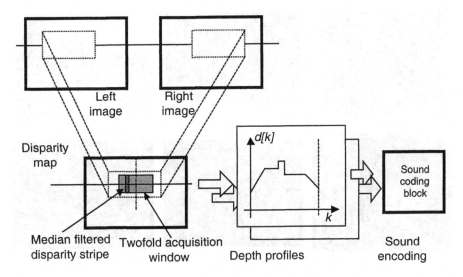

Fig. 5. Information processing diagram. Disparity is computed only in the acquisition window, then filtered and passed to the sound encoding block in two sound channels

5 Experimental Results

The information that is received at the end of the system is a depth-modulated noise that can be easily learned and personally adjusted for navigation among surrounding objects. Experiments were performed by means of the laboratory built software that implements all blocks depicted in Fig. 1. Each of the processing blocks is divided further into specialized objects that are responsible for a particular action. For example, stereo processing can be computed in many different ways by exchanging only one object keeping other intact. Hardware version of this system is planned to be built after final refinements of the software. The biggest improvements of the system speed can be achieved by a custom hardware for stereo processing [15].

Fig. 6 depicts experimental results of a depth recovery obtained with an area-based version of the tensor stereo method, augmented by a detector of uniform places.

The experimental disparity maps in Fig. 6 are shown for the whole images, but in this system computations at a given time are restricted only to the acquisition window (see Fig. 5).

It was already pointed out that the whole stereo algorithm, as well as its settings, such as size of each window, can be changed during operation of the system. The same holds for settings of the Sound Coding Block.

Because the system is not absolutely calibrated, at its output one observes only relative and not an absolute depth. This is a trade-off between computational complexity and abilities of the system to compute absolute depths. It turns out however, that it can be quite easily adjusted (or acoustically calibrated) by a user, simply by remembering noise (sound) intensity of objects located at known distances.

Fig. 6. Experimental results of depth recovery (d,e,f) from real images (a,b,c) obtained with an area-based version of the tensor stereo method improved by the detector of uniform places. Whiter places in depth images (d,e,f) are closer to an observer; black – infinity or "don't know"

6 Conclusions

The presented system can by itself be a part of an enhanced vision aid system, for example such as the one described in [7], in which there are additional image processing channel that encode also intensity values and position of edges. However, the presented system can be sufficient in many practical applications. Its main benefits can be stated as follows:

– No camera calibration, except assurance of a canonical setup.
– Safe (passive vision, low power) and comfortable system (can be in a size of a walkman).
– Not too many software setting parameters, except for few threshold values.
– Greatly improved computation time because of small acquisition window.
– Low cost of hardware (laptop or custom hardware and small camera setup).
– Easy extensions to the existing software (upgrades).

At the other hand, the system is by no means an ultimate solution and the work must be still done to make necessary improvements. The known drawbacks of the presented system are as follows:

– Not for each real scene stereo algorithms produce disparity map with an acceptable quality. One solution is to change the algorithm or change its settings. However, from the output sound alone it is usually not possible to judge the quality of the stereo matching process.
– There is only one value (a median) chosen for a given vertical image stripe in the acquisition window (Fig. 5).
– Due to limitations of stereo algorithms and system information bandwidth, the depth signal is strongly lowpass filtered. This can be considered as a feature.

The presented system exposed its usefulness during experiments. However, the whole domain of visual aids needs further research, since many people can directly benefit such results – this is what the science is certainly for.

References

1. Cyganek, B.: Novel Stereo Matching Method That Employs Tensor Representation of Local Neighborhood in Images, Machine Graphics & Vision, Vol.10, No.3 (2001) 289–316
2. Cyganek, B., Borgosz, J.: A Comparative Study of Performance and Implementation of Some Area-Based Stereo Algorithms, 9th International Conference on Computer Analysis of Images and Patterns CAIP'2001, Warsaw, Poland (2001) 709–716
3. Cyganek, B.: Computer Processing of 3D Images, (in Polish) Academic Publisher House EXIT, Series: Problems in Contemporary Science. Computer Science, Warsaw (2002)
4. Edmund Industrial Optics™. Optics and Optical Instruments Catalog (2001)
5. Faugeras, O.: Three-dimensional computer vision. A geometric viewpoint. MIT (1993)
6. Hartley, R.I., Zisserman, A.: Multiple View Geometry in Computer Vision. Cambridge University Press (2000)
7. Korohoda, P.: Treatise on possibilities of acoustic representation of selected 3D objects. Polish Research Grant No. 8 T11E 009 10 (1999)
8. Molton, N., Se, S., Brady, J.M., Lee, D., Probert, P.: A Stereo Vision-Based Aid for the Visually Impaired. Image and Vision Computing, Vol. 16, No.4 (1998) 251–263
9. Molton, N.D.: Computer Vision as an Aid for the Visually Impaired. PhD Thesis. University of Oxford, (1998)
10. Scharstein, D., Szeliski, R.: A Taxonomy and Evaluation of Dense Two-Frame Stereo Correspondence Algorithms. IEEE Workshop on Stereo and Multi-Baseline Vision, (2001)
11. Se, S., Brady, M.: Stereo Vision-Based Obstacle Detection for Partially Sighted People. Third Asian Conference on Computer Vision ACCV'98, Vol. I (1998) 152–159
12. Se, S., Brady, M.: Vision-Based Detection of Stair-Cases. Fourth Asian Conference on Computer Vision ACCV 2000, Vol. I (2000) 535–540
13. Se, S., Brady, M.: Zebra-crossing Detection for the Partially Sighted. Technical Report. University of Oxford (2000)
14. Szeliski, R., Zabih, R.: An Experimental Comparison of Stereo Algorithms. Vision Algorithms: Theory and Practice. Lecture Notes in Computer Science 1883. Springer-Verlag, Berlin Heidelberg New York (2000)
15. Woodfill, J., Von Herzen, B.: Real-Time Stereo Vision on the PARTS Reconfigurable Computer. IEEE Symposium on FPGAs for Custom Computing Machines (1997)
16. Zabih, R., Woodfill, J.: Non-parametric Local Transforms for Computing Visual Correspondence. Computer Science Department, Cornell University, Ithaca (1998)

A Real-Time Multisensory Image Segmentation Algorithm with an Application to Visual and X-Ray Inspection

Yuhua Ding[1], George J. Vachtsevanos[1], Anthony J. Yezzi Jr.[1], Wayne Daley[2], and Bonnie S. Heck-Ferri[1]

[1]School of Electrical and Computer Engineering, Georgia Institute of Technology, Atlanta, GA 30332, USA
{yhding,george.vachsevanos,ayezzi,
bonnie.heck}@ece.gatech.edu,
Tel. (404) 894-6252   Fax. (404) 894-7358
http://icsl.marc.gatech.edu/
[2]Food Processing Technology Division, Electro-Optics, Environment and Materials Laboratory, Georgia Tech Research Institute, Atlanta, GA 30332-0837, USA
wayne.daley@gtri.gatech.edu
Tel. (4040) 894 3693   http://www.gtri.gatech.edu/

Abstract. A new multisensory image segmentation algorithm is presented. In this algorithm, the images from different sensors are segmented in a sequential manner using curve evolution methods. There are no fusion rules involved and no controlling weights to adjust. It is effective in eliminating errors in single modality segmentation, and is fast enough for segmentation in real-time applications. The algorithm is applied to real-time fan bone detection in deboned poultry meat based on visual and x-ray images. Results show that the fusion-based inspection algorithm is efficient, accurate, and robust to registration errors.

1   Introduction

Computer vision techniques have been widely used in detecting the presence of undesirable objects or defects in a variety of products. However, most of the inspection algorithms are based on monosensory image data, which may not produce satisfactory performance due to the intrinsic ambiguity and incompleteness associated with the data. Images acquired by different sensors are generally partially redundant and partially complementary, which is helpful to reduce imprecision and to provide a more complete description of the scene. Therefore, the inspection performance based on multisensory image data is expected to be better than the monosensory performance.

In contrast to monosource algorithms, multisensory algorithms extract the segmentation features directly from all sensor images, which facilitates the further processing steps of feature extraction and classification. An important goal of multisensory image segmentation is to improve the segmentation performance. Segmentation accuracy has a significant effect on feature distributions and classification performance [4]. In monosensory image segmentation, each image generates false regions or edges. Several approaches ([2,5,8,11,14]) have been developed to increase segmentation accuracy on monosensory images. However, the processing times of these methods are multiple times longer than that of a single algorithm and thus cannot be used in real-time applications. In [4], a real-time recursive segmentation and classification scheme is proposed to achieve accurate segmentation, where the segmentation result needs to be refined only when the result is found to be inaccurate by the classifier. However, the final achievable accuracy largely depends on the classification performance. Instead of trying to improve segmentation accuracy on monosensory images, the multisensory image segmentation algorithms seek to combine the information from different modalities to resolve the ambiguity and eliminate the imprecision in monosensory information. By combining different modalities in segmentation, we expect to achieve the following goals:

· Locate more accurate boundaries for the objects in the scene.
· Eliminate false edges/regions as much as possible.
· For the false edges/regions that cannot be totally eliminated, the significant difference between the segmentation results on individual modalities can be utilized to further discriminate false edges/regions from true edges/regions.

In this paper, a PDE-based curve evolution scheme is presented for multisensory image segmentation. In this algorithm, the images of different modalities are segmented in a serialized manner. The energy functional for each curve evolution model is constructed based on that image's characteristics and, therefore, the method is applicable to the case where the objects in the scene exhibit totally different views between images. Moreover, since the initial estimation of the segmentation is from the segmentation results of the registered peer images, the overall speed is faster than segmenting each modality independently. Besides, there are no fusion rules involved and no controlling weights to adjust. The algorithm is useful in reducing segmentation errors in single modality segmentation, and is fast, reliable, and robust to registration errors.

The paper is organized as follows: First, the multisensory image segmentation methods are briefly reviewed. Then, a real-time serialized segmentation approach is presented. Finally, the approach is applied to the visual- and x-ray-based inspection of fan bones in deboned poultry meat and the results are presented.

2   Multisensory Image Features and Segmentation Methods

Depending on the characteristics of the physical sensors and target objects, the definition for edge and region on multisensory images may vary. Bonnin [1] defines multi-spectral edge point as a pixel where there are important variations at least in one direction in its local neighborhood of a property, in at least one spectral image. This definition implies a logical OR between the different spectral images of edge points. But it does not solve the problem of the obvious displacement of an edge between two spectral images. This problem has to be taken into account and solved in the thinning edge and chaining edge steps. In addition, the false edges caused by artifacts and noise are not considered. By applying the logical OR operation, the false edges will be accumulated in the final edge map. Therefore, caution needs to be taken when fusing edge maps. The majority voting rule in [12] can eliminate false edges if they are only observed in a limited range of bands. However, only the most important edge information is preserved. Similarly, the region of homogeneity implies a logical AND between the homogeneity predicates in all spectral images. The homogeneity criteria are usually thresholdings of the homogeneity measures. The measures can vary largely with different sensors, and even for the same measure, the thresholds may be different. The choice of the homogeneity measure and the adjustment of its thresholds are usually guided by the knowledge of the sensors' physical characteristics.

To address the problem of multisensory image segmentation, one common scheme, as shown in Fig. 1(a), is to obtain features from individual sensor images, then combine these monosensory features using simple fusion rules or within the mathematical frameworks of Bayesian Theorem, Fuzzy Theory, and Dempster-Shafer (DS) Theory. Note that in order to utilize the rules in such frameworks, the fusion problem first has to be modeled in that framework. Another typical way is to build a segmentation map directly on all images using some segmentation algorithm without obtaining individual features beforehand (Fig. 1(b)).

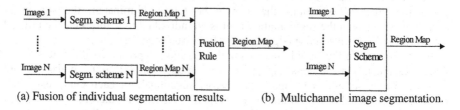

(a) Fusion of individual segmentation results.   (b) Multichannel image segmentation.

Fig. 1. Common schemes for multisensory image segmentation

An example of the first method can be found in [6], where SAR and optical images are fused to achieve better performance to detect urban areas. The fusion of individually segmented images is modeled as a nonlinear optimization problem whose solution leads to the optimally fused versions of each segmented image. The objective function is the sum of two terms: the mismatch between the two fused segmentation maps and the discrepancies between corresponding fused and original segmentations. The unmatched monosource features are controlled by the penalization parameters on the second term. Small parameters result in fused images with more evident characteristics from both the SAR and the optical images, while larger ones result in "less merged" images where the boundary locations of the fused images are marked with more evidence. One concern about this method is that *ad hoc* calibrations of several parameters are necessary. Another issue is that the nonlinear optimization problem is hard to solve and can be too slow to be used in real-time.

One can also build a segmentation map directly on all images using some segmentation algorithm. For example, in [7], multisensory data are classified pixel by pixel using DS theory to produce a labeled image (segmentation map). However, the segmentation map needs to be further refined to remove speckle errors. Another interesting example is the method proposed by Koepfler etc. in [9], where a simplified Munford-Shah functional-based region grow algorithm is adopted for segmentation of the multichannel images generated by any textured image. Although this method is presented for segmentation of monosensor textured images, the notation and methodology can be applied to multisensory image segmentation. It assumes the image in each channel is smooth within individual regions. The variations allowed in each region in different channels are controlled by the weights in the norm. For multisensory images, where intensity variances can be significantly different across images, the choice of the weights will be a demanding task. Moreover, registration errors tend to cause over-segmentation errors by this method. Besides, it is well known that the curve evolution based on Mumford-Shah functional model is extremely slow. Even if a region grow scheme is adopted in this paper, the reported processing times on 512x512 gray-level images range from 10 seconds to 6 minutes.

3   Serialized Segmentation of Multisensory Images

The proposed multisensory image segmentation scheme employs the PDE-based curve evolution method, where the contour evolves according to the optimal flow derived from the energy functional. The reason for segmentation errors is mainly that the images do not satisfy the assumptions on which the energy functional is constructed. Because this type of method is local in nature, the curves tend to get trapped by unexpected features before they reach the true edges in the image, which causes under- or over- segmentation errors. Since the unexpected feature that entrapped the contours may show itself differently in images acquired by other sensors, it may function as a driving force to push the contour toward the true edge and thus reduce the error in monosensory segmentation.

In the serialized segmentation scheme (Fig. 2), multiple images are segmented sequentially. Since no information exchange occurs during the segmentation on individual images, the energy functional can be chosen according to that image only. When proceeding to the next image, not only the contours, but also the values of the energy functional, are passed along.

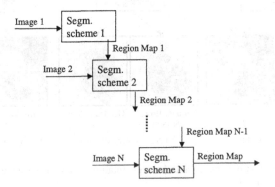

Fig. 2. Serialized segmentation scheme

This scheme is robust to registration error because the snake segmentation algorithm can pull the contour to accommodate a small registration mismatch. The computational load is small and is lower than the total load of segmenting individual images independently thanks to the more accurate initial estimate of contours.

Simulation of this scheme is performed on the gray-scale test images shown in Fig. 3(a), where I_0 is the root image and I_A and I_B are the two gray-scale test images generated by diffusing and shading I_0, respectively. In I_A, the edge information is totally lost during diffusion, while in I_B, although edge is well preserved, the region R cannot be differentiated from its background $\overline{R}$ simply based on the intensity information. Since I_A and I_B have totally different characteristics, they cannot be segmented satisfactorily using one single segmentation algorithm. To show this, we applied the following two flows on both I_A and I_B: the region-based binary flow ([15])

$$\frac{d\psi}{dt} = \{(v-u)(\frac{I-u}{A_u}+\frac{I-v}{A_v}) + \alpha \cdot \mathrm{div}(\frac{\nabla \psi}{\|\nabla \psi\|})\}\|\nabla \psi\| \tag{1}$$

where Ψ is the level set, I is the pixel intensity, $\alpha \in [0, 1]$ is a constant weight, and u, v, and A_u, A_v are the mean intensities and areas inside and outside the contour, respectively; and the geodesic flow

$$\frac{d\psi}{dt} = \phi \cdot \mathrm{div}(\frac{\nabla \psi}{\|\nabla \psi\|})\}\|\nabla \psi\| + \nabla \phi \cdot \nabla \psi \tag{2}$$

where $\phi = \dfrac{1}{1+\|\nabla I\|^2}$ is the edge feature metric. It can be seen from the results, which are shown in Fig. 3(b) and (c), that the binary flow is effective only on I_A, while the geodesic flow is effective only on I_B.

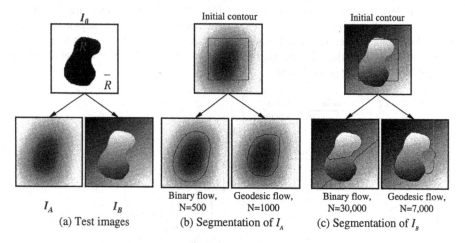

(a) Test images (b) Segmentation of I_A (c) Segmentation of I_B

Fig. 3. Gray-scale test images (a) and the segmentation results using binary flow and geodesic flow on both I_A (b) and I_B (c)

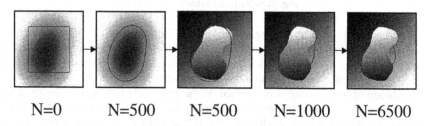

N=0   N=500   N=500   N=1000   N=6500

Fig. 4. Result on test images using the serialized segmentation scheme

The serialized segmentation is performed as follows: the binary flow is first applied on I_A to obtain a contour that separates the darker region from the brighter background. Then starting from this contour, the geodesic flow is applied to I_B. From the simulation results shown in Fig. 4, we can see that the contour found in I_A is refined to catch the exact boundary of the region R. The final contour obtained is obviously superior than results derived individually. Also, the segmentation on the first image actually serves as a contour initialization module for the second image in this scheme.

4   Application — Real-Time Fan Bone Inspection of Deboned Poultry Products

4.1   Problem Description

The application of bone detection in deboned meat is motivated by the dramatic increase in the demand for deboned meat over the last few years. The end users of the deboned product, especially fast food companies, are requesting zero bones in meat [11]. X-ray-based equipment has been used to detect large, embedded bones such as pulley bones, but it has difficulty detecting thin surface bones, such as fan bones, surface bones with fan-like shape. Fan bones are typically less dense and of lower thickness perpendicular to the x-ray beam than other bones normally found in the meat. In this paper, we apply the proposed multisensory segmentation techniques to visual and x-ray inspection so that the overall inspection performance is improved.

The visual image of the deboned chicken breast contains various features, such as meat, fat, blood, bruise, bone, white membrane, among others. Although the contrast between fan bone and meat is prominent, there are other spots on the image that may appear similar in color and shading to bones. These include shadows and edge characteristics that must be distinguished from fan bones. In x-ray images, the local bone-meat contrast is good, but the fan bone regions have similar intensity levels as the thicker meat does and, therefore, is very difficult to segment.

The visual-based inspection algorithm, which is described in detail in [3], consists of four steps: preprocessing, segmentation, feature extraction, and classification. The region-based snake algorithm with the optimal flow (2) is applied, and only 75.5% of all fan bone regions are segmented accurately. For the remaining fan bone regions, segmentation errors are generated because of the closeness of fan bone to other similar features, resulting in a low detection rate of 40.91% on these regions.

4.2   Inspection through Fusion of Visual and X-Ray Modalities

4.2.1   Image Registration

X-ray and visual images are manually aligned before fusion by computing the transform matrix using manually selected control points (CP). An example of the registration results is shown in Fig. 5., where (a) and (b) are the clips of the visual and x-ray images, respectively, for the same fan bone-contaminated chicken part. The fan bone is marked out with a circle in each image. The x-ray image and the red channel of the visual image are overlapped to form the synthesized image in (c). Significant registration errors (mismatch between the transformed x-ray image and the visual image) are observed in the registered images. The main reason is that the assumption of linear conformal transform between the two images is not totally valid. Besides, error is introduced during manual selection of CPs due to distinct sensor sensitivities: one common subject (such as a fan bone) may have various views in the images of different modalities.

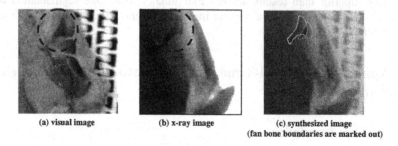

(a) visual image   (b) x-ray image   (c) synthesized image
                                                     (fan bone boundaries are marked out)

Fig. 5. An example of registered visual and x-ray images

4.2.2   Visual-Feature-Based Segmentation of X-Ray Images

In x-ray images, the local contrast between the fan bone and the meat is good, but the intensity levels inside and outside the fan bone regions are very close due to the uneven thickness of chicken meat. In order to compensate for this effect, we adopted the feature extraction method proposed in [9]. The raw image is first filtered using the Laplacian of Gaussian and then binarized. The feature image is obtained by adding all the binarized images. A polar pair of pixels of the edge polarity represents edge features. Bar features are represented by single pixels of the corresponding polarity. The x-ray clip in Fig. 5 and its visual feature image are shown in (a) and (b) of Fig. 6. Fig. 6 (c) is the segmentation result using the binary flow curve evolution method on the feature image. The segmentation algorithm captured the fan bone, but it did not separate the fan bone region totally from the darker regions nearby and, therefore, the fan bone cannot be identified successfully by the classifier.

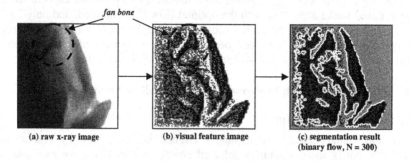

(a) raw x-ray image   (b) visual feature image   (c) segmentation result
                                                               (binary flow, N = 300)

Fig. 6. The feature image of x-ray image and its segmentation result

4.2.3   Segmentation Using the Serialized Segmentation Scheme

The serialized segmentation scheme is applied on the x-ray feature image and the red channel of the corresponding visual image. The same binary flow in (2) is used throughout the segmentation procedure, which is illustrated in Fig. 7. The initial contour (a) is obtained from thresholding the red channel of the visual image. Then, the contour evolved for 50 iterations and the result is shown in (b). Starting from this contour (c), the x-ray feature image is used in computing the binary flow and the results after 150 and 300 iterations are shown in (d) and (e), respectively.

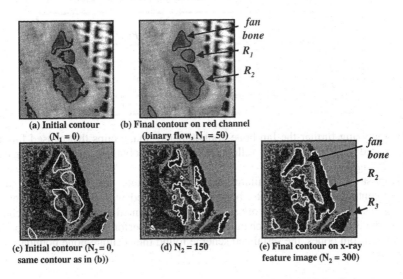

(a) Initial contour
(N$_1$ = 0)

(b) Final contour on red channel
(binary flow, N$_1$ = 50)

(c) Initial contour (N$_2$ = 0,
same contour as in (b))

(d) N$_2$ = 150

(e) Final contour on x-ray
feature image (N$_2$ = 300)

Fig. 7. The procedure of serialized segmentation scheme

It can be seen from the example that the scheme is effective in allocating the boundaries of fan bones in both visual and x-ray feature images. In spite of the significant registration error, the snake algorithm is able to pull the contour to the exact boundary of the fan bone. Note also that R_1, the first shadow region found in the visual image, is totally eliminated in (e), while R_2, the other shadow region, is changed completely by the algorithm. A new region (R_3) is generated in x-ray segmentation. Both R_2 and R_3 can be identified easily as false regions because of the significant difference of the regions in two modalities.

The algorithm is tested on 160x160 image clips cut from the registered visual and x-ray images taken on-line in a poultry plant. There are totally 106 clips, out of which 51 contain fan bones and the others contain shadow features that look similar to fan bones on visual images.

Out of the 55 fan bone-free clips, 48 result in totally different segmentation results between the visual-based segmentation and the serialized segmentation. For the 51 fan bone-contaminated clips, the segmentation results are assessed visually and classified as *Good*, *Fair*, and *Poor* according to the closeness of the contour to the true boundary. Each clip is assigned two assessments: G_v and G_{xf}, for the monosensory contour and multisensory contour, respectively. For clips that contain fan bones, the total number of clips with the same G_v and G_{xf} are listed in Table 1.

From the table, we can see that the serialized segmentation scheme achieved good results on 32 clips, while the visual-based segmentation only 26 clips. In particular, out of the 22 clips that visual-based segmentation totally failed, the serialized segmentation scheme successfully corrected the results in 9 clips. In contrast, out of the 26 clips that the visual-based segmentation results are good, only 1 failed by the serialized scheme. These preliminary results show that the proposed serialized segmentation scheme is more accurate than the one based on visual information only.

Table 1. Segmentation accuracy on fan bone regions

G_v \ G_{xf}	Good	Fair	Poor	Total
Good	21	4	1	26
Fair	2	0	1	3
Poor	9	0	13	22
Total	32	4	15	51

By analyzing further the fan bone-contaminated image clips that caused failure in visual-based segmentation, the following results are obtained, whose examples are shown in Fig. 8:

- Almost all of the 22 failures from red channel segmentation are under-segmentations where the fan bone regions merged with their neighboring dark regions. Nine of these clips are successfully segmented by the serialized scheme.
- On the 3 clips that the red channel segmentation performs poorly due to partially covered fan bones, the serialized scheme found the accurate bone boundaries in 2 clips.

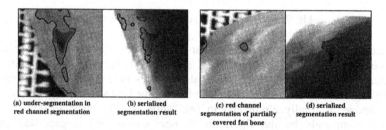

(a) under-segmentation in red channel segmentation (b) serialized segmentation result (c) red channel segmentation of partially covered fan bone (d) serialized segmentation result

Fig. 8. Comparison of results obtained from visual-based segmentation and serialized segmentation

The above two observations further confirm that the contention that the proposed multisensory segmentation algorithm not only is effective in improving segmentation accuracy, but also corrects the errors caused by inaccurate information involved in monosensory data.

5   Conclusions

In this paper, a serialized scheme for multisensory image segmentation is presented. The experimental results suggest that the algorithm is effective in achieving high segmentation accuracy. The scheme is fast, reliable and, thus, suitable for segmentation tasks in real-time inspection applications.

Acknowledgements. The authors would like to express their appreciation to the State of Georgia and the Governor's Food Processing Advisory Council for their support in the conduct of this research. The authors also wish to thank Tyson Foods, Inc. and Cagle's Inc. for supplying chicken parts during the development and testing of the system.

References

1. Bonnin, P., Hoeltzener-Douarin, B., Pissaloux, E.: A New Way of Image Data Fusion: The Multi-Spectral Cooperative Segmentation. Proc Intl Conf Image Processing, 3 (1995) 572–575

2. Charroux, B., Phillipp, S., Cocquerez, J-P.: Image Analysis: Segmentation Operator Cooperation Led by the Interpretation. Proc. Intl. Conf. Image Processing, Vol. 3, (1996) 939 – 942

3. Ding, Y., Yezzi, A., Heck, B., Daley, W., Vachtsevanos, G., Zhang, Y.: An On-line Real-time Automatic Visual Inspection Algorithm for Surface Bone Detection in Poultry Products. 2nd WSEAS Intl. Conf. Signal, Speech, and Image Processing (WSEAS ICOSSIP 2002), Sept. 2002.

4. Ding, Y., Vachtsevanos, G., Yezzi, A., Zhang, Y., Wardi, Y.: A Recursive Segmentation and Classification Scheme for Improving Segmentation Accuracy and Detection Rate in Real-Time Machine Vision Applications. Proc. 14th Intl. Conf. Digital Signal Processing (DSP2002), 2 (2002), 1009–1014

5. Falah, R. K., Bolon, P., Cocquerez, J.P.: A Region-Region and Region-Edge Cooperative Approach of Image Segmentation. First IEEE Intl. Conf. Image Processing, Vol. 3, (1994) 470–474

6. Fatone, L., Maponi, P., Zirilli, F.: Fusion of SAR/Optical Image to Detect Urban Areas. IEEE/ISPRS Joint Workshop on Remote Sensing and Data Fusion over Urban Areas, (2001) 217–221

7. Hegarat-Mascle, S. L., Bloch, I., Vidal-Madjar, D.: Application of Dempster-Shafer Evidence Theory to Unsupervised Classification in Multisource Remote Sensing. IEEE Trans. Geoscience and Remote Sensing, 35 (1997) 1018–1031

8. Huet F., Philipp, S.: Fusion of Images after Segmentation by Various Operators and Interpretation by a Multi-Scale Fuzzy Classification. Proc. 14th Intl Conf. Pattern Recognition, Vol.2, (1998) 1843–1845

9. Koepfler, G., Lopez, C., Rudin, L.: Data Fusion by Segmentation. Application to Texture Discrimination," Actes du 14me Colloque GRETSI, (1993) 707–710

10. Peli, E.: Feature Detection Algorithm Based on a Visual System Model. Proceedings of the IEEE, 90 (2002) 78 –93

11. Smith, D.: Bones in Boneless Broiler Breast Meat Is a Legitimate Concern. World Poultry, 15 (1999) 35–36

12. Solaiman, B., Koffi, R. K., Mouchot, M-C, Hillion, A.: An Information Fusion Method for Multispectral Image Classification Postprocessing. IEEE Trans. Geoscience and Remote Sensing, 36 (1998) 395–406

13. Spinu, C., Garbay, C., Chassery, J. M.: A Multi-Agent Approach to Edge Detection as a Distributed Optimization Problem. Proc. 13th Intl. Conf. Pattern Recognition, 2 (1996) 81–85

14. Stewart, D., Blacknell, D., Blake, A., Cook, R., Oliver, C.: Optimal Approach to SAR Image Segmentation and Classification. IEE Proc. Radar, Sonar Navigation, 147 (2000) 134–142

15. Yezzi, A., Tsai, A., Willsky, A.: Medical Image Segmentation via Coupled Curve Evolution Equations with Global Constraints. Mathematical Methods in Biomedical Image Analysis, 2000. Proc. IEEE Workshop on Biomedical Image Analysis, (2000) 12–19

An Attentive, Multi-modal Laser "Eye"

Simone Frintrop, Erich Rome, Andreas Nüchter, and Hartmut Surmann

Fraunhofer Institut für Autonome Intelligente Systeme, Schloss Birlinghoven,
53754 Sankt Augustin, Germany
{simone.frintrop, erich.rome, andreas.nuechter,
hartmut.surmann}@ais.fraunhofer.de
http://www.ais.fhg.de/

Abstract. In this paper we present experimental results on a novel application of visual attention mechanisms for the selection of points of interest in an arbitrary scene. The imaging sensor used is a multi-modal 3D laser scanner. In a single 3D scan pass, it is capable of providing range data as well as a gray-scale intensity image. The scanner is mounted on top of an autonomous mobile robot and serves control purposes. We present results achieved by applying the visual attention system of Itti et al. [8] to recorded scans of indoor and outdoor scenes. The vast majority of the primary attended locations pointed to scene objects of potential interest for navigation and object detection tasks. Moreover, both sensor modalities complement each other, resulting in a greater variety of points of interest than one modality alone can provide.

1   Introduction

Common tasks in the control of autonomous mobile robots are collision avoidance, navigation, and the manipulation of objects. In order to execute these tasks correctly, the robot needs to detect objects and free space in its environment fast and reliably. One method to find potential points of interest in the environment is to model human visual attention.

In human vision, attention helps to identify relevant data and so to efficiently select information from the broad sensory input. These effects are even more desired in computational applications like image processing. Our work is based on the model of visual attention by Itti et al. [8]. In this model, different features like intensity, color and orientation are evaluated in parallel and fused into a single saliency map that topographically codes salient locations in a visual scene. These locations can be analyzed later by object recognition modules and the found objects can help to accomplish robot control tasks.

This model, like many others, includes no depth feature, although in robotic applications depth is often employed for object detection tasks. Objects usually have range discontinuities at their borders which can help to detect them. Models comprising depth as a feature typically use stereo vision to compute it [10,2]. But stereo vision is computationally expensive, and only a fraction of the image pixels contribute to the computed 3D point clouds.

J.L. Crowley et al. (Eds.): ICVS 2003, LNCS 2626, pp. 202–211, 2003.

As an alternative, 3D laser scanners are a class of sensors suitable for the fast acquisition of precise and dense depth or range information. The multi-modal 3D laser scanner used for our work [12] provides the technical means to acquire both range data as well as an intensity image of a scene in a single 3D scan pass. Since the data from the different sensor modalities result from the same measurement, we know exactly which remission or intensity value belongs to which range data. There is no need to establish correspondence by complex algorithms.

Such a multi-sensor offers new algorithmic possibilities. It is to be expected that range data and remission values complement each other, providing some redundancy that can be exploited. Contrasts in range and in intensity need not necessarily correspond for one object. That is, an object producing the same intensity like its background may not be detected in a gray-scale image, but probably in the range data. On the other hand a flat object on a flat background – e.g. a poster on a wall or a letter on a desk – that could be clearly distinguished in an intensity image, may be too flat to be detected in the range data.

In this paper we use the data from the 3D laser scanner as input to the attentional model by generating a special input image by combining range and intensity data in a suitable way. We show the applicability of the laser data for attentional mechanisms and compare these results to the ones from corresponding camera images. For our experiments, we used recorded scan data from indoor and outdoor scenes. The 3D laser scanner is mounted on top of a robot (Fig. 1), and data acquisition is steered by the robot's CPU.

The remainder of this article is structured as follows. We start with analyzing the state of the art in robotic 3D scene imaging and in models of visual attention. Then we describe our system setup, that is, the multi-modal 3D scanner and our use of the visual attention system of Itti et al. In the main section we describe the acquisition and evaluation of the data and analyze the results. Finally, we summarize the arguments and give an outlook on future work.

2   State of the Art

Some groups have developed methods to build 3D volumetric representations of environments using 2D laser range finders. Thrun et al. [7], Früh et al. [6] and Zhao et al. [16] combine two 2D laser scanners for acquiring 3D data. One scanner is mounted horizontally, one vertically. Since the vertical scanner is not able to scan lateral surfaces of objects, Zhao et al. use two additional vertically mounted 2D scanners shifted by 45° to reduce occlusions [16]. The horizontal scanner is employed to compute the robot pose. The precision of 3D data points depends on that pose and on the precision of the scanners. All of these approaches have difficulties to navigate around 3D obstacles with jutting out edges. They are only detected while passing them.

A few other groups use true 3D laser scanners that are able to generate consistent 3D data points within a single 3D scan. The RESOLV project aimed at modelling interiors for virtual reality and tele-presence [11]. They employed a RIEGL laser range finder. The AVENUE project develops a robot for modelling urban environments [1]. This robot is equipped with an expensive CYRAX 3D laser scanner.

The multi-modal 3D laser range finder employed for this work [12] is a precise, fast scanning, reliable, and cost effective multi purpose sensor. Range data and remission images are acquired in one 3D scan pass. The interpretation of these data may require exhaustive time ressources. One approach to reduce these is to use attentional machanisms that help to find regions of interest in the data.

Many computational models of human visual attention are based on the psychological work of Treisman et al., known as *feature-integration theory* [13], and on the *guided search* model by Wolfe [15]. The first explicit computational architecture for controlling visual attention was proposed by Koch and Ullman [9]. It already contains the main properties of the more elaborated model of Itti et al. [8] which forms the basis of our work. This model belongs to the group of *feature-based models* that use classical linear filter operations for feature extraction, what makes them especially useful to real-world scenes. Another approach provide the connectionist models, e.g. the *selective tuning model* by Tsotsos et al. [14].

Attentional systems using depth information can be found in [10] and [2], where stereo vision is applied to retrieve depth information. In robotics, attentional mechanisms are often used to direct the gaze (i.e. a camera) to interesting points in the environment. In [4], a robot shall look at people or toys and in [3] it uses attention to play at dominoes. However, the use of attentional mechanisms for robot control tasks is rarely considered.

3   Experimental Setup

3.1   The Multi-modal Custom 3D Laser Scanner

For the data acquisition in our experiments, we used a custom 3D laser range finder (Fig. 1, left). The scanner is based on a commercial SICK 2D laser range finder. In [12], the custom scanner setup is described in detail. The paper also describes reconstruction and scan matching algorithms and their use for robot applications. Here, we provide only a brief overview of the device.

A 3D scan is performed by step-rotating the 2D scanner around a horizontal axis by a total of up to 105 degrees. The 2D scanner is very fast (processing time about 13 ms for a 180° scan with 181 measurements) and precise (typical range error - 1 cm). A typical medium resolution 3D scan producing 256 layers of 362 values each, with an angular resolution of 0.5 degrees both horizontally and vertically, takes about 7.5 seconds and yields 92 672 data points. In lowest resolution mode, a 3D scan measures 128×180 points in about 1.75 seconds, in highest resolution mode, it yields 256×720 measurements in about 15 seconds.

The scanner can operate in two modes. In the usual mode, it returns range data in a predefined resolution. In an alternative mode, it is able to yield two different kinds of data for each measured point in a single scan pass: A distance value and a remission value that quantifies the intensity of the reflected laser

Fig. 1. Left: The custom 3D range finder mounted on top of the mobile robot KURT 2. Right: An office scene imaged with the 3D scanner in remission value mode. Medium resolution, 256×360 pixels

light. The latter data type can directly be converted into a gray scale intensity image of the scanned parts of the scene. Compared to a normal camera image, the remission value image is spherically distorted (Fig. 1, right). This effect is due to the different measuring principle. The scanner has only one light sensitive element, which receives a beam reflected by a rotating mirror (for horizontal scanning), and is then rotated around a horizontal axis (for vertical scanning).

The current scanner software processes only the range data yielding, e.g., a rough 3D surface approximation of the environment [12]. For robot control tasks this needs to be processed further in order to identify objects and free space for navigation. The attention system shall be used to quickly identify points of interest as starting points for further segmentation and object detection tasks.

3.2   The Artificial Visual Attention System

Our experiments are based on an available implementation of the attentional model of Itti et al. [8] (large central box in Fig. 2). In their model, input is provided in the form of static color images taken from any kind of camera. The input is first decomposed into a set of topographic feature maps usually using intensity, color and orientation as feature dimensions. Each feature is computed by a set of linear *center-surround* operations, which are particularly well-suited to detecting locations which locally stand out from their surroundings. The feature maps are fed into a master *saliency map* (SM) which combines salient points from all feature maps. The most salient point in this map is found by a winner take all network (WTA). After shifting the focus of attention (FOA) to this location, local inhibition is activated in the SM, in the area of the FOA. This mechanism models the *inhibition of return* (IOR) phenomenon observed in humans. It yields dynamical shifts of the FOA and prevents the FOA from immediately returning to a previously attended location.

In our system (Fig. 2), input images are generated from the range data and remission values provided by the 3D scanner. The latter ones can immediately be used as a gray-scale image in a straightforward manner. The depth values from

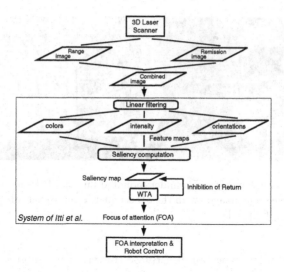

Fig. 2. Simplified system architecture diagram

the range data require a more elaborate transformation. The basic approach is to interpret the depth values of the range data as intensity values, representing small depth values as light intensity values and large depth values as dark ones. Since close objects are considered more important for robot applications, we introduced an additional double proximity bias. Firstly, we consider only objects within a radius of 10 m of the robot's location. Secondly, we code the depth values by using their square roots, so pixel p computes from depth value d by:

$$p = \begin{cases} I - (\sqrt{d/max} * I) & : \quad d \leq max \\ 0 & : \quad d > max \end{cases} \tag{1}$$

with $I = 255$ denoting the maximum intensity value and $max = 1000$ the maximum distance in cm. This measure leads to a finer distinction of range discontinuities in the vicinity of the robot and works better than a linear function.

In order to generate salient locations from both sets of scanner data in one processing stage, we fuse a range and a remission image into one colorized image which serves as input to the model of Itti et al. To accomplish this, the transformed range data are treated as intensity values of the new input image, but the remission values are coded as color (hue) information of the new input image, i.e. we utilize the so far unused color feature dimension. High intensities are coded in red hues, low intensities in greens (Fig. 3). This results in suitable color images because the color feature map takes into account blue-yellow contrasts as well as red-green contrasts. This mapping enables us to utilize the attentional system as is without the need to adapt it. It would be also possible to code remission as intensity and depth as color but for implementation reasons our versions yields slightly better results. Of course, it is also still possible to use only either the range or the remission image as input to the system.

Fig. 3. From left to right: A remission image, the corresponding range image and the combined colorized image. In gray-scale its hardly possible to see the red-green components from the remission image, so the image is very similar to the range image.

4   Results

We have tested our approach on scans of indoor as well as outdoor scenes. In Fig 3, we show a remission image, a range image, and the combined color image. Since the color image does not print well in gray-scale, we have decided to display only the separately processed range and remission images in later figures (Fig. 4, 5). The circles indicate the FOAs, showing only the first resp. the first two FOAs. If there is more than one FOA shown, the arrow indicates their order of detection.

In a first test set we show the general applicability of the 3D laser scanner as a sensor for attentional mechanisms (Fig. 4). In the remission images (left column) the presented objects are detected at the first try in almost all cases except in the first row, where the cable reel is not regarded as an attentional point. In the range images (middle column), the FOAs always find the presented objects, because they are well separated from the background. These results show, that data from the 3D-laser scanner is generally well-suited to find attentional points as long as objects have a popping-out intensity or a certain distance to their background. More difficult is the detection of objects in crowded scenes like office environments (cf. Fig. 1) where these conditions are often not met.

The second test set shows a comparison of attentional points in either laser sensor mode and in corresponding camera images (Fig. 5). The columns show, from left to right, the remission, range and camera images each with some FOAs. The first row shows an example where all modes obtain the same results: the traffic sign is always detected by the first FOA.

An advantage of the laser data over the camera image can be found in row 2, where the traffic sign is easily detected by remission and range image but missed in the camera image. However the fire extinguisher in row 4 is only detected in the camera image because of its red color (1. FOA).

The complementary effect of the two laser modes is illustrated in rows 3 and 4. In row 3, the 2nd FOA in the remission image is placed on the icon on the ground marking a parking space for disabled people, which is impossible to be detected in the depth image. On the other hand, range shows its value in the last row, where the cable reel is detected immediately but missed completely

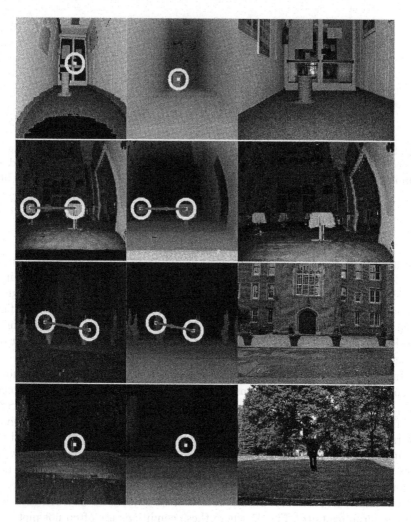

Fig. 4. Test result set 1: Attentional points in laser data. Columns from left to right: Laser remission images with attentional points, laser range images with attentional points, reference scene images.

in the remission image. The presented examples show in a convincing way the advantage of having different sensor modes at hand.

To evaluate the performance of our system, we generated the first 5 FOAs of 15 scenes and tested whether they showed an object of potential interest (OPI). An OPI is an object the robot could derive benefit from, e.g. obstacles like the cable reel or landmarks like the fire extinguisher. The FOAs were generated for remission and range images yielding $5 * (2 * 15) = 150$ FOAs. Of these FOAs, 81 (54%) pointed to OPIs. Regarding this results one should consider that in most of our scenes the number of salient spots that generate FOAs is greater than

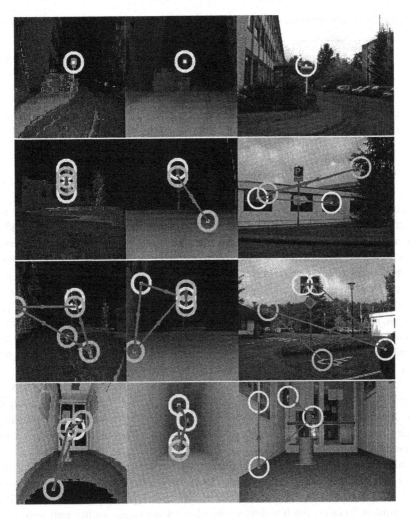

Fig. 5. Test result set 2: Comparison of attentional points in camera images and in laser data. Columns from left to right: Laser remission images, laser range images, camera images. 1. row: same results in all modes. 2. row: traffic sign not found in camera image. 3. row: lower traffic sign not found in camera image, handicapped person sign not found in range image. 4. row: fire extinguisher only found in camera image, cable reel only found in range image.

the number of OPIs, so usually not all foci point to OPIs. Furthermore, if there is only one OPI in a scene, at most three of the first five FOAs can lie on an OPI, because IOR forces the focus to go away from the OPI before it can return again.

Tab. 1 shows the distribution of the FOAs. Of the first attended locations, 86% show a potential object of interest. The 2nd and 3rd ranked FOAs find less objects, because there are frequently only one or two objects in the scene. The

Table 1. Distribution of the 5 most salient FOAs on a test set of 30 images.

Number of the FOA (decreasing saliency)	1.	2.	3.	4.	5.
Attended objects of potential interest [%]	86	56	30	53	43

4th and 5th FOAs have higher values than the 3rd one, because an inhibited object often attracts the focus again after a while.

5   Conclusion and Outlook

We have introduced a new application of visual attention algorithms for robot control purposes. The input images for the attentional system were provided by a 3D laser scanner. We have shown that the attentional system was able to generate a high number of salient locations, both in indoor and outdoor real-world scenes. It was demonstrated that under certain conditions range and remission values complement each other.

Multi-modality of a 3D sensor opens a wide range of new algorithmic possibilities, as we have demonstrated in this work. More expensive laser range finders are able to yield up to two more data qualities, namely color and temperature. These data could also be fed into the attention model, and it is to be expected that this setup would yield even more complementary points of interest.

A limiting factor for the application of a scanning device is the low scan speed. The minimum speed of 1.7 seconds for a low resolution 3D scan does not allow for its use as single sensor for robot navigation in quickly changing environments. But it is well-suited for applications like security inspection tasks in facility maintenance and interior survey of buildings, for instance.

Since the scan speed is determined mostly by the scan mechanics, it makes sense to consider doing without it. Currently, several research prototypes of non-scanning 3D laser "cameras" are under development, e.g. at KTH [5] and at DaimlerChrysler. Such a device can also return range values and a gray-scale image, too, but faster than a scanning device.

Concerning visual attention a next step will be to use the laser scanner in combination with a camera which can be used to utilize additional color information. Additionally it can be directed to points of potential interest to do further processing like object recognition. The found objects can support collision avoidance, navigation and the manipulation of objects.

We also plan to develop a new system that combines both bottom-up, feature-based generation of FOAs, and top-down modulating mechanisms. For robot control, bottom-up attention is well-suited for exploring unknown environments, whereas top-down modulation may alter scan paths in order to effectively search for expected objects with known features like particular landmarks.

Acknowledgements. The authors wish to thank Laurent Itti for providing access to his attention modelling software. This support is gratefully acknowledged.

References

1. Allen, P., Stamos, I., Gueorguiev, A., Gold, E. and Blaer, P. AVENUE: Automated Site Modelling in Urban Environments. In: Proc. 3rd Int'l Conf. on 3D Digital Imaging and Modeling (3DIM '01) (2001).
2. Backer, G. and Mertsching, B. Integrating depth and motion into the attentional control of an active vision system. *Baratoff, G.; Neumann, H. (eds.): Dynamische Perzeption. St. Augustin (Infix)* (2000) 69–74.
3. Bollmann, M. Entwicklung einer Aufmerksamkeitssteuerung für ein aktives Sehsystem. PhD thesis Universität Hamburg (1999).
4. Breazeal, C. A context-dependent attention system for a social robot. In: Proc. 16th Int'l Joint Conf. on Artifical Intelligence (IJCAI 99) (1999) 1146–1151.
5. Carlsson, T. E., Gustafsson, J. and Nilsson, B. Development of a 3D camera. In: Practical Holography XIII, S. A. Benton (Ed.) volume 3637 of *Proc. SPIE* (1999) 218–224.
6. Früh, C. and Zakhor, A. 3D Model Generation for Cities Using Aerial Photographs and Ground Level Laser Scans. In: Proc. Computer Vision & Pattern Recognition Conference (CVPR '01) (2001).
7. Hähnel, D., Burgard, W. and Thrun, S. Learning Compact 3D Models of Indoor and Outdoor Environments with a Mobile Robot. In: Proc. 4th European Workshop on Advanced Mobile Robots (EUROBOT '01) (2001).
8. Itti, L., Koch, C. and Niebur, E. A Model of Saliency-Based Visual Attention for Rapid Scene Analysis. *IEEE Trans. on Pattern Analysis & Machine Intelligence* **20** (11, 1998) 1254–1259.
9. Koch, C. and Ullman, S. Shifts in selective visual attention: towards the underlying neural circuitry. *Human Neurobiology* (1985) 219–227.
10. Maki, A., Nordlund, P. and Eklundh, J.-O. Attentional Scene Segmentation: Integrating Depth and Motion. *CVIU* **78** (3, 2000) 351–373.
11. Sequeira, V., Ng, K., Wolfart, E., Goncalves, J. and Hogg, D. Automated 3D reconstruction of interiors with multiple scan–views. In: Proc. SPIE, Electronic Imaging '99, SPIE's 11th Annual Symposium (1999).
12. Surmann, H., Lingemann, K., Nüchter, A. and Hertzberg, J. A 3D laser range finder for autonomous mobile robots. In: Proc. 32nd Intl. Symp. on Robotics (ISR 2001) (April 19–21, 2001, Seoul, South Korea) (2001) 153–158.
13. Treisman, A. and Gelade, G. A feature integration theory of attention. *Cognitive Psychology* **12** (1980) 97–136.
14. Tsotsos, J. K., Culhane, S. M., Wai, W. Y. K., Lai, Y., Davis, N. and Nuflo, F. Modeling Visual Attention via Selective Tuning. *AI* **78** (1-2, 1995) 507–545.
15. Wolfe, J., Cave, K. and Franzel, S. Guided Search: An Alternative to the Feature Integration Model for Visual Search. *J. of Experimental Psychology: Human Perception and Performance* **15** (1989) 419–433.
16. Zhao, H. and Shibasaki, R. Reconstructing Textured CAD Model of Urban Environment Using Vehicle-Borne Laser Range Scanners and Line Cameras. In: 2nd Int'l Workshop on Computer Vision System (ICVS '01) (2001) 284 – 295.

Navigating through Logic-Based Scene Models for High-Level Scene Interpretations

Bernd Neumann and Thomas Weiss

FB Informatik, Universität Hamburg, Voigt-Kölln-Str. 30
22527 Hamburg, Germany
{neumann, weiss}@informatik.uni-hamburg.de

Abstract. This paper explores high-level scene interpretation with logic-based conceptual models. The main interest is in aggregates which describe interesting co-occurrences of physical objects and their respective views in a scene. Interpretations consist of instantiations of aggregate concepts supported by evidence from a scene. It is shown that flexible interpretation strategies are possible which are important for cognitive vision, e.g. mixed bottom-up and top-down interpretation, exploitation of context, recognition of intentions, task-driven focussing. The knowledge representation language is designed to easily map into a Description Logics (DL), however, current DL systems do not (yet) offer services which match high-level vision interpretation requirements. A table-laying scene is used as a guiding example. The work is part of the EU-project CogVis.

1 Introduction

This contribution presents a framework for high-level scene interpretation based on logic-based conceptual models. Model-based scene interpretation in general is a well-known methodology, and various kinds of models - notably relational, frame-based, rule-based, neural and probabilistic models - have been investigated for their utility to capture and apply generic knowledge for Computer Vision systems. In this paper, logic-based models are explored because (i) high-level vision needs an interface to general knowledge and thus to AI-type knowledge representation, (ii) there exist powerful logic-based theories for qualitative spatial and temporal reasoning [1], [2] which may be useful for vision, (iii) little is known about the usefulness of logic-based models for scene interpretation [3], [4], [5], [6], [7] and (iv) even less is known about the use of logic-based models for the particular requirements of a "cognitive vision system" which is understood to exploit context, recognise intentions, apply task-driven focussing, and exploit past experiences.

The paper addresses high-level scene interpretations in the sense that the main interest is in interpretations above the level of single-object recognition. We consider indoor scenes, and a table-setting scene is used as a guiding example. Observed by stationary cameras, a human agent places covers onto a table. An interpretation sum

J.L. Crowley et al. (Eds.): ICVS 2003, LNCS 2626, pp. 212–222, 2003.

marising an evolving scene as "An agent is setting the table" is typical for high-level scene interpretation and exemplifies several characteristics:

- The interpretation describes the scene in qualitative terms, omitting details.
- The interpretation may include inferred facts, unobservable in the scene.
- The scene is composed of several occurrences
- Occurrences are spatially and temporally related.

One of the guiding ideas of this paper is to model constituents of a scene together with their perceptual correlates as "co-occurrence relations" which take the form of aggregates and parts in an object-oriented knowledge representation formalism. In our guiding example, placing a cover is such an aggregate. The approach is inspired by Barwise and Perry [8] who model coherent pieces of 3D scenes and their percepts by relations. The approach also allows to model intentions - mental states of agents in a scene - as parts of an aggregate.

The following section describes the structure of the knowledge base. In Section 3, interpretation strategies are presented for several different cognitive situations. Section 4 explores the usefulness of a DL system for representing the knowledge base and for providing interpretation services. Finally, Section 5 presents the conclusions.

2   Conceptual Structure

The basic building blocks for high-level scene interpretation are shown in Figure 1. A dynamic scene is captured by several cameras and processed essentially bottom-up to the level of geometric scene descriptions (GSD) [9]. It is assumed that at this level the scene is described by (partial) views of objects ("blobs"). Furthermore it is assumed that moving blobs can be tracked and grouped into blob motions. We are well aware of the problem of providing a perfect GSD. It will be shown further down that high-level processes can cope with degraded information at the GSD level and even support lower-level processes.

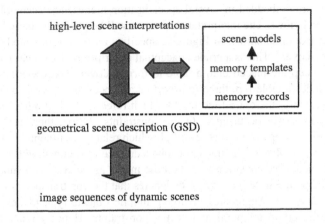

Fig. 1. Basic high-level vision architecture

Blobs and blob motions constitute the visual evidence which is used for high-level interpretations. The conceptual framework for interpretations is provided in terms of scene models which range from single object models to complex occurrence models. Scene models are linked to the records of a vision memory and are considered the result of a learning process. However, this aspect will not be discussed in detail in this paper.

The main conceptual entities are aggregates. An aggregate consists of a set of parts tied together to form a concept and satisfying certain constraints. As an example, consider the conceptual model of a plate in a scene, where the physical plate and two views are combined as an aggregate. Figure 2 shows the concept in a frame-like notation:

name:	scene-plate
parents:	:is-a scene-object
parts:	scpl-body :is-a plate with scpl-body-preds
	scpl-view-A :is-a sc-view-A
	with scpl-view-A-preds
	scpl-view-B :is-a sc-view-B
	with scpl-view-B-preds
constraints:	(scpl-view-constraints)

Fig. 2. Conceptual model of a plate in a scene

The concept "scene-plate" is a specialisation of the concept "scene-object" and consists of three parts: "scpl-body" describes the physical body, "scpl-view-A" and "scpl-view-B" describe two plate views by camera A and B, respectively. The parts are specialisations of their respective parent concepts and fulfill certain predicates, e.g. shape predicates required for plate views. The constraints section contains constraints which relate parts to each other, e.g. ensuring that the views are compatible with a 3D shape of the physical object (which is, of course, not trivial). Note that the aggregate and its parts are embedded in several specialisation hierarchies: scene-objects, physical bodies, and views. The interpretation process will be guided by these hierarchies.

The next example, shown in Figure 3, specifies an occurrence model of the type "scene-place-cover". This is a crude conceptual description of a scene where a plate, a saucer and a cup are placed onto a table to form a cover. The scene-place-cover aggregate includes a table top, three transport occurrences and a cover configuration as parts. Furthermore, there are time marks which refer to the beginning and ending of the scene-place-cover occurrence. In the constraints section, there are identity constraints, such as pc-tp1.tp-ob = pc-cv.cv-pl, which relate constituents of different parts to each other (the plate of the transport suboccurrence is identical with the plate in the cover) and qualitative constraints on the time marks associated with sub-occurrences. For example, pc-tp3.tp-te $\geq$ pc-tp2.tp-te denotes that the cup transport should end after the saucer transport. Aggregates involving mobile objects typically require that the objects fulfill certain temporal and spatial constraints. Hence temporal and spatial constraint solving will be an important part of the interpretation process.

The transport occurrences of the scene-place-cover aggregate are examples of conceptual entities embedded in a hierarchy of motion concepts. This hierachy is built on top of primitive occurrences which are generated as parts of the GSD. A primitive occurrence extends over a time interval where a qualitative predicate is fulfilled [10].

name:	scene-place-cover
parents:	:is-a scene-agent-activity
parts:	pc-tt :is-a scene-table-top
	pc-tp1 :is-a scene-transport
	with (tp-obj :is-a scene-plate)
	pc-tp2:is-a scene-transport
	with (tp-obj :is-a scene-saucer)
	pc-tp3 :is-a scene-transport
	with (tp-obj :is-a scene-cup)
	pc-cv :is-a scene-cover
time marks:	pc-tb, pc-te :is-a timepoint
constraints:	pc-tp1.tp-ob = pc-cv.cv-pl
	...
	pc-tp3.tp-te $\geq$ pc-tp2.tp-te
	pc-tb $\leq$ pc-tp3.tb
	pc-te $\geq$ pc-cv.cv-tb

Fig. 3. Conceptual model of a place-cover scene

As stated above, aggregates describe entities which tend to co-occur in a scene, regardless of whether the entities are visible or not. In fact, they provide the means to hypothesise parts without evidence. Hence it is natural to use aggregates which include mental states of agents, in particular intentions, as parts along with occurrences in a scene. The aggregate in Figure 4 is a sketch of an "intended place-cover", specifying an agent along with the place-cover occurrence and an intended cover configuration as the mental state of the agent.

name:	scene-intended-place-cover
parents:	:is-a scene-intended-action
parts:	sipc-pc :is-a scene-place-cover
	sipc-ag :is-a scene-agent
	sipc-cv :is-a scene-cover
constraints:	sipc-ag.desire = sipc-cv
	(and other constraints)

Fig. 4. Conceptual model for an intended action

As a summary of this section, Figure 5 gives on overview of the conceptual structure of the high-level vision system, restricted to static concepts for the sake of simplicity. The arrows denote is-a relationships. Dotted arrows indicate is-a relationships over several specialisation stages. Aggregates are shown as boxes with their parts as interior boxes. In general, parts represent concepts restricted by constraints specified by the enclosing aggregate (see the examples above). Hence parts are specialisations of the corresponding unconstrained concepts and linked accordingly.

As stated eralier, there are different hierarchies for physical objects and scene objects. The former are concepts independent of a scene, whereas the latter are described by aggregates containing physical objects together with the views provided by sensors. Separate hierarchies are also provided for important descriptive entities such as 3D bodies and trajectories and their 2D counterparts, regions and 2D trajectories. Parts which constitute a region description, e.g. colour, shape, texture, are not shown explicitly. Concepts of these hierarchies provide indices for the interpretation process. As an example, "oval-region" is linked to "oval-view-B" which in turn is linked to the scene objects "scene-plate" and "scene-saucer" which may have an oval view (among others). Trajectories describe consecutive locations of a physical bodies, including constant locations for static bodies, and also form a separate hierarchy.

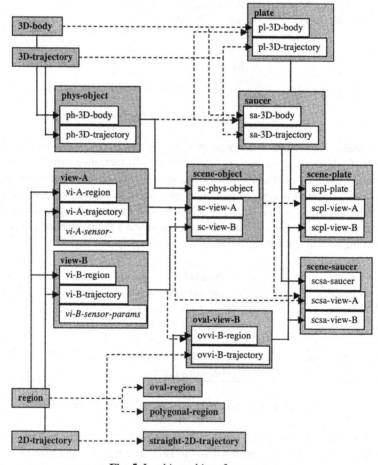

Fig. 5. Is-a hierarchies of concepts

Note that higher-level aggregates may be expanded until they contain only scene objects by resursively replacing aggregate parts by their conceptual descriptions. The expanded form of an aggregate includes all view entities which may support the aggregate based on visual evidence.

3 Model-Based Interpretation of a Scene

This section describes how scene interpretation can be guided by the conceptual structure presented above. In particular we want to demonstrate that different cognitive situations can be treated with interpretation strategies based on the same conceptual basis. This is an important feature which distinguishes our approach from rule-based or deduction-based approaches where interpretation strategies are much narrower defined. The following cognitive situations will be considered:

- Context-free interpretation
- Exploiting spatial context
- Exploiting temporal context
- Exploiting domain context
- Exploiting focus of attention
- Intention-guided interpretation

Before dealing with these tasks, we present the framework of the incremental interpretation process.

3.1 Framework of Interpretation Process

An interpretation of a scene is a partial description in terms of instances of concepts of the knowledge base. It is partial because, in general, only parts of the scene and a subset of the concepts are interesting, depending on the cognitive situation. The interpretation process can be viewed as an incremental information gathering process with the goal to verify interesting instances. The increments are based on the internal structure of the concepts and the is-a structure in which they are embedded. Let I be an instance of a concept C, PC_1 ... PC_N the parent concepts of C, IP_1 .. IP_K instances of its parts, and CE_1 ... CE_K the concept expressions associated with the parts. Then a verification of I with respect to C has the following logical structure:

$$
\begin{aligned}
\mathrm{Ver}(I, C) = \quad & \mathrm{Ver}(I, PC_1) \ \& \ ... \ \& \ \mathrm{Ver}(I, PC_N) \ \& \\
& \mathrm{Ver}(IP_1, CE_1) \ \& \ ... \ \& \ \mathrm{Ver}(IP_K, CE_K) \ \& \\
& \mathrm{Ver}(I, \mathrm{constraints}(C))
\end{aligned}
$$

Note that the verification of I w.r.t. C is recursively defined in terms of the verification of I w.r.t. the parents of C, and in terms of the verification of its parts. A recursion terminates successfully either at the root of a taxonomy (which by definition contains the instance) or when instances of the concept are already known and can be merged with the instance in question. The latter case includes the important step when an expected view instance is merged with one of the views generated from the GSD. As the GSD will not be perfect, parts may be occluded, and models may be too crude etc., it is mandatory that verification provides graded results. The operator "&" will combine graded partial results. Details of the grading scheme are outside the scope of this paper.

The actual interpretation procedure differs from the recursive structure in that (i) the execution order of the verification subtasks is subject to an independent control, and (ii) constraints are partially evaluated and used to restrict the selection of missing parts. The control will be based on a probabilistic rating scheme currently under development. The interpretation procedure is composed of 3 types of interpretation steps. The first is *aggregate instantiation*. This step transforms an interpretation as shown in Figure 6.

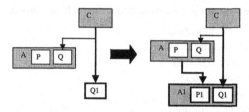

Fig. 6. Aggregate instantiation

In the figure, thin arrows denote is-a links, bold arrows instance links. Similarly, thin boxes denote concepts and bold boxes instances. Aggregate instantiation can be carried out when an instance Q1 of a concept C exists which may be part of an aggregate A. Instantiation of an aggregate causes the aggregate with all additional parts to be instantiated. This step corresponds to part-whole reasoning where a part gives rise to a hypothetical larger structure.

It may seem somewhat arbitrary that by this step aggregates are only instantiated if one part is already instantiated. However, this does not prevent aggregates to be instantiated as a whole via instance refinement (with no parts already instantiated) or as a part of a higher-level aggregate.

A second type of interpretation step is *instance refinement*. With this step one tries to find a more special concept for some instance. In general, instances are parts of some aggregate, hence instance refinement can be illustrated as in Figure 7.

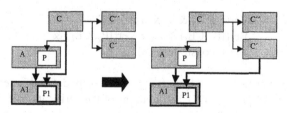

Fig. 7. Instance refinement

The figure shows an instance P1 which is reclassified from C to C′. As indicated with the alternative concept C″, there may be many possible refinements. A control scheme will be required to avoid arbitrary guesses.

A third interpretation step is *instance merging*. As is evident from the aggregate instantiation step, new instances are generated as parts of a new aggregate irrespective of existing instances which could be used to build the aggregate bottom-up. Hence merging may be necessary. Roughly, two instances P1 and Q1 may be merged, if they have the same class and their expansions are grounded in the same views. We indicate instance merging graphically by assigning a common name, see Figure 8.

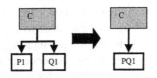

Fig. 8. Instance merging

3.2 Cognitive Situations

We now address the cognitive situations listed earlier and describe how the tasks can be realised by the repertoire of interpretation steps.

By *context-free interpretation* we mean interpretation based initially solely on visual evidence and without other restricting information. Hence this situation essentially tests bottom-up interpretation facilities. We assume that blobs and blob motions are available from the GSD and automatically mapped into instances of views of the respective sensors, constituting the initial state of the interpretation.

The next step may be to carry out an aggregate instantiation step and create a "scene-object" with views as parts. Alternatively, a region could be specialised - say to an "oval-region" - by an instance refinement step. An "oval-region" is known to be a part of an "oval-view", hence another aggregate instantiation step can be carried out. The same result can be achieved by specialising the corresponding view with an instance refinement step. An "oval-view" may be part of several scene-objects, including a plate and a saucer. Aggregate instantiation steps will generate the corresponding instances. Again,there may be alternate paths leading to the same instantiations, for example successive instance refinement steps in the scene-object hierarchy. In summary, context-free interpretation is achieved by classifying low-level evidence via successive refinements and by instantiating scene-objects and aggregates based on the classified evidence.

As a second cognitive situation we consider exploitation of *spatial context*. In our framework, context is understood as an instantiated aggregate which specifies constraints between entities, including scene objects. Hence, if a spatial context is given, this is equivalent to an instantiated aggregate which specifies spatial constraints. As an example, consider a given context in terms of a kitchen bordering the living room scene. In our framework, this context will be modelled by an instantiated aggregate specifying the spatial relationship of the two rooms and including typical occurrences. Thus aggregates such as "bring-plate-from-kitchen" may become possible as the kitchen context supports the corresponding part-whole-reasoning. Note that within an aggregate, spatial constraints between parts may provide a dynamic spatial context provided by one part for another.

Exploitation of *temporal context* is very similar to the exploitation of spatial context. Temporal constraints in aggregates relate parts, e.g. occurrences, temporally to each other. Temporal properties of instantiated parts, e.g. begin and end, can be propagated to restrict the temporal window of expected parts. An efficient temporal constraint mechanism for temporally related occurrences has been presented in [9].

By *domain context* we mean thematic knowledge restricting the possible contents of a scene, for example, knowledge that the scene will show a living-room or a dinner-table. Domain context is brought to bear by instantiating a corresponding aggregate. In this case, aggregates typically express co-occurrence relationships at a high abstraction level with potentially many alternative choices for parts.

We examine now how the interpretation process can be controlled by a *focus of attention*. One obvious way to express a thematic focus of attention is by instantiating concepts of interest and using the interpretation steps to elaborate these instances. This is similar to providing a domain context. To provide a temporal or spatial focus, a concept for temporally or spatially restricted interpretations may be instantiated.

Finally, we consider the role of recognised *intentions* for predicting the development of a scene. As shown in Section 2, the intention of an agent is modelled as a mental state which may be ascribed to an agent, given certain occurrences. Our interpretation process can instantiate intentions by part-whole reasoning (aggregate instantiation) and thus provide information about the goal state intended by the agent.

It is outside the scope of this paper to deal with other aspects of the interpretation process, in particular uncertainty management and preference ranking of hypotheses. We are developing a ranking system based on the statistics of recorded experiences which guides the possible choices for interpretation steps.

4 Translating into a Description Logic (DL)

In this section we sketch how the frame-like modelling formalism introduced above and the interpretation steps can be translated into the formal language of the highly expressive description logic *SHIQ* [11] implemented by the system RACER [12]. The purpose is to investigate to which extent inference mechanisms available in DL systems may be used to support the interpretation process. *SHIQ* is the basic logic *ALC* augmented with qualifying number restrictions, role hierarchies, inverse roles, and transitive roles. In addition to these basic features, RACER also provides concrete domains for dealing with min/max restrictions over the integers and linear polynomial (in-)equalities over the reals.

The aggregate structure as shown in Figures 2 - 4 maps into the RACER concept language roughly as follows.

- the name of an aggregate is a RACER concept name
- the parents of an aggregate are concept names defining unary predicates
- part names are roles defining binary predicates
- with-expressions are role qualifications
- constraints map into concrete domain predicates

Currently, only inequality constraints can be handled by RACER´s concrete-domain facilities. This is sufficient, for example, to implement a qualitative temporal constraint system for a time point algebra. Other constraint schemes, e.g. for qualitative spatial contraints, would require extensions.

Assuming that these extensions can be provided, we will examine the interpretation process now. It should be clear that automatic instance classification cannot be employed since concrete views do not provide logically sufficient conditions for hgher-level classification. As shown by [3] and further elaborated in [5], image interpretation can be formally described as partial model construction ("model" in the logical sense). In fact, RACER offers an ABox consistency check which amounts to model construction. Given an ABox with concrete views as individuals, model construction generates an interpretation including all additional individuals which are required to satisfy the conceptual framework.

Unfortunately, model construction in RACER (and other reasoning systems) is conceived as an open-world consistency check where any model means success and additional individuals are hypothesised liberally without consideration of missing visual evidence. Hence this process cannot be employed without severe changes. For example, partial evidence for a cover in terms of a plate should only be extended to a full cover if the possible views of missing objects are compatible with the actual scene. Furthermore, as in general many models are possible, a ranking is required so that "preferred interpretations" can be delivered.

RACER can be used, however, in support of one of the more modest interpretation steps outlined in Section 3: Instance refinement is available in RACER as individual classification. Also general services such as a TBox consistency checking may be used.

5 Conclusions

A conceptual framework for high-level vision has been presented using a representational formalism which easily maps into an expressive description logic. The main conceptual units are aggregates which represent co-occurring physical bodies and their percepts. Guided by the need to deal with various cognitive situations, interpretation steps have been proposed which support flexible interpretation strategies. As it turns out, current DL reasoning systems do not (yet) provide the services which would optimally support high-level vision. In particular, a ranking scheme should guide possible choices.

References

1. Cohn, A.G., Hazarika, S.M.: Qualitative Spatial Representation and Reasoning: An Overview, Fundamenta Informaticae,46 (1–2) (2001) 1–29
2. Vila, L.: A Survey on Temporal Reasoning in Artificial Intelligence", AI Communications, Vol. 7, (1994) 4–28
3. Reiter, R., Mackworth, A.: The Logic of Depiction, TR 87–23, Dept. Computer Science, Univ. of British Columbia, Vancouver, Canada (1987)
4. Matsuyama, T., Hwang, V.S.: SIGMA – A Knowledge-Based Aerial Image Understanding System, Advances in Computer Vision and Machine Intelligence, Plenum (1990)
5. Schröder, C.: Bildinterpretation durch Modellkonstruktion: Eine Theorie zur rechnergestützten Analyse von Bildern, Dissertation, DISKI 196, infix (1999)
6. Nagel, H.-H.: From Video to Language – a Detour via Logic vs. Jumping to Conclusions, Proc. Integration of Speech and Image Understanding, IEEE Computer Society (1999) 79–99
7. Möller, R., Neumann, B., Wessel, M.: Towards Computer Vision with Description Logics: Some Recent Progress, Proc. Integration of Speech and Image Understanding, IEEE Computer Society (1999) 101–116
8. Barwise, J., Perry, J.: Situations and Attitudes, Bradford (1983)
9. Neumann, B.: Description of Time-Varying Scenes, Semantic Structures, Lawrence Erlbaum (1989) 167–206
10. Neumann, B.: Conceptual Framework for High-Level Vision, FBI-HH-B-241/02, FB Informatik, Universität Hamburg (2002)
11. Horrocks, I., Sattler, U., Tobies, S.: Reasoning with Individuals for the Description Logic SHIQ, Proc. 17th Int. Conf. on Automated Deduction (CADE-17). LNCS Springer (2002)
12. Haarslev, V., Möller, R.: RACER User's Guide and Reference Manual Version 1.7, http://www.fh-wedel.de/˜mo/3214/racer-manual-1-7.pdf

A Real-World Vision System: Mechanism, Control, and Vision Processing

Andrew Dankers and Alexander Zelinsky

Robotic Systems Laboratory,
Research School of Information Sciences and Engineering,
The Australian National University
Canberra ACT 0200 Australia
{andrew,alex}@syseng.anu.edu.au
http://syseng.anu.edu.au/rsl

Abstract. This paper reports on the development of a multi-purpose active visual sensor system for real-world application. The Cable-Drive Active-Vision Robot (CeDAR) has been designed for use on a diverse range of platforms, to perform a diverse range of tasks. The novel, biologically inspired design has evolved from a systems based approach. The mechanism is compact and light-weight, and is capable of motions that exceed human visual performance and earlier mechanical designs. The control system complements the mechanical design to implement the basic visual behaviours of fixation, smooth pursuit and saccade, with stability during high speed motions, high precision and repeatability. Real-time vision processing algorithms have been developed that process stereo colour images at $30Hz$, resulting in a suite of basic visual competencies. We have developed a scheme to fuse the results of the visual algorithms into robust task-oriented behaviours by adopting a statistical frame-work. CeDAR has been successfully used for experiments in autonomous vehicle guidance, object tracking, and visual sensing for mobile robot experiments.

1 Introduction

In recent years, increased hardware performance versus component cost has brought vision firmly into the realm of practical robot sensors. The domain of computer vision has sufficiently matured to enable researchers to build and experiment with systems that model and interact with what they observe. We concern ourselves with refining a multi-purpose visual sensor system for real-world, real-time, task-directed robotic applications. The vision system must be fit for use on a diverse range of platforms, performing a diverse range of tasks. It must be able to intelligently gather data from its environment in a sufficiently timely fashion for it to make the decisions for task-oriented behaviour.

A truly useful system is required to react to the real world in real-time. We define real-time as a time period commensurate to the rate of change of the environment. The real world is an unstructured, possibly cluttered, dynamic environment that extends beyond sensor range. A vision system operating in the

J.L. Crowley et al. (Eds.): ICVS 2003, LNCS 2626, pp. 223–235, 2003.

real world must therefore be equipped with mechanisms to fixate its attention on that which is important within the time-frame of its relevance, while simultaneously disregarding background irrelevancies. Attention should be directed to what can loosely be described as "interesting", including that which may be useful to the completion of goal-directed behaviour. The sensory system must therefore be capable of shifting focus to the location of interest and maintain focus even if the target is moving. In addition, as the environment is large, it may be necessary that the architecture of the vision system allow it to extend its field of awareness via searching behaviour. Appropriate sensory and processing resources must be selected with these considerations in mind.

Such requirements point strongly towards the use of a visual system able to adjust its visual parameters to aid task-oriented behaviour (an approach labeled *active* [1] or *animate* [3] vision). An active vision approach can offer impressive computational benefits for scene analysis in realistic environments [2]. We believe that active vision is one of the best sensing modalities for task-oriented behaviour.

The concept of controlled camera movements to facilitate vision undoubtedly originated from observations of the biological world. And with few exceptions, animals have developed active visual abilities. The human eye achieves extraordinary performance through its low weight and low inertia muscle actuation. Accordingly, existing synthetic vision systems have been built that have endeavoured to mimic the properties of biological vision systems.

1.1   Related Work

A brief overview of previous active vision devices reveals a trend towards smaller, more agile systems. In the past the goals were to experiment with different configurations using large systems with many degrees-of-freedom like the KTH active head [13] with its 13 degrees-of-freedom and Yorick 11-14 [14] with a 55*cm* baseline[1] and re-configurable joints. Although useful for experimentation, these systems were excessively cumbersome for agile motion, and not easily configurable for mobility. More recently, developers of smaller active heads such as the palm-sized Yorick 5-5C [14] and ESCHeR [10] with an 18*cm* baseline have reported on light-weight systems suitable for mobile robot navigation and for teleprescence applications. Internationally, the trend towards smaller active vision systems comparable to the size of the human head is pushing the limit of motor, gear box and camera design. In most systems, the size of the motors and cameras limits the compactness of the active head and the motors themselves add to the inertia of the moving components. A notable exception is the Agile Eye [8] where no motor carries the mass of any other. All three versions of Yorick as well as ESCHeR use harmonic-drive technology. A disadvantage of the technology is an unavoidably large speed-reduction ratio that limits the output speed to less than 100*rpm*.

We aim to improve upon such past mechanical designs, to manifest a mechanism that is light-weight, and more agile than previous approaches.

---

[1] Distance between camera retinas.

2   CeDAR's Evolution

A multi-modal systems approach was adopted where the mechanism [Fig. 1], its control, and vision processing modules were developed in parallel, but with integration in mind [4]. From the outset, it was desired that the system be capable of out-performing existing synthetic vision systems and replicating the abilities of the human vision system, while incorporating reasonably sized payloads (two $700g$ cameras). The mechanism and control modules have been conceived with the purpose of having a high level of mechanical performance to allow rapid motion and short reaction times, as well as being re-configurable for application to many situations with minimal modification. The control and vision processing modules have been developed for use with standard digital visual hardware operating at a $30Hz$ frame rate. Low cost and ease of reproduction were also significant factors in the evolution of the design.

Fig. 1. CeDAR (C̲able-D̲rive A̲ctive-Vision R̲obot) mechanism.

2.1   Mechanism

The mechanism has incorporated aspects of design from other groups and the mechanics of the human visual system. As seen in nature, muscles are lightweight, exhibit high accelerations and do not suffer from the common problem encountered in serial active head designs whereby each degree of freedom requires sufficiently powerful actuators to move all previous degrees of freedom, including their actuators. It was shown that by relocating the motors to a fixed base and thereby reducing the inertia of the active component to essentially a camera, problems inherent in serial design were alleviated [5]. This biologically inspired concept is an important feature of CeDAR's novel mechanical design.

Additionally, because backlash-free speed reduction is essential for high-speed performance, the choice of transmission system for the parallel architecture is important. During high-speed movements such as saccades[2] – where motors are driven at maximum acceleration – velocity saturation for harmonic-drive gear

---

[2] Saccade is the ability to rapidly transfer fixation from one visual target to another

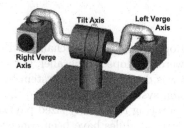

Fig. 2. Left: The Helmholtz configuration. Right: Early prototype.

boxes is of concern. Cable drive is a novel alternative for use with repeated bounded motions that does not induce speed limitations, operates lubricant-free with low friction, exhibits high torque transmission, and is low-cost.

An earlier prototype [5] [Fig. 2] proved the usefulness of cable drive transmissions and parallel mechanical architectures in a two-degree-of-freedom active 'eye' system. The prototype was fast, responsive and accurate. In 2000, the prototype's architecture was transferred to a stereo Helmholtz configuration [12] [Fig. 2], resulting in the present mechanical design of CeDAR [Fig. 3]. Actuation has been transferred through cable drive circuits that seamlessly integrate with the parallel architecture.

Fig. 3. CAD model rear view of CeDAR showing parallel architecture and cable drive.

An important kinematic property of the design is that the axes intersect at the optical centre of each camera, minimising kinematic translational effects. This property of the stereo camera configuration aids development of stereo algorithms such as depth re-construction through image disparity calculations, a competency that some biological vision systems exhibit [15].

2.2 Control

Research has shown that gaze control can be broken down into three tasks: gaze fixation, saccade, and smooth pursuit[3] [12]. CeDAR's control routines are an

---

[3] Smooth pursuit involves gaze fixation upon a moving target.

extension of work undertaken by [12] on Trapezoidal Profile Motion (TPM). In particular, our approach allows for the implementation of a single algorithm for both saccade and smooth pursuit, enhancing the simplicity and compactness of the controller design.

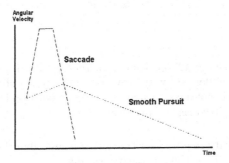

Fig. 4. Trapezoidal Profile Motion velocity profiles.

The essence of the TPM problem is to catch the target gaze point a distance from the image centre either in the shortest time possible (saccade) or as smoothly as possible (smooth pursuit). Both the joints' and target's starting velocity are potentially non-zero and disparate. Specifically, we cause an axis to accelerate constantly to a calculated ceiling velocity[4], coast at this velocity for a given period, then decelerate at the same constant rate as the acceleration until the target velocity is reached [Fig. 4]. Mathematically, it is a four-dimensional problem where the acceleration a, ceiling velocity v, move time T and total distance traveled x are unknown. The initial joint velocity v_1, target velocity v_2 and the target's initial distance from the image centre x_0 are the givens.

If the acceleration a is assumed to be constant, the time taken by the head to accelerate from its initial velocity to the ceiling velocity is

$$T_a = \frac{s \cdot v - v_1}{s \cdot a},\tag{1}$$

Where s is positive for $v_1 < v$ and negative for $v_1 > v$. Similarly, the time to decelerate to target velocity is

$$T_d = \frac{s \cdot v - v_2}{s \cdot a}.\tag{2}$$

Note that acceleration and deceleration rates are equal. If T_c is the time spent coasting at the ceiling velocity, the total time for TPM is

$$T = T_a + T_c + T_d.\tag{3}$$

The distance traveled by the head in time T is

$$x = \frac{s \cdot v + v_1}{2}T_a + s \cdot vT_c + \frac{s \cdot v + v_2}{2}T_d,\tag{4}$$

---

[4] The maximum absolute velocity of the TPM trajectory

but can also be considered as the sum of the initial distance of the target from the foveal centre x_0 and the distance traveled by the target during the move

$$x = x_0 + Tv_2. \tag{5}$$

These general equations can be used to develop the case for saccade and smooth pursuit.

Saccade involves changing the head's current position and velocity state to that of the target, as inferred by its previous states, in the shortest time possible. Motion smoothness is not a concern and hence acceleration is set to its maximum possible magnitude. Two cases can arise:

- The ceiling velocity required for the action is less than the maximum allowed velocity and hence no time is spent coasting
- The theoretical ceiling velocity required for the action is greater than the maximum allowed velocity and hence some time must be spent coasting.

It is useful to assume T_c is initially zero so that (1)-(5) yield

$$s \cdot v = v_2 \pm \frac{1}{2}\sqrt{4sx_0a - 2(v_1^2 + v_2^2 - 4v_1v_2}, \tag{6}$$

where the smaller value is taken for $v_2 > v_1$ and vice-versa. If v exceeds the maximum allowed velocity, a and v are replaced by their maxima. Then

$$T_c = \frac{1}{v_2 - s \cdot v}\left(\left(\frac{s \cdot v + v_1}{2} - v_1\right)T_a + \left(\frac{s \cdot v + v_2}{2} - v_2\right)T_a - x_0\right), \tag{7}$$

is calculated to deduce T. Equation (6) also defines the value of s so that the operand of the radical is greater than or equal to zero

$$s = 1 \quad \text{for} \quad (v_1 - v_2)^2 + 4x_0a \geq 0 \quad \text{and} \quad s = -1 \quad \text{otherwise.}$$

Smooth Pursuit involves moving from one position and velocity state to the next in a given amount of time with optimal smoothness. To achieve this, the acceleration in moving to and from the ceiling velocity must be as small as possible. Again both the coasting and non-coasting cases are relevant. With the assumption that the coasting velocity is initially zero, (1)-(5) yield

$$v = \frac{x}{T} \pm \frac{1}{2T}\sqrt{4x^2 - 4Tx(v_1 + v_2) + 2T^2(v_1^2 + v_2^2)}. \tag{8}$$

If these values are in excess of the maximum allowable velocity of the head, the time constraint is unrealisable. In this instance, a saccade is initiated.

2.3   Vision Processing

Our previous work revealed that a comprehensive collection of basic visual behaviours may be more suitable for investigation of an unknown, complex unstructured environment - such as the real world - than a high-level processing
technique constructed for a specific situation [4]. An objective is the implementation of such a suite of elementary competencies. As low-level mechanisms, the
algorithms should attempt to minimise assumed knowledge in the form of explicit
world or object models and high-level decision making. However, they should be
designed in such a way as to be bases suitable for having these abstractions applied on top of them. They should be general-purpose in order to maximise their
applicability to real-world layouts and situations, and should be suitable for use
either in serial or parallel. Finally, the algorithms should be designed for use in
combination while exhibiting real-time performance by addressing the trade-offs
between accuracy and speed.

Competencies that have been implemented include motion segmentation,
edge detection, depth mapping, zero disparity filtering [6], colour detection, and
template matching. All have been implemented using C++ algorithms that take
advantage of MMX[5] CPU architecture for pipelined processing performance.

With the aid of such competencies, relevant information can be extracted
from a scene so that intelligent gaze fixation can be effected. For example, the
system has successfully tracked the template of facial features and coloured objects.

The use of multiple cues in parallel has enabled more robust object tracking.
A multiple cue object tracking algorithm has been implemented that incorporates four simple cues - colour, edge detection, texture detection and motion. A
cue voting scheme is adopted to identify pixel locations in the view frame that
appear target-like. A simple Zero Disparity Filter using virtual horopters[6] then
visually extracts the object from its surroundings, as well as mapping its position in three-dimensional space. The processing of all visual information takes,
on average, only $8ms$ per frame on a dual Pentium III computer - well below
the required $30Hz$ frame-rate set by the digital camera image capture frequency.
Unfiltered operation was susceptible to distractions due to target-like regions in
the camera's views. Kalman Filtering reduced the effect of these distractions significantly. The algorithm allows successful real-time tracking of arbitrary objects
through a cluttered environment [Fig. 5].

Intuitively, however, it is not sensible to assume all cues or competencies
should be relied upon equally for different tasks in changeable environments.
Consequently, a framework has been developed to adaptively allocate computational resources over multiple cues. Bayesian Markov Localisation probability
theory provides the framework for sensor fusion, and resource scheduling is used
to intelligently allocate the limited computational resources across the suite of
cues. Each cue's expected utility and resource requirement is taken into account,
and the system can accommodate for cues running at different frequencies to al-

---

[5] Intel's Multi-Media Extension CPU architecture.
[6] The Horopter defines the locus of points in space that map to a stereo image pair
with identical coordinates.

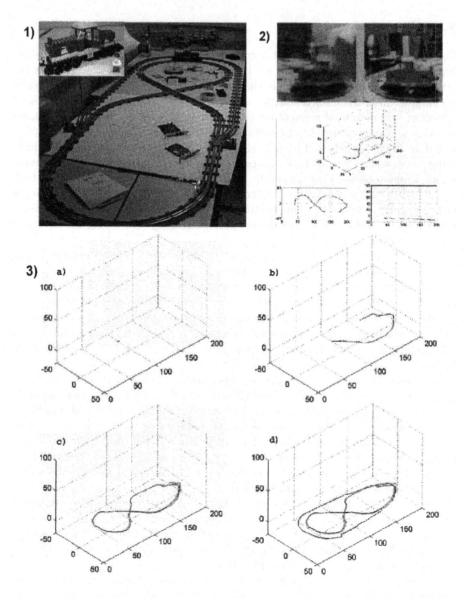

Fig. 5. 1) Scenario. 2) Screenshot: left and right camera views and trajectory. 3) Target trajectory at t=0s, 10s, 20s and 30s (units in *cm*).

low cues performing less well to be run slowly in the background. A particle filter [9] is adopted to maintain multiple hypotheses of the target location and orientation in three-dimensional state space.

A number of cues are calculated from image and state information and combined to provide evidence strengthening or attenuating the belief in each hypothesis. Fig. 6 shows the structure of the system. It consists of two subsystems: a particle filter and a cue processor, each of which cycle through their loops once per frame. These subsystems interact as shown by the thick arrows. The particle filter passes the current particle locations to the cue processor. The cue processor determines probabilities for the particles and passes these back to the particle filter. Intricacies of this adaption fusion architecture are clarified in [11].

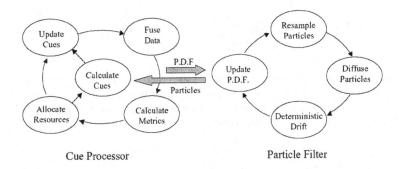

Cue Processor   Particle Filter

Fig. 6. Adaptive fusion architecture [11].

This framework has enabled tracking of a person moving in a cluttered environment, as well as real-time tracking of lane position and orientation for an autonomous vehicle [Fig. 7].

2.4   System Integration

The interaction between the motion control and vision processing routines is summarised in Fig. 8. A Firewire card captures images from each of the Sony DFW-VL500 cameras every $33ms$. The images are processed to determine the desired gaze. The gaze controller routines calculate the desired visual trajectory and visual parameters. A MEI[7] or Server To Go[8] card delivers actuation instructions to CeDAR via a PWM[9] amplifier and acquires positional feedback. All coding has been developed with C++ in a LINUX environment. QT[10] libraries were used to develop CPU thread and GUI frameworks.

3   Performance Evaluation

The performance figures traditionally reported for active vision mechanisms consist of maximum angular velocity, maximum angular acceleration, angular resolution and axis range. While the latter two are highly relevant, we consider the

---

[7] Motion Engineering Inc.
[8] Server To Go Inc.
[9] Pulse Width Modulation.
[10] Programming toolkit developed by Trolltech.

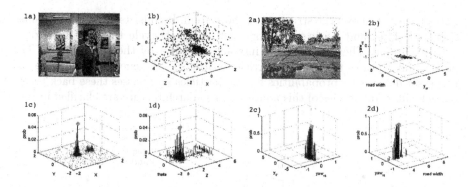

Fig. 7. 1) A frame from a face tracking sequence showing particles in the image (a), in three-dimensional space (b), and in particle distributions over x, y (c) and $z, theta$ (d) states [11]. 2) A frame from a lane tracking sequence showing a) perceived lane, b) lane width and orientation, c) yaw, offset and d) yaw, width distributions [7].

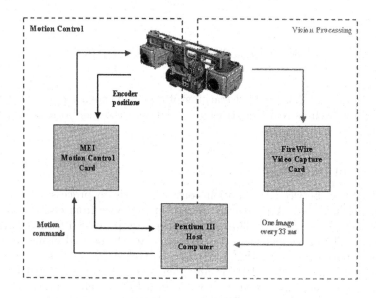

Fig. 8. System integration.

others to be not especially useful in that they do not detail any form of specific task competency. Four additional specifications for an active vision system which not only involve the speed and acceleration of the axes, but also express the usage intention of the system in the form of a functional requirement, are given in Table 1.

The tabled values need to be achieved in order to satisfy constraints related to desired motion abilities with respect to the usual $30Hz$ visual input. CeDAR's maximum allowable full-speed saccade time was required to be $0.18s$ to enable

Table 1. Performance specifications and test results.

Specification	Test Tilt	Vergence	Specification Tilt	Vergence
Max velocity	$600^o s^{-1}$	$800^o s^{-1}$	$600^o s^{-1}$	$600^o s^{-1}$
Max acceleration	$18,000^o s^{-2}$	$20,000^o s^{-2}$	$10,000^o s^{-2}$	$10,000^o s^{-2}$
Saccade rate	$5s^{-1}$	$6s^{-1}$	$5s^{-1}$	$5s^{-1}$
Ang repeatability	0.01^o	0.01^o	0.01^o	0.01^o
Ang resolution	0.01^o	0.01^o	0.01^o	0.01^o
Max range	90°	90°	90°	90°
Payload	Two $700g$ cameras			
Baseline	$30cm$			

three 90° gaze shift saccades, with an allowance for each to be preceded by four target location video frames and succeeded by one stabilisation video frame, per second. Just over 5 frames are captured during the saccade itself.

The minimum allowable full-speed stop-to-stop angular change within one video frame was required to be 15°, which equates to the ability to predictively track an object moving past the cameras at up to $4ms^{-1}$ at a distance of $1m$ (allowing for the discarding of every second frame as required by some visual algorithms). The angular resolution has been selected with the aim of allowing the platform to perform meaningfully small camera movements and to allow single pixel selection.

The required maximum range, payload and baseline specifications were based on the desire to use larger motorised-zoom cameras. The saccade rate and pointing accuracy were chosen based on the desired performance of the device in its intended applications. Real-time tracking was the most basic desired task and there is a direct relationship between the task-oriented specifications and the maximum requirements for effective tracking [4].

Speed performance was determined by driving the joints to their maximum range, speed and acceleration in a cyclical fashion (repeated saccades). The command positions and actual positions of the joints were logged at millisecond intervals. The position data was then differentiated using a three-point rule and filtered using a seven-point moving average to obtain velocity and acceleration profiles.

A series of accuracy tests were also conducted using laser pointers mounted on the head. Repeatability, the ability to return to an absolute position after a series of complex movements, was demonstrated by moving the joints to an arbitrary position, relocating to another location and then returning to the original point. In systems that suffer from backlash, friction, or poor compliance, the return point differs from the original. Angular resolution, the smallest angle that can be actuated was measured by moving the joints a minimal increment. Coordinated motion, the joints' ability to move in unison in both time and space, was demonstrated by verging both laser pointers to the same location on a wall then commanding the system to follow a predetermined trajectory. Coordination was evaluated according to how closely the lasers were converged throughout the motion.

Table 1 lists results of the accuracy tests along with results from the speed tests and the design specifications. All of the mechanical design specifications were met. CeDAR's mechanical performance compares favourably to similar systems [Table 2].

Table 2. Performance of world-class vision systems.

	Max Vel.	Max Accel.	Approx. Mass (inc. payload)
CeDAR	$800^{o}s^{-1}$	$20,000^{o}s^{-2}$	$3.5kg$
Yorick 8-11	$600^{o}s^{-1}$	$38,000^{o}s^{-2}$	$9.0kg$
Yorick 85CR	$660^{o}s^{-1}$	$10,000^{o}s^{-2}$	$3.0kg$
ESCHeR	$400^{o}s^{-1}$	$16,000^{o}s^{-2}$	$2.0kg$
Agile Eye	$1,000^{o}s^{-1}$	$20,000^{o}s^{-2}$	
KTH	$180^{o}s^{-1}$		$15kg$

4 Conclusion

Philosophies important to the evolution of a multi-purpose active visual sensor system for real-world application have been presented. Our multi-modal approach has resulted in a high-performance visual agent that integrates excellent mechanical, control and vision processing architectures.

We have developed a biologically inspired, novel mechanical design capable of out-performing state-of-the art active mechanisms. Generalised Trapezoidal Profile Motion control routines effect stable, precise and repeatable gaze control. A suite of basic visual competencies has been created, and a statistical framework for allocating computational resources across multiple cues for general task-specific behaviours has been developed. Guidelines for task competency performance evaluation of the system have been presented.

The vision system has been successfully used in object tracking, lane-tracking for autonomous vehicle guidance, and visual sensing for mobile robots.

Web Footage

Footage from work with the CeDAR system can be found on the RSL demonstrations page:

http://www.syseng.anu.edu.au/rsl

References

1. Aloimonos, J., Weiss, I., Bandopadhay, A.: Active vision. International journal on Computer Vision 1 (1988) 333–356

2. Bajczy,R.: Active Perception. Proceedings of the IEEE (1988) 76(8):996–1005
3. Ballard, D.: Animate vision. Artificial Intelligence 48 (1991) 57–86
4. Brooks, A., Abdallah, S., Zelinsky, A., Kieffer, J.: A multimodal approach to real-time active vision. International Conference on Intelligent Robotics (1998)
5. Brooks, A., Dickins, G., Zelinsky, A., Kieffer, J., Abdallah, S.: A high-performance camera platform for real-time active vision. First International Conference on Field and Service Robotics (1997)
6. Coombs, D., Brown, C.: Real-time smooth pursuit tracking for a moving binocular robot. In Proc., International Conference on Computer Vision and Pattern Recognition (1992) 23–28
7. Fletcher, L., Apostoloff, N., Chen, J., Zelinsky, A.: Computer vision for vehicle monitoring and control. Australian Conference on Robotics and Automation (2001)
8. Gosselin, C., St-Pierre, E., Gagne, M.: On the development of the agile eye. IEEE Robotics and Automation Magazine (1996) 29–37
9. Isard, M., Blake, A.: Condensation – conditional density propagation for visual tracking. International Journal of Computer Vision 29(1) (1998) 5–28
10. Kuniyoshi, Y., Kita, N., Rougeaux, S., Suchiro, T.: Active stereo vision system with foveated wide angle lenses. Asian Conference on computer vision (1995)
11. Loy, G., Fletcher, L., Apostoloff, N., Zelinsky, A.: An adaptive fusion architecture for target tracking. Fifth International Conference on Automatic Face and Gesture Recognition (2002)
12. Murray, W.W., Du, F., McLauchlan, P.F., Reid, I.D., Sharkey, P.M., Brady, M.: Active Vision (1992) 155–172
13. Pahlavan, K., Eklundh, J.O.: A head-eye system – analysis and design. CVGIP: Image Understanding: Special issue on purposive, qualitative and active vision (1992)
14. Sharkey, P.M., Murray, D.W., Heuring, J.J.: On the kinematics of robot heads. IEEE Transactions on Robotics and Automation (1997) 437–442
15. Wilson, H.R., Cowan, J.D.: Excitatory and inhibitory interactions in localized populations of model neurons, Biophys. J. 12 (1972) 1–24

Learning Optimal Parameters for Self-Diagnosis in a System for Automatic Exterior Orientation

Wolfgang Förstner and Thomas Läbe

Institute for Photogrammetry, University of Bonn
Nussallee 15, 53115 Bonn, Germany
wf|laebe@ipb.uni-bonn.de,
http://www.ipb.uni-bonn.de/staff/wf|laebe.html

Abstract. The paper describes the automatic learning of parameters for self-diagnosis of a system for automatic orientation of single aerial images used by the State Survey Department of Northrhine–Westfalia. The orientation is based on 3D lines as ground control features, and uses a sequence of probabilistic clustering, search and ML-estimation for robustly estimating the 6 parameters of the exterior orientation of an aerial image. The system is interpreted as a classifier, making an internal evaluation of its success. The classification is based on a number of parameters possibly relevant for self-diagnosis. A hand designed classifier reached 11 % false negatives and 2 % false positives on appr. 17 000 images. A first version of a new classifier using support vector machines is evaluated. Based on appr. 650 images the classifier reaches 2 % false negatives and 4 % false positives, indicating an increase in performance.

1 Motivation and Goal

Vision systems are nearly always embedded systems and are often the bottle neck of an automation chain. Their performance therefore is crucial for their usefulness within the embedding system. Independent of the output type of the vision system, e. g. reading bar codes, detecting passengers, tracking objects, or determining ego-motion, the vision system may be successful and produce one of these outputs, or it may fail and not deliver its output. Acceptable failure rates of systems may vary between 25 % e. g. in automatic image retrieval, and 0.0001 % in visual control of production processes. Many applications allow an efficient reaction to self-diagnosis of the vision system. Self-diagnosis is the internal evaluation of the system based on redundant information within the image analysis process. However, often such redundancy is intentionally introduced into the design of the vision system only to enable self-diagnosis.

An increase in efficiency of a system with self-diagnosis could be achieved by eliminating failures in case the system actually predicts a failure based on internal self-diagnosis. A system with self-diagnosis therefore can be interpreted as a classifier with respect to its ability to succeed or to fail, independent of the type of its output within the embedding system. The situation is sketched in fig. 1. A vision module in a first instance uses input data, preferably with measures on

J.L. Crowley et al. (Eds.): ICVS 2003, LNCS 2626, pp. 236–246, 2003.

their quality and - using a vision algorithm - produces output data, preferably with measures on their quality, which allows chaining of vision modules based on the exchange of evaluated data. Decisions to use certain modules need to be made subject to the success of the module, this would require active checking. Using an algorithm for self-diagnosis could produce values characterizing the internal prediction of success, again preferably with quality measures. Together with the quality of the output data, the self-diagnosis can be used by the control module. The distinction between the quality of the output data and the result of the self-diagnosis algorithm is motivated by the inability or reduced ability of the control module to interpret the details of the output characteristics of the vision module.

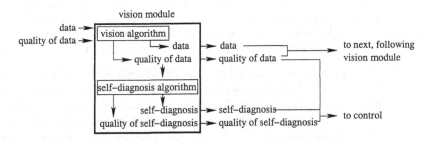

Fig. 1. Components of a vision module with self-diagnostic capabilities.

Characterizing the performance of a system therefore may also refer to characterizing the performance of its self-diagnostic abilities, on top of the performance of the output of the vision system as such.

We are concerned with the automatic determination of the parameters of the exterior orientation of single aerial images being the basis for ortho-photo maps. Being able to orient single images avoids the need for digitizing all images of a flight for bundle block adjustment, but enables to restrict digitization and storage to a single image (appr. 25 Mbyte) per map sheet (cf. fig. 2). In a country like Nordrhein-Westfalen, with appr. 8 000 map sheets in 1 : 5 000 this is a significant cost saving. The orientation of aerial images is supported by the global positioning system (GPS) giving sufficiently accurate projection centers, however allows no precise determination of the rotation parameters. As ortho-photo map update is done on a regular basis, the Survey Department already decided to build up a control point data base in the 70's, mainly consisting of buildings, especially the 3D coordinates of two of their roof points. Automating the process of ortho-photo production requires automation of the up to recently manual orientation procedure. The database therefore has been newly built up in the years 1992-1996, each control point consisting of a set of 3D line segments for each building, actually being derived from a manually measured wire-frame model of the buildings. The matching of the 3D line segments with 2D image line segments allows to determine the orientation parameters automatically (SESTER & FÖRSTNER 1989). The system has recently been integrated and now is in use at the Survey Department.

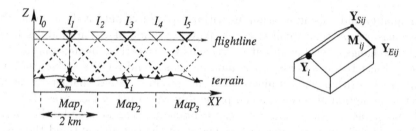

Fig. 2. Left: Setup of externally checking a procedure for automatic orientation of aerial images. Given: Images $I_0, ...,$ control points (reference coordinates $\mathbf{Y}_i$) (black filled triangle), terrain surface. *In practice* every second image is oriented and rectified. *Here* we orient all images individually by automatic mensuration of the control points. The same images and manually measured control points are used for a bundle adjustment. Evaluation is based on the difference of ground point coordinates $\mathbf{X}_m$ (black circle) determined with single image orientation and bundle orientation. Right: Structure of a control point. Set of 3D-line segments $\{\mathbf{M}_{ij}\}$ and reference point $\mathbf{Y}_i$.

This paper reports attempts to evaluate the self-diagnostic tools of the system and to improve them by automatic learning techniques, while not changing the automatic procedure for orientation. The paper is organized as follows: Section 2 describes the system, however, only to such a detail that the reader can locate and assess the self-diagnosis within the system. The manually designed self-diagnosis and its evaluation, based on 17 000 images is discussed in Section 3. Learning the relevant criteria for self-diagnosis is the topic of Section 4. Based on appr. 650 images it is shown that an improvement of the self-diagnosis can be achieved by using the result of a support vector machine classifier.

2   The System for Automatic Model Based Orientation

The core algorithm of the system for automatic model based orientation of aerial images consists of three robust techniques. A feature extraction procedure precedes these steps, the self-diagnosis finalizes the processing chain.

2.1   Preprocessing

Prediction of approximate image coordinates: Based on approximate values for the orientation of the aerial image the system selects those control points which are likely to appear in the image. The approximate projection matrix P is derived from the GPS-coordinates, the calibration parameters of the cameras and the knowledge, that the viewing direction is nearly towards nadir. Each control point P_i consists of a set $\{\mathbf{M}_{ij}\} = \{(\mathbf{Y}_S, \mathbf{Y}_E)_{ij}\}$ of 3D-line segments $\mathbf{M}_{ij}$ and has a reference point $\mathbf{Y}_i = (X, Y, Z, 1)_i^{\mathsf{T}}$ attached to it. It predicts the image coordinates $\mathbf{y}'_i = \mathrm{P} \mathbf{Y}_i$ of the reference point $\mathbf{Y}_i$ and of all starting and end points $\mathbf{y}'_{Sij}$ and $\mathbf{y}'_{Eij}$, leading to predicted 2D-line segments $\mathbf{m}'_{ik}$.

Line segment extraction: In a pre-defined window around the predicted reference point $\mathbf{y}'_i$, with 250^2 pixel covering appr. 0.3 % of the image area, a set

$\{l'_{ik}\} = \{(\mathbf{x}'_S, \mathbf{x}'_E)_{ik}\}$ of line segments are extracted. No correspondence to the control point line segments $\mathbf{M}_{ij}$ is available at this stage. Their quality is characterized by the standard deviations of their position component orthogonal to the line segment and of their direction. In a first approximation the standard deviation of their position component is $\sigma_{x'}/\sqrt{l}$ and of their direction $\sigma_{x'}\sqrt{12/l^3}$, where $\sigma_{x'}$ is the positional accuracy of an edge pixel, say 0.3 [pel], and l is the length of the line segment measured in pixels.

2.2   Automatic Orientation

1. step: Probabilistic clustering. For finding good approximate values for the projected control point features a probabilistic clustering, described in (SESTER & FÖRSTNER 1989) determines the position $\widehat{\mathbf{y}}_i$ of each individual *reference point separately*. This is achieved by integrating, realized by an accumulator, the likelihoods of each observed image segment l'_{ik} matching to each projected model line segment $\mathbf{m}'_{ij}$. In this context a parallel projection for the small image windows is sufficient, and only a translation $\mathbf{t}$, between the predicted model set and the observed segments is determined. Only line segments $(l'_{ik}, \mathbf{m}'_{ij})$ with similar direction give rise to a range of translation values $\mathbf{t}_i$ their likelihood depending on the length difference, on the uncertainty of the observed line segments and on the assumed uncertainty of the translational model.

2. step: Orientation with points. The resulting set $\{\widehat{\mathbf{y}}_i\}$ of estimated reference points may contain blunders. This mostly occurs due to similar line segment patterns in the vicinity of the building caused by shadows or due to bad image contrast. Using these initial matches $\{\mathbf{Y}_i, \widehat{\mathbf{y}}_i\}$, namely the reference coordinates $\mathbf{Y}_i$ of each control point and its measured image coordinates $\mathbf{y}'_i$, we determine the six orientation parameters. Here we implemented two versions:

A For all *quadruples of control points* we determined the orientation parameters by minimizing the reprojection error using a bundle adjustment. In case the geometric configuration is acceptable (see sect. 2.3) the smallest robust sum $\sum_l \min(\widehat{e}_l^2, t_e^2)$ of the square of all remaining residuals $\widehat{e}_i$ indicated the most likely set of outliers, which then do not take part in the last step. The tolerance t_e was set to 10 pixels. In this version the initial approximate values or the orientation parameters are used for the final step 3.

B Here we attempt to perform a *complete search for the erroneous control points*. In case of N control points this requires $M = \sum_{i=4}^{N} \binom{N}{i} = 2^N - (1 + N + \binom{N}{2} + \binom{N}{3}))$ trials, as a minimum of 4 points is necessary to obtain a check on errors. In order to reduce the number of trials, we first compute the exterior orientation with *all* N control points. If this rectification yields an acceptable precision, i. e. the estimated reprojection standard deviation $\widehat{\sigma}_{x'} < 1.5$ [pel], the search is stopped and no error has been found. In all other cases we continue to evaluate all N cases with $N - 1$ control points (and one error), then all $\binom{N}{2}$ cases with $N - 2$ points, etc. until the threshold 1.5 [pel] has been reached.

All erroneous control points are re-projected by using the determined orientation to get a new set of matching image line segments for these control point models. The resulting orientation parameters are used as initial values for the following final step.

3. step: Estimation for orientation with line segments. In the last step we use all the line segments l'_{ik} of *all* control point models and perform a robust maximum-likelihood-type bundle adjustment for the image, minimizing the weighted reprojection error. The re-weighting scheme of the ML-estimation is required in order to eliminate wrong matches of line segments. The weights of the line segments are taken from the feature extraction. All available information is used, not only the reference points as in the last step.

2.3   Self-Diagnosis

Self-diagnosis requires performance measures and criteria for their evaluation. The following two types of measures can be used for both steps, the estimation with points and the estimation with line segments, cf. (FÖRSTNER 2001):

Measuring the precision for self-diagnosis: The first performance measure reflects the achieved precision, namely the influence of random errors between observations and assumed model. The estimated variance factor $\widehat{\sigma}_0^2$ is derived from the reprojection errors by (MIKHAIL & ACKERMANN 1976)

$$\widehat{\sigma}_0^2 = \frac{\sum_{ik} \widehat{e}_{ik}^{\mathsf{T}} \Sigma_{l_{ik}l_{ik}}^{-1} \widehat{e}_{ik}}{R} \qquad \widehat{\sigma}_0 \leq T_P \qquad (1)$$

where $\widehat{e}_{ik}$ is the reprojection error of the k-th image feature, point or line segment, at control point i, $\Sigma_{l_{ik}l_{ik}}$ the a priori covariance matrix of the image feature, again point or line segment, and $R = \mathrm{rank}(\Sigma_{ll}) - 6$ the redundancy of the single image bundle adjustment.

In case the coordinates of the observed features are normally distributed, the a priori covariance matrix is chosen realistically, and the model $\mathbf{x}' = \mathrm{P}\mathbf{X}$ holds, the estimated variance factor will have an expected value 1, following a $F_{R,\infty}$ distribution. However, as all types of errors in the underlying model may have an influence on the estimated variance factor and the model only holds approximately, the Fisher-test, if applied rigorously, almost always leads to a rejection of the model. It has been found empirically, that assuming the standard deviation $\sigma_{x'}$ to be larger by a factor 2 or 3 is reasonable.

Measuring the quality of the configuration for self-diagnosis: The second performance measure evaluates the difference between the geometric configuration of the control point models and a reference configuration. It actually measures the closeness of the geometric configuration to a critical configuration.

The standard reference configuration for this application consists of 4 control points located in the corners of the image. This configuration would guarantees a reliable determination of the exterior orientation. The measure compares the expected precision reachable with both configurations. It uses the largest possible variance $\sigma_g^{(est)2}$ of a function $g = \boldsymbol{f}^\mathsf{T}\widehat{\boldsymbol{p}}$ (BAARDA 1973)

$$\lambda_{\max} = \max_g \left(\frac{\sigma_g^{(est)}}{\sigma_g^{(ref)}}\right)^2 = \max_f \frac{\boldsymbol{f}^\mathsf{T}\boldsymbol{\Sigma}_{\widehat{p}\widehat{p}}^{(est)}\boldsymbol{f}}{\boldsymbol{f}^\mathsf{T}\boldsymbol{\Sigma}_{\widehat{p}\widehat{p}}^{(ref)}\boldsymbol{f}} \qquad \lambda_{\max} \leq T_C \qquad (2)$$

of the orientation parameters $\widehat{\boldsymbol{p}}$ in relation to that variance $\sigma_g^{(ref)2}$ reachable with the reference configuration i. e. with covariance matrix $\boldsymbol{\Sigma}_{\widehat{p}\widehat{p}}^{(ref)}$. The maximum at the same time is the maximum eigenvalue of the matrix $\boldsymbol{\Sigma}_{pp}^{(est)}[\boldsymbol{\Sigma}_{pp}^{(ref)}]^{-1}$.

In case the configuration is close to a critical one, then $\lambda_{\max}$ would be very large. A threshold $T_C = 10$ for the configuration measure $\lambda_{\max}$ has been found to be reasonable, as then the achievable standard deviations stay below approx. 3 times the standard deviations of the desired reference situation, being consistent with a three-fold larger measuring standard deviation $\sigma_{x'}$ above.

3   Evaluation of the Manually Designed Self-Diagnosis

3.1   External Evaluation

In order to decide, whether the self-diagnosis was successful or not one needs an external reference, or ground truth. To establish a reference data set playing the role of ground truth is usually an enormous effort. Here we evaluated the automatic procedure with the result of a simultaneous bundle block adjustment of *all* available images, and manually measured ground control points. The complete set of images shows an overlap of at least 60 %, not only of about 20 %, as this is the case for the images used for ortho-photo production, which, when used alone, would not allow a bundle adjustment. This reference bundle adjustment results in highly reliable orientation parameters.

As the final goal is the computation of ortho-photos, i. e. the rectification of the aerial images to the geometry of the map, we measure the *maximum* of the *planimetric distortion* $\Delta \boldsymbol{X} = \boldsymbol{X}^{(est)} - \boldsymbol{X}^{(bundle)}$ at the ground by re-projecting a 3×3-grid from the images to the ground (cf. fig. 2) using both the orientation parameters $\widehat{\boldsymbol{p}}^{(est)}$ of the automatic procedure and the orientation parameters $\widehat{\boldsymbol{p}}^{(bundle)}$ of the complete bundle adjustment:

$$D_{\max} = \max \sqrt{(X_m^{(est)} - X_m^{(bundle)})^2 + (Y_m^{(est)} - Y_m^{(bundle)})^2}\,, \quad D_{\max} \leq T_D \quad (3)$$

Following the requirements of the application, the average planimetric distortion should not exceed $T_D = 1.5$ m.

3.2   Empirical Evaluation of the Self-Diagnosis

A first evaluation of the quality of the self-diagnosis used the two criteria for precision and configuration in version A, thus just the thresholded mean reprojection errors and the thresholded configuration measure. The external evaluation was based on the distortion.

The result of appr. 17 000 samples, i. e. image orientations is shown in the following table: 69 % orientations were correct and this was reported by the self-diagnosis. In 18 % of the cases the orientation was incorrect, which was detected by the analysis. The percentage of false negatives with 11 % is high. Though the percentage of false positives with 2 % is quite low, this still represents appr. 340 images!

Table 1. Result of an empirical test using appr. 17000 aerial images.

		reality	
		correct	wrong
self-diagnosis	correct	69 % (correct decision)	2 % (false positives)
	wrong	11 % (false negatives)	18 % (correct decision)

In nearly all cases, the wrong orientations resulted from errors in the second step (cf. sect. 2.2), namely the error detection using the reference coordinates of the control points.

This result, especially the low success rate of 69 %, was the motivation to increase the quality of the self-diagnosis.

4 Learning Criteria for Self-Diagnosis Using SVM

In order to improve the performance of the orientation procedure we tried to use the result of the second step, i. e. the orientation with points, to predict the final result and at the same time to automatically learn the criteria for self-diagnosis using support vector machines (SVM, (SCHÖLKOPF et al. 1998)). We also used version B, i. e. all meaningful orientations per image.

For finding a good predictor we used the following four features $x = (x_1, x_2, x_3, x_4)^\mathsf{T}$, which are available after the second step, and which can be expected to be useful for predicting the final result:

1. x_1: the number N of control points in the image, because we expect larger numbers N to increase the performance
2. x_2: the number E of control points eliminated for the final estimation process, as we expect smaller numbers E to increase the performance.
3. x_3: the precision measure $\widehat{\sigma}_0$, as we expect smaller $\widehat{\sigma}_0$ to increase the performance. Actually we used logarithm, which is identical to the negative self-information $-I(\widehat{\sigma}_0) = \log \widehat{\sigma}_0$.
4. x_4: the configuration measure $\lambda_{\max}$, as we assume smaller $\lambda_{\max}$ to increase the performance. In this case we actually used the logarithm $\log(\lambda_{\max})$ too.

For training we used *all M trials* of the orientation with points in step 2. They are used for determining the best decision function $d(\boldsymbol{x})$ for a given sample $(\boldsymbol{x}, y)_i$. For labeling the images as y =correct or y =wrong we performed the ML-estimation of step 3 and evaluated the orientation using the distortion $D_{\max}$ at ground level.

We used the support vector machine implementation LIBSVM of Chang and Lin (CHANG & LIN 2002) for determining a decision function $d(\boldsymbol{x})$. As it is a binary decision problem, the decision function determines an optimal evaluation using the score function $s(\boldsymbol{x}) = \text{abs}(d(\boldsymbol{x}))$, thus thresholding at 0: if $d(\boldsymbol{x}) < 0$ the case is wrong, otherwise it is correct. The resultant support vector classifier determines whether a sample is correct or wrong.

Actually we are not interested in the classification of each of the M trials per image, but only in the best achievable result per image. Looking for the best score per image leads to an unacceptable result, as some of the M cases get a very high score for being wrong, which might be higher than the maximum score of the correct cases.

Therefore we use the original decision function $d(\boldsymbol{x})$ for classification. Instead of thresholding at 0, we choose a threshold T_d leading to the classifier:

$$y = \text{correct, if } d(\boldsymbol{x}) > T_d, else wrong \tag{4}$$

The choice of T_d can be used to optimize the classifier, e. g. minimizing expected costs for the classification result.

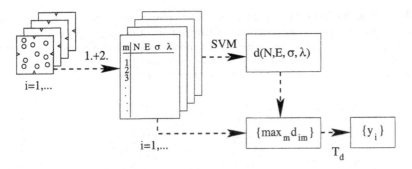

Fig. 3. The procedure for optimizing self-diagnosis: for each image i a set of alternative orientations is calculated in steps 1 and 2 of the procedure, using the N reference points of the control points. The result depends on the number E of eliminated control points. The numbers N and E and the two performance measures $\hat{\sigma}_0$ and $\lambda_{\max}$ for precision and configuration are used to automatically determine a decision function $d(\boldsymbol{x})$ using binary support vector machines. The best orientation per image is used for classification, leading to a binary y_i, thus $y_i \in \{\text{correct}, \text{wrong}\}$.

4.1 Empirical Accuracy of the Self-Diagnosis Based on SVM Decision Function

We tested this procedure on two sets of images of blocks with 60 % overlap covering two areas in Nordrhein-Westfalen. The 436 images from Area I show good quality, in the sense that all images are of good quality and contain enough control points, whereas the 243 images from Area II do not have good image quality and partially contain badly identifiable control points.

As we now have one free parameter for classification, namely the threshold T_d for deciding between correct and wrong orientations we give the confusion tables for four values of T_d.

We give the result as confusion tables with the number of images for the four cases $(self diagnosis : \mathsf{correct}|reality : \mathsf{correct})$, $(self diagnosis : \mathsf{correct}|reality : \mathsf{wrong})$ etc. The confusion tables are obtained by using approximately half the data set for training of the SVM and the other half for testing.

To evaluate the quality of the resulting confusion tables we might use the expected cost. They depend on the costs for each case $\{\mathsf{cc}, \mathsf{cw}, \mathsf{wc}, \mathsf{ww}\}$ (abbreviating the labels). The expected cost is

$$E(C) = P_{cc}C_{cc} + P_{cw}C_{cw} + P_{wc}C_{wc} + P_{ww}C_{ww}$$

which requires a specification by the user. For a first evaluation we use the additional costs $C_{cc} = 0$, $C_{cw} = 40$, $C_{wc} = 5$, $C_{ww} = 10$. The expected cost is given below the confusion tables.

Table 2. Results from Area I. In each table, column index (c, w): result of self-diagnosis, row index (c, w): reference. Changing the threshold T_d may be used to increase performance, e. g. by reducing the number of false positives (upper right). Expected cost below tables. First row of tables: training data set: 240 images, test set: 196 images. Second row of tables: exchange of test and training data.

	$T_d = 0$		$T_d = 1$		$T_d = 2$		$T_d = 3$	
	c	w	c	w	c	w	c	w
1 — 2	c 173	21	c 172	17	c 166	5	c 140	5
	w 0	2	w 1	6	w 7	18	w 33	18
	$E(C)=4.39$		$E(C)=3.80$		$E(C)=2.11$		$E(C)=2.78$	
	c	w	c	w	c	w	c	w
2 — 1	c 233	7	c 229	6	c 217	5	c 172	0
	w 0	0	w 4	1	w 16	2	w 61	7
	$E(C)=1.17$		$E(C)=1.13$		$E(C)=1.25$		$E(C)=1.56$	

Choosing a threshold of $T_d = 2$ appears to be optimal. The expected cost, averaged over both versions 1—2 and 2—1, with $E(C) = 1.64$ is lower than the expected cost for the earlier version of the classification, where the expected cost is $E(C) = 3.15$. The result for the image set II shows significant worse results (cf. table 3). There appears to be no clear minimum of the expected cost in that range of thresholds. We also investigated whether the classifiers could be generalized to other data sets. We trained the classifier with one data set, I or II, and tested it on the other one. The two data sets turned out to be too different.

Table 3. Results from Area II. For each confusion table, column: result of self-diagnosis, row: reference. Expected cost below tables. First row of tables: training data set: 99 images, test set: 124 images. Second row of tables: exchange of test and training data.

	$T_d = 0$			$T_d = 1$			$T_d = 2$			$T_d = 3$	
		c	w		c	w		c	w		c	w
1 — 2	c	72	35	c	64	21	c	45	10	c	25	4
	w	1	16	w	9	30	w	28	41	w	48	47
	$E(C)$=12.62			$E(C)$=9.55			$E(C)$=7.66			$E(C)$=7.01		
		c	w		c	w		c	w		c	w
2 — 1	c	66	18	c	55	9	c	21	4	c	1	0
	w	1	14	w	12	23	w	46	28	w	66	32
	$E(C)$=8.74			$E(C)$=6.56			$E(C)$=6.76			$E(C)$=6.56		

4.2 Simplifying the Classifier

The scatterplots of pairs of features suggest that the two performance measures for precision and configuration might be sufficient. The scatterplot for these two features shows that a linear decision boundary with a slope of -0.5 might do. The normal of this line approximately is $w = (2, 1)$. Therefore we investigated the following single feature $x = 2x_3 + x_4 = 2\log \hat{\sigma}_0 + \log \lambda_{max} = \log(\hat{\sigma}_0^2 \lambda_{max})$. This appears reasonable, as $\hat{\sigma}_0^2 \lambda_{max}$ is the maximum increase in variance compared to the reference configuration due to both the estimated precision and the configuration.

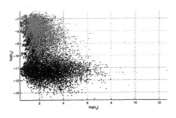

Fig. 4. Cluster of $\log \hat{\sigma}_0$ (right) and $\log \lambda_{max}$ (up)

However, using only this feature for classification leads to slightly worse results: The expected cost in the good data set decreased by nearly a factor 2, whereas the expected cost in the bad data set II did not change very much.

5   Conclusions

Integrating self-diagnosis into a system for automatic orientation enabled to increase its performance by training the self-diagnosis using support vector machines. The setup appears general enough and may be transferred to any type of vision system, even if its primary output is not the result of a classifier.

References

CHANG, C.-C. & LIN, C.-J. (2002): LIBSVM: a Library for Support Vector Machines (Version 2.33), *Technical report*, Dep. of Computer Science and Information Engineering, National Taiwan Univ., Taipei 106, Taiwan: last update: January, 2002.

BAARDA, W. (1973): S-Transformations and Criterion Matrices, *Netherlands Geodetic Commission*, Ser. 1, Vol **5**.

FÖRSTNER, W. (2001): Calibration and orientation of cameras in computer vision, *in* A. GRÜN & T. HUANG (Eds.), *Generic Estimation Procedures for Orientation with Minimum and Redundant Information*, Springer.

MIKHAIL, E. M. & ACKERMANN, F. (1976): Observations and Least Squares, University Press of America, 1976

SCHÖLKOPF, B., BURGES, C. J. C. & SMOLA, A. J. (1998): Introduction to Support Vector Learning, *in* B. SCHÖLKOPF ET AL. (EDS.), *Advances in Kernel Methods: Support Vector Learning*, MIT Press, Cambridge, chapter 1, pp. 1–15.

SESTER, M. & FÖRSTNER, W. (1989): Object Location Based on Uncertain Models, *Mustererkennung 1989*, Springer Informatik Fachberichte, **219**, pp. 457–464

Multi-agent Activity Recognition Using Observation Decomposed Hidden Markov Model

Xiaohui Liu and Chin-Seng Chua

Nanyang Technological University, Block S1,
Nanyang Avenue, 639798, Singapore.
ECSChua@ntu.edu.sg

Abstract. A new approach of modeling/recognizing multi-agent activities from image sequences is presented. In recent years, Hidden Markov Models (HMMs) have been widely used to recognize activity units ranging from individual gestures to multi-people interactions. However, traditional HMMs meet many problems when the number of agents increases in the scene. One significant reason for this inability is the fact that HMMs require their 'observations' to be of fixed length and order. Unlike conventional HMMs, a new algorithm to model multi-agent activities is proposed. This has two sub-processes: one for modelling the activity based on decomposed observations and the other for recording the 'role' information of each agent in the activity. This new algorithm allows changing of the observations' length, and does not require initial agent assignment. The experimental results show that this algorithm is also robust when the agents' information is only partially represented.

1 Introduction

Recently, there is a surge in interest in recognizing human activities. This interest is mainly driven by the large potential applications, such as surveillance, content-based video indexing and human-computer interfaces, that may arise from the recognition of activities. With activity recognition techniques, computers can explain what they 'see', and even suggest plausible interpretations according to some prior knowledge.

Multi-people interaction is an important branch of activity recognition. Although there has been relative success in gesture and individual action recognition, there is significant work to be done for multi-agent activities. A new method for multi-agent activity recognition based on Hidden Markov Models (HMMs) is presented in this paper. We call this the Observation Decomposed HMM (ODHMM). Unlike former HMM related works, this new HMM is designed to alleviate the constraints on observations in conventional HMMs. The key idea of our method is to decompose the original observation into sub-observations belonging to each agent respectively. The advantage of this newly designed HMM is that it can reduce the dimensionality of the feature space and allows changes in the number of agents.

J.L. Crowley et al. (Eds.): ICVS 2003, LNCS 2626, pp. 247–256, 2003.
© Springer-Verlag Berlin Heidelberg 2003

Since the observations are decomposed, information of the sub-observations' order is neglected. In order to compensate for this undesirable property, we add extra 'role' models to our proposed HMM. The role of each agent in an activity is stored in a statistical table established within the HMM decoding result.

Four simulated three-people activities were used to test the performance of the proposed algorithm. The average recognition rate is about 97 percent. Simulations have also been done in situations where only partial information of the agents is available. The results show that the recognition rate only decreases a little, and thus prove that the algorithm is not sensitive to a change in the number of activity agents.

1.1   Outline

The rest part of this paper is arranged as follows. Previous works are reviewed in Section 2. Section 3 describes the difficulties in multi-agent activity recognition and presents the proposed method. Simulation results are given in Section 4. Lastly the conclusion and discussion of this work is presented in section 5.

2   Review of Previous Work

During the past decade, researchers have achieved great success in activity recognition ranging from individual gestures to people's interaction. Good surveys of this area are [1] and [2]. However, unlike the work presented in this paper, which can recognize activities containing multiple agents, previous works mainly focused on activities containing no more than two agents.

Many works have been done for gesture recognition. Campbell et al. [3] applied Hidden Markov models to recognize 18 Tái Chi gestures. Starner et al. [4] combined HMMs with a strong grammar to recognize American Sign Language on the sentence level. Wilson and Bobick [5] proposed a novel Parametric HMM and applied it to distinguish similar gestures with variations. An HMM-based threshold model was proposed by Hyeon-Kyu Lee and Jin H. kim [6]. Superior to other models, this threshold model can distinguish between meaningful and meaningless gestures, whereas other models have to assume that any input gesture is meaningful. Unlike those works using HMMs for gesture recognition, Ming-Hsuan Yang et al. [7] applied Time-delay Neural Network to classify gesture patterns based on motion trajectories.

Much effort have also been invested into individual action recognition. Yamato et al. [8] first use HMMs to recognize tennis swings using mesh features. Krahnstöver et al. [9] established a unified framework for tracking and analysis of human motions based on HMMs and a low-dimensional description of spatial information obtained by PCA. Instead of using first order HMMs, Galata et al. [10] applied Variable-length Markov models to model human behaviors. Bobick and Davis [11] applied Motion Energy Image(MEI) and Motion History Image(MHI) to aerobic action recognition by using a template matching approach. Toshikazu Wada and Takashi Matsuyama [12] used Non-deterministic

Finite Automata (NFA) to activity recognition, being aware of the shortcomings of deterministic models such as HMMs.

However, most of these works only concentrated on one or two agents. Their approaches cannot be extended to multi-agent activity recognition directly. Oliver et al. [13] applied Coupled HMMs to model interactions between two agents. But their method needs to assign each agent a hidden-state process respectively. This requirement increases the complexity of HMMs greatly and makes the estimation of HMM parameters intractable when applied to activities containing more than two agents. The work of Somboon Hongeng and Ramakant Nevatia [14] is also a multi-agent activity recognition related work. But this work requires complex temporal description and is difficult to be applied to the case where there is a large number of agents.

3   Problem Description and Proposed Method

3.1   Difficulties

The complexity of multi-agent activity lies in the large number of agents and complex interactions between these agents.

The first difficulty is the *large feature space problem*. In computer vision system, an agent's information in each frame is often represented by a feature vector, which describes the agent's position, speed, shape or other distinctive characteristics. In the case of multi-agent activity recognition, the dimension of the feature vector increases in proportion to the number of agents in each frame and is often very long. Longer feature vectors usually cause more error in the processes of vector quantization or distribution estimation. Therefore, a way to decrease the length of these feature vectors is needed in multi-agent activity recognition. The second difficulty is *the changing number of agents*. Unlike the recognition of individual activity or gesture, which have a constant number of agents throughout the whole activity sequence, multi-agent activity recognition faces the problem of changing number of agents. This change may be caused by occlusion by objects or tracking failure, which often happen in multi-agent activities. This change also exists in some particular activities in which the number of agents is inherently changing, depending on the characteristic of the activities we are interested in. The last difficulty is about *agent assignment*. Agent assignment is a special problem of multi-agent activity recognition. Unlike single-agent activity recognition, multi-agent activity recognition has to align each agent in the dataset with one agent in the model. For an activity that includes N agents, there are N! pairs of possible alignments. Therefore, before matching with stored models, a computational search for the optimal agent assignment should be taken. It would be better if we can avoid this search since this will decrease the system's efficiency.

3.2   Proposed Observation Decomposed HMM

Hidden Markov Models is adopted in this work because of their outstanding ability to offer non-linear matching between two sequences. However, in order to solve the problems mentioned in Section 3.1, a structural modification of conventional HMMs is proposed. In conventional HMMs, each state should only have one fixed-length observation whose elements are arranged in a fixed order. However, in multi-agent activity, this requirement inhibits the use of HMMs directly due to the problems described in Section 3.1. The key idea of our method is to decompose each original observation, according to the number of agents, into a set of sub-observations that are assumed to be independent for the sake of simple computation. Thus in the hidden Markov chain, each state emits a set of sub-observations rather than a single observation. The illustration of this Observation Decomposed HMM(ODHMM) is shown in Fig. 1. The white circles represent the states, while the black circles represent the sub-observations. The number of sub-observations under each state equals to the number of agents in that scene.

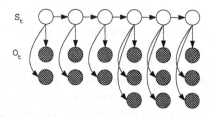

Fig. 1. Illustration of the Observation Decomposed HMM: S_t is the state sequence, O_t is the decomposed observation sequence

This ODHMM has many advantages. Firstly, each sub-observation belongs to an agent, and there is no limitation on how many sub-observations a state should contain. Thus, ODHMM allows changes of the number of agents in the chain process. Secondly, since we assume that all sub-observations are independent, there is no need for us to give an initial agent assignment. For example, vectors $[A, B, C]$, $[A, C, B]$ and $[B, A, C]$ will be treated as the same, since they all produce the same set of sub-observations $[A]$, $[B]$ and $[C]$. Finally, and obviously, by decomposing the original observations, the ODHMM reduces the dimensionality of the feature space considerably.

Since we do not change the state structure of HMMs, there is no need to change the re-estimation formulas of state initialization and transition probabilities. Only the output probability re-estimation formula needs to be modified.

In conventional HMM, the probability of observing observation k in state j is computed using a lookup table B.

$$b_{s_j}(O_t) = P[O_t = k, s_t = j|\lambda] = B(j, k) \tag{1}$$

However, in ODHMM the output probability is a joint output probability of the sub-observations. Since all the sub-observations are of equal length and arranged in the same order, table B can still be used. But the output probability is computed by calculating the joint output probability of all the sub-observations in each frame. This is given by

$$b_{s_j}(O_t) = \prod_{r=1}^{R_t} b_{s_j}(o_t^r) = \prod_{r=1}^{R_t} B(j, k_r), k_r = o_t^r \tag{2}$$

where $O_t = \{o_t^1, o_t^2, \ldots, o_t^{R_t}\}$, O_t is the original observation, o_t^r is the sub-observation belonging to agent r in O_t and R_t is the total number of sub-observations at time t.

Based on Eq. 2, the new re-estimation formula of each element in the output probability table can be obtained following a similar way of the original EM algorithm of HMMs [15]

$$\bar{b}_j(k) = \frac{\displaystyle\sum_{t \in \{\delta(O_t, k) = 1\}} N_t(k) \gamma_t(j)}{\displaystyle\sum_k \sum_{t \in \{\delta(O_t, k) = 1\}} N_t(k) \gamma_t(j)} \tag{3}$$

where, $\bar{b}_j(k)$ refers to the element $B(j, k)$ in the output probability table; $\gamma_t(j) = P[q_t = s_i | O, \lambda]$ [15]; $N_t(k)$ is the number of sub-observations that are equal to k in frame t. The δ function used in this formula is defined by

$$\delta(O_t, k) = \begin{cases} 1 \text{ if } O_t \text{ contains sub-observations that are equal to } k; \\ 0 \text{ otherwise.} \end{cases}$$

Although the non-requirement of agent assignment is an advantage in the proposed ODHMM, a drawback of ODHMM is that it may confuse activities that are different inherently but have similar decomposed observations, since it only preserves the information of the activity happening but neglects the role of each agent in the activity. In order to compensate for this undesirable property, additional 'role' models are built for each agent involved in the activity. By neglecting each agent's role, the ODHMM of each activity is trained using a set of training sequences. After training, the optimal state sequences of all training sequences are derived based on the ODHMM which they are associated to. Then all the training sequences are converted to sequences of state-observation pairs (s_i, o_t^r). Finally, the probability of obtaining each state-observation pair (s_i, k) in role r is calculated and stored in a role table. Thus every agent in the activity has an additional role table. Table 1 shows the typical structure of a role table. Elements in this table are calculated using

$$R_\lambda^h(i, k) = Pr[(s_i, k) | role = h, \lambda] = \frac{T_\lambda[(s_i, k), h]}{\displaystyle\sum_{h=1}^{H} T_\lambda[(s_i, k), h]} \tag{4}$$

where function $T_\lambda[(s_i, k), i]$ denotes the number of times of obtaining (s_i, k) under role h in model λ.

Table 1. The illustration of the role table

	Observation Codewords		
	1	$2 \cdots$ K	
State 1	$R_\lambda^h(1,1)$	$R_\lambda^h(1,2)$	$\cdots R_\lambda^h(1,K)$
State 2	$R_\lambda^h(2,1)$	$R_\lambda^h(2,2)$	$\cdots R_\lambda^h(2,K)$
$\cdots$	$\cdots$	$\cdots\cdots\cdots$	
State N	$R_\lambda^h(N,1)$	$R_\lambda^h(N,2)$	$\cdots R_\lambda^h(N,K)$

Then given an input activity, the probability that agent i plays a role j in model λ can be calculated using these role tables. The results are listed in an agent assignment table as shown in Table 2, which is built for a three-agent activity

Table 2. Agent assignment table

	Role 1	Role 2	Role 3
Agent 1	$P_\lambda(1,1)$	$P_\lambda(1,2)$	$P_\lambda(1,3)$
Agent 2	$P_\lambda(2,1)$	$P_\lambda(2,2)$	$P_\lambda(2,3)$
Agent 3	$P_\lambda(3,1)$	$P_\lambda(3,2)$	$P_\lambda(3,3)$

where, $P_\lambda(i,j)$ represents the probability that agent i plays role j in the activity

$$P_\lambda(i,j) = \prod_{t \in \{o_t^i \neq \phi\}} R_\lambda^j(s_t, o_t^i) \tag{5}$$

The final likelihood is calculated by searching for the optimal agent assignment H that maximizes

$$Pr[S,O|H,\lambda] = \prod_{r=1}^{R} Pr[S,O^r|h_r,\lambda] \tag{6}$$

$$= \prod_{r=1}^{R} P_\lambda(r,k_r), (\forall i,j \in [1,R], k_i \neq k_j) \tag{7}$$

For computational efficiency, we use this $\max\{Pr[S,O|H,\lambda]\}$ as the criteria for classification instead of using $Pr[O|\lambda]$ which is frequently used in conventional HMM-based works.

4   Simulation

Four simulated street activities are selected as test activities. Each activity contains three players, who are divided into two groups: two players A and B for group 1 and single player C for group 2. The details of each activity is described as follows and illustrated in Fig. 2

- Act.1: The two groups approaches in the same way on opposite directions. When they meet, they stop for a while. Then A and C form a new group and turn to a new direction while B keeps going in his original direction.
- Act.2: The two groups walk in the same way and direction, but group 1 is ahead of group 2. For some reason group 2 speeds up and catches up with group 1 after a while. After stopping for a while, A and C form a new group and turn back while B keeps going in his original direction.
- Act.3: The beginning of this activity is similar to Act.1. After meeting, both A and C turn back, whereas B keeps going in the original direction and forms a new group with C.
- Act.4: This activity also begins with the two groups approaching each other as in Act.1. After meeting, both groups turn to new(still opposite) directions. No new group is formed in this activity.

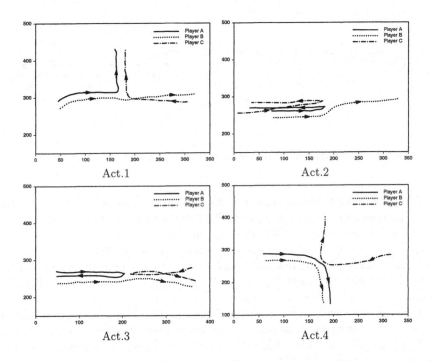

Fig. 2. Trajectories of each agents in the four tested three-agent activities

In our simulations, the agent is defined as a pair of players. Due to not having any initial agent assignment, we take player pair AB and player pair BA as different agents in order to avoid confusion. The feature vector of each agent is a five dimensional vector. For example, the feature vectors of AB and BA are derived from their raw position as follows:

$$[\frac{|A_t A_{t+1}|}{|A_t B_t|}, \frac{|B_t B_{t+1}|}{|A_t B_t|}, \frac{|A_{t+1} B_{t+1}|}{|A_t B_t|}, \cos(\theta_A), \cos(\theta_B)]$$

$$[\frac{|B_t B_{t+1}|}{|A_t B_t|}, \frac{|A_t A_{t+1}|}{|A_t B_t|}, \frac{|A_{t+1} B_{t+1}|}{|A_t B_t|}, \cos(\theta_B), \cos(\theta_A)]$$

The definition of θ_A and θ_B are shown in Fig. 3(a). These feature vectors are then used as the input to the ODHMMs. 10 sequences are used for training each of the models. The number of states in each model is 10. We use a typical left-right topology with one additional skip transition for each state. The topology of the state-to-state connection is illustrated in Fig. 3(b).

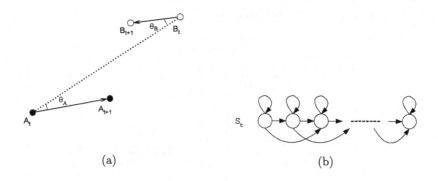

(a)   (b)

Fig. 3. (a) Illustration of feature extraction (b) State transition topology

After obtaining the trained models, 30 'unseen' new sequences are used as the test sequences for each activity model. The total number of test sequences is 120. The performances of using ODHMM only and using additional role models are compared. Their recognition results are shown in Table 3. The results show that ODHMMs cannot distinguish Act.3 and Act.4 without the help of role models. Thus it is shown that adding role tables to reduce the ambiguities between similar activities is necessary.

Experiments have also been done in situations where only partial information of the agents is available. One player is randomly selected and deleted in $\frac{1}{4}$ frames in the test sequences. This is equivalent to deleting 4 agents in these frames. The results are shown in Table 4. The results show that there is no significant decrease in the recognition rate in most of the situations, and prove that the proposed

Table 3. Recognition results 1

	Act.1	Act.2	Act.3	Act.4
ODHMM only	95%	100%	50%	50%
Add role table	97%	100%	100%	93%

method is not sensitive to a change in the number of agents. The relative lower accuracy of Act.4 is driven by the similarity between Act.4 and Act.3. In some difficult situations, for example in deleting a player in the last quarter of the sequences, the loss of information increases the ambiguity in Act.4, and thus results in a lower recognition rate.

Table 4. Recognition results 2

Deleted frames	Act.1	Act.2	Act.3	Act.4
0 to $\frac{1}{4}$	97%	97%	100%	83%
$\frac{1}{4}$ to $\frac{1}{2}$	100%	100%	97%	83%
$\frac{1}{2}$ to $\frac{3}{4}$	97%	100%	97%	90%
$\frac{1}{4}$ to $\frac{1}{2}$	87%	100%	90%	60%

5 Conclusion and Discussion

A new method for multi-agent activity recognition based on Observation Decomposed Hidden Markov Model is presented. Using this model, the feature space can be greatly reduced and changes in the number of agents in activities are allowed. This method also does not require any initial assignment for the agents. In order to reduce the ambiguities that may arise from observation decomposition, additional role models are proposed. The test results show that this method offers an average recognition rate of 97.5% in situations of no loss of information, which is quite acceptable. In situations where only partial information is available, this method can still offer a high average accuracy of about 92.4%.

Although tests have been based on simulated data, it should be easy to apply this algorithm with real data by combining it with some robust multi-object tracking methods. Since this method only requires the raw position of each player, the computational cost of preprocessing is quite small and the complexity of the required tracking system can be relatively low.

References

1. Aggarwal, J.K., Cai, Q.: Human Motion Analysis: A Review. Computer vision and image understanding, Vol. 73, No. 2, March, (1999) 428–440
2. Gavrila, D.M.: The Visual Analysis of Human Movement: A survey. Computer and image understanding, Vol. 73, No. 1, January, (1999) 82–98
3. Campbell, L.W., Becker, D.A., Azarbayejani, A., Bobick, A.F., Pentland, A.: Invariant feature for 3-D gesture recognition. Proceedings of the Second International Conference on Automatic Face and Gesture Recognition, (1996) 157–162
4. Starner, T., Weaver, J., Pentland, A.: Real-time American Sign Language Recognition Using Desk and Wearable Computer Based Video. IEEE Trans. PAMI, Vol. 20, No, 12, December, (1998) 1371–1375
5. Wilson, A.D., Bobick, A.F.: Parametric Hidden Markov Models for Gesture Recognition. IEEE Trans. PAMI, Vol.21, No. 9, Sep, (1999) 884–899
6. Lee, H.K., Kim, J.H.: An HMM-Based Threshold Model approach for Gesture Recognition. IEEE Trans. PAMI, Vol. 21, No. 10, (1999) 961–973
7. Yang, M.H., Ahujia, M., Tabb M.: Extraction of 2D Motion Trajectories and Its Application to Hand Gesture Recogntion. IEEE Trans. PAMI, Vol.24, No.8, Aug, (2002) 1061–1074
8. Yamato, J., Ohya, J., Ishii, K.: Recognizing human action in time-sequential images using hidden Markov model. IEEE CVPR, (1992) 379–385
9. Krahnstöver, N., Yeasin, M., Sharma, R.: Towards a Unified Framework for Tracking and Analysis of Human Motion. IEEE Workshop on Detection and Recognition of Events in Video, (2001) 47–54
10. Galata, A., Johnson, N., Hogg D.: Learing Variable-length Markov Models of Behavior. Comuter Vision and Image Understanding, Vol. 81, No. 3, (2001) 398–413
11. Bobick, A.F., Davis, J.W.: The recognition of Human Movement Using Temporal Template. IEEE Trans. PAMI, Vol.23, No. 23, (2001) 257–267
12. Toshikazu, W., Takashi, M.: Multiobject Behavior Recognition by Event Driven Selective Attention Method. IEEE Trans. PAMI, Vol. 22, No. 8, Aug. (2000) 873–887
13. Oliver, N.M., Rosario, B., Pentland, A.: A Bayesian Computer Vision System for Modeling Human Interactions. IEEE Trans. PAMI, Vol. 22, No.8, August, (2002) 831–843
14. Hongeng, S., Nevatia, R.: Multi-agent event recognition. Eighth ICCV, Vol. 2, (2001) 84–91
15. Rabiner L. R.: A Tutorial on Hidden Markov Models and Selected Applications in Speech Recognition. IEEE, Vol. 77, No.2, (1989) 257–286

VICs: A Modular Vision-Based HCI Framework

Guangqi Ye, Jason Corso, Darius Burschka, and Gregory D. Hager

The Johns Hopkins University
Computational Interaction and Robotics Laboratory
cips@cs.jhu.edu

Abstract. Many Vision-Based Human-Computer Interaction (VB-HCI) systems are based on the tracking of user actions. Examples include gaze-tracking, head-tracking, finger-tracking, and so forth. In this paper, we present a framework that employs no user-tracking; instead, all interface components continuously observe and react to changes within a local image neighborhood. More specifically, components expect a predefined sequence of visual events called Visual Interface Cues (VICs). VICs include color, texture, motion and geometric elements, arranged to maximize the veridicality of the resulting interface element. A component is *executed* when this stream of cues has been satisfied.

We present a general architecture for an interface system operating under the VIC-Based HCI paradigm, and then focus specifically on an appearance-based system in which a Hidden Markov Model (HMM) is employed to learn the gesture dynamics. Our implementation of the system successfully recognizes a button-push with a 96% success rate. The system operates at frame-rate on standard PCs.

1 Introduction

The promise of computer vision for human-computer interaction (HCI) is great: vision-based interfaces would allow unencumbered, large-scale spatial motion. They could make use of hand gestures, movements or other similar input means; and video itself is passive, (now) cheap, and (soon) nearly universally available. In the simplest case, tracked hand motion and gesture recognition could replace the mouse in traditional applications. But, computer vision offers the additional possibility of defining new forms of interaction that make use of whole body motion, for example, interaction with a virtual character [17].

A brief survey of the literature (see Section 1.1) reveals that most reported work on vision-based HCI relies heavily on *visual tracking* and *visual template recognition algorithms* as its core technology. While tracking and recognition are, in some sense, sufficient for developing general vision-based HCI, one might ask if they are always necessary and if so, in what form. For example, complete, constant tracking of human body motion, while difficult because of complex kinematics [21], might be a convenient abstraction for detecting that a user's hand has touched a virtual "button," but what if that contact can be detected using simple motion or color segmentation? What if the user is not in a state

J.L. Crowley et al. (Eds.): ICVS 2003, LNCS 2626, pp. 257–267, 2003.

where he or she is interacting at all? Clearly, we don't want to perform these operations except when needed, and then hopefully within a context that renders them reliable.

1.1 Related Work

The Pfinder system [29] and related applications [17] is a commonly cited example of a vision-based interface. Pfinder uses a statistically-based segmentation technique to detect and track a human user as a set of connected "blobs." A variety of filtering and estimation algorithms use the information from these blobs to produce a running state estimate of body configuration and motion [28]. Most applications make use of body motion estimates to animate a character or allow a user to interact with virtual objects.

More broadly, from the point of view of vision, there has been a great deal of interest in tracking of human body motion, faces, facial expression, and gesture, e.g. [2,10,23,5,30,8,3,19,16,7,4], with the general goal of supporting human-computer interaction.

From the HCI perspective, there have also been a wide class of "demonstration systems" that make use of vision as their input. The ZombiBoard [18] and BrightBoard [24] are examples of extensions of classical 2-D "point-and-click" style user interfaces to desktop/blackboard style interactions. They allow, for example, the selection, capture, or manipulation of items viewed by a video camera on a whiteboard or desktop. Input is usually via special written tokens; vision processing is based on simple background subtraction or thresholding followed by binary image processing, much as with Pfinder. More extensive proposals for mixing virtual and physical documents on the desktop include work on the Digital Desk [27] and on the "office of the future" [20]. A good example of a gesture-based interface is GestureVR [23].

It is clear that general-purpose vision tools for HCI is a nascent technology – systems are quite limited in scope, slow, or lack flexibility and robustness. In our work, we present a general architecture for an interface system operating under the VIC-Based HCI paradigm (Section 2). To the best of our knowledge, it is the first proposed general-purpose framework for vision-based HCI. We then focus on an appearance-based system using a Hidden Markov Model to learn user-input dynamics. This system operates under the VIC paradigm.

2 The VIC Paradigm

2.1 Modeling Interaction

Current interface technology, Windows-Icons-Menus-Pointers (WIMP) [26], is modeled with a simple state-machine (Figure 1). The dominant interface component in these *third-generation interfaces* is the *icon*. Typically, these icons have one pre-defined action associated with them that is triggered upon a mouse click.

We extend the functionality of a traditional icon by increasing its number of associated actions that can be triggered by the user. For standard WIMP

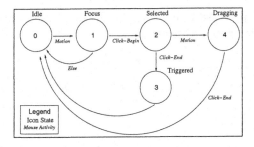

Fig. 1. The icon state model for a WIMP interface.

interfaces the size of this set is 1: point-and-click. For *super*-WIMP[1] interfaces, the size of this set is larger, but still relatively small; it is limited by the coarse nature of mouse input. Our vision-based extension greatly increases the set of possible user inputs. To allow for such an extension, the notion of the icon must change: we define a VIC-based interface component (VICon) to be composed of three parts. First, it contains a visual processing engine. This engine is the core of the VICon as it replaces the current point-and-click nature of third-generation interfaces. Second, it has the ability to display itself to the user, and lastly, it has some application specific functionality.

As mentioned earlier in Section 1, the VICon does not rely on tracking algorithms to monitor the user and detect actions. Instead, the VICon watches a region-of-interest (ROI) in the video stream and waits for recognizable user-input. For instance, if we model a simple push-button, the VICon might watch for something that resembles a human-finger in its ROI.

The obvious approach to detect user interaction is one of template-matching in which the VICon is aware of a set of possible gestures and uses image processing techniques to analyze the ROI in every frame of video. However, in practice, such a method is prone to false-positives by spurious template matches. Also, a template matching approach, alone, is potentially wasteful because it is more expensive than other simpler tasks like motion detection and color segmentation that may easily indicate a negative match.

If one observes the sequence of cues that precede a button-push, for instance, one notices that there are distinct stages preceding the actual button push: motion, color-blob, rough edges. This sequence of cues, ordered from simple to complex, can be used to facilitate efficient, accurate user-input detection. Define a *selector* to be a vision component that computes some measure on a local region of an image, and returns either nothing, indicating the absence of a cue or feature, or values describing a detected feature [11]. For example, a motion selector might return nothing if there is no apparent image motion or a description of the size and magnitude of a region of detected motion. Thus, at

---

[1] We call a *super*-WIMP interface any interface that extends the traditional functionality of the mouse to include multi-button input or mouse-gesture input. One such example is the SKETCH framework [31].

its core, the visual processing engine of the VICon is a sequence of selectors: we call it a *visual interaction cue parser* or just a parser.

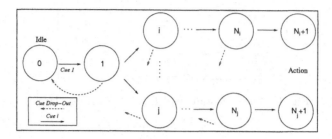

Fig. 2. The state model for a VIC-based interface component.

Formally, we define a visual interaction cue parser (Figure 2). It is a component with the following structure:

1 A finite set of discrete states $s_1, s_2, ...s_n$.
2 A distinguished initial state s_1.
3 Associated with each state s_i, a function f_i on the incoming input stream that defines a continuous state variable x.
4 For each state s_i, a set of transition rules that associates an event $e_{i,j}$, $j = 1 ... m \leq n$ (informally, the output of a selector) with either a state of higher index, or s_1. By convention, the first transition event to fire defines the transition for that state.

We return to the example of a button push from above. Using a parser, we create a possible sequence of selectors: (1) a simple motion selector, (2) a coarse color and motion selector, (3) a selector for color and cessation of motion, and (4) gesture recognition. It is easy to see that processing under this framework is efficient because of the selector ordering from simple to complex wherein parsing halts as soon as one selector in the sequence is not satisfied. More powerful and sophisticated parsing models are plausible under this paradigm: an example showing the use of a Hidden Markov Model is presented in Section 3.

The intent of the framework is that a parser will not only accept certain input, but might return other relevant information: location, duration. The key factor differentiating the VIC paradigm from traditional interface components is that there may be multiple exit cases for a given VICon determined by different streams through the parser each triggering a different event. The lexicon of possible triggers is an order of magnitude larger than WIMP and *super*-WIMP interfaces.

2.2 Interaction Modes

The notion of a VIC-based interface is broad and extensible to varying application domains. In this section we enumerate the set of interaction modes in which a VICon may be used.

1. **2D-2D Projection** - Here, one camera is pointed at a workspace, e.g. table-top. One or many projectors are used to project interface components onto this surface while the video-stream is processed under the VIC paradigm. This mode has been proposed in [32]. We feel incorporating VIC-based interface components will increase is effectiveness and broaden the domain of applications.

2. **2D-2D Mirror** - In this mode of interaction, one camera is aimed directly at the user and the image stream is displayed in the background of the user-interface for the user. Interface components are then composited into the video stream and presented to the user. This interface mode could also be used in a projection style display to allow for a group to collaborate in the shared space.

3. **3D-2D Projection** - This mode is similar to the first (2D-2D Projection) except that 2 or more cameras will be aimed at the workspace and the set of possible selectors is increased to include more robust 3d geometry.

4. **2.5D Augmented Reality** - Both video-see-through and optical-see-through augmented reality are possible if the user(s) wear stereo head-mounted displays (HMD) [1]. With stereo cameras mounted atop the HMD, knowledge of a governing surface can be extracted from the view, e.g. planar surface [6]. All VICons can then be defined to rest on this governing surface and interaction is defined with respect to this surface. One possible application is a piano where each key is a separate VICon.

5. **3D Augmented Reality** - In this case, we remove the constraint that the interface is tied to one governing surface and allow the VICons to be fully 3D. An example application would be a motor-function training program for young-children in which they would have to organize a set of blocks whose shapes and colors differ according to some rubric.

2.3   Prior State of the Art in VIC Technology

In this section we show a small set of example interfaces built under the VIC paradigm: interaction through a stream of local-based selectors. First, we show a simple button-based VICon in a calculator setting (Figure 3-left). In this case, the VICon used a motion-based cue, a color-segmentation cue, and enforced that the color remain present for a static time-interval. Next, we show multiple triggers based on user-input (Figure 3-middle). Here, the user can select the ball, drag it, and release. The parser incorporates a simple-gesture recognition stage; it's state-model follows Figure 2. As mentioned earlier, motion and dynamics can be added to the VICons. Figure 3-right shows a $Breakout^{TM}$ like program where the ball is a VICon. During play, the ball, the VICon, travels through the workspace. The user attempts to prevent the ball from falling through the bottom of the workspace while deflecting it toward the colored bricks at the top of the workspace; notice the VICon is not anchored.

The previous three VIC-based interface examples employ the 2D-2D Mirror mode of operation. Our current focus is the 2.5D Augmented Reality mode of operation. We have developed a set of fast surface recovery techniques [6]

Fig. 3. (left) A VIC-based calculator using a motion-color parser. (middle) Gesture-based demonstration of multiple interaction triggers for a single VICon. (right) VIC-Based 2D-2D mirror mode interface for a *Breakout*^{TM} style game.

allowing us to anchor the interface to a planar surface. In the next section, we present an extension of the parsers presented above through the incorporation of background-foreground modeling and stochastic parsing.

3   Focus: A Stochastic VICon via HMM

We designed and implemented a real-time VICs-based interaction system to identify a button-pushing action. This module can be easily incorporated into a larger system that allows the user to interact with the computer through gesture and finger movement. We use a static camera to supervise a virtual button, which is represented by a graphical icon. The user is expected to move his finger toward the button and stay on the button for a short period of time to trigger it. The system will decide whether the user has triggered the button. Thus, fast and robust foreground segmentation and action recognition are two key elements of our system.

3.1   Background Modeling and Image Segmentation Based on Hue Histogram

Background subtraction, gray-scale background modeling [12], color appearance modeling [25], color histogram [15] and combining of multiple cues [22] are among the most widely used methods to model the background and perform foreground segmentation. We propose to use a hue histogram for two reasons: speed and relative color invariance. This scheme employs a very fast on-line learning process, which is an advantage for this specific application since the area surrounding the button may change between sessions. Furthermore, hue is a good color invariant model that is relatively invariable to translation and rotation about the viewing axis, and changes slowly under change of angle of view, scale and occlusion [9].

We assume that the background is static for a given session. We split the background image into an array of equal-sized sub-images. For each sub-image, we build a hue histogram to model it. We process the foreground image in a similar way and perform pairwise histogram matching between background and foreground image histograms. Here, we employ histogram intersection [25] as the comparison criterion.

$$H(I, M) = \frac{\sum_{j=1}^{n} min(I_j, M_j)}{\sum_{j=1}^{n} M_j} \tag{1}$$

Here I and M refer to model and measure histogram respectively. If the matching value is below the threshold, which is determined empirically, the corresponding image region is classified as foreground; otherwise, it is background. Our experiments show that combining hue color model and histogram intersection can achieve relative invariance to illumination changes and obtain good segmentation results. After employing a median filter on this binary image to reduce possible noise, we perform the segmentation on the original image according to the identity of each region. Figure 1 shows an example.

Fig. 4. An example of background image, unsegmented image and segmentation result. The leftmost image is the background. The second image shows when the hand has entered the scene. The final segmentation result is shown in the third image. The last image demonstrates our feature space definition.

3.2 HMM-Based Human Activity Recognition

In our experiment, we employ a simple HMM [13] [14] to train and recognize the button-pushing action. The basic idea is to define a finite feature space onto which the image is mapped. Then based on captured training image sequences, we can construct HMMs for each class of actions and train them using the Baum-Welch[14] algorithm. The probability that each HMM generates the given feature sequence is the criterion of recognition.

We propose a computationally efficient and robust feature extraction scheme. This feature indicates the direction and distance of the finger from the center of the button. In principle, we split the contiguous region of the button into a 5 by 5 grid. According to the segmentation result, we can tell whether a certain cell is foreground or background. By comparing the number of cells touched by the hand in each direction, we know from which direction the hand is coming. It's also easy to tell the distance of the finger to the button by checking the nearest cell covered by the hand. Combination of all possible direction and distance forms our feature space.

For each feature state, we define a basic HMM to represent it. And for each of the four classes of actions (i.e., pushing from up, down, left and right, respectively), we will find a representative sequence. Based on this standard sequence, we build the HMM for this class by concatenating, with null transitions, all the basic HMMs corresponding to each symbol in the sequence.

Since it is difficult to capture all possible patterns of non-pushing actions, we use a threshold on the highest possibility of the classes to perform rejection. However, the duration of the action may vary significantly and thus the possibilities that each class generates such a sequence, even though the action pattern is still the same. To overcome this time variation, we perform sequence aligning in training and recognition. That is, we choose a fixed length, for example, 20 frames, to be the standard duration. For any sequence longer than this, we re-sample the sequence to get a new sequence with standard length. We will discard those sequences that are shorter than standard length.

4   Experiment Results

In our current experiment, we use a color camera with image size of 640×480 as the imaging sensor. The system can achieve a frame rate of about 10 fps on a Pentium III PC. If we reduce the resolution to 320×240, the system can run at over 20 fps.

4.1   Background Modeling and Segmentation Result

To test our segmentation scheme, we captured image pairs of the background and foreground. By comparing the segmentation result and the ground-truth classification image, which is generated by manually marking the foreground part of the scene, we are able to evaluate this algorithm. We captured more than 20 pairs of background/foreground images with different background scenes and carried out the experiment on these images. The test set also includes 6 pairs of images that undergo illumination changes. As a result, the average correct ratio is 98.16%, with average false positive ratio of 1.55% and false negative ratio of 0.29%.

We also compare the segmentation result with different sub-window size and with different number of bins of the hue histogram. The result shows that histograms with at least 8 bins perform better than those with less, while increasing the bins to 16 or more does not bring any performance enhancement. Figure 5 shows the relationship between segmentation result and size of sub-images. It can be seen that for a histogram with only 4 bins, the more samples, the better the result. While with 8 bins, the correct ratio and false positive doesn't change much. For both cases, false negative ratio increases with the tile size.

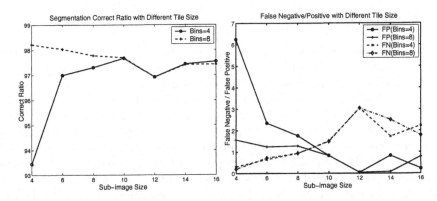

Fig. 5. Segmentation correct ratio/false positive/false negative with different sub-image size.

4.2   Action Recognition Result

For training and testing of our HMMs, we recorded over 300 action sequences by 6 different people, 76 of them used for training. An offline procedure is carried out to find the best characteristic sequence for each class. After training, the system can achieve a correct ratio of 100% on the training set. We tested the system on a set of 277 well-segmented sequences, including both valid and invalid button-triggering actions. The length of these sequences varies significantly, ranging from 30 to over 220. Our test set includes some sequences with illumination changes, which are also segmented successfully. The overall correct ratio on this test set is 96.8%. The result demonstrates the robustness and correctness of our system.

The standard length of the category characteristic sequence will influence the system performance and speed. Along with the increase of the size of primary sequence, the time needed to carry out the recognition will also grow linearly. However, since a longer sequence contains more information and thus, has a larger HMM, the total system performance will improve. The following table shows the experimental results with category primary sequences of different sizes.

Table 1. Experiment results with different length of characteristic sequence

L	Average fps	Accuracy of Training Set	Accuracy of Test Set
10	10.3	100.0%	86.8%
20	10.0	100.0%	94.2%
30	9.8	100.0%	96.8%

5   Conclusion

We have introduced the VICs approach to vision-based interaction. VICs stems from our experience using locally activated iconic cues to develop simple vision-driven interfaces. In particular, we have identified two central problems to be solved: developing reliable foreground-background disambiguation, and incorporating dynamics into gestures. We have shown that, given good solutions to the former problem, the latter can be addressed using standard HMM techniques.

Our immediate goal for the VICs project is to create 2.5D surface-anchored interfaces. To this end, we have developed a set of fast surface recovery techniques to place two rectified images in correspondence [6], and we are currently extending the results reported in this paper to a two-camera system. In the latter case, the HMM input will be data from both images, and the goal will be to recognize that the user is pressing a button as if it appears on the underlying surface.

References

1. R. Azuma. A survey of augmented reality. *Presence: Teleoperators and Virtual Environments 6*, pages 355–385, 1997.
2. S. Basu, I. Essa, and A. Pentland. Motion regularization for model-based head tracking. In *Proc. Int. Conf. Pattern Recognition*, 1996.
3. M.J. Black and Y. Yacoob. Tracking and recognizing rigid and non-rigid facial motions using local parametric models of image motion. *Int. J. Computer Vision*, 25(1):23–48, 1997.
4. G. Bradski. Computer vision face tracking for use in a perceptual user interface. *Intel Technology Journal*, April 1998.
5. C. Bregler and J. Malik. Tracking people with twists and exponential maps. In *Proc. Computer Vision and Pattern Recognition*, pages 8–15, 1998.
6. Jason Corso and Gregory D. Hager. Planar surface tracking using direct stereo. Technical report, The Johns Hopkins University, 2002. CIRL Lab Technical Report.
7. Y. Cui and J. Weng. View-based hand segmentation and hand-sequence recognition with complex backgrounds. In *ICPR96*, page C8A.4, 1996.
8. D. Gavrila and L. Davis. Towards 3-d model-based tracking and recognition of human movement: A multi-view approach. In *Proc. Int. Conf. Automatic Face and Gesture Recognition*, 1995.
9. Theo Gevers. Color based object recognition. *Pattern Recognition*, 32(3):453–464, 1999.
10. L. Goncalves, E. Di Bernardo, E. Ursella, and P. Perona. Monocular tracking of the human arm in 3-d. In *Proc. Int. Conf. Computer Vision*, pages 764–770, 1995.
11. G. Hager and K. Toyama. Incremental focus of attention for robust visual tracking. *International Journal of Computer Vision*, 35(1):45–63, November 1999.
12. Thanarat Horprasert, David Harwood, and Larry S. Davis. A robust background substraction and shadow detection. In *Proc. ACCV'2000, Taipei, Taiwan*, January 2000.
13. K. Ishii J. Yamota, J. Ohya. Recognizing human actions in time-sequential images using hidden markov model. In *IEEE Proc. CVPR 1992, Champaign, IL*, pages 379–385, 1992.

14. Frederick Jelinek. In *Statistical Methods for Speech Recognition*, MIT Press, 1999.
15. Michael J. Jones and James M. Rehg. Statistical color models with application to skin detection. *International Journal of Computer Vision*, 46(1):81–96, 2002.
16. R. Kjeldsen and J.R. Kender. Interaction with on-screen objects using visual gesture recognition. In *CVPR97*, pages 788–793, 1997.
17. P. Maes, T.J. Darrell, B. Blumberg, and A.P. Pentland. The alive system: Wireless, full-body interaction with autonomous agents. *MultSys*, 5(2):105–112, March 1997.
18. T. Moran, E. Saund, W. van Melle, A. Gujar, K. Fishkin, and B. Harrison. Design and technology for collaborage: Collaborative collages of information on physical walls. In *Proc. ACM Symposium on User Interface Software and Technology*, 1999.
19. V.I. Pavlovic, R. Sharma, and T.S. Huang. Visual interpretation of hand gestures for human-computer interaction: A review. *PAMI*, 19(7):677–695, July 1997.
20. R. Raskar, G. Welch, M. Cutts, A. Lake, L. Stesin, and H. Fuchs. The office of the future: A unified approach to image-based modeling and spatially immersive displays. In *Proc. SIGGRAPH*, 1998.
21. J.M. Rehg and T. Kanade. Visual tracking of high DOF articulated structures: An application to human hand tracking. In *Computer Vision – ECCV '94*, volume B, pages 35–46, 1994.
22. Christopher Richard Rwen, Ali Azarbayejani, Trevor Darrell, and Alex Paul Pentland. Pfinder: Real-time tracking of the human body. *IEEE Transactions on Pattern Analysis and Machine Intelligence 19(7)*, 19(7):780–784, 1997.
23. J. Segen and S. Kumar. Fast and accurate 3d gesture recognition interface. In *ICPR98*, page SA11, 1998.
24. Quentin Stafford-Fraser and Peter Robinson. Brightboard: A video-augmented environment papers: Virtual and computer-augmented environments. In *Proceedings of ACM CHI 96 Conference on Human Factors in Computing Systems*, pages 134–141, 1996.
25. M. J. Swain and D. H. Ballard. Color indexing. *International Journal of Computer Vision 7(1)*, pages 11–32, 1991.
26. Andries van Dam. Post-wimp user interfaces. *Communications Of The ACM*, 40(2):63–67, 1997.
27. Pierre Welner. Interacting with paper on the digital desk. *Communications of the ACM*, 36(7):87–96, 1993.
28. C. Wren and A. Pentland. Dynamic modeling of human motion. In *Proc. Int. Conf. Automatic Face and Gesture Recognition*, 1998.
29. C.R. Wren, A. Azarbayejani, T.J. Darrell, and A.P. Pentland. Pfinder: Real-time tracking of the human body. *PAMI*, 19(7):780–785, July 1997.
30. M. Yamamoto, A. Sato, and S. Kawada. Incremental tracking of human actions from multiple views. In *Proc. Computer Vision and Pattern Recognition*, pages 2–7, 1998.
31. Robert C. Zeleznik, Kenneth P. Herndon, and John F. Hughes. Sketch: an interface for sketching 3d scenes. In *Proceedings of the 23rd annual conference on Computer graphics and interactive techniques*, pages 163–170. ACM Press, 1996.
32. Zhengyou Zhang, Ying Wu, Ying Shan, and Steven Shafer. Visual panel: Virtual mouse keyboard and 3d controller with an ordinary piece of paper. In *Workshop on Perceptive User Interfaces*. ACM Digital Library, November 2001. ISBN 1-58113-448-7.

A Miniature Stereo Vision Machine for Real-Time Dense Depth Mapping

Yunde Jia, Yihua Xu, Wanchun Liu, Cong Yang, Yuwen Zhu,
Xiaoxun Zhang, and Luping An

Department of Computer Science and Engineering, Beijing Institute of Technology,
Beijing 100081, P. R. China
yjiar@bit.edu.cn

Abstract. We have developed a miniature stereo vision machine (MSVM-2) to generate high-resolution dense depth map for application to portable intelligent robots and smart visual interface. The machine uses multiple cameras, each with a very wide field of view, to synchronously capture stereo image sequences, and then computes dense depth maps in real time. The whole algorithm, including radial distortion correction, LoG filtering, correspondence finding, and dense depth map computation, is compactly implemented in a single FPGA. The machine also has an IEEE 1394 port for video-rate data transferring to PCs and a parallel data interface port to other user-systems. The machine could achieve more than 30 frame-per-second processing rate for 640×480 dense depth map with a 64-pixel disparity search range and 8-bit depth precision, and up to 50 frame-per-second for a 320×240 depth map.

1 Introduction

Real-time stereovision has been widely used in various fields, such as robot navigation, visual surveillance, 3D reconstruction, and 3D measurement. Real-time stereovision machine should be the ideal alternative of human eyes to simultaneously provide gray, color and depth information of 3D scene for autonomous systems.

Much work has been reported over the past decade on the development and implementation of real-time stereo vision systems with PCs or common hardware. Hardware-based, especially DSP- or FPGA-based, stereo vision systems usually achieve much higher processing rate than homochronous PCs [1]. In 1993, Faugeras et al. [2, 3] developed a binocular stereo system (MD96) using DSPs, and Nishihara [6] designed an FPGA-based binocular stereo system named PRISM-3. In 1996, Kanade et al. [4] developed a five-eye video-rate stereo vision machine (CMU machine) based on the multi-baseline stereo algorithm with a C40 DSP array, which was the most advanced and fast real-time stereo vision machine of the age. In 1997, Konolige [5] developed a DSP-based binocular stereo system that uses an ADSP2181 chip, and Woodfill [7] designed an FPGA-based reconfigurable computing device (PARTS)

This work is partially supported by Chinese Natural Science Foundation K60075005.

J.L. Crowley et al. (Eds.): ICVS 2003, LNCS 2626, pp. 268–277, 2003.
© Springer-Verlag Berlin Heidelberg 2003

that uses 16 FPGAs as main processors and communicates with host computers via PCI buses. Dunn [8] also developed an FPGA-based stereo system in 1997 that uses 7 FPGA chips. In 1999, Kimura et al. [9] designed an FPGA-based stereo vision system (SAZAN) with a nine-camera head (arranged in 3×3) for real-time computing dense depth map. All these systems are most advanced, however, none of them is small enough, or providing real-time dense depth maps with a wide field of view for application to miniature autonomous systems and smart visual interface.

We have developed a miniature stereo vision machine (MSVM-2) with a multiple-camera stereo head (from 2 to 8 cameras) for real-time dense depth mapping as shown in Figure 1. The full size of the machine is about 10 centimeters and its cameras can match lenses with a very wide field of view (diagonal FOV up to 140 degree). The processing rate of the machine can achieve more than 30 frame-per-second for a 640×480 dense depth mapping with a 64-pixel disparity search range and 8-bit depth precision, and up to 50 frame-per-second for 320×240. The machine also has an IEEE 1394 port for real-time data transferring to PCs and a parallel data interface port to other user-systems. In this paper, we present the architecture and implementation of the machine. The algorithm includes lens distortion correcting, LoG filtering, corresponding, and depth computing, which could be implemented in custom hardware.

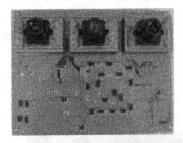
(a) Image capturing card

(b) Stereo processing card

(c) The whole view of the system

Fig. 1. Miniature stereo vision machine (MSVM-2)

2 Stereo Vision Algorithm

Similar to systems [4,9], we also employ multi-baseline stereo algorithm. However, we use cameras with a very wide field of view to increase sensing efficiency. So it is necessary to correct distorted images before computing SAD (the sum of absolute differences) and SSAD (the sum of SADs). In the following part, we will describe the algorithm in detail. For simplification, let the camera number of the machine be K ($K \geq 3$) and one of these cameras be the base camera. The image of the base camera is called base image, and the pixel of the base image is base pixel.

2.1 Lens Distortion Correction

We use the lens with a very wide field of view ($\sim 140^0$) to capture a wide range scene, but it introduces significant image distortions [10]. In our system we only consider the radial distortion, where the pixels are distorted along radial directions. The distortion correction model is

$$u' = u + (u - u_0)\left(k_1 r^2 + k_2 r^4\right)$$
$$v' = v + (v - v_0)\left(k_1 r^2 + k_2 r^4\right) \tag{1}$$
$$r = \sqrt{\alpha^2 (u - u_0)^2 + \beta^2 (v - v_0)^2}$$

where u', v' are the coordinates in the corrected image, u, v are ones in real image, u_0, v_0 represent the position of optical center, α, β are the camera's internal parameters, k_1, k_2 are the radial distortion coefficients. Figure 2 shows the results of the radial distortion correction.

(a) Original image   (b) Corrected image
Fig. 2. Radial distortion correction

2.2 LoG Filtering

LoG (Laplacian of Gaussian) filter can reduce image noise, enhance texture features, and diminish the global intensity difference between image pairs. For implementation using an FPGA, we decompose the LoG filter into a 2D Gaussian filter and a Laplacian filter, and furthermore disintegrate the 2D Gaussian filter into a horizontal and a vertical 1D filter.

The pixel values after LoG filtering mainly concentrate on a small range near 0, it is possible to represent them with fewer bits. This will significantly reduce the amount of data needed to be processed, and hereby reduce the required hardware resource. By

using nonlinear histogram transformation, we reduce the output image of LoG filter
from 10 bits to 4 bits, as shown in Figure 3.

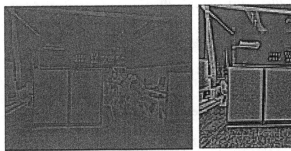

(a) The LoG filtered image of Fig.2b   (b)   Transformed image

Fig. 3. Nonlinear histogram transformation

2.3 Correspondence Finding

SAD computation needs to find the correspondence to any candidate depth value and
any base pixel in other images. Due to the high time complexity, it is very time consuming to implement this step using either PCs or DSPs. Moreover, this step involves
certain complex matrix operations and multiplication/division operations, so it is also
logic consuming to be implemented in programmable logic devices (such as FPGA).
So, both CMU machine and SAZAN system use a huge look-up-tables to avoid the
correspondence computation. In our system, we use a compact correspondence computation algorithm which needs small FPGA resource and is able to precisely generate
dense depth maps.

Suppose that the absolute coordinate system coincides with base camera coordinate
system. Consider a point $P(x,y,z)$ in the absolute coordinate, its projection in the
base image plane $p(c',r')$ is determined by

$$
z \cdot \begin{bmatrix} c' \\ r' \\ 1 \end{bmatrix} = \begin{bmatrix} f' & & 0 \\ & a'f' & 0 \\ & & 1 & 0 \end{bmatrix} \cdot \begin{bmatrix} x \\ y \\ z \\ 1 \end{bmatrix} \tag{2}
$$

where f', a' are the internal parameters of the base camera. Also, the projection of
$P(x,y,z)$ in other image plane $p(c,r)$ is determined by

$$
z_c \begin{bmatrix} c \\ r \\ 1 \end{bmatrix} = \begin{bmatrix} fr_{11} & fr_{12} & fr_{13} & ft_1 \\ afr_{21} & afr_{22} & afr_{23} & aft_2 \\ r_{31} & r_{32} & r_{33} & t_3 \end{bmatrix} \begin{bmatrix} x \\ y \\ z \\ 1 \end{bmatrix} \tag{3}
$$

where f, a, r_{ij}, t_k are the internal or external parameters of this camera.

Combining (3) and (2), we get

$$
\frac{z_c}{z}\begin{bmatrix} c \\ r \\ 1 \end{bmatrix} = \begin{bmatrix} \dfrac{fr_{11}}{f'} & \dfrac{fr_{12}}{a'f'} & fr_{13}+\dfrac{ft_1}{z} \\ \dfrac{afr_{21}}{f'} & \dfrac{afr_{22}}{a'f'} & afr_{23}+\dfrac{aft_2}{z} \\ \dfrac{r_{31}}{f'} & \dfrac{r_{32}}{a'f'} & r_{33}+\dfrac{t_3}{z} \end{bmatrix}\begin{bmatrix} c' \\ r' \\ 1 \end{bmatrix} = H\begin{bmatrix} c' \\ r' \\ 1 \end{bmatrix}
$$

(4)

And the positions of the correspondence are

$$
\begin{cases} c = \dfrac{h_{11}c' + h_{12}r' + h_{13}}{h_{31}c' + h_{32}r' + h_{33}} \\[2mm] r = \dfrac{h_{21}c' + h_{22}r' + h_{23}}{h_{31}c' + h_{32}r' + h_{33}} \end{cases}
$$

(5)

There are totally 6 additions, 6 multiplications, and 2 divisions in Eqs (5). In the practice of SAD computation, c' and r' always increase progressively. So the 6 multiplications can be replaced by 6 accumulations. In addition, when the image planes are approximately aligned in parallel (this is not a strict requirement and most existing stereo systems conform well), the denominator $h_{31}c' + h_{32}r' + h_{33} = z_c/z$ is approximately equal to 1, and only fluctuates in a small range. Building a small look-up-table to save all reciprocals of the denominator in necessary precision, we can transform the 2 divisions in Eqs (5) to 2 multiplications. Hence the whole correspond-ing finding step needs only 2 multiplications and 12 additions.

2.4 SSAD Computation

The direct computation of SSAD is obviously very time-consuming and hence unacceptable. Since the subsequent subpixel depth computation step needs to consecutively scan different SSAD values of the same base pixel under different candidate depths, it is desirable to perform SSAD computation in the same order. We use a 2D iterative algorithm whose outputs are SSAD values in this order, while signifi-cantly reducing required buffer memories and hereby simplifying the system design. This is a major differ-ence of our system from others including CMU ma-

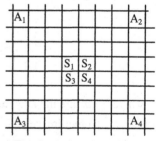

Fig. 4. 2D Iterative SSAD

chine and the SAZAN system. As shown in Figure 4, $A_i (i = 1 \sim 4)$ are the SAD val-ues, $S_j (j = 1 \sim 4)$ are the SSAD values (the window size is 7×7), and S_4 is com-puted by the following iterative form:

$$
S_4 = S_2 + S_3 - S_1 + A_1 - A_2 - A_3 + A_4
$$

(6)

2.5 Subpixel Depth Computation

After computing SSAD, we can obtain the correspondences and calculate the depth values in subpixel precision. We need to find the minimum among SSAD values first, and then do sub-pixel interpolation. Scanning SSAD values of the same base pixel under all candidate depths, we get the minimal SSAD value y_0, and its corresponding depth value $d^*(i,j)$. Let the two SSAD values neighboring to y_0 be y_{-1} and y_{+1}. By parabolic interpolation, the depth value in subpixel precision is given by

$$d_{sub}(i,j) = d^*(i,j) + \frac{y_{+1} - y_{-1}}{2(2y_0 - y_{-1} - y_{+1})} \tag{7}$$

3 Implementation

3.1 Architecture

Our machine uses an FPGA chip as the main processor to perform real-time image preprocessing and find out correspondence for depth recovery. According to the use of external RAMs, the algorithm is divided into a few modules as shown in Figure 5. There is also a manager module that is responsible to system management, e.g., to make other modules run in pipeline, and to make the adjacent modules mutually and exclusively access shared the RAMs. Figure 5 is the architecture of the machine, where the parentheses indicate the contents saved in RAMs. There are totally $K-1$ RAMs to save LoG outputs, where K is the number of cameras.

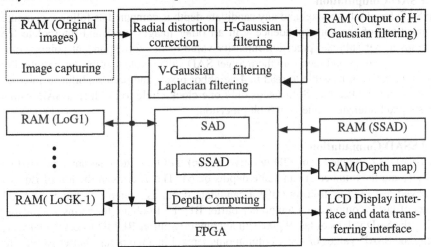

Fig. 5. Miniature stereo vision machine architecture

3.2 Image Preprocessing

The image preprocessing module contains six submodules: radial distortion correction, horizontal Gaussian filtering, vertical Gaussian filtering, Laplacian filtering, data reducing, and data combining. The results of distortion correction are passed directly to horizontal Gaussian filtering submodule, which outputs 8-bit precision data. The subsequent vertical Gaussian filtering produces 10-bit precision data. These two submodules share a set of logic gates because they always run exclusively. The output is fed to Laplacian module and then to data reducing submodule, which uses a look-up-table to perform data transformation from 10-bit to 4-bit. The look-up-table is much smaller and can be saved in the FPGA internal RAMs.

The subsequent SAD computation module needs to read 4-neighbor pixels for bilinear interpolation to get subpixel-precision intensity value in non-base images. To reduce memory access times, we combine 4-neighbor pixels together and save it in a 16-bit memory. This enables SAD module to read them in only one time of memory access, which significantly improves system performance because the bottleneck of the whole system lies in memory access time. Notice that for the base image, we also combine 4 pixels in 4-neighboring columns together to reduce memory accessing on base pixels.

3.3 Depth Recovery

The depth recovery module includes three submodules: SAD, SSAD, and subpixel-precision depth computation.

3.3.1 SAD Computation

The SAD for any base pixel and any candidate depth is computed as follows: compute the positions of the correspondence y in all other images, read and interpolate the positions to get subpixel-precision intensity value of the correspondent points, compute the AD values and then sum them to get SAD value. Note that the data combining procedure makes it possible to read in 4-neighbor pixels and perform bilinear interpolation in one clock cycle. So it needs only one clock circle to produce a SAD value. The subpixel intensity value is in 6-bit precision.

3.3.2 SSAD Computation

The SSAD is computed using 2D iterative Eq. (6). Let the size of summation window be 9×9, and the number of candidate depths be 64. The 7 terms in the left of Eq. (6) are saved and read as follows (take a candidate depth as example): saving the SAD values of last 9 columns in a temporary buffer BUFF1 to obtain the terms A_1 and A_2, saving the SAD values of last 9 pixels in a temporary buffer BUFF2 to get the term A_3, saving the SSAD values of last 1 column plus 1 pixel in a temporary buffer BUFF3 to find the terms S_1, S_2 and S_3. To guarantee enough access time of the BUFF1, we combine three neighboring SAD values together and then save them into the BUFF1 in one clock circle. This spares two clocks to read out A_1 and A_2, which are also in the forms of the combination of 3 neighboring values. Note that the above procedure needs to continuous compute 3 neighboring SSAD values under the same candidate depth.

3.3.3 Depth Computation in Subpixel-Level

The first step of depth computation is to find the minima of SSAD curves in pixel-level, and the next step is to calculate the minima location using parabolic interpolation in subpixel-level. The output sequence of SSAD computation module is shown in Figure 6, where the numbers indicate base pixel indexes, and the subscripts indicate candidate depth indexes. It can be seen that the interval between the SSAD values of a same base pixel is 2 clock cycles, when the SSAD values of 2 neighboring base pixels are output. So the minima can be found out by using 3 parallel modules. Since only one interpolation operation is needed for every 32 SSAD values, these 3 modules can share one parabolic interpolation module. The interval of the outputs of these 3 modules is 4 clocks. We increase the interval to 8 clocks because the interpolation module can only accept one input every 8 clock cycles.

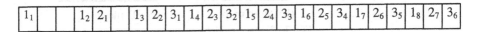

Fig. 6. The output sequence of the SSAD computation module

4   Experimental Results and Discussion

The system clock of the MSVM-2 is 80 MHz. There are six modules running in the system in pipeline, the system work cycle is the maximum of the sum of two neighboring modules time. Table 1 shows the time spent by these modules in 3-camera, 5-camera, and 8-camera stereo machines. It shows that the maximal time is the sum of vertical filtering and stereo computation modules: 27ms, 29ms, and 31ms for 3, 5, and 8-camera, respectively. That is, the speed of the system is greater than 30 frame/second, and the depth recovery performance is greater than 84 MDPS. Actually the system performance is not heavily dependent on the number of cameras, as long as there is enough logic resource to run the algorithm. If the number of cameras is less than or equal to 8, the speed changes little. If the number is greater than 8, the speed decreases linearly as the number increases.

The stereo system using multiple cameras with a normal field of view can produce highly accurate dense depth maps. Hence they are suitable for the applications such as object modeling and accurate object localization. Figure 7 is the face modeling result with a normal field of view. Note that patterned lighting is used only to improve scene textures. Stereo vision machine with a very wide field of view can recover depth information very efficiently and fit the application such as real-time object tracking, surveillance, obstacle detection, and so on. Figure 8 shows the dense depth map with a view of 140 degree.

276   Y. Jia et al.

Table 1. Time cost of different modules in our stereovision machine with 3, 5, and 8 cameras

	Original image capturing	Distortion correction and H-filter	V-filter	Stereo computation	Depth map
Number of clock cycles	3(5, 8) × 640×480	3(5, 8) ×4× 640×480	3(5, 8) × 640×480	64× 640×480	1× 640×480
Time (ms)	2.3(3.8, 6.1)	9.2(15.4, 24.58)	2.3(3.8, 6.1)	24.58	0.77

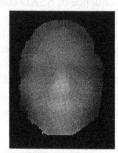

(a)Intensity image　　　(b)Depth map　　　(c) 3D mesh

Fig. 7. 3D face modeling

(a) Original image　　　(b) Undistorted image

(c) Depth map

Fig. 8. Depth recovery with a very wide field of view

5   Conclusion

This paper presents the architecture and implementation of a miniature stereovision machine for real time dense depth mapping. The miniaturization design, a very wide field of view, and real-time computation are the substantial features of our machine. This machine includes an IEEE 1394 port to transfer data in real time with PCs, and a common data interface to communicate with other user systems. Therefore, it can be used in autonomous systems, especially miniature robots, to perform efficient vision perception, navigation, object location and recognition. It can also be designed as 3D video camera, for applications such as real-time object modeling, object tracking, and vision-based interface. Some of these applications are just being conducted in our vision lab.

References

1. L. Di Stefano, M. Marchionni, S. Mattoccia, G. Neri, A Fast Area-Based Stereo Matching Algorithm, in Proc. of the 15th IAPR-CIPPRS International Conference on Vision Interface, Calgray, CA,May 2002.
2. O.Faugeras, et al. Real-time Correlation-based Stereo: Algorithm, Implementations and Applications. Technical Report 2013, INRIA, August 1993.
3. Herve Methieu. A Multi-DSP96002 Board. Technical Report 153, INRIA, May 1993.
4. T.Kanade, A.Yoshida, K.Oda, H.Kano, and M.Tanaka. A Stereo Machine for Video-Rate Dense Depth Mapping and Its New Applications. Proc. of IEEE Int. Conf. on Computer Vision and Pattern Recognition, pp.196-202, June 1996.
5. Kurt Konolige. Small Vision Systems: Hardware and Implementation. In 8th International Symposium on Robotics Research, Hayamn, Japan, October 1997.
6. H.K.Nishihara. Real-time Stereo- and Motion-based Figure-ground Discrimination and Tracking Using LoG Sign-correlation. Proc. of IEEE 27th Asilomar Conf. on Signals, Systems, and Computers, pp.95-100, Nov 1993.
7. Paul Dunn, Peter Corke. Real-time Stereopsis Using FPGAs. Proc. of IEEE Region 10 Annual International Conference, pp.235-238, Dec 1997.
8. J.Woodfill, B.V.Herzen. Real-time Stereo Vision on the PARTS Reconfigurable Computer. IEEE Workshop on FPGAs for Custom Computing Machines, pp.242-252, April 1997.
9. Shigeru Kimura, Tetsuya Shinbo, H Yamaguchi, E Kawamura, and K Nakano. A Convolver-based Real-time Stereo Machine (SAZAN). Proc. of IEEE Int. Conf. on Computer Vision and Pattern Recognition, pp.457-463, June 1999.
10. J.Weng, P.Cohen, and M.Herniou. Camera calibration with distortion models and accuracy evaluation. IEEE Trans. On Pattern Analysis and Machine Intelligence, Vol.14,No.10,Oct.1992

Performance Evaluation Metrics and Statistics for Positional Tracker Evaluation

Chris J. Needham and Roger D. Boyle

School of Computing, The University of Leeds, Leeds, LS2 9JT, UK
{chrisn,roger}@comp.leeds.ac.uk
http://www.comp.leeds.ac.uk/chrisn

Abstract. This paper discusses methods behind tracker evaluation, the aim being to evaluate how well a tracker is able to determine the position of a target object. Few metrics exist for positional tracker evaluation; here the fundamental issues of trajectory comparison are addressed, and metrics are presented which allow the key features to be described. Often little evaluation on how precisely a target is tracked is presented in the literature, with results detailing for what percentage of the time the target was tracked. This issue is now emerging as a key aspect of tracker performance evaluation.

The metrics developed are applied to real trajectories for positional tracker evaluation. Data obtained from a sports player tracker on video of a 5-a-side soccer game, and from a vehicle tracker, is analysed. These give quantitative positional evaluation of the performance of computer vision tracking systems, and provides a framework for comparison of different methods and systems on benchmark data sets.

1 Introduction

There are many ways in which the performance of a computer vision system can be evaluated. Often little evaluation on how *precisely* a target is tracked is presented in the literature, with the authors tending to say for what percentage of the time the target was tracked. This problem is beginning to be taken more seriously, and an annual workshop on performance evaluation of tracking and surveillance [5] has begun recently (2000).

Performance evaluation is a wide topic, and covers many aspects of computer vision. Ellis [1] discusses approaches to performance evaluation, and covers the different areas, which include how algorithms cope in different physical conditions in the scene, i.e. weather, illumination and irrelevant motion, to assessing performance through ground truthing and the need to compare tracked data to marked up data, whether this be targets' positions, 2D shape models, or classification of some description.

In previous work [4] , mean and standard deviations of errors in tracked data from manually marked up data has been presented, with simple plots. Harville [2] presents similar positional analysis when evaluating the results of person tracking using plan-view algorithms on footage from stereo cameras. In certain

J.L. Crowley et al. (Eds.): ICVS 2003, LNCS 2626, pp. 278–289, 2003.

situations Dynamic Programming can be applied to align patterns in feature vectors, for example in the speech recognition domain as Dynamic Time Warping (DTW) [6]. In this work trajectory evaluation builds upon comparing equal length trajectories having frame by frame time steps with direct correspondences.

When undertaking performance evaluation of a computer vision system, it is important to consider the requirements of the system. Common applications include detection (simply identifying if the target object is present), coarse tracking (for surveillance applications), tracking (where reasonably accurate locations of target objects are identified), and high-precision tracking (for medical applications, reconstructing 3D body movements). This paper focuses on methods behind *positional* tracker evaluation, the aim being to evaluate how well a tracker is able to determine the position of a target object, for use in tracking and high-precision tracking as described above.

2 Metrics and Statistics for Trajectory Comparison

Few metrics exist for positional tracker evaluation. In this section the fundamental issues of trajectory comparison are addressed, and metrics are presented which allow the key features to be described. In the following section, these metrics are applied to real trajectories for positional tracker evaluation.

2.1 Trajectory Definition

A **trajectory** is a sequence of positions over time. The general definition of a trajectory T is a sequence of positions (x_i, y_i) and corresponding times, t_i:

$$T = \{(x_1, y_1, t_1), (x_2, x_2, t_2), \dots, (x_n, y_n, t_n)\} \tag{1}$$

Fig. 1. Example of a pair of trajectories.

In the computer vision domain, when using video footage, time steps are usually equal, and measured in frames. Thus, t_n may be dropped, as the subscript on the positions can be taken as time, and Equation 1 becomes:

$$T = \{(x_1, y_1), (x_2, x_2), \dots, (x_n, y_n)\} \tag{2}$$

i.e. trajectory T is a sequence of (x_i, y_i) positions at time step i, as illustrated in Figure 1. **Paths** are distinguished from trajectories by defining a path as a trajectory not parameterised by time.

To evaluate the performance of the tracker, metrics comparing two trajectories need to be devised. We have two trajectories T_A and T_B which represent the trajectory of a target from the tracker, and the ground truth trajectory - which is usually marked up manually from the footage. Metrics comparing the trajectories allow us to identify how *similar*, or how *different* they are.

2.2   Comparison of Trajectories

Consider two trajectories composed of 2D positions at a sequence of time steps. Let positions on trajectory T_A be (x_i, y_i), and on trajectory T_B be (p_i, q_i), for each time step i. The displacement between positions at time step i is given by $\mathbf{d}_i$:

$$\mathbf{d}_i = (p_i, q_i) - (x_i, y_i) = (p_i - x_i, q_i - y_i) \tag{3}$$

And the distances between the positions at time step i are given by d_i:

$$d_i = |\mathbf{d}_i| = \sqrt{(p_i - x_i)^2 + (q_i - y_i)^2} \tag{4}$$

Fig. 2. Comparison of displacement between two trajectories.

A metric commonly used for tracker evaluation is the mean of these distances [4,2]. We shall call this metric m_1.

$$m_1 = \mu(d_i) = \frac{1}{n} \sum_{i=1}^{n} d_i \tag{5}$$

m_1 gives the average distance between positions at each time step. Figure 2 shows two trajectories and identifies the distance between corresponding positions. The distribution of these distances is also of significance, as it shows how the distances between trajectories (tracker error) are spread, as illustrated in Figure 3, where a skewed distribution can be seen.

Other statistics provide quantitative information about the distribution. Here we identify the mean, median (expected to be lower than the mean, due to the

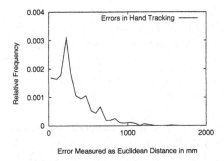

Fig. 3. Distribution of distances between positions.

contribution to the mean of the furthest outliers), standard deviation, minimum and maximum values as useful statistics for describing the data. Let us define $\mathcal{D}(T_A, T_B)$ to be the set of distances d_i between trajectory A and B. The above statistics can be applied to this set:

Mean $\mu(\ \mathcal{D}(T_A, T_B)\ ) = \frac{1}{n}\sum_{i=1}^{n} d_i$

Median $median(\ \mathcal{D}(T_A, T_B)\ ) = d_{\frac{n+1}{2}}$ if n odd,

$= \frac{1}{2}(d_{\frac{n}{2}} + d_{\frac{n}{2}+1})$ if n even

Standard deviation $\sigma(\ \mathcal{D}(T_A, T_B)\ ) = \sqrt{\frac{1}{n}\sum_{i=1}^{n}(d_i - \mu(d_i))^2}$

Minimum $min(\ \mathcal{D}(T_A, T_B)\ ) = $ the smallest d_i

Maximum $max(\ \mathcal{D}(T_A, T_B)\ ) = $ the largest d_i

$$(6)$$

2.3 Spatially Separated Trajectories

Some pairs of trajectories may be very similar, except for a constant difference in some spatial direction (Figure 4). Defining a metric which takes this into account may reveal a closer relationship between two trajectories.

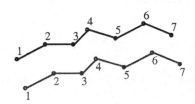

Fig. 4. Two spatially separated trajectories.

Given the two trajectories T_A and T_B, it is possible to calculate the optimal spatial translation $\hat{\mathbf{d}}$ (shift) of T_A towards T_B, for which m_1 is minimised. $\hat{\mathbf{d}}$ is the average displacement between the trajectories, and is calculated as:

$$\hat{\mathbf{d}} = \mu(\mathbf{d}_i) = \frac{1}{n} \sum_{i=1}^{n} \mathbf{d}_i \qquad (7)$$

Now we can define $\mathcal{D}(T_A + \hat{\mathbf{d}}, T_B)$ to be the set of distances between a translated trajectory T_A (by $\hat{\mathbf{d}}$) and T_B. The same statistics can be applied to this set, $\mathcal{D}(T_A + \hat{\mathbf{d}}, T_B)$, to describe the distances. $\mu(\mathcal{D}(T_A + \hat{\mathbf{d}}, T_B)) < \mu(\mathcal{D}(T_A, T_B))$ in all cases, except when the trajectories are already optimally spatially aligned.

When $\mu(\mathcal{D}(T_A + \hat{\mathbf{d}}, T_B))$ is significantly lower than $\mu(\mathcal{D}(T_A, T_B))$, it may highlight a tracking error of a consistent spatial difference between the true position of the target, and the tracked position.

2.4   Temporally Separated Trajectories

Some pairs of trajectories may be very similar, except for a constant time difference (Figure 5). Defining a metric which takes this into account may reveal a closer relationship between two trajectories.

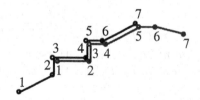

Fig. 5. Two temporally separated trajectories.

Given the two trajectories T_A and T_B, it is possible to calculate the optimal temporal translation j (shift) of T_A towards T_B, for which m_1 is minimised. When the time-shift j is positive $T_{A,i}$ is best paired with $T_{B,i+j}$, and when j is positive $T_{A,i+j}$ is best paired with $T_{B,i}$. Time-shift j is calculated as:

$$j = \arg \min_k \left(\frac{1}{n - |k|} \sum_{i=Q}^{R} |(p_{i+k}, q_{i+k}) - (x_i, y_i)| \right) \qquad (8)$$

if $k \geqslant 0$ then $Q = 0$ else $Q = -k$. $R = Q + n - |k|$.

Now we can define $\mathcal{D}(T_A, T_B, j)$ to be the set of distances between a temporally translated trajectory T_A or T_B, depending on j's sign. The same statistics as before can be applied to this set, $\mathcal{D}(T_A, T_B, j)$, to describe the distances.

$\mu(\ \mathcal{D}(T_A, T_B, j)\ ) < \mu(\ \mathcal{D}(T_A, T_B)\ )$ in all cases, except when the trajectories are already optimally temporally aligned.

When $\mu(\ \mathcal{D}(T_A, T_B, j)\ )$ is significantly lower than $\mu(\ \mathcal{D}(T_A, T_B)\ )$, it may highlight a tracking error of a consistent temporal difference between the true position of the target, and the tracked position. In practice j should be small; it may highlight a lag in the tracked position (Figure 5).

2.5   Spatio-Temporally Separated Trajectories

Combining the spatial and temporal alignment process identifies a fourth distance statistic. We define $\mathcal{D}(T_A + \hat{\mathbf{d}}', T_B, j)$ to be the set of distances between the spatially and temporally optimally aligned trajectories, where $\hat{\mathbf{d}}' = \hat{\mathbf{d}}(T_A, T_B, j)$ is the optimal spatial shift between the temporally shifted (by j time steps) trajectories.

The procedure for defining this set is similar to above; calculate the optimal j for which the mean distance between space (translation of $\hat{\mathbf{d}}'$) and time (time-shift of j) shifted positions is minimised, using an exhaustive search. Once j has been calculated, the set of distances $\mathcal{D}(T_A + \hat{\mathbf{d}}', T_B, j)$ can be formed, and the usual statistics can be calculated.

When the trajectories are spatio-temporally aligned, the mean value, $\mu(\ \mathcal{D}(T_A + \hat{\mathbf{d}}', T_B, j)\ )$ is less than or equal to the mean value of the three other sets of distances; when the trajectories are unaltered, spatially aligned, or temporally aligned.

2.6   Area between Trajectories

The area between two trajectories provides time independent information. The trajectories must be treated as paths whose direction of travel is known.

Given two paths A and B, the area between them is calculated by firstly calculating the set of crossing points where path A and path B intersect. These crossing points are then used to define a set of regions. If a path crosses itself *within* a region, then the loop created is discarded by deleting the edge points on the path between where the path crosses itself. This resolves the problem of calculating the area if a situation where a path crosses itself many times occurs, as illustrated in Figure 6. Now the area between the paths can be calculated as the summation of the areas of the separate regions. The area of each region is calculated by treating each region as an n-sided polygon defined by edge points (x_i, y_i) for $i = 1, \ldots, n$, where the first point is the intersection point, the next points follow those on path A, then the second crossover point, back along path B to the first point. i.e. the edge of the polygon is traced. Tracing the polygon, the area under each edge segment is calculated as a trapezoid, each of these is either added to or subtracted from the total, depending on its sign, which results from the calculation of $(x_{i+1} - x_i)(y_i + y_{i+1})/2$ as the area between the x-axis and the edge segment from (x_i, y_i) to (x_{i+1}, y_{i+1}). After re-arrangement

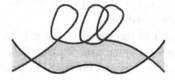

Fig. 6. Regions with self crossing trajectories. The shaded regions show the area calculated.

Equation 9 shows the area of such a region. (It does not matter which way the polygon is traced, since in our computation the modulus of the result is taken).

$$A_{region} = \left| \frac{1}{2} \left(\left(\sum_{i=1}^{n-1} x_{i+1}y_i \right) + x_1 y_n \right) - \left(\left(\sum_{i=1}^{n-1} x_1 y_{i+1} \right) + x_n y_1 \right) \right| \quad (9)$$

The areas of each of the regions added together gives the total area between the paths, and has dimensionality L^2 i.e. mm^2. To obtain a useful value for the area metric, the area calculated is normalised by the average length of the paths. This gives the 'area' metric on the same scale as the other distance statistics. It represents the average time independent distance (in mm) between the two trajectories, and is a **continuous average distance**, rather than the earlier discrete average distance.

3   Evaluation, Results, and Discussion

Performance evaluation is performed on two tracking systems; a sports player tracker, [4] and a vehicle tracker [3]. Figure 7 shows example footage used in each system. First, the variability between two hand marked up trajectories is discussed.

Fig. 7. Example footage used for tracking.

3.1   Comparison of Two Hand Marked up Trajectories

This section compares two independently hand marked up trajectories of the same soccer player during an attacking run (both marked up by the same person, by clicking on the screen using the mouse). There are small differences in the trajectories, and they cross each other many times. The results are shown in Table 1, and the trajectories are shown graphically in Figure 8 with the area between the two paths shaded, and dark lines connecting the positions on the trajectories at each time step. The second row of Table 1 identifies an improvement in the similarity of the two trajectories if a small spatial shift of $\hat{\mathbf{d}} = (-58, 74)$ in mm, is applied to the first trajectory. As expected in hand marked up data, the two trajectories are optimally aligned in time (time-shift $j = 0$).

Fig. 8. Two example hand marked up trajectories, showing the area between them, and the displacements between positions at each time step.

Table 1. Results of trajectory evaluation. All distances are in mm.

Metric	mean	median	min	max	s.d	'area'
$\mathcal{D}(T_A, T_B)$	134	115	0	444	89	56
$\mathcal{D}(T_A + (-55, 74), T_B)$	110	92	10	355	72	42
$\mathcal{D}(T_A, T_B, 0)$	134	115	0	444	89	56
$\mathcal{D}(T_A + (-55, 74), T_B, 0)$	110	92	11	355	72	42

3.2   Sports Player Tracker Example

This section compares a tracked trajectory, T_C, to a hand marked up trajectory T_B. The sports player tracker [4] identifies the ground plane position of the players, which is taken as the mid-point of the base of the bounding box around the player, and is generally where the players' feet make contact with

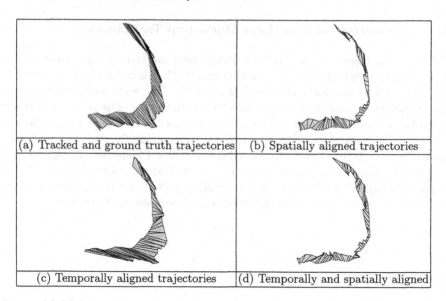

(a) Tracked and ground truth trajectories	(b) Spatially aligned trajectories
(c) Temporally aligned trajectories	(d) Temporally and spatially aligned

Fig. 9. (a)-(d) Example trajectories over 70 frames. Trajectory T_C from tracker compared to T_B - the hand marked up trajectory. The figures show the area between them, and the displacements between positions at each time step.

the floor. Figure 9 qualitatively illustrates the shifted trajectories, whilst Table 2 quantitatively highlights the systematic error present in this sequence.

If T_C is shifted by 500mm in the x-direction, and $600 - 700$mm in the y-direction, the differences between the trajectories fall significantly. This may be due to an invalid assumption that the position of the tracked players is the midpoint of the base of the bounding box around the player. This may be due to the player's shape in these frames, tracker error, or human mark up of the single point representing the player at each time step.

Table 2. Results of trajectory evaluation. All distances are in mm.

Metric	mean	median	min	max	s.d	'area'
$\mathcal{D}(T_C, T_B)$	890	859	393	1607	267	326
$\mathcal{D}(T_C + (510, -710), T_B)$	279	256	40	67	145	133
$\mathcal{D}(T_C, T_B, -9)$	803	785	311	1428	237	317
$\mathcal{D}(T_C + (551, -618), T_B, -2)$	263	230	52	673	129	138

3.3   Car Tracker Example

This section compares trajectories from a car tracker [3] with manually marked up ground truth positions. In this example, the evaluation is performed in image plane coordinates (using 352×288 resolution images), on a sequence of cars on an inner city bypass, a sample view is shown in Figure 7.

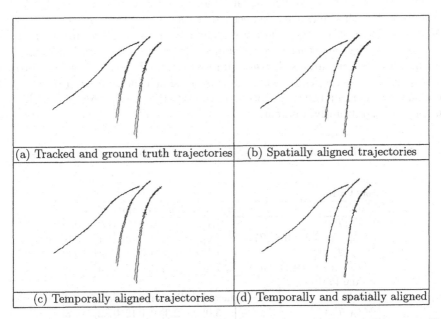

(a) Tracked and ground truth trajectories   (b) Spatially aligned trajectories

(c) Temporally aligned trajectories   (d) Temporally and spatially aligned

Fig. 10. (a)-(d) Three pairs of example trajectories over 200 frames. Trajectory T_A from tracker compared to T_B - the hand marked up trajectory, with the area between them shaded.

Trajectory comparison is performed on three trajectories of cars in the scene, each over 200 frames in length. Figure 10 displays these trajectories along with the ground truth, and Table 3 details the quantitative results, from which it can be seen that there is little systematic error in the system, with each car's centroid generally being accurate to between 1 and 3 pixels.

4   Summary and Conclusions

Quantitative evaluation of the performance of computer vision systems allows their comparison on benchmark datasets. It must be appreciated that algorithms can be evaluated in many ways, and we must not lose target of the aim of the evaluation. Here, a set of metrics for positional evaluation and comparison of trajectories has been presented. The specific aim has been to compare two trajectories. This is useful when evaluating the performance of a tracker, for quantifying the effects of algorithmic improvements. The spatio/temporally separated metrics give a useful measure for identifying the precision of a trajectory, once the systematic error is removed, which may be present due to a time lag, or constant spatial shift. There are many potential obvious uses for trajectory comparison in tracker evaluation, for example comparison of a tracker with Kalman Filtering and without [4] (clearly this affects any assumption of independence).

It is also important to consider how accurate we require a computer vision system to be (this may vary between detection of a target in the scene and precise location of a targets' features). Human mark up of ground truth data is also subjective, and there are differences between ground truth sets marked up by different individuals. If we require a system that is at least as good as a human, in this case, the tracked trajectories should be compared to how well humans can mark up the trajectories, and a statistical test performed to identify if they are significantly different.

Table 3. Results of trajectory evaluation. All distances are in pixel units.

Left Path

Metric	mean	median	min	max	s.d	'area'
$\mathcal{D}(T_A, T_B)$	1.7	1.3	0.1	7.1	1.3	0.6
$\mathcal{D}(T_A + (-0.2, -0.8), T_B)$	1.6	1.3	0.2	6.5	1.1	0.5
$\mathcal{D}(T_A, T_B, 1)$	1.5	1.3	0.1	5.1	0.8	0.6
$\mathcal{D}(T_A + (0.8, -0.1), T_B, 1)$	1.3	1.2	0.1	5.2	0.8	0.5

Middle Path

Metric	mean	median	min	max	s.d	'area'
$\mathcal{D}(T_A, T_B)$	3.0	2.3	0.4	12.4	2.2	1.8
$\mathcal{D}(T_A + (1.9, -0.9), T_B)$	2.3	1.9	0.1	11.2	2.0	0.9
$\mathcal{D}(T_A, T_B, 1)$	2.9	2.3	0.5	8.7	1.4	1.8
$\mathcal{D}(T_A + (3.1, 1.8), T_B, 3)$	1.3	1.3	0.1	3.6	0.7	0.6

Right Path

Metric	mean	median	min	max	s.d	'area'
$\mathcal{D}(T_A, T_B)$	3.2	2.9	0.3	9.7	1.8	2.1
$\mathcal{D}(T_A + (2.3, -0.2), T_B)$	2.5	2.3	0.1	8.6	1.4	1.2
$\mathcal{D}(T_A, T_B, 0)$	3.2	2.3	0.3	9.7	1.8	2.1
$\mathcal{D}(T_A + (2.9, 2.0), T_B, 2)$	1.7	1.6	0.1	6.0	0.9	1.0

References

1. T. J. Ellis. Performance metrics and methods for tracking in surveillance. In *3rd IEEE Workshop on Performance Evaluation of Tracking and Surveillance*, Copenhagen, Denmark, 2002.
2. M. Harville. Stereo person tracking with adaptive plan-view statistical templates. In *Proc. ECCV Workshop on Statistical Methods in Video Processing*, pages 67–72, Copenhagen, Denmark, 2002.

3. D. R. Magee. Tracking multiple vehicles using foreground, background and motion models. In *Proc. ECCV Workshop on Statistical Methods in Video Processing*, pages 7–12, Copenhagen, Denmark, 2002.
4. C. J. Needham and R. D. Boyle. Tracking multiple sports players through occlusion, congestion and scale. In *Proc. British Machine Vision Conference*, pages 93–102, Manchester, UK, 2001.
5. IEEE Workshop on Performance Evaluation of Tracking and Surveillance. `http://visualsurveillance.org/PETS2000` Last accessed: 18/10/02.
6. H. Sakoe and S. Chiba. Dynamic Programming optimization for spoken word recognition. *IEEE Trans. Acoustics, Speech and Signal Processing*, 26(1):43–49, 1978.

On the Application of the Concept of Dependability for Design and Analysis of Vision Systems

Christof Eberst[1] and Thomas Herbig[2]

[1] Profactor Produktionsforschungs GmbH, Steyr, Austria
Christof.Eberst@profactor.at
[2] Ingenieurbüro Herbig, Munich,Germany
IbHerbig@aol.com

Abstract. Dependability is the property of a computer system such that reliance can justifiably be placed on the service it delivers[28]. In safety- and mission-critical systems such as in space or avionics the concept of dependability has become imperative for the specification, design and assessment. Dependability evaluation techniques allow to estimate the availability and reliability of highly complex systems prior to their implementation. Thus, it supports rapid development by reducing late corrections of design and implementation.

This paper aims to introduce the dependable system theory for vision-systems and discusses its applicability and limitations. Models are provided for analyzing the structural robustness of computer vision systems and demonstrated in the exemplary analysis of a voting-based multi-cue tracking-system.

1 Motivation

Principle ideas of dependable systems, such as redundancy, have been applied extensively in multi-cue/-view vision systems. Even though that dependability theory could support composite evaluation, modular design, and a-priori performance assessment and therfore rapid development expecially of multi-cue vision systems, it has only been applied very limited in design and analysis. One reason might be that proven approaches in "dependability"-literatur are not instantaneously applicable to vision systems, since highly reliable modules, very structured systems, and uncoupled faults are assumed. The main topic of the presented paper is therefore to introduce the dependability concepts for the analysis and design of vision systems and to discuss their applicability. The remaining sections present: State of art(Sec.2), usage of appropriate aspects of dependabiltiy for reliability modeling of an exemplary vision system (Sec.3 and Sec.4), model-evaluation and effects of different modelling accuracy (Sec.5), and the conclusion (Sec.6). The paper ignores control aspects, precision and the aspect of robustness by redundancy vs. tracking-rate[1].

---

[1] A study of processing-time and robustness is presented in [25]

J.L. Crowley et al. (Eds.): ICVS 2003, LNCS 2626, pp. 290–303, 2003.
© Springer-Verlag Berlin Heidelberg 2003

2 Related Work

2.1 Robust Vision: Systems, Design, and Evaluation

Besides correctness, effectiveness, and stability of employed vision algorithms, such as the robust and selective generation and verification of hypotheses [19, 16], the promotion of uncertainties [26], and mathematical stability, redundancy is a major key to robust vision [50,24,39,46,2]. Redundancy involved in multi-cue [50,24,39] multi-cue/-sensor/-view [2,50] approaches allows to overcome missed detection or failure of complete modules in vision, such as in tracking [24,39,46] (see Fig. 1 for a typical multi-cue tracking system) or recognition [50,44] and is therefore a major key for robust vision systems. However, the usage and evaluation of advanced vision system structures (e.g. including redundancy) on one hand, and the analysis and forecast of their effects/robustness on the other hand are unbalanced: While experimental [14,9, 45], analytical [37,40], or combined [4] evaluation of vision-algorithms form a fundamental step for the selection of algorithms, the actual design-phase of vision

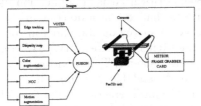

system structures is not represented according to its importance. Especially modularized approaches which employ composite evaluation seem to lack in computer vision (see also [37]). Vision-system designers only find examples for accurate evaluation of very restricted structures [37], or coarse guidelines for design of multi-cue systems, employing simple reliability analysis for *k-out-of-n*/voting systems [39].

Fig. 1. Exempl. multi-cue tracking system from [24]. By courtesy of D. Kragic.

2.2 Dependable Computing Systems

In this section, a survey of the comprehensiveness of dependable computing systems and technical terminology is presented. We will adopt a generic concept of dependability that integrates **impairments, means,** and **attributes** [27].

Impairments are *faults, errors* and *failures*. In [28], faults and failures are classified and the evolution and manifestation mechanisms are summarized.

The dependability of a HW/SW system can be improved by different **means:** Fault-prevention, fault removal, fault tolerance (FT), and fault forecasting. *Fault prevention* must accompany the design of complex systems to achieve the goal of dependability. Formal methods permit to proof the correctness of system specifications during the initial design phase [43]. *Fault removal* covers the steps verification, diagnosis, and correction. Verification activities ensure that a specified function was implemented correctly. Static verification utilizes inspection and walkthrough [34], data flow analysis [35], complexity analysis [31] or proof-of-correctness [10]. Dynamic verification can take place by symbolic execution [52] or through structural, functional, and fault-based testing[48][33]. *FT strategies* *and mechanisms* enable a system to operate in the presence of a given number of faults. FT is realized through redundancy in HW[36], SW[5], information[32], or computations[15] and is carried out by error processing and fault treatment[1].

Fault forecasting is achieved by performing an evaluation of the system behavior with respect to fault incidence. For this measure essential **attributes** are estimated. Physical fault injection techniques can be used to evaluate the error detection coverage of FT algorithms/mechanisms [3] on HW/SW target architectures. Qualitative evaluation relates to security- and safety-assessment. In [30] an introduction to safety criteria, hazard analysis, and risk analysis is given. Quantitative attributes like reliability and availability are defined as measures of dependability. Reliability modeling and analysis during the architectural design of a system helps to meet the requirements [42].

2.3   Introduction on Dependability in Vision and Robotics

Robotic systems are used increasingly in safety critical fields of application like space, nuclear, and surgery or in environments that are hazardous or inaccessible. Therefor dependability is imperative. For a survey on standards in robot reliability and fault-tolerance see [7]. Vision systems with their HW/SW components are used as sensor subsystems in robotic systems. Thus a vision system can not guarantee the qualitative attributes of dependability from itself.

In order to prevent accidental or intentional human interaction faults that obstruct the correct system operation security policy services must be integrated independently of the vision system. It is therefore not further regarded here.

Also there are restrictions regarding the qualitative attribute safety. The safety-assessment can be executed only for the complete system reviewing the components, assemblies, and subsystems by means of the Failure Mode, Effects, and Criticality Analysis (FMECA) [22]. Failure rates are then ascribed to each component/subsystem level failure mode and the totals for each of the overall modes can be calculated. For an integrated vision module an failure rate has to be determined. A failure such as a failed detection, tracking, and recognition or false alarm is mostly caused by design faults, i.e. not all characteristically complex environmental conditions can be considered. Physical faults (hardware) are in contrast of subordinated importance. Due to this circumstances the means for dependability (computing systems) cannot be applied without reservation. Since the implemented algorithms embodies the bottleneck, fault tolerance strategies and mechanisms on vision module level [17] are only suitable for long term operation in environments that provide suitable sensing conditions, outherwise the fault tolerance must be implemented through multi-sensor systems [49,13] and fault-tolerant control units which executes the essential voting algorithms [38]. On the foundation of redundant information the error detection, error diagnosis, and fault treatment can be performed [47]. In contrast, the information redundancy available within multi-cue systems does not serve for fault tolerance, rather it is needed for a reliable function.

However, the remaining means for dependability provide procedures to increase the reliability of a vision system substantially: Fault prevention, fault removal, and fault forecasting. The application of reliability modeling, analysis and prediction procedures considering the dependence of environmental influences is of crucial importance. The application of parts-count models, combinatorial reliability block diagrams and Markov models (for repairable fault tolerant systems) is shown in [42]. The adaptation of notions and techniques from fuzzy logic to fault trees and Markov models admits the use of approximate failure rates during the design process of robot system [LeWaCa96].

3   Modeling Vision Systems

In this section, we present the application of dependability concepts for an exemplary voting-based multi-cue tracking-system.

3.1   Exemplary Multi-cue System

The models we provide are applicable to rather general multi-cue systems. However, to allow for a feasible and in detailed analysis, we will discuss one exemplary (simplified!) multi-cue tracking-system, with uneven number of cues (3 and 5).This system reflects the principle structure of many known tracking systems (see also Fig. 1). A cue[2] is considered to operate improperly if its output, i.e. its pose estimate, does not correspond to the presented input within the limits that are tolerable for successful tracking. The system combines the information from all cues by a weighted, inexact voting in a totally ordered (metric) space. The system is reinitializing itself, i.e. setting non coinciding cues to the trusted value, if the vote includes a predefined minimum number of consistent cues. It must be noted, that the criteria/strategies for considering a cue operating correctly/incorrectly, for voting, or for re-initialization, can easily be exchanged in the model. We first analyze the principle structure of the system with simple models from reliability modeling. The system is interpreted as a $k\text{-}out\text{-}of\text{-}n$ system which is operational if at least k cues provide the correct result.

3.2   Coarse Models

For the practical applications[3] the HW failures can be neglected compared to failures of vision-modules. **Combinatorial models** of the parallel multi-cue system in which the probability for proper system operation P_{sys} is expressed by the probabilities of the individual units P_i according to a $k\text{-}out\text{-}of\text{-}n$ system

$$P_{sys} = P_{mc} * P_{voting} \; ; P_{mc} = \sum_{m=k}^{n} \binom{n}{m} P^m * (1 - P)^{(n-m)} \qquad (1)$$

---

[2] We use the expression cue also for the related vision-module that processes the information

[3] Except industrial image processing applications

for identical probability ratings $(P_1 = P_2 = .. = P_n)$[4] allow for a identification of dependability bottlenecks, especially for more complex systems, but is not applicable due to lower accuracy and problems to model the entire process in a combinatoric fashion, such as repair/recovery. **Markov-models** are proper models for repairable, memoryless behaviors. Its two basic elements are the state and the state transition. The states represent all distinguishable states in which the system can be at any given point in time. For reliability models each state represents a combination of faulty and fault-free system units. The state transitions are characterized by probabilities which represent occurred failures or the process of repair/recovery. Markov-models are memory-less, i.e. the probabilities depend only on the direct predecessor state, independent of the time and history. An exponentially distributed life- and downtime meet this condition. With a constant failure/recovery rate λ/μ the probability for a state transition within the time period Δt is approximated through $\lambda * \Delta t$ respectively $\mu * \Delta t$. The probability of being in any given state s at time t depends on the probability that the system was in a state from which it could transit to state s and its probability. Extracting a state transition matrix from the Markov chain for discrete time-steps ($t = n * \Delta T$; ΔT is 1/frame-rate) leads to a compact eq. 2.

$$P(n+1) - P(n) = (\Lambda + M) * P(n) \qquad (2)$$

Λ is the state transition matrix due to failing cues, M specifies the transition matrix due to spontaneous recovery of faulty cues. The later respects the fact that an incorrect cue can track the correct object again (by random), if the object did not leave the observed scene, or re-appears. Distinguishing only between $n + 1$ states referring to the number (0..n) of incorrect cues does not allow for precise modeling of the states or the

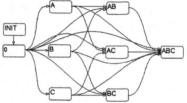

Fig. 2. Fine Markov model. In state AB cue A and B provide incorrect estimations.

voting process, since it ignores the high diversity of the individual cues in computer vision. For a system with heterogenous cues, the states of individual cue must be modeled. The state vector $x(n)$ of the system determines the probability of the system being in state x_s with combined cue-failures (see Fig. 2, for better readability, only the λ-transitions are plotted).

4   Advanced Model

The latter basic approaches do not consider: the optional implementation of re-initialization, failures and failure-rates which are dependent on different environmental conditions, possible correlation of failure-rates, the specific implementation of the voting, such as static and adaptive weighting, the imperfect identification of the correct and faulty cues. The advanced model deals with these topics.

---

[4] For the general case see [18].

4.1   Overview and Extensions

In this section we describe an analytic representation of the probability for a correct tracking result $R(n)$ (eq.4) as a function of failure-rates λ of the single cues (eq.3). The actual, situation-dependent failure-probabilities of the cues are expressed in matrix Λ. From that probability we derive the probability $R(n)$ for a correct vote result over time which is a measure for the reliability. v describes the probability of a correct vote for each state (with the probability x to be in that state) of the multi-cue system. $x_r(n)$ is the probability for each state of the system after reinitialization (eq.5). RI specifies the probability for transitions between the states due to correct/incorrect reinitialization. For better readability, actual probabilities such as $P(R(n)), P(R(n)|U_i), P(x)$ are described as $R(n), (R(n)|U_i), x$.

$$x(n+1) - x(n) = (\Lambda + M) * x(n) \qquad (3)$$
$$R(n) = v * x(n) \qquad (4)$$
$$x_r(n) = RI * x(n) \qquad (5)$$

Extension: The following extensions are modeled:

1. dependencies on scene/environmental conditions (see sec. 4.2 and 4.3),
2. a detailed model of voting (see sec. 4.4),
3. a detailed model of re-initialization (see sec. 4.5).

4.2   Scene/Environmental Conditions

Comparing the performance of vision systems under very controlled conditions (e.g. industrial vision systems) with general cases, it is obvious that scene and environmental conditions must be explicitly considered. First, critical conditions must be identified, such as defocussation, occlusion, or the presence of similar objects. Then the likelihood of their appearance (U_1, U_2, U_3 and $NONE$ (with index $-$)[5]) must be measured or estimated. Assuming that the conditions appear independently, the probability of their combined occurrences $P(U)$ is $U = (U_1 U_2 U_3, U_1 U_2, ., U_3, -)^T, DIM(U) = 8$.

Modeled are the effects of the conditions on the following aspects:

1. The failure rates (see sec. 4.3).
2. The uniform/non-uniform distribution of incorrect cues' output (sec. 4.4).
3. The confidence of the cues (see sec. 4.4).

In order to break down resulting correlations of failures – a requirement of Markov-modeling – Λ, v, RI, are modeled dependent on the (combined) occurrence of these dominant conditions U. The total probability $R(n)$ is then combined from the conditioned probabilities: $R(n) = \sum_{i=1}^{i=DIM(U)}(P(U_i) * (R(n)|U_i))$. While the conditions U_i are non-overlapping, the assumption that all (environmental) conditions are completely independent does not hold. Thus, $R(n)$ is an approximation. However, equation 6 conserves the dominant dependencies exemplary for $R(n)$.

$$R(n+1) = \sum_{i=1}^{i=DIM(U)} (v(U_i) * (\Lambda(U_i) + M(U_i)) * x(n) + x(n)) * P(U_i) \qquad (6)$$

---

[5] Simulation cost is exponential to the number of conditions

In equation 6 continous changes of environmental/scene conditions are considered. The conditioned probabilities are accumulated to the total probability after each step (n). In opposite, equation 7 considers the second extreme occurrence pattern, that is static conditions for all N sensor readings of one experiment. The system performance will be bounded by these two cases for most occurrences of conditions.

$$R(N) = \sum_{i=1}^{i=DIM(U)} (P(U_i) * (R(N)|U_i)) \tag{7}$$

4.3 Λ - M - Model of Cues

In order to construct the accurate failure-transition matrix $\Lambda = \Lambda(U)$, we approximate λ_j, the failure-rate of the cue $j, (j \in A, B, C)$, by its (measured or estimated) inverse MTBF (mean-time between failure, in frames) for each separate condition U_i, $i(i \in 1, 2, 3)$. We hereby assume that the dominant dependencies among failure-rates of different cues can be traced back on a correlation over scene/environmental conditions.

Then, the failure rate λ_j for a constellation of conditions U is modeled as an independent, serial combinatoric system, such as: $\lambda_j(U_iU_l) = 1 - \bar{\lambda}_j(U_i) * \bar{\lambda}_j(U_l)$ (with $\bar{\lambda} = 1 - \lambda$).

It is imperative **not** to derive the "average" failure-rate $\lambda = (\lambda_a(U), \lambda_b(U), \lambda_c(U))^T$ by multiplying the distribution $\lambda(U)$ with the combined occurrence of the environmental conditions $(U))^6$ prior to the voting for defining the Λ matrix, as presented in eq. 8, since it would hide the common dependency of the failure-rate of the two or more cues on the occurrence of one condition.

$$R(n+1) = V * \sum_{i=1}^{i=8} (\Lambda(U_i) + \mu(U_i) * P(U_i)) * x(n) + X(n) \tag{8}$$

The spontaneous recovery of a faulty cue is specified by the M-matrix, similarly to Λ. In difference to most applications in dependability theory, which consider limited resources for repairing multiple faulty modules, e.g. due to limited maintenance capacities, proper models for tracking must focus on restricted time for spontaneous recovery: The object must be still in the visual field. This implies that the object has been tracked successfully in one of the last l sensor readings, with l specified by the size of the observed area and the speed of the tracked object in image space. Thus, the matrix M is a function of the result of tracking $M(n) = M(R(n-1), R(n-2), .., R(n-l))$.

4.4   Cue-State to Voting Model – Stability

This model describes the possible implementations of the voting. $R(n) = v * x(n)$ with $v = v(U)$ presents the probability of a correct vote according to the

---

[6] of separate environmental conditions $(U_1, U_2, U_3)^T$

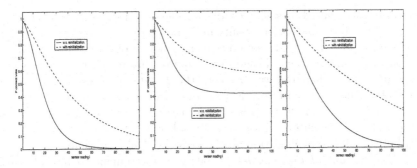

Fig. 3. Plausibility for a correct vote over time, without spontaneous recovery, with permanent recovery, with recovery restricted on 3 frames after loosing the target (left to right).

probability $v = [v_{ABC}, v_{BC}, ...v_A, v_0]^T$ of obtaining a correct vote for a specific state s and its probability x_s: v_s is the probability of obtaining a correct vote when the actual state of the system is s. v represents the implemented voting strategy, including potential adaptive weighting. We calculate the probability v for each specific state of the multi-cue system, by multiplying the probability for misinterpreting a specific state and a specific distribution/grouping of the incorrect values with the probability of the latter. We model this probability for correct identification of the correct cues as the probability that the grouped correct cues have the greater adapted weight than the incorrect ones, separate ones and/or coinciding and grouped ones. The probability that several subgroups of the incorrect cues' output will be grouped is non-zero and must be considered!

Let $v(j)$ $(\bar{v}(j) = 1 - v(j))$ be the probability for obtaining an correct (incorrect) result $R(n)$ at time-step n for the cue-failure state j, i.e. vote correctly (incorrectly).(With $j, k, l \in ABC \land j \neq k \neq l$).

One simple model for the case $\bar{v}(j)$ is that the weight of the faulty cue j is higher than the weight of the two correct cues k and l. $\bar{v}(jk)$ would then be the probability that the state jk leads to an incorrect vote, i.e. that the weight of one of the cues j and k, or the weight of randomly coinciding cues j and k, is higher than the weight of the correct cue l (see equation **??**).

$\bar{v}(jkl)$ is set to 1: If all cues provide incorrect results, the voting will also lead to an incorrect result with very high likelihood. $\bar{v}(0)$ is set to 0, i.e. if all cues provide the correct result, the voting will provide the correct result (thus $v(0) = 1$). Potential errors in the voting algorithm itself are handled as an sequential "error-source" for all cases.

The correct identification of correct cues is complicated by the following topics on which special attention is spent for accurate modeling:

Non-uniform distribution of the output: For several environmental conditions, such as for the presence of one ore more similar objects in the observed area, the output of incorrect cues, can not be assumed distributed uniformly. The output of a faulty cue is focused on the equivalent image region if the failure was caused/dominated by such a condition. The obvious modeling of such a system with the cue-states correct, faulty uniform distribution, faulty non-uniform-distribution (for each condensation-point), is not applicable, since changes in the considered environmental conditions requires changes in the structure of the cue-state model. Therefore we stay with the 2 states per cue (correct, wrong) and subsequently calculate for each incorrect cue j the probability of returning a uniformly/non-uniformly distributed output. Simplified, this is a function of the $\lambda_j(U_i)$ of the subset of the actual conditions i that cause a non-uniform distribution (and its strength) and $\lambda_j(U_i)$ of all actual conditions.

Self-evaluation of the modules: A powerful instrument to improve voting is the usage of weights that are adapted according to the confidence-values of each module. However, modeling suffers from incorrect confidence values i.e. a faulty cue considers itself as trustworthy while a correct one does not. As an approximation of the possible widely differing adaptations, we model the *incorrect* decrease/increase of the weight of a correct/incorrect cue in addition to its *correct* increase/decrease. Both with probabilities that depend on the conditions, and in a manner that preserves possible correlations between the non-uniform distribution and the erroneous confidence value.

4.5   Reinitialization

To improve the robustness of multi-cue systems, cues whose outputs are identified to be incorrect are reseted/re-initialized by an "external expert", e.g. the voter. Prior to the next sensor-reading, the search windows of these cues are set according to the merged result of the cues that were considered correct. The reliable identification of the correct cues is however critical. In case of a correct identification, the state $x(n)$ is set to $x(0)$, resembling the repair of all faulty system-components in dependability-theory with duration 0. In case of the an incorrect identification, $x(n)$ is set to state ABC, i.e. all cues operate incorrect. Since these aspects resemble the stability problem in voting, its modeling resembles sec. 4.4. However since a state-transition from $x(n)$ to $x_r(n)$ is described, it is expressed in matrix-form $x_r(n) = RI * x(n)$

5   Validation and Applicability

5.1   Model Properties and Validation

This section compares the model with and without consideration of environmentally induced effects. Evaluation is done as Matlab simulation. In an extreme coarse check for plausibility, effects of correlated failure rates, non-uniform distribution of incorrect outputs, and incorrect confidence values, will be studied qualitatively in order to justify the usage of the advanced model.

Cue-state to voting model:

The identification of the (in)correctly operating cues by weighted voting is strongest impaired by the incorrect confidence values and the non-uniform distribution of incorrect outputs. Fig. 4 shows the probability for a correct vote at

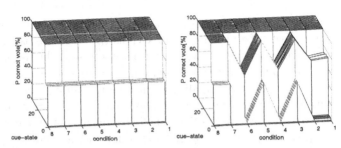

Fig. 4. Probability [%] for a correct vote (z-axis) with adaptive weights for the states of the 2^5 cues (y-axis) and 8 combined conditions (x-axis). *Left/right*: Without/with modeling of imperfect confidence estimation and non-uniform distribution of wrong outputs.

each cue-state and environmental/scene condition. The *left/right* plot represents the case that these effects are *ignored / modeled* for one separate condition only. The right plot demonstrates qualitatively correctly that the impairment is stronger if this condition appears separately (Fig.5: condition 6) than in combination with other impairing conditions (4,2,1).

Spontaneous Recovery: The effect of spontaneous recovery on the performance over time, restricted on l sensor-readings after loosing the tracked object (case temp. restricted), is presented in Fig. 5, left image couple. As to expect, the impact is bounded by no recovery and by permanent recovery that ignores that the object can leave the image region. Fig. 5 (right 2 plots) show the effect

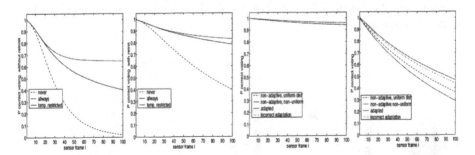

Fig. 5. Performance over sensor readings ($P_{tracking}$). *Left image couple*: Spontaneous recovery *with/without* reinitialization (*inner/outer plot*). *Right image couple*: Performance for differently detailed models, *with/without* consideration of correlations (*outer/inner*).

of considering adapted weighting and non-uniform distribution of incorrect outputs and confidence values. The inner/outer image shows the "reliability" over time for ignored/considered failure correlations.

5.2   Application in System Design

The model extensions allow to apply reliability modeling to vision systems. Various aspects of a vision system, such as the structure, the required cue quantity and quality, voting strategies and parameters can be inspected.

Parameter selection: Simulation make the influence of parameters and/or their limits on the overall performance predictable and allows tuning starting with promising values. E.g. the influence of weight-selection on the state-specific and overall vote-correctness (Fig.6 left image-couple) can be visualized.

Reliability forecasting: Reliability forecasting allows to estimate the system performance based on estimated (or measured) failure rates of single cues. In the following simulation, 3 design alternatives of vision systems are compared (only cues D and E are varied):

1. Case "normal, high correlation": $\phi\lambda_d = 0.0644, \phi\lambda_e = 0.08161, r_{ad} = 0.9834$, $r_{ae} = 0.9814$ is the the original system (dotted).
2. Case "good, high correlation" is the design alternative with cues that posses a smaller average failure-rate: $\phi\lambda_d = 0.0344, \phi\lambda_e = 0.0516, r_{ad} = 0.9741, r_{ae} = 0.9497$ $\phi\lambda_i,\phi\lambda_i$ but similar correlation r_{ij} between λ_i, λ_j,
3. Case "bad, low correlation": $\phi\lambda_d = 0.0441, \phi\lambda_e = 0.2686, r_{ad} = -0.0884, r_{ae} = -0.7959$ is a design alternative with cues selected according to smaller correlation values r_{ij} but similar average failure rates $\phi\lambda_i,\phi\lambda_j$ indicates that the extended model.

For comparison: $\phi\lambda_a = 0.0644, \phi\lambda_b = 0.0558, r_{ab} = 0.9832$. A comparison of the two right images show that disregarding the correlation of cue-failure rate over environmental conditions let different design alternatives appear better (see Fig. 6, right image-couple).

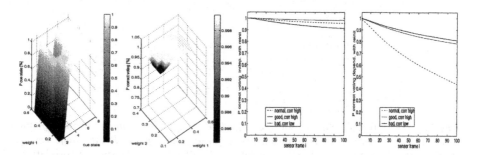

Fig. 6. *Left couple:* State-specific (*outer*) and overall (*inner plot*) probability of a correct vote for weights w(1), w(2), (w(3)=1.0-w(1)-w(2)). *Right couple:* Performance forecast over 100 frames for different failure rates and correlations. Model with/without (*outer/inner plot*) consideration of dependencies.

6   Conclusion and Future Work

In the paper we introduced the concept of dependability and motivated the application of reliability modeling, analysis, and prediction procedures for a simplified exemplary multi-cue tracking system. An extended model, which does consider common properties of vision systems, such as stability, self-evaluation and dependencies of failure-rates and the impact of environmental condition was developed. The model has been tested in simulation so far. A very powerful tool for rapid design of vision systems, that allows assessment in detail would be available – in case it proves in real experiments, that prediction from simulation coincides with real system behavior.

References

1. T. Anderson and P. A. Lee. *Fault Tolerance – Principles and Practice*. Prentice Hall, 1981.
2. K. Arbter, J. Langwald, G. Hirzinger, G. Q. Wei, and P. Wunsch. Proven Techniques for Robust Visual Servo Control. In *IEEE Int. Conf. on Robotics and Automation (ICRA'98) Workshop on Robust Vision for Vision-Based Control of Motion*, May 1998.
3. J. Arlat, Y. Crouzet, P. Folkesson, J. Karlsson, and G. Leber. Integration and Comparison of Three Physical Fault Injection Techniques. In *Predictably Dependable Computing Systems, Basic Research Series*. Springer Verlag, 199.
4. J. P. Baretto, P. Peixoto, and J. Batista ans H. Araujo. Evaluation of the Robustness of Visual Behaviors through Performance Characterization. In *IEEE Int. Conf. on Robotics and Automation (ICRA'98) Workshop on Robust Vision for Vision-Based Control of Motion*, May 1998.
5. A. Bondavalli, F. D. Giandomenico, and J. Xu. A Cost-Effective and Flexible Scheme for Software Fault Tolerance. *Journal of Computer Systems Science and Engineering*, 8(4): 234–244, 1993.
6. W. C. Carter. A time for reflection. In *Proc. 12th IEEE Int. Symp. on Fault Tolerant Computing (FTCS-12)*, pages 9–1 – 9–15. Springer Verlag, January 1982.
7. R. Cavallaro and I. D. Walker. A Survey of NASA and Military Standards on Fault Tolerance and Reliability Applied to Robotics. In *Proc. AIAA/NASA Conference on Intelligent Robots in Field, Factory, Service, and Space*, pages 282–286, Mar 1994.
8. S. C. Cheung and J. Kramer. An integrated method for effective behaviour analysis of distributed systems. In *Proc. 16th Int. Conf. on Software engineering*, pages 309–, 1994.
9. A. Cozzi, B. Crespi, F. Valentinotti, and F. Wörgötter. Perfromance of Phase-Based Algorithms for Disparity Estimation. In *IAPR Machine Vision and Applications*, 1997.
10. D. Craigen. FM 89: Assessment of Formal Methods For Trustworthy Computer Systems. In *Proc. 12'th Int. Conf. on Software Engineering*, pages 233–235, 1990.
11. B. Curtis, H. Krasner, and N. Iscoe. "A field study of the software design process for large systems. *Commun. ACM*, 31(11):1268–1287, 1988.
12. A. J.van de Goor and C. A.Verruijt. An overview of deterministic functional RAM chip testing. *ACM Comput. Survey*, 22, 1990.

13. H. F. Durrant-Whyte. Sensor Models and Multisensor Integration . *Int. Journal of Robotics Research*, Vol. 7 No. 6:97–113, 1988.
14. D. W. Eggert, A. Lorusso, and R. B. Fisher. Estimating 3D Rigid Body Transformations: a Comparision of four Major Algorithms. In *IAPR Machine Vision and Appli.*, 1997.
15. G. Färber and F. Demmelmeier. Taskspecific assignment of redundancy in the fault-tolerant multicomputer system future. In D. R. Wilson et al, editor, *Micro-Computers: Developments in industry, business and education. Prepr. from the 9th EUROMICRO Sympos*, pages 245–255. Euromicro, North Holland Publishing Company, 1983.
16. O. D. Faugeras and M. Hebert. The Representation, Recognition, and Locating of 3-d objects. *Int. J. Robotics Research*, 5(3):27–54, 1986.
17. J. A. Fayman, E. Rivlin, and D. Mosse. Real-Time Active Vision with Fault Tolerance. In *Int. Conf. on Pattern Recognition*, 1996.
18. K.W: Gaede. *Zuverlaessigkeit, Mathematische Modelle.* Carl Hanser Verlag, Muenchen, Wien, 1977.
19. W. Eric L. Grimson and T. Lozano-Perez. Localizing Overlapping Parts by Searching the Interpretation Tree. *IEEE Trans. on Pattern Analysis and Machine Intelligence*, 9(4):469–482, July 1987.
20. D.L. Hamilton, J.K. Bennett, and I.D. Walker. Parallel fault-tolerant robot contro. In *Proc. 1992 SPIE Conf. on Cooperative Intelligent Robotics in Space III*, pages 251–261. SPIE, Nov. 1992.
21. J. Herbsleb, A. Carleton, J. Rozum, J. Siegel, and D. Zubrow. Benefits of CMM-Based Software Process Improvement: Initial Results. Technical Report CMU/SEI-94-TR-013, Carnegie Mellon, 1994.
22. IEEE. *Institute of Electrical and Electronics Engineers, ANSI/IEEE-Std-352, IEEE Guide for General Principles of Reliability Analysis of Nuclear Power Generating Station Protecting Systems.* IEEE, 1975.
23. H. Kopetz, A. Damm, C. Koza, M. Mulazzani, W. Schwabl, C. Senft, and R. Zailinger. Distributed Fault-Tolerant Real-Time Systems: The Mars Approach. *IEEE Micro*, 9(1):25–40, 1989.
24. D. Kragic and H. I. Christensen. Integration of Visual Cues for Active Tracking of an End-Effector. In *Proc. IEEE/RSJ Int. Conf. on Intelligent Robots and Systems (IROS)*, pages –, 1999.
25. P. Krautgartner and M. Vincze. Optimal Image processing Architecture for Active Vision Systems. In *Proc. 1st International Conf. on Computer Vision Systems (ICVS'99)*, pages 331–343, January 1999.
26. S. Lanser and T. Lengauer. On the Selection of Candidates for Point and Line Correspondences. In *International Symposium on Computer Vision*, pages 157–162. IEEE Computer Society Press, 1995.
27. J.-C. Laprie. Dependability: Basic Concepts and Terminologie in English, French, German, Italian and Japanese. In J.-C. Laprie, editor, *Dependable Computing and Fault Tolerance,5.*Springer Verlag Vienna, Austria, 1992.
28. J.-C. Laprie. Dependability -Its Attributes, Impairments and Means. In *Predictably Dependable Computing Systems, Basic Research Series*. Springer Verlag Vienna, Austria, 1995.
29. M. I. Leuschen, I. D. Walker, and J. R. Cavallaro. Robot Reliability Using Fuzzy Fault Trees and Markov ModelsThrough Markov Fuzzy Models.
30. N. G. Leveson. *Safeware: System Safety and Computers.* Addison-Wesley, 1995.
31. T. J. McCabe and C. W. Butler. Design Complexity Measurement and Testing. *Commun. ACM*, 32(12):1415–1425, 1989.

32. M. Misra and I. Mitrani. Analysis of Data Replication with Two Levels of Consistency. In *Proc. of the 2nd Int. Comp. Perform. and Dependability Symp. (IPDS 96)*. IEEE, 1996.
33. L.J. Morell. A Theory of Fault-Based Testing. *IEEE Trans. on Software Engineering*, 16(8):844–857, 1990.
34. G. J. Myers. *The Art of Software Testing*. John Wiley and Sons, 1979.
35. G. Naumovich, G. S. Avrunin, L. A. Clarke, and L. J. Osterweil. Applying Static Analysis to Software Architectures. In *Proceedings of the 6th Europ. Conf. held jointly with the 5th ACM SIGSOFT Symp. on Software engineering*, pages 77–93, 1997.
36. Victor P. Nelson. Fault-Tolerant Computing: Fundamental Concepts. *IEEE Computer*, 23(7):19–25, 1990.
37. N. Thacker P. Courtney and A. F. Clark. Algorithmic Modelling for Performance Evaluation. In *IAPR Machine Vision and Applications*, 1997.
38. Behrooz Parhami. Voting algorithms. *IEEE Transactions on Reliability*, 43(4):617–629, December 1994.
39. P. Pirjanian and H. I. Christensen. Improving Task Reliability by Fusion of Redundant Homogeneous Modules Using Voting Schemes. In *Proc. IEEE Int. Conf. on Robotics and Automation (ICRA'97)*, pages 425–430, April 1997.
40. V. Ramesha and R. M. Haralick. Random Perturbation Models for Boundary Extraction Sequence. In *IAPR Machine Vision and Applications*, 1997.
41. B. Randell, J.-C. Laprie, H. Kopetz, and B. Littlewood (Eds.). *Predictably Dependable Computing Systems*. Springer Verlag, 1995.
42. A. L. Reibman and M. Veeraraghavan. Reliability Modeling: An Overview for Systems Designers. *IEEE Computer*, 24(4):49–57, 1991.
43. J. Rushby. Formal Specification and Verification for Critical Systems: Tools, Achievements, and Prospects. In *EPRI Workshop on Methodologies for Cost-Effective, Reliable Software Verification and Validation, EPRI TR-00294*. 9–1 to 9–15, 1992.
44. G. D. Sullivan S. Zhang and K. D. Baker. Using Automatically Constructed View-Independent Relational Model in 3D Object Recognition. In *European Conf. on Computer Vision*, pages 778–768, May 1992.
45. J. Sheinvald and N. Kiryati. On the Magic of Slide. In *IAPR Machine Vision and Applications*, 1997.
46. Y. Shirai, R. Okoda, and T. Yamane. Robust Visual Tracking by Integrating Various Cues. In *IEEE Int. Conf. on Robotics and Automation (ICRA'98) Workshop on Robust Vision for Vision-Based Control of Motion*, May 1998.
47. M. Soika. Grid Based Fault Detection and Calibration for Sensors on Mobile Robots. In *Proc. of the IEEE Int. Conf. on Robotics and Automation*, pages 2589–2594, 1997.
48. R. N. Taylor, D. L. Levine, and C. D. Kelly. Structural Testing of Concurrent Programs. *IEEE Trans. on Software Engineering*, 18(3):206–215, 1992.
49. P. K. Varshney. Distributed Detection With Multiple Sensors: Part I - Fundamentals. *Proceedings of the IEEE*, Vol. 85 No. 1:3–4, 1997.
50. S. Vinther and R. Cipolla. Active 3D Object Recognition using 3D Affine Invariants. In *European Conf. on Computer Vision*, pages 16–24, May 1994.
51. Jeffrey M. Voas and Keith W. Miller. Software Testability: The New Verification. *IEEE Software*, 12(3), 1995.
52. C. Wang and D. R. Musser. Dynamic verification of C++ generic algorithms. *IEEE Trans. on Software Engineering*, 23(5):314–323, 1997.

The CSU Face Identification Evaluation System: Its Purpose, Features, and Structure

David S. Bolme, J. Ross Beveridge, Marcio Teixeira, and Bruce A. Draper

Computer Science Department Colorado State University

Abstract. The CSU Face Identification Evaluation System provides standard face recognition algorithms and standard statistical methods for comparing face recognition algorithms. The system includes standardized image pre-processing software, three distinct face recognition algorithms, analysis software to study algorithm performance, and Unix shell scripts to run standard experiments. All code is written in ANSI C. The preprocessing code replicates feature of preprocessing used in the FERET evaluations. The three algorithms provided are Principle Components Analysis (PCA), a.k.a Eigenfaces, a combined Principle Components Analysis and Linear Discriminant Analysis algorithm (PCA+LDA), and a Bayesian Intrapersonal/Extrapersonal Classifier (BIC). The PCA+LDA and BIC algorithms are based upon algorithms used in the FERET study contributed by the University of Maryland and MIT respectively. There are two analysis. The first takes as input a set of probe images, a set of gallery images, and similarity matrix produced by one of the three algorithms. It generates a Cumulative Match Curve of recognition rate versus recognition rank. The second analysis tool generates a sample probability distribution for recognition rate at recognition rank 1, 2, etc. It takes as input multiple images per subject, and uses Monte Carlo sampling in the space of possible probe and gallery choices. This procedure will, among other things, add standard error bars to a Cumulative Match Curve. The System is available through our website and we hope it will be used by others to rigorously compare novel face identification algorithms to standard algorithms using a common implementation and known comparison techniques.

1 Introduction

The The System was created to evaluate how well face identification systems perform. In addition to algorithms for face identification, the system includes software to support statistical analysis techniques that aid in evaluating the performance of face identification systems. The current system is designed with identification rather than verification in mind. The identification problem is: given a novel face, find the most similar images in a gallery of known people/images. The related verification problem is: given a novel image of specific person, confirm whether the person is or is not who they claim to be.

For simplicity sake, the CSU Face Identification and Evaluation System will henceforth be called the System. The System assumes, as did the earlier FERET evaluation[7], that a face recognition algorithm will first compute a similarity measure between images, and

J.L. Crowley et al. (Eds.): ICVS 2003, LNCS 2626, pp. 304–313, 2003.

second perform a nearest neighbor match between novel and stored images. When this is true, the complete behavior of a face identification system can be captured in terms of a similarity matrix. The System will create these similarity matrices and provides analysis tools that utilize them generate cumulative match curves and recognition rate sample probability distributions. This document describes version 4.0 of the System that is available through our website[2].

2 System Overview

The System functionality can be split into four basic phases: image data preprocessing, algorithm training, algorithm testing and analysis of results: see Figure1. Preprocessing reduces unwanted image variation by aligning the face imagery, equalizing the pixel values, and normalizing the contrast and brightness. The three algorithms in this distribution have a training phase and a testing phase. The training phase reads training data and creates a subspace into which test images will be projected and matched. The testing phase reads the subspace information, projects images into this subspace, and generates a distance matrix. Typically the testing phase creates a distance matrix for the union of all images to be used either as probe images or gallery images in the analysis phase. The fourth phase performs analyzes on the distance matrices. This include computing recognition rates (csuAnalyzeRankCurve), conducting virtual experiments (csuAnalizePermute), or performing other statistical analysis on the data.

Sections 3 and 4 describe this functionality in greater detail. Before proceeding to discuss functionality further, there are four data structures commonly used to pass information between components of the System. These are imagery, image sets, algorithm training configurations, and distances matrices.

2.1 Imagery

The System was developed using frontal facial images from the FERET data set. Images are stored in an image file that contains pixel values in a binary floating point format (Big Endian / Sun byte order). The current system generates ".sfi" files. SFI stands for Single Float Image. Each image file contains a single line (record) ASCII header that contains the format specifier, "CSU_RASTER", followed by the column dimension, followed by the row dimension, followed by the number channels of data. The remainder of the file contains raw pixel values in row major order. Most images are single channel, but for multi-channel images the pixel value for channel two follows directly the pixel value for one, etc. The floating point portion of a single channel SFI file is identical to the NIST FERET image format. The only difference is our addition of a header. The The System also supports this NIST format and identifies such images with a ".nrm" suffix.

Preprocessing

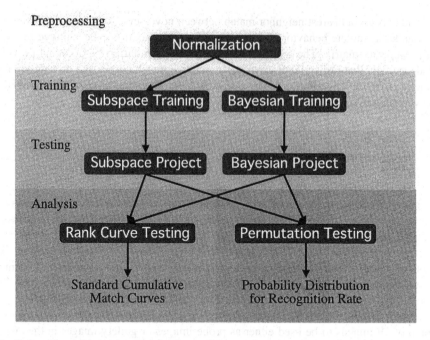

Fig. 1. Overview of execution flow for the csuSubspace system, which includes a standard PCA identification algorithm and also a PCA+LDA identification algorithm.

2.2   Image Sets

It is impossible to run experiments without first identifying sets of images to be used to train and test algorithms. This distribution includes many common image lists, including the training images, gallery images, and four standard probe sets used in the FERET evaluations. While image lists are always ASCII files enumerating filenames of image files, they are used to represent training image sets, test image sets, probe image sets and gallery image sets. When running experiments, it is important to keep track of how distinct lists are being used. The actual FERET training, gallery and probe set lists are available at: http://www.cs.colostate.edu/evalfacerec/data.html

2.3   Training Configuration Files

These files contain subspace basis vectors, associated eigenvalues, along with algorithms specific meta-data such as an ASCII copy of the command line used to generate the training data. The training files are a combination of binary and ASCII data: an ASCII header followed by binary data. Specifically, the basis vectors are stored as 64 bit floating point values. These files are inputs to the testing algorithms and carry all the necessary information generated by the algorithm training phase.

2.4 Distance Matrices

Each algorithm produces a distance matrix for all of the images in the testing list. All algorithms assume that smaller distances are a closer match. In many cases the base metric will yield a similarity score, where higher scores indicate more similarity. When this is the case the similarity values are negated to produce a "distance like" metric. Some examples of this are the Correlation and MahAngle distance metrics in csuSubpace, and the Bayesian and Maximum Likelihood Metric in the csuBayesian code.

3 Preprocessing

Preprocessing is conducted using the executable csuPreprocessNormalize. The executable performs five steps in converting a PGM FERET image to a normalized image. The five steps are summarized in Figure2 and an sample normalized image is shown. The eye coordinates are required for geometric normalization. These are available for the FERET images from NIST and are included in the System.

1. Integer to float conversion - Converts 256 gray levels into floating point equivalents.

2. Geometric normalization -- Lines up human chosen eye coordinates.

3. Masking -- Crops the image using an elliptical mask and image borders such that only the face from forehead to chin and cheek to cheek is visible.

4. Histogram equalization -- Equalizes the histogram of the unmasked part of the image.

Sample Normalized Image

5. Pixel normalization -- scales the pixel values to have a mean of zero and a standard deviation of one.

Fig. 2. Image Normalization

Our csuPreprocessNormalize code accomplishes many of the same tasks performed by code originally written at NIST called "facetonorm". However, it is not identical to the NIST version. For example, histogram equalization is done only within the unmasked portions of the face. Our code is more robust and we recommend using it in place of the NIST version.

4 Algorithms

Version 4.0 of the System comes with three face identification algorithms. These algorithms where chosen because they are well known and had high scores on the FERET Phase 3 test. The algorithms are intended to perform as a test platform for evaluation techniques and to serve as a common baseline for algorithm comparisons.

4.1 Principle Components Analysis (csuSubspace/PCA)

The first algorithm released by CSU was based on Principle Components Analysis (PCA)[5]. This system is based on a linear transformation in feature space. Feature vectors for the PCA algorithm are formed by concatenating the pixel values from the images. These raw feature vectors are very large (~20,000 values) and are highly correlated. PCA rotates feature vectors from this large, highly correlated subspace to a small subspace which has no sample covariance between features.

PCA has two useful properties when used in face recognition. The first is that it can be used to reduce the dimensionality of the feature vectors. This dimensionality reduction can be performed in either a lossy or lossless manor. When applied in a lossy manor, basis vectors are truncated from the front or back of the transformation matrix. It is assumed that these vectors correspond to not useful information such as lighting variations (when dropped from the front) or noise (when dropped from the back). If none of the basis vectors are dropped it is called a lossless transformation and it should be possible to get perfect reconstruction for the training data based on the compressed feature vectors.

The second useful property is that PCA eliminates all of the statistical covariance in the transformed feature vectors. This means that the covariance matrix for the transformed (training) feature vectors will always be diagonal. This property is exploited for some distance measures such as L1, MahAngle, and Bayesian based classifiers.

Training. PCA training is performed by the csuSubspaceTraining executable. The PCA is the default mode (it can also perform LDA training). The PCA basis is computed by the snapshot method using a Jacobi eigensolver from the Intel CV library. The basis vectors can be eliminated from the subspace using the cutOff and dropNVectors command line options. These methods are described in detail in[9]. The training program outputs a training file that contains a description of the training parameters, the mean of the training image, the eigenvalues or fisher values, and a basis for the subspace.

Distance Metrics. The csuSubspaceProject code is used to generate distance files. It requires a list of images and a subspace training file. The code projects the feature vectors onto the basis. It then computes the distance between pairs of images in the list. The output is a set of distance files containing the distance from each image to all other images in the list. The distance metrics include city block (L1), Euclidean (L2), Correlation, Covariance, versus Angle (PCA only), and LDA Soft (LDA only). We have published a study comparing PCA to PCA+LDA using these different distance metrics[1]

4.2 Linear Discriminant Analysis (csuSubspace/PCA+LDA)

The second algorithm is Linear Discriminant Analysis (PCA+LDA) based upon that written by Zhao and Chellapa[10]. The algorithm is based on Fischer's Linear Discriminants. LDA training attempts to produce a linear transformations that emphasize differences between classes while reducing differences within classes. The goal is to form a subspace that is linearly separable between classes.

When used in the Face Identification and Evaluation System each human subject forms a class. LDA training requires training data that has multiple images per subject. LDA training is performed by first using PCA to reduces the dimensionality of the feature vectors. After this LDA is performed on the training data to further reduces the dimensionality in such a way that class distinguishing features are preserved. A final transformation matrix is produced by multiplying the PCA and LDA basis vectors to produce a full raw to LDA space transformation matrix.

The final output of the LDA training is the same as PCA. The algorithm produces a set of LDA basis vectors. These basis vectors produce a transformation of the feature vectors. Like the PCA algorithm, distance metrics can be used on the LDA feature vectors.

Training. Like PCA, LDA training is performed by the csuSubspaceTraining executable. This algorithm is enabled using the -lda option. PCA is first performed on the training data to determine an optimal basis for the image space. The training images are projected onto the PCA subspace to reduce their dimensionality before LDA is performed. Computationally LDA follows the method outlined by [3]. A detailed description of the implementation can be found in[4]. The subspace generated using the -lda option is the composition of the PCA followed by the LDA projection matrices. LDA generates one fewer basis vectors than there are training classes, i.e. training subjects.

Distance Metrics. The csuSubspaceProject generate distance files for PCA+LDA. Please see the PCA distance metrics section for more information.

4.3 Bayesian Intrapersonal Classifier (csuBayesian/BIC)

The third algorithm in the CSU distribution is based on an algorithm developed by Moghaddam and Pentland[6]. There are two variants of this algorithm, a *maximum a posteriori* (MAP) and *maximum likelihood* (ML) classifier. This algorithm is interesting for several reasons, including the fact that it examines the difference image between two photos as a basis for determining whether the two photos are of the same subject. Difference images which originate from two photos of different subjects are said to be *extrapersonal* whereas images which originate from two photos of the same subject are said to be *Intrapersonal*.

The key assumption in Moghaddam and Pentland's work is that the particular difference images belonging to the Intrapersonal and extrapersonal difference images originate from distinct and localized Gaussian distributions within the space of all possible difference images.

The actual parameters for these distributions are not known, so the algorithm begins by extracting from the training data, using statistical methods, the parameters that define the Gaussian distributions corresponding to the Intrapersonal and extrapersonal difference images. This training stage, called density estimation, is performed through Principle Components Analysis (PCA). This stage estimates the statistical properties of two subspaces: one for difference images that belong to the Intrapersonal class and another for difference images that belong to the extrapersonal class. During the testing phase, the classifier takes each image of unknown class membership and uses the estimates of the the probability distributions as a means of identification.

Training. In the current CSU implementation, the extrapersonal and intrapersonal difference images for training are generated using the "csuMakeDiffs" program and subsequently the parameters of the two subspaces are estimated by running PCA ("csuSubspaceTrain"). This is done independently for the intrapersonal and extrapersonal difference images. Unlike in our earlier distribution, the current distribution does *not* include a separate and independent program for training the Bayesian classifier.

Distance Metrics. The "csuBayesianProject" code is used to generate distance files. It requires a list of images and two subspace training files (one for the extrapersonal difference images and another for the intrapersonal difference images). The code projects the feature vectors onto each of the two sets of basis vectors and then computes the probability that each feature vector came from one or the other subspace. The output is a set of distance files containing the similarity from each image to all other images. The similarities may be computed using the maximum a posteriori (MAP) or the maximum likelihood (ML) methods. From a practical standpoint, the ML method uses information derived only from the intrapersonal images, while the MAP method uses information derived from both distributions.

5   Standardizing Algorithm Analysis

The primary motivation in developing the System is to analyze the performance of different algorithms. Many publications in the face identification domain compare recognition rates between different algorithms. However, different implementations of even such apparently simple algorithms as a PCA face identification algorithm can produce different outcomes, particularly if image preprocessing, training and choice of distance metric is not controlled. For example, in[1], the comparison of different PCA distance metrics showed that using PCA with L2 distance can create a false impression that an alternative algorithm is doing well: our studies as well as FERET, show PCA should be used with Mahalanobis Angle as the preferred distance metric.

It is therefore important that Our System provides not only standardized algorithms, but also standardized preprocessing, standardized scripts that include details such as choice of distance metric, and finally standardized ways of analyzing results. In this section we will explain in more detail the two analysis tools included in the System.

5.1   Rank Curve Generation

Rank curve analysis was used in the FERET evaluations as one basis for algorithm comparison. It provides a method of analyzing recognition rates of an algorithm f recognition rank. Although this analysis is simple it can provide interesting information not apparent in a rank one recognition rate. Figures 3 and 4 show the rank curves generated for the standard FA and FC FERET probe sets. The System comes with a set of Unix Scripts that run a portion of the original FERET evaluation for the three algorithms including all four of standard probe sets. This experiment is not identical to that done in FERET. Differences include new algorithm implementations, new image preprocessing code and perhaps most importantly different training image sets. Keeping those caveats in mind, the script will preprocess the FERET imagery, train the algorithms, run the algorithms to generate distance matrices, and finally build cumulative match curves for the standard set of FERET gallery images and each of the four standard FERET probe image sets. This script is intended as a baseline, or point of departure, for people wanted understand what was done in the FERET evaluation and wanting to adapt it to their own purposes.

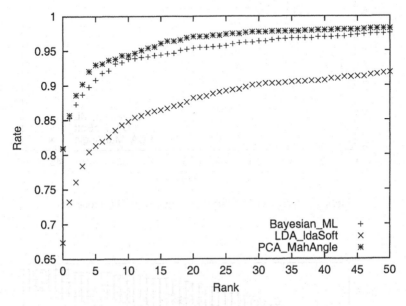

Fig. 3. Comparison of the three algorithms on the FB probe set.

5.2   Permuting Probe and Gallery Image Choices

A weakness of comparing recognition rates in cumulative match curves is they lack standard error bars. The question of what one really wants standard error bars to represent, and thus how to compute them, can become more involved that at first it might appear. We have developed a Monte Carlo based method that is described fully in [1]. An alternative means of computing error bars has been developed by Ross Micheals and Terry Boult[8]. Our csuPermute code performs virtual experiments using the distance files. It does this by taking random permutations of the probe and gallery sets and then performs nearest neighbor classification. It then generates a sample probability distribution for recognition rate under the assumption that probe and gallery images are interchangeable for subjects. Figure 5 shows an example comparing the PCA and BIC algorithms on a set of 640 FERET images of 120 subjects. Observe that average performance of the PCA algorithm is higher than BIC, but that relative to standard error bars derived from the sample distributions, the difference does not appear significant relative to changes in the choice of probe and gallery images.

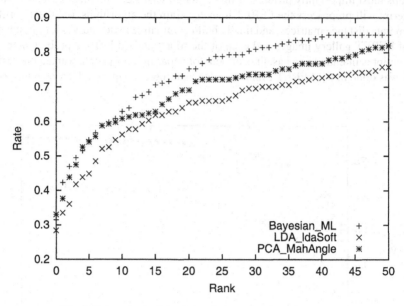

Fig. 4. Comparison of the three algorithms on the FC probe set.

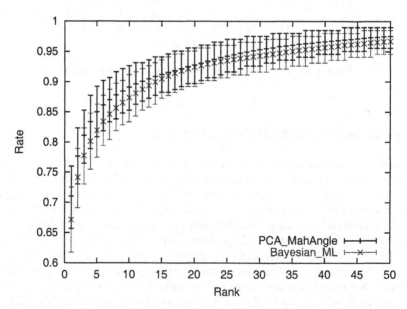

Fig. 5. This figure compares our PCA and Bayesian algorithms. The rank curves include 95% error bars that were estimated by csuPermute. The error bars show that there is no significant difference between PCA and Maximum Likelihood when trained on the FERET training set.

References

1. J. Ross Beveridge, Kai She, Bruce Draper, and Geof H. Givens. A nonparametric statistical comparison of principal component and linear discriminant subspaces for face recognition. In *Proceedings of the IEEE Conference on Computer Vision and Pattern Recognition*, pages 535–542, December 2001.
2. Ross Beveridge. Evaluation of face recognition algorithms web site. http://cs.colostate.edu/evalfacerec.
3. Richard O. Duda, Peter E. Hart, and David G. Stork. *Pattern Classification*. John Wiley & Sons, second edition edition, 2001.
4. J. Ross Beveridge. The Geometry of LDA and PCA Classifiers Illustrated with 3D Examples. Technical Report CS-01-101, Computer Science, Colorado State University, 2001.
5. M. A. Turk and A. P. Pentland. Face Recognition Using Eigenfaces. In *Proc. of IEEE Conference on Computer Vision and Pattern Recognition*, pages 586–591, June 1991.
6. B. Moghaddam, C. Nastar, and A. Pentland. A bayesian similarity measure for direct image matching. *ICPR*, B:350–358, 1996.
7. P.J. Phillips, H.J. Moon, S.A. Rizvi, and P.J. Rauss. The FERET Evaluation Methodology for Face-Recognition Algorithms. *T-PAMI*, 22(10):1090–1104, October 2000.
8. Ross J. Micheals and Terry Boult. Efficient evaluation of classification and recognition systems. In *IEEE Computer Vision and Pattern Recognition 2001*, page (to appear), December 2001.
9. Wendy S. Yambor. Analysis of pca-based and fisher discriminant-based image recognition algorithms. Master's thesis, Colorado State University, 2000.
10. W. Zhao, R. Chellappa, and A. Krishnaswamy. Discriminant analysis of principal components for face recognition. In *In Wechsler, Philips, Bruce, Fogelman-Soulie, and Huang, editors, Face Recognition: From Theory to Applications*, pages 73–85, 1998.

The Imalab Method for Vision Systems

Augustin Lux

Laboratoire GRAVIR/IMAG
Institut National Polytechnique de Grenoble
Augustin.Lux@imag.fr

Abstract. We propose a method to construct computer vision systems
using a workbench composed of a multi-faceted toolbox and a general
purpose kernel. The toolbox is composed of an open set of library modules. The kernel facilitates incremental dynamic system construction.
This method makes it possible to quickly develop and experiment new
algorithms, it simplifies the reuse of existing program libraries, and allows to construct a variety of systems to meet particular requirements.
Major strong points of our approach are: (1) Imalab is a homogeneous environment for different types of users, who share the same basic code with
different interfaces and tools. (2) Integration facility: modules for various scientific domains, in particular robotics or AI research (e.g. Bayesian
reasoning, symbolic learning) can be integrated automatically. (3) Multi-
language integration: the C/C++ language and several symbolic programming languages - Lisp(Scheme), Prolog, Clips - are completely integrated. We consider this an important advantage for the implementation
of cognitive vision functionalities. (4) Automatic program generation, to
make multi-language integration work smoothly. (5) Efficiency: library
code runs without overhead.
The Imalab system is in use for several years now, and we have started
to distribute it.

1 Introduction

We propose to construct computer vision systems using a workbench composed
of a large set of reusable modules, and a set of sophisticated tools for system construction, including an interactive programming shell, and a program generator
to automatically integrate C++ source code into the shell.

We illustrate this method with the Imalab system, which is a research system
combining all major features that are available in the workbench:

- A large set of C++ libraries (some 100 classes with more than thousand
  methods and functions) makes it easy to experiment algorithms on new
  images, and to develop new algorithms.
- An interactive shell, with a large subset of C++ as a shell language.
- Homogeneous environment: the same programming language is used for interactive experimentation in the shell, for writing scripts to automate sequences of commands, and to extend the system's native code.

J.L. Crowley et al. (Eds.): ICVS 2003, LNCS 2626, pp. 314–322, 2003.
© Springer-Verlag Berlin Heidelberg 2003

- Automatic library linkage: New libraries written in C++ can be added to the system, provided the header files are available.
- Incremental dynamic system construction, making it extensible according to user needs.

Comparison with Existing Systems

There is a large spectrum of vision oriented software [12]. On one end of the spectrum, one finds libraries with code for image processing operations providing functionalities to be used in an application program. Important examples of libraries are the Image Understanding Environment[2] defining a large hierarchy of C++ classes modelizing all data structures necessary in computer vision in a general way, and Intel's Open Source Computer Vision Library[3] providing numerous C procedures with code written for efficiency. On the other end of the spectrum, one can find complete systems built around such libraries, containing sophisticated tools for the development of vision applications. One outstanding example of this kind is the Khoros system [4][15], which includes the *Cantata* visual programming environment [16].

The Imalab project lives on a much smaller scale; it places the main emphasis on *interactive development* and *modularity*, it aims to be particularly useful for the development of new algorithms, and for experimentation with new applications. In this respect, we have the same motivations as the authors of the ScilImage system[17]: "The immediate feedback interactive systems provide reduces the time needed to develop new applications" and "the ability to see the result of processing and to modify code or parameters within seconds brings new insights, such as how sensitive an algorithm is to a small change in the image, or how parameters should be tuned in response to certain shapes". However, in spite of so similar motivations, there is very little concrete resemblance between Imalab and ScilImage. One major reason for this is the use of C++ and object oriented programming, rather than using C, which completely changes the system architecture. The use of C++ as command language implies an important facility that an experimental environment "ideally" should provide [12]: "An essential facility during testing and debugging is the ability to monitor and examine both data and the interaction of system components".

Another specific characteristic of the Imalab approach is the concern to integrate external libraries; this is useful e.g. to compare different solutions to a given problem, to combine vision with other domains, to extend vision with AI programming.

Outline of the Paper

In section 2, we present the Imalab system as it is currently being used: a highly interactive programming environment featuring a large number of vision-related data structures and algorithms. Section 3 presents the underlying method for constructing vision systems, available modules, and module generation tools.

2   The Imalab System

Imalab is an interactive programming shell for computer vision research. Its most prominent features are:

- A large choice of data structures and algorithms
- A subset of C++ statements as interaction language
- Extensibility through dynamic loading
- A multi language facility including Scheme, Clips, Prolog

By the use of standard or personalized scripts, the user initializes the system in a way that places him/her in a comfortable environment where he can efficiently work on a particular problem; the initial environment includes a set or a sequence of images, a window for image display, and a number of global variables allowing the detailed exploration of all data structures at any time during a session.

Any shell is characterized by an interaction language and an environment, which must have in common a set of data types: the Imalab shell uses C++ statements as interaction language, including a subset of C++ expressions which is "complete" in the sense that it gives access to all functionalities of the programs.

2.1   Data Structures and Algorithms

The standard Imalab environment contains about a hundred classes with a total of several thousand methods to be used for work on vision problems. A *help* command is available to get information on all class and function definitions; this is particularly useful to explore external libraries, and also helps to remember about your own programs.

Important basic classes are:

- Image classes. There is a hierarchy of image classes trying to realize a reasonable trade-off between efficiency, generality, genericity, and simplicity. Abstract classes provide a large number of virtual or generic methods for image management and basic processing (input/output, conversions, thresholding, histograms, etc.), base classes provide for one-, three-, or four-band images with byte, int, or float pixels. We do not use template classes for images in order to assure maximum portability, and a certain kind of simplicity.
- Image processing algorithms. Every user has a large set of algorithms to work on, so these modules are fluctuating quickly. In particular, we use fast algorithms for Gaussian filters[18] useful for working with scale space, a "color" module providing standard color encodings; a connectivity analysis module for image segmentation.
- Classes for image display and graphics. Using specific classes for windows and events, rather than giving direct access to the underlying system functions, simplifies shell programming: these system functions tend to have a large number of parameters, most of which have "natural" default values in the current environment.
- Objects of 2-D geometry: points, lines, rectangles, etc.
- Numerical routines, in particular matrix computations.

2.2   Friends

Excellent software exists for graphical plotting of numerical data, and for 3-D display. We can easily profit from these using a light interface through pipes. For example, Imalab communicates in this way with gnuplot and geomview, and there is a series of Imalab commands generating input for gnuplot and geomview, visualizing e.g. gradient, laplacian, or other filter values as curves or surfaces.

For the construction of graphical user interfaces, there are special provisions to simplify the use of FLTK[1] and QT[6].

2.3   Extensibility and Dynamic Loading

As can be seen from the enumeration of basic classes and algorithms, there is no point in trying to have a complete collection: the number of potentially useful algorithms is illimited. A vision system must be extensible in order to add new algorithms as they become available. One essential aspect of extensibility is dynamic loading. The Imalab command *require* loads the given module into the shell, making all classes, methods, and functions of the module source code available in the current shell environment.[1]

2.4   Basic Shell Interaction

The use of C++ as interaction and scripting language makes the shell easy to use and powerful, because the shell language is the same as the programming language for the source code[2]. In the shell, one can create objects, activate methods/functions, and inspect any data objects as can be done inside the source code.

Thus the shell gives the same feeling as writing a main procedure; in fact, it is much simpler, because a large number of initializations are carried out on starting the shell. These initializations, based on Unix-command parameters, define global variables that are handily used later on. In particular:

- The variable *CurrentImage* holds an image as a C++ object, shielding the user from details of image acquisition/conversion
- The variable *Screen* holds a window to be used for all kinds of image display.

As all initializations are programmed in a script file, one can define a personnalized version of Imalab with complements to this script.

Using the same language for programming in the shell, for script files and source code is an essential feature to make the system practical and convenient: one can work out a sequence of image operations interactively, then put the same code into a script file (copying from the history file), and when it works correctly, "promote" this code into a compiled module, or as part of some library.

---

[1] Module generation can be more sophisticated, see section 3.

[2] We will take up the multi language aspect in the next paragraph.

The shell language is a carefully chosen subset of C++, which is semantically much closer to Java: there is no pointer arithmetic, no indirection or reference operator, no casts[3]. Restrictions of this kind are necessary because C++ was designed for compilation, not for an interpretive shell.

2.5   Multi Language Feature

In the Imalab system, the term "multi-language" has two distinct meanings:

- A syntactic meaning. In the shell, the user can choose the syntax for his commands. The default syntax for the Imalab shell is C++, but one can just as well use Lisp (Scheme), or Prolog. One can switch from one syntax to another at any time; this changes the input reader, but not the shell interpreter.
- Source code language. The source code in any file may be written in any of Imalab's languages; being a collection of source files, a module may combine source code in different languages; there is a provision for easy cross-language calls.

Seamless integration in this respect is a strong feature: when creating an object, calling a method or a function, the shell user does not have to know which source language has been used to implement this particular code. Of course, this is possible only inasmuch as different programming languages share the same basic concepts, like object, method, function.[4] A basic step to achieve this integration was the extension of Scheme with a new data type *c-object* for "handles" to C++ data. Inversely, to access Scheme data from C++, nothing has to be done, because Scheme is implemented in C++.

As a consequence, Imalab can appear as a C++ shell (extended with Scheme), or as a Scheme shell (extended with C++), with the same functionalities. In practice, all Imalab users have knowledge of C++, and this is sufficient to use the shell, and to extend Imalab with new algorithms. Few users have knowledge of Scheme. In fact, Scheme becomes important to understand internal shell programming, and the tools of the workbench presented in section 3.

If the multi-language feature appears strange to you, you may consider it just an internal feature of the system. However, we firmly believe that it adds much power to a vision system workbench.

2.6   Beyond C++: Memory Management and Advanced Features

One good reason for combining C++ and Scheme is that Scheme, as a dialect of Lisp, includes important high level features one expects from a programming shell, which are not found in C++.

---

[3] Even though our goal always has been to implement a "comfortable C"++ shell", a fairly complete C++ interpreter progressively gets into reach. See the Ravi webpage for a discussion on this point.

[4] Much more shall be said on this in another paper.

- Automatic storage management through garbage collection is precious for interactive use: in complex situations, it is impossible for a human to remember precisely which data structures still are in use. However, garbage collection in a Scheme system only concerns Scheme data, special care has to be taken if we also want to manage general C++ objects like images, windows, and the like. For this reason, the Scheme garbage collector has been extended to handle c-objects containing reference pointers, or to delete objects directly. Information about the way C++ objects are handled by the garbage collector has to be supplied during module generation.
- Dynamic typing allows for dynamic type checking. Indeed, the shell verifies all arguments for calls to C++ methods or functions. Dynamic typing also is an important ingredient for introspection and other reflective capacities.
- Error recovery and signal handling can be carried out by the virtual machine on which the Scheme implementation is based. This adds important functionality to the shell; for instance, the shell stays alive after a segmentation fault, so the user can go through all data to look for the problem. A control-C suspends a computation and recursively calls the shell in the interrupted environment: the user can inspect the situation, and then continue or abort the suspended computation.

3   The Imalab Workbench for System Building

The description in the preceding section clearly shows that the Imalab system is constructed in a highly modular fashion. The main point we want to make in this paper is that the Imalab system is just one example of the use of a very general workbench which allows to efficiently design and construct a large variety of vision systems with different behaviors.

This workbench is our response to the fact that it is impossible to construct a universal vision system: only a workbench can, eventually, be universal on the meta-level, enabling us to construct a state-of-the-art vision system for a given problem specification with little effort.

A workbench should propose a set of reusable modules, tools to create new modules from newly available software, and support for writing a system toplevel responsible for module integration, control, and other global aspects. These three points are taken up in the following subsections.

3.1   Building Blocks: Existing Libraries

Section 2.2 has mentioned some of the vision related modules. The entire set of available modules is much larger, and also includes modules not directly related to vision. There are modules for

- learning algorithms
- language modules for Clips, Prolog, and a frame language
- Bayesian inference
- general data structures (tables, numerics, ...)

There may be redundancy in the modules. For instance, there are several modules implementing image classes which are quite equivalent. This eases the problem of portability: when importing new code, it is easier to import it with its data structures than to adapt the algorithms to our "standard" image structures. In fact, different implementations may coexist within Imalab - this is very useful for prototyping, and for testing combinations of different algorithms. In many cases, conversion between different image classes turns out to be trivial, because the pixel data are the same.

3.2   Tools for Creating New Modules

The major technical problem for the generation of new modules concerns the integration of "raw" C++ programs, which may be available as source code, or as dynamic libraries. Using C++ programs inside an interactive shell requires a fair amount of highly technical "interface code". The modern solution to this requirement is automatic interface generation. This role is played by the Ravi Interface Generator[5] which produces all necessary code by analysing C++ header files. Module generation does neither modify nor need the source code for libraries[6], nor does it need a special interface file[7]. However, it does need some informations that cannot be deduced from header files, e.g. about the use of reference counters, about the existence of output parameters, templates to be instantiated, etc.

3.3   Constructing a Vision System

We now are able to sketch the basic steps of the Imalab method for constructing a vision system.

- Define the modules you want; you may (re-)use existing modules, or create new ones. Creation of new modules may take some time, even if all algorithmic problems are solved.
- According to the kind of system you want to create, write the basic script. Two typical situations are:
  - A stand-alone application system. In this case, the system structure is fixed. The modules can be linked statically, there is no interactive shell, or the shell will just be used by the system engineer.
  - An interactive system for use in teaching or research, as is the case with Imalab. The system structure is as open as possible, so we define a basic kernel, and each user loads dynamically whatever he needs.
- Work the system's overall behavior. The workbench furnishes several language modules that make it possible to give a system a particular twist with little effort; for instance by using the production system module (Clips like) with an appropiate set of rules.

---

[5] Ravi[7] is the name of the system shell Imalab is built on.

[6] as is the case with OpenC++[10]

[7] as is the case with Swig[8]

The workbench does not provide solutions to all problems, but gives important help to combine pieces for a solution into a single system.

One important point to note is that the whole workbench uses C++ as the basic implementation language. The source code for all tools and modules is available. We may also note that work on the tools never is finished!

4 Conclusion: Perspectives for Cognitive Vision

4.1 About the Multi Language Feature

Do we need AI languages for cognitive vision systems?

A system is more than just the sum of its parts: a system ties together the functionalities provided by its components, adding control and other high-level characteristics. We don't believe a single programming language can be well adapted for the implementation of all aspects of a vision system. We rather contend that, given that different programming languages each have their strengths and weaknesses, one should carefully choose the right programming language for each component of a system.

Argumenting about this point is subtle: from a theoretical standpoint, all programming languages have equal power, being all equivalent to a Turing machine. However, it also is true that programming languages differ in important aspects. In particular, each programming language proposes a type system which may be more or less adapted to a given problem. A good choice of programming language may greatly simplify the solution. For example:

- Lisp provides symbolic list structures, automatic memory management, functional programming, and dynamic typing. These properties are precious for the implementation of sophisticated object models, for the representation of knowledge within vision programs.
- C++ provides a rich set of tools for efficient implementation of sophisticated data structures. This is essential for image processing, all problems of "low-level" vision, and much more.
- Prolog provides unification and automatic backtracking. Our users don't seem to need this ... for the moment.

The proof will be in the eating - our feeling is that dialects of logic programming languages, like Prolog and Clips, will show themselves useful to introduce symbolic processing and knowledge manipulation into vision systems. Significant work of this kind has been done long time ago [13][9], and should be taken up in current work.

4.2 The Imalab Method

The essential assets of our approach are

- The set of libraries, usable as interactive modules
- The system kernel with the C++ interpreter
- The interface generator RIG

The set of libraries contains the basic building blocks that make up a vision system, as well as numerous user-specific libraries which generally are evolving at a very fast rate. The system tools also simplify the reuse of libraries, which is important given the tendency of research teams to produce new software at each generation of students. It is encouraging to see that the Imalab modules and libraries are now combining the work of three generations of thesis students.

The system kernel and RIG are not specific to computer vision. They are general tools, just as language processors are general tools. However, adapting such general tools for vision research will pave the way for progress in vision systems.

The Imalab system is in use for several years now, with a total of several dozen users in several research teams. We have started to distribute it under GPL (see the Imalab homepage[5]).

References

1. http://www.fltk.org/
2. http://www.aai.com/AAI/IUE/IUE.html
3. http://www.intel.com/research/mrl/research/opencv/
4. http://www.khoral.com/khoros/
5. http://www-prima.inrialpes.fr/lux/Imalab/
6. http://doc.trolltech.com/3.0/
7. http://www-prima.inrialpes.fr/Ravi/
8. http://www.swig.org/index.html.
9. D.H.Ballard, C.M.Brown, J.A.Feldman. *An approach to knowledge-directed image analysis.* in [13].
10. Shigeru Chiba. *OpenC++ 2.5 Reference Manual.* University of Tsukuba.
11. V. Colin de Verdière and J. L. Crowley (1998) *Visual Recognition using Local Appearance.* European Conference on Computer Vision ECCV'98, Freiburg, June 1998.
12. J.L.Crowley and H.Christensen (editors). *Experimental Environments for Computer Vision and Image Processing.* World Scientific, Machine Perception Artificial Intelligence Series, Vol. 11, 1994.
13. A.R.Hanson, E.M.Riseman (eds.) *Computer Vision Systems.* Academic Press 1978.
14. Augustin Lux (2001). *Tools for automatic interface generation in scheme.* In *2nd workshop on Scheme and Functional Programming,* Florence, Italy, September 2001.
15. J.Rasure, S.Kubica (1994). *The Khoros Application Development Environment* In [12].
16. J.Rasure, M.Young (1995). Cantata: *Visual Programming Environment for the Khoros system.* Computer Graphics, A Publication of the ACM Siggraph, 29:22–24.
17. R.van Balen et al. (1994) ScilImage: *A Multi-Layered Environment for Use and Development of Image Processing Systems.* In [12].
18. I.T.Young, L.J. van Vliet (1995). Recursive Gaussian Filtering In *SCIA'95.*

Dynamically Reconfigurable Vision-Based User Interfaces

Rick Kjeldsen, Anthony Levas, and Claudio Pinhanez

IBM T.J. Watson Research Center
PO Box 704
Yorktown Heights, NY 10598
{fcmk, levas, pinhanez}@us.ibm.com

Abstract. A significant problem with vision-based user interfaces is that they are typically developed and tuned for one specific configuration – one set of interactions at one location in the world and in image space. This paper describes methods and architecture for a vision system that supports dynamic reconfiguration of interfaces, changing the form and location of the interaction on the fly. We accomplish this by decoupling the functional definition of the interface from the specification of its location in the physical environment and in the camera image. Applications create a user interface by requesting a configuration of predefined widgets. The vision system assembles a tree of image processing components to fulfill the request, using, if necessary, shared computational resources. This interface can be moved to any planar surface in the camera's field of view. We illustrate the power of such a reconfigurable vision-based interaction system in the context of a prototype application involving projected interactive displays.

1 Introduction

Vision-based user interfaces (VB-UI) are an emerging area of user interface technology where a user's intentional gestures are detected via camera, interpreted and used to control an application. Although the recognition of human gesture and action has been the topic of many workshops and conferences [1-3], and the focus of much of our previous work [4, 5], the problem of design and implementation of these applications as well as the integration of computer vision has received, comparatively, less attention. Most real-life vision interface systems incorporate the vision system as a module that is hard-coded to operate under a fixed set of circumstances. In this paper we describe a system where the application sends the vision system a description of the user interface as a *configuration* of widgets (describing *What* the interface is). Based on this, the vision system assembles a set of image processing components that implement the interface, sharing computational resources when possible. To change the interaction, a new interface description can be sent to the system at any time.

The architecture also provides for the deployment of an interface onto different real-world planar surfaces. The parameters of the surfaces where the interface can be realized are defined and stored independently of any particular interface. These

J.L. Crowley et al. (Eds.): ICVS 2003, LNCS 2626, pp. 323–332, 2003.

include the size, location and perspective distortion within the image and characteristics of the physical environment around that surface, such as the user's likely position while interacting with it. *When* the application requests a interface be activated on a particular surface (that is, *Where* the interaction should happen in the environment) the system propagates the surface parameters down the assembly of image processing components that implements that interface.

By explicitly decoupling the information describing the characteristics of *Where* an interface happen in an environment, i.e., surface-specific information, we facilitate (1) the porting an application to a new environment where the interaction surfaces are different; (2) the use of one surface for multiple applications; and (3) the use of the same interface on multiple surfaces.

These issues are very important in our current work that investigates steerable, projected interactive user interfaces, as described later in this paper (see also [6]). However, the framework presented in this paper should be seen as a way that vision-based applications can easily adapt to different environments. Moreover, the proposed vision-system architecture is very appropriate for the increasingly common situations where the interface surface is not static (as, for instance in the cardboard interface described in [7]), when a pan/tilt camera is used to make an interface follow the user (as in [8]), or when the camera is attached to the user as in applications involving augmented reality or wearable computers(see [9]).

The main contribution of this paper is the system architecture for the support of these *dynamically reconfigurable vision-based user interfaces*, both from the application point of view and in the inner workings of the vision system.

2   Basic Elements of Dynamically Reconfigurable VB-UIs

We start the discussion of our framework by describing three primitive concepts: configurations, widgets, and surfaces.

2.1   Configurations and Widgets

In our framework, a vision-based user interface is composed of a set of individual interaction dialogs referred to as *configurations*. Each configuration is a collection of interactive *widgets*, in a structure similar to how a traditional window-based application is defined as a set of dialog windows, each containing elements such as scroll bars, buttons and menus. In the case of a VB-UI, each widget provides an elemental user interaction, such as detecting a touch or tracking a fingertip. Widgets generate events back to the controlling application where they are mapped to control actions such as triggering an event or establishing the value of a parameter. Some of our earlier work describes the individual widget types we use and how they are implemented [10, 11]. Here we will focus on how they are dynamically combined to create a user interface.

In addition to defining the widgets, a configuration specifies a *boundary* area that defines the configuration coordinate system. The boundary is used during the process of mapping a configuration onto a particular surface, as described later.

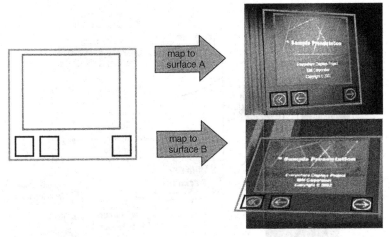

Fig. 1. Mapping a configuration onto two different surfaces.

2.2 Surfaces

An application needs to be able to define the spatial layout of widgets with respect to each other and the world, as that is relevant to the user experience, but should not be concerned with details of the recognition process, such as exactly where these widgets lie within the video image. To provide this abstraction we use the concept of named interaction *surfaces*. A surface is essentially the camera's view of a plane in 3D space.

When a configuration is defined, its widgets are laid out using the coordinate system defined by the boundary area. A configuration is mapped to a surface by warping that coordinate system into the image with a perspective transformation (homography). When the configuration is activated, the region of the image corresponding to each widget is identified and examined for the appropriate activity, which in turn will trigger events to be returned to the application. Figure 1 shows a configuration with three buttons (blue squares) and a tracking area (green rectangle) being mapped onto different surfaces. The process of determining the homography and establishing other local surface parameters is described in the next section.

3 Architecture of a Dynamically Reconfigurable Vision System

In order to efficiently support dynamic reconfiguration of vision-based interfaces, a flexible internal architecture is required in the vision system. In addition, the vision system must support operations that are not visible to the application, such as calibration, testing, and tuning. This section will describe this internal architecture.

In our system, each widget is represented internally as a tree of *components*. Each component performs one step in the widget's operation. For example the component tree of a "touch button" widget is circled in figure 2. There are components for

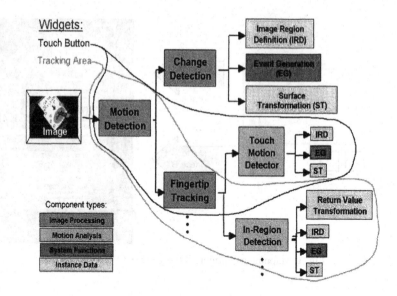

Fig. 2. Tree of components for two widgets.

finding the moving pixels in an image (Motion Detection), finding and tracking fingertips in the motion data (Fingertip Tracking), looking for touch-like motions in the fingertip paths (Touch Motion Detection), generating the touch event for the application (Event Generation), storing the region of application space where this widget resides (Image Region Definition), and managing the transformation between application space and the image (Surface Transformation).

Information is passed into the trunk of this tree and propagates from parent to child. During image processing, images are passed in. In this example, the Motion Detection component takes in a raw camera image and generates a motion mask image for its child components. Fingertip Tracking takes the motion mask and generates a path for the best fingertip hypothesis. Touch Motion Detection examines the fingertip path for a motion resembling a touch inside the image region of this button. When it detects such a motion, it triggers the Event Generation component. A similar structure is used by the "tracking area" widget, also circled in figure 2. Because of the structured communication between components, they can easily be reused and rearranged to create new widget types with different behavior.

3.1   Shared Components

When an application activates a configuration of widgets, the vision system adds the components of each widget to the existing tree of active components. If high-level components are common between multiple widgets, they may either be shared or duplicated. For example, if there are multiple Touch Button components, they can share the motion Detection and Fingertip Tracking components, or each may have its own copy. The advantage of shared components is that expensive processing steps need not be repeated for each widget. Unfortunately this can sometimes lead to undesirable interactions between widgets, so the application has the option of specifying that these components be shared or not as needed.

A good example of the trade-offs of shared components is when using touch-sensitive buttons. If there are multiple buttons active at one time, these buttons generally share the Motion Detection component. When the Fingertip Tracking component is shared, however, the behavior of the widgets can change. Recall that the Fingertip Tracker component tracks fingertip hypotheses within a region of the image. If this component is shared by more than one button, these widgets will both use the same fingertip hypothesis, meaning that only one of them can generate an event at a time. This may be desirable in some circumstances, say when implementing a grid of buttons, such as telephone keypad. In other circumstances, however, the application may not want activity in one button to prevent operation of another, so the widgets should each have their own fingertip tracker.

3.2   Communication and Control

When components are combined in a tree, widgets loose their individuality. However, it is still necessary to have a mechanism able to send information to and from widgets both individually and in groups (e.g. all widgets in a configuration). Information is propagated down the tree by Posting typed data to the root nodes. Data is retrieved from components in the tree by Querying for some data type. Both Post and Query use a fully qualified *address* including Configuration Name and Widget Name, either of which can be "all". As Post and Query data structures flow through a component, the address and data type of the structure are examined to determine if it should be handled or ignored by that component.

For example, during operation, image data addressed to all widgets is posted to the root components of the tree.   As the data flows from parent to child, some components, such as the Motion Detector, may choose to modify the image before they post it to their children. Others, like the Fingertip Tracker, may create a new type of data (in this case a fingertip path) and post that to their children instead.

3.3 Surface Calibration

Applications identify surfaces by name, but each surface must be calibrated to determine where it lies in the video image. A surface is calibrated by identifying the points in the image that correspond to the corners of a configuration's boundary. These points can be located either manually or automatically, and then are saved with the surface. When a configuration is mapped to a surface, the point pairs for each boundary corner are posted to the component tree.   Each widget has a Surface Transformation (ST) component that computes a homography from the four point-pairs, and then uses it to convert the widget's configuration coordinates into image coordinates.   The other components of the widget query the ST component to determine what image region to examine.

3.4 Vision System Parameters

In order to get the best performance from the vision system, a number of internal parameters can be adjusted. We keep these parameters hidden from the application so that the application need not be concerned with the specifics of visual recognition, and so the internal implementation of the widgets can change without requiring changes to the application.

The system maintains a local record of all configurations and surfaces that have been defined, and parameters are maintained independently for each one. The developer of an application can manually adjust (and test) the parameters from the vision system local GUI. When a configuration is mapped to a surface and activated, the parameters of both the configuration and the surface are retrieved.

Configurations maintain parameters for each widget component, allowing control of image-processing aspects such as sensitivity to motion. This allows the application designer to adjust each configuration for different recognition characteristics. For example, one configuration may need a higher recognition rate at the expense of a higher false positive rate, while in another a high false positive rate may not be acceptable. Surfaces maintain parameters about the physical environment, such as where a user is typically located with respect to the surface during an interaction, which can be used by the widgets during processing

4 An XML API for a Dynamically Reconfigurable VB-UI System

To create a VB-UI an application must define the What, When and Where of each interaction. Defining What and When is similar to developing standard non VB-UI applications. One or more configurations must be defined, specifying the spatial layout of the widgets in each. The sequence of configurations (and of the non-UI aspects of the application) must be defined as a function of the events returned from the widgets and the application state. Unique to VB-UI interactions, the Where of each interaction must also be defined, meaning on which surface a configuration is to be displayed.

To give the application the needed control we have defined an API based on a dialect of XML we call VIML (Vision Interface Markup Language). VIML defines a set of visual interface objects and methods. Three basic objects are: *VIsurface* for defining attributes of a surface; *VIconfiguration* for defining widgets, their spatial relationships and elaborating their behavior; and *VIevent* for communicating events, such as a button press back to the application. In this paper we are concerned only with three methods for VIconfigurations and VIsurfaces: "Set", used for setting values of objects; and "Activate/Deactivate" for activation.

"Set" commands can be issued to adjust the external parameters of objects, e.g. the location and size of a button, the resolution of a tracking area, etc. Once an object has been configured with "Set", it can be started and stopped as needed with "Activate" and "Deactivate" commands. Once activated, visual interface widgets begin to monitor the video stream and return relevant events to the application.

The following XML string exemplifies a typical VIML-based command. It directs the VB-UI system to set the parameters of the VIconfiguration called "cfg" so that the boundaries of the internal coordinate frame are 500 units in x and y. It also sets the parameters of two widgets in the configuration, a button named "done", which is located at x=200, y=200 and is 50 units large, and a track area which is 100 units in x and y and located at the origin (0,0) of the configuration coordinate frame.

```
<set id="uniqueID1001">
  <VIconfiguration name="cfg" left="0" right="0" top="500" bottom="500">
    <VIbutton name="done" x="200" y="200" size="50" />
    <VItrackArea name="T1" left="0" right="0" top="50" bottom="50" />
  </VIconfiguration>
</set>
```

When a widget detects a user interaction, it returns a VIML event to the application. VIML events are XML valid strings that can be parsed by the application. These events are interpreted and handled by the application to control the flow of execution. The syntax of VIML events, as well as other objects and methods, is beyond the scope of this paper, and will be available soon in a publication format.

5 Example Application: A Multi-surface Projected Store Index

One example of the experimental applications developed with this framework uses a device called an Everywhere Display projector (ED) to provide information access in retail spaces. This application provides a good example of how our dynamically reconfigurable vision system is used in practice.

5.1 The Everywhere Display

The ED is a device that combines steerable projector and camera, dynamic correction for oblique distortion, and a vision-based user interface system so it can direct a projected interactive interface onto virtually any planar surface. This allows visual information and interaction capabilities to be directed to a user when and where they are needed, without requiring the user to carry any device or for the physical environment to be wired. Figure 3 shows the current ED prototype (see [6] for details and other applications).

The current ED software consists of a three-tier architecture composed of a Services Layer, an Integration Layer and an Application Layer. The Services Layer contains the modules that control the projector, the gesture recognition system (the

Fig. 3. The ED projector.

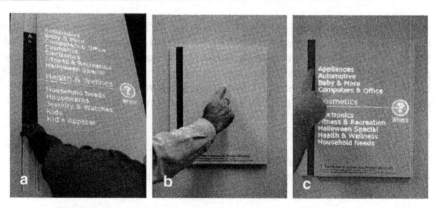

Fig. 4. The Product Finder application mapped onto different surfaces.

subject of this paper), and other system functions. Each of the modules in the Services layer exposes a set of core capabilities through a specialized dialect of XML, e.g. VIML for the vision component. An ED interaction is accomplished by orchestrating the modules in the Service layer through a sequence of XML commands.

5.2 The Product Finder Application

The goal of this application is to allow a customer to look up products in a store directory, and then guide her to where the product is. This *Product Finder* is accessed in two forms. At the entrance to the store there is a table dedicated to this purpose, much like the directory often found at the entrance to a mall. Here there is a physical slider bar the user manipulates to navigate the projected index (see figure 4.a). Note that the slider has no physical sensors; its motion is detected by the vision system. Elsewhere in the store the Product Finder can be accessed using wall signs that look like the table at the entrance, with a red stripe on the left instead of a moving slider but with no image projected on them (figure 4.b). When a sign is touched (figure 4.b), the projector image is steered towards it, the store index is projected, and product search is accomplished in much the same way as on the table, except that moving the physical slider is replaced by the user sliding her finger on the red stripe (figure 4.c).

This application uses two vision interface configurations: a "call" configuration to request the Product Finder to be displayed on a particular surface; and a "selection" configuration to perform the product search. The "call" configuration consists of a touch button that covers the whole sign or table. The selection configuration consists of three widgets (figure 5). On the left of the configuration there are a widget designed to track the physical slider (red) and a widget designed to track the user's fingertip (green). Only one of these will be active at a time. On the right is a touch button for the user to request directions to the selected item. The widgets are located with respect to the surface/configuration boundary area (the blue rectangle in figure 5). The corners of this area correspond to the corners of the wall signs.

In the current system, a single pan/tilt camera monitors the call surfaces using the information from a person tracking system. It automatically aims the camera to the sign or table nearest to the user (the current prototype is setup for a single shopper at a time). Then, it activates the "call" configuration on that sign's surface. In this way the system is always ready for the user to "call" the Product Finder.

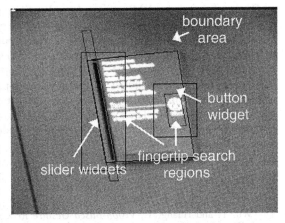

Fig. 5. Widgets mapped onto the surface of a wall sign.

When the user touches a sign or table, the "call button" widget sends an event to the application, which then projects the "selection" graphics on the sign, while activating the corresponding configuration on the sign's surface. If the Product Finder is being displayed on the table, the Physical Slider Tracker widget is activated and the Fingertip Tracker widget deactivated. On the wall signs, the reverse is true.

At this point the Product Finder is ready for use. The tracking widget sends events back to the application whenever the shopper moves their finger on the red stripe (or moves the slider), and the application modifies the display showing the product she has selected. When the user touches the "request directions" button, the application projects arrows on hanging boards that guide the shopper through the store, while the camera/vision system returns to monitoring signs.

This example demonstrates how the vision system can be easily switched between different configurations, how configurations are used on different surfaces, and how configurations are dynamically modified (by activating and deactivating widgets) to adapt to different contexts. The vision system architecture makes adding additional wall signs as easy as hanging the sign and defining a new surface for it.

6   Conclusion

The system described in this paper provides an application the ability to dynamically reconfigure a vision system that implements user interfaces. Interaction widgets recognize atomic interaction gestures, widgets are combined into configurations to support more complex interactions, and configurations are sequenced to create complete applications. These vision-based interactions can be created on the fly by an application that has little or no knowledge of computer vision, and then placed onto any calibrated planar surface in the environment.

The underlying architecture of the system, consisting of a dynamic tree of image processing components, combines flexibility, efficiency (through shared use of computational results), and easy code reuse and upgrading. Different applications and interactions can reuse the parameters of any given surface, which needs to be calibrated only once. Each widget can be tuned for best performance by parameters saved locally for each configuration and surface. The result is an "input device" that can be dynamically configured by an application to support a wide range of novel interaction styles.

Our work in using a XML protocol for describing dynamically reconfigurable VB-UIs is part of a larger effort to develop similar protocols for the communication between an application and input/output service modules. So far we have also defined a protocol for controlling camera positions and movements (CAML) and another for the description and control of assemblies of projected images and video streams (PJML). In both cases a similar philosophy was applied, that is, decoupling of What, Where, and When; and run-time system structures that assemble input/output components on the fly. The system has been deployed in our laboratory and in two university laboratories where it is being used by graduate students and researchers.

References

1. Wu, Y. and Huang, T., *Vision-Based Gesture Recognition: A Review*. Lecture Notes in Artificial Intelligence **1739**, 1999.
2. *Proc. of the 5th International Conference on Automatic Face and Gesture Recognition (FG 2002)*. 2002, IEEE Computer Society: Washington, DC.
3. Turk, M., ed. *Proc. of the Workshop on Perceptual/Perceptive User Interfaces*. 2001: Orlando, Florida.
4. Kjeldsen, F., *Visual Recognition of Hand Gesture as a Practical Interface Modality*. 1997, Columbia University: New York, New York.
5. Pinhanez, C.S. and Bobick, A.F., *"It/"*: *A Theater Play Featuring an Autonomous Computer Character*. To appear in Presence: Teleoperators and Virtual Environments, 2002.
6. Pinhanez, C. *The Everywhere Displays Projector: A Device to Create Ubiquitous Graphical Interfaces*. in *Proc. of Ubiquitous Computing 2001 (Ubicomp'01)*. 2001. Atlanta, Georgia.
7. Zhang, Z., et al. *Visual Panel: Virtual Mouse, Keyboard, and 3D Controller with an Ordinary Piece of Paper*. in *Proc. ACM Perceptual/Perceptive User Interfaces Workshop (PUI'01)*,. 2001. Florida, USA.
8. Pingali, G., et al. *User-Following Displays*. in *Proc. of the IEEE International Conference on Multimedia and Expo 2002 (ICME'02)*. 2002. Lausanne, Switzerland.
9. Starner, T., et al., *Augmented Reality through Wearable Computing*. Presence **6**(4), 1997: p. 386–398.
10. Kjeldsen, F. and Hartman, J. *Design Issues for Vision-based Computer Interaction Systems*. in *Proc. of the Workshop on Perceptual User Interfaces*. 2001. Orlando, Florida.
11. Kjeldsen, F., et al. *Interacting with Steerable Projected Displays*. in *Proc. of the 5th International Conference on Automatic Face and Gesture Recognition (FG'02)*. 2002. Washington, DC.

From a CORBA-Based Software Framework to a Component-Based System Architecture for Controlling a Mobile Robot*

Stefan A. Blum

Institute for Real-Time Computer Systems
Technische Universität München
Germany
Stefan.Blum@rcs.ei.tum.de
http://www.rcs.ei.tum.de/persons/blum.html

Abstract. We present the general purpose system architecture OSCAR (Operating System for the Control of Autonomous Robots) for mobile robots that completely relies on a software framework embedding several component types and the related "glue code". The underlying framework defines the necessary infrastructure in several ways: interfaces and data flow are standardized as well as configuration, booting, shutdown and several development constraints and facilities. All communication issues are covered by employing the CORBA middle-ware standard. The architecture itself defines a behavior-based control system that easily can be adapted to different tasks of a mobile robot if the related components are available. A network established between several laboratories will support the exchange of components for rapid software development for robotic systems.

1 Introduction

The necessity of adopting an architecture for software running e.g. on a mobile robot is indisputable. Even smaller tasks and projects are accelerated in development if there exists a guideline about how to handle decomposition, coding, communication and integration. Larger projects are not manageable at all without an underlying architecture that should also be able to take care of multi developer integration. In short, the architecture serves as backbone of robotic systems [13]. Architectures in the application field of robotics and computer vision usually combine at least two issues: a communication framework and a control system. Since architectures may not only be utilized for development and execution, there may be additional infrastructure required to specify and validate tasks and applications.

---

* The work presented in this paper was supported by the *Deutsche Forschungsgemeinschaft* as part of the project *Exploration von Innenräumen mit optischen Sensoren auf mehreren, aufgabengerechten Abstraktionsebenen*(Fa109/14).

J.L. Crowley et al. (Eds.): ICVS 2003, LNCS 2626, pp. 333–344, 2003.

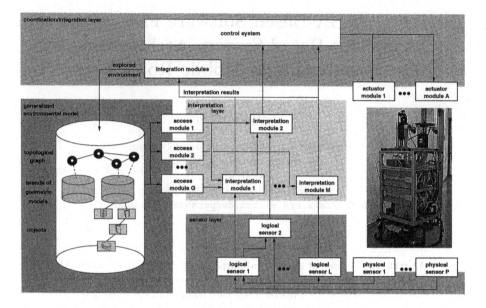

Fig. 1. System structure

The key issue of architectures is modularization whose benefits are self-evident: It enables testing facilities, development by different persons and, of course, reusability. Furthermore, since an autonomous robot must perceive its environment, sensor data may be obtained from several sensor devices or may be processed distributed in several ways. Modularization is the smartest way to handle this parallelization issue that is easy to argue: modularization allows the development of sensor processing modules without e.g. considering any explicit time constraints between different sensors or processing modules. However, this has then to be carried out by higher level scheduling instances within the control system and can be performed in a more abstract and universally valid way. Modularization leads to component-based systems if the encapsulation and reusability aspects are emphasized [26]. Components are considered as black box modules with well-defined interfaces since they are distributed as binaries.

Besides, there are other criteria for software architectures in the context of robotics. Furthermore, Arkin [3] specifies timeliness in development (e.g. provided using specialized tools), niche targetability, robustness regarding exceptions of components, run-time flexibility and reconfigurability as well as performance effectiveness.

In this paper we present the system architecture OSCAR (Operating System for the Control of Autonomous Robots) that is developed for the autonomous mobile robot MARVIN [8,9] (see Figure 1) at our institute [6,7]. Originally, OSCAR has been designed for the autonomous exploration of indoor environments (see Section 2). We started in 1997 to define a system structure for this class of applications. We decided to constrain our own software framework to integrate different categories of modules to employ the very promising new middleware technology CORBA (see section 3). Thereby, we first excluded the issue of a centralized control system by arguing that it may be developed almost independently. Within the last two years, the design and implementation of a behavior-based control system including resource management was started (see Section 4). To establish a "component market", OSCAR was redesigned to cope with similar application fields. Infrastructure for exchanging software components between several institutes was created [5]. The remaining sections present a survey of related work (Section 5) and conclude the paper (Section 6).

2   System Structure and Application Example

Thus we started with a focus on application in the context of exploration of indoor environments with a mobile robot equipped with several sensors, our system structure (Figure 1) mainly emphasizes on data processing and standardization. Therefore, the system structure defines different processing units as basic elements in several layers. Within the logical sensor and interpretation layer, a hierarchical arrangement of processing units may also be applied. We distinguish *physical sensors, logical sensors, interpretation modules, integration modules* and *actuator modules*. As a global data base for world modeling, we use *GEM* (Generalized Environmental Model) [17]. GEM is able to register environment data hierarchically in symbolic, topological and geometric instances. Envoronmental GEM data can be accessed by *GEM access modules* that serve as local data caches.

Information processing in the system structure can be described as follows: Sensor raw data is handled by physical sensors. Logical sensors extract and abstract features in a way that the interpretation modules can interpret it using GEM access modules for obtaining model data. As a result, e.g. different object and localization hypotheses are generated that may be fused in integration modules, which themselves supply GEM with new achieved environmental information. The available actuators that are encapsulated by *actuator modules* obtain commands by the control system. The coordination layer contains a central control system which is described in detail in Section 4. The coordination layer may also enclose HMI facilities which are left out in Figure 1. The concept makes the system employable for different devices and robots by exchanging physical sensors and actuator modules. In general, the design renders the system structure highly scalable in a way that it supports exchanging modules with identical functions, but different implementations, processing speed, accuracy, etc.

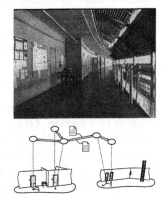

Fig. 2. Application example: Doorway and structure of the model to be gained

At the beginning of the project "Exploration of Indoor Environments" we defined an exploration task in a doorway scenario for our mobile robot MARVIN, which is equipped with four PCs running under the Linux operating system. Sensors and actors are described in more detail e.g. in [7]. The task MARVIN has to fulfill is to detect all doors and register their position together with their room number in GEM. Therefore, a geometric model of the mission relevant object door is a-priori given and can be accessed from GEM.

The typical action sequence to detect and register an instance of the object door in the model is processed as follows: After the robot has found the main wall of the doorway, it starts following the wall creating a temporary local map of obstacles that is applied for short-term planning movements of the platform. In case of a door detection, the platform targets a position from where the related door can completely be captured by the CCD cameras for relative localization purpose. Based thereupon, the platform moves in front of the predicted door plate and utilizes OCR to read the room number. After the position of the door, plate number and an additional driving command list are stored in the model, the cycle starts again.

3   Communication Issues and Component-Based Framework

A system architecture that totally relies on software components needs a strong unification of all interfaces. Therefore, OSCAR allows several kinds of component types which are similar in their nature. All processing units mentioned in the previous section are to be mapped to OSCAR components.

Considering the data flow between components, data that is transmitted mainly in the bottom-up direction is referred as *cue flow*. Consequently, *cues* encompass sensor raw data, extracted features, hypotheses, etc. Cues are container-like typed data and enclose always a sequence of timestamps to monitor e.g. the point in time of their generation or fusion with other cues. Data generated from the control systems is referred as *configuration flow* in the following.

3.1   General Component Model

Since we distinguish several kinds of OSCAR components, a common view is given in this section. Generally, a component may have input/output interfaces for cue flow, a configuration interface, a control interface and an interface to a related GEM access module.

A component mainly serves for "data processing" and is therefore always in one of the following states that must be configured a-priori or can be controlled by a coordination instance in the control system:

- *deactivated*: The component has released all resources such as devices, computing time and not necessarily allocated memory.
- *continuous mode*: The component processes data continuously, i.e. either as fast as possible or in a quasi-constant time interval.

– *single-step mode*: Data processing is only performed when the component is triggered from "outside", i.e. cues are queried or delivered (see below).

Data processing is generally done "stepwise", i.e. an atomic procedure has to be defined and implemented in each component. Except for components which fuse cues from different sources and/or over time, this fact means that the atomic procedure is exactly processing cues generated at a certain timestamp.

From the developer's perspective, a component defines a lean application programming interface (API) that is realized with an abstract C++ class. To implement a component, several virtual methods have to be overridden: the main information processing (*Step* method) and actions to be performed for reconfiguration, activation and deactivation, etc. Furthermore, the component's designer defines cue-typed input and output channels.

The OSCAR framework specifies different component types for processing units in the system's hierarchy, for which only the amount of interfaces provided is concerned: physical sensors do not provide input channel facilities as well as integration modules and behavior components (see Section 4) do not have output channel facilities; behavior components, integration and interpretation modules may have an interface to GEM access modules. Actuator components additionally have specific control interfaces, for which a part of the functionality of an actuator is standardized (e.g. move commands for a camera head), another part is generic (e.g. acceleration parameter for camera movements if configuration of a certain camera head is provided). Consequently similar actuators are exchangeable within the system architecture.

3.2 CORBA

The communication issue can be seen as one of the most crucial topics related to distributed system architectures. While some architectures come with their own communication layer (see e.g. [15]), OSCAR fully relies on the middleware standard CORBA 2.3 [21] specified by the OMG (Object Management Group) consortium. The benefits of CORBA are – besides the incorporation of the object-oriented design paradigm to the client-server approach – its interoperability, scalability and independence of programming language and hardware platform. This simplifies porting to other operating systems e.g. to real-time OS in the future. We are using the CORBA implementation from IONA Technologies [20], as it has a full support for threaded applications. Figure 3 shows the measured performance of a simple client/server application: By request, a server delivers a defined

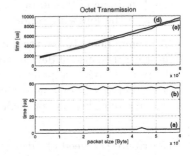

Fig. 3. Performance

amount of transparent data (so-called `octets`). Depending on the relative location of client and servers different latency times are to be expected. In Figure 3, we have applied four measurements with different package sizes averaged over time. Thereby, client and server reside within the same thread (a), in different threads within one process (b), in different processes on the same host (c) or on different hosts (d).[1] The results show the importance of collocation of two instances communicating via CORBA: Larger data packages such as images may therefore not be transmitted over process borders. This has consequences for the design of OSCAR communication mechanisms and component embedding (see next section).

3.3   Component Embedding and OSCAR Modules

The granularity of decomposition on component level, i.e. the "amount" of data processing algorithms has to be determined considering a trade-off between reusability and the possibility to be distributed on one side and the time and memory consuming overhead caused by data copying, communication, thread or process context switch on the other side. OSCAR's component embedding framework tries to minimize this overhead in a way that fine-grained components are feasible.

Since components running in single-step mode behave synchronously, they can be integrated in a single thread of a process if the following conditions are considered:

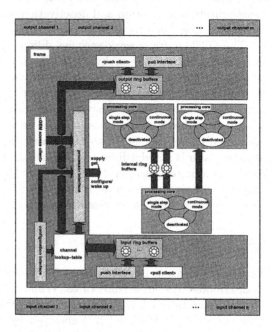

Fig. 4. OSCAR module embedding components

- All components to be integrated in a process must be runnable on the same host e.g. because of device location constrains.
- Only up to one component may run in continuous mode, all others are deactivated or run in single-step mode for synchronization purpose.
- The use of either pull or push cue transport mechanism (see next section) is allowed.

To contribute the need of infrastructure to store a history of cues, the OSCAR component embedding framework provides ring buffers for each input and output

---

[1] Both hosts (Celeron@400MHz, Linux2.4) are located on the robot MARVIN, connected via a switched 100Mbit/s Ethernet. The applied Object Request Broker ORBacus4.1 uses TCP/IP.

channel of a component. In case of synchronous running components, the output channel's ring buffer of a hierarchically lower located component is merged with the corresponding input channel's ring buffer of the hierarchically higher located one. If no need for buffering is required, the ring buffer may be left out totally; thus cues are not copied but transmitted "by reference".

An agglomeration of synchronously running components builds the *processing core* of a OSCAR module. Besides, the OSCAR modules consist of a unified *frame* that provides all infrastructure related to buffering and communication issues (see Figure 4). An internal ring buffer i.e. a ring buffer between two components within a core may be externalized in a way that other components in different modules can access cues from it.

A module is mapped onto a UNIX process consisting of two threads: one for all processing cores and one for the frame. All components always reside in a module except actuator components which are implemented as "pure" CORBA servers. A module itself always contains at least one component.[2] Therefore, OSCAR communication infrastructure encapsulates a polymorphic transport mechanism that supports all cases enumerated above. Since the composition of components into modules is not defined at compile time, modules employ a dynamic plug-in concept relying on the dynamic linking library *libdl*. Therefore, components as well as cue type stubs and skeletons are only available as shared objects. Parallel and asynchronous processing can be achieved using OSCAR modules.

3.4   Data Flow

As stated before, data flow between components encompasses cue and configuration flow. Since configuration data, which is represented by a pair of a token and a numeric or string value, obeys the classical client/server principles[3], cue flow considers also the public/subscribe approach. Thus two mechanisms for cue transmissions are implemented, which are referred as *pull* and *push* resp. in the following:

Applying a pull method, a hierarchically lower located component delivers the requested cues that may – depending on the state of module – have to be processed first. Push methods underlie a controversial logic: The hierarchically lower located component actively delivers cues after they have been processed to all components that are subscribed.

Since cue data flow in a channel may underlay a 1-n or n-1 relationship (for pull and push resp.), double buffering of cues prevents the loss of data in some cases, especially if cues are processed with strong different time rates.

Besides pull and push, it is possible to access cues with a timestamp as index and chronologically ordered arrays of cues that avoid the additional offset

---

[2] In early OSCAR versions, a module was restricted to exactly one core, which had severe consequences for the decomposition vs. performance issue.

[3] Configurees are meant to be servers.

of a CORBA method invocation (approx. 1.6 ms, see Figure 3). Non-blocking triggering of cue processing from lower-level components is also supported.

For the distribution of components to modules, it also has to be considered that avoiding communication overhead in larger modules leads to longer responding times of data requested to be processed. In contrary, older cues can be requested ad hoc, since the module consists of two threads.

3.5   Infrastructure

OSCAR can be seen as an abstract operating system providing an assemblage of infrastructure. A boot routine starts and initially configures all modules; related components are registered in a centralized registry. Monitors installed on each PC hosting a OSCAR module keep the related processes under surveillance. Components may be exchanged at run-time, if e.g. a component has run into an error state.

From the developer's point of view, several facilities are provided for analyzing, component testing and debugging purposes including generic cue loggers, a simulation environment and graphical tools for application configuration and component management. Employing CVS and environment variables, a multi developer environment was designed supporting release management and developer testbeds.

Future Work. will also include an automated mapping of components to employable hosts regarding load balancing issues. The cue flow as well as the processing state of a component shall be automatically configured. Therefore, the Flow Scheduling Framework [16] delivers interesting aspects.

4   Behavior-Based Control System

As stated before, a keynote by designing the OSCAR architecture was the strict separation of data processing components and control system. This decoupling enables the exchange of the control system for different purposes on the one hand and allows a more abstract formulation of application on the other hand. Since OSCAR was originally designed for the exploration of indoor environments, we chose to adopt a behavior-based approach that provides better flexibility while reacting in dynamic and partly unknown environments.

An elementary behavior is defined as a "coupling" between the current sensor state and actions to be performed [3]. In more detail, if activated it uses the current abstracted sensor reading to generate adequate commands for related actuator components. From the architectural perspective, an elementary behavior is mapped into a *behavior component* for reuse and exchange purposes. An elementary behavior (recursively) depends on a set of given physical and logical sensors, interpretation and integration modules. The connectivity structure of sensor, interpretation and integration components together with cue and configuration flow emerges from the used behavior components for a scenario.

Therefore, this approach is behavior specification-centered, in contrary to most architectures that define their system structure by parsing a configuration file that contains a linear list of processing units (see e.g. [19]).

The overall behavior of the mobile robot is determined by an arbitration module that coordinates all applied elementary behaviors. By coordination we mean "controlling" the *activity variable* of each elementary behavior for the following reasons:

- Each two behaviors may not work correctly together since they want to access the same resources with different goals.
- The activation of an elementary behavior only makes sense if a certain "state" of the task to fulfill is reached. Hereby, coordination serves in the sense of sequencing.
- Besides, each behavior $B_i, i \in \{1, 2, \ldots, n\}$ calculates a pre-defined *context variable* $C_i \in [0, 1]$ which is an abstracted sensor reading independent from other behaviors. A sensor context $C_i \approx 1$ is a precondition for the activation of the behavior.

An adequate framework called the *Dynamic Approach* was introduced by Steinhage and Bergener [25]. Pairwise relationships (requirement and inhibition) between each two elementary behaviors B_i and B_j, $i \neq j \in \{1, 2, \ldots, n\}$ can be defined. Both relationships are coded in two $n \times n$ matrices within an arbitration module.

The activation of each elementary behavior is controlled by a set of differential equations evaluating both matrices and considering the individual context for each behavior.

Within the context of exploration[7] with a mobile robot, elementary behaviors serve to achieved sub-goals in the sense of enabling the sensor system to gather informa-

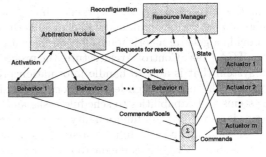

Fig. 5. Structure of the control system

tion about the environment. Therefore, we use the terms *abstract state* and *resource* as follows: The *abstract state* $\sigma \in \mathcal{S}$ describes the current state of the robot. It encompasses all degrees of freedom (pose and velocities) of the actors, discrete modes of all the sensors[4] as well as CPU and memory consumption of the used PCs referred as *state space* $\mathcal{S}$. The activity of behavior B_i requests *resources* $\mathcal{R}_i \subset \mathcal{S}$. A resource conflict activating B_i and B_j occurs if $\mathcal{R}_i \cap \mathcal{R}_j = \emptyset$. In this case, additional inhibition relationships will temporary be introduced to the arbitration module by a resource manager. The resource manager also keeps track of violations of sub-goals by observing the states of all actuators (see Figure 5).

---

[4] E.g. an IEEE1394 camera may run with different rates.

Future Work. We are currently implementing a high-configurable rule-based resource managing system. Future work will also encompass the exploitation of redundant degrees of freedom using e.g. several movable cameras as well as automatic determination of resources by learning strategies.

5   Related Work

Most intelligent mobile robot systems rely upon a more or less distinctive software architecture. Publications like e.g. [3] or [13] enumerate and classify many systems which might be seen as concurrents of our architecture. In this section, we try to compare some of them with OSCAR whenever this is possible at all.

The term *architecture* is often used in several different ways: it describes the chosen approach to control the robot (deliberative, behavior-based or hybrid) [3] or relates to the way algorithms have to be integrated and emphasizes communication issues (see e.g. [23]). OROCOS [12] is an open software project concerning all related aspects in an early state of progress.

In [1] RCS (Real-time Control System) is proposed as a reference architecture for intelligent systems. RCS consists of hierarchically layered processing nodes with a strong distribution of deliberative and reactive functionality as well as of world modeling in contrast to OSCAR that propagates a more centralized view of these issues. Despite the strong hierarchically top-down control approach that restricts run-time flexibility, RCS may suffer from consistency problems regarding the world model. OSCAR provides integration component infrastructure and a general environmental model to overcome these problems, but of course cannot provide a general algorithmic solution for data fusion and integration.

TCA (Task Control Architecture, the proceeder of TDL/IPC) [24] introduces a system that is able to handle information processing from the perspective of tasks. TCA includes high-level methods for passing messages between distributed systems and capabilities to schedule tasks and manage their resources. OSCAR still does not provide functionality that can be related to this. Mid- and long-term planning and scheduling classically conflicts to reacting flexibly on external events. Since OSCAR is meant to cover a wider range of application fields than "pure" exploration tasks, bridging this gap will be a main challenge in the future.

Saphira provides with its C-like programming language COLBERT [18] a flexible "interface" for task composition on a middle level of abstraction. Besides the behavior-centered task specification, OSCAR does not provide such "programming facilities" yet.

Behavior-based control mechanisms, first introduced in [11], find their representative in several software architectures: In [2] a schema-based behavior coordination approach is proposed. BERRA [19] is a behavior-based architecture for service robots integrating a human-computer interface in its deliberative planner. In [4] an architecture is described where behavior modules are controlled by an arbiter deploying a real-time operating system. A similar approach provides the DD-Designer environment for behavior engineering for RoboCup mobile platforms [10]. The related Dual Dynamics architecture includes a framework for a specification-centered design approach. OSCAR's control system belongs to this class of behavior-based systems.

Mobility [22] is a commercial available system that is shipped with RWI robot platforms and theirfore supports unfortunately only a certain class of robots. Moreover, no explicit framework for a control system is provided. Also, the application designer is not completely separated from CORBA issues. In contrary, the OSCAR API provides easier to understand infrastructure and interfaces. In our opinion, the acceptance and application of frameworks and architectures mainly depends on their easiness. Besides, easy to built components accelerate time-to-market since the application developer may implement and integrate his/hers contributed components contemporary.

6 Conclusion

We have presented the design of the system architecture OSCAR for autonomous mobile systems. OSCAR proposes a definition for domain-specific interfaces for data processing and behavior units. The underlying framework provides efficient embedding structures for components and takes care of all communication issues. Although the architecture is still under development and only about 60 components are available, we are confident that more components will emerge by realizing more use-cases also for other robotic platforms.

An external evaluation of OSCAR can be found in [14]. Currently, we are about to establish a network of OSCAR users [5]. Besides exchanging components, we hope to get further input for requirements also related to architectural issues.

References

1. J. S. Albus and A. M. Meystel. A Reference Model Architecture for Design and Implementation of Intelligent Control in Large and Complex systems. *Int. J. of Intelligent Control and Sytems*, 1(1):15–30, 1996.
2. R. C. Arkin. Motor schema-based mobile robot navigation. *International Journal of Robotics Research*, 8(4), 1989.
3. R. C. Arkin. *Behavior-Based Robotics*. MIT Press, 1998.
4. Thomas Bergener and Axel Steinhage. An Architecture for Behavioral Organization using Dynamical Systems. In C. Wilke, S. Altmeyer, and T. Martinetz, editors, *Third German Workshop on Artificial Life*. Verlag Harri Deutsch, 1998.
5. Stefan Blum. OSCAR-Homepage. http://www.oscar-net.org.
6. Stefan Blum. OSCAR - Eine Systemarchitektur für den autonomen, mobilen Roboter MARVIN. In *Autonome Mobile Systeme*, Informatik aktuell, pages 218–230. Springer-Verlag, November 2000.
7. Stefan Blum. Towards a Component-based System Architecture for Autonomous Mobile Robots. In *Proc. IASTED Int. Conf. Robotics and Applications (RA'01)*, pages 220–225, Tampa, FL, USA, November 2001. IASTED.
8. Stefan Blum, Darius Burschka, Christof Eberst, Tobias Einsele, Alexa Hauck, Norbert O. Stöffler, and Georg Färber. Autonome Exploration von Innenräumen mit der Multisensorik-Plattform MARVIN. In *Autonome Mobile Systeme*, Informatik aktuell, pages 138–147. Springer-Verlag, 1998.

9. Stefan Blum, Tobias Einsele, Alexa Hauck, Norbert O. Stöffler, Georg Färber, Thorsten Schmitt, Christoph Zierl, and Bernd Radig. Eine konfigurierbare Systemarchitektur zur geometrisch-topologischen Exploration von Innenräumen. In *Autonome Mobile Systeme*, Informatik aktuell, pages 378–387. Springer-Verlag, November 1999.

10. Ansgar Bredenfeld and Giovanni Indiveri. Robot behavior engineering using DD-designer. In *Proc. IEEE/RSJ Int. Conf. on Intelligent Robots and Systems (IROS'01)*, Seoul, Korea, May 2001.

11. R. A. Brooks. A Robust Layered Control System For a Mobile Robot. *IEEE Journal of Robotics and Automatisation*, RA-2, No. 1:14–23, 1986.

12. Herman Bruyninckx. The OROCOS Project. http://www.orocos.org.

13. Ève Coste-Manière and Raid Simmons. Architecture, the backbone of robotic systems. In *Proc. IEEE Int. Conf. on Robotics and Automation (ICRA'00)*, San Franciso CA, USA, April 2000.

14. Markus Vincze et al. ActIPret: Interpreting and Understanding Activities of Expert Operators for Teaching and Education. http://actipret.infa.tuwien.ac.at.

15. C. Fedor. TCX - An Interprocess Communication System for Building Robotic Architectures. Carnegie Mellon University, Pittsburg, Pennsylvania, 1993.

16. Alexandre R.J. François and Gérard G. Medioni. A Modular Software Architecture for Real-Time Video Processing. In *Proceedings of the International Workshop on Computer Vision Systems*, pages 35–49, Vancouver, B.C., Canada, July 2001.

17. A. Hauck and N. O. Stöffler. A Hierarchic World Model Supporting Video-based Localization, Exploration and Object Identification. In *Proc. 2nd Asian Conf. on Computer Vision (ACCV'95)*, volume 3, pages 176–180, 1995.

18. Kurt Konolige. COLBERT: A Language for Reactive Control in Saphira. In *German Conference on Artificial Intellgence*, Freiburg, 1997.

19. M. Lindström, A. Orebäck, and H.I. Christensen. Berra - a behaviour based robot architecture. In *Proc. IEEE Int. Conf. on Robotics and Automation (ICRA'00)*, San Francisco, CA, USA, 2000.

20. Object Oriented Concepts. *Orbacus*. http://www.ooc.com/ob/.

21. OMG. CORBA/IIOP 2.3 specification. http://www.omg.org/corba, 1998.

22. Real World Interfaces, Inc. Mobility. http://www.rwii.com/rwi/software_mobility.html, 1998.

23. C. Schlegel, J. Illmann, H. Jaberg, M. Schuster, and R. Wörtz. Integrating Vision Based Behaviours with an Autonomous Robot. In *International Conference on Vision Systems (ICVS)*, volume 1542 of *Lecture Notes in Computer Science*. Springer-Verlag, 1999.

24. Reid Simmons. An architecture for coordinating planning, sensing, and action. In *Proc. of the DAPRA workshop*, pages 292–297, 1990.

25. A. Steinhage and T. Bergener. Dynamical Systems for the Behavioral Organization of an Anthropomorphic Mobile Robot. In *From animals to animats 5: Proceedings of the Fifth International Conference on Simulation of Adaptive Behavior*, pages 147–152. MIT Press, 1998.

26. Clemens Szyperski. *Component Software, Beyond Object-Oriented Programming*. Addison-Wesley Publishing Company, 1997.

A Framework for Visual Servoing

Danica Kragic and Henrik I. Christensen

Centre for Autonomous Systems,
Royal Institute of Technology,
S-10044 Stockholm, Sweden,
{danik,hic}@nada.kth.se
http://www.nada.kth.se/~danik

Abstract. We consider typical manipulation tasks in terms of a service robot framework. Given a task at hand, such as "Pick up the cup from the dinner table", we present a number of different visual systems required to accomplish the task. A standard robot platform with a PUMA560 on the top is used for experimental evaluation. The classical *approach-align-grasp* idea is used to design a manipulation system. Here, both visual and tactile feedback is used to accomplish the given task. In terms of image processing, we start by a recognition system which provides a 2D estimate of the object position in the image. Thereafter, a 2D tracking system is presented and used to maintain the object in the field of view during an approach stage. For the alignment stage, two systems are available. The first is a model based tracking system that estimates the complete pose/velocity of the object. The second system is based on corner matching and estimates homography between two images. In terms of tactile feedback, we present a grasping system that, at this stage, performs power grasps. The main objective here is to compensate for minor errors in object position/orientation estimate caused by the vision system.

1 Introduction

Robotic visual servoing and manipulation has received significant attention during the past few years. Still, most of the existing systems rely on one visual servoing control strategy or one sensory modality. This commonly limits the system to concentrate on one of the *approach-align-grasp* steps. It has been pointed out that one of the key research areas in the field of visual servoing is the integration of existing techniques, regarding both the estimation and control, [1].

In terms of robotic appliances for service robotics, it is of inevitable importance to observe the complete robotic task. Assuming basic *fetch-and-carry* tasks, there are varying demands for precision and degrees of freedom in control depending on complexity. As proposed in [2], a key to solving robotic hand-eye tasks efficiently and robustly is to identify how precise control is needed at a particular time during task execution. The required level of precision should then be matched with appropriate sensory input. This is also one of the main ideas pursued in our work.

We consider three levels for an object manipulation sequence, see Fig.1:

- **Transport** considers motion of the robot platform and/or the robot arm to the vicinity of the object. From this position, the arm should be able to reach the object without moving the base.

J.L. Crowley et al. (Eds.): ICVS 2003, LNCS 2626, pp. 345–354, 2003.
© Springer-Verlag Berlin Heidelberg 2003

- **Alignment** of the hand with the object such that a grasp can be performed.
- **Grasping** of the object which can be performed using tactile feedback or in a predefined open–loop manner.

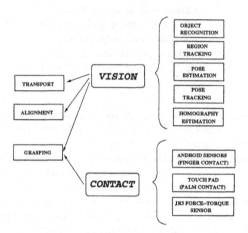

Fig. 1. Robot control versus sensory feedback hierarchy. The required complexity and type of feedback depends on the current step of a manipulation task.

Our main goal is to present a number of different techniques that allow robots to perform manipulation tasks in real world scenarios according to the above. We will show how visual and tactile feedback can be used together with a number of visual servoing strategies to manipulate simple, everyday objects. We do not offer a general solution from a system point of view, rather a first step towards it. Compared to our previous work [3], where the main consideration was the overall control framework and systems integration, here we concentrate on the actual building blocks. In particular, visual and tactile feedback and underlying servoing strategies are studied. We believe that our approach is relatively easy to build upon - each of the individual techniques can easily be extended and combined to perform more complex tasks. Similarly, in human physiology there is a differentiation between identification of the object, ballistic motion to the proximity of the object, preshaping of the hand, alignment, and interaction. Here, the identification and ballistic motion are fused into a single task for convenience.

The paper is organized as follows. In Section 2 basic control strategies for visual servoing are presented together with commonly facilitated camera/robot configurations. In Section 3 image processing algorithms currently used in the system are briefly presented. The strategies for using tactile feedback for grasping are discussed in Section 4. The experimental platform and few experiments are presented in Section 5. And finally, Section 6 discusses the current limitations of the system and provides topics for future research.

2   Visual Servoing

In terms of the design of visual servoing systems, there are three major issues that have to be considered: i) the choice of control law, ii) camera-robot configuration, and iii) the choice algorithms used to provide the feedback for the control loop. We will touch upon the first two issues briefly in Section 2.1 and Section 2.2. Section 3 outlines the image processing algorithms currently available in our system.

2.1   Control Design

There are two basic approaches to visual servo control [4]: i) image–based visual servoing (IBVS) and position–based visual servoing (PBVS). In IBVS, an error signal is measured in the image and then mapped directly to robot motion commands. In PBVS, features are extracted from the image and then used to compute a partial or a complete pose/velocity of the object. An error is then computed in the task space and thereafter used by the control system. To overcome the problems of IBVS and PBVS systems, several hybrid systems have been proposed [10], [11]. In general, these systems decouple the translational and rotational part of the control signal achieving the desired stability of the system even for cases where the difference between the start and desired pose of the robot is significant. In our system, all three strategies are used.

2.2   Camera-Robot Configurations

Fig. 2 shows some of the most common camera-robot configurations typically used in visual servoing systems. In our system, according to the figure, we are using a combination of VM1 and VM4 which is a special case of VM5. The available configuration usually determines the design of the feedback system. For example, an eye–in–hand camera configuration commonly requires fast image processing (since the image changes with each motion of the arm) as well as the flexibility in terms of scale. Since there is a significant difference between the start and the destination pose, 2 1/2 D approach is commonly adopted control strategy [10], [12]. A stereo stand–alone system requires less features per image and, for the case of static targets, the appearance of the features may remain almost constant throughout the visual servo sequence.

There are numerous examples where one or the other control approach or configuration will perform better. To that end, we have decided to use a number of different systems and use them depending on the task at hand and at the level of detail/complexity needed to perform the given task.

3   Transportation and Alignment

The following sections give a short overview of the image processing methods currently exploited in the system.

Fig. 2. Most common camera–robot configurations: monocular eye–in–hand, monocular stand–alone, binocular eye–in–hand, binocular stand–alone and redundant camera system. In our system, we are using a combination of VM1 and VM4 which is a special case of VM5.

3.1   Recognition

The object to be manipulated is first recognized using the view-based SVM (support vector machine) system presented in [7]. The recognition step delivers the image position and approximate size of the image region occupied by the object. This information is then used i) either by the tracking system to track the part of the image, the *window of attention*, occupied by the object while the robot approaches it, or ii) by the stereo system to provide a rough estimate of the object's 3D position. Recent research on human vision has clearly demonstrated that *re*-cognition of prior known objects can be efficiently modeled as a view based process [16], [17], which motivates our use of an SVM based approach to recognition.

3.2   Region Tracking

Our tracking system is based on integration of multiple visual cues using *voting*, [5]. The visual cues used are motion, color, correlation and intensity variation. Cues are fused using weighted super-position and the most appropriate action is selected according to a winner-take-all strategy. The advantage of the voting approach for integration is the fact that information of different cues can be easily combined without the need for explicit models as it is for example is the case in Bayesian approaches. Lots of perceptual experiments support the idea that when it comes to aspects of visual scenes, people most likely mention color, form and motion as being quite distinct. There is a believe that information about form, color, motion and depth is processed separately in the visual system. However, it has also been shown that the segregation is not complete and there is a cross-talk among different cues [18].

3.3   Pose Estimation and Tracking

Our model-based tracking system integrates the use of both appearance based and geometrical models to estimate the position and orientation of the object relative to the camera/robot coordinate system, [6]. There are basically three steps in the system:

- *Initialization* - here, Principle Component Analysis (PCA) is used to provide an approximation to the current object pose.

- *Pose Estimation* - To estimate the true pose, the initialization step is followed by a local fitting method that uses a geometric model of the object. This is made possible by the fact that we deal with an object that has already been recognized and thus its model is known. The method used here was proposed in [8].
- *Pose Tracking* - If the object or the camera start to move, the system will provide a real–time estimate of the object pose. Again, the method proposed in [8] is used.

It has been shown in [20] that visuo-motor actions such as grasping, use the actual size of the object and that the position and orientation are computed in egocentric frames of reference. Thus, human reaching movements are planned in spatial coordinates, not in joint space. If an accurate pose of the target is available together with a good arm model (which is true in our case), one can use the ideas proposed in [19] to generate human–like arm trajectories. In our case, both IBVS and PBVS are used as demonstrated in [5].

3.4 Homography Based Matching

Using a stored image taken from the reference position, the manipulator can be moved in such a way that the current camera view is gradually changed to match the stored reference view (*teach–by–showing* approach). Accomplishing this for general scenes is difficult, but a robust system can be made under the assumption that the objects are piecewise planar. In our system, a wide baseline matching algorithm is employed to establish point correspondences between the current and the reference image [12]. The point correspondences enable the computation of a homography relating the two views which is then used for 2 1/2D visual servoing.

4 Grasping

The following sections give a short overview of the current grasping strategies where tactile and force-torque feedback are considered. The grasping system is still in its initial phase and does not perform any intelligent grasp planning. The main objective here was to design a system which will be able to perform a grasp even if the pose of the object is not perfectly known. Therefore, the current implementation considers only power grasps.

4.1 Grasp Modeling

After the arm (hand) is aligned with the object, grasping can be performed. Using the available pose estimate and tactile feedback, the grasping system compensates for minor errors in the pose estimate. The grasping strategy is formulated using finite state machines (FSM) [14]. Using the general idea proposed by [15], the basic states, q_i of a FSM are shown in Fig.3. These states basically mimic the human grasping procedure. In addition, Fig.3 shows the actions, a_i, needed to execute the grasp. Also, basic conditions, e_i under which the actions, a_i are running are outlined.

For the control of grasping, our three–fingered Barrett hand has been equipped with two types of tactile sensors. The palm is equipped with a touch pad for detection of palm contacts. In addition, each link of the three fingers have basic sensors for detection of

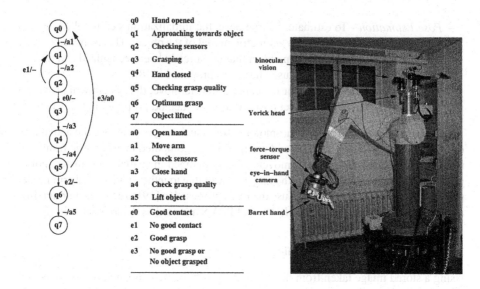

q0	Hand opened
q1	Approaching towards object
q2	Checking sensors
q3	Grasping
q4	Hand closed
q5	Checking grasp quality
q6	Optimum grasp
q7	Object lifted
a0	Open hand
a1	Move arm
a2	Check sensors
a3	Close hand
a4	Check grasp quality
a5	Lift object
e0	Good contact
e1	No good contact
e2	Good grasp
e3	No good grasp or No object grasped

Fig. 3. Left) Minimized abstract representation of the grasping process, and Right) XR4000 equipped with an eye–in–hand camera, stereo head, JR3 force–torques sensor, and Barret hand with tactile sensors.

contact. In addition, the arm has a force torque sensor for overall sensing of hand forces. The details of the setup are described in Section 5.1. To achieve the desired flexibility of the system, ideas from behavior–based planning were used, see [13] for details.

5   Experimental Evaluation

In this section, a few examples are presented to demonstrate the system. Since the task is given (i.e. "Robot, pick up the raisins."), the object to be dealt with is known in advance as well as the transport-align-grasp strategy to be used. This is explained in more detail with each of the examples.

5.1   Experimental Platform

The experimental platform is a Nomadic Technologies XR4000 equipped with a Puma 560 arm for manipulation (see Fig. 3). The robot has two rings of sonars, a SICK laser scanner, a wrist mounted force/torque sensor (JR3), and a color CCD camera mounted on the gripper (Barrett Hand). On the robot shoulder, there is a Yorick robot head providing a stereo visual input. The palm of the Barrett hand is covered by a VersaPad sensor. The Versa Pad was designed to be used as a touch pad on a laptop. It reports the following: i) a Boolean value if the pad is active (contact occurred), ii) the coordinates of the contact point , and iii) pressure at the contact point. On each finger link, an Android sensor is placed. It reports the pressure applied on the link. The wrist mounted JR3 force–torque sensor is here primarily used as a "safety–break" for the system: if the contact occurs on the VersaPad's "blind" spot, it can still be felt by the JR3 sensor.

5.2 Example 1

This example shows the basic idea for "Robot, pick up the raisins" task. The object is first located in the scene using the recognition system, see Fig. 4. The object is polyhedral and in this case a homography based approach is used during the align step. The current image is compared with the stored image of the object as presented in Section 3.4. 2 1/2 D visual servoing is the used to control the motion of the robot. After the hand is aligned with the object, an open–loop grasp strategy is performed to pick-up the object. A few example images during servoing onto and grasping a package of raisins are shown in Fig. 5.

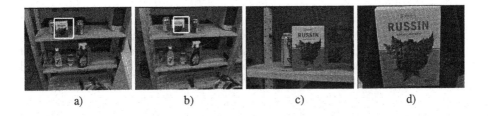

a)   b)   c)   d)

Fig. 4. a) and b) Images observed by the left and right head camera, respectively. The windows show the position of the raisins package estimated by the recognition system. c) image observed by the eye–in–hand camera, and d) destination image used for 2 1/2 D visual servoing.

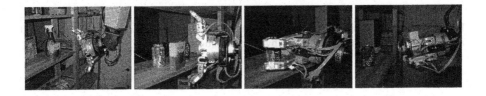

Fig. 5. A few example images during servoing onto and grasping a package of raisins.

5.3 Example 2

Fig.6 shows an example where model-based pose estimation/tracking system is used to estimate the complete pose of the object and then align the gripper with it. After that, the the object can be grasped. Since the model of the object is available, it is enough to use one camera during the whole servoing sequence.

5.4 Example 3

Fig. 7 shows the image position of two example objects (a soda bottle and a cleaner item) estimated by the visual recognition system. Using the knowledge of the head camera

Fig. 6. The basic idea of our approach: after the object is recognized, 2D tracking is used to approach the object. After that, the appearance based approach followed by a local fitting stage is used to estimate the current pose of the object. After that, simple grasping can be performed.

intrinsic and extrinsic parameters, an approximate 3D position of the object is estimated. It is assumed that the object is in vertical position. The arm is then aligned with the object so that the palm of the hand is facing the object, see Fig.8. Finally, the hand is moved towards the object in the direction orthogonal to the palm plane.

a)   b)   c)   d)

Fig. 7. a) and b) The position of a soda bottle, and c) and d) the position of a cleaner bottle in left and right head camera images estimated by the recognition system.

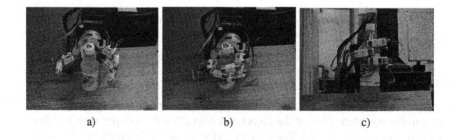

a)   b)   c)

Fig. 8. a) Approaching the bottle, b) Grasping, and c) Lifting.

5.5   Example 4

Fig.9 shows an example grasping sequence where the Android sensors on the hand's fingers are used during grasping. Here, a contact with one of the fingers occurs before the contact with the palm. The hand is driven in the horizontal plane to center the object inside the hand. The hand is moved until contact with each of the fingers is reported. If no contact is reported from one of the sensors, the principle described in the previous experiment is used.

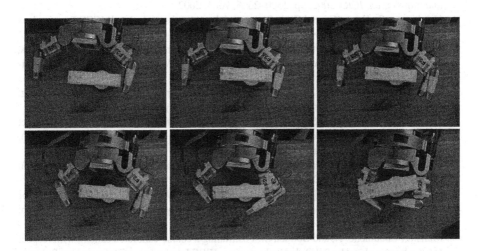

Fig. 9. Grasping a cleaner bottle (see text for a detailed description).

6   Conclusions and Future Work

We have discussed major building blocks of a typical manipulation tasks in terms of a service robot. Assuming a task such as "Pick up the cup from the dinner table", we have presented a number of different visual systems required to accomplish the task. The classical transport-align-grasp strategy was used to choose between available feedback systems. Both visual and tactile feedback were used to accomplish the given task.

In terms of image processing used during the transportation step, we have presented a recognition system which provides a position estimate of the object, and a 2D tracking system used to keep the object in the field of view. For the alignment step, two systems are available. The first is a model based tracking system that estimates the complete pose/velocity of the object. The second system is based on corner matching and estimates homography between two images. In terms of tactile feedback, we have presented a grasping system that currently performs power grasps. The main objective here was the design of a system capable of compensating for minor errors in object position/orientation estimate caused by the vision system.

References

1. Workshop on visual servoing, *IEEE International Conference on Intelligent Robots and Systems, IROS2002*, Lausanne, Switzerland, 2002
2. Dodds, Z., Jägersand, M., Hager G., and Toyama K.: A hierarchical vision architecture for robotic manipulation tasks, *International Conference on Computer Vision Systems, ICVS'99*, pp. 312–331, 1999
3. Petersson, L., Jensfelt, P., Tell, D., Strandberg, M., Kragic, D. and Christensen, H.: Systems Integration for Real-World Manipulation Tasks, *IEEE International Conference on Robotics and Automation, ICRA 2002*, pp. 2500–2505, vol 3, 2002
4. Hutchinson, S., Hager, G., and CorkeP.: A tutorial on visual servo control, *IEEE Transactions on Robotics and Automation*, 12(5), pp. 651–670, 1996.
5. Kragic, D.: Visual servoing for Manipulation: Robustness and Integration Issues, PhD thesis, Computational Vision and Active Perception Laboratory (CVAP), Royal Institute of Technology, June, 2001.
6. Kragic, D. and Christensen, H.: Model Based Techniques for Robotic Servoing and Grasping, *IEEE International Conference on Intelligent Robots and Systems, IROS2002*, pp. 2002
7. Roobaert, D.: Pedagogical Support Vector Learning: A Pure Learning Appr oach to Object Recognition, PhD thesis, Computational Vision and Active Perception Laboratory (CVAP), Royal Institute of Technology, May, 2001.
8. T.W. Drummond and R. Cipolla. Real-time tracking of multiple articulated structures in multiple views. *ECCV'00*, 2:20–36.
9. L. Petersson, D. Austin, and H.I. Christensen. "DCA: A Distributed Control Architecture for Robotics", *IEEE International Conference on Intelligent Robots and Systems, IROS2001*, pp. 2361–2368, vol 3, 2001
10. Malis,E., Chaumette, F., and Boudet, S.: Positioning a coarse-calibrated camera with respect to an unknown object by 2-1/2-d visual servoing. *IEEE International Conference on Robotics and Automation, ICRA98*, pp. 1352–1359, 1998.
11. Deguchi, K.: Optimal motion control for image-based visual servoing by decoupling translation and rotation, *IEEE International Conference on Intelligent Robots and Systems, IROS1998*, pp. 705–711, 1998.
12. Tell, D.: Wide baseline matching with applications to visual servoing, PhD thesis, Computational Vision and Active Perception Laboratory (CVAP), Royal Institute of Technology, June, Stockholm, Sweden, 2002.
13. Crinier, S.: Behavior-based Control of a Robot Hand Using Tactile Sensors, Master thesis, Centre for Autonomous Systems, Royal Institute of Technology, December, 2002.
14. Katz, R.H.: Contemporary logic design, Benjamin Cummings/Addison Wesley Publishing Company, 1993
15. Horswill, I.D.: Behavior-Based Robotics, Behavior Design, Technical report CS 395, Northwestern University, 2000
16. Tarr, M.J., and Bulthoff,H.: Object recognition on man, monkey and machine, *International Journal of Cognitive Science*, Vol. 69, No. 1–2, July 1998.
17. Edelman, S.: Representation and Recognition in Vision, *MIT Press*, Cambridge, MA. 1999.
18. Palmer, S.E.: Vision Science: Photons to Phenomenology, *MIT Press*, Cambridge, MA. 1999
19. Goodman, S.R. and Gottlieb, G.G.: Analysis of kinematic invariances of multijoint reaching movements, *Biological Cybernetics*, vol 73, pp.311–322, 1995
20. Hu, Y. and Goodale, M.: Constraints in Human visuomotor systems, *IEEE International Conference on Intelligent Robots and Systems, IROS 2000*, pp. 1633–1638, vol 2, 2000

Automatic Mapping of Settlement Areas Using a Knowledge-Based Image Interpretation System

Bernd-Michael Straub[1], Markus Gerke[1], and Martin Pahl[2]

[1] Institute of Photogrammetry and GeoInformation (IPI), University of Hannover,
Nienburger Str. 1, D-30167 Hannover, Germany
{straub, gerke}@ipi.uni-hannover.de

[2] Institute of Communication Theory and Signal Processing (TNT), University of Hannover, Appelstr. 9A, D-30167 Hannover, Germany
geoaida@tnt.uni-hannover.de

Abstract. We introduce the knowledge-based image interpretation system GeoAIDA and give examples for an image operator, extracting trees from aerial imagery. Moreover we present a generic grouping approach, based on the Relative Neighborhood Graph. The application of the tree operator to a test site shows that the introduced approach for the delineation of trees using Active Contour Models leads to good results. The grouping algorithm is used in order to identify building rows. In the paper we shortly describe the theory of the image operator, and the performance of the whole system is demonstrated by means of examples. Results from a test area show that the information about building rows can be used for the enhancement of the building reconstruction.

1 Introduction

One main task when aerial images of settlement areas have to be interpreted automatically is the reconstruction of trees and buildings [7]. In this paper we present how object extraction from high-resolution aerial images can be supported by structural scene analysis. The knowledge-based image interpretation system GeoAIDA (**Geo A**utomatic **I**mage **D**ata **A**nalyser) [cf. 4] acts as a control unit: It calls *top-down* operators and the respective *bottom-up* operators. Finally it checks the consistency of the results. The *top-down* extraction modules "know" how the objects in the scene appear in the images and generate hypotheses of these objects. In the data-driven phase (*bottom-up*) the structural knowledge about the scene is used to refine these hypotheses.

After a short introduction of the concept of GeoAIDA in section 2 of the paper, we describe two types of operators in detail. In section 3.1 a *top-down* operator dealing with the extraction of single trees, an advancement of the approach introduced in [22]. Furthermore we introduce a *bottom-up* operator for the structural analysis of objects in section 3.2. It considers topological relations, represented by the Relative Neighborhood Graph [23], and geometric constraints in order to find rows of buildings. This information is then used to refine the reconstruction. Finally we present results to demonstrate the performance and potential of these two operators in section 4.

J.L. Crowley et al. (Eds.): ICVS 2003, LNCS 2626, pp. 355–364, 2003.

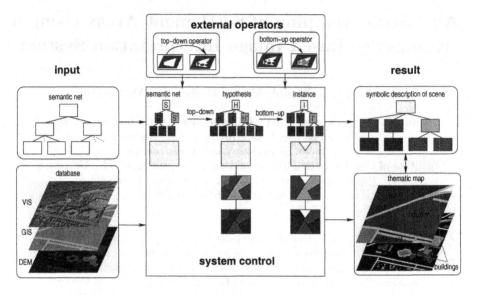

Fig. 1. GeoAIDA design

2   The Concept of GeoAIDA

Image interpretation systems are often restricted to segmentation and classification of images into one or few different classes. They are highly specialized and optimized for a certain task or have difficulties processing large images. Especially methods which follow a strict structural approach [14, 17, 24], i.e. working with primitive objects extracted from the image data, are not capable of handling whole aerial images due to the large number of extracted primitives in such images. GeoAIDA is designed for the automatic extraction of objects from remote sensing data. On the input side the system consists of the components *database* and *semantic net* (refer to Fig. 1 for an overview). Semantic nets provide a formalism for knowledge representation using nodes and links as basic elements. Nodes represent objects, while relations between these nodes are described by links. The a priori knowledge about the scene under investigation is stored in a generic semantic net. This net is called concept net and includes the objects expected in the input data. The nodes of the net are ordered strictly hierarchically, i.e. each node has exactly one parent node. Attributes can be assigned to each node dynamically, common attributes are *name*, *class* and the associated *top-down* and *bottom-up* operators.

The scene interpretation is handled by *top-down* and *bottom-up operators*, which are called by the system control unit. Results are shown in an interactive map which consists of a *symbolic description of the scene* and a *thematic map*.

The core *system control* queries the image database, reads the semantic net as well as project descriptions and generates hypotheses by calling *top-down* operators. A *top-down* operator associated with a node is capable of detecting objects of this kind of node (called *class*) in the given input data. For each object, which is expected in the scene, a hypothesis node is instantiated. The *bottom-up* operator investigates the relationship between the subnodes and groups them into consistent objects of the class given by the node the operator is connected to.

3   Interpretation Process

In this section two external operators for the extraction and grouping of objects are described. Three different semantic levels are used for the creation of the hypotheses: On the highest abstraction level the scene is segmented into *GroupOfTrees*, *BuildingAreas* and the background. The segmentation is based on thresholds in the Difference Normalized Vegetation Index (NDVI) and the normalized Digital Surface Model (DSM). The normalized DSM is the difference between the Terrain Model and the Surface Model, i.e. the ground topography is removed from the height dataset. Using these data sources as input information, the classification of the segmented regions leads to sufficient results in our test site. In more complex situations it can be useful to formulate the segmentation as a statistical classification problem; for example the use of a Markov random field is proposed by [2]. The detection of trees is performed together with the detection of buildings, in some cases as a pre-processing step for the building reconstruction, as described in [10]. An excellent overview of the recent research work in the domain of the automatic extraction of objects from remote sensing data is given in [3]. The second abstraction level is the object level. Based on the first segmentation the system calls a *top-down* operator for the instantiation of trees and buildings. Instances of *Trees* are generated as child nodes of the *GroupOfTrees* areas in the scene, and finally the contour of the tree's *Crown* – representing the third abstraction level – is delineated. This *top-down* operator is described in section 3.1 of this paper.

Instances of *Buildings* are created by the system according to the approach presented in [9] using a histogram analysis for the detection of buildings inside the *BuildingArea*, followed by the use of invariant geometric moments for the reconstruction of single buildings. The last step is the grouping of all the buildings in the scene, with the aim to find buildings arranged in a straight line. This is done with the *bottom-up* operator described in section 3.2.

Aerial color infrared (CIR) images and height data of a test site in Grangemouth, Scotland were used for the investigations. The CIR images were acquired in summer 2000 by the French company ISTAR. The image flight was carried out with 80% overlap along and across the flight direction using an analogue aerial film camera. The image scale is 1 : 5000, which leads to a GSD (Ground Sampling Distance) of 10 cm at a scanning resolution of 21 μm. Based on these images ISTAR has produced a DSM and a true orthoimage mainly automatically, using the approach described in [8]. The orthoimage and the DSM cover an area of $4 \, \mathrm{km}^2$, the GSD of the DSM is about $0.2 \, \mathrm{m}$.

3.1   A *top-down* Operator for the Extraction of Trees

The *top-down* operator for the extraction of trees is described in this section. The extraction is subdivided into two phases, first the detection of trees is performed, and in the second phase the crown perimeter is delineated. The precise delineation of the crown's contour is an important task within the reconstruction of a tree. The outline can be used for the estimation of the position and the radius of the stem; which are relevant parameters of a tree from a forestry point of view [11]. Furthermore, it is useful for a precise estimation of texture and color values without having the problem of mixed pixels, which is helpful for a more detailed classification of the type of the tree or its vitality.

The delineation of the individual crowns is done using Active Contour Models, also called Snakes. Snakes were introduced by Kass et al. [13] as mid-level algorithm which combines geometric and/or topologic constraints with the extraction of low-level features from images. The principal idea is to define a contour with the help of mechanic properties like elasticity and rigidity, to initialize this contour close to the boundary of the object one is looking for, and then let the contour move into the direction of the boundary of the objects. The original energy based approach for the contour can be reformulated to a pure geometry based approach, called Geodesic Active Contours [6]. Recent developments combine Geodesic Active Contours with level set methods [18], then the topology of the Active Contour can change during the optimization.

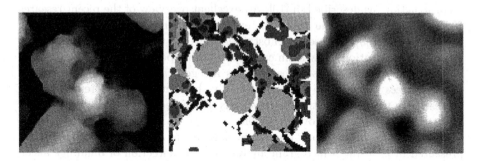

Fig. 2. The left image shows three different trees in the DSM. The optimal local scale is coded in the middle image, grey values assign the diameter of the corresponding region. The second derivative used for the extraction of the crown positions is printed on the right side using light grey for negative values and dark grey for positive values. The scale parameter used for the computation of the second derivative is selected according to the regions in the middle image.

In our approach one Active Contour Model is initialized for every tree as a circular shaped closed contour with an approximate value for the radius and the center position. The computation of these approximate values can be looked upon as the critical point in the whole extraction process.

A segmentation of the DSM into regions having the same diameter is used for the estimation of the radius. The segmentation is performed using morphological bandpass filters with a circular structuring function as proposed in [15]. The maximum value of the normalized response of the bandpass filters gives the local optimal scale for the appropriate pixel (Fig. 2). The optimal scale for the extraction of crowns in linear scale space [16] can be selected with this information about the diameter of the corresponding region. The sigma of the Gaussian - being the filter function in linear scale space - is proportional to the diameter of the region [20]. This property is used for the extraction of tree hypothesis. The minima of the DSM's second derivative in scale space are valid hypothesis of the searched tree positions, if the scale is selected correctly. These steps are depicted in Fig. 2: The left image shows the original DSM, the optimal local scale in morphological scale space is presented in the middle, and the respective second derivative in linear scale space is presented in the right image. The final result of the reconstruction using Active Contour Models is depicted in Fig. 4.

3.2   Grouping Approach Based on Neighborhood Graphs

In this section we present a generic approach based on neighborhood graphs for the grouping of objects and show how this approach can be used to create instances of building-rows. These rows are used to refine the orientation of the automatically extracted buildings.

Neighborhood graphs play an important role in many image analysis tasks and geographic applications [cf. 12, Ch. 7]. In the field of road extraction the network characteristic, i.e. the connection of single road segments to a road network represented by a graph is of substantial importance [cf. 21]. In [19] neighborhood relations between cars are used to detect parking lots. An other example is the clustering of geographic data to support generalization [1]. This clustering - provided by graph approaches - is necessary to obtain information about the structure of the data.

We use a Relative Neighborhood Graph (RNG) as introduced by Toussaint [23] to represent the topological relations between instances of the *Building* class; members of an arrangement like a row have to be connected by the edges of the RNG. We call constraints reflecting the topological relations of an arrangement *topological constraints*. In [23] the proximity definition of "relatively close" can be found:

> If we consider a set of distinct points $P = \{p_1, p_2, \ldots, p_n\}$ in the plane two points p_i and p_j are supposed to be "relatively close" if $d(p_i, p_j) \leq \max[d(p_i, p_k), d(p_j, p_k)] \forall k = 1, \ldots, n, k \neq i, j$, where d denotes the distance.

The edges of the RNG are connecting each pair of points which are "relatively close". Generally the RNG belongs to the family of *proximity graphs*; other representatives of this family are the Delaunay Triangulation (DT) or the Minimum Spanning Tree (MST). Whereas the DT is a superset of the RNG and the MST

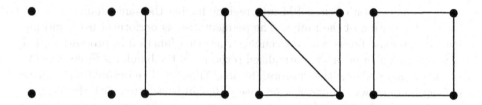

Fig. 3. Four points in the plane and the MST, DT and RNG of these points, from [23]

is a subset of it [23]. In Fig. 3 the differences between the three representatives
of proximity graphs are pointed out: On the left side a set of four points in the
plane is shown. The MST of these points is depicted in the second picture, besides the DT and the RNG. Our perception would "do" the same like the RNG
and connect the four points in order to yield a rectangle. Besides the *topological
constraints* we define geometric constraints which reflect the particular arrangement, e.g. for a row: "All instances have to be aligned to a straight line". We call
these constraints *global geometric constraints*. Additionally some *local geometric
constraints* may be formulated, for example "all buildings in a row must have
the same orientation".

  We use the RNG as an adequate representative of the topology. The distance
between two buildings is the shortest distance between the appropriate region.
This distance is assigned to the edges of the RNG as a weight. In order to express
the condition that buildings may not exceed a given distance from each other a
maximum weight for the edges can be required. Additionally the number n_s of
nodes in this graph can be restricted, and a minimum can be required. We define
the minimum number of buildings in a row is $n_{s_{\min}} = 3$. Then we demand that
the neighbored buildings should lie on a straight line. This is a global geometric
constraint, because it concerns all buildings in one row. Every buildings center
of gravity may not exceed a maximum distance $d_{\max}$ to a common straight line.
This maximum distance $d_{\max}$ is set to $d_{\max} = 3$m. Additionally we want all
buildings belonging to a row of buildings to have the same orientation, this is a
local geometric constraint.

4   Results

In this chapter we show some results of the introduced operators. The test site
on which we concentrate is a small part of the Grangemouth data set (cf. Sec. 3).

4.1   Results of Tree Extraction

The results of the described algorithm are depicted in Fig. 4. On the left image
the perimeter of a *GroupOfTree* instance is superimposed to the optical image.

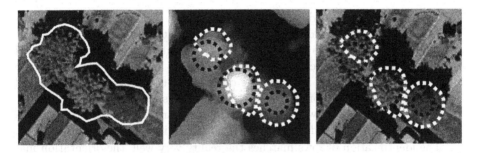

Fig. 4. Exemplary results of the tree extraction operator are depicted in these three pictures

Fig. 5. Reconstructed buildings with marked centers of gravity and row of buildings (left), buildings after orientation enhancement (right)

The initial contour for the Snakes are depicted as black dotted lines, and the final solution as white dotted lines superimposed onto the DSM in the center of Fig. 4 and onto the optical image to the right.

Three typical cases can be explained with the help of this small group of three trees. The left crown in Fig. 4 consists of a clear "mountain", which is correctly delineated in the DSM, but the optical image shows, that the crown is larger than this one "mountain". The middle crown is not extracted correctly, the lower left part of the contour is too far away from the center. The right tree in the example group is correct. Another case, which is not depicted here, occurs sometimes: If the initialization of the Snake is bad, the contours contracts to a length of zero.

4.2 Results of Building Extraction and Building Row Identification

We applied our approach for building extraction to the used image data. For more detailed results concerning the building extraction operator see [9]. The results for our subset are depicted on the left image in Fig. 5. Besides the outlines of reconstructed buildings, the centers of gravity of the buildings and the identified row of buildings is displayed. The orientation of buildings is needed for the fulfillment of a local geometric constraints. Now, after identifying the rows, it can be enhanced. This can be observed in the images: In the original reconstruction result the orientations of the buildings in the row oscillate. After the identification of the row all concerned buildings are oriented accordingly to a common average. This leads to the outlines depicted in the right image in Fig. 5.

The identification of rows matches the reality very well, the orientation manipulation results in a significant improvement of the reconstruction result.

5   Conclusions

We have presented an approach for the automatic extraction of trees in settlement areas and a generic grouping algorithm using neighborhood relations. The GeoAIDA-System allows the combination of several image analysis operators together with structural analysis. The process of the generation of hypothesis and their evaluation can be clearly separated. Moreover the possibility to integrate external operators makes the system modular and allows the combination of very complex operators. In the near future GeoAIDA will be utilized in the framework of a project initiated by the German Federal Agency for Cartography and Geodesy (BKG). In this project a system for the image based automated quality control of the Germany-wide available topographic vector data set ATKIS DLM-Basis is being developed [5]. Here GeoAIDA will be the main system integrating several operators.

While the essential part of the algorithm for the extraction of buildings was introduced in [9] the algorithm for tree extraction as described in this paper is a further development of the algorithm presented in [22]. The example for the grouping approach shows that the building reconstruction process can be supported by the structural analysis. The process of building orientation adjustment after identifying a building row obviously leads to an improved reconstruction result. Nevertheless a verification of building edges in the image data is indispensable for a further result enhancement. In the future we will test our grouping approach using a larger dataset in order to learn more about the algorithms limitations. The Active Contour Model for the delineation gives the possibility to introduce knowledge about the object *Tree* on a very general level. The problem of finding approximate values for the initialization of the Snake was solved by means of the estimation of the local optimal scale in morphological scale space. The interrelationship between the optimal scale in morphological and in linear scale space was used for an estimation of the optimal position and radius of tree-crowns.

Acknowledgment. Parts of this work were developed within the IST Program CROSSES financed by the European Commission under the project number

IST-1999-10510. The development of GeoAIDA is partly funded by BKG. Aerial Images, DEM and True Orthoimages © ISTAR. DEM and True Orthoimages made by ISTAR.

References

[1] Anders, K.H., Sester, M.: Parameter-Free Cluster Detection in Spatial Databases and its Application to Typification. In: International Archives of Photogrammetry and Remote Sensing. Vol. XXXIII (A4), Amsterdam (2000) 75–82

[2] Baillard, C., Maitre, H.: 3-D Reconstruction of Urban Scenes from Aerial Stereo Imagery: A Focusing Strategy. In: Computer Vision and Image Understanding. **76**, No. 3. (1999) 244–258

[3] Baltsavias, E., Grün, A., van Gool, L.: Automatic Extraction of Man-Made Objects from Aerial and Space Images (III). Balkema Publishers, Rotterdam (2001) 415 pages

[4] Bückner, J., Pahl, M., Stahlhut, O., Liedtke, C.-E.: A Knowledge-Based System for Context Dependent Evaluation of Remote Sensing Data. In: Pattern Recognition, 24th DAGM Symposium, Nr. 2449 in LNCS. Springer, Zurich, Switzerland (2002) 58–67

[5] Busch, A., Willrich, F.: Quality Management of ATKIS Data. In: Proceedings of OEEPE/ISPRS Joint Workshop on Spatial Data Quality Management. Istanbul (2002) 30–42

[6] Casselles, V., Kimmel, R., Sapiro, G.: Geodesic Active Contours. International Journal of Computer Vision. **22**. (1997) 61–79

[7] Fuchs, C., Gülch, E., Förstner, W.: OEEPE Survey on 3D-City Models. In: OEEPE Publications, Bundesamt für Kartographie und Geodäsie, No. 25, Frankfurt (1998) 9–123

[8] Gabet, L., Giraudon, G., Renouard, L.: Construction automatique de modèles numériques de terrain haute résolution en milieu urbain. Société Française de Photogrammétrie et Télédétection. **135**. (1994) 9–25

[9] Gerke M., Heipke C., Straub B.-M.: Building Extraction From Aerial Imagery Using a Generic Scene Model and Invariant Geometric Moments. In: Proceedings of the IEEE/ISPRS Joint Workshop on Remote Sensing and Data Fusion over Urban Areas, IEEE Piscataway (2001) 85–89

[10] Haala, N., Brenner, C.: Extraction of Buildings and Trees in Urban Environments. In: ISPRS Journal of Photogrammetry and Remote Sensing. **54**, No. 2-3. (1999) 130–137

[11] Hyyppä, J., Hyyppä, H., Ruppert, G.: Automatic Derivation of Features to Forest Stand Attributes Using Laser Scanner Data. In: International Archives of Photogrammetry and Remote Sensing. Vol. XXXIII (B3), Amsterdam (2000) 421–428

[12] Jaromczyk, J., Toussaint, G.: Relative neighborhood graphs and their relatives. In: Proceedings IEEE. **80**, No. 9. (1992) 1502–1517

[13] Kass, M., Witkin, A., Terzopoulus, D.: Snakes: Active Contour Models. In: International Journal of Computer Vision. **32**, No. 1. (1988) 321–331

[14] Kummert, F., Niemann, H., Prechtel, R., Sagerer, G.: Control and explanation in a signal understanding environment. In: Signal Processing, special issue on 'Intelligent Systems for Signal and Image Understanding'. **32**. (1993) 111–145

[15] Köthe, U.: Local Appropriate Scale in Morphological Scale-Space. In: R. C. B. Buxton(ed.): 4th European Conference on Computer Vision (1). Springer, Lecture Notes in Computer Science 1064. Berlin (1996) 219–228

[16] Lindeberg, T.: Scale-Space Theory in Computer Vision. Kluwer Academic Publishers, Boston (1994) 423 pages
[17] Niemann, H., Sagerer, G., Schröder, S., Kummert, F.: ERNEST: A Semantic Network System for Pattern Understanding. In: IEEE Trans. on Pattern Analysis and Machine Intelligence. 12, No. 9. (1990) 883–905
[18] Paragios, N., Deriche, R.: Geodesic Active Regions and Level Set Methods for Supervised Texture Segmentation. In: International Journal of Computer Vision. 46, No. 3. (2002) 223–247
[19] Quint, F.: MOSES: A Structural Approach to Aerial Image Understanding. In: Automatic Extraction of Man-Made Objects from Aerial and Space Images (II), Birkhäuser, Basel. (1997) 323–332
[20] Steger, C.: Extraction of Curved Lines from Images, In: 13th International Conference on Pattern Recognition. (1996) 251–255
[21] Steger, C., Mayer, H., Radig, B.: The Role of Grouping for Road Extraction. In: Automatic Extraction of Man-Made Objects from Aerial and Space Images (II). Birkhäuser, Basel. (1997) 245–256
[22] Straub, B.-M., Heipke, C.: Automatic Extraction of Trees for 3D-City Models from Images and Height Data. In: Automatic Extraction of Man-Made Objects from Aerial and Space Images (III). Balkema Publishers, Rotterdam. (2001) 267–277
[23] Toussaint, G.: The relative neighbourhood graph of a finite planar set. Pattern Recognition. 12. (1980) 261–268
[24] Tönjes, R., Growe, S., Bückner, J., Liedtke, C.-E.: Knowledge-Based Interpretation of Remote Sensing Images Using Semantic Nets. Photogrammetric Engineering and Remote Sensing. 65, No. 7. (1999) 811–821

A Software Architecture for Distributed Visual Tracking in a Global Vision Localization System[*]

Siniša Šegvić and Slobodan Ribarić

University of Zagreb,
Faculty of Electrical Engineering and Computing,
Unska 3, 10000 Zagreb, Croatia,
sinisa.segvic@fer.hr,
http://www.zemris.fer.hr/~ssegvic/index.html

Abstract. The paper considers detecting and tracking multiple moving objects in real time by a multiagent active vision system. The main objective of the envisioned system is to maintain an explicit comprehensive representation of the scene by combining individual views obtained from several autonomous observer nodes. In order to allow for a near real time performance, each observer agent has been assigned a separate computer system, while an additional coordination agent is introduced for relieving the observers from correspondence and coordination tasks. The proposed architecture is specially suited for monitoring ground objects whose dimensions are relatively small when compared to the dimensions of the scene. This assumption makes it possible to speculate a ground object 3D position from the single view, which consequently allows a robust correspondence approach. The architecture has been implemented in an experimental global vision system, whose final objective is to provide localization information for a group of simple robots without vision sensors. The system was preliminary tested in the laboratory environment, and the obtained experimental results are presented.

1 Introduction

Visual tracking is an important field of computer vision, in which the movement of the objects in the scene is inferred from the acquired sequence of image frames. Many applications in this field deal with complex 3D scenes, in which approaches based on single point of view face considerable limitations. The problems include limited coverage of complex scenes, speculative and imprecise 3D tracking results, and various occlusion ambiguities and failures. Some of these limitations may be alleviated by using active vision [1] or panoramic sensors [2], but the most robust solution can be achieved only in a distributed vision system, by combining evidence obtained from several adequately placed observer nodes.

Most of the existing distributed visual tracking (DVT) systems focus on tracking humans in indoor environments [3,1,4,2,5]. These designs have been

---

[*] This work has been supported by the Croatian Ministry of Science and Technology, Contract Number 2001-072.

J.L. Crowley et al. (Eds.): ICVS 2003, LNCS 2626, pp. 365–375, 2003.

motivated either by surveillance [1,4,5] or general human-computer interaction [3,2] applications. An another important application field of DVT is the real time monitoring of various sport events. The information about the game status can be used for augmenting a broadcast TV edition by an overlay image showing the positions of the players or the ball [6], which are difficult to estimate from the current view. Additionally, the obtained data could be employed for a semi-automated direction of the TV edition. In such an arrangement, the viewing directions of all cameras covering the scene might be adjusted by the automated control system, in order to achieve an acceptable presentation of the event.

The proposed work has been directly inspired by a yet another application of DVT, and that is providing localization information to a group of simple autonomous mobile robots with modest equipment (see fig.1). This approach has been called global vision [7,8], distributed vision [9,10] and sensor network for mobile robotics [11], and has been classified with artificial landmark localization techniques [12], since it requires special interventions to the environment in which the navigation takes place. The approach is particularly suitable for applications requiring a large number of autonomous vehicles (e.g. an automated warehouse), because it allows trading fixed cost vision infrastructure for a per-vehicle savings in advanced sensor accessories [7]. Recently, global vision has become a popular method for coordinating "players" in small robot soccer teams (see e.g. [8]).

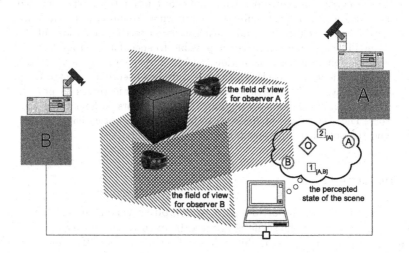

Fig. 1. Overview of a global vision localization system.

In most realistic global vision applications, it is feasible and favourable to place the cameras above the navigation area so that the objects appear relatively small in images acquired from each viewpoint (see fig.1). The proposed architecture therefore assumes that the position of each tracked ground object can be estimated from a single view. In order to improve the tracking quality and simplify the implementation of the overall control, it is advantageous to consider autonomous observers, capable of adjusting the viewing direction according to the movement of the tracked objects. Consequently, the observers are organized in a multiagent system [13], in which some of the actions are taken autonomously while others are done in coordination with other observers.

The following section gives a brief overview of the previous work in related research directions. The proposed multiagent architecture is outlined in section 3, while sections 4 and 5 provide some of the implementation details for the two types of agents within the system. Experimental results are shown in section 6, while section 7 contains a short discussion and directions for the future work.

2   Previous Work

Previous researchers identified many useful design patterns and ideas for building DVT systems. Multiple viewpoints have been employed because they allow: disambiguating occlusions [5]; monitoring structured scenes (e.g. corridors) [3, 1]; determining exact 3D position of the tracked object [6,10]; solving difficulties tied to the limited field of view [9,5,4,10]; fault tolerance [2]. In order to ensure the flexibility and openness of the system, it has been assumed that the observers are not mutually synchronized and that they have different processing performance [3,2,10]. Consequently, a special protocol has been needed to synchronize the clock of each observer to the referent time. Active vision [1,10] and panoramic cameras [2] have been used in order to enlarge the visible portion of the scene from each viewpoint. The most significant DVT architectures are outlined in the following list, in the decreasing order of centralization:

1. Monolithic system: raw images from all cameras are processed within the same program, there is no per-view autonomous processing [1,11].
2. Hierarchical division of responsibility: each observer node is assigned a dedicated computer system, while the observations are gathered and processed in a centralized fashion within a higher level program [2,5].
3. Decentralized common view: observers communicate the tracking results to all peers, so that each observer stores a copy of the common view [3].
4. Society of independent watchers: observers independently localize the objects within the visible portion of the navigation area; the tracking is performed within per-object agents by combining evidence from relevant observers [9].
5. Society of cooperative agents: each observer tracks a single object and adjusts the viewing direction accordingly [10]; observers dynamically form groups tracking a single object, and are ignorant of the movement of other objects.

Different architectures suite different configurations with respect to the parameters such as count of observers n_{obs}, count of tracked objects n_{to} and whether active cameras are available [10]. In general, the decentralized approaches are more flexible with respect to scalability and fault tolerance. However, the intelligent behaviour of the system tends to be more complicated to express through control protocol between peer components, than within a single component of the hierarchical structure. Thus, architectures 4) and 5) have been employed in systems for which $n_{obs} \gg n_{to}$, in which suboptimal resource allocation is affordable. The architecture proposed in this paper aims at many realistic applications for which $n_{obs} \leq n_{to}$ and consequently combines the effectiveness of the hierarchical structure with the flexibility of autonomous observers.

Multiagent organization [13] has recently become an often proposed software architecture paradigm. Building systems in terms of intelligent anthropomorphic components is appropriate when the communication between the large parts of a system becomes complex enough, so that it becomes useful to model it after the human interaction. A good description of the multiagent paradigm has been articulated as the agenthood test [14], which states that a system containing one or more reputed agents should change substantively if another reputed agent is introduced to the system. The test stresses that the operation of a multiagent system depends on mutual awareness of its components.

3   The Proposed Architecture

According to fig.1, the desired system should possess the following capabilities:

- tracking objects of interest within a single observer by an active camera;
- integration of the data obtained from several observers to the common scene representation, by assuming different observer performances;
- coordination of the viewing directions of the observers for the purpose of achieving a good tracking of the state in the scene;
- robustness with respect to the removal of existing or adding new observers;
- soft real time performance.

The architecture design is mostly determined by the requirement that a computer vision algorithm is required to operate in the real time environment. Because of the complexity of vision algorithms, it is favourable to ensure that each observer agent gets most of the time of a dedicated processor, and to assign data integration and coordination tasks to the coordinator agent running on a separate computer. The resulting architecture is outlined in fig.2: observers send measurements to the coordinator, which integrates the data into the common view and controls the observers behaviour in an opportunistic manner.

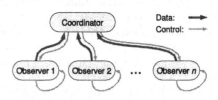

Fig. 2. The top level view of the multiagent architecture.

The system organized after fig.2 satisfies the agenthood test cited in the Introduction, if the coordinator is viewed as a part of communication infrastructure. Whenever a new observer registers with the coordinator, the responsibilities of all observers are rescheduled in order to obtain a better coverage of the scene.

4 Implementation Details for the Observer Agents

Observer agents are responsible for detection and tracking of objects of interest, as well as for adjusting the viewing direction of the associated camera with the purpose of following the current object or searching for new objects. The desired system consists of several observers so that, besides coordinate systems of the image (o, x, y) and the camera (C, X, Y, Z), it is necessary to define the common referent coordinate system of the scene (O, K, L, M). An important property of considered scenes is that the objects of interest move within the horizontal ground plane π. It is therefore convenient to align the pan axis of the camera with the normal of π, and to choose the camera and the world coordinate systems for which the upright axes Z and M coincide with that direction (see fig.3).

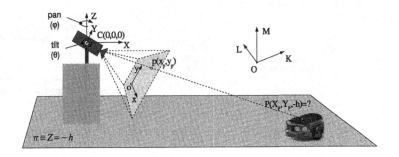

Fig. 3. The observer agent imaging geometry.

In order to speculate the 3D position in camera coordinates $P(X_P, Y_P, -h)$ from the position of the object in the image plane $p(x_p, y_p)$, it is necessary to perform several transformations, based on precalibrated intrinsic and extrinsic [15] camera parameters and the known angular position of the camera (ϕ, θ). In theory, the only error of the obtained position is caused by the finite height of the tracked object, but in practice several other errors come into effect. These errors are due to imperfect estimations of camera parameters and compensations of lens distortions and geometric inadequacies of the camera controller (offset of the projection center from the crossing of pan and tilt axes).

The main requirement for observer agents is the real time detection and tracking of objects of interest within the current field of view. Additionally, they are required to exchange the following data with the coordinator: (i) clock synchronization and extrinsic camera parameters (at the registration time), (ii) the current viewing direction (after each change), and (iii) the time stamped list of detected objects in camera coordinates (after each processed image). Observers operate in one of the following modes with respect to autonomous camera movement: seeking (camera seeks for an object and then the mode is switched to 'tracking'), tracking (viewing direction follows the active object), or immobile (viewing direction does not change). Finally, they listen for control messages from the coordinator and switch operating modes or move the camera accordingly.

5   Implementation Details for the Coordinator

The basic responsibilities of the coordinator encompass integration and analysis of individual object positions reported by the observers. The integration task sums up to repetitive updating of the common representation of the scene. The data structure holding the representation is the central component of the coordinator, and is organized in four hierarchical levels with gradual increase of abstraction: (i) object positions (measurements), (ii) individual trajectories, (iii) top level objects, and (iv), trajectories of top-level objects (see fig.4).

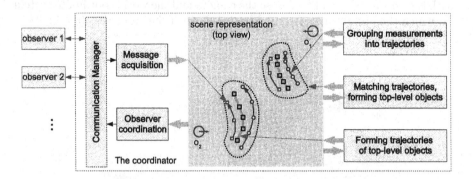

Fig. 4. Block diagram of the coordinator agent.

5.1   Overall Architecture

The five basic procedures of the coordinator agent are (see fig.4): message acquisition, grouping measurements into trajectories (temporal integration), matching trajectories into top-level objects (spatial integration), formation of top-level trajectories, and observer coordination. These procedures transform the lower level structure components into the higher level ones, and their activation order depends on run-time detected conditions, such as the arrival of a new measurement, or when a certain observer looses the tracked object from its visual field. The required opportunistic activation can be adequately expressed within the blackboard [16,17] design pattern, which is often used in the distributed solving of the complex problems. The main subjects in such organization are knowledge sources (the basic procedures), the central data structure or blackboard (common view of the scene) and the control component which triggers the activation of knowledge sources (see fig.5).

5.2   Matching Individual Trajectories

An individual trajectory is a temporal sequence of measurements reported by a certain observer, for which it is believed that they correspond to the same object. Each measurement contains the object position converted to world coordinates,

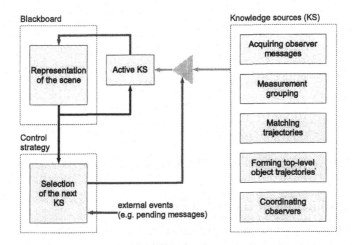

Fig. 5. The proposed coordinator architecture.

as well as the acquisition time of the image in which the object was detected. The matching procedure establishes correspondence between recent segments of trajectories containing measurements obtained within the last two seconds. Each of the obtained correspondence sets defines a 3D position of the top level blackboard object which should correspond to a real object in the scene. The correspondence procedure is different from clustering because, during the procedure, some trajectories become mutually incompatible and can not be grouped together. This occurs whenever the trajectories belong to the two correspondence sets both of which contain trajectories reported by the same observer.

The main difficulty in matching a pair of recent trajectory segments reported by different observers is caused by the assumption that the observers are not synchronized, i.e. that single measurements in corresponding trajectories have different acquisition times. The problem has been solved by (i) finding the time interval for which both segments are defined, (ii) taking N equidistant time instants within that interval, and (iii) interpolating representative points in both trajectories within that instants. The procedure is illustrated for $N=5$ in fig.6, where the synchronized representative points are designated with crosses.

As described in section 4, measurements of the same object recorded by different observers may systematically differ due to multiple sources of error. Experiments have shown that the dominant effect of these errors to short trajectory segments can be modeled as a simple translation. The matching is therefore based on a distance function computed as a weighted sum of mean value and standard deviation of the displacements between the corresponding representative points. The correspondence procedure follows a greedy iterative approach, such that in each iteration the least distant pair of matchable trajectories is associated together until the distance is greater than a predetermined threshold.

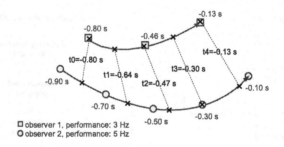

Fig. 6. Finding synchronized sets of representative points in two trajectory segments.

5.3   Coordination of the Observers

In general, the coordination of the observers is a complex task since it is composed of at least the following two contradictory requirements: (i) precise position determination for each tracked object, and (ii), monitoring the empty parts of the scene for appearance of new objects. The optimal coordination strategy is necessarily application specific, since it depends on many parameters such as the counts of observers and objects of interest, the priority of individual objects, whether all observers can "see" the entire scene, etc. The following terms may prove useful in the design of a strategy:

- an object tracked by exactly one observer is defined as *weak*;
- an observer tracking a weak object is defined as *bound*;
- an observer tracking an object which is tracked by exactly one additional observer is defined as *important*;
- an observer tracking 0 objects is defined as *idle*;
- an observer which is neither important nor bound nor idle, is defined as *free*.

It seems that the real time performance will remain the most challenging requirement for quite some time, so that the communication protocol between the coordinator and the observers should not prescribe waiting for confirmation messages. This can be achieved by scheduling the activation of the coordination procedure in regular time intervals (e.g. 2 seconds). In such an arrangement, the procedure in each invocation examines the situation on the blackboard, issues one or more control messages to the observers, and returns to the blackboard control component (no answer from the observer is required). The following minimalistic strategy has been devised for robust (although suboptimal) coordination in partially occluded scenes containing a small number of objects.

1. observers in seeking operating mode, bound, important, free and idle observers are assigned priorities of 0, 0, 1, 2 and 3, respectively;
2. if there are no observers with a non-zero priority, no action is performed;
3. otherwise, the highest ranked observer (round robin scheme is used to choose among observers with the same priority) is chosen and is denoted as O_C;
4. if there is a weak object A positioned outside the field of view of O_C (otherwise, A is occluded from O_C), O_C is assigned the tracking of A;
5. otherwise, only if O_C is not important, it is switched to the seeking mode.

6   Experimental Results

The experimental system was tested in a heterogeneous environment, with three observers running under different operating systems connected to the Ethernet LAN. Individual applications within the system (the agent program, the observer program, calibration and testing utilities) were built from the version control system managed library containing about 50000 lines of C++ source code.

Fig. 7 shows experimental results for the two observers tracking the same object. In the experimental implementation, the objects are detected on the basis of their colour and the colour of the surrounding background. For each observer, the figure shows the original image with the designated detected object (a,e), the saturation-value mask used for eliminating regions that are too dark or too light (b,f), and connected regions which are, according to the hue of the corresponding pixels, classified as objects (c,g) or background (d,h).

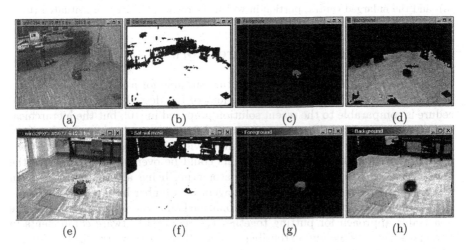

Fig. 7. Experimental results for observers A (a-d) and B (e-h); see text for details.

One of the observers was running on a multiprocessor computer which made it possible to run the coordinator on the same computer without a performance hit. Simple but effective procedures for object detection and tracking allowed for high observer performance of 12.5 Hz and 9.1 Hz on computers with approximate single processor SPEC CINT2000 base performances of 710 and 530, respectively.

Fig. 8 shows the top view of the scene with two objects moving at speeds of about 0.5 m/s, which is computed in real time within the coordinator agent. The figure background contains the referent one-metre grid and the walls of the lab in which the experiment takes place. Each of the three registered observers is designated with the circle indicating the observer position, the short line showing its orientation, and the polygonal area designating the respective fields of view. Finally, the detected objects are designated with their last positions and recent trajectory segments (as reported by observers), as well as with positions, approximate areas and trajectories of the respective top level blackboard objects.

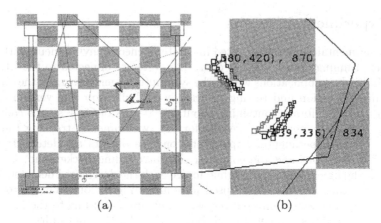

Fig. 8. The top-level view of the scene with three observers and two tracked objects (a), and the enlarged central portion in which the detected objects are situated (b).

7   Conclusions and the Future Work

A hierarchical multiagent DVT architecture suitable for a large class of realistic problems has been proposed. The behaviour of the described coordination procedure is comparable to the recent solution proposed in [10], but the hierarchical coordination approach has a great potential for more sophisticated behaviours due to the availability of the explicit common view. Eventual network congestion problems arising for large observer counts could be overcome by extending the architecture with a "recursive" coordinator type, being able to perform as an observer responsible to the coordinator agent at a higher hierarchical level.

The obtained experimental results confirmed that the proposed architecture is a viable approach for putting together the required software components in a manageable, flexible and extensible manner. The future work will be directed towards refinements to the existing architecture in order to achieve more involved coordination schemes, as well as towards dealing with procedures for diminishing the systematic error in observer measurements, and ensuring robustness of the system in the view of the physical contact of tracked objects.

References

1. Cai, Q., Aggarwal, J.: Tracking human motion in structured environments using a distributed-camera system. IEEE Transactions on Pattern recognition and Machine Intelligence **21** (1999) 1241–1247
2. Karuppiah, D., Zhu, Z., Shenoy, P., Riseman, E.: A fault-tolerant distributed vision system architecture for object tracking in a smart room. In: Proceedings of the International Workshop on Computer Vision Systems, Vancouver, Canada (2001) 201–219
3. Nakazawa, A., Kato, H., Inokuchi, S.: Human tracking using distributed vision systems. In: Proceedings of the International Conference on Pattern Recognition. Volume I., Brisbane, Australia, IEEE (1998) 593–596

4. Khan, S., Javed, O., Rasheed, Z., Shah, M.: Human tracking in multiple cameras. In: Proceedings of the International Conference on Computer Vision, Vancouver, Canada, IEEE (2001) I: 331–336
5. Dockstader, S.L.; Tekalp, A.: Multiple camera tracking of interacting and occluded human motion. Proceedings of the IEEE **89** (2001) 1441–1455
6. Guéziec, A.: Tracking pitches for broadcast television. Computer **35** (2002) 38–43
7. Kay, M., Luo, R.: Global vision for intelligent AGVs. SME Journal of Vision **9** (1993)
8. Veloso, M., Stone, P., Han, K., Achim, S.: The CMUnited-97 small robot team. In Kitano, H., ed.: RoboCup-97: Robot Soccer World Cup I. Springer Verlag, Berlin (1998) 242–256
9. Sogo, T., Ishiguro, H., Ishida, T.: Mobile robot navigation by distributed vision agents. In Nakashima, H., Zhang, C., eds.: Approaches to Intelligent Agents. Springer-Verlag, Berlin (1999) 96–111
10. Matsuyama, T., Ukita, N.: Real-time multitarget tracking by a cooperative distributed vision system. Proceedings of the IEEE **90** (2002) 1136–1150
11. Hoover, A., Olsen, B.D.: Sensor network perception for mobile robotics. In: Proceedings of the International Conference on Robotics and Automation. Volume I., San Francisco, California, IEEE (2000) 342–348
12. Borenstein, J., Everett, H.R., Feng, L.: Navigating Mobile Robots: Sensors and Techniques. A. K. Peters, Ltd., Wellesley, MA (1996)
13. Wooldridge, M.: Intelligent agents. In Weiss, G., ed.: Multiagent Systems. MIT Press (1999) 27–79
14. Huhns, M.N., Singh, M.P.: The agent test. Internet Computing **38** (1997) 78–79
15. Mohr, R., Triggs, B.: Projective geometry for image analysis. A tutorial given at the International Symposium of Photogrammetry and Remote Sensing, Vienna (1996)
16. Pfleger, K., Hayes-Roth, B.: An introduction to blackboard-style systems organization. Technical Report KSL-98-03, Stanford University, California (1998)
17. Huhns, M.N., Stephens, L.M.: Multiagent systems and societies of agents. In Weiss, G., ed.: Multiagent Systems. MIT Press (1999) 79–121

Multi-object Tracking Based on a Modular Knowledge Hierarchy

Martin Spengler and Bernt Schiele

Perceptual Computing and Computer Vision Group
Computer Science Department
ETH Zurich, Switzerland
{spengler,schiele}@inf.ethz.ch

Abstract. An important goal of research in computer vision systems is to develop architectures which are general and robust and at the same time transparent and easily transferable from one domain to another. To this extent this paper discusses and demonstrates the versatility of a multi-object tracking framework based on the so called *knowledge hierarchy*. The systematic description and analysis of a priori knowledge provides means not only for reducing the complexity of the multi-object tracking problem but also for building modular systems for solving it. The modularity of the framework, an essential ingredient for versatility, allows to replace individual parts of an existing system without altering the rest of the system or the overall architecture. The paper presents the modular framework including the knowledge hierarchy for multi object tracking. In order to demonstrate the transferability of the proposed approach the tracking framework is then applied to three different tracking scenarios (parking lot surveillance, people interaction monitoring, and dining table setup).

1 Introduction

Any versatile computer vision system should be able to cope with a variety of tasks. Furthermore, it should also be transferable from one domain to another. Most often vision systems are designed for one particular task in one specific domain. However the real value of any system architecture is fundamentally linked to the ability to reconfigure and reuse the system in order to meet the needs of another task or problem domain. The art and science of designing versatile computer vision systems and architectures thus aims to find the optimal trade-off between flexibility and transparency on the one side and robustness and performance on the other side.

As in other areas, the key to versatility for vision systems is a well structured and modular architecture. In order to get a system that is easily reconfigured, its individual subsystems have to be well-separated and self-contained. Only if function and responsibility of each single module are precisely defined, one can achieve effective and transparent exchange of any particular subsystem. By following a modular design, the resulting architecture will allow to substitute

J.L. Crowley et al. (Eds.): ICVS 2003, LNCS 2626, pp. 376–385, 2003.

individual parts without any negative impact on the system's overall correctness. Simple replacement of modules can adapt a system to new tasks or incorporate new algorithms and methods. Such versatility ultimately provides significant increase in reusability of the system's framework and its components.

The problem domain of this paper is multi-object tracking. More specifically the Bayesian formulation of the multi-object tracking problem is cast into a general framework where the use of knowledge is made explicit through the so called *knowledge hierarchy* [1]. In contrast to pure single-object tracking systems [2,3,4,5] – often using elaborate object models – the presented appearance based multi-object tracking system is able to track an almost arbitrary number of objects simultaneously with only elementary means. Like other Bayesian multi-object trackers [6,7,8,9,10,11], the presented system uses *sequential Monte Carlo* methods [12] for Bayesian inference. Though the idea of hierarchically organized prior knowledge can also be found in previous work, e.g. [13,14], the idea of a more general and versatile vision system is only marginal in these approaches.

Tracking multiple objects simultaneously within a single tracker allows to model not only the behavior of each individual object but also their interactions. This additional capability can be exploited to increase the robustness and reliability of the tracking algorithm. Unfortunately, simultaneous tracking of multiple objects increases not only robustness and reliability but also complexity. Modeling inter-object relations makes the situation even worse since the complexity of the problem's search space is increased. Prior knowledge will thus be essential for the reduction of the complexity, making the problem computationally tractable again. The above mentioned knowledge hierarchy provides us with means for analyzing and evaluating potentially useful knowledge.

As pointed out above, any computer vision system architecture should be versatile so that it can be transferred easily to other tasks and domains by replacing only individual modules and models. This paper demonstrates that the proposed framework of Bayesian multi-object tracking based on the novel knowledge hierarchy can be effectively and easily transferred between different tasks. After a short introduction of the Bayesian formulation of the multi-object tracking problem (sec. 2), section 2.1 introduces the knowledge hierarchy. The hierarchy is a theoretical framework that supports the systematic description and analysis of a priori knowledge. Prior knowledge is essential to reduce the complexity of the multi-object tracking problem. At the same time the knowledge hierarchy also allows to get a modular architecture for solving the multi-object tracking problem. In order to stress the domain transferability of the approach, it is applied to three different tasks in vision-based tracking in section 3. The first scenario is far-range surveillance (parking lot surveillance). The second scenario is mid-range monitoring (human interaction monitoring). The third scenario is short-range observation as it is familiar with robotics (dining table observation). The adaptation from one domain to the other only requires to exchange some of the applied models while the rest of the system remains untouched. Although the used models and methods are rather simple the results are promising and the concept of a modular hence versatile tracking system is strongly supported.

2   Multi-object Tracking

Single-object tracking in a Bayesian framework is defined as sequential estimation of an object's state θ_t at any time t [1]. Based on a sequence of observations
$\mathbf{z}_{1:t} = \{\mathbf{z}_1, \mathbf{z}_2, \ldots, \mathbf{z}_t\}$ up to this time t, the object's state is repetitively esti-
mated by determining the maximum a posteriori solution for $p(\theta_t|\mathbf{z}_{1:t})$.

When tracking multiple objects in parallel, the state vector θ_t of a single
object is replaced with the concatenation Θ_t of m individual objects: $\Theta_t =
\{\theta_t^{(1)}, \theta_t^{(2)}, \ldots, \theta_t^{(m)}\}$, where m is the variable number of objects a particular
concatenation consists of. Using such *object compounds* allows not only to model
the individual object's state but also their relations.

Assuming that tracking can be regarded as Markovian process, the observa-
tion likelihood $p(\mathbf{z}_t|\Theta_t)$, the initial distribution $p(\Theta_0)$ and the compound state
transition $p(\Theta_t|\Theta_{t-1})$ are sufficient to propose a recursive formulation of the
tracking problem:

Prediction (MOT):

$$p(\Theta_t|\mathbf{z}_{1:t-1}) = \int p(\Theta_t|\Theta_{t-1})p(\Theta_{t-1}|\mathbf{z}_{1:t-1})d\Theta_{t-1} \tag{1}$$

Update (MOT):

$$p(\Theta_t|\mathbf{z}_{1:t}) = \frac{p(\mathbf{z}_t|\Theta_t)p(\Theta_t|\mathbf{z}_{1:t-1})}{\int p(\mathbf{z}_t|\Theta_t')p(\Theta_t'|\mathbf{z}_{1:t-1})d\Theta_t'} \tag{2}$$

Observation likelihood $p(\mathbf{z}_t|\Theta_t)$, state transition $p(\Theta_t|\Theta_{t-1})$ and distribution
$p(\Theta_0)$ are the elements where a priori knowledge may be introduced into a sys-
tem. Careful design of the appropriate knowledge representations is crucial for
the reliability of a tracker. As will become clear in Sec. 2.1, these probability
distributions have tight relations with the knowledge hierarchy.

If observation likelihood $p(\mathbf{z}_t|\Theta_t)$ as well as state transition $p(\Theta_t|\Theta_{t-1})$ and
initial distribution $p(\Theta_0)$ were Gaussians, the well-known Kalman filter would
solve the maximum a posteriori problem. However, in most cases the distributions are non-gaussian and thus (1) and (2) have no analytical solution.

A common solution is thus the *approximation* of the posterior $p(\Theta_t|\mathbf{z}_{1:t})$
and to solve this numerical problem with a computationally efficient algorithm.
Sequential Monte Carlo methods [12], also known as *particle filtering, bootstrap
filtering* or CONDENSATION [15] have proofed to be suitable for this purpose.

2.1   Knowledge Hierarchy

The complexity of the problem increases non-linearly with every additional object, since object compounds are not only able to model the state of individual
objects but also their interactions and group behavior. Bayesian multi-object
trackers are therefore likely to be trapped by the *curse of dimensionality*. In [1]

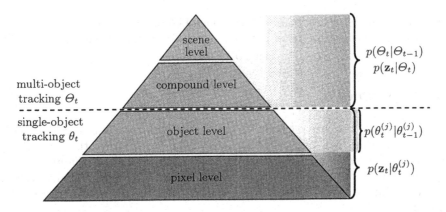

Fig. 1. Knowledge Hierarchy. See text for details about the four knowledge levels.

we proposed the *knowledge hierarchy*, a framework for analyzing and classifying a priori knowledge given to a Bayesian multi-object tracker.

The knowledge hierarchy (Fig. 1) consists of four levels for classifying prior knowledge. The *pixel* knowledge, the *object* knowledge, the *compound* knowledge and the *scene* knowledge. The hierarchy levels are tightly coupled to the observation likelihoods and the state transitions in (1) and (2).

Pixel knowledge. Pixel knowledge is the lowest level of the hierarchy. Usually this type of knowledge is local to one particular pixel and does neither influence its even directest neighbors nor does it rely on its neighbors. Typical examples for pixel knowledge are background models used for foreground segmentation. In Bayesian multi-object tracking systems pixel knowledge is represented as object observation likelihood $p(\mathbf{z}_t|\theta_t^{(j)})$ which is part of the compound observation likelihood $p(\mathbf{z}_t|\Theta_t)$.

Object knowledge. Although object knowledge is one level above pixel knowledge, it is also represented by the object observation likelihood $p(\mathbf{z}_t|\theta_t^{(j)})$ and additionally by the object state transition model $p(\theta_t^{(j)}|\theta_{t-1}^{(j)})$. In analogy to $p(\mathbf{z}_t|\theta_t^{(j)})$, $p(\theta_t^{(j)}|\theta_{t-1}^{(j)})$ is often part of compound state transition $p(\Theta_t|\Theta_{t-1})$. Object knowledge is specific to a particular object or object type, e.g. an object's motion model. The behavior of an object is considered to be object knowledge as long as it is independent from other objects.

Compound knowledge. In contrast to the first two hierarchy levels, compound knowledge models entire *compounds* of objects, i.e an agglomeration of multiple objects. Behavior of object groups as well as the interaction between two or more objects are part of the compound knowledge level. In Bayesian multi-object tracking systems, compound knowledge is represented by the observation likelihood $p(\mathbf{z}_t|\Theta_t)$ as well as by the compound transition model $p(\Theta_t|\Theta_{t-1})$. Compound knowledge is scene-independent and thus reusable.

Scene knowledge. The top most knowledge, the scene knowledge, models all the knowledge about one particular scene. It is only valid for one particular scene or family of scenes. Similar to compound knowledge, scene knowledge goes into the observation likelihood $p(\mathbf{z}_t|\Theta_t)$ and the compound transition likelihood $p(\Theta_t|\Theta_{t-1})$.

3   Experiments

In this section, the general multi-object tracking framework introduced in the previous sections will be applied to three different scenarios: the *surveillance* sequence, the *human interaction monitoring* sequence and the *dining table* sequence. The successful application to tracking tasks in different domains stresses the versatility of multi-object tracking systems based on the novel knowledge hierarchy.

3.1   Tracking Framework

The tracking algorithm used in the following experiments models object compounds Θ_t as concatenations of an arbitrary number of m individual objects: $\Theta_t = \{\theta_t^{(1)}, \theta_t^{(2)}, \ldots, \theta_t^{(m)}\}$. An object j is parameterized by a state vector $\theta_t^{(j)} = [x, y, dx, dy, \sigma(x, y), \kappa]^{\mathrm{T}}$, where x and y are the object's position in image coordinates, dx and dy the corresponding velocities and $\sigma(x, y) > 0$ a predetermined position-dependent scaling function for the object template κ. The object templates κ as well as the scaling functions $\sigma(x, y)$ were learned during a training period and remain constant for the experiments. The object state transition $p(\theta_t^{(j)}|\theta_{t-1}^{(j)})$ is defined as a simple linear motion model superimposed with Gaussian noise. The observation likelihood $p(\mathbf{z}_t|\theta_t^{(j)})$ uses template matching for estimating how well the scaled object model $\sigma_{x,y} \cdot \kappa^{(j)}$ fits the measurement $\mathbf{z}_t$ at image coordinates (x, y).

The compound state transition $p(\Theta_t|\Theta_{t-1})$ is held constant. There is no dynamic change of the configuration's size (number of objects) and no motion model at compound-level. The configuration likelihood $p(\mathbf{z}_t|\Theta_t)$ consists of three components: The observation likelihood $p(\mathbf{z}_t|\theta_t^{(j)})$ of the configuration's individual objects, a term measuring the compounds compactness and measure how well the compound covers the detected foreground regions. In order to deal with appearing and disappearing objects, new compound hypotheses are injected into the set of compound hypotheses that approximates $p(\Theta_t|\mathbf{z}_t)$. The size of the newly injected hypotheses is variable and modeled as normal distribution $\mathcal{N}(\mu, \sigma)$.

3.2   Parking Lot Surveillance

The first experiment is an excerpt of the PETS2000 dataset which shows the view of a surveillance camera overlooking a parking lot [1]. In order to cope with this specific scenario, the general multi-object tracker is equipped with task-specific knowledge: the set $\mathcal{K}$ of expected object types is fixed to $\mathcal{K} = \{\text{car}, \text{person}\}$.

Fig. 2. Two frames from the PETS2000 dataset. Column one shows the input frame, column two the foreground/background segmentation, and column three the top 1% of the 5000 configuration hypotheses.

Both object types have an object-specific shape template κ and a corresponding scaling function $\sigma(x, y)$. For evaluating the shape templates, background subtraction is applied to every single frame in advance. the background is modeled pixel-wise as a single Gaussian and held static after the initial training phase. In addition, the expected size of the object compounds is modeled as Gaussian distribution $\mathcal{N}(3, 1)$, i.e. in average compounds with 3 objects will explain the scene best.

Figure 2 shows two exemplary frames of the PETS2000 dataset together with the foreground segmentation and the best 50 compound hypotheses. In the first row two persons approach a car on the parking lot. Since the other cars are part of the background model they wont be considered as objects by the tracking algorithm. The algorithm correctly generates and reinforces hypotheses which explain the scene best. In the next time step they are replicated and propagated, reinforcing "proper" hypotheses even more. Compounds consisting of cars and persons at the same time are possible and explain the situation well. The system is thus not only able to deal with multiple objects but also with multiple object types. The second row of Fig. 2 demonstrates the system's capability to deal with newly emerging objects. Due to the continuous injection of new hypotheses, it is likely that new objects are incorporated into the set of compound hypotheses.

The parking lot surveillance scenario demonstrated that our Bayesian multi-object tracking system is able to track multiple objects simultaneously. In addition, this sequence showed the architecture's ability to cope with mixed compounds, i.e. compounds consisting of objects of different type.

3.3   People Interaction Monitoring

Next, the versatility of our approach should be demonstrated by switching to a different domain – monitoring interacting people. The sequence analyzed below shows two persons meeting within the field of view of a static camera, shacking

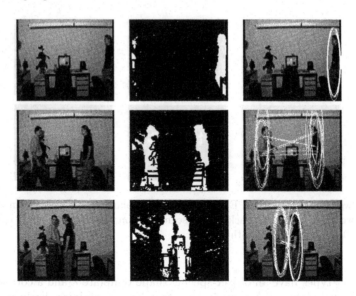

Fig. 3. Three frames from the human interaction sequence. Column one shows the input frame, column two the foreground/background segmentation, and column three the top 2% of the 1000 configuration hypotheses.

hands, crossing and leaving the scene in opposite directions. Figure 3 displays three representative frames of the sequence.

In order to deal with the different domain, the object models have to be adapted. The set $\mathcal{K}$ of available object models is reduced to one since the sequence will only have people as objects: $\mathcal{K} = \{\text{person}\}$. A corresponding shape template has been learned together with the scaling function $\sigma(x, y)$. The background model has been learned off-line as well and the expected compound size is modeled as $\mathcal{N}(2, 1)$ since one expects that in most frames two persons are visible. No further adaptations were required in order to transfer the tracker from the surveillance domain to human interaction monitoring.

At the beginning of the sequence no person is present. The initial set of 1000 hypotheses consists therefore of randomly injected compounds, distributed over the whole image. Once the first person enters at the right side of the camera's field of view (Fig. 3, first row), the single-object hypotheses start to accumulate, explaining the first person as expected. After a few frames, the second person starts to enter the scene. With a short delay of three frames, two-object compounds emerge, explaining both persons simultaneously (Fig. 3, second row). Due to the poor background subtraction in the region of the subjects' legs, some hypotheses are biased vertically.

The two subjects are correctly tracked by the system to the point where they meet and start to shake hands (Fig. 3, third row). When the two subjects cross, the ratings of the two-object compound hypotheses decrease and single-object hypotheses are considered to be better. After only a few frames, the persons have separated and the two-objects compounds dominate the top 2% hypotheses again. They keep a high rating until the first subject disappears at the left side of the view field. Within a short period the tracker correctly reinforces single-object compounds and continues to track the remaining subject. When the second subject has left the scene as well, random hypotheses emerge and the system start to "seek" for new objects.

Besides demonstrating the ease of transferring the original tracking system from one domain to another, the human interaction monitoring task shows that tracing a wide variety of possible hypotheses at any time is important for successful tracking in multi-object scenes. The analyzed system has the capability to cope with newly appearing objects as well as with disappearing objects without handling these events as special cases. The model implicitly expects objects to vanish or to emerge. Nevertheless, the assumption that objects may occur and be deleted at every position in the view field is rather coarse. Introducing a better model for object addition and deletion might stabilize the system's performance further.

3.4   Dining Table

The dining table scenario is the third task the multi-object tracking system was applied to. A static camera overlooks a round table, onto which an arm puts up to three cups, moves them around and also removes some again. Scenes with one, two or three cups are possible whereas scenes without any object do not appear. Figure 4 displays three frames of the dining table sequence.

The domain transfer to the dining table scenario again consists of altering the used object models, adjusting the background model and assigning a proper compound size model. Since only cups were expected to appear, the set of possible object models was reduced to a single object: $\mathcal{K} = \{\texttt{cup}\}$. As will be seen later, this expectation turned out to be inappropriate. The background model is learned during a separate training period and held static afterward. The compound size is modeled as $\mathcal{N}(2, 1)$.

After an initial period with only one cup on the table, an arm puts a second cup onto the table. Almost immediately corresponding two-object compound hypotheses emerge explaining the presence of two cups in the scene (Fig. 4, first row). Since the hand that holds the cup fits pretty well into the cup's object model, some of the hypotheses have the hand and arm as part of the compound. However, the top 2% compounds model all the first cup and the second cup or the hand respectively. That is, no "arm-only" compound gets high rating and thus will be suppressed after a few iterations. But as mentioned in the beginning, neglecting the object type $\texttt{arm}$ turned out to be a problem in this scenario.

After the arm withdraws, the scene remains static for a certain period and the two cups cause an accumulation of appropriate two-object compound hypotheses. When the arm next grasps one of the cups, moving it to another position, many wrong hypotheses are generated, resulting in many two- and three-object compounds containing one or two false-positive objects from the arm. After withdrawing again, the arm puts a third cup onto the table, moving

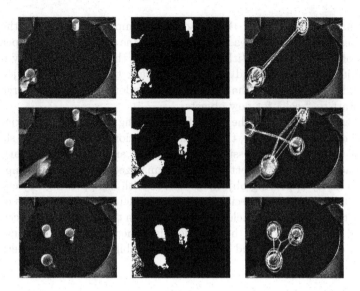

Fig. 4. Three frames from the dining table sequence. Column one shows the input frame, column two the foreground/background segmentation, and column three the top 2% of the 1000 configuration hypotheses.

it toward the other two cups (Fig. 4, second row). Though the arm is a distractor, the compound hypotheses recover when it withdraws, reinforcing the two- and three-object compound hypotheses explaining the three cup scene best (Fig. 4, third row). The arms enters the scene twice in the rest of the sequence, grasping the cups and moving them around. In both cases the tracking system is able to recover from the instabilities the arm introduced into the set of compound hypotheses.

Although the tracker performed well in the case of "cups-only" scenes, it destabilized whenever an arm was part of the scene. The reason for this weakness is not a principal failure of the tracking framework but the result of inadequate modeling and knowledge representation. Apparently, disregarding the fact that the scene consists of more than cups had a significant impact on the system's performance. Although a partial failure, the dining table sequence provides a very valuable lesson as it demonstrates the importance of analyzing and modeling any new domain carefully.

4   Conclusion

In this paper we discussed the versatility of a multi-object tracking system with respect to different domains. The analyzed system fits into an overall framework where the use of knowledge is made explicit through the novel knowledge hierarchy. A modular architecture allows to easily transfer the system from one domain to another without touching the majority of the system. In order to stress the importance of versatility the proposed multi-object tracker was applied to three different domains: the parking lot scenario, the human interaction monitoring scenario and the dining table scenario. The system was successful in all three domains. Nevertheless, the dining table sequence made explicit that careful analysis of a particular domain and the choice of proper a priori knowledge is crucial for successful domain transfer.

References

1. Spengler, M., Schiele, B.: Multi-object tracking: Explicit knowledge representation and implementation for complexity reduction. In: Cognitive Vision Workshop, Zurich, Switzerland (2002)
2. Fablet, R., Black, M.J.: Automatic detection and tracking of human motion with a view-based representation. In: European Conference on Computer Vision. (2002) 476–491
3. Isard, M., Blake, A.: ICondensation: Unifying low-level and high-level tracking in a stochastic framework. Lecture Notes in Computer Science **1406** (1998) 893–??
4. Vermaak, J., Pérez, P., Gangnet, M., Blake, A.: Towards improved observation models for visual tracking: Selective adaptation. In: European Conference on Computer Vision. (2002) 645–660
5. Spengler, M., Schiele, B.: Towards robust multi-cue integration for visual tracking. In: International Workshop on Computer Vision Systems. (2001) 94–107
6. Koller-Meier, E., Ade, F.: Tracking multiple objects using the condensation algorithm. Journal of Robotics and Autonomous Systems **34** (2001) 93–105
7. Maskell, S., Rollason, M., Salmond, D., Gordon, N.: Efficient particle filtering for multiple target tracking with application to tracking in structured images. In: SPIE Vol 4728, Signal and Data Processing of Small Targets. (2002)
8. Isard, M., MacCormick, J.: BraMBLe: A bayesian multiple-blob tracker. In: Internation Conference on Computer Vision ICCV. (2001)
9. Hue, C., Le Cadre, J.P., Pérez, P.: Sequential monte carlo methods for multiple target tracking and data fusion. IEEE Transactions on Signal Processing **50** (2002) 309–325
10. Pérez, P., Hue, C., Vermaak, J., Gangnet, M.: Color-based probabilistic tracking. In: European Conference on Computer Vision. (2002) 661–675
11. Tao, H., Sawhney, H.S., Kumar, R.: A sampling algorithm for tracking multiple objects. In: Workshop on Vision Algorithms. (1999) 53–68
12. Doucet, A., de Freitas, N., Gordon, N., eds.: Sequential Monte Carlo Methods in Practice. Statistics for Engineering and Information Science. Springer (2001)
13. Buxton, H., Gong, S.: Visual surveillance in a dynamic and uncertain world. Artificial Intelligence **78** (1995) 431–459
14. Buxton, H.: Generative models for learning and understanding dynamic scene activity. In: 1st International Workshop on Generative-Model-Based Vision, Copenhagen, Denmark (2002)
15. Blake, A., Isard, M.: Active Contours. Springer Verlag (1998)

Monkeys – A Software Architecture for ViRoom – Low-Cost Multicamera System

Petr Doubek, Tomáš Svoboda, and Luc Van Gool

Computer Vision Laboratory, ETH Zürich, Switzerland

Abstract. This paper presents a software architecture for a software-synchronized multicamera setup. The software allows consistent multi-image acquisition, image processing and decision making. It consists of several programs that perform certain tasks and communicate with each other through shared memory space or TCP/IP packets. The software system can easily accommodate different number of FireWire digital cameras and networked computers. Minimal hardware requirement is the main advantage of the system which makes it flexible and transportable. The functionality of the system is demonstrated on a simple telepresence application.

1 Introduction

Smart multicamera systems are becoming more common due to the decreasing prices of powerful computers and digital cameras. Some of them were developed for creating realistic 3D models [4] or virtual views [5]. In late 1990's, new kinds of multicamera setups appeared. The main goal was not so much reconstruction but action recognition and interpretation. These applications mostly need real-time performance and current computers are capable of running wide range of image processing algorithms in real-time.

Cameras were often combined with microphone arrays for voice recognition and/or navigation. The EasyLiving project is developing an intelligent room that will be able to unobtrusively interact with a user [3]. The AVIARY project uses cameras and a microphone array for finding moving and/or speaking person. The detected speaker is then tracked and the best camera is chosen. A limited number of basic events are recognized [12]. Very recent project called M4 [1] tries to develop system that enables structuring, browsing and querying of an archive of analyzed meeting. In an addition to the projects creating whole environments, monocular methods are being extended to multiple views, especially tracking [7].

However, most of the systems are fixed to one room and they are still expensive for a casual user. Our goal is to develop a real-time multicamera system which would be flexible in terms of camera types and their number, easy to setup so that it can be moved from one place to another within hours, able to run on standard consumer hardware and affordable for almost anyone who already has a computer. The basic service that it should provide is a synchronized image capturing and the possibility to easily integrate both image processing

J.L. Crowley et al. (Eds.): ICVS 2003, LNCS 2626, pp. 386–395, 2003.
© Springer-Verlag Berlin Heidelberg 2003

algorithms working on single images as well as algorithms which use information from multiple cameras. Appropriate algorithms can be plugged-in for any particular application without the need to rebuild the whole system.

The mobility allows to move the system to the environment where the activities take place instead of moving the activities to the lab with the camera system. The production of training videos or the visual supervision of a machine maintenance in a factory are only two examples of applications of such a mobile multicamera system.

2   Hardware

We decided to use IEEE 1394 (FireWire) digital cameras which are now available in a large variety of types and prices. It is easy and cheap to add a FireWire card to a computer and new computers often already have FireWire ports included. Linux was chosen as an operating system for ViRoom because of its support for networking. We use several PCs connected by Ethernet and communicating over the TCP/IP protocol. Any Linux/PC computer connected to Internet can become a part of our system.

To keep the price of the whole setup low we use mainly simple webcams such as ADS[1] PYRO or Unibrain[2] Fire-i without precluding attaching higher quality cameras. Prices for the simple FireWire cameras start around 100 Euro which makes them affordable even for an occasional user or for home usage and it also allows to build systems with a high number of cameras. The main drawback is that they lack the external synchronization feature, so the software synchronization described have to be used. We describe it briefly in this paper, more details can be found in [11]. Although it is not as accurate solution as the hardware synchronization it requires no additional hardware or cables and thus helps to keep the system mobile and flexible.

3   Software Architecture

The overall software architecture is determined by the need for a software synchronization. The main control process, called Orangutan, synchronizes image capturing servers (CameraD) and collects the results from the image processing servers (Tamarin). The three processes mentioned above are necessary for any application and they will be described in this section. Inter-process communication and dataflow are explained in Fig. 1. Application-dependent multiple view algorithms are separate processes and they will be described in Sec. 4.

3.1   CameraD – Capturing Server

CameraD is a capturing server running on every computer with cameras attached. Its job is to wait for commands to capture images from the camera(s).

---

[1] http://www.adstech.com
[2] http://www.unibrain.com

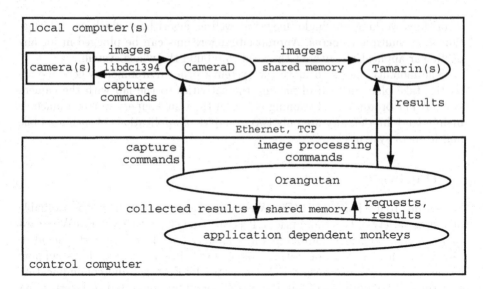

Fig. 1. Monkeys for the ViRoom. The top box shows processes running on the local computers with attached cameras. The bottom one shows the control computer with the control process. Arrows indicate commands and data exchanged between processes.

Captured images are stored in a cyclic buffer in a shared memory. This shared memory space is being accessed by other processes running on the same computer. Sending images over the network or saving them to the local disk are also possible options. Each stored image is identified by a camera number and a frame number. The frame number is a part of the capture command and serves for the time synchronization.

3.2 Tamarin – Image Processing Server

Tamarin is an image processing server running on computers with cameras attached. One Tamarin is started for each camera. It waits for commands to process images captured by CameraD. The frame number is attached to each command and Tamarin waits until the frame with this number appears in the shared memory. The commands for each frame are sent all at once, but results are sent back separately as soon as they are available.

The operations that Tamarin performs are supposed to be quite elementary. Currently image resampling, histogram calculation, background segmentation and silhouette extraction have been implemented. These operations may be combined to form more advanced tasks, e.g. sending extracted silhouettes from a segmented downsampled image together with a part of that image.

The required frame rate and output resolution or precision may vary for each application. Computationally expensive algorithms are performed on a downsampled image while the same frame in the original resolution can still be used for another task.

3.3   Orangutan – The Main Control Process

Orangutan is the main control process. It synchronizes CameraDs and collects the results from Tamarins. It parses a XML configuration file which specifies the desired application. The file contains instructions about processes to start, connection points (addresses, ports and shared memory keys) and commands to send, see Table 1 for an example. Its first task is to start all other processes including those running on remote computers. Orangutan passes the same configuration file to every process it starts so that they can establish necessary connections.

After this starting phase, it begins to send capturing commands to all CameraDs to synchronize them and immediately after that commands to the Tamarins to process the images. Then it gathers the results and stores them into shared memory. It does not run any algorithms on the results to ensure an undelayed sending of commands and gathering of results. Orangutan can run on any computer and we usually attach also one or two of the cameras to the computer with Orangutan.

Table 1. An example of a simple configuration file. Orangutan starts the mentioned processes – CameraD and two Tamarins on host viroom02 and Lemur (will be discussed later) on the local computer. Tamarins will be asked to send downsampled images which will be stored locally by Orangutan and displayed by Lemur.

```
<orangutan id="255" start_rid="1" shmkey="22000" period="66">

  <image start="yes" downscale="1"/>
  <lemur display_info="0" display_areas="1"/>

  <camerad id="2" name="viroom02" port="6666" shmkey="21005">
    <tamarin id="20" node="0" port="6700" mode="rgb"/>
    <tamarin id="21" node="1" port="6701" mode="rgb"/>
  </camerad>

</orangutan>
```

4   Multiple View Algorithms

The three processes described in Sec. 3 are necessary for any application. Their output is stored in the shared memory. We need also process(es) which display or further work out the results. The Lemur process has been developed for displaying. It can display images stored in the shared memory as well as other results, such as segmented images, silhouettes, histograms or virtual 3D objects etc. Algorithms using multiple image information run as another process and use also the same shared memory as Lemur for an input. Their results can be displayed, stored or they can pass requests back to Orangutan.

4.1   Gibbon – Closest View Selection for Telepresence

Gibbon is an example of a process working with information from multiple cameras. Its task is to select the closest view of a person moving in ViRoom. Teleteaching or teletraining are motivations for this specific application. The main goal is to provide an immersive video stream of an action that is being performed in a relatively large environment, a classroom or an assembly booth, for instance. One camera suffers from a limited and often occluded field of view. The main ViRoom idea is to place several cameras around or even inside the working volume and to let Gibbon keep the person optimally visible in the videostream throughout his or her action.

Gibbon runs on the same computer as Orangutan and has access to the shared memory where Orangutan stores results from the Tamarins, see Fig. 2. Tamarin runs background segmentation on each frame, based on [6] and [2]. Silhouettes are extracted from the segmented image using algorithm based on marching squares. Tamarin also computes the bounding box of the silhouette. The decision making process, Gibbon, selects the silhouette with the largest

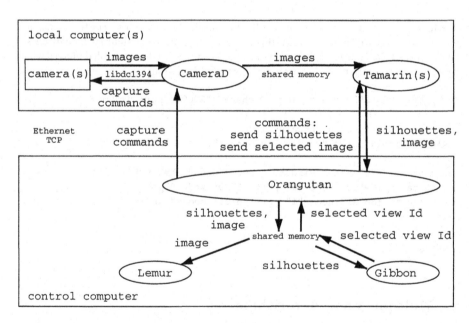

Fig. 2. Dataflow for the closest view selection application is shown in this figure. Compared to the general software architecture scheme in Fig. 1 there are two new processes on the control computer. Gibbon selects the closest view and Lemur displays it.

bounding box $s_{i,t}$ for each camera i and time frame t. A camera candidate for the best view is selected as $c_t = \arg\max_i area(s_{i,t})$. To prevent rapid and thus disturbing switching between views, when a person has about an equal size in two or more cameras, we set the switching resistance $r > 1$. To switch the view, the inequality $area(s_{c_t,t}) > r * area(s_{c_{t-1},t})$ has to be satisfied, otherwise c_t is set back to c_{t-1}.

Another feature offered by Lemur is virtual zooming. When it is turned on, Gibbon finds a rectangle inside the view c_t which contains the silhouette and has a specified aspect ratio. This information (selected view and zoom-in rectangle) is passed back to Orangutan. Orangutan then asks Tamarin to send only the requested rectangle from the next frame and Lemur will show the zoomed image of the person moving in ViRoom, see Fig. 3. The whole image is sent and displayed in the case that the virtual zoom is turned off.

It should be noted that this view selection is fairly simple and does not take into account changes in the background (for example a moved chair would be selected), or heading of the person (the closest view is not useful if we do not see the face). These drawbacks are currently being solved by the integration of a human tracker [9].

Fig. 3. Zoomed-in image of the segmented object is shown on the top, small images on the bottom line show available views and extracted silhouettes in them.

The application currently works with 320x240 pixel images which are downsampled to 160x120 pixels for the segmentation and silhouette extraction because higher resolution silhouettes are not needed for this application. However, the selected view is sent in the original 320x240 resolution using JPEG compression. The image processing itself including the compression (which takes about half of the time) is fast enough to run at 30 frames per second, but because of the delays caused by the network and the capturing a framerate of 15 fps is used for a stable performance (on Pentium III 1 GHz processor). An alternative is to use 640x480 pixel resolution at 7.5 fps which presented in Fig. 3. There is space for improving the framerate or resolution by using faster compression, code optimizations or up-to-date CPUs.

4.2   Synchronization Error Measurement

In this experiment, the error of the software synchronization managed by Orangutan (see Sec. 3.3) is roughly measured for two cameras. The main limitations of this synchronization are network delay on a loaded network, latency of the Linux scheduler and unknown delays caused by camera drivers and hardware [11].

We point the cameras at a computer screen and display a simple box counter on the screen, see Fig. 4. The window on a screen is completely black at the start. Every 10 ms one white box is added in a line until they reach end of the screen and counting starts over. Tamarin segments the foreground white boxes, counts them and sends the result to Orangutan. The results from both Tamarins are stored in shared memory and compared against each other.

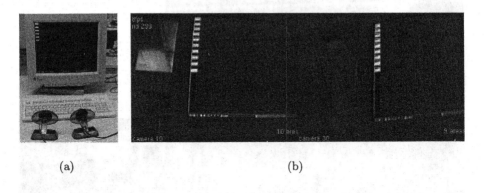

(a)   (b)

Fig. 4. Synchronization error measurement. Both cameras (a) should capture at the same time and therefore see the same number of boxes (b). However, the left camera captured later and captured one box more compared to the right one.

This measurement is not entirely precise due to the limited refresh rate of the monitor (the refreshing period is 12-17 ms depending on settings used) and errors in the segmentation caused by noise. The length of a camera exposure is another limitation – during the exposure time box may light up which makes box count ambiguous. Nevertheless, calculating the difference between counted boxes for a large number of frames gives us idea how big the synchronization error is. An average value of about 20 ms was measured for typical frequencies we use (15 and 7.5 frames per second), which may be considered significant. However, our older experiments [11] showed that it is acceptable even for such a synchronization sensitive task as the self-calibration by a moving object.

5   System Setup

As already mentioned, the flexibility of the whole system is one of the main features. The system configuration is expected to change often by accommodating new cameras and computers or just simply changing the camera positions. Though many multiview algorithms may run with a totally uncalibrated system, the knowledge about its parameters may be very helpful or even necessary for many applications. Our geometric self-calibration and color alignment methods are sketched in the following two sections.

5.1   Self-Calibration

The theoretical basis can be found in [10]. Here, we describe briefly the practical realization. A person waves a standard laser pointer around the whole working volume. The very bright projections of the laser pointer can be detected in each image with subpixel precision by fitting an appropriate point spread function. These particular positions are then merged together over time, creating thus projections of a virtual 3D object. This virtual object is then projectively reconstructed. The final step is the Euclidean stratification that converts the projective reconstruction into Euclidean structures. More details can be found in [11]. The whole process runs without any user interaction, requires no special calibration object with known 3D coordinates and produces the complete linear camera models, ie. intrinsic and extrinsic parameters. All cameras are calibrated with respect to one common world frame.

5.2   Color Alignment

Having the same color characteristics across all cameras is necessary for a disturbance-free impression of the automatic camera selection algorithm described in Sec. 4.1. The color alignment would also ease correspondence search and color based tracking.

Our cameras have an auto-adjustment feature which changes gain, brightness and white balance dynamically. But this feature cannot be used, because it changes the camera parameters during the runtime without any notice to the software. An appearance of a large object in the camera view – for instance a person moving close to the camera – can cause a significant change in the parameters and affect the segmentation method.

The most precise way to align camera parameters would be to use some object with a known color for the calibration or use common parts of the scene and adjust the parameters to match their colors. Unfortunately, the use of some calibration object for the color adjustment is not suitable for a flexible and mobile system with such a large working volume.

Therefore, so called "medium gray world" is assumed and the algorithm described in [8] is applied. This algorithm changes the brightness, the gain and the white balance parameters of the camera to make the mean value in each color separation (R,G,B) equal to a predefined value (usually 50% of the maximal value), see Fig. 5. The parameters are adjusted for each view separately, because we do not have information about view overlap. We can either adjust the parameters each time the system starts or adjust them and save for later use.

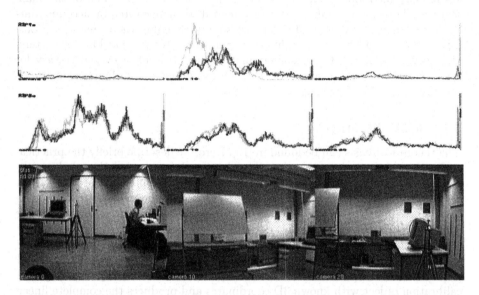

Fig. 5. Image color histograms before (top) and after (middle) the color alignment between three views. At the start the left image was too dark, the middle one lacks one color and the right one is too bright. The color alignment adjusts camera parameters so that colors are balanced and the mean intensity value is at 50% of the maximal value. The resulting images are shown on the bottom. A large number of high intensity pixels in the middle and left view is caused by the light reflected from white walls.

6   Conclusions

Monkeys for the ViRoom — the software architecture for software-synchronized multicamera system — were presented. This architecture allows to build low-cost systems for the applications where multiple views are essential. Moreover, it permits frequent reconfiguration, thus making the multicamera setup very flexible. We argue that the synchronization error — although it is high compared to hardware synchronization — is acceptable for a wide range of applications and we introduce the closest view selection for telepresence as a first application of the architecture.

The results were achieved with relatively simple image processing algorithms and the reliability of our self-calibration motivate us to upgrade our system by integrating new tracking algorithms such as [9] and by using 3D information. We are also working on improving reliability of the capturing software, especially in the case that more cameras are attached to one computer.

Acknowledgment. This work has been supported by ETH Zürich project BlueC and European Union project STAR.

References

1. M4 — multi-modal meeting manager. http://www.idiap.ch/~mccowan/meeting/, Last visited on 25th October 2002. European project, 5th Framework Programme, IST.
2. Til Aach and André Kaup. Bayesian algorithmus for adaptive change detection in image seuences using Markov random fields. *Image Communication*, 7:147–160, 1995.
3. Barry Brumitt, Brian Meyers, John Krumm, Amanda Kern, and Steven Shafer. Easyliving: Technologies for intelligent environments. In *Proceedings of the 2nd International Symposium on Hanheld and Ubiquitos Computing*, pages 12–29, September 2000.
4. Takeo Kanade, P.J. Narayanan, and Peter W. Rander. Virtualized reality: Concepts and early results. In *IEEE Workshop on the Representation of Visual Scenes*, pages 69–76, June 1995.
5. I. Kitahara, H. Saito, S. Akimichi, T. Onno, Y. Ohta, and T. Kanade. Large–scale virtualized reality. In *Computer Vision and Pattern Recognition, Technical Sketches*, June 2001.
6. Rudolf Mester, Til Aach, and Lutz Dümbgen. Illumination-invariant change detection using statistical colinearity criterion. In R. Radig and Florczyk S., editors, *DAGM2001*, number 2191 in LNCS, pages 170–177. Springer–Verlag, 2001.
7. Anurag Mittal and Larry S. Davis. M2tracker: A multi-view approach to segmenting and tracking people in a cluttered scene using region-based stereo. In A. Heyden, G. Sparr, M. Nielsen, and P. Johansen, editors, *The seventh European Conference on Computer Vision, ECCV2002*, volume 1 of *LNCS*, pages 18–36. Springer, May 2002.
8. Harsh Nanda and Ross Cutler. Practical calibrations for a real-time digital omnidirectional camera. In *Technical Sketches, Computer Vision and Pattern Recognition*, December 2001.
9. K. Nummiaro, E. B. Koller-Meier, and L. Van Gool. An adaptive color-based particle filter. *Image and Vision Computing*, page 3, 2002. To appear.
10. Mark Pollefeys, Reinhard Koch, and Luc Van Gool. Self-calibration and metric reconstruction inspite of varying and unknown intrinsic camera parameters. *International Journal of Computer Vision*, 32(1):7–25, August 1999.
11. Tomáš Svoboda, Hanspeter Hug, and Luc Van Gool. ViRoom — low cost synchronized multicamera system and its self-calibration. In Luc Van Gool, editor, *Pattern Recognition, 24th DAGM Symposium*, number 2449 in LNCS, pages 515–522. Springer, September 2002.
12. Mohan M. Trivedi, Ivana Mikic, and Sailendra K. Bhonsle. Active camera networks and semantic event databases for intelligent environments. In *IEEE Workshop on Human Modeling, Analysis and Synthesis (in conjunction with CVPR)*, June 2000.

Hierarchical Bayesian Network for Handwritten Digit Recognition

JaeMo Sung and Sung-Yang Bang

Department of Computer Science and Engineering,
Pohang University of Science and Technology,
San 31, Hyoja-Dong, Nam-Gu, Pohang, 790-784, Korea
{emtidi, sybang}@postech.ac.kr

Abstract. To recognize the handwritten digit, this paper proposes a hierarchical Gabor features extraction method using a hierarchical Gabor filter scheme and hierarchical structure encoding the dependencies among the hierarchical Gabor features for a hierarchical bayesian network(HBN). Hierarchical Gabor features represent a different level of information which is structured such that, the higher the level, the more global information they represent, and the lower the level, the more localized information they represent. This is accomplished by a hierarchical Gabor filter scheme. HBN is a statistical model whose joint probability represents dependencies among the features hierarchically. A fully connected HBN may include irrelevant information which is useless for recognition. Pruning method can remove this irrelevant information so that the complexity of HBN can be reduced and the recognition can be accomplished more efficiently. In the experiments, we show the results of handwritten digit recognition by HBN with the hierarchical Gabor features and we compare with the naive bayesian classifier, the back-propagation neural network and the k-nearest neighbor classifier. Our proposed HBN outperforms all these methods in the experiments.

1 Introduction

We believe that human beings use structured information rather than non-structured information and use the relations among the structured information by some mechanism for recognition. We assume that this structured information is hierarchical and that the relations are limited by hierarchical dependencies. With the above assumption, we propose a hierarchical bayesian network(HBN) having the hierarchical Gabor features as the values of nodes. The hierarchical structure represents dependencies among the hierarchical Gabor features for classification. Also, we propose a pruning method to reduce the complexity of HBN. Fig.1 shows the diagram of the proposed method for recognition.

J.L. Crowley et al. (Eds.): ICVS 2003, LNCS 2626, pp. 396–406, 2003.

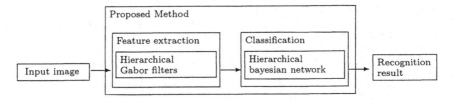

Fig. 1. Diagram of the proposed method

2 Hierarchical Gabor Features Extraction

2.1 Gabor Filter

The Gabor filter which is represented in the spatial-frequency domain is defined as

$$G(x, y, \omega_0, \sigma, r, \theta) = \frac{1}{\sqrt{\pi r \sigma}} e^{-\frac{1}{2}\left[\frac{(rR_1)^2 + R_2^2}{(r\sigma)^2}\right]} e^{i\omega_0 R_1} , \qquad (1)$$

where $R_1 = x\cos\theta + y\sin\theta$, $R_2 = -x\sin\theta + y\cos\theta$, ω_0 is the radial frequency in radians per unit length, θ is the orientation in radians and σ is the standard deviation of elliptical gaussian envelope along the x axes. The Gabor filter is centered at $(x = 0, y = 0)$ in the spatial domain. Also, the elliptical gaussian envelope of the Gabor filter has the aspect ratio $\sigma_y/\sigma_x = r$ and the plane wave's propagating direction along the short axis, where σ_x, σ_y are the standard deviations of elliptical gaussian envelope along the x, y axes[1].

2.2 Hierarchical Gabor Filter Scheme

To structure features hierarchically, the features must be able to represent different level information such that the features in the higher level represent more global information and the features in the lower level represent more localized information. To accomplish this, a hierarchical Gabor filter scheme is planned.

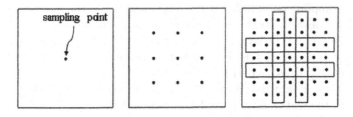

Fig. 2. Sampling points of each level, with level, 1, 2, 3 from left to right. In level 3, rows and column of sampling points surrounded by rectangles denote common sub-sampling points of the adjacent sampling points in level 2

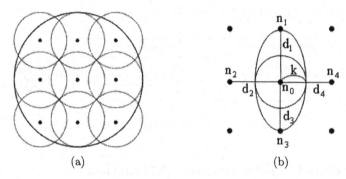

Fig. 3. (a) A big circle is a region covered by a gaussian envelope of the upper sampling point and smaller nine circles are regions covered by gaussian envelopes of sub-sampling points (b) A Circle is half of the max of the circular gaussian envelope, where its radius is $k = \text{mean}(d_1, d_2, d_3, d_4)/2$. In the case of ellipse, aspect ratio $r = 2$

In this scheme, the Gabor filter banks whose Gabor filters can represent the global or the localized information are defined. Next, the optimal Gabor filters are selected from the Gabor filter banks by a fisher score, and then hierarchical Gabor features are extracted from the optimal Gabor filters.

To define the Gabor filter banks, recursively from the highest level which has only one sampling point at the center in the image plane, a sampling point is decomposed into nine sub-sampling points in the level beneath. This sub-sampling decomposition is shown in Fig.2. The position of the sampling point in the image plane becomes the center of the Gabor filter in the spatial domain.

In order to extract information having the global property at the high level and the localized property at the low level from the Gabor filters(See the Fig.3(a)), the standard deviation σ^{ls} of gaussian envelope of the Gabor filter can be restricted such that the contour's radius having half of max of the circular gaussian envelope becomes k. From the equation (1), the σ^{ls} becomes

$$\sigma^{ls} = \frac{k}{\sqrt{ln2}} \, , \qquad (2)$$

where $l = 1, \ldots, N_L$, $s = 1, \ldots, N_{lS}$. l is a the level index and N_L is the level size. s is a sampling point index at the level l and N_{lS} is the number of sampling points of the level l. Next, the k which is near the $\text{mean}(d1, d2, d3, d4)/2$ is selected to represent the localized information which is not included in the higher level, where d_1, d_2, d_3, d_4 are distance from a sampling point to its four neighbor sampling points, n_1, n_2, n_3, n_4 (See Fig.3(b)).

After the standard deviation σ^{ls} and the aspect ratio r of Gabor filter are determined, the Gabor filter bank $\mathbf{FB}_j^{ls}$ can be defined as

$$\omega_i \in \Omega \quad \text{and} \quad \Omega = \{\omega_1, \ldots, \omega_{N_\omega}\}, \quad i = 1, \ldots, N_\omega$$
$$\theta_j \in \Theta \quad \text{and} \quad \Theta = \{\theta_1, \ldots, \theta_{N_\theta}\}, \quad j = 1, \ldots, N_\theta$$
$$\mathbf{FB}_j^{ls} = \{f_1, \ldots, f_{N_\omega}\}, \quad f_i(x, y) = G(x^{ls} - x, y^{ls} - y, \omega_i, \sigma^{ls}, r, \theta_j) \, , \quad (3)$$

where Ω is a set of spatial frequencies, Θ is a set of the orientations, and f_i is a Gabor filter centered at (x^{ls}, y^{ls}) from the equation (1). (x^{ls}, y^{ls}) is xy-coordinates of the sampling point in the image plane. Thus, for each sampling point and orientation, the Gabor filter bank $\mathbf{FB}_j^{ls}$ is a set of Gabor filters which have different frequencies in the Ω. For classification, an optimal Gabor filter F_j^{ls} from $\mathbf{FB}_j^{ls}$ is selected by the fisher score from the training images (See the Appendix for fisher score). A preclassified training image is defined by (h_d, I_d), where $h_d \in \mathbf{C}$ and $I_d \in \mathbf{I}$. $\mathbf{C} = \{c_i : i = 1, \cdots, N_c,\ N_c :$ the number of classes$\}$ is a set of class hypotheses and $\mathbf{I}$ is a set of training images. An optimal Gabor filter F_j^{ls} is selected such as

$$f_i \in \mathbf{FB}_j^{ls}, \quad i = 1, \ldots, N_f, \quad N_f = |\mathbf{FB}_j^{ls}|$$

$$\mathbf{G}_i = \{(h_1, g_1), \ldots, (h_{N_I}, g_{N_I})\}, \quad g_d = \sum_{\{x\}}\sum_{\{y\}} I_d(x, y) f_i(x, y)$$

$$F_j^{ls} = \underset{f_i \quad \{i\}}{arg\ max}\,(FScore_i), \quad FScore_i = FisherScore\,(\mathbf{G}_i), \quad (4)$$

where g_d is the Gabor filter response of the image and N_I is the number of training images. For each Gabor filter f_i in Gabor filter bank $\mathbf{FB}_j^{ls}$, the Gabor filter responses of all the training images are calculated. Next, the Gabor filter whose frequency maximizes the fisher score is selected as the optimal filter F_j^{ls}.

After obtaining optimal Gabor filter F_j^{ls}, a Gabor feature of a sampling point about the image I is defined as

$$\mathbf{a}^{ls} = [a_1^{ls}\ a_2^{ls}\ \ldots\ a_{N_\theta}^{ls}]^T, \quad a_j^{ls} = \sum_{\{x\}}\sum_{\{y\}} I(x, y) F_j^{ls}(x, y) \quad (5)$$

The Gabor feature $\mathbf{a}^{ls}$ of a sampling point becomes an N_θ-dimensional vector whose elements are responses of optimal Gabor filters of all the orientations about the image I. Also, the hierarchical Gabor features $\mathbf{a}$ of the image I consists of the Gabor features of all the sampling points.

$$\mathbf{a} = \{\mathbf{a}^1, \mathbf{a}^2, \ldots, \mathbf{a}^{N_L}\}, \quad \mathbf{a}^l = \{\mathbf{a}^{l1}, \mathbf{a}^{l2}, \ldots, \mathbf{a}^{lN_{ls}}\}, \quad (6)$$

where $\mathbf{a}^l$ is a set of Gabor features of level l.

3   Hierarchical Bayesian Network

3.1   Bayesian Networks

About a finite set of random variables, $\mathbf{U} = \{A_1, \ldots, A_n\}$, a bayesian networks[2][3][4] is generally defined by $< G, \mathbf{P}_c >$. The $G = (\mathbf{V}, \mathbf{E})$, that is a directed acyclic graph(DAG), defines the structure of bayesian networks. $\mathbf{V} = \{A_1, \ldots, A_n\}$ is a set of vertices (nodes) and $\mathbf{E} = \{(A_i, A_j) : A_i, A_j \in \mathbf{V}, \text{where } i \neq j\}$ is a set of direct edges, where (A_i, A_j) denotes directed edge from A_i to

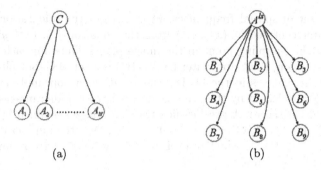

Fig. 4. (a) Structure of bayesian network for naive bayesian classifier (b) Sub-structure of HBN

A_j which imply that the node A_i affect the node A_j directly. There is a one-to-one correspondence between elements of $\mathbf{V}$ and $\mathbf{U}$. A directed edge set $\mathbf{E}$ represent directed dependencies between the random variables in $\mathbf{U}$. $\mathbf{P}_c$ is a set of conditional probability distributions of nodes. The conditional probability distribution of a node A_i in G is defined by $P(A_i|\,\mathbf{\Pi}_{A_i})$, where $\mathbf{\Pi}_{A_i}$ denotes the set of parents of A_i in G. Also, the joint probability distribution $P(\mathbf{U})$ explained by bayesian networks is factorized by conditional probability distributions in the $\mathbf{P}_c$ and is followed as

$$P(A_1,\dots,A_n) = \prod_{i=1}^{n} P(A_i|\,\mathbf{\Pi}_{A_i}) \tag{7}$$

For examples, the structure of the naive bayesian classifier[5], which does not represent any dependencies among the feature nodes, is shown the Fig.4.(a) and the joint probability is factorized such as $P(A_1,\dots,A_N,C) = \prod_{i=1}^{N} P(A_i|\,C)P(C)$

3.2   Hierarchical Bayesian Network

The hierarchical structure of HBN represents the dependencies among the hierarchical Gabor features of the adjacent levels. It is assumed by the hierarchical structure that the Gabor features at a given level affect the Gabor features at their below level having a more local property.

The structure of HBN is defined by the $G_H =<\mathbf{V}_H,\mathbf{E}_H>$, which represents the dependencies among the hierarchical Gabor features excluding the class node. There is a one-to-one correspondence between a sampling point in the hierarchical Gabor filter scheme and an element of $\mathbf{V}_H$. Let A^{ls} to the node in $\mathbf{V}_H$ or the random variable in $\mathbf{U}_H$ corresponding to the sampling point s at the level l. Thus, the node set $\mathbf{V}_H$ becomes

$$\mathbf{V}_H = \mathbf{A}^1 \cup \dots \cup \mathbf{A}^{N_L}, \quad \mathbf{A}^l = \{A^{l1},\dots,A^{lN_{ls}}\}, \tag{8}$$

where $\mathbf{A}^l$ is a set of nodes at level l. A set $\boldsymbol{\Phi}^{ls}$, which has elements as the nodes corresponding to the nine sub-sampling points of the sampling point corresponding to the node A^{ls}, is defined as

$$\boldsymbol{\Phi}^{ls} = \{B_1^{ls}, \dots, B_9^{ls}\}, \quad B_i^{ls} \in \mathbf{A}^{l+1} , \tag{9}$$

where $l = 1, \dots, N_L - 1$. Thus, a directed edge set $\mathbf{E}_H$ is defined as

$$\mathbf{E}_H = \mathbf{E}^1 \cup \cdots \cup \mathbf{E}^{N_L-1}, \quad \mathbf{E}^l = \mathbf{E}^{l1} \cup \dots \cup \mathbf{E}^{lN_{ls}},$$
$$\mathbf{E}^{ls} = \{(A^{ls}, B_1^{ls}), \dots, (A^{ls}, B_9^{ls})\} , \tag{10}$$

where $B_i^{ls} \in \boldsymbol{\Phi}^{ls}$ and level $l = 1, \dots, N_L - 1$.

In the hierarchical structure G_H of HBN, the node A^{ls} affects the nodes in $\boldsymbol{\Phi}^{ls}$ corresponding to its nine sub-sampling points at level $l + 1$ (See Fig.4(b)). Thus, directed dependencies from a node to nodes in the below level are limited to nodes corresponding to the nine sub-sampling points.

For classification, the hierarchical structure G_H must be modified to $G_H{}'$. $G_H{}' =< \mathbf{V}_H{}', \mathbf{E}_H{}' >$, which includes the class node C, is defined as

$$\begin{aligned}
\mathbf{V}_H{}' &= \mathbf{U}_H{}' = \mathbf{V}_H \cup \{C\} \\
\mathbf{E}_H{}' &= \mathbf{E}_H \cup \mathbf{E}^c, \qquad \mathbf{E}^c = \{(C, V_i) : V_i \in \mathbf{V}_H, \text{ for all } i\} \\
\boldsymbol{\Pi}^{ls'} &= \boldsymbol{\Pi}^{ls} \cup \{C\} \qquad \text{for all } l, s ,
\end{aligned} \tag{11}$$

where $\mathbf{E}^c$ denotes a set of directed edges from the class node C to all nodes in the set $\mathbf{V}_H$, $\boldsymbol{\Pi}^{ls'}$ denotes to a set of parents of a node A^{ls} in $G_H{}'$ and $\boldsymbol{\Pi}^{ls}$ denote to a set of parents of a node A^{ls} in G_H. All nodes in $G_H{}'$ excepting node C have node C as its parent. This modified structure of HBN ensures that in the learned network, the probability $P(C|\mathbf{V}_H)$, the main term determining the classification, will take into account all the hierarchical Gabor features[5].

For the complete definition of HBN with hierarchical structure $G_H{}'$, a set of conditional probability distributions, denoted by $\mathbf{P}_c$, must be defined. HBN has mixed types of continuous and discrete variables, where the variables of the hierarchical Gabor features in set $\mathbf{U}_H$ are continuous and only the class variable C is discrete. Thus, for each continuous Gabor feature variable A^{ls}, the conditional probability distribution $P(A^{ls}|\boldsymbol{\Pi}_{ls}{}')$ is defined as conditional multivariate gaussian[3]. Also, for the discrete class variable C which does not have any parents, the conditional probability distribution $P(C)$ is defined as the multinomial distribution[4]. The joint probability distribution of $\mathbf{U}_H{}'$ is factorized by the conditional probability distributions such as equation (7).

Using HBN defined as $< G_H{}', \mathbf{P}_c >$, inference can be made by a belief propagation algorithm in [3]. As the interesting variable is the class variable C for classification, inference is performed for $P(C|\mathbf{U}_H = \mathbf{a})$, where $\mathbf{a}$ is an instance of the hierarchical Gabor features of image from (6). Afterwards, the instance $\mathbf{a}$ is assigned to a class label maximizing $P(C|\mathbf{U}_H = \mathbf{a})$ for classification.

3.3   Pruning Method of Hierarchical Bayesian Network

The pruning assumption is that some of the nodes of HBN are possibly irrelevant or redundant so that these nodes may be not helpful for classification. Although the irrelevant nodes increase the complexity of HBN, they may not increase the correct classification rate significantly. Pruning irrelevant nodes make HBN compact to represent information for classification. The number of nodes to be pruned is a tradeoff between complexity and the classification rate. Nevertheless, it is shown in the simulation result that pruning many nodes does not decrease the classification rate significantly.

The pruning method is that the first, the fisher score of all nodes is calculated from the hierarchical Gabor features of the training data set independently. Then from the full connected structure of HBN, nodes are pruned by a fisher score (See the Appendix) with starting a node of the lowest score gradually. If a node has more child nodes than one, pruning is delayed until it has at most one child by pruning. Because a particular node is needed to give correlations among its child nodes, if a node has at most one child and must be pruned by a fisher score it is not needed. When a node is pruned, all directed edges connected with the pruned node are removed and directed edges from each parent node of the pruned node to the child node of the pruned node are added. After pruning nodes, the assumed hierarchical bayesian network structure encoding dependencies between levels can be maintained.

Pruning nodes play a role like the relevant feature selection. By ignoring the irrelevant nodes by pruning, the complexity of HBN can be reduced without a significant decrease in the classification rate. A compact hierarchical bayesian network structure can be determined from the separate validate set taking into account the tradeoff between complexity and classification rate.

4   Experiments

Our HBN was simulated about binary handwritten numerical data set for recognition. This numerical data set was obtained from the UCI(University of California, Irvine) databases[6]. 32×32 UCI handwritten numeral characters were centered and normalized. Fig.5 shows some of these characters.

The experiments were conducted with the following conditions for comparison with other methods. The training data set consisted of a randomly chosen 500 samples(50 per class) and testing data set consisted of the remaining 1,943 samples. The configuration of training and testing data set is same with the paper [9] in which the recognition of handwritten numeral data was simulated using a tolerant rough set and backpropagation neural networks having different features from hierarchical Gabor features. The number of testing data set per class is shown in Table.1. For extracting the hierarchical Gabor features, the hierarchical Gabor filter scheme uses the imaginary part of Gabor filters. The parameters of Gabor filter banks were set up such as $\Omega = \{0.025, 0.05, 0.075, 0.1, 0.15, 0.2, 0.4, 0.6, 0.8, 1, 1.2\}$ for frequencies, $\Theta = \{0, \frac{1}{4}\pi, \frac{1}{2}\pi, \frac{3}{4}\pi\}$ for orientations, aspect ratio $r = 2$ and

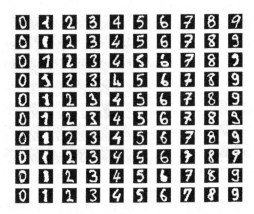

Fig. 5. 100 samples out of handwritten numerical character data set

Table 1. The number of testing data per class

Class	0	1	2	3	4	5	6	7	8	9	Total
N_{class}	189	198	195	199	186	187	195	201	180	204	1934

$k = \text{mean}(d1, d2, d3, d4)/2$ which determine the σ in the equation (2), and level size $N_L = 3$.

Experiment 1 : Our proposed HBN without a pruning method was simulated. Without pruning, the number of nodes of HBN of $N_L = 3$ is 60 of 59 feature nodes and a class node. From the training handwritten numerical character images, the hierarchical Gabor features were extracted by hierarchical Gabor filter scheme. Fig.6 shows the optimal Gabor filters of sampling points from Gabor filter banks using training image set. After constructing the hierarchical structure of HBN, the parameters of the conditional probability distributions of HBN were learned by maximum likelihood(ML) method from hierarchical Gabor features of training images[2][3][4]. After hierarchical Gabor features of testing images were extracted, these hierarchical Gabor features were classified for testing by HBN.

Experiment 2 : The naive bayesian classifier[5](See Fig.4(a)), which had exactly same nodes of HBN and the hierarchical Gabor features in the experiment 1, was simulated.

Experiment 3 : For the inputs of the k-nearest neighbor classifier[7], the hierarchical Gabor features in the experiment 1 were modified to a $236(=59 \times 4)$ dimensional feature vector, where 59 was the number of the Gabor features in the hierarchical Gabor features and 4 was the dimension of the Gabor feature of a sampling point. In these experiments the k-nearest neighbor classifiers with $k = 1, 4, 8$ were simulated. From the results, the case of the $k = 4$ showed the best recognition rate.

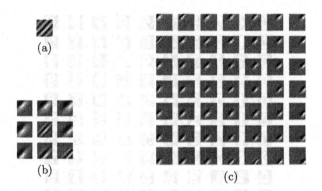

Fig. 6. Optimal Gabor filters of sampling points with orientation $\theta_j = \frac{1}{4}\pi$, aspect ratio $r = 2$ and $k = \text{mean}(d1, d2, d3, d4)/2$ (a) level 1 (b) level 2 (c) level 3

Table 2. Recognition rate. HBN : hierarchical bayesian network, NBC : naive bayesian classifier, KNN : k-nearest neighbor classifier, NN : backpropagation neural network

Experiment 1	Experiment 2	Experiment 3	Experiment 4
HBN	NBC	KNN with $k = 4$	NN
0.9741	0.9657	0.9609	0.9481

Experiment 4 : The number of input nodes of backpropagation neural networks[7] were set up to 236(=59 × 4) to use the same hierarchical Gabor features in experiment 1. Also, the parameters of backpropagation neural networks were set up such as 150 hidden units, learning rate $\eta = 0.01$, momentum rate $\alpha = 0.5$, number of learning iteration = 10,000.

In the paper [9], for these training and testing sets, it was reported that the correct classification rate was $0.911(= \frac{1762}{1934})$ by using tolerant rough set and $0.906(= \frac{1753}{1934})$ by using the backpropagation neural network. The recognition rate of our HBN having hierarchical Gabor features was $0.9741(= \frac{1884}{1934})$. From this result, our HBN outperformed the methods in the paper [9], which used different features and classification methods from ours.

Comparisons with the results of the above four experiments are shown in Table.2. A comparison between HBN and naive classifier in the experiment 2 shows that the performance of HBN is not only due to hierarchical Gabor features but also due to the hierarchical dependencies. In addition, comparing with a k-nearest neighbor classifier and backpropagation neural network having the same hierarchical Gabor features shows that the hierarchical dependencies represented in the HBN have a robust effect on recognition. From the above experiments, our proposed HBN outperformed all the methods in experiments.

The recognition rate with the proposed pruning method, where training and testing data set are the same with the above experiments, is shown in Fig.7. Because there are small changes along the axis of number of pruned nodes if

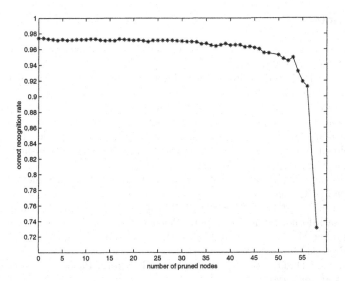

Fig. 7. Pruning effect of HBN.

nodes are not pruned excessively, the complexity of HBN can be controlled with a tradeoff between the recognition rate and complexity from a separate validation set.

5   Conclusion

In this paper, we assume that humans recognize an object using structured information by some mechanism such that if the object is so complex that it is not easily distinguished from others, the localized information, which can distinguish from others, is used. To represent the above assumption, we proposed a hierarchical bayesian network with hierarchical Gabor features.

Our proposed HBN was applied to the problem of handwritten digit recognition and compared with other methods, such as the naive classifier, k-nearest neighbor classifier, backpropagation neural networks. Results of simulations show the hierarchical dependencies of HBN have a effect on recognition. Comparison with the method in the paper [9], whose features and classification method are different from our method, shows that our structured hierarchical Gabor features are more suitable for recognition. Also, the proposed pruning method could reduce the complexity of HBN without a significant decrease in the classification rate.

Although we applied HBN to the problem of handwritten digitre cognition, we believe our method can be extended to a general recognition system.

References

1. Tai Sing Lee.: Image Representation Using 2D Gabor Wavelets. IEEE trans. PAMI, vol. 18. no. 10. (1996) 959–971
2. Pearl, J. : Probabilistic Inference in Intelligent Systems. Morgan Kaufmann, San Mateo, California, (1988)
3. Robert G. Cowell, A. Philip Dawid, Steffen L. Lauritzen, David J, Spiegelhalter.: Probabilistic Networks and Expert Systems. Springer (1999)
4. Heckerman, D.: A tutorial on learning with Bayesian networks. In 'Learning in Graphical Models'. (ed. M. I. Jordan). Kluwer Academic Publishers, Dordrecht, The Netherlands, (1998) 301–354
5. N. Friedman, D. Geiger, M Goldszmidt.: Bayesian network classifiers. Mach. Learn 29 (1997) 131–163
6. C. L. Blake and C. J. Merz.: UCI Repository of Machine Learning Databases. Dept. of Information and Computer Science, Uive. of California, Irvine, (1998)
7. Chistopher M. Bishop.: Neural Networks for Pattern Recognition. Oxford University Press (1995)
8. Richard O. Duda, Peter E. Hart, David G. Strok.: Pattern Classification. John Wily and Sons. (2001)
9. Daijin Kim, Sung-Yang Bang.: A Handwritten Numeral Character Classification Using Tolerant Rough Set. IEEE trans. PAMI, vol. 22. no. 9. (2000) 923–937

Appendix: Fisher Score

The fisher score is a measure to how certain information is efficient for discrimination. The fisher score is defined by a within-class scatter matrix and a between-class scatter matrix. A good fisher score is one which within the one class, scatter of information are the smaller and among the classes, the scatter of information are the larger[8].

For the c-class problem, suppose that a set of n d-dimensional instances, $\mathcal{X}$, have its elements such as $\mathbf{x}_1, \ldots, \mathbf{x}_n$, n_i in the subset $\mathcal{X}_i$ labeled c_i. Thus within-class scatter matrix $\mathbf{S}_W$ is defined by

$$\mathbf{S}_i = \sum_{\mathbf{x} \in \mathcal{X}_i} (\mathbf{x} - \mathbf{m}_i)(\mathbf{x} - \mathbf{m}_i)^T, \qquad \mathbf{m}_i = \frac{1}{n_i} \sum_{\mathbf{x} \in \mathcal{X}_i} \mathbf{x} \qquad \mathbf{S}_W = \sum_{i=1}^{c} \mathbf{S}_i ,$$

where T is matrix transpose. After defining a total mean vector $\mathbf{m}$, between-class scatter matrix $\mathbf{S}_B$ is defined.

$$\mathbf{m} = \frac{1}{n} \sum_{\mathbf{x} \in \mathcal{X}} \mathbf{x} = \frac{1}{n} \sum_{i=1}^{c} n_i \mathbf{m}_i, \qquad \mathbf{S}_B = \sum_{i=1}^{c} n_i (\mathbf{m}_i - \mathbf{m})(\mathbf{m}_i - \mathbf{m})^T$$

A simple scalar measure of scatter is the determinant of the scatter matrix. From this scatter measure, $FisherScore$ is

$$FisherScore = \frac{|\mathbf{S}_B|}{|\mathbf{S}_W|}, \text{ where } |\cdot| \text{ denotes determinant.}$$

A Spectral Approach to Learning Structural Variations in Graphs

Bin Luo, Richard C. Wilson, and Edwin R. Hancock

Department of Computer Science, University of York,
York, Y01 5DD, UK.

Abstract. This paper investigates the use of graph-spectral methods for learning the modes of structural variation in sets of graphs. Our approach is as follows. First, we vectorise the adjacency matrices of the graphs. Using a graph-matching method we establish correspondences between the components of the vectors. Using the correspondences we cluster the graphs using a Gaussian mixture model. For each cluster we compute the mean and covariance matrix for the vectorised adjacency matrices. We allow the graphs to undergo structural deformation by linearly perturbing the mean adjacency matrix in the direction of the modes of the covariance matrix. We demonstrate the method on sets of corner Delaunay graphs for 3D objects viewed from varying directions.

1 Introduction

Many shape and scene analysis problems in computer vision can be abstracted using relational graphs. Examples include the use of shock graphs[7] to represent the differential structure of boundary contours and view graphs to represent 3D object structure. The main advantage of the graph-representation is that it captures the structural variation of shape in a parsimonious way. However, the task of learning structural descriptions from sets of examples has proved to be an elussive one. The reasons for this are three-fold. First, graphs are not vectors and hance the apparatus of statistical pattern recognition may not be applied to them directly to construct shape-spaces. Before vectorisation can be performed, correspondences between nodes must be established. This task is fustrated by the fact that graphs are notoriously susceptible to the effects of noise and clutter. Hence, the addition or loss of a few nodes and edges can result in graphs of significantly different structure, and this in turn frustrates the task of correspondence analysis and hence vectorisation. As a result it is difficult to characterise and hence learn the distribution of structural variations in sets of graphs.

The ability to learn the modes of variation of the adjacency matrix is an important one. The reason for this is that it allows the statistical significance of changes in the edge-structure of graphs to be assessed. This is crucial capability in measuring the similarity of graphs, matching them to one-another or clustering them. There have been several previous attempts to solve this problem. One of the earliest of these was to extend the concept of string edit distance to

J.L. Crowley et al. (Eds.): ICVS 2003, LNCS 2626, pp. 407–417, 2003.

graphs. Here Fu and his co-workers[5] introduced edit costs associated with the re-labelling, insertion and deletion of edges. However, the costs were selected on an ad-hoc basis and there was no method for learning the edit costs. Moreover, the theory underlying graph-edit distance lacks the formality and rigour of that for strings. However, some steps have recently been taken by Bunke[1], who has shown the relationship between edit distance and the size of the maximum common subgraph. Christmas, Kittler and Petrou[2] have taken a probabilistic approach to the problem. They develop a Gaussian model for edge structure, which is used to compute compatibility function for relaxation labelling. Again, there is no methodology for learning the model from data.

The aim in this paper is to overcome this problem by developing statistical methods for analysing the modes of structural variation in sets of graphs. We pose the problem as that of estimating a covariance matrix for the edge-sets of the graphs. To do this we require a means of vectorising the graphs. We do this using correspondence matches to permute the adjacency matrices onto a standard reference order. We estimate the required correspondences using a recently reported EM algorithm[4], in which the correspondences are located using a singular value decomposition in the maximisation step. The standardised adjacency matrices are vectorised by stacking the columns to form long-vectors. We model the pattern-space for the standardised long-vectors using a Gaussian mixture model. The EM algorithm is used to make maximum likelihood estimates for the mean-vectors and covariance matrices for the mixture components.

From the covariance matrices for the standardised vectors, there are a number of ways in which to construct pattern-spaces. The simplest of these is to construct an eigenspace by projecting the standardised adjacency matrix long-vectors onto the leading eigenvectors of the covariance matrix. The distribution of graphs so produced can be further simplified by fitting a manifold or a mixture model. However, here we use the eigenvectors of the covariance matrix to construct a linear model for variations in the adjacency matrices. To do this we borrow ideas from point distribution models. Here Cootes and Taylor[3] have shown how to construct a linear shape-space for sets of landmark points for 2D shapes. We use a variant of this idea to model variations in the long-vectors for the standardised covariance matrices. We commence by computing the leading eigenvectors for the cluster covariance matrices. The graphs deformed by displacing the mean adjacency matrix long-vectors in the directions of the leading eigenvectors of the covariance matrix. Our method allows the pattern of edge-deformations to be learned and applied at the global level. In principal edge edit costs can be obtained from our model via a process of averaging the deformations. In this way we construct a generative model of graph-structure. This model may be both fitted to data and sampled.

2   Background

In this paper we are concerned with the set of graphs $G_1, G_2, .., G_k, ..., G_N$. The kth graph is denoted by $G_k = (V_k, E_k)$. where V_k is the set of nodes and $E_k \subseteq V_k \times V_k$ is the edge-set. Our approach in this paper is a graph-spectral one.

For each graph G_k we compute the adjacency matrix A_k. This is a $|V_k| \times |V_k|$ matrix whose element with row index i and column index j is

$$A_k(i,j) = \begin{cases} 1 & \text{if } (i,j) \in E_k \\ 0 & \text{otherwise} \end{cases}.$$ (1)

To construct our generative model of variations in graph structure, we will convert the adjacency matrices into long-vectors where the entries have a standardised order. To do this we need to permute the order of the rows and columns of the adjacency matrices. We represent the set of correspondences between the nodes in pairs of graphs using a correspondence matrix. For the graphs indexed k and l, the correspondence matrix is denoted by $S_{k,l}$. The elements of the matrix convey the following meaning

$$S_{k,l}(i,j) = \begin{cases} 1 & \text{if node } i \in V_k \text{ is in correspondence with node } j \in V_l \\ 0 & \text{otherwise} \end{cases}$$ (2)

To recover the correspondence matrices, we use the EM algorithm recently reported by Luo and Hancock [4]. This algorithm commences from a Bernoulli model for the correspondences indicators which are treated as missing data, From this distribution an expected log-likelihood function for the missing correspondence indicators is developed. In the maximisation step a singular value decomposition method is used to recover the correspondence matrix which satisfies the condition

$$S_{k,l} = \arg\max_{S} Tr[A_k^T S A_l S^T]$$ (3)

In other words, the maximum likelihood correspondence matrices are those that maximise the correlation of the two adjacency matrices.

2.1 Preclustering

To establish initial clusters, we perform clustering using the pairwise distance between spectral feature-vectors extracted from the graphs. From the adjacency matrices $A_k, k = 1...N$ at hand, we can calculate the eigenvalues λ_k by solving the equation $|A_k - \lambda_k I| = 0$ and the associated eigenvectors ψ_k^ω by solving the system of equations $A_k \psi_k^\omega = \lambda_k^\omega \psi_k^\omega$. We order the eigenvectors according to the decreasing magnitude of the eigenvalues, i.e. $|\lambda_k^1| > |\lambda_k^2| > ... |\lambda_k^{|V_k|}|$. With the eigenvalues and eigenvectors of the adjacency matrix to hand, the spectral decomposition for the adjacency matrix of the graph indexed k is

$$A_k = \sum_{i=1}^{|V_k|} \lambda_k^i \psi_k^i (\psi_k^i)^T$$ (4)

Our vector of spectral features is constructed from the ordered eigenvalues of the adjacency matrix. For the graph indexed k, the vector is $B_k = (\lambda_k^1, \lambda_k^2, ..., \lambda_k^n)^T$. For the pair of graphs indexed k and l, the squared Euclidean distance between the spectral feature vectors is $d_{k,l}^2 = (B_k - B_l)^T (B_l - B_l)$ From the set of distance, we can construct a pairwise representation of the affinity of different graphs. The affinity is captured using an $N \times N$ matrix whose element with row k and column l is $W_{k,l}^{(0)} = \exp[-\mu d_{k,l}^2]$.

We apply a pairwise clustering method to the matrix W. The initial set of clusters are defined by the eigenmodes of the link-weight matrix W. Here we follow Sarkar and Boyer [6] have shown how the positive eigenvectors of the matrix of link-weights can be used to assign objects to perceptual clusters. Using the Rayleigh-Ritz theorem, they observe that the scalar quantity $\underline{x}^t W \underline{x}$ is maximised when $\underline{x}$ is the leading eigenvector of W. Moreover, each of the subdominant eigenvectors corresponds to a disjoint pairwise cluster. They confine their attention to the same-sign positive eigenvectors (i.e. those whose corresponding eigenvalues are real and positive, and whose components are either all positive or are all negative in sign). If a component of a positive same-sign eigenvector is non-zero, then the corresponding object belongs to the associated cluster of segmental entities. The eigenvalues $\lambda_1, \lambda_2 \ldots$ of W are the solutions of the equation $|W - \lambda I| = 0$ where I is the $|V| \times |V|$ identity matrix. The corresponding eigenvectors $\underline{x}_{\lambda_1}, \underline{x}_{\lambda_2}, \ldots$ are found by solving the equation $W \underline{x}_{\lambda_i} = \lambda_i \underline{x}_{\lambda_i}$. With this notation, the set of positive same-sign eigenvectors is represented by $\Omega = \{\omega | \lambda_\omega > 0 \wedge [(\underline{x}_\omega^*(i) > 0 \forall i) \vee \underline{x}_\omega^*(i) < 0 \forall i])\}$.

To develop our pairwise clustering method further, we require a cluster membership indicator $s_{i\omega}$ which convey the following meaning

$$s_{i\omega} = \begin{cases} 1 & \text{if node } i \text{ belongs to cluster } \omega \\ 0 & \text{otherwise} \end{cases} \tag{5}$$

We use the link-weight matrix and the cluster membership indicator variables to develop an iterative maximum likeihood clustering algorithm. To do this we draw on assumption that the cluster membership indicators are drawn from the Bernoulli distribution

$$p(W_{k,l}|\omega) = W_{k,l}^{s_{i\omega} s_{j\omega}} (1 - W_{k,l})^{1 - s_{k\omega} s_{l\omega}} \tag{6}$$

This distribution takes on its largest values when either the affinity weight $W_{k,l}$ is unity and $s_{k\omega} = s_{l\omega} = 1$, or if $W_{i,j} = 0$ and $s_{k\omega} = s_{l\omega} = 0$. The log-likelihood function for the cluster configuration is

$$\mathcal{L} = \ln\left\{ \prod_{\omega \in \Omega} \prod_{k=1}^{N} \prod_{l=1}^{N} p(W_{i,j}|\omega) \right\} = \sum_{\omega \in \Omega} \sum_{k=1}^{N} \sum_{l=1}^{N} \left\{ s_{k\omega} s_{l\omega} \ln W_{k,l} + (1 - s_{k\omega} s_{l\omega}) \ln(1 - W_{k,l}) \right\} \tag{7}$$

The log-likelihood can be maximised with dual update steps for the cluster-indicator variables and the link-weights. This is reminiscent of the EM algorithm. The updated link weights are found by solving the equation $\frac{\partial \mathcal{L}}{\partial W_{k,l}} = 0$. As a result the updated elements of the weight matrix are given by

$$\hat{W}_{kl} = \frac{1}{|\Omega|} \sum_{\omega \in \Omega} s_{k\omega} s_{l\omega} \tag{8}$$

The analogous maximisation step is not tractable in closed form for the cluster membership indicators. Hence we use a soft-assign method instead. To do this we compute the derivatives of the expected log-likelihood function with respect to the cluster-membership variable

$$\frac{\partial \mathcal{L}}{\partial s_{k\omega}} = \sum_{l=1}^{T} s_{l\omega} \ln \frac{W_{kl}}{1 - W_{kl}} \tag{9}$$

The soft-assign update procedure involves exponentiating the partial derivatives of the expected log-likelihood function. The resulting update equation is

$$\hat{s}_{k\omega} = \frac{\Pi_{l=1}^{N} \left\{ \frac{W_{k,l}}{1-W_{k,l}} \right\}^{s_{l\omega}}}{\sum_{i=1}^{N} \Pi_{j=1}^{N} \left\{ \frac{W_{k,l}}{1-W_{k,l}} \right\}^{s_{l\omega}}} \tag{10}$$

The two update equations are interleaved and interated until convergence is reached. We initialise the cluster memberships using the components of the same-sign positive eigenvectors and set

$$s_{iw} = \frac{|\mathbf{x}_\omega^*(i)|}{\sum_{i \in V_\omega} |\mathbf{x}_\omega^*(i)|} \tag{11}$$

3 Graph Clustering

We use the pairwise clusters to seed our EM algorithm. For each cluster, we identify the modal graph. This is the graph for which $l_\omega = \arg\max_i s_{i\omega}$. The modal graphs for the different clusters are used to establish a reference order for the nodes. We use the correspondence matrices to permute the node-order of the graphs into the reference order for the different clusters. For the graph indxexed k, the permuted adjacency matrix relevant to the cluster ω is $M_k^\omega = S_{k,l_\omega}^T A_k S_{k,l_\omega}$.

Once the adjacency matrices have been permuted, then we can convert them into pattern-vectors. We do this by stacking the columns of the adjacency matrix to form a long-vector. For the graph-indexed k and the cluster the long-vector is ω, the $V_k^\omega = (M_k^\omega(1,1), M_i^\omega(1,2), ..., M_k^\omega(n,n))$. Using the pairwise cluster-membership indicators we can compute the mean long-vectors and the covariance matrices for each cluster. These will be used to seed our EM algorithm. For the cluster indexed ω, the mean-vector and covariance matrix are

$$U_\omega^{(0)} = \sum_{k=1}^{N} s_{k\omega} V_k^\omega \qquad \Sigma_\omega^{(0)} = \sum_{k=1}^{N} s_{k\omega} (V_k^\omega - U_\omega)(V_k^\omega - U_\omega)^T \tag{12}$$

With this initialisation to hand, we use a Gaussian mixture model to iteratively recover improved estimates of the mean long-vector and the associated covariance matrix. We commence by assuming that the long-vectors are drawn from the Gaussian distribution

$$p(V_k^\omega | U_\omega, \Sigma_\omega) = \frac{1}{(2\pi)^{\frac{n}{2}} \sqrt{|\Sigma|}} \exp\left[-\frac{1}{2} (V_k^\omega - U_\omega)^T \Sigma^{-1} (V_k^\omega - U_\omega) \right] \tag{13}$$

In the maximisation step of the algorithm, the mean long-vector and the covariance matrices for each of the clusters are updated. The updated mean is

$$U_\omega^{(n+1)} = \sum_{k=1}^{N} P(k \in \omega | V_k^\omega, U_\omega^{(n)}, \Sigma_\omega^{(n)}) V_k^\omega \qquad (14)$$

While the updated estimate of the covariance matrix is

$$\Sigma_\omega^{(n+1)} = \sum_{k=1}^{T} P(k \in \omega | U_\omega^{(n)}, \Sigma_\omega^{(n)}, V_k^\omega)(V_k^\omega - U_\omega^{(n)})(V_k^\omega - U_\omega^{(n)})^T \qquad (15)$$

In the expectation step the *a posteriori* cluster membership probabilities are updated using the Bayes rule. The update equation is

$$P(k \in \omega | U_\omega^{(n)}, \Sigma_\omega^{(n)}, V_k^\omega) = \frac{\alpha_{k\omega} p(V_k^\omega | U_\omega^{(n+1)}, \Sigma_\omega^{(n)})}{\sum_{\omega \in \Omega} \alpha_{k\omega} p(V_k^\omega | U_\omega^{(n+1)}, \Sigma_\omega^{(n)})} \qquad (16)$$

where

$$\alpha_{k\omega} = \frac{1}{N} \sum_{k=1}^{N} P(k \in \omega | U_\omega^{(n)}, \Sigma_\omega^{(n)}, V_k^\omega) \qquad (17)$$

4   Modal Analysis

Our aim is to use the covariance matrix delivered by the EM algorithm to analyse the modes of variation for the long-vectors representing the adjacency matrices of the graphs. To do this we use a simple linaer model which has been used to great effect in represent the modes of variations for sets of point patterns.

We commence by computing the eigenvalues and eigenvectors for the covariance matrix Σ_ω. The eigenvalues $\lambda_1, \lambda_2, ...$ are found by solving the polynomial equation $|\Sigma_\omega - \lambda I| = 0$, where I is the identity matrix. The assoiciated eigenvectors $\phi_1^\omega, \phi_2^\omega, ...$ are found by solving the linear eigenvector equation $\Sigma_\omega \phi_l^\omega = \lambda_l \phi_l^\omega$ From the eigenvectors we construct a modal matrix. The eigenvectors are ordered in decreasing eigenvalue order to form the columns of the modal matrix $\Phi_\omega = (\phi_1^\omega | \phi_2^\omega | .... | \phi_n^\omega)$. The linear deformation model allows the components of the adjacency matrix long-vectors to undergo displacement in the directions of the eigenvectors of the covariance matrix. For the long-vector of the graph G_k and the cluster indexed ω, the displaced vector is given by

$$\tilde{V}_k^\omega = U_\omega + \Phi_\omega b_{k\omega}^* \qquad (18)$$

The degree of displacement for the different vector components is controlled by the vector of parameters $b_{k\omega}$.

The linear deformation model may be fitted to data. This is done by searching for the least squares parameter vector. Suppose that the model is to be fitted to the graph with standardised adjacency matrix V_k. The least-squares parameter vector which satisfies the condition

$$b^*_{k\omega} = \arg\min_b (V^\omega_k - U_\omega - \Phi_\omega b)^T (V^\omega_k - U_\omega - \Phi_\omega b) \tag{19}$$

and the solution is

$$b^*_{k\omega} = \frac{1}{2}\left[\Phi^T_\omega \Phi_\omega\right]^{-1} \Phi^T_\omega \left\{V^\omega_k - U_\omega\right\} \tag{20}$$

5 Experiments

Our experimental vehicle is provided by 2D views of 3D objects. We have collected sequences of views for a number of objects. For the different objects the image sequences are obtained under slowly varying changes in viewer angle. From each image in each view sequence, we extract corner features. We use the extracted corner points to construct Delaunay graphs. In our experiments we use three different sequences. Each sequence contains images with equally spaced viewing directions. For each sequence we show a sample of 5 images. Figure 1 shows example images from the three sequences and the associated graphs. The number of feature points varies significantly from image to image, for the first (CMU) sequence there are about 30 points, for the second (MOVI) sequence there are about 140 and for the final (Chalet) sequence there are about 100. There are a number of "events" in the sequences. For instance in the MOVI sequence, the right-hand gable wall disappears after the 12th frame, and the left-hand gable wall appears after the 17th frame. Several of the background objects also disappear and reappear. In the Swiss chalet sequence, the front face of the house disappears after the 15th frame.

We commence by providing some examples to illustrate the behaviour of the learning process when it applied The top-left panel of Figure 2 shows the modal graph from the sequence. This graph is the one which has the largest cluster membership probability in the pre-clustering step. The top-right panel shows the test graph which is generated from the $8th$ image in the sequence. The mean graph is displayed in bottom-left panel. This graph is generated using the method described in section 4. The model fitting result is shown in the bottom-right panel. In the lower two panels of the figure, the darkness of the edges is proportional to the magnitude of the corresponding element of the adjacency matrix. In the case of the mean-graph, this quantity is proportional to the number of times the corresponding edge appears in the training data. It is interesting to note the similarities and differences in the structure of the mean and modal graphs. In the first instance, all the strong edges in the mean graph are common with the modal graph. Second, in the mean graph edges are pruned away from the high degree nodes. Hence, the learning process would appear to locate common salient structure, but remove ephemeral detail.

Next, we turn our attention to the clusters delivered by the learning proces. For each graph k we select the cluster of maximum probability $\theta_k =$

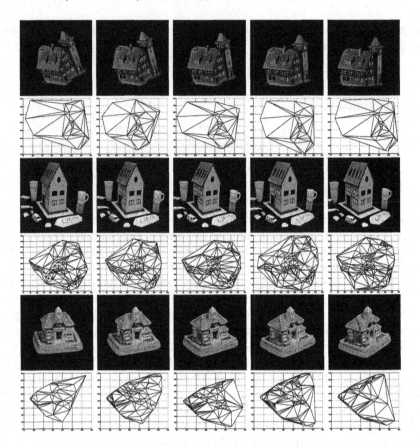

Fig. 1. Image sequences and corresponding graphs

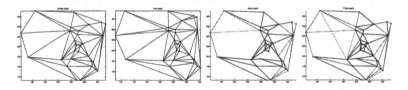

Fig. 2. Modal graph, test graph, mean graph and fitted graph for the CMU sequence

$\arg\max_\omega P(k \in \omega | U_\omega, \Sigma_\omega, V_k^\omega)$ For the maximum probability cluster, we compute the best-fit long-vector $V_k^* = \tilde{V}_k^{\theta_\omega}$. For each pair of graphs with indices k_1 and k_2, we compute the $L2$ distance $D(k_1, k_2) = (V_{k_1}^* - V_{k_2}^*)^T(V_{k_1}^* - V_{k_2}^*)$. We visualise the graphs by applying multidimensional scaling to the matrix of distances D and placing a thumbnail image at the point defined by the leading two components of the resulting embedding. We compare the results with those obtained using a simple spectral representation. Here we compute distances between the vectors of adjacency matrix eigenvectors B_k extracted using the method outlined in Section 3.1. This is simply the input to our preclustering method. The left-hand panel in Figure 3 shows the MDS visualisation of preclustering generated from the spectral vectors. The righthand panel shows the corresponding result generated from the fitted long-vectors. The clustering of the graphs is much tighter and there is less overlap between the different sequences.

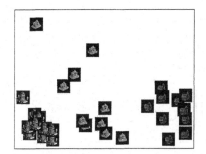 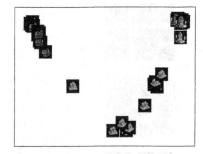

Fig. 3. Spectral pre-clustering (left) and final clustering (right) visualised using multidimensional scaling.

In the final set of experiments, we investigate the different image sequences separately. Here the aim is to determine whether the methods explored in the previous section can identify the finer view structure of the different objects. At this point it is important to note that we have used Delaunay graphs to abstract the corner features. Our view-based analysis explores how the edge-structure of the graphs changes with varying object pose. Since the Delaunay graph is the neighbourhood graph of the Voronoi tessellation, i.e. the locus of the median line between adjacent points, it may be expected to reflect changes in the shape of the arrangement of corner features. We investigate which combination of spectral feature-vector and embedding strategy gives the best view manifold for the different objects. In particular, we aim to determine whether the different views are organised into a well structured view trajectory, in which subsequent views are adjacent to one-another.

In Figure 4 the top row shows the results obtained for the CMU sequence, the second row those for the MOVI house and the bottom row shows those for the chalet sequence. In the left-hand column of each figure, we show the matrix of pairwise $L2$ distances between the projected vectors $\tilde{V}_k^\omega$. The second column we show the eigenspace found by projecting the fitted long-vectors onto the basis spanned by the leading three eigenvectors of the cluster covariance matrix, i.e. the vector $Z_k^\omega = (\phi_1^\omega|\phi_2^\omega|\phi_3^\omega)^T \tilde{V}_k^\omega$. The third column shows the eigenspace generated by applying ICA to the covariance matrix. Finally, the right-hand column shows the result of applying MDS to the matrix of $L2$ distances.

First, we compare the structure of the view-spaces obtained using PCA and MDS. Generally speaking, they are rather different. In the case of PCA, a cluster structure emerges. By contrast, in MDS the different views execute smooth trajectories. Hence, the output of PCA would appear to be best for locating clusters of similar views, while MDS provides information which might be more useful in constructing parametric eigenspaces.

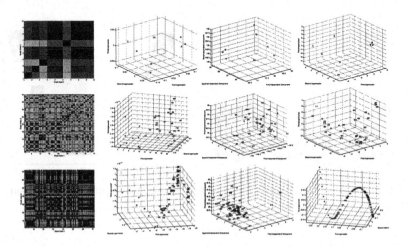

Fig. 4. Eigenspaces from graphs belonging to separate sequences.

6 Conclusions

In this paper, we have presented a framework for leaning a linear model of the modes of structural variation in sets of graphs. We commence by locating correspondences between the nodes in different graphs and using the correspondence order to vectorise the adjacency matrices. We cluster the vectors using the EM algorithm. From the eigenmodes of the cluster covariance matrices we construct a linear model of the modes of structural variation in the graphs.

There are a number of ways in which we intend to develop this work. First, we aim to integrate the correspondence and clustering steps into a single process. Second, we aim to use the cluster covariance matrices to construct piecewise subspace models for the graphs.

References

1. H. Bunke and K. Shearer. A graph distance metric based on the maximal common subgraph. *Pattern Recognition Letters*, 19:255–211;259, 1998.
2. W.J. Christmas, J. Kittler, and M. Petrou. Structural matching in computer vision using probabilistic relaxation. *IEEE Transactions on Pattern Analysis and Machine Intelligence*, 17(8):749–211;764, 1995.
3. T.F. Cootes, C.J. Taylor, D.H. Cooper, and J. Graham. Active shape models - their training and application. *Computer Vision and Image Understanding*, 61(1):38–211;59, 1995.
4. B. Luo and E.R. Hancock. Structural graph matching using the em algorithm and singular value decomposition. *IEEE PAMI*, 23(10):1120–211;1136, 2001.
5. A. Sanfeliu and K.S. Fu. A distance measure between attributed relational graphs for pattern recognition. *IEEE Transactions Systems, Man and Cybernetics*, 13(3):353–211;362, May 1983.
6. S. Sarkar and K.L. Boyer. Quantitative measures of change based on feature organization: Eigenvalues and eigenvectors. *CVIU*, 71(1):110–211;136, July 1998.
7. K. Siddiqi, A. Shokoufandeh, S.J. Dickinson, and S.W. Zucker. Shock graphs and shape matching. *IJCV*, 35(1):13–211;32, November 1999.

Sigmoidal Weighted Vector Directional Filter

Rastislav Lukac[1], Bogdan Smolka[2],
Konstantinos N. Plataniotis[3], and Anastasios N. Venetsanopoulos[3]

[1] Slovak Image Processing Center,
Jarkova 343, 049 25 Dobsina, Slovak Republic
lukacr@ieee.org

[2] Department of Automatic Control,
Silesian University of Technology, Akademicka 16 Str., 44-101 Gliwice, Poland
bsmolka@ia.polsl.gliwice.pl

[3] Edward S. Rogers Sr. Department of Electrical and Computer Engineering,
University of Toronto, 10 King's College Road, Toronto, Canada
{kostas, anv}@dsp.toronto.edu

Abstract. In this paper, we provide and analyze a sigmoidal optimization of a recently developed class of weighted vector directional filters (WVDFs) outputting the input multichannel sample associated with the minimum sum of weighted angular distances to other input samples. Because the WVDFs can perform a number of smoothing operations in dependence on the weight coefficients, the aim of this paper is to adapt the WVDF behavior to statistical properties of noise and original color image. The filtering results and the complete analysis of the sigmoidal function based WVDF optimization are also provided.

1 Introduction

The field of color image filtering still takes the growth research interest, because colors provide important information about the objects on the scene. In the last decade, a rich family of vector filtering algorithms was developed to suppress noisy samples in multichannel signals such as color images and simultaneously to preserve thin image details and color chromaticity. This capability is required not only by a human visual system, however, the same demand is requested in applications [7] such as computer and robot vision systems, recognition/ interpretation systems, automatic analysis, etc.

An important task related to nonlinear image filtering is to build a unified filter theory, develop a generalization of a variety of existing nonlinear filters and provide a versatile optimization. In this paper, we provide a generalized class of vector directional filters for color image filtering and also the sigmoidal optimization algorithm taking the advantage of weighted median filters and stack filters. By using the sigmoidal optimization, it is possible to adapt the WVDF weight coefficients to varying statistics of useful signal and noise. The proposed optimization is fast, saves the memory space and is easy to implement. After the optimization, the proposed optimal WVDFs are sufficiently robust and useful for practical image/video applications.

J.L. Crowley et al. (Eds.): ICVS 2003, LNCS 2626, pp. 418–427, 2003.

2 Directional Processing of Color Images

Let $y(x): Z^l \to Z^m$ represent a multichannel image, where l is an image dimension and m characterizes a number of channels ($m = 3$ for color images). Let $W = \{ \mathbf{x}_i \in Z^l ; i = 1, 2 ..., N \}$ represent a filter window of a finite size N, where $\mathbf{x}_1, \mathbf{x}_2, ..., \mathbf{x}_N$ is a set of noisy samples. Note that the position of the filter window is determined by the central sample $\mathbf{x}_{(N+1)/2}$.

Since each multichannel sample represents a vector of color channel intensities, it is exactly determined by its magnitude and direction in the vector space. Usually, the standard images are characterized by a high spatial correlation between neighborhood samples. This correlation is significantly dislocated by introducing the noise into the image, especially during the image scanning or the transmission through noisy information channel. If introduced noise has a character of bit errors or random changes affecting only a number of samples, whereas other samples remain unchanged, it is a kind of impulsive noise.

In order to suppress impulsive noise or outliers in color images, the last decade was accompanied with a large research interest in the field of nonlinear filtering based on the robust order-statistic theory. The purpose of the ordering operation in vector-valued signals is to select the lowest ranked sample associated with the minimum sum of specific distance measure to other input samples, whereas atypical samples, i.e. noise, are usually represented by the input samples associated with the maximum sum of distance measures computed to other samples in the filter window.

The most commonly used measure to quantify the distance between two m-channel samples is the generalized Minkowski metric [7]. The typical filtering example based on the Minkowski metric is the well-known vector median [1] utilizing usually the Euclidean (L_2 norm). If the distance measure is expressed through the angle between two multichannel samples, it is the case of directional processing, because the angle determines the orientation of multichannel samples in the vector space. A class of vector directional filters (VDFs) performing directional processing of noisy samples was investigated in [8]. The minimization of the sum of angles to other input eliminates the image vectors with atypical directions in the vector space so that the VDFs result in optimal estimates in the sense of vectors' directions. Note that the direction of multichannel image vectors signifies their color chromaticity. The theory including the study of statistical and deterministic properties was described in [9].

2.1 Basic Vector Directional Filter

Let each input vector $\mathbf{x}_i$ be associated with the angular measure α_i given by

$$\alpha_i = \sum_{j=1}^{N} A(\mathbf{x}_i, \mathbf{x}_j) \quad \text{for } i = 1, 2, ..., N \tag{1}$$

where

$$A(\mathbf{x}_i, \mathbf{x}_j) = \cos^{-1}\left(\frac{\mathbf{x}_i.\mathbf{x}_j^T}{|\mathbf{x}_i|.|\mathbf{x}_j|}\right) \tag{2}$$

$$= \cos^{-1}\left(\frac{x_{i1}x_{j1} + x_{i2}x_{j2} + ... + x_{im}x_{jm}}{\sqrt{x_{i1}^2 + x_{i2}^2 + ... + x_{im}^2}\sqrt{x_{j1}^2 + x_{j2}^2 + ... + x_{jm}^2}}\right) \tag{3}$$

represents the angle between two m-dimensional vectors $\mathbf{x}_i = (x_{i1}, x_{i2}, ..., x_{im})$ and $\mathbf{x}_j = (x_{j1}, x_{j2}, ..., x_{jm})$.

If $\alpha_1, \alpha_2, ..., \alpha_N$, i.e. the sums of vector angles, serve as an ordering criterion, i.e.

$$\alpha_{(1)} \leq \alpha_{(2)} \leq ... \leq \alpha_{(r)} \leq ... \leq \alpha_{(N)} \tag{4}$$

and the same ordering is applied to the input set $\mathbf{x}_1, \mathbf{x}_2, ..., \mathbf{x}_N$, this operation results in the following expression:

$$\mathbf{x}^{(1)} \leq \mathbf{x}^{(2)} \leq ... \leq \mathbf{x}^{(r)} \leq ... \leq \mathbf{x}^{(N)} \tag{5}$$

The sample $\mathbf{x}^{(1)}$, i.e. the sample that minimizes the sum of angles to other vectors, represents the output of the basic vector directional filter (BVDF) [8]. The BVDF filtering algorithm can be stated as follows:

```
Inputs:    NumberOfRows × NumberOfColumns noisy image
           Window size N
           Moving window spawning the input set {x₁,x₂,...,xₙ}
Output:    NumberOfRows × NumberOfColumns image
```

For $a = 1$ to $NumberOfRows$
  For $b = 1$ to $NumberOfColumns$
    Determine the input set $W(a,b) = \{\mathbf{x}_1, \mathbf{x}_2, ..., \mathbf{x}_N\}$
    For $i = 1$ to N
      For $j = 1$ to N
        Compute the angle $A(\mathbf{x}_i, \mathbf{x}_j)$
      end
      Compute the sum $\alpha_i = A(\mathbf{x}_i, \mathbf{x}_1) + A(\mathbf{x}_i, \mathbf{x}_2) + ... + A(\mathbf{x}_i, \mathbf{x}_N)$
    end
    Sort $\alpha_1, \alpha_2, ..., \alpha_N$ to the ordered set $\alpha_{(1)} \leq \alpha_{(2)} \leq ... \leq \alpha_{(N)}$
    Apply the same ordering to $\mathbf{x}_1(\alpha_1), \mathbf{x}_2(\alpha_2), ..., \mathbf{x}_N(\alpha_N)$
    Store ordered sequence as $\mathbf{x}^{(1)} \leq \mathbf{x}^{(2)} \leq ... \leq \mathbf{x}^{(N)}$
    Let the filter output $\mathbf{y}(a,b) = \mathbf{x}^{(1)}$
  End
End

2.2 Generalized Vector Directional Filter

In order to improve the noise attenuation capability of the BVDF, the generalized vector directional filter (GVDF) was introduced [8]. The GVDF output is given by the set of r samples associated with the minimum sum of angles to other input samples. Mathematically, the GVDF operation can be expressed by

$$\mathbf{y}_{GVDF} = \left\{ \mathbf{x}^{(1)}, \mathbf{x}^{(2)}, ..., \mathbf{x}^{(r)} \right\} \tag{6}$$

where $\mathbf{x}^{(1)}, \mathbf{x}^{(2)}, ..., \mathbf{x}^{(r)}$ is the set of the lowest r vector directional order-statistics that are characterized by the similar direction in the vector space.

To determine the output sample, works [8],[9] brought another GVDF extensions such as double window GVDF (GVDF_DW) followed by an α–trimmed mean and GVDF_DW followed by a multistage max/median filter. These methods perform directional processing at the first stage and magnitude processing at the second stage.

Another improvement was achieved by vector median-vector directional hybrid filters introduced in [3], fuzzy VDF provided by [6] and directional distance filter (DDF) [4] combining the properties of the VMF and BVDF. However, all the above-mentioned BVDF extensions significantly increased the computational complexity of their filtering operation in the comparison with the BVDF.

3 Weighted Vector Directional Filters

The aim of this paper deals with a recently introduced class of weighted vector directional filters (WVDFs) [5] that can offer significantly improved preservation of image-details and color chromaticity, a higher flexibility of the filter design and a less computational complexity in comparison with the BVDF extensions. In addition, the WVDFs perform pure directional processing similarly the BVDF, exclude the use of the additional filter such as in the GVDF design and provide only one sample on the filter output.

The idea of WVDFs outcomes from the weighted vector median filters [2],[10] that utilize the weighted distances and the choice of a multivariate sample associated with the minimum sum of weighted distances.

Let $\mathbf{x}_1, \mathbf{x}_2, ..., \mathbf{x}_N$ be an input set of multichannel samples and N a window size. Let us consider that $w_1, w_2, ..., w_N$ represent a set of positive real weights, where each weight w_j, for $j = 1, 2, ..., N$, is associated with the input sample $\mathbf{x}_j$. Then, the sum of weighted angular distances β_i [5] associated with the input sample $\mathbf{x}_i$ is given by

$$\beta_i = \sum_{j=1}^{N} w_j A(\mathbf{x}_i, \mathbf{x}_j) \quad \text{for } i = 1, 2, ..., N \tag{7}$$

where $A(\mathbf{x}_i, \mathbf{x}_j)$ is the angle between two m-dimensional vectors $\mathbf{x}_i$ and $\mathbf{x}_j$ given by Eq. (2) and (3). The ordering criterion is given by ordered set

$$\beta_{(1)} \leq \beta_{(2)} \leq \ldots \leq \beta_{(N)} \tag{8}$$

The output of the proposed WVDFs corresponds to the sample $\mathbf{x}^{(1)} \in \{\mathbf{x}_1, \mathbf{x}_2, \ldots, \mathbf{x}_N\}$ associated with the minimum weighted angular distance $\beta_{(1)} \in \{\beta_1, \beta_2, \ldots, \beta_N\}$. Thus, the WVDFs are outputting the sample from the input set, so that the local distortion is minimized and no color artefacts are produced. The WVDFs algorithm can be written as follows:

```
Inputs:   NumberOfRows × NumberOfColumns noisy image
          Window size N
          Moving window spawning the input set {x₁,x₂,...,xₙ}
          The set of weight coefficients {w₁,w₂,...,wₙ}
Output:   NumberOfRows × NumberOfColumns image
```

```
For a =1 to NumberOfRows
  For b =1 to NumberOfColumns
    Determine the input set W(a,b) = {x₁,x₂,...,xₙ}
    For i =1 to N
      For j =1 to N
        Compute the angle A(xᵢ,xⱼ)
      end
      Compute the sum βᵢ = w₁A(xᵢ,x₁) + w₂A(xᵢ,x₂) + ... + wₙA(xᵢ,xₙ)
    end
    Sort β₁,β₂,...,βₙ to the ordered set β₍₁₎ ≤ β₍₂₎ ≤...≤ β₍ₙ₎
    Apply the same ordering to x₁(β₁),x₂(β₂),...,xₙ(βₙ)
    Store ordered sequence as x⁽¹⁾ ≤ x⁽²⁾ ≤...≤ x⁽ᴺ⁾
    Let the filter output y(a,b) = x⁽¹⁾
  End
End
```

A class of the WVDFs holds not only the practical filtering importance, however, the WVDFs also represent the BVDF generalization. If all weight coefficients are set to the same value, all angular distances will have the same importance and the WVDF operation will be equivalent to the BVDF. If only the center weight is alternated, whereas other weights remain unchanged, i.e.

$$w_i = \begin{cases} N - 2k + 2 & \text{for } i = (N+1)/2 \\ 1 & \text{otherwise} \end{cases} \quad \text{for } k = 1, 2, \ldots, (N+1)/2 \tag{9}$$

then, the WVDFs perform the center weighted vector directional filtering (CWVDF). In the case of the smoothing parameter $k = 1$, the central weight $w_{(N+1)/2}$ has the maximum possible value, i.e. $w_{(N+1)/2} = N$ and the CWVDF performs the identity operation. Thus, no filtering is provided and the CWVDF output is given by the input central sample $\mathbf{x}_{(N+1)/2}$. The increased value k increases the smoothing capability of the CWVDF. For the maximum value of k, i.e. $k = (N+1)/2$, the CWVDF provides the maximum amount of the smoothing equivalent to the BVDF operation.

Clearly, the WVDFs can be designed to perform a variety of smoothing operations. For that reason, the optimization of the weight vector or weight coefficients represents the most important task in the filter design.

4   Sigmoidal Optimization of Weighted Vector Directional Filters

The similar problems are related to the optimization of standard weighted median (WM) filters [2],[10]. Because the WM filters are usually applied to the gray-scale images, i.e. the scalar case, the optimization is relatively simple.

Consider the input set of scalar samples written as $\{x_1(n), x_2(n), ..., x_N(n)\}$ and the original (desired) sample $o(n)$, all for the time position n of running filter window. In the case of sigmoidal approximation, the adaptive optimization algorithm derived from the stack filter design [2],[10] can be simplified to the following expression

$$w_i(n+1) = P\left[w_i(n) + 2\mu(o(n) - y(n))\mathrm{sgn}_s(x_i(n) - y(n))\right] \tag{10}$$

where $w_i(n)$, for $i = 1,2,...,N$, is the filter weight, $y(n)$ is the filter output, μ is the iteration constant, $P(.)$ characterizes a projection operation and $\mathrm{sgn}_s(.)$ is a sign function approximated by sigmoidal function defined by

$$\mathrm{sgn}_S(a) = \frac{2}{1+e^{-a}} - 1 \tag{11}$$

If the actual WM output is smaller than the original value, the weights corresponding to the samples which are larger than the actual output are incremented. In the case of sigmoidal approximation of the sign function, the convergence to a global optimal solution cannot be guaranteed [10]. In general, the adaptive WM algorithms save the memory space, they are easy to implement and provide good results for the time-varying statistics.

In the case of vector-valued samples such as multichannel image samples, the main difficulty is given by a sign function, because it is not possible to determine the polarity of the distance measure between two multichannel samples. The reason why we will select just the sigmoidal optimization from possible WM optimization approaches [10] such as nonadaptive optimization, adaptive optimizations based on linear and sigmoidal approximation of the sign function is the fact that the sigmoidal optimization utilizes the filter output. Thus, the update of the weight vector related to the WVDF will incorporate some information about the correlation between channels of the output sample.

Let $\{\mathbf{x}_1(n), \mathbf{x}_2(n), ..., \mathbf{x}_N(n)\}$ be the input set of m-channel samples and $\mathbf{o}(n)$ the desired multichannel sample. Note that N is the window size and n characterizes the time position of the running filter window. Let also each input sample $\mathbf{x}_i(n)$ be associated with the nonnegative real weight w_i, for $i = 1,2,...,N$. Then, the sigmoidal optimization extended for the multichannel case can be expressed as follows:

$$w_i(n+1) = P\left[w_i(n) + 2\mu f_C(\mathbf{o}(n),\mathbf{y}(n))\,\mathrm{sgn}_s\left(f_C(\mathbf{x}_i(n),\mathbf{y}(n))\right)\right] \qquad (12)$$

where $\mathbf{y}(n)$ is the WVDF output (computed according to Eq.(8) and Eq.(9)) related to the actual weight coefficients $w_1(n), w_2(n),...., w_N(n)$ and time position n. Description $f_C(\mathbf{x}_i(n),\mathbf{x}_j(n))$ $f_C(\mathbf{x}_i(n),\mathbf{x}_j(n))$ characterizes the component-wise subtraction of two m-dimensional vectors $\mathbf{x}_i = (x_{i1},x_{i2},...,x_{im})$ and $\mathbf{x}_j = (x_{j1},x_{j2},...,x_{jm})$ so that the Eq.(12) can be redefined as

$$w_i(n+1) = P\left[w_i(n) + 2\mu\sum_{j=1}^{m}\left((o_j(n) - y_j(n))\left(\frac{2}{1+e^{-(x_{ij}(n)-y_j(n))}} - 1\right)\right)\right] \qquad (13)$$

The sigmoidal optimization is starting with the initialization of the weight vector as the vector of any positive values. Note that the iteration constant μ should be set to a small value, e.g. $\mu = 0.0001$. The rest of the optimization algorithm is written as

```
Inputs:    NumberOfRows × NumberOfColumns noisy image
           NumberOfRows × NumberOfColumns original image
           Window size N
           Moving window spawning the input set {x₁,x₂,...,x_N}
           Weight vector w(0) set to any positive values
           Adaptive stepsize μ
Output:    Weight vector w = {w₁,w₂,...,w_N}
```

```
For  a =1  to  NumberOfRows
  For  b =1  to  NumberOfColumns
    Determine the input set  W(a,b) = {x₁,x₂,...,x_N}
    Determine the original sample  o  in position  (a,b)
    For  i =1  to  N
      For  j =1  to  N
        Compute the angle  A(xᵢ,xⱼ)
      end
      Compute the sum  βᵢ = w₁A(xᵢ,x₁) + w₂A(xᵢ,x₂) +...+ w_N A(xᵢ,x_N)
    end
    Sort  β₁,β₂,...,β_N  to the ordered set  β_(1) ≤ β_(2) ≤...≤ β_(N)
    Apply the same ordering to  x₁(β₁),x₂(β₂),...,x_N(β_N)
    Store ordered sequence as  x⁽¹⁾ ≤ x⁽²⁾ ≤...≤ x⁽ᴺ⁾
    Let the filter output  y = x⁽¹⁾
    Let actual  wᵢ  is given by Eq.(13), for  i =1,2,...,N
  End
End
Output  w = {w₁,w₂,...,w_N}
```

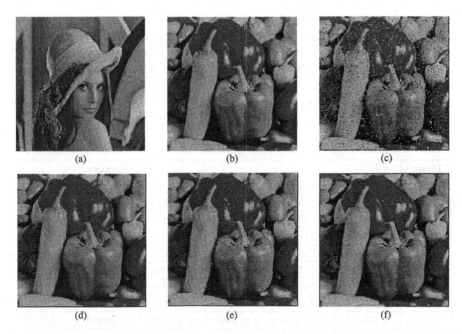

Fig. 1. (a) Original image Lena, (b) original image Peppers, (c) noisy image $p = 0.10$ (10% impulsive noise) (d) VMF output, (e) BVDF output, (f) Output of optimal WVDF

5 Experimental Results

To evaluate the efficiency of the new method we used the color test images Lena (Fig. 1a) and Peppers (Fig. 1b) distorted by impulsive noise (Fig. 1c) [7]. The performance of the proposed optimal WVDFs will be compared with the BVDF, the non-optimal WVDFs with selected weight vector and well-known standard vector filters such as the vector median (VMF) [1] and the directional distance filter (DDF) [4]. The objective results were evaluated by commonly used measures [7] such as mean absolute error (MAE), mean square error (MSE) and normalized color difference (NCD). These criteria provide a good mirror of the signal-detail preservation (MAE), the noise attenuation capability (MSE) and the measure of the color distortion (NCD) presented in the noisy or resulting image, respectively.

All achieved results are related to a square 3×3 filter window. In the case of VMF and DDF we used the Euclidean distance (L_2 norm). The sigmoidal WVDF optimization started with the same initial weight vector $\mathbf{w}(0) = [1,1,1,1,1,1,1,1,1]$ that corresponds to the BVDF operation. Concerning the results present in Tables 1-3 we used always the fixed iteration constant $\mu = 0.0001$ related to Eq.(13). For smaller value of μ, the sigmoidal WVDF filter provides worse preserving characteristics and after some critical point dependent on statistical properties of the training sequence, it will converge to the BVDF.

The optimal weights achieved by using various training images are presented in Table 1. Note that each achieved weight vector was normalized by its maximum weight. In order to compare the performance of the method, we provide Tables 2-3. The descriptions $WVDF_1$ and $WVDF_2$ characterize the non-optimized WVDFs with weight vectors $\mathbf{w} = [3,2,3,2,5,2,3,2,3]$ and $\mathbf{w} = [1,2,1,4,3,4,1,2,1]$, respectively. The optimal WVDFs with weight vectors presented in the columns "Lena, $p = 0.10$" and "Peppers, $p = 0.05$" of Table 1 are denoted as $WVDF_3$ and $WVDF_4$.

Table 1. Optimal weights related to training images with the impulsive noise corruption p

Image	Lena			Peppers		
Weight	$p = 0.05$	$p = 0.10$	$p = 0.20$	$p = 0.05$	$p = 0.10$	$p = 0.20$
w_1	0.133424	0.170721	0.296759	0.340823	0.385124	0.493880
w_2	0.366566	0.420953	0.562738	0.466587	0.517015	0.605439
w_3	0.178661	0.211257	0.358347	0.266013	0.330582	0.452581
w_4	0.192818	0.218979	0.356750	0.459833	0.510709	0.606587
w_5	1.000000	1.000000	1.000000	1.000000	1.000000	1.000000
w_6	0.198828	0.231475	0.345636	0.376208	0.449896	0.551736
w_7	0.187104	0.220442	0.344647	0.264374	0.327760	0.447986
w_8	0.367654	0.440867	0.547669	0.365318	0.426939	0.541525
w_9	0.133156	0.183260	0.307718	0.153024	0.206036	0.335968

Table 2. Results achieved related to the test image Lena

Noise	$p = 0.05$			$p = 0.10$			$p = 0.20$		
Method	MAE	MSE	NCD	MAE	MSE	NCD	MAE	MSE	NCD
Noisy	3.762	427.3	0.0445	7.312	832.0	0.0840	14.019	1604.6	0.1625
VMF	3.430	50.8	0.0403	3.687	56.5	0.0429	4.335	80.3	0.0492
BVDF	3.818	58.6	0.0407	4.099	67.6	0.0432	4.859	107.8	0.0499
DDF	3.509	52.3	0.0402	3.733	57.3	0.0424	4.321	78.8	0.0483
$WVDF_1$	2.954	44.7	0.0317	3.241	54.5	0.0343	4.037	98.7	0.0413
$WVDF_2$	2.643	41.5	0.0283	2.989	56.3	3.734	4.113	131.3	0.0414
$WVDF_3$	1.514	22.7	0.0159	1.883	41.2	0.0193	3.299	155.8	0.0325
$WVDF_4$	2.093	28.9	0.0223	2.401	42.1	0.0250	3.360	107.2	0.0338

Table 3. Results achieved related to the test image Peppers

Noise	$p = 0.05$			$p = 0.10$			$p = 0.20$		
Method	MAE	MSE	NCD	MAE	MSE	NCD	MAE	MSE	NCD
Noisy	3.988	486.1	0.0441	7.677	943.3	0.0870	14.912	1832.0	0.1694
VMF	3.169	43.9	0.0452	3.503	55.0	0.0494	4.232	85.7	0.0600
BVDF	3.740	60.7	0.0438	4.151	82.7	0.0484	5.111	152.9	0.602
DDF	3.182	44.6	0.0431	3.512	56.6	0.0475	4.254	90.4	0.0580
$WVDF_1$	2.861	48.5	0.0333	3.242	68.9	0.0377	4.317	149.3	0.0504
$WVDF_2$	2.197	38.1	0.0257	2.659	65.9	0.0325	4.275	206.5	0.0503
$WVDF_3$	1.160	31.9	0.0194	2.124	73.1	0.0247	4.090	267.9	0.0466
$WVDF_4$	1.985	34.1	0.0239	2.364	55.6	0.0284	3.776	177.8	0.0444

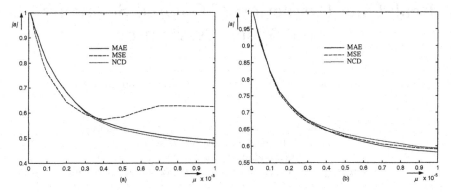

Fig. 2. Normalized measures of the optimized WVDF in the dependence on the iteration stepsize μ: (a) image Lena with 10% impulse noise, (b) image Peppers with 5% impulse noise

6 Conclusions

In this paper, a sigmoidal optimization of the generalized class of WVDFs for the noise suppression in color images has been proposed. The results show the excellent adaptive behavior of the new approach and the excellent performance in terms of objective quality measures. The optimized WVDFs are sufficiently robust, and can often outperform the standard vector filters such as VMF, BVDF and DDF.

References

1. Astola, J., Haavisto, P., Neuvo, Y.: Vector Median Filters. Proceedings of the IEEE 78 (1990) 678–689
2. Astola, J., Kuosmanen, P.: Fundamentals of Nonlinear Digital Filtering. CRC Press (1997)
3. Gabbouj M., Cheickh F.A., Vector Median-Vector Directional Hybrid Filter for Color Image Restoration. Proceedings of EUSIPCO-96 (1996) 879–881
4. Karakos, D.G., Trahanias, P.E.: Generalized Multichannel Image-Filtering Structure. IEEE Transactions on Image Processing 6 (1997) 1038–1045
5. Lukac, R.: Adaptive Impulse Noise Filtering by Using Center-Weighted Directional Information. Proc. CGIV'2002 in Poitiers, France, (2002) 86–89
6. Plataniotis, K.N., Androutsos, D., Venetsanopoulos, A.N.: Color Image Processing Using Adaptive Vector Directional Filters. IEEE Trans. Circ. Syst. II, 45 (1998) 1414–1419
7. Plataniotis, K.N., Venetsanopoulos, A.N.: Color Image Processing and Applications. Springer Verlag (2000)
8. Trahanias, P.E., Venetsanopoulos, A.N.: Vector Directional Filters - a New Class of Multichannel Image Processing Filters. IEEE Trans. on Image Processing, 2 (1993) 528–534
9. Trahanias, P.E., Karakos, D., Venetsanopoulos, A.N.: Directional Processing of Color Images: Theory and Experimental Results. IEEE Trans. Image Processing, 5 (1996) 868–881
10. Yin, L., Yang, R., Gabbouj, M., Neuvo, Y.: Weighted Median Filters: A Tutorial. IEEE Transactions on Circuits and Systems -II, 43 (1996) 157–192

Real-Time Extraction of Colored Segments for Robot Visual Navigation[*]

Pedro E. López-de-Teruel[1], Alberto Ruiz[2], Gines García-Mateos[2], and
Jose M. García[1]

[1] Dpto. de Ingeniería y Tecnología de Computadores
[2] Dpto. de Informática y Sistemas
Universidad de Murcia (Spain)
{pedroe,jmgarcia}@ditec.um.es,{aruiz,ginesgm}@um.es

Abstract. We propose an image representation method appropriate for
real-time visual geometry applications. If the expressive power of raw segments is augmented with robust color information from their two sides,
the most relevant geometric and photometric structure in the image can
be concisely captured. In this paper we describe an efficient algorithm to
compute this kind of representation, which can be successfully exploited
in several projective geometry problems, such as 3D reconstruction, motion estimation or calibration, and in interpretation related tasks. We
also show how these enhanced primitives are powerful enough to recover a very acceptable approximation of the original image, especially
for partially structured scenes, like interior of buildings, man-made objects, and so on. The algorithm works at frame rate for medium size
images (PAL/2), using low-cost hardware, such as an off-the-self image
acquisition card and a standard PC. This makes it very useful as an *on-
line* feature extraction method for robot visual navigation, where more
elaborated (and slower) methods can not be used. We describe some
applications of the algorithm in this kind of tasks.

1 Introduction

3D reconstruction and scene interpretation have been active research topics in
the last years, mostly due to significant advances in the application of projective
geometry to computer vision [8]. This approach typically uses points, lines and
segments as working primitives when trying to perform scene reconstruction,
autocalibration, and object localization and recognition tasks. In the robotics
community, however, some authors have highlighted the fact that successful
achievements in reconstruction of scenes from image sequences have not been
accompanied by advances in real-time methods [5]. This is due to the complexity of some of the involved methods, as well as their inherent *batch* methodology,
where sequences of images are first acquired and then analysed *off-line*.

---

[*] This work has been partially supported by the Spanish CICYT under grants DPI-
2001-0469-C03-01 and TIC-2000-1151-C07-03.

Color information, on the other hand, has also been successfully used in several real-time vision problems, such as segmentation [2], tracking [12], or learning and classification [3]. But these approaches usually discard geometric information, often working only with unstructured sets of spatially related pixels.

In this paper we propose a computationally efficient algorithm to reduce images to sets of colored segments, trying to take advantage of both the color information and the geometric structure of the scene. We justify that the obtained representation effectively summarizes the contents of the input data, by showing how the original image can be recovered with high accuracy using only the extracted information. Finally, we show a number of applications in a machine vision system with strong real-time requirements: the visual calibration and guidance of a robot through an indoor environment, that performs *on-line* reconstruction and interpretation of the scene while navigating.

2   Color Augmented Segment Extraction

Finding lines or segments in an image is a basic problem frequently studied in the computer vision literature. Most of the available methods are variations of the well known Hough Transform [10]. Other authors prefer to find segments by locally grouping edge pixels into contours (for example, using the Canny operator [4]), which are then split using piecewise linear polygonal approximations [13]. A drawback of many of these methods is that they only account for geometric properties of the segment (i.e. position in the image), thus discarding other visual information useful for tracking or interpretation, such as color or texture of the local vicinity of each segment. Of course, there are some exceptions (see, for example, [14]), but using the neighborhood of the features often slows the process down, making it unusable under real-time constraints.

An alternative is to describe the segment vicinity in a simple, robust and accurate way, for example, sampling color from both sides of the segment. Color information is obtained in the segment extraction phase itself, with negligible additional computational effort. This is especially appropriate for real-time applications. In the following we explain the fundamentals of our approach, including a detailed algorithm description.

Preprocessing: Most of the existing edge segmentation methods rely on a preprocessing stage to remove noise from the input image, for example by means of a Gaussian or median filter. Then, the image gradient is approximated using a pair of perpendicularly oriented masks, such as Roberts' or Sobel's, and this output is postprocessed to estimate both the magnitude and the orientation of the gradient. This information is finally used to group pixels into lines, or any other edge primitive (circles, contours, etc). This is the basis of the extensively used Canny edge detector [4], and similar line extractor procedures [1].

Instead, we only perform a simple high-pass filtering of the input image, to minimise computational effort. This filtering will be followed by an efficient sequential grouping stage that takes into account the local orientation of the edges, and that, at the same time, has a noise suppression effect (see next paragraph). Therefore, the input (gray converted) image must only be preprocessed using a simple 3×3 mask (see Fig. 1a), alleviating the computational burden of image

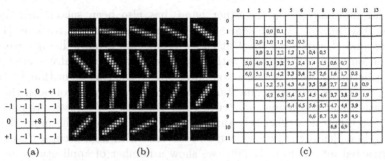

Fig. 1. (a) High-pass mask. (b) Density plot (0-1 valued) of the orientation masks for $R = 5$, $A = 20$ and $W_{edg} = 2.80$. (c) Table of pixel positions for the vicinity of width $W_{seg} = 5.0$ of the segment $((y_1, x_1), (y_2, x_2)) = ((3, 2), (8, 11))$, (a pair (i, j) in position (y, x) means that table position (i, j) stores image position (y, x)).

preprocessing. Fig. 3b shows the result of applying the mask to the input image of Fig. 3a. If the input image is very finely textured, a previous noise removal filtering of the monochrome image (3×3 median or Gaussian, for example) could also be useful. This would still be faster than the preprocessing stages of classical methods.

Local orientation and grouping: To find segments in the high-pass image obtained in the previous step, we look for local alignments of pixels around the edge input points (that is, those with high response to the filter). For this, our method computes the response to a set of adequate masks (see Fig. 1b) centered in those pixels. These masks have been designed to estimate a local orientation with the desired accuracy from noisy input edge images. This is an alternative to traditional gradient based methods. To control its sensitivity, the masks are generated depending on three parameters: R, the radius in pixels of each mask, W_{edg}, the expected *edgel* width, and A, the number of discrete orientations to be considered. For example, the set of masks of Fig. 1b has been generated using $R = 5$, $W_{edg} = 2.80$ and $A = 20$. Reasonable values for these parameters are in the ranges $R \in \{3, 4, 5\}$, $W_{edg} \in [1.50, 3.0]$ and $A \approx 4R$. In general, the smaller the values of R, W_{edg} and A, the faster the algorithm, but also the less accurate.

The grouping method proceeds as follows: if a pixel value in the edge image is greater than a given threshold τ_h, the masks in every orientation are applied centered on it, to get A output values, of which only the maximum is taken into account. Therefore, the filter is a nonlinear robust estimator, despite of the linear nature of the individual orientation detectors. A new segment is then created, and a grouping process is initiated in the selected orientation, following a precomputed pixel ordering, beginning in the mask center and towards the extremes. This process is recursively repeated in each segment extreme, clustering points with high-pass response greater than another lower threshold τ_l, in both directions. Thus, parameters τ_h and τ_l are analogous to those of the Canny hysteresis procedure [4]. An additional parameter is n_{min}, the minimum number of collected points in a window to keep on grouping edge pixels for that segment before stopping. The process also finishes if orientation in the current segment extreme differs from the original one in more than one step. This is a tolerance threshold to cope with slight variations caused by noise. Captured points are marked as visited to be discarded in subsequent processing. Note that the masks are not applied to all the pixels, but only to a small number of the active ones in the edge image. Finally, the centroid and main eigenvector of the covariance matrix of the set of points are used to accurately adjust the segment extremes. The grouping and segment refinement processes are summarized in the corresponding sections of the algorithm, shown in Fig. 2.

Color sampling and postprocessing: When a segment is found, the next step is to label it with robust color information. We use the median red, green and blue values of image pixels in both sides of the segment. Our experiments provide extensive evidence that, contrary to intuition, independent estimation of median color channels does not generate color artifacts. The obtained color models are, for all practical purposes, perceptually indistinguishable from the original ones. Therefore, the computational overhead of a more complex robust multivariate estimator is not justified.

Color sampling is performed by scanning the pixels in the vicinity of the segment, using an access table computed to this effect. The table contains image positions located along both sides of the segment (see Fig. 1c for an example). Its generation is based on Bresenham's algorithm, a standard computer graphics method for drawing lines on pixel grids [7]. We extend this algorithm to "thicken" the segment, by replicating the pixels in both sides. The algorithm uses only $O(W_{seg}L)$ integer operations, being L the segment length and W_{seg} the desired width. So, even though the table must be recalculated for each new segment, this will not be a computational bottleneck.

Tables computed with this algorithm have two advantages. First, they cover the segment neighborhood *densely*, that is, without leaving uncovered pixels. Second, they also arrange the pixels in an *orderly* fashion, by means of a rectangular array of positions with r rows and c columns, $((7, 10)$, respectively, in the example table of Fig. 1c). These tables will be used for two complementary tasks, as can be seen in the last section of the algorithm in Fig. 2: First, to find the median value of the color channels for each side of the segment, using rows 0 to $\lfloor \frac{r}{2} \rfloor - 1$ for the left side, and $\lfloor \frac{r}{2} \rfloor + 1$ to $r - 1$, for the right one. Second, to clean up the surroundings of the segment of possible edge points that were not caught during the grouping process, marking them as visited. This avoids the extraction of spurious small segments close to the good ones. For this, we can take the central rows of the table (for example, covering a width of $W_{seg}/3$).

Performance evaluation: Fig. 2 outlines the colored segment extraction algorithm. We have implemented it using the OpenCV and Intel Image Processing Libraries [9] for the basic operations (RGB to gray conversion, high-pass filtering, median or Gaussian previous smoothing for noisy images, and so on). These libraries are optimized to run on the different Pentium processors. The procedure works at 15-25 fps (depending on the complexity of the scene) for 288×384 (PAL/2) images, running on a 533 MHz Pentium III. For more modern ($\sim$1 GHz) processors, it works always at the camera frame rate (25 fps). We show an example of the segments obtained in an indoor scene in Fig. 3c.

Due to space limitations, we cannot include here an exhaustive study of the execution time and precision of the algorithm. Nevertheless, to give a flavor of

INPUT:
- RGB image (I^{RGB}).
- Algorithm parameters (τ_h, τ_l, W_{seg}, and n_{min}, see text).
- Weighting masks and pixel paths for each orientation (see Fig. 1b).

OUTPUT:
- Set of S segments with left and right color information.

ALGORITHM:

Initialisation and preprocessing:
- Initialize the segment counter, $S := 0$.
- Convert the RGB image, I^{RGB}, to get the gray image I^{gray}.
- Filter I^{gray} using the high-pass mask (Fig. 1a), to get I^{hp} (use absolute value).
- Mark all the pixels in the edge image I^{hp} as "not visited".

High-pass image traversal:
for each image position (y, x) *do*
   if $I^{hp}_{(y,x)} \geq \tau_h$ *and* (y, x) is marked as "not visited" *then*
      - Increment the segment counter, $S := S + 1$.

   Local orientation and grouping:
      - Apply the set of orientation masks (Fig. 1b) to I^{hp}, centered on (y, x). Let a^{max} be the mask index with maximum response.
      for $i := 1$ *to* 2 *do* (both directions)
         - Initialize current orientation, $a^{cur} := a^{max}$.
         - Initialize current segment extreme, $(y_i, x_i) := (y, x)$.
         repeat
            - Using the precomputed pixel path for orientation a^{cur} and current direction i, centered on (y_i, x_i), keep on capturing image pixels with $I^{hp} > \tau_l$, marking them as "visited".
            - Update current segment extreme with the last captured point in the previous step, $(y_i, x_i) := (y^{last}, x^{last})$.
            - Apply the set of masks (Fig. 1b) to I^{hp} again, but now centered on (y_i, x_i). Let a^{cur} be the new mask index (orientation) with maximum response.
         until (Number of captured points in this step $< n_{min}$) *or*
                (Distance from a^{cur} to $a^{max} > 1$)
      endfor

   Segment refinement:
      - Compute the centroid, covariance matrix and major eigenvector of the set of points captured for the current segment S.
      - Update segment extremes (y_1, x_1) and (y_2, x_2) by projecting them onto the principal direction computed in the previous step.

   Color sampling and postprocessing:
      - Compute access table (Fig. 1c) corresponding to segment S.
      - Compute the median of the RGB channels of image I separately, for the set of pixels whose position is indicated by rows $0 \ldots \lfloor \frac{r}{2} \rfloor - 1$ of the access table. The obtained vector $(r^S_{left}, g^S_{left}, b^S_{left})$ is the left color information for segment S. Repeat the process for rows $\lfloor \frac{r}{2} \rfloor + 1 \ldots r - 1$ to get $(r^S_{right}, g^S_{right}, b^S_{right})$.
      - Mark pixels pointed by rows $\lfloor \frac{r}{2} \rfloor - \lfloor \frac{r}{6} \rfloor \ldots \lfloor \frac{r}{2} \rfloor + \lfloor \frac{r}{6} \rfloor$ of the table as "visited".
   endif
endfor

Fig. 2. Algorithm that extracts colored segments from a RGB image.

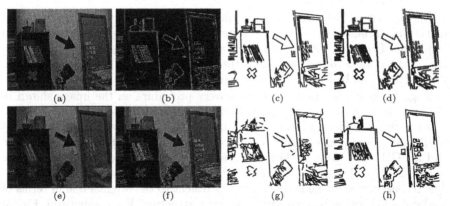

Fig. 3. Results in a typical indoor image: (a) Original image. (b) High-pass filtered image. (c) Segments extracted by our method. (d) Segments with color information. (e) Recovered image. (f) JPEG image with the same compression ratio. (g) Segments extracted by PPHT. (h) Segments extracted by polygonal approximation.

the advantages of our approach, we will compare it with two popular segment extractors, representing the alternatives mentioned at the beginning of the section. Anyway, a direct comparison is difficult, since, to the best of our knowledge, methods dealing with color have not been previously described in the literature. First, we tested the *Progressive Probabilistic Hough Transform (PPHT)*, a modern variant of the classical HT adapted to run in real-time applications [11]. For the same image size, scene and CPU, the PPHT method, as implemented in the OpenCV, obtains qualitatively worse segments (see Fig. 3g) while running at only 3-5 fps on average, including the necessary edge detection stage using the Canny operator. The second method is based on polygonal approximations [13] of the contours obtained by the Canny procedure. Though not directly implemented in the OpenCV, this alternative obtains better solutions than those of the PPHT (see Fig. 3h), but still worse than our segment extractor (Fig. 3c), and at a lower rate (7-9 fps). Observe also that, besides being faster and more robust, our method adds color information to the segments, making them more useful for many applications, as we will show in the next sections.

3   Expressive Power of Colored Segment Representation

The color augmented segment is a very powerful visual representation primitive, whose main advantages can be exploited in a number of general image processing and computer vision tasks:

Image compression: Image data can be concisely represented in terms of such primitives without significant loss of 'large scale' photometric information. A simple iterative diffusion procedure can be used to recover a good approximation to the original pixel array. The pixels located immediately to the left and right of each segment are initialized and fixed (using tables like the one shown in Fig. 1c) with their respective RGB median values (see Fig. 3d). The rest of pixels are marked as uninitialized. Then, in each iteration a RGB pixel value

434   P.E. López-de-Teruel et al.

is recomputed as the mean of its initialized neighbors in a 3×3 window, and marked as initialized too. The procedure acts as an iterative linear interpolation technique. Typically, 200-400 iterations are enough to get a good result, depending on the number of segments and the desired precision. In image sequences, initialization can be based on the previous frame, speeding up convergence.

Fig. 3e shows the results of the recovery procedure on the image shown in Fig. 3a. The original, uncompressed RGB image size is $288 \times 384 \times 3 = 324$ KB. The compressed information is formed by 261 segments, each labelled with two RGB values. A segment extreme can be coded using $\lceil \log_2(288 \times 384) \rceil = 17$ bits, and a RGB value using 24 bits. Therefore, the whole set of segments will use $261 \times ((2 \times 17) + 2 \times 24) = 21402$ bits $= 2.61$ KB, i.e. a 99.2% compression factor. The reconstructed image is essentially equivalent to the original one in terms of medium and large scale color and geometric structure. For comparison, Fig. 3f shows a JPEG image with the same compression ratio.

Of course, explicit recovery of the image is rarely needed. It is shown here only to illustrate the expressive power of the representation. For many applications, once the colored segments have been obtained, the original image is not needed for any subsequent processing. This can be exploited if we want to send the sequence of compressed data through a low bandwidth network, for example.

Segment tracking: Reliable matching and tracking of features (points or segments) is essential to carry out 3D reconstructions from multiple views of the scene. Some tracking methods only take into account the position of the feature in successive images [16]. But tracking is more robust if the local neighborhood of the feature is also taken into account. For isolated points, one of the best methods is to compare local neighborhoods of candidates through intensity correlation, perhaps taking into account a previous warping [15]. For segments, this kind of technique can be applied to individual points along them. For example, in [14] the epipolar restriction is used to obtain corresponding points in candidate matching segments, and a correlation measure is computed for the pixels paired this way. But this method needs robust estimates of the involved fundamental matrices [8], which is computationally hard for real-time operation.

We propose to simplify the characterisation of the feature, making it adequate for faster processing, as needed by *on-line* applications such as robot navigation. The median RGB values on the sides of each segment can be used to compute a similarity measure between candidate pairs of segments, taking into account both geometric distance and photometric information. Hence, tracking becomes more robust without reducing the speed of the system.

Segment classification: The obtained median color values could also be useful in interpretation. For example, if we search for objects with a characteristic, *a priori* known color, we can use the color information of each segment in order to directly associate it with a real world object.

Contour following: Finally, even if we do not know *a priori* the color of an object, we can still find closed contours by looking for segments with nearby extremes and similar colors, grouping and sorting them without being disturbed by other segments in the vicinity that have different colors.

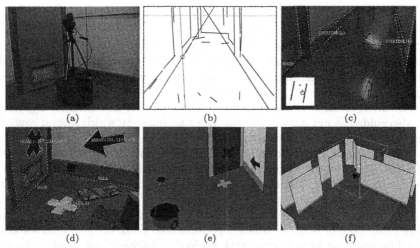

Fig. 4. Color segments for robot navigation: (a) *GeoBot*. (b) Calibration. (c) Typical situation (corridor). (d) Walls, doors, and signs detection in the presence of clutter. (e) 3D reconstruction corresponding to (d). (f) 3D reconstruction of the environment during a visually guided walk.

4   Colored Segments for Visual Robot Navigation

Taking advantage of the above properties, the algorithm described in this paper is being successfully used in a mobile robot which builds and interprets structured 3D world representations in real-time from pure visual information. Fig. 4a shows *GeoBot*, the mobile platform in which we are currently developing our research. *GeoBot* is a Pioneer AT equipped with a monocular visual sensor (a Mitsubishi 400-E camera) and an on-board Pentium 200 MMX PC.

The first application of the colored segment extractor is the autocalibration of the robot-camera system. To accomplish this task, the height of the horizon is first determined by detecting two parallel floor lines. The camera intrinsic and extrinsic (robot-relative) parameters are then easily obtained by tracking just one line and one point in the scene during a controlled movement. These minimal requirements for a full calibration of the system (position and orientation of the camera with respect to the robot, and focal length) are possible due to availability of odometric (egomotion) information, and a few realistic simplifications on the camera model [6]. Fig. 4b shows how, using the extracted segments, the system finds the horizon and the line and point to track in order to perform the calibration. Color is essential to interpret the segments as belonging to the floor or a door, and to robustly track these segments during the movement.

Using the estimated camera parameters, and following reasonable clues obtained from the geometric and color information of the segments, *GeoBot* can detect relevant planes (floor, walls, doors) in indoor environments. This information is used to categorize different high level typical situations (rooms, corridors, corners, and so on), that allow the robot to exhibit a non-reactive behaviour, depending on abstract properties of the environment. Fig. 4c shows one of these situations, when the robot is entering a corridor. Observe how a door and the left and right walls are located, while the spurious segments caused by reflections are adequately rejected. A calibrated sensor allows for the metric rectification of the relevant planes of the scene (the floor and the walls, in this case). The system is then able to construct an abstract interpretation of the scene (see the bottom left part of the image) to give the adequate control orders to navigate through the corridor.

The interpretation is extended to handle obstacles and external signs that can also guide the navigation. Fig. 4d shows an image in which several contours of different colors are located and recognized as signs (arrows and crosses), without being disturbed by other objects, that are simply categorized as unknown obstacles. The contour following procedure outlined in the previous section is used for this purpose. The exact position (in mm) of the interpreted signs has been superimposed in the original image for clarity. The signs can be metrically rectified, again using the calibration information, by determining the plane of the image (wall, floor or door) in which it is contained. Thus, the sign interpretation procedure does not have to cope with projective deformations. Rather, simpler similarity-invariant sign classification is performed once the metric rectification of the contour has been accomplished. Fig. 4e shows the 3D reconstruction of the interpreted elements in the scene, without any scale ambiguity.

Finally, the robot is able to accumulate the reconstruction of the visited environment as it navigates, using odometry and tracking. Fig. 4f shows a 3D reconstruction of a large portion of a building, as interpreted by *GeoBot* during a visually guided walk.

Though *GeoBot*'s processor has become somewhat obsolete, our efficient implementation of the segment extractor still allows for an overall 5 Hz perception-action cycle, including calibration, reconstruction, interpretation, and motion control. This is enough to robustly navigate at $\sim$20 cm/s.

We conclude the discussion with an example of how the compression capabilities of the colored segments can also be exploited in autonomous agents. *GeoBot* is equipped with an on-board PC connected to the outside world through a Radio Ethernet interface. This kind of interfaces are usually very slow (1 Mb/s bandwidth in our case). This is not enough to send images of moderate sizes at video rates of 25 fps. But, if segments are extracted in the robot PC, and then sent through the network, the only bottleneck is the local CPU speed, not the radio interface. The rest of the processing can be performed in an external, more powerful and unloaded computer, from which the control orders are sent back to the robot. This way, we save CPU time for possible additional tasks.

5   Conclusions

We have described an efficient image representation algorithm for visual geometry applications. It works by detecting relevant segments that are then labelled with color information. Images can be compressed down to a $\sim$1% of the original size, while capturing the essential structure of the scene: the original image can be easily recovered by means of a simple diffusion procedure. The compression factor is interesting by itself, but the main advantages of the algorithm are computational efficiency and the convenience of colored segments for further geometric processing. Finally, we have shown several applications in real-time vision tasks, such as robot navigation and environment reconstruction and interpretation in indoor scenarios. Nevertheless, the procedure is not limited to this field, and can be successfully used in many other computer vision domains.

References

1. M. Aste and M. Boninsegna. A fast straight line extractor for vision-guided robot navigation. Technical Report I-38050, Ist. Ric. Sci. e Tecn., Trento (Italy), 1993.
2. J. Bruce, T. Balch, and M. Veloso. Fast and inexpensive color vision for interactive robots. In *Proceedings of the Intelligent Robots and Systems*, 2000.
3. S.D. Buluswar and B.A. Draper. Color machine vision for autonomous vehicles. *Engineering Applications of Artificial Intelligence*, 11(2):245–256, 1998.
4. J. Canny. A computational approach to edge detection. *IEEE Transactions on Pattern Analysis and Machine Intelligence*, 8(6):679–698, 1986.
5. A.J. Davison and N. Kita. Sequential localisation and map-building for real-time computer vision and robotics. *Robotics and Auton. Systems*, 36(4):171–183, 2001.
6. P.E. López de Teruel and A. Ruiz. Closed form self-calibration from minimal visual information and odometry, 2003. (*Submitted*).
7. J.D. Foley, A. Van Dam, S. Feiner, and J.F. Hughes. *Computer Graphics: Principles and Practice*. Addison-Wesley, 1990.
8. R. Hartley and A. Zisserman. *Multiple View Geometry in Computer Vision*. Cambridge University Press, 2000.
9. Intel Corporation. The open source computer vision library (OpenCV) homepage, 2002. http://www.intel.com/research/mrl/research/opencv/.
10. V.F. Leavers. Survey: Which hough transform? *Computer Vision, Graphics, and Image Processing: Image Understanding*, 58:250–264, 1993.
11. J. Matas, C. Galambos, and J. Kittler. Robust detection of lines using the progressive probabilistic Hough transform. *Comp. Vis. & Im. Und.*, 78:119–137, 2000.
12. S.J. McKenna, Y. Raja, and S. Gong. Tracking colour objects using adaptive mixture models. *Image and Vision Computing*, 17:223–229, 1999.
13. P.L. Rosin. Techniques for assesing polygonal approximation of curves. *IEEE Transactions on Pattern Analysis and Machine Intelligence*, 19:659–666, 1997.
14. C. Schmid and A. Zisserman. Automatic line matching across views. In *Proceedings of the Computer Vision and Pattern Recognition*, pages 666–671, 1997.
15. T. Tommasini, A. Fusiello, E. Trucco, and V. Roberto. Making good features to track better. In *Proceedings of the Comp. Vis. and Pattern Recognition*, 1998.
16. Z. Zhang. Token tracking in a cluttered scene. *International Journal of Image and Vision Computing*, 12(2):110–120, 1994.

A Multiple Classifier System Approach to Affine Invariant Object Recognition

Alireza R. Ahmadyfard and Josef Kittler

Center for Vision, Speech and Signal Processing
University of Surrey, Guildford GU2 7XH,UK
{A.Ahmadyfard,J.Kittler}@eim.surrey.ac.uk

Abstract. We propose an affine invariant object recognition system which is based on the principle of multiple classifier fusion. Accordingly, two recognition experts are developed and used in tandem. The first expert performs a course grouping of the object hypotheses based on an entropy criterion. This initial classification is performed using colour cues. The second expert establishes the object identity by considering only the subset of candidate models contained in the most probable coarse group. This expert takes into account geometric relations between object primitives and determines the winning hypothesis by means of relaxation labelling. We demonstrate the effectiveness of the proposed object recognition strategy on the Surrey Object Image Library database. The experimental results not only show improved recognition performance but also a computational speed up.

1 Introduction

The recognition of objects from their 2D image has applications in robot vision and remote sensing. There is also a lot of interest in object recognition in the context of image retrieval from large databases.

Among the many methods which address the problem of 3D object recognition from 2D views[7], some represent the image of an object using geometric features[12]. During matching, the correspondence between the features from the test image and those of object model is sought by exploiting the geometric constraints. The object model which best matches the test image defines the identity of the object in the scene.

The other end of the methodological spectrum is occupied by appearance-based approaches in which the image of an object is represented using the raw pixel information[5]. In contrast with the former methods, the matching between two image of an object is accomplished by comparing the image descriptors in a feature space[1]. As a result, the matching in these methods is much faster than establishing feature correspondences. This is why the appearance-based approach has recently received a lot of attention for image retrieval. Unfortunately, the matching in feature space may fail to interpret a scene image unambiguously. This is likely to happen, in situations where different objects have similar appearance, or the appearance is distorted by occlusion and the background clutter

J.L. Crowley et al. (Eds.): ICVS 2003, LNCS 2626, pp. 438–447, 2003.

is complex.In such situations, these methods can be used only to identify a number of candidate models which may match the test image.

In pattern recognition the multiple classifier system approach has been used successfully to solve many recognition tasks. In this paper we shall investigate the merits of this approach in the context of object recognition in computer vision. We shall show that by combining two distinct object recognition approaches in a tandem, we can improve the overall recognition performance . For the two cooperating object recognition experts we choose one from among the appearance based methods and one based on features correspondence matching.

The appearance-based approach is used to prune the list of object models in the model database. The resulting candidate models are then involved in the matching based on feature correspondences to determine the identity of the object in the scene.

More specifically in the first stage of this system we coarsely classify the objects in the database into two groups, *candidate* and *rejected* objects. This initial classification is performed using colour cues. For this purpose we measure dissimilarity between colour structure in the scene image and each of the object models. The grouping of the object hypotheses is then performed based on an entropy criterion. As the second stage of the recognition task we apply an Attributed Relational Graph (ARG) matching to identify the correct object in the test image among the list of candidates obtained from the first stage.

The simplicity of extracting colour features as well as the capability of such features for representing colour objects motivated us to use this cue for object grouping. Among the early efforts, Swain and Ballard[11] introduced a method based on the colour histogram.The sensitivity of this histogram approach to illumination changes was later reduced by Funt and Finlayson[4]. They advocated the use of relative colour rather than absolute colour for indexing. But as histogram matching is, in essence, a global approach, it cannot entirely overcome the sensitivity to changing background clutter. In order to improve robustness to background changes, the use of local colour invariant features has recently been receiving increasing attention. For instance Matas et al[10] proposed a method based on the matching of invariant colour features computed from multimodal neighbourhoods. The method is called Multimodal Neighbourhood Signature (MNS). It has been tested in image retrieval and object recognition applications with promising results[10]. Although colour-based methods in general are remarkably fast and for this reason they are popular in image retrieval, in the object recognition context they are not very reliable. The reason is that these methods match the features of object images in the colour space regardless of any spatial correspondence between them. Clearly, colour features alone cannot capture the structure of an object in the scene. Nevertheless we use them to reduce the classification entropy of the entire recognition system. Accordingly, in this paper we use the MNS method as a pre-matching stage for the ARG method. An ARG method is then applied to identify, from among the remaining candidates, the model which matches the object in the scene image.

The matching in the second stage is performed by establishing a correspondence between regions segmented from the scene image and the corresponding regions from the model of the correct object. In this method the regions of the image are represented by an Attributed Relational Graph (ARG) where each node and link between a pair of nodes are described using unary and binary features respectively[2]. These measurements characterise regions in an image in terms of geometric and appearance properties. Object recognition is achieved by comparing the scene ARG to the graph of object models using probabilistic relaxation labelling technique [13] adapted to the problem.

We refer to the new system using two recognition experts the MNS and ARG method as the MNS-ARG method. The results of experiments carried out with the new method show that the recognition rate of the MNS-ARG system is better than for the stand alone ARG system. We also demonstrate that the model pruning performed by the MNS method significantly improves the speed of our object recognition system.

The paper is organised as follows. In the next section we briefly describe the MNS method[10]. In Section 2 we overview the ARG method [2]. The proposed recognition system based on combining the MNS and ARG matching is introduced in Section 4. The experimental results are reported in Section 5. In the last section we draw the paper to conclusion.

2   MNS Method

In the MNS method proposed by Matas et al[10] an image is described using a number of local invariant colour features computed on multimodal neighbourhoods detected in the image. In the first step of the MNS representation, the image plane is covered by a set of overlapping windows. For every neighbourhood defined in this manner, the modes of the colour distribution are computed with the mean shift algorithm[3]. The neighbourhoods are then categorised according to their modality as unimodal, bimodal, trimodal, etc. The invariant features are only computed from the multimodal neighbourhoods. For every pair of mode colours m_i and m_j in a multimodal neighbourhood, a 6-dimensional vector $v = (m_i, m_j)$(in RGB^2 domain) is constructed. The computed vectors are then clustered in RGB^2 space using the mean shift algorithm[3]. As an output of this process, for each detected cluster its representative vector is stored. The collection of all cluster representatives constitutes the image signature.

During recognition, the signature of a test image is matched to each model signature separately. As the outcome of this process, each model is given a score according to the dissimilarity between its signature and the test image signature. The models are then rank ordered according to their scores.

The details of the matching process between a test signature D and a model signature Q are as follow: Consider the test and model signatures as sets of features $D = \{f^i_D : i = 1..m\}$ and $Q = \{f^j_Q : j = 1..n\}$. Recall that each feature in these sets is a 6-dimensional vector in the RGB^2 space. For every pair f^i_D, f^j_Q the distance $d(f^i_D, f^j_Q) \equiv d_{ij}$ is used as the similarity measure between the two features. Now the test and model signatures D and Q are considered as a bipartite graph where the edge between pair of nodes i and j is described by the distance d_{ij} ($d_{ij} = d_{ji}$). A match association function $u(i) : Q \rightarrow 0 \bigcup D$ is defined as a mapping of each model feature i to a proper test feature or to 0 (in case none of the test features matches). In the same manner a test association function $v(j) : D \to 0 \bigcup Q$ maps each test feature in D to a feature in Q or to 0. A threshold T_h is used to define the maximum allowed distance between two matched features. The algorithm can be summarised as follows:

Algorithm 1: **MNS Matching**

---

1. Set $u(i) = 0$ and $v(j) = 0$ $\forall i, j$.
2. From each signature s compute the invariant features f_D^i, f_Q^j according to the colour change model dictated by the application.
3. Compute all pairwise distances $d_{ij} = d(f_D^i, f_Q^j)$ between the test and model features.
4. Set $u(i) = j$, $v(j) = i$ if $d_{ij} < d_{kl}$ and $d_{ij} < T_h$ $\forall k, l$ with $u(k) = 0$ and $v(l) = 0$.
5. Compute signature dissimilarity as
$$\Delta(D, Q) = \sum_{(\forall i : u(i) \neq 0)} d_{ij} + \sum_{(\forall i : u(i) = 0)} T_h$$

In summary function Δ measures the dissimilarity between the test image and model signatures. This measurement consists of two parts. The first term represents the goodness of fit between the features of the candidate model and the test image features. The second term penalises any unmatched model features. The models are then ranked in the increasing order of their signature dissimilarities.

3   ARG Object Recognition

In this method an object, or more specifically an image of the object is represented in terms of its segmented regions. The extracted regions are described individually and in pairs using their geometric and colour features. The entire image is then represented in the form of an Attributed Relational Graph(ARG)where each node corresponds to one of the regions and the edges between the nodes capture the region adjacency information.

The segmentation of an image into regions is based on colour homogeneity of the pixels. For this purpose we use the region growing method proposed in [6]. Each extracted region R_i is characterised individually using its (RGB) colour vector and we refer to this description as unary measurement vector $\overline{\mathbf{X}_i}$. The relationship between a pair of regions R_i, R_j is described using geometric and colour measurements which constitute a so called binary measurement vector, $\overline{\mathbf{A}_{ij}}$, defined as follows: Let us consider a pair of regions R_i and R_j in Fig 1. The line which connects the centroid points c_i and c_j intersects with the regions boundaries at a_i, b_i, a_j and b_j. Under affine transformation assumed here, the ratio of segments on a line remains invariant. Using this property, we define $m_1 = \frac{a_i b_i}{c_i c_j}$ and $m_2 = \frac{a_j b_j}{c_i c_j}$ as two elements of the binary measurement vector. In addition, the area ratio $AreaRatio = A_i/A_j$ and the distance between colour vectors $\overline{ColourDis} = \overline{C_i} - \overline{C_j}$ are used as complementary components of the bi-

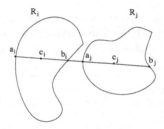

Fig. 1. Binary measurements associated with pair of regions

nary measurement vector $\overline{\mathbf{A}}_{ij}$. All the elements used in the binary measurement vector are affine invariant.

Using the extracted regions and the associated measurement vectors we construct a Relational Attributed Graph in which a graph node O_i represents region R_i. The measurement vector, $\overline{\mathbf{X}}_i$, embodies the node unary attributes. The binary measurement vector $\overline{\mathbf{A}}_{ij}$ describes the link between the pair of nodes O_i, O_j.

Using this approach an object is modelled in the recognition system by an attributed relational graph constructed from its representative image. The graphs of all objects in the model database are collected in a single graph referred to as the composite model graph. The content of an imaged scene is interpreted by constructing an ARG for the scene image. The resulting representation is referred to as the scene graph. Scene objects are then identified by matching the composite model and scene graphs.

The matching is accomplished using the relaxation labelling technique[13] which has been modified for the object recognition application[2]. In order to recognise objects in the scene image, the scene graph is matched against the composite model graph. This is in contrast with the methods in which the scene graph is matched against one object model at a time. By this matching strategy, we provide a unique interpretation for each part of the scene[2].

Before describing the algorithm for matching two ARGs let us introduce the necessary notation and the definitions required. We allocate to each node of the scene graph a label. Set $\theta = \{\theta_1, \theta_2, \cdots, \theta_N\}$ denotes the scene labels where θ_i is the label for node O_i. Similarly we use $\Omega = \{\omega_0, \omega_1, \cdots, \omega_M\}$ as the label set for the nodes of the composite model graph. In this label set, ω_0 is the null label which does not refer to any real node. It is added to be assigned to the scene nodes for which no other label in Ω is appropriate[13]. The contextual information in a graph is conveyed to a node from a small neighbourhood. In this regard, node O_j is a neighbour of O_i if the Euclidean distance between the associated regions is below a predefined threshold. We use set $\mathcal{N}_i$ to refer to the nodes in a neighbourhood of O_i. Similarly the labels in the neighbourhood of ω_α are referred to by set Ω_α.

By labelling we mean the assignment of a proper label from set Ω to each node of the scene graph. In this regard, $P(\theta_i = \omega_\alpha)$ denotes the probability that node O_i in the scene graph takes label ω_α. Obviously the majority of labels in Ω are not admissible for O_i. Therefore in the first stage of matching we compile a list of admissible labels for any scene node O_i denoted by Ω^i. This list is constructed by measuring the mean square error between the unary measurement vector for scene node O_i and the vectors of unary relation for all nodes in the model graph. Note that we include the null label in the label list of all the scene nodes, as it can potentially be assigned to any node in the scene. In the second stage of matching the modified labelling probability updating formula is applied[2]:

$$P^{(n+1)}(\theta_i = \omega_\alpha) = \frac{P^{(n)}(\theta_i = \omega_\alpha)Q^{(n)}(\theta_i = \omega_\alpha)}{\sum_{\omega_\lambda \in \Omega} P^{(n)}(\theta_i = \omega_\lambda)Q^{(n)}(\theta_i = \omega_\lambda)} \tag{1}$$

$$Q^{(n)}(\theta_i = \omega_\alpha) = \prod_{j \in \mathcal{N}_i} \{ \sum_{\omega_\beta \in \{\Omega^j \cap \Omega_\alpha\}} P^{(n)}(\theta_j = \omega_\beta)P(A_{ij}|\theta_i = \omega_\alpha, \theta_j = \omega_\beta)$$
$$+ \sum_{\omega_\beta \in \Omega^j - \{\Omega^j \cap \Omega_\alpha\}} P^{(n)}(\theta_j = \omega_\beta)\eta \} \tag{2}$$

The relaxation labelling technique updates the labelling probabilities in an iterative manner using the contextual information provided by the nodes of the graph. In this formulation $Q(\theta_i = \omega_\alpha)$ is the support function which measures the consistency of the label assignments to the scene nodes in the neighbourhood of O_i assuming O_i takes label ω_α. The labelling consistency is expressed as a function of the binary measurement vectors associated with the centre node O_i and its neighbours. The support function consists of two parts: the first part measures the contribution from Ω_α neighbours (the main support) and the second part is added to balance the number of contributing terms via the other labels in $\Omega[2]$. η is a parameter which plays the role of the binary relation distribution function $P(A_{ij}|\theta_i = \omega_\alpha, \theta_j = \omega_\beta)$ when the model nodes ω_α and ω_β are not neighbours.It takes a fixed value which is determined experimentally.

Upon termination of the relaxation labelling process, we have a list of correspondences between the nodes of the scene and model graphs. We count the number of scene nodes matched to the nodes of each object model and this measure is used as an object matching score.

4   MNS-ARG Matching

Now we construct a recognition system by combining the two recognition experts, MNS and ARG matching. It is well known that a classifier performance declines with the increasing number of classes (objects in the database). Our objective is to reduce the probability of incorrect assignments in ARG matching due to the increased entropy of the interpretation which is a function of the number of possible interpretations. For this purpose we use the MNS method as the first stage of our system to compile the list of hypothesised objects from the object models in the database. This list is then passed to the second stage of the system in which the ARG method establishes a correspondence between the scene content and the model of correct object among the hypothesised objects. Apart from improvement in the recognition rate we expect significant gains in speed of ARG matching due to reducing the dimensionality of the model graph. In the first stage, we use dissimilarity measures associated with the object models in the database to classify the objects into two groups, candidate and rejected objects. Recalling the MNS method, we denote the dissimilarity between the scene and the object models in the database by set $\mathcal{D} = \{\Delta_i, i \in \{1, \cdots, K\}\}$. Δ_i is the dissimilarity between the scene and the model of the i th object in the database and K denotes the number of objects in the database. The probability that the object in the test image is the i th object in the database given the test image signature $\overline{x}$, can be written as follows:

$$p(\omega_i | \overline{x}) = \frac{P(\overline{x}|\omega_i)p(\omega_i)}{P(\overline{x})} \tag{3}$$

where $P(\overline{x}|\omega_i)$ is the density function of observation $\overline{x}$ conditional on class ω_i. $p(\omega_i)$ is the prior probability of class ω_i and $P(\overline{x})$ denotes the density function of the measurements. It is worth nothing that as this latter density function remains the same for all a posteriori probabilities we ignore this term for the computation of $p(\omega_i | \overline{x})$. We also assume that a priori class probabilities are equal. Accordingly, the only term influencing the above formula is the conditional distribution function $P(\overline{x}|\omega_i)$. We use a folded Gaussian function to model the dissimilarity between the test image signature, $\overline{x}$, and the model of hypothesised object $\hat{\overline{x}}_i$. Accordingly $\hat{\overline{x}}_i$ is given as:

$$P(\overline{x}|\omega_i) = \sqrt{\frac{2}{\pi \sigma^2}} \exp\left(-\Delta_i / 2\sigma^2\right) \tag{4}$$

where σ^2 is the variance of the dissimilarity measures. Having provided the set of a posteriori probabilities $\mathcal{P} = \{p(\omega_i | \overline{x}), \forall i \in \{1 \cdots K\}\}$, we rank them in the descending order. Our objective is to compile a list of hypothesised objects based on their likelihood being in the scene $(\mathcal{P})$. For this purpose we use the entropy of the system as a criterion. Let us consider the list, $\mathcal{O}$ of objects arranged according to the descending order of their probabilities being in the scene. If $\mathcal{O}$ is split into two groups O_1 and O_2 corresponding to the m most likely objects in the scene and the remaining objects in the database respectively, the entropy of the system is evaluated as follows [9]:

$$E = \alpha E(O_1) + (1 - \alpha)E(O_2) \tag{5}$$

where $E(O_1)$ and $E(O_2)$ are the entropies associated with groups O_1 and O_2 respectively and α is the probability that the present object in the scene exists in the group O_1. By searching the range of possible configurations, $(m = \{1 \cdots K\})$, the grouping with the minimum entropy is selected and the group of the hypothesised objects, O_1, is passed to the next expert (ARG).

In the second stage of our recognition system we apply ARG matching to identify the identity of the object in the test image.

5   Experimental Results

We designed an experiment to demonstrate the effect of model pruning on the performance of the ARG method. We compared ARG with the MNS-ARG

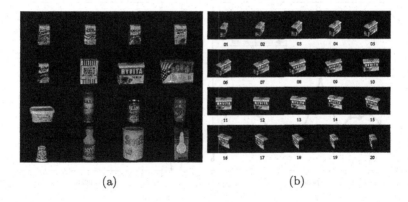

(a)   (b)

Fig. 2. a) The frontal view of some objects in the SOIL47 database b) 20 views of an object used for the test

method from the recognition rate and the recognition speed points of view. The experiment was conducted on the SOIL-47 (Surrey Object Image Library) database which contains 47 objects each of which has been imaged from 21 viewing angles spanning a range of up to ± 90 degrees. Fig2(a) shows the frontal view of the objects in the database. The database is available online[8]. In this experiment we model each object using its frontal image while the other 20 views of the objects are used as test images.(Fig 2(b)). The size of images used in this experiment is 288×360 pixels.

For each test image we applied the MNS method to determine the hypothesised objects matched to it. The results of the experiment are shown in Fig 3. In this figure we plot the percentage of cases in which the list of hypothesised objects includes the correct model. This rate has been shown as a function of object pose. For comparison we plot the percentage of cases in which the correct object has the highest probability among the other candidates, referred to as the recognition rate. The results illustrate that the recognition rate for the MNS method is not very high. In contrast, as seen from Fig 3 in the majority of cases the hypothesised list includes the correct object. It is worth noting that the average size of the list of hypothesised objects is 16 which is near to one third of the database size(47 objects).

The ARG method was then applied to identify the object model based on the list of hypothesised objects generated by the MNS method. This recognition procedure was applied to all test images in the database. In Fig 4 we have plotted the recognition rate for the MNS-ARG method as a function of object pose. For comparison we have shown the recognition rate when ARG method is applied as a stand alone expert. As a base line we added the rate of correct classification of the MNS method. The results show that the object grouping using the MNS method improves the recognition rate particularly for extreme object views. For such views the hypotheses at a node of the test graph do not receive a good

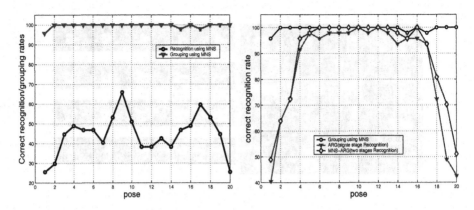

Fig. 3. The likelihood of the correct model being in the list of hypothesised objects generated MNS method

Fig. 4. The percentage of correct recognition for the ARG and the MNS-ARG methods

support from its neighbours (problem of distortion in image regions). Moreover a large number of labels involved in the matching increases the entropy of labelling. When the number of candidate labels for a test node declines by virtue of model pruning the entropy of labelling diminishes. Consequently it is more likely for a test node to take its proper label (instead of the null label).

We now consider the computational advantage of the model pruning. As the model images in both the ARG and MNS methods are represented off-line we do not consider the cost of model construction in the recognition system processing. In the ARG method the recognition task consists of two stages: the representation of the test image in an ARG form and the graph matching. We refer to the associated process times as t_{GR} and t_{GM} respectively. By analogy, MNS matching also involves two stages: the extraction of the image MNS signature and the signature matching. The corresponding process times are referred as t_{SR} and t_{SM} respectively. The total recognition time for the ARG matching is $T_{ARG} = t_{GR} + t_{GM}$. When we deploy MNS for model pruning, the total MNS-ARG process time is $T_{MNS-ARG} = t_{SR} + t_{SM} + t_{GR} + t_{GM}$. Among the terms in $T_{MNS-ARG}$ only the graph matching time t_{GM} varies with the size of the list of candidates. In fact this process time depends on the number of nodes in the model graph which is a function of the number of models and their complexity. Table 1 shows the average process time for the MNS-ARG method in comparison to a single stage recognition using the ARG method. The processing time is given in central processor units. The results demonstrate that the speed gain obtained by pruning the model list is more than two.

6   Conclusion

The problem of object recognition from 2D views was addressed. A new object recognition system which combines the Attributed Relational Graph(ARG) and Multimodal Neighbourhood Signature (MNS) methods was proposed. In the

Table 1. The process times for ARG and MNS-ARG methods in CPU units

Methods	t_{SR}	t_{SM}	t_{GR}	t_{GM}	$Tot.$
ARG (Single stage recognition)	-	-	2.57	31.01	33.58
MNS-ARG	0.90	1.52	2.57	7.66	12.67

proposed system first we perform non-contextual matching using MNS to prune the number of candidate models.In the next stage ARG matching is applied to identify the correct model for each object in a test image. The results of experiments showed an improvement in the recognition rate in comparison to the ARG method being used in the stand alone mode. As the experimental results showed, the model pruning using the MNS method also speeds-up the matching process significantly.

References

1. Leonardis A. and Bischof H. Robust recognition using eigenimages. *Computer Vision and Image Understanding*, 78(1):99–118, 2000.
2. A. Ahmadyfard and J. Kittler. Enhancement of ARG object recognition method. In *Proceeding of 11 the European Signal Processing Conference*, volume 3, pages 551–554, September 2002.
3. D. Comaniciu and P. Meer. Mean shift analysis and applications. In *Proceedings of ICCV*, pages 1197–1203, 1999.
4. Funt B. Finlayson G. and Barnard J. Color constant color indexing. *IEEE Transaction on PAMI*, 17((5):522–529, 1995.
5. Murase H. and Nayar S. Visual learning and recognition of 3d objects from appearance. *International Journal of Computer Vision*, pages 5–24, 1995.
6. R. Haralick and L. Shapiro. Image segmentation techniques. *Computer Vision, Graphics and Image Processing*, pages 100–132, 1985.
7. Wolfson H.J. Model-based object recognition by geometric hashing. In *Proceedings of ICCV*, pages 526–536, 1990.
8. http://www.ee.surrey.ac.uk/Research/VSSP/demos/colour/soil47/.
9. Ianakiev K. and V. Govindaraju. Architecture for classifier combination using entropy measures. In *IAPR International Workshop on Multiple Classifier Systems*, Lecture Notes in Computer Science, pages 340–350, June 2000.
10. J. Matas, D. Koubaroulis, and J. Kittler. Colour image retrieval and object recognition using the multimodal neighbourhood signature. In *Proceedings of ECCV*, pages 48–64, 2000.
11. Swain M.J. and Ballard D.H. Colour indexing. *Intl. Journal of Computer Vision*, 7(1):11–32, 1991.
12. Pope R. Model-based object recognition a survey of recent research. Technical report, 1994.
13. Christmas W.J., Kittler J., and Petrou M. Structural matching in computer vision using probabilistic relaxation. *IEEE Transactions on PAMI*, pages 749–764, 1995.

Measuring Scene Complexity to Adapt Feature Selection of Model-Based Object Tracking*

Minu Ayromlou, Michael Zillich, Wolfgang Ponweiser, and Markus Vincze

Institute of Automation and Control, Vienna University of Technology
Gusshausstr. 27-29/376, 1040 Vienna, Austria
ma@acin.tuwien.ac.at, www.acin.tuwien.ac.at

Abstract. In vision-based robotic systems the robust tracking of scene features is a key element of grasping, navigation and interpretation tasks. The stability of feature initialisation and tracking is strongly influenced by ambient conditions, like lighting and background, and their changes over time. This work presents how robustness can be increased especially in complex scenes by reacting to a measurement of the scene content. Element candidates are proposed, to indicate the scene complexity remaining after running a method. Local cue integration and global topological constraints are applied to select the best feature set. Experiments show in particular the success of the approach to disambiguate features in complex scenes.

1 Introduction

Since beginning of computer vision research the main limitations of visual tracking in real-world applications have been the lack of robustness while accomplishing real-time. Instability of tracking is caused especially by varying background, lighting and occlusion conditions. In model-based tracking these difficulties impede the problem of matching features found in the image to the according model features. Cluttered background or close features produce ambiguous results and full matching of image to model features is not applicable in real-time due to its combinatorial explosion. Nevertheless, matching techniques are of interest since correct matching enhances significantly the reliability of tracking. Successful results of different approaches in feature matching have been presented in model-based object recognition [4,17,1,15].

To make matching applicable for real-time tracking, strategies for restriction of feature matching have to be implemented. One common way is to use windowing techniques [6,5,16]. Though, in complex environments more than one feature is found in a tracking window and matching of features remains ambiguous. To avoid matching expenses, it is a usual method to project the model into the image and to consider the closest feature found as the one searched [6,7,10,14]. The redundancy of using many control points along the edges for pose estimation

---

* This work has been supported by the EU-Project ActIPret under grant IST-2001-32184.

J.L. Crowley et al. (Eds.): ICVS 2003, LNCS 2626, pp. 448–459, 2003.

compensates for inaccuracies and mismatching. The trade-off is the decreasing reliability with fast motions and cluttered or structured environments.

[13] counters the problem of sensitivity to mismatching by running intermediate filters for outlier detection of edges and pose fitting. Another approach for limiting matches is the application of cues [9]. Cues are characteristics found or derived from image data, which specify additional properties of features. [11] uses the integration of depth and colour cues for tracking of heads. In [16] image cues, like colour or intensity, are extracted from features found to reduce the number of edgels to edgels with strong likelihood for easier re-finding of the features in the subsequent cycle.

The examples above show that the difficulty of robust model-based tracking increases with the number of possibilities for matching image to model features. This paper introduces a simple scene complexity measure to specialise processing for tracking. The number of element candidates is used to estimate scene complexity. In a first step multiple cues help to reduce the number of edgels, which diminishes the also the number of possible feature candidates. In more complex scenes this approach is not sufficient. Reasons can be environmental conditions like disadvantageous lighting, cluttered background or repeated objects. A different reason is the lack of tracking information either because the feature was searched for the first time (initialisation) or because tracking failed in the previous cycle (track lost). In these cases the high complexity causes the application to select a second approach. Using topological constraints the consistency and validity of whole sets of feature candidates are examined to achieve a plausibility measure in a more global context. Since matching of all possible combinations is not feasible, only probabilistic samples of candidate sets are chosen and examined according to their topological constraints.

Section 2 gives an overview of the main elements of the tracking tool V4R. In Section 3 the complexity measure is introduced and its role for tracking is demonstrated. The results of enhanced tracking based on the complexity measure are presented in Section 4. The summary with outlook concludes the paper.

2   Tracking with V4R

The tool Vision for Robotics (V4R) tracks the 3D pose of objects through a sequence of images [16]. It uses model-based tracking of edge features to detect the 2D feature positions, which are input to the pose calculation algorithm for 3D-pose estimation. Since tracking has to be performed in real-time a window-based approach is used, where the size of the window is kept fixed by subsampling along the main feature extension. The search window position is given through tracking, prediction or the projection of the initialisation/last pose into the image. Hence, the matching of image features to their according model is constrained by the candidates extracted from the search window.

The idea developed in this paper is that feature candidates are selected at different levels depending on scene complexity to ensure robust tracking. On the local level of single features cues like colour, intensity or texture of the regions adjacent to the edges give a clue about the local confidence of the candidates. In global context, the exploitation of relational constraints given by the model provides confidence measures for sets of candidates. According to the contextual scope the basic entities used in V4R can be divided into two groups of features:

- *Simple Features* are edges (*lines* and *ellipses*) that are searched in the image.
- *Composite Features* are features representing the topological relationship of simple features. Composite features, like *junctions* and *parallel lines*, are not searched as entities but rather deliver model constraints to be proven.

The whole set of visible features in the scene is referred to as *object view*, which delivers the structure for a final consistency check of topological constraints validated. In the two following sub-sections a short overview of the techniques for feature candidate evaluation is given.

2.1   Local Feature Tracking – EPIC

The goal of Edge Projected Integration of Cues (EPIC) is to use different cue values (e.g. intensity, colour) extracted from the previous tracking cycle to pre-select candidate edgels coming from the search windows. This means that for further processing only edgels with cue values similar to the cue values of previously found edges are taken into account. Additional robustness is achieved by incorporating knowledge about the expected view of the object, which enables to determine if the regions on either side of edges belong to the object or the background. Only cue values belonging to the object are evaluated.

The remaining good edgels are input to the RANSAC voting scheme [2] to fit the edgels to the feature geometry and to generate edge candidates. Samples for edges are chosen probabilistically and the edgels within a certain distance to the hypothetical edges are regarded as edge members. The calculation of an overall likelihood $\mathcal{L}_E$ provides a confidence measure for each hypothetical edge:

$$\mathcal{L}_E = \frac{\bar{l}_e \cdot N_E}{H} \tag{1}$$

where the average cue likelihood of edgels is given by $\bar{l}_e$ for all edgels e of the edge. N denotes the number of edgels located on the hypothetical edge and H is the length of the edge in pixels. With this likelihood calculation the overall edge likelihood depends not only on the number of edgels on the edge [3] but also on the likelihoods of the participating edgels, hence incorporating the cue values.

Independent of the specific thresholds to select a feature candidate it is observed that in a simple scene the correct feature is salient while in more complex scenes it is increasingly difficult to make the correct selection. Using the scene complexity measure the necessity for invoking more constraints is validated. Thus, data can be reduced to relevant elements in simple scenes, whereas in ambiguous cases more instances for element evaluation have to be applied.

2.2   Object View Tracking – Topology Validation

The idea is to use topological and image constraints to evaluate, which set of candidate features best describes the model description and expected appearance. The use of topological information is related to work in computer vision using Gestalt criteria (e.g.[10]) where image edges are grouped using the Gestalt rules for tracking or object recognition. However, the bottom-up approach suffers from the difficulty to limit the combinatorial explosion of matching image to model features. Using the Gestalt properties of the model to disambiguate the candidates coming from local tracking makes topology validation feasible. The composite features junction and parallel lines represent the Gestalt constraints.

The validation process is divided into two stages. First, local consistency check of composite features is performed by examining the constraint rules on their underlying feature candidates. Sets of feature candidates fulfilling the constraints are stored as *composite feature candidates*. The main criteria tested to create the candidates can be summarised as follows.

1. Junctions:

   - Edge candidates do intersect in one point.
   - Edge candidates end in the intersection calculated.
   - No related edge candidates are the same, parallel or collinear.
   - For junctions with three or more edges: the clockwise order of edge candidates is according to the model description.

2. Parallel lines:

   - The related line candidates are not the same.
   - Line candidates are parallel (deviations due to perspective are considered).
   - Edge candidates have the appropriate order in the image.

After determining the local topological properties of the edge candidates, global consistency has to be examined. To circumvent the complete search of all possible candidate combinations probabilistic samples of candidates are taken [2], where the selection of the candidates is biased according to their likelihoods $\mathcal{L}_E$. These samples represent hypothetical object views. By taking probabilistic samples the performance of validation increases only linearly with the number of features.

Finally the resulting object view candidates are evaluated to find the candidate with maximum global consistency. The number of met relational constraints as well as the similarity of properties of the relations to the ones found in previous steps, provide measures for validation. The set of candidates with best overall likelihood and maximum consistency is then selected. Since the selection is mainly based on relation checks between features, tracking incorporating validation is also referred to as *object view tracking*.

3   Scene Dependent Feature Selection

The last section gave an overview about the two major strategies to fit image features to their according model features. The aim in this section is to introduce a simple measure for scene complexity and to demonstrate the application of these strategies depending on the estimated complexity.

3.1   A Measure of Scene Complexity

Assuming S denotes the occurrence of selecting a certain element candidate out of a set of candidates and R the presence of the correct candidate, the probability of a correct candidate selection can be formulated as follows:

$$P(S \cap R) = P(S|R) \cdot P(R) \qquad (2)$$

This formula indicates that the probability of choosing the correct candidate depends on the abilities of candidate extraction and element selection. In general the performance of element selection is directly dependent on the number of candidates for one element. The more candidates are available the more complex is the task to choose the right entity and probability of selecting the right candidate decreases. Because of this fact we can define a simple yet efficient measure for scene complexity C by relating the candidates with an appropriate reference

$$C = \frac{\text{number of element candidates}}{\text{reference number}}. \qquad (3)$$

Specifically for the feature level the complexity C_{feat} is given by the average number of candidates per feature

$$C_{feat} = \frac{k}{n - m} \qquad (4)$$

where k is the number of all candidates in the scene, n denotes the number of all features that should be visible and m the subgroup of n, which does not have candidates either due to bad edges or because of occlusions.

Fig. 1 depicts examples for a simple scene opposed to a complex one. In the simple scene the number of candidates is almost restricted to the number of features searched. Local candidate extraction with simple gradient search provides unambiguous results. Therefore matching of image to model features is trivial and the correctness of the solution remains only dependent on the probability of extracting the right feature. This is not the case for the complex scene. In the local feature window several line candidates for the same feature are found. Matching of image to model features is now also dependent on the probability of each candidate being selected and therefore the probability of selecting the searched solution drops. The increasing tracking instability of local tracking with rising complexity is demonstrated in Fig. 4.

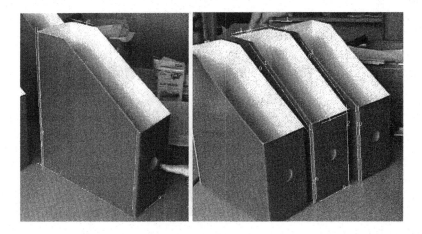

Fig. 1. Left: A simple scene with easy matching of image to model features ($C = 1.22$); Right: A complex scene with several different candidates for each feature ($C = 2.22$)

3.2   Feature Selection

In Section 2 two methods for tracking at different levels were introduced. Each of them play a distinct role in dealing with scene complexity. The integration of local cues in EPIC is mainly a means to restrict the number of element candidates to the most relevant for tracking. This means that with EPIC we intend to reduce complexity and simplify the scene as much as possible. The simplification on feature level is demonstrated in Figure 2. The number of candidates of the complex scene of Figure 1 is reduced to edge candidates most similar to the edges extracted in the previous tracking cycle. Though, reduction of complexity can also be observed on edgel level. Complexity is then given by the ratio of all extracted edgels to the length of the edge in pixels. An example for the capabilities of EPIC at edgel level is given in Figure 3.

However, in some situations reduction of scene complexity with EPIC is either not applicable (e.g. in the initialisation phase or after loss of features, where no cue information is available) or complexity can not sufficiently be reduced (e.g. due to repeated patterns in the image). Complexity remains high and feature selection based only on the local likelihoods is not feasible. Then, validation of topological constraints is a second method to counter ambiguity of matching.

Validation aims to bias candidate selection in favour of the solution searched by adding more global knowledge derived from the topology of the model. The local likelihood of each single candidate is extended to an evaluation value within the context of neighbouring candidates to get a preference of candidate combinations. The set of candidates (i.e. object view) with maximum belief and consistency determines then the particular feature selections. The success of global topology validation in the complex case of Figure 1 is shown in Figure 4.

Fig. 2. The complex scene of Figure 1 (right) simplified through EPIC ($C = 1.22$)

Fig. 3. Complexity at edgel level. Left: Edgels extracted with a gradient filter and with $C = 4.3$. Right: Edgels diminished by EPIC to the number of relevant edgels. Complexity is reduced to $C = 1.16$. Yellow indicates the feature edgels selected, cyan is the colour of other candidates and black denotes the remaining edgels extracted

To summarise, EPIC enables the simplification of complex scenes and validation provides the means to handle remaining complexity. Now the question is if it is necessary to apply validation regardless of complexity. This question is of interest because additional usage of computing power should be restricted to cases where significant enhancements can be obtained. Thus, the output of simple scenes were examined. An example of typical feature selection results are shown in Fig. 5. Obviously in the simple case validation achieves no enhancement of feature selections. The remaining deficiencies are rather due to shortcomings in feature candidate extraction that are mostly caused by weak edges.

These experiments show that topology validation obtains adequate improvement only when either reduction of scene complexity is not successful or no local cue knowledge can be applied for feature selection. Therefore geometrical constraint validation is only used complementary to EPIC and is restricted to the following situations:

– *High complexity of the scene*: This is mostly caused by structured objects or due to ambiguous background.

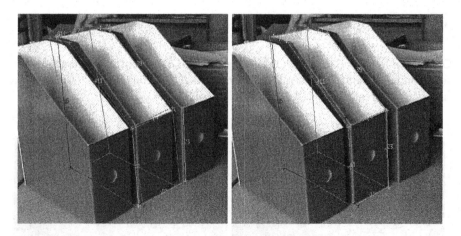

Fig. 4. Left: Feature initialisation in a complex scene using only local constraints (Fig. 1); Right: Initialisation incorporating validation. Yellow features with numbers indicate lines selected and green lines are the final projection of the calculated pose

- *Initialisation*: No tracking information is available and feature candidates fulfil only the minimum constraint of being an edge. Local likelihoods do not express the correctness of candidate representing the according model. Thus, initialisation is treated as a separate case regardless of scene complexity.
- *High complexity at edgel level*: High edgel complexity is mostly given when tracking of one or several features is lost. Again, like in the initialisation process restriction of candidates by applying cues is not possible and validation compensates for the lack of feature specific candidate selection on local level.

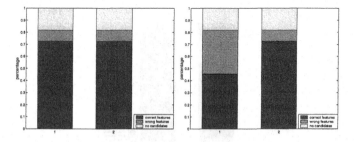

Fig. 5. The feature selection results of the simple scene (left), versus the complex case (right) of Fig. 1. (1) shows the results with the use of gradient edgels only (2) depicts the results applying validation. In the complex case validation gives 27.3% improvement.

4 Experimental Results

One example for the role of the decrease of scene complexity to enhance feature selection is already demonstrated in Section 3.2. For comparison, the initialisation in a different scene and its results is depicted in Fig. 6 and Fig. 7.

Fig. 6. Left: Result of initialising a book using only gradients. The two vertical faces have both close parallel lines which can not be disambiguated locally. Right: Feature selection incorporating validation. Matching is performed successfully.

The main difficulty in this scene is the closeness of several object features with similar cue properties. The feature windows overlap and the same edges become candidates for more than one feature. When no validation is applied features are selected locally regardless of arising inconsistencies in the global object view. In these cases only topology validation is able to disambiguate close similar edges and can deliver the correct matching to the model.

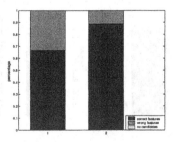

Fig. 7. Comparing results of tracking initialisation of the book (1) using only gradients and (2) including validation. Feature selection is improved by 22.2%

The performance of tracking is demonstrated in Figure 8 and 9. Adaptive feature selection is compared to the results of EPIC and to classical edge extraction using only gradient edgels. To provide the comparability of the outcome, features are initialised to the best candidates delivered by validation, regardless of the actual method applied. Analysing the results of correct feature matching it can be seen that adaptive feature selection shows the best performance. Furthermore, it can be observed that in general tracking runs more stable as soon as EPIC is incorporated. Once a feature is found the probability of re-finding the feature is high. The trade-off is that a wrong selection tends to propagate throughout several cycles of the sequence. In these cases the simple gradient approach can achieve better results. Figure 8 shows that the application of validation is the only means, which improves ambiguity of close features significantly.

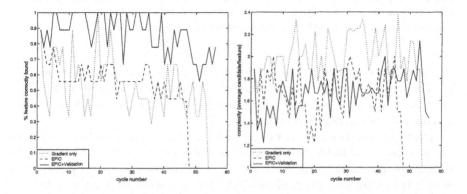

Fig. 8. Comparison of tracking with three different strategies: gradient only, EPIC and adaptive feature selection. With EPIC and gradient, tracking is lost before the end of the sequence. Right: Correct feature identification through a sequence of the moving book. Left: The development of complexity

As expected, scene complexity has its highest values when applying the simple gradient approach. Complexity is only reduced with EPIC, therefore both methods, EPIC and adaptive selection show values in about the same range. The difference of the values is caused by the fact that tracking evolves differently dependent on the method. To enable an easier comparison of the complexity measures, only the values of the gradient approach are compared to adaptive feature selection in Figure 9.

5   Conclusion and Outlook

The paper presented a first implementation of a concept to use an estimate of the scene complexity perceived to select appropriate processing routines for a tracking application. Scene complexity is estimated with the ratio of element

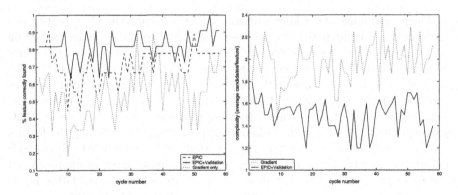

Fig. 9. Comparison of tracking with three different strategies: Gradient only, EPIC and adaptive feature selection. Right: Correct feature identification through a sequence of a moving magazine box. Left: The development of complexity

candidates versus the reference expected. The use of two methods to improve gradient based tracking is demonstrated. EPIC reduces the number of feature candidates at local level, while topological feature validation can disambiguate if many feature candidates remain.

The work proposes to estimate scene complexity as a measure to self-evaluate the performance of methods in the context of the scenes viewed. The complexity measure is subjective to the methods. After EPIC the complexity perceived is smaller than after a simple gradient method. Hence the complexity measure can be utilised to describe the complexity reduction achieved by a certain method. The experiments show how too many candidates are handled and additional processing is requested. This relates to findings of human vision, where simple patterns or patterns different to the background stick out as salient while repeated patterns require additional or sequential processing [8,12].

The validation method can discriminate the local occurrence of one object to similar objects. Further work needs to take dynamic effects into account such as identical objects occluding each other. Another extension is to handle cases where the complexity measure indicates that too few candidates have been found. This means that the method applied is too restrictive and more sensitive methods need to be used. It is stressed in this work that self-evaluation of the performance with respect to the scene context can be utilised to improve tracking robustness.

References

1. J.S. Beis, D.G. Lowe. Indexing without Invariants in 3D object recognition. *IEEE Trans. on Pattern Analysis and Machine Intelligence* 21(10), pp.1000–1015, 1999.
2. M.A. Fischler and R.C. Bolles. Random sample consensus: A paradigm for model fitting with applications to image analysis and automated cartography. *Communications of the ACM*, 24(6):381–395, 1981.

3. W. Förstner. 10 Pros and Cons Against Performance Characterization of Vision Algorithms. *Workshop on Perf. Characteristics of Vis. Algorithms*, Cambridge, 1996.

4. W.E.L. Grimson. Object Recognition by Computer: The Role of Geometric Constraints. *MIT Press*, 1990.

5. G.D. Hager, K. Toyama. The XVision-System: A Portable Substrate for Real-Time Vision Applications, *CV and Image Understanding* 69(1), pp. 23–37, 1998.

6. C. Harris. Tracking with rigid models, A. Blake, A. Yuille, eds., Active Vision, *MIT Press*, pp 59–73, 1992.

7. S. Jörg, J. Langwald, J. Stelter, and G. Hirzinger. Flexible robot-assembly using a multi-sensory approach. *IEEE ICRA*, pp.3687–3694, 2000.

8. B. Julesz. *Early Vision and focal attention;* Reviews of Modern Physics 63(3), pp.735–772, 1991.

9. D. Kragic, A. Miller, P. Allen. RealTime Tracking Meets Online Grasp Planning. *IEEE Int. Conference on Robotics and Automation*, pp.2460–2465,2001

10. D.G. Lowe. Robust Model-Based Motion Tracking Through the Integration of Search and Estimation. *Int. J. of Computer Vision Vol.8(2)*, pp.113–122, 1992.

11. F. Moreno, A. Tarrida, J. Andrade Cetto, A. Sanfeliu. 3D real-time head tracking fusing color histograms and stereovision. *Int. Conf. on Pattern Recognition*, 2002.

12. S.E. Palmer. *Vision Science: Photons to Phenomenology.* MIT Press, Cambridge, MA, 1999.

13. R.L. Thompson, I.D. Reid, L.A. Munoz, D.W. Murray. Providing synthetic views for teleoperation using visual pose tracking in multiple cameras. *IEEE SMC Part A* 31(1), 43–54, 2001.

14. M. Tonko, N.H. Nagel. Model-based Stereo-Tracking of Non-Polyhedral Objects for Automatic Disassembly Experiments. *Int. J. of Comp. Vision* 37(1):99–118, 2000.

15. K. Toyama, A. Blake. Probabilistic Tracking of a Metric Space. *Int. Conference on Computer Vision*, pp.50–59, 2001

16. M. Vincze, M. Ayromlou, W. Ponweiser, and M. Zillich. Edge-projected integration of image and model cues for robust model-based object tracking. *Int. Jounal of Robotics Research*, 20(7):533–552, 2001.

17. A. Zisserman, D. Forsyth, J. Mundy, and C. Rothwell at.al. 3D object recognition using invariance. *Artificial Intelligence*, 78:239–288, 1995.

A Framework for Robust and Incremental Self-Localization of a Mobile Robot

Matjaž Jogan, Matej Artač, Danijel Skočaj, and Aleš Leonardis

Faculty of Computer and Information Science,
University of Ljubljana,
Tržaška 25, Ljubljana, Slovenia,
matjaz.jogan@fri.uni-lj.si,
http://www.lrv.fri.uni-lj.si

Abstract. In this contribution we present a framework for an embodied robotic system that is capable of appearance-based self-localization. Specifically, we concentrate on the issues of robustness, flexibility, and scalability of the system. The framework presented is based on a panoramic eigenspace model of the environment. Its main feature is that it allows for simultaneous localization and map building using an incremental learning algorithm. Further, both the learning and the training processes are designed in a way to achieve robustness and adaptability to changes in the environment.

1 Introduction

With the increase of interest for autonomously navigating mobile robots, which are not any more limited to operate in production halls, but are able to function in the unconstrained environment, several new issues regarding the design and implementation of such machines arose. The need for systems that would be capable of operating in unstructured and dynamically changing environments shifted the focus of robotics research away from the classical artificial intelligence reasoning towards new fields like embodied intelligence, reactive learning, and distributed thinking. The same definition of an intelligent system now means that it is capable of operating in changing conditions, which includes the capability of continuous and unsupervised learning, generalization of knowledge, and robustness against random changes, which can occur in the environment during interaction.

Mobile robot self-localization is an important part of the navigation task (besides defining the goal and planning). Obviously, to estimate the current position, there is a need for a reference model of the environment to which the momentary sensory data has to be compared. The recent decade saw a gradual shift from the systems that use 3D models towards appearance-based approaches. In fact, supported by the findings of psychologists, theories awoke that describe the visual process as a task of recognizing and associating 2D imagery [15,16, 14,11]. Instructive collections of work that stresses the relation between the 3D

J.L. Crowley et al. (Eds.): ICVS 2003, LNCS 2626, pp. 460–469, 2003.

Fig. 1. Mobile robot equipped with a catadioptric panoramic sensor.

reconstruction approach and the appearance-based visual recognition can be found in [18] and [1].

In this contribution we present a framework for an embodied robotic system that is capable of appearance-based self-localization. The framework presented is based on a panoramic eigenspace model of the environment. The eigenspace model of appearance is essentially a model of memory that, besides storing compressed imagery, allows also for pictorial retrieval.

Although distributed systems give a solution to limited physical resources, most of the autonomous robots are expected to be embodied, therefore allowing for a limited processing capability and speed. When storing large collections of visual cues, the storage demands can become quickly prohibitive. It is therefore of extreme importance for the model to be optimized in both the terms of descriptive power and compactness. While dealing with these issues, the notions of local vs. global models and modularity arise.

Further, the robot should be capable to use the model in any time, i.e., the classical divide between the learning and the training stage, typical for the appearance-based recognition methods, should be overcome by introducing an open-ended incremental model capable of dynamic updating and splitting into local representations.

Another important issue of an intelligent embodied system is the fashion in which new knowledge is being acquired. As Rolf Pfeifer argues [17], classical AI models suffer from a number of fundamental problems, such as symbol grounding and dependance on the knowledge of the designer, rather than being environmentally conditioned, knowledge being acquired only through interaction with the environment. The robot should be therefore capable of independent exploration without any intervention of the human operator or other displaced intelligent units. As we show, eigenspace recognition methods comply with the latter requirements, being essentially unsupervised learning schemes.

This paper is organized as follows: in Section 2 we give a general overview of the framework for embodied intelligent self-localization, first describing the hardware and the software used and then concentrating on the overall structure of the system. In Section 3 we first describe the learning stage, which is designed to be a robust procedure. We continue with a description of the recognition part of the system. After emphasizing the importance of constant interaction between the learning and localization scenarios, we introduce the on-line methods, that enable us to use a SLAM (Simultaneous Learning and Map Building) approach. Finally, in Section 4, we give an overview of experimental results and end up with a conclusion and an overview of future work.

2   A Framework for Embodied Intelligent Self-Localization

The robot that we use as a testing platform for the appearance-based self-localization is a Magellan Pro with a Pentium II based onboard computer, manufactured by the iRobot company (Figure 1). The software part of the system is written based on the *Mobility* system, which uses CORBA for distributed computing.

Although the robot comes equipped with a variety of sensors, our goal is to enable localization using only a vision sensor. A schema of the system's framework is depicted in Figure 2. The cognitive part of the system consists of models and routines needed to perform simultaneous localization and map building. Although the learning stage and the localization (recognition) stage are depicted as divided entities, with further development of the system, they will presumably become more and more interconnected, finally becoming a unique cognitive model, using common mechanisms and methods.

As the primary source of external information about the environment, panoramic snapshots enter the system and are encoded in the eigenspace model and/or used for localization. To enhance the accuracy of localization, we further use short range readings from the odometry, which helps us to calculate a probabilistic function for the momentary positional estimate.

The software part of the system is implemented such that it allows for distributed computing. However, since the robot is linked to the network using a slow wireless LAN connection, we tend to run all of the data processing on the robotic platform, so that there is no need to transfer the images over the network.

2.1   The Model of the Environment

As we have already mentioned, we use panoramic images acquired from a catadioptric panoramic camera. Panoramic images are becoming more and more popular in the area of computer vision, their primary advantage being a wide field of view. Further, they provide an efficient representation of the surrounding

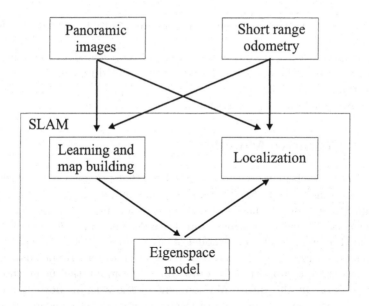

Fig. 2. The framework of the localization system.

and their special properties allow for an efficient encoding in the eigenspace [8,9, 4]. On the top of the robot we mounted a catadioptric panoramic camera, which was the only visual sensor used. We used two different mirrors in the catadioptric camera. The first mirror was of a spherical shape, while the second mirror had a hyperbolical reflective surface of a $r = 1.9$ ratio.[1]

2.2   Learning and Recognition

The images that are to be learned as depictions of the environment the robot is navigating in are represented in a compressed form using the eigenspace representation [21,15]. The major advantage of the eigenspace method is that it allows to perform image matching in a much lower-dimensional space. As one can deduce from the experimental evidence from previous work, the covariance between two panoramic images drops with the distance between positions where they were taken. Position could be therefore inferred by finding the image in the training set that shows the largest covariance with the momentary panoramic view. However, it can be shown that when projecting an image onto the eigenspace, the L_2 norm and the covariance produce the same result as when calculated on original images, when using the complete set of eigenvectors. It is therefore possible to match images in a much lower-dimensional space by representing all the images by their projections in the eigenspace and then by adopting the L_2 norm or the Mahalanobis distance between the projections as the distance metric. Furthermore, it is possible to densely interpolate the set of points in the eigenspace to

---

[1] For a review of catadioptric cameras see [5].

obtain a hyperplane that represents an approximation of an arbitrary dense set of images [15].

The model of the environment is therefore represented by the eigenvectors representing the optimized subspace where the trained images lie in and the representations of positions, which are derived from projections of training images or from interpolation between them.

3   The Cognitive Modules

In this Section we briefly describe the modules that provide the routines needed to perform simultaneous localization and map building. As we have already mentioned, the system consists of two separate modules. The learning module implements the learning routines, which are designed in order to allow for an open-ended, incrementally built model of environment. The localization module implements routines needed for robust recognition of panoramic snapshots and robust localization, supported by a probabilistic computation using short-range odometry data. In the future development of the system, both modules will presumably become more and more interconnected, finally becoming a unique cognitive model, using common mechanisms and methods.

3.1   The Learning Module

The standard approach to eigenspace learning is by the eigen-decomposition of the covariance matrix of the training images. Such a method is susceptible to outliers, occlusions, and varying illumination. However, PCA can be considered as a limiting case of a linear Gaussian model, when the noise is infinitesimally small and equal in all directions. From this observation one can derive an algorithm for calculating principal axes, which is based on the EM (expectation-maximization) algorithm [19]. This algorithm consists of two steps, E and M, which are sequentially and iteratively executed:

- **E-step**: Estimate the coefficients using computed eigenvectors
- **M-step**: Compute the new eigenvectors which maximize expected joint likelihood of the estimated coefficients and the training images

Since the EM algorithm can run on subsets of image pixels, our system implements it in order to obtain a consistent subspace representation in the presence of outlying pixels in the training images. By treating the outlying points as missing pixels, we arrive at a robust PCA representation [20].

Another issue in learning is how to represent images that are taken under different orientation of the robot. Such panoramic images have the same pictorial content, since they represent the same view, yet they are rotated for an angle (phase) of ϕ. To solve this problem, our system implements a specific eigenspace representation, called *"eigenspace of spinning–images"* [7,9], which achieves insensitivity to the rotation of the sensor by integrating multiple rotated versions of a single panoramic image. The representation exploits the fact that a set of

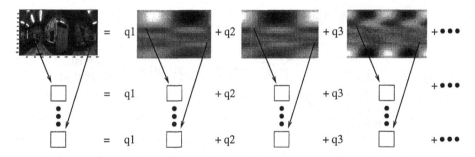

Fig. 3. Calculating the coefficients from a set of linear equations.

rotated templates carrying identical pictorial information can be compressed in the eigenspace in an efficient way. By doing so, we have the advantage of being able to match the incoming image directly to the whole set of rotated images in the recognition phase.

3.2   Adaptable Robust Recognition Module

To localize the robot we have to find the coefficients of the input image and then search for the nearest point on the interpolated hyperplane, which represents the model built on the basis of the images in the training set. The standard method to recover the coefficients is to project the image vector onto the eigenspace [15]. However, this way of calculation of parameters is non-robust[2] and thus not accurate in the case when the input image locally deviates from the image approximated in the environment map.

To overcome the erroneous calculation of image parameters when the visual content deviates from the learning examples, we use the robust approach [11], that, instead of using the image vectors as a whole, generates and evaluates a set of hypotheses r as subsets of k image points $r = (r_1, r_2, \ldots, r_k)$. In fact, the coefficients can be retrieved by solving a set of linear equations on $k = n$ points, where n denotes the dimensionality of the eigenspace.

The principle of such computation is clearly illustrated in Figure 3, where q_i are the image parameters.

By selecting only p, $p \leq n$ eigenimages as our basis we have to solve an over-constrained system in a robust way. We solve the system on $k, k > p$ points, where k is significantly smaller than the total number of image points. After the robust solving of the set of equations, we first perform an α–trimming step, in order to allow only the points on which the error is arbitrary small to contribute to the further computation of the parameters. To further increase the probability of avoiding points that are noise or represent occlusion, several different subsets of points are generated, resulting in multiple hypotheses. A hypothesis consists of

---

[2] Robustness is defined as the extent of the ability of a method to give expected results despite the deviations of the input data.

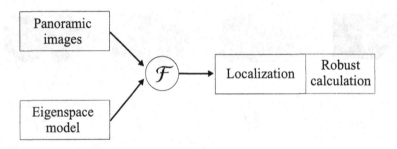

Fig. 4. Schema of the robust localization subsystem.

a set of parameters, an error vector ϵ calculated as the squared difference between the original image and its reconstruction, and the domain of compatible points that satisfy an error margin constraint. These hypotheses are then subject to a selection procedure, based on the *Minimal Description Length* principle, as described in [11].

Illumination artifacts are another problem that influence the overall robustness of the system. A straightforward approach to the problem of illumination in appearance-based learning and recognition is to learn the appearance under all of the possible light conditions [13]. However, an object in the environment can produce so many different images that it is not clear how to sample all of them.

Instead of this, we employ an extended schema of robust calculation of parameters: by convolving the eigenimages with linear filters, we significantly remove the illumination artifacts [10]. As the eigensystem is a linear equation, both the eigenspace and the input image can be convolved with linear filters without changing the results of computation. The important notion here is that the model itself does not depend on filters at all - filtering can be done just in the process of localization, using an arbitrary number and type of filters, or even using none of them, when the illumination conditions are equal to those encoded in the eigenspace.

The overall schema of the robustified localization system is depicted in Figure 4. $\mathcal{F}$ denotes the bank of linear filters applied. Note that the also robust calculation can be turned on or off, according to the momentary conditions.

3.3   The SLAM Approach

The eigenspace learning and recognition method applied in the standard way has its drawbacks. One of them is the fact that the localization stage is strictly separated from the learning stage. In the learning stage we capture all images first, and only then can we construct the model. The model built in this way can not be modified unless we keep the original images. To update the model with new images, we have to construct a new one from the scratch. Therefore, standard approaches are not optimal for performing simultaneous learning (environment exploration) and localization (SLAM [3]).

To overcome these problems, we developed an incremental method for building the subspace. Incremental computation of eigenvectors has been considered before [6]. However, for a method to be completely on-line, we have to simultaneously update both the eigenvectors and the low-dimensional representations of images. In this way, we can discard the original images immediately after the updating of the subspace. One has to be aware, however, that the low-dimensional representations of the images are only approximations of the originals.

With our approach [2] we are able to perform simultaneous exploration and localization, which means that from the very first moment of the exploration (learning) phase, the robot can use the momentary model of the environment, as it is built incrementally. By collecting new pictorial evidence, the model grows, and by applying a multiple eigenspace growing procedure [12], it can be segmented into logical submodels.

4   Experimental Results

In this section we give the experimental results that show how our self-localization system performs in navigation. In an incremental training phase, the robot explored an indoor environment, storing snapshots at positions that are depicted as empty squares on Figure 5. Then, we positioned the robot on an arbitrary position and sent an order to navigate to a position which was determined by a previously acquired panoramic image. In order to navigate to the goal, the robot performs the following steps: first he estimates his momentary position and orientation, then he estimates the goal's position and determines the vector which points in its directions. He then moves for 70cm in the direction of the goal and again performs localization. According to the new estimate, he recalculates the homing vector and moves for another 70cm.

We present the results as the odometry of the path that the robot followed during his navigation to the goal. In order to demonstrate robustness, we performed tests in both static and dynamic conditions, both with normal and robust techniques.

The leftmost map on Figure 5 illustrates the path of the robot in the case when there are no occlusions in the environment. The filled squares denote the estimated training positions, while the circles denote the positions where the robot stopped to perform self-localization. One can associate the estimated and the actual positions by their numbering. Please note that the information on the odometry accumulated a large amount of error. In truth, the actual ending position differed from the expected one for less than 5cm.

The map in the center illustrates the path of the robot in the presence of significant occlusions and change in illumination. The navigation was in this case performed without employing any of the robust features of the localization system. The rightmost map illustrates, how the robust features of the system improve the performance in harsh conditions.

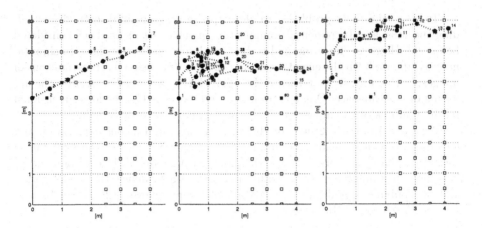

Fig. 5. Localization results in point-to-point navigation.

5 Conclusions

In this contribution we presented a framework for an embodied robotic system that is capable of appearance-based self-localization using a parametric eigenspace model built from panoramic snapshots of the environment.

The eigenspace approach for appearance-based learning and recognition proved itself to be a suitable core for the self-localization system. It provides an efficient representation of the environment, which can be stored in the robot's onboard memory. Further, it allows for a true on-line learning process, enabling simultaneous localization and map building. As we showed in the description of our system, the eigenspace method can be extended with mechanisms that provide robustness both in the learning and in the localization process.

We concluded the paper with a set of experiments which demonstrate the effectiveness of the system. In future work we intend to enhance the accuracy of localization by introducing more knowledge on short range odometry, implement the probabilistic framework and enhance the process of incremental learning with the support for building modular local representations. Further, we are investigating how to build reliable maps with a fully unsupervised procedure in order to achieve a genuine SLAM approach.

References

1. *IEEE Computer Society Workshop on Models versus Exemplars in Computer Vision,* Kauai, Hawaii. IEEE Computer Society, December 2001.
2. Matej Artač, Matjaž Jogan, and Aleš Leonardis. Mobile robot localization using an incremental eigenspace model. In *ICRA 2002,* pages 1025–1030. IEEE Robotics and Automation Society, 2002.
3. A. J. Davison and N. Kita. Sequential localisation and map-building for real-time computer vision and robotics. *Robotics and Autonomous Systems,* 36(4):171–183, 2001.

4. José Gaspar, Niall Winters, and José Santos-Victor. Vision-based navigation and environmental representations with an omnidirectional camera. *IEEE Transaction on Robotics and Automation*, 16(6), December 2000.
5. Chris Geyer and Kostas Daniilidis. Catadioptric projective geometry. *International Journal of Computer Vision*, (43):223–243, 2001.
6. P. Hall, D. Marshall, and R. Martin. Incremental eigenanalysis for classification. In *British Machine Vision Conference*, volume 1, pages 286–295, September 1998.
7. Matjaž Jogan and Aleš Leonardis. Robust localization using eigenspace of spinning-images. In *IEEE Workshop on Omnidirectional Vision*, pages 37–44. IEEE Computer Society, June 2000.
8. Matjaž Jogan and Aleš Leonardis. Robust localization using panoramic view-based recognition. In *15th International Conference on Pattern Recognition*, volume 4, pages 136–139. IEEE Computer Society, September 2000.
9. Matjaž Jogan and Aleš Leonardis. Robust localization using an omnidirectional appearance-based subspace model of environment. *Accepted for publication in Robotics and Autonomous Systems*, 2002.
10. Matjaž Jogan, Aleš Leonardis, Horst Wildenauer, and Horst Bischof. Mobile robot localization under varying illumination. In *ICPR 2002*, volume II, pages 741–744. IEEE Computer Society, 2002.
11. Aleš Leonardis and Horst Bischof. Robust recognition using eigenimages. *Computer Vision and Image Understanding - Special Issue on Robust Statistical Techniques in Image Understanding*, 78(1):99–118, 2000.
12. Aleš Leonardis, Horst Bischof, and Jasna Maver. Multiple eigenspaces. *Pattern Recognition*, 35(11):2613–2627, 2002.
13. Hiroshi Murase and Shree K. Nayar. Illumination planning for object recognition using parametric eigenspaces. *IEEE Trans. on Pattern Analysis and Machine Intelligence*, (12):1219–1227, 1994.
14. Hiroshi Murase and Shree K. Nayar. Detection of 3D objects in cluttered scenes using hirearchical eigenspace. *Pattern recognition letters*, (18):375–384, 1997.
15. S. K. Nayar, S. A. Nene, and H. Murase. Subspace methods for robot vision. *IEEE Trans. on Robotics and Automation*, 12(5):750–758, October 1996.
16. S.K. Nayar and T. Poggio, editors. *Early visual learning*. Oxford University Press, 1996.
17. Rolf Pfeifer and Christian Scheier. *Understanding Intelligence*. MIT Press, Cambridge, 2001.
18. J. Ponce, A. Zisserman, and M. Hebert, editors. *Object Representation in Computer Vision II, ECCV'96 Int. Workshop, Cambridge*, volume 1114 of *Lecture Notes in Computer Science*. Springer, 1996.
19. Sam Roweis. EM algorithms for PCA and SPCA. In *Neural Information Processing Systems 10 (NIPS'97)*, pages 626–632, 1997.
20. Danijel Skočaj, Horst Bischof, and Aleš Leonardis. A robust PCA algorithm for building representations from panoramic images. In *Proc. ECCV02*, volume IV, pages 761–775. Springer, 2002.
21. M. Turk and A. Pentland. Face recognition using eigenfaces. In *Proc. Computer Vision and Pattern Recognition, CVPR-91*, pages 586–591, 1991.

Discriminant Isometric Mapping for Face Recognition

Ming-Hsuan Yang

Honda Research Institute
Mountain View, CA 94041
myang@honda-ri.com

Abstract. Recently the Isometric mapping (Isomap) method has demonstrated promising results in finding low dimensional manifolds from data points in the high dimensional input space. While classical subspace methods use Euclidean or Manhattan metrics to represent distances between data points and apply Principal Component Analysis to induce linear manifolds, the Isomap method estimates geodesic distances between data points and then uses Multi-Dimensional Scaling to induce low dimensional manifolds. Since the Isomap method is developed based on reconstruction principle, it may not be optimal from the classification viewpoint. In this paper, we present a discriminant isometric method that utilizes Fisher Linear Discriminant for pattern classification. Numerous experiments on three image databases show that our extension is more effective than the original Isomap method for pattern classification. Furthermore, the proposed method shows promising results compared with best methods in the face recognition literature.

1 Motivation and Approach

Subspace methods can be classified into two main categories: either based on reconstruction (i.e., retaining maximum sample variance) or classification principle (i.e., maximizing the distances between samples). Principal Component Analysis (PCA) and Multidimensional Scaling (MDS) have been applied to numerous applications and have shown their abilities to find low dimensional structures from high dimensional samples [4]. Oftentimes these unsupervised methods are effective in finding compact representations and useful for data interpolation and visualization with appropriate distance metrics. On the other hand, Fisher Linear Discriminant (FLD) and alike have shown their successes in pattern classification when class labels are available [2] [4]. Contrasted to PCA which finds a projection direction that retains maximum variance, FLD finds a projection direction that maximizes the distances between cluster centers. Consequently, FLD-based methods have been shown to perform well in classification problems such as face recognition [1] [13] [10].

Two dimensionality reduction methods have recently been proposed for learning complex embedding manifolds using local geometric metrics within a single global coordinate system [7] [11]. The Isomap (or isometric feature mapping)

J.L. Crowley et al. (Eds.): ICVS 2003, LNCS 2626, pp. 470–480, 2003.
© Springer-Verlag Berlin Heidelberg 2003

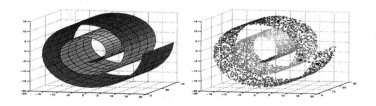

Fig. 1. A complex manifold that shows why Euclidean distances may not be good metrics in pattern recognition.

method argues that only the geodesic distance reflects the intrinsic geometry of the underlying manifold [11]. Figure 1 shows one example where data points of different classes are displayed in distinct shaded patches (left) and data points sampled from these classes are shown (right). For a pair of points on the manifold, their Euclidean distance may not accurately reflect their intrinsic similarity and consequently is not suitable for determining intrinsic embedding or pattern classification. The Euclidean distance between circled data points (e.g., x_1 and x_2 in Figure 1) may be deceptively small in the three-dimensional input space though their geodesic distance on a intrinsic two-dimensional manifold is large. This problem can be remedied by using geodesic distance (i.e., distance metrics along the surface of the manifold) if one is able to compute or estimate such metrics. The Isomap method first constructs a neighborhood graph that connects each point to all its k-nearest neighbors, or to all the points within some fixed radius ϵ in the input space. For neighboring points, the input space distance usually provides a good approximation to their geodesic distance. For each pair of points, the shortest path connecting them in the neighborhood graph is computed and is used as an estimate of the true geodesic distance. These estimates are good approximations of the true geodesic distances if there are sufficient number of data points (See Figure 1). The classical multidimensional scaling method is then applied to construct a low dimensional subspace that best preserves the manifold's estimated intrinsic geometry.

The Locally Linear Embedding (LLE) method captures local geometric properties of complex embedding manifolds by a set of linear coefficients that best approximates each data point from its neighbors in the input space [7]. LLE then finds a set of low dimensional points where each can be linearly approximated by its neighbors with the same set of coefficients that was computed from the high dimensional data points in the input space while minimizing reconstruction cost. Although these two methods have demonstrated excellent results in finding the embedding manifolds that best describe the data points with minimum reconstruction error, they are suboptimal from the classification viewpoint. Furthermore, these two methods assume that the embedding manifold is well sampled which may not be the case in some classification problems such as face recognition since there are typically only a few samples available for each person.

In this paper, we propose a method that extends the Isomap method with Fisher Linear Discriminant for classification. The crux of this method is to estimate geodesic distance, similar to what is done in Isomap, and use pairwise geodesic distances as feature vectors. We then apply FLD to find an optimal projection direction to maximize the distances between cluster centers. Experimental results on three databases show that the extended Isomap method consistently performs better than the Isomap method, and performs better than or as equally well as some best methods in the face recognition literature.

2   Discriminant Isometric Mapping

Consider a set of m samples $\{\mathbf{x}_1, \ldots, \mathbf{x}_m\}$ and each sample belongs to one of the c class $\{Z_1, \ldots, Z_c\}$, the first step in the extended Isomap method is, similar to the Isomap method, to determine the neighbors of each sample $\mathbf{x}_i$ on the low dimensional manifold M based on some distance metrics $d_X(\mathbf{x}_i, \mathbf{x}_j)$ in the input space X. Such metrics can be Euclidean distance that is often used in face recognition [12] or tangent distance that has been shown to be effective in hand digit recognition [9]. The assumption is that input space distance provides a good approximation to geodesic distance for neighboring points (See Figure 1). Consequently, input space distance metric can be utilized to determine whether two data points are neighbors or not. The k-Isomap method uses a k-nearest neighbor algorithm to determine neighbors while the ϵ-Isomap method includes all the points within some fixed radius ϵ as neighbors. These neighborhood relationships are represented in a weighted graph G in which $d_G(\mathbf{x}_i, \mathbf{x}_j) = d_X(\mathbf{x}_i, \mathbf{x}_j)$ if $\mathbf{x}_i$ and $\mathbf{x}_j$ are neighbors, and $d_X(\mathbf{x}_i, \mathbf{x}_j) = \infty$ otherwise.

The next step is to estimate geodesic distance $d_M(\mathbf{x}_i, \mathbf{x}_j)$ between any pair of points on the manifold M. For a pair of points that are far away, their geodesic distance can be approximated by a sequence of short hops between neighboring data points. In other words, $d_M(\mathbf{x}_i, \mathbf{x}_j)$ is approximated by the shortest path between $\mathbf{x}_i$ and $\mathbf{x}_j$ on G, which is computed by the Floyd-Warshall algorithm [3]:

$$d_G(\mathbf{x}_i, \mathbf{x}_j) = \min\{d_G(\mathbf{x}_i, \mathbf{x}_j), d_G(\mathbf{x}_i, \mathbf{x}_k) + d_G(\mathbf{x}_k, \mathbf{x}_j)\}$$

The shortest paths between any two points are represented in a matrix D where $D_{ij} = d_G(\mathbf{x}_i, \mathbf{x}_j)$.

The main difference between extended Isomap and the original method is that we represent each data point by a feature vector of its geodesic distance to any points, and then apply Fisher Linear Discriminant on the feature vectors to find an optimal projection direction for classification. In other words, the feature vector of $\mathbf{x}_i$ is an m dimensional vector $\boldsymbol{f}_i = [D_{ij}]$ where $j = 1, \ldots, m$ and $D_{ii} = 0$.

The between-class and within-class scatter matrices in Fisher Linear Discriminant are computed by:

$$\begin{aligned} S_B &= \sum_{i=1}^{c} N_i(\boldsymbol{\mu}_i - \boldsymbol{\mu})(\boldsymbol{\mu}_i - \boldsymbol{\mu})^T \\ S_W &= \sum_{i=1}^{c} \sum_{\boldsymbol{f}_k \in Z_i} (\boldsymbol{f}_k - \boldsymbol{\mu}_i)(\boldsymbol{f}_k - \boldsymbol{\mu}_i)^T \end{aligned}$$

where μ is the mean of all samples f_k, μ_i is the mean of class Z_i, S_{Wi} is the covariance of class Z_i, and N_i is the number of samples in class Z_i. The optimal projection W_{FLD} is chosen as the matrix with orthonormal columns which maximizes the ratio of the determinant of the between-class scatter matrix of the projected samples to the determinant of the within-class scatter matrix of the projected samples:

$$W_{FLD} = \arg\max_W \frac{|W^T S_B W|}{|W^T S_W W|} = [\mathbf{w}_1 \ \mathbf{w}_2 \ \ldots \ \mathbf{w}_m]$$

where $\{\mathbf{w}_i | i = 1, 2, \ldots, m\}$ is the set of generalized eigenvectors of S_B and S_W, corresponding to the m largest generalized eigenvalues $\{\lambda_i | i = 1, 2, \ldots, m\}$. The rank of S_B is $c-1$ or less because it is the sum of c matrices of rank one or less. Thus, there are at most $c-1$ nonzero eigenvalues [4]. Finally, each data point $\mathbf{x}_i$ is represented by a low dimensional feature vector computed by $\mathbf{y}_i = W_{FLD} \, f_i$. The extended Isomap algorithm is summarized in Figure 2.

---

1. **Constructing neighboring graph**
   First compute Euclidean distance, $d_X(\mathbf{x}_i, \mathbf{x}_j)$ between any two points $\mathbf{x}_i$ and $\mathbf{x}_j$ in the input space X. Next connect neighbors of any point $\mathbf{x}_i$ by finding its k-nearest neighbors or all the points that are within ϵ radius of $\mathbf{x}_i$. The procedure results in a weighted graph $d_G(\mathbf{x}_i, \mathbf{x}_j)$ where

$$d_G(\mathbf{x}_i, \mathbf{x}_j) = \begin{cases} d_X(\mathbf{x}_i, \mathbf{x}_j) & \text{if } \mathbf{x}_i \text{ and } \mathbf{x}_j \text{ are neighbors} \\ \infty & \text{otherwise.} \end{cases}$$

2. **Computing shortest path between pairs of points**
   Compute shortest path between any pair of points $\mathbf{x}_i$ and $\mathbf{x}_j$ on d_G using Floyd-Warshall algorithm, i.e.,

$$d_G(\mathbf{x}_i, \mathbf{x}_j) = \min\{d_G(\mathbf{x}_i, \mathbf{x}_j), d_G(\mathbf{x}_i, \mathbf{x}_k) + d_G(\mathbf{x}_k, \mathbf{x}_j)\}$$

   The shortest paths between any two points are represented in a matrix D where $D_{ij} = d_G(\mathbf{x}_i, \mathbf{x}_j)$.

3. **Determining most discriminant components**
   Represent each point $\mathbf{x}_i$ by a feature vector f_i where $f_i = [D_{ij}]$, $j = 1, \ldots, m$. Determine a subspace where the class centers are separated as far as possible by using the Fisher Linear Discriminant method.

Fig. 2. Extended Isomap Algorithm.

The computational complexity and memory requirement of the Isomap and the extended Isomap are dominated by the calculation of all pair shortest paths. The Floyd-Warshall algorithm requires $O(m^3)$ operations and stores $O(m^2)$ elements of estimated geodesic distances for straightforward implementations. On the other hand, the MDS procedure in the Isomap method can be time consuming as a result of its iterative operations to detect meaningful underlying dimensions that explain the observed similarities or dissimilarities (distances) between data points.

It can be shown that the graph $d_G(\mathbf{x}_i, \mathbf{x}_j)$ provides increasing better estimates to the intrinsic geodesic distance $d_M(\mathbf{x}_i, \mathbf{x}_j)$ as the number of data points increases [11]. In practice, there may not be sufficient number samples at one's disposal so that the geodesic distances $d_G(\mathbf{x}_i, \mathbf{x}_j)$ may not be good approximates. Consequently, the Isomap may not be able to find intrinsic dimensionality from data points and not suitable for classification purpose. In contrast, the extended Isomap method utilizes the distances between the scatter centers and thus may perform well for classification problem in such situations. While the Isomap method uses classical MDS to find dimensions of the embedding manifolds, the dimensionality of the subspace is determined by the number of class (i.e., $c - 1$) in the extended Isomap method.

To deal with the singularity problem of within-scatter matrix S_W that one often encounters in classification problems, we can add a multiple of the identity matrix to the within-scatter matrix, i.e., $S_W + \varepsilon I$ (where ε is a small number). This also makes the eigenvalue problem numerically more stable. See also [1] for a method using PCA to overcome singularity problems in applying FLD to face recognition.

3   Experiments

We applied the proposed discriminant isometric method to the classical appearance-based face recognition, and compared its performance with the original Isomap methods using three databases. In the appearance-based face recognition approach, each face image provides a rich description of one's identity and as a whole (i.e., holistic) is usually treated as a pattern without extracting features explicitly. We tested both the original and extended Isomap methods against LLE [7], Eigenface [12] and Fisherface [1] methods using the publicly available AT&T [8], Yale[1], and UMIST [5] databases. The face images in these databases have several unique characteristics. While the images in the AT&T database contain facial contours and vary slightly in pose as well as scale, the face images in the Yale database have been cropped and aligned. The face images in the AT&T database were acquired under well controlled lighting conditions whereas the images in the Yale database were acquired under varying lighting conditions. On the other hand, the UMIST database contains face images acquired under large varying pose (from profile to frontal view). We used the first two databases to analyze their performance since they comprise dense samples and allow both the original and extended Isomap method to approximate geodesic distance well. Then we used the third one to evaluate face recognition methods under varying lighting conditions where only sparse samples are available. Note also that we apply a simple nearest neighbor classifier to all the projected samples in all the experiments for baseline studies. The recognition rates achieved by these methods can certainly be improved by using more sophisticated classifier such as k-nearest neighbor classifier or alike.

3.1 Face Recognition: Variation in Pose and Scale

The AT&T (formerly Olivetti) face database contains 400 images of 40 subjects (http://www.uk.research.att.com/facedatabase.html). To reduce computational complexity, each face image is downsampled to 23 × 28 pixels for experiments. We represent each image by a raster scan vector of the intensity values, and then normalize them to be zero-mean unit-variance vectors. Figure 3 shows images of a few subjects. In contrast to images of the Yale database shown in Figure 7, these images include facial contours, and variations in pose as well as scale. However, the lighting conditions remain relatively constant.

Fig. 3. Face images in the AT&T database.

The experiments were performed using the "leave-one-out" strategy (i.e., m fold cross validation): To classify an image of a person, that image is removed from the training set of $(m - 1)$ images and the projection matrix is computed. All the m images in the training set are projected to a reduced space and recognition is performed using a nearest neighbor classifier. The parameters, such as number of principal components in Eigenface and LLE methods, were empirically determined to achieve the lowest error rate by each method. For Fisherface and extended Isomap methods, we project all samples onto a subspace spanned by the $c - 1$ largest eigenvectors. The experimental results are shown in Figure 4. Among all the methods, the extended Isomap method with ϵ radius implementation achieves the lowest error rate and outperforms the Fisherface method by a significant margin. Notice also that two implementations of the extended Isomap (one with k-nearest neighbor, i.e., extended k-Isomap, and the other with ϵ radius, i.e., extended ϵ-Isomap) to determine neighboring data points) consistently perform better than their counterparts in the Isomap method by a significant margin.

3.2 Face Recognition: Large Variation in Pose

The UMIST face database (publicly available at http://images.ee.umist.ac.uk/danny/database.html) comprises 564 images of 20 people where each set covers a range of pose from profile to frontal views (See Figure 5). Each image is downsampled to 23 × 28 pixels for computational efficiency and then represented by a normalized zero-mean unit variance vector.

It is known that the variation of face images of different people with the same pose is much less than the variation of face images of the same person

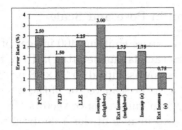

Method	Reduced Space	Error Rate (%)
Eigenface	40	2.50 (10/400)
Fisherface	39	1.50 (6/400)
LLE, # neighbor=70	70	2.25 (9/400)
Isomap, # neighbor=100	45	3.00 (12/400)
Ext Isomap, # neighbor=80	39	1.75 (7/400)
Isomap, ε=10	30	1.75 (7/400)
Ext Isomap, ε=10	39	0.75 (3/400)

Fig. 4. Results with the AT&T database.

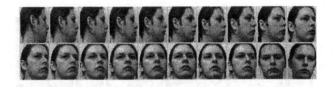

Fig. 5. Face images in UMIST database.

with different pose [5] [6]. Note that even though the UMIST database contains dense samples of face images with pose variation, the Isomap method Figure 6 summarizes the experimental results using leave-one-out setup. Similar to the results presented in the previous sections, the proposed discriminant isometric method outperforms their counterparts.

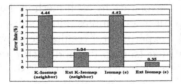

Method	Reduced Space	Error Rate (%)
Isomap, # neighbor=10	30	4.44 (25/565)
Ext Isomap, # neighbor=10	19	1.24 (7/565)
Isomap, ε=12	30	4.42 (25/565)
Ext Isomap, ε=12	19	0.35 (2/565)

Fig. 6. Results with the UMIST database.

3.3   Face Recognition: Variation in Lighting and Expression

The Yale database contains 165 images of 11 subjects with facial expression and lighting variations (available at http://cvc.yale.edu/). For computational efficiency, each image has been downsampled to 29×41 pixels. Similarly, each face image is represented by a centered vector of normalized intensity values. Figure 7 shows closely cropped images of a few subjects which include internal facial structures such as the eyebrow, eyes, nose, mouth and chin, but do not contain facial contours.

Fig. 7. Face images in the Yale database.

Using the same leave-one-out strategy, we varied the number of principal components to achieve the lowest error rates for Eigenface and LLE methods. For Fisherface and extended Isomap methods, we project all samples onto a subspace spanned by the $c - 1$ largest eigenvectors. The experimental results are shown in Figure 8. Both implementations of the extended Isomap method perform better than their counterparts in the Isomap method. Furthermore, the extended ϵ-Isomap method performs almost as well as the Fisherface method (which is one of the best methods in the face recognition literature) though the original Isomap does not work well on the Yale database.

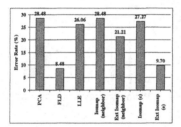

Method	Reduced Space	Error Rate (%)
Eigenface	30	28.48 (47/165)
Fisherface	14	8.48 (14/165)
LLE, # neighbor=10	30	26.06 (43/165)
Isomap, # neighbor=50	50	28.48 (47/165)
Ext Isomap, # neighbor=25	14	21.21 (35/165)
Isomap, ϵ=20	60	27.27 (45/165)
Ext Isomap, ϵ=12	14	9.70 (16/165)

Fig. 8. Results with the Yale database.

Figure 9 shows more performance comparisons between Isomap and extended Isomap methods in both k-nearest neighbor as well as ϵ radius implementations. The extended Isomap method consistently outperforms the Isomap method with both implementations in all the experiments.

As one example to explain why extended Isomap performs better than Isomap, Figure 10 shows training and test samples of the Yale database projected onto the first two eigenvectors extracted by both methods. The projected samples of different classes are smeared by the Isomap method (Figure 10(a)) whereas the samples projected by the extended Isomap method are separated well (Figure 10(b)).

4 Concluding Remarks

In this paper, we present an extended Isomap method for pattern classification when the labels of data points are available. The Isomap method is developed

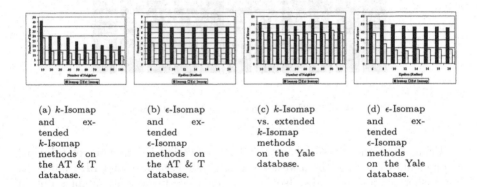

(a) k-Isomap and extended k-Isomap methods on the AT & T database.

(b) ϵ-Isomap and extended ϵ-Isomap methods on the AT & T database.

(c) k-Isomap vs. extended k-Isomap methods on the Yale database.

(d) ϵ-Isomap and extended ϵ-Isomap methods on the Yale database.

Fig. 9. Performance of the Isomap and the extended Isomap methods.

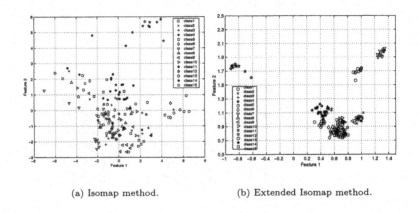

(a) Isomap method.

(b) Extended Isomap method.

Fig. 10. Samples projected by the Isomap and the extended Isomap methods.

based on reconstruction principle, and thus it may not be optimal from the classification viewpoint. Our extension is based on Fisher Linear Discriminant which aims to find an optimal project direction such that the data points in the subspace are separated as far away as possible.

Our experiments on face recognition suggest a number of conclusions:

- The extended Isomap method performs consistently better than the Isomap method in classification (with both k nearest neighbor and ϵ radius implementations).
- Geodesic distance appears to be a better metric than Euclidean distance for face recognition in all the experiments.
- The extended Isomap method performs better than one of the best methods in the literature on the AT &T database. When there exist sufficient number of samples so that the shortest paths between any pair of data points are good

approximates of geodesic distances, the extended Isomap method performs well in classification.

- The extended Isomap method still performs well while the Isomap method does not in the experiments with the Yale database. One explanation is that insufficient samples result in poor approximates of geodesic distances. However, the discriminant isometric method still manages to finds a subspace where the samples are separated as much as possible.
- Though the Isomap and LLE methods have demonstrated excellent results in finding the embedding manifolds that best describe the data points with minimum reconstruction error, they are suboptimal from the classification viewpoint. Furthermore, these two methods assume that the embedding manifold is well sampled which may not be the case in face recognition since there are typically only a few samples available for each person.

Our future work will focus on efficient methods for estimating geodesic distance, and performance evaluation with large and diverse databases. We plan to extend our method by applying the kernel tricks, such as kernel Fisher Linear Discriminant, to provide a richer feature representation for pattern classification. We also plan to compare the extended Isomap method against other learning algorithms with UCI machine learning databases, as well as reported face recognition methods using FERET and CMU PIE databases.

References

1. P. Belhumeur, J. Hespanha, and D. Kriegman. Eigenfaces vs. Fisherfaces: Recognition using class specific linear projection. *IEEE Transactions on Pattern Analysis and Machine Intelligence*, 19(7):711–720, 1997.
2. C. M. Bishop. *Neural Networks for Pattern Recognition*. Oxford University Press, 1995.
3. T. H. Cormen, C. E. Leiserson, and R. L. Rivest. *Introduction to Algorithms*. The MIT Press and McGraw-Hill Book Company, 1989.
4. R. O. Duda, P. E. Hart, and D. G. Stork. *Pattern Classification*. Wiley-Interscience, New York, 2001.
5. D. B. Graham and N. M. Allinson. Characterizing virtual eigensignatures for general purpose face recognition. In H. Wechsler, P. J. Phillips, V. Bruce, F. Fogelman-Soulie, and T. S. Huang, editors, *Face Recognition: From Theory to Applications*, pages 446–456. Springer-Verlag, 1998.
6. B. Raytchev and H. Murase. Unsupervised face recognition from image sequences based on clustering with attraction and repulsion. In *Proceedings of IEEE Conference on Computer Vision and Pattern Recognition*, volume 2, pages 25–30, 2001.
7. S. T. Roweis and L. K. Saul. Nonlinear dimensionality reduction by locally linear embedding. *Science*, 290(5500), 2000.
8. F. Samaria and S. Young. HMM based architecture for face identification. *Image and Vision Computing*, 12(8):537–583, 1994.
9. P. Simard, Y. Le Cun, and J. Denker. Efficient pattern recognition using a new transformation distance. In S. J. Hanson, J. D. Cowan, and C. L. Giles, editors, *Advances in Neural Information Processing Systems*, volume 5, pages 50–58. Morgan Kaufmann, San Mateo, CA, 1993.

10. D. L. Swets and J. Weng. Hierarchical discriminant analysis for image retrieval. *IEEE Transactions on Pattern Analysis and Machine Intelligence*, 21(5):386–401, 1999.

11. J. B. Tenenbaum, V. de Silva, and J. C. Langford. A global geometric framework for nonlinear dimensionality reduction. *Science*, 290(5500), 2000.

12. M. Turk and A. Pentland. Eigenfaces for recognition. *Journal of Cognitive Neuroscience*, 3(1):71–86, 1991.

13. W. Zhao, R. Chellappa, and A. Krishnaswamy. Discriminant analysis of principal components for face recognition. In *Proceedings of the Third International Conference on Automatic Face and Gesture Recognition*, pages 336–341, 1998.

Extracting Salient Image Features for Reliable Matching Using Outlier Detection Techniques

Dimitri Lisin, Edward Riseman, and Allen Hanson

Department of Computer Science, UMASS - Amherst, Amherst, MA, USA

Abstract. This paper presents an efficient method for finding salient differential features in images. We argue that the problem of finding salient features among all the possible ones is equivalent to finding outliers in a high-dimensional data set. We apply outlier detection techniques used in data mining to devise a linear time algorithm to extract the salient features. This yields a definition of saliency which rests on a more principled basis and also produces more reliable feature correspondences between images than the more conventional ones.

1 Introduction

Extracting *salient* features is often a crucial preprocessing step for image analysis. Many vision tasks, such as object recognition, object detection, and stereo matching require establishing correspondences between point features from different images. Most often it is infeasible to consider potential features at every pixel in the image, so only a key subset, called *salient features*, are used.

In the worst case the salient features are identified by hand [2], but more often a general definition of saliency is used. Often corners, are considered salient [14], and also edges and blobs can be added to the set of salient features [9].

In this paper we define an image feature the same way as in [9], as a vector of Gaussian derivative responses at a pixel over a range of scales, In particular, we use the first and the second derivatives over three consecutive scales. Thus, a feature is defined at every pixel of every scale of the image, except for the topmost and the bottom-most scales. We use the normalized inner product between two feature vectors as a measure of similarity between the corresponding features. The normalization provides a degree of invariance to linear changes in intensity.

We argue that the space of all features in an image can be viewed as a large multi-dimensional data set, and the *salient points correspond to the outliers of the set*. We show that density-based outlier detection techniques [5], [1] used in data mining are applicable to the problem of finding salient features. We use these techniques together with the smoothness property of the feature space described in section 4 to devise a linear time algorithm to detect the salient features. Our definition of saliency rests on a more principled basis, and intuitively it seems

---

[1] This work was funded in part by a Fellowship from Eastman Kodak Company Research Labs.

J.L. Crowley et al. (Eds.): ICVS 2003, LNCS 2626, pp. 481–491, 2003.
© Springer-Verlag Berlin Heidelberg 2003

to be more natural than those commonly used because it is derived from the structure of the feature space itself.

We present experiments in which we establish correspondences between features in pairs of images using only the feature similarity and the self-consistency constraint described in section 7. No other constraints are assumed. The experiments show, that features that are salient according to our definition produce more reliable correspondences than ones defined by more traditional means. Of course, many systems that require correspondences do use other constraints to successfully disambiguate the matches [14], [9]. However, extracting features that are salient according to our definition can be a useful preprocessing step, which may improve the overall accuracy of such systems and it may reduce the time required for disambiguating the matches.

2   Salient Features as Outliers

The problem of finding outliers in high-dimensional data sets arises in data mining. It is assumed that points in a data set form clusters, and outliers are points that do not belong to any of the clusters. In the context of data mining outliers represent unusual cases, such as fraud and other criminal activity in e-commerce.

Hawkins [4] defines an outlier as "an observation that deviates so much from other observations as to arouse suspicion that it was generated by a different mechanism." On the other hand, the word *salient* is defined by the Webster's Dictionary as *prominent*. It is the opinion of the authors that the two definitions really point to the same concept. In particular, a multi-dimensional space of image features is really nothing more than a large data set. Intuitively we can see that features similar to many others would form clusters, while distinct features, which we might call *salient*, would be the outliers.

In contrast, one could also examine the clusters that exist in the feature space, as opposed to the outliers. Patterns formed by these clusters also carry information about the appearance of the scene in an image, and may be useful for recognition. Such an approach would be similar to the histogram-based technique described in [10], which uses the global distribution of differential features for recognition. However, this paper deals with point features, which may be used in applications other than object recognition, such as stereo matching and object detection. Point feature correspondences also offer ways to recover the three dimensional structure of scenes and objects, which is not possible with purely appearance-based approaches. Therefore, it is not the clustering, but the outlier detection algorithms that interest us.

In this paper we examine two such algorithms: the distance-based $DB(p, D)$ scheme [5], and the Local Outlier Factor approach [1]. We will show that with minor modifications both are applicable to our problem, and that the latter yields superior results.

3   Related Work

This work has been inspired by [9], which presents a system for learning differential features to recognize objects. In this paper, however, we only focus on the problem of establishing correspondences between point features. We propose methods for finding features that are likely to be matched correctly, and we defer the question of how to use them to the future work. We will present an overview of the existing definitions of salient point features, but we consider salient edges, curves, etc. to be outside the scope of this paper.

3.1   Saliency

Most often salient point features are defined as the local extrema of some function of the image. One example is using corners, or points of high curvature as salient [14]. Also, local maxima of "blobs" (the trace of the Hessian) and the gradient magnitude can be used [9]. Since such functions are combinations of image derivatives they can be computed very fast. Another interesting example is presented in [12], where a multiscale decomposition of an image is computed using a 1D wavelet at various orientations, and the local maxima of the sum of the wavelet responses are used as salient features.

A definition of saliency most similar to the one presented by this paper is given is [13]. In this work the feature components are the differential invariants at a pixel over a range of scales, and the Mahalanobis metric is used as feature distance. The saliency is defined in terms of the density of the feature space. Lower density regions correspond to higher saliency. This makes sense, because features at the low density regions of the space are unlike most others, and therefore are less likely to be mismatched.

In [13] a multivariate Gaussian mixture model of the feature space is used as a density function, whose local minima are considered salient. The main drawback of this approach is its time complexity, which is quadratic in the total number of features in the space. The problem can be alleviated by modeling a randomly sampled subset of the features instead of the entire space. This reduces the number of features that need to processed, but the time complexity is still $O(n^2)$.

The approach described in this paper is similar to that of [13] in that it uses the density of the feature space to define saliency. However, we use local outlier detection techniques which give us a more precise and well-founded definition of saliency. We also use the smoothness property of the feature space to reduce the time complexity to linear.

3.2   Multiscale Differential Features

The Gaussian and its derivatives are a family of kernels used to generate a linear isotropic scale-space of an image, which has been studied extensively under scale-space theory [8]. Image derivatives define the local behavior of the intensity surface, which makes them useful for describing the image features. Using Gaussian derivative filters at a range of σ's allows us to analyze the surface patches of varying sizes.

Our definition of a feature at a pixel and a particular scale σ_i is a vector of Gaussian derivative responses at three scales: $\sigma_{i-1}, \sigma_i, \sigma_{i+1}$. We use the first and the second derivatives [9]. Since we have 2 components of a first derivative, and 3 components of the second over 3 scales, our feature space has 15 dimensions. Using multiple scales increases the specificity of a feature.

This feature representation is not invariant to in-plane rotation. For the purpose of this paper we set up our experiments so that such invariance is not required. If, however, it is required the steerability property of the Gaussian derivative filters can be used as in [9], or, alternatively, the rotationally invariant combinations of derivatives can be used as in [13]. Our definition of saliency should still be applicable in these cases, but more experiments are needed to be certain.

4   Fast Density Estimation Using Smoothness

The outlier detection techniques that we consider in this paper use a notion of density of the data points in the space to find the outliers. We therefore need a way to compute the density of our feature space at every feature. One example of such a method is presented in [13], and it has been discussed in section 3.1. Recall that it takes $O(n^2)$ time, where n is the number of features.

A simpler way to estimate local density at a particular feature f is to compute the distance to the farthest of its k nearest neighbors, for some natural number k. We will denote the farthest neighbor as f_d, and the distance from f to f_d as $r(f)$, which is the radius of the smallest hyper-sphere containing the k nearest neighbors of f. Since we use a similarity measure rather than distance between features, in our case $r(f)$ is the similarity to the least similar of the neighbors. The problem with this approach is that first we need to determine what the k nearest neighbors of a feature are. This would require comparing each feature to every other feature, and would also take $O(n^2)$ time.

In this section we will show that our feature space is smooth, such that features that are neighbors in the image, also tend to be neighbors in the feature space. This will allow us to treat the nearest neighbors of a feature in the image as its nearest neighbors in the feature space, and reduce the time complexity of the density estimation to $O(n)$.

A Gaussian derivative response at some pixel (x, y), and some scale σ is obviously a function of x, y, and σ. Therefore, the features form a 3D manifold in a 15D space. Because we use Gaussian derivatives, the image at each scale σ is blurred which causes its derivatives to be smooth. As a result, the whole manifold has to be smooth, especially for the coarser scales. Figure 1 illustrates this idea. The top row shows the image of a mobile robot at 3 scales, and the bottom row shows a plot of the first x derivative (I_x) vs. the first y-derivative (I_y) of each corresponding scale plane. Each plot is a 2D projection of a plane's submanifold. We can see that the sub-manifolds, as expected, become progressively smoother as we move to coarser scales.

The smoothness property directly implies that features that are neighbors in the image (*image-neighbors*) also tend to be neighbors in the feature manifold (*actual-neighbors*). We make a stronger assumption:

Conjecture 1. 8 *immediate* neighbors of a feature in the image are also its 8 *nearest* neighbors in the feature manifold.

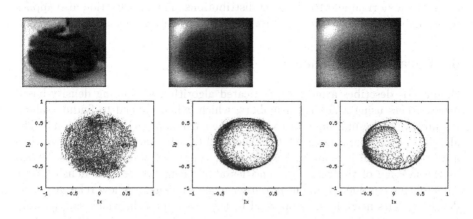

Fig. 1. Scale planes 1, 5, and 9, with $\sigma = \sqrt{2}, 4\sqrt{2}, 16\sqrt{2}$ respectively, and their corresponding feature sub-manifolds

Conjecture 1 gives us 8-nearest actual-neighbors of a feature, "for free" without us having to search the entire feature space. This is what allows us to reduce the time complexity to linear. Experimental results supporting the conjecture are given in [7]. This assumption would not hold true for images with high contrast repetitive patterns. Because of this our approaches may not work well for the natural outdoor scenes, but they should be quite suitable for the indoor ones.

5   A Naive Approach to Outlier Detection

A simple approach to find outliers is to compute the density, $r(f)$, for each feature f at every pixel in the image at every scale to create a density map. The local minima of the density correspond to salient features. We call this approach naive, because we present a more sophisticated scheme in section 6.

This algorithm runs in linear time in the number of features. It takes $8N$ feature comparisons to compute $r(f)$ for every feature f and $26N$ comparisons of floating point numbers to find the local minima across scales, where N is the total number of features. The dimensionality of the feature space only affects the time it takes to compare two features, and this dependency is also linear.

This algorithm is related to the distance-based $DB(p, D)$ outlier detection scheme presented in [5]. In the scheme a data point o in a data set T is considered an outlier if at least fraction p of the points in T lie greater than distance D from o. Essentially, a DB outlier minimizes the number of neighbors it has within a fixed hyper-sphere, and a naive salient feature maximizes the hyper-sphere containing its 8 nearest neighbors. In effect, they both minimize the ratio of the number of neighbors to the volume of the hyper-sphere containing them, i. e. the local density of the space.

[5] formally shows that the DB scheme is a generalization of statistical outlier tests for the normal and the Poisson distributions. This justification also applies to our naive approach, since we have shown its essential equivalence to DB.

6   Local Outlier Factor

Breunig [1] describes a more sophisticated algorithm for finding density-based local outliers using k-nearest neighbors, which, when applied to finding salient features, yields results superior to that of the naive approach from section 5. The algorithm computes a Local Outlier Factor (LOF) for each data point, which is a degree to which it is an outlier. $LOF(p)$, where p is a data point, is defined as the average of the ratios of densities at p's neighbors to the density at p. This scheme considers a point an outlier when its density is low relative to the densities at its neighbors, as opposed to the DB approach, which simply looks for low absolute density. It is more reasonable, because low density alone may not necessarily be characteristic of an outlier, e.g. in a case when the whole data set is very sparse.

We use the same procedure to compute the local density for this algorithm as we do for the naive approach, so the time complexity is still $O(n)$. The details of our implementation of LOF are described in [7]. In section 7 we show empirical justification for preferring LOF over the naive approach.

7   Results

During testing we establish correspondences between pairs of images using the self-consistency constraint, similar to the one in [6] and [11]. Let F_1 and F_2 be the sets of salient features from two images. We call $f \in F_1$ and $f' \in F_2$ a self-consistent match if features f and f' are mutually maximally similar. This ensures that the matches are bidirectional between the two images, and increases their reliability.

We tested our approach using synthetic images, where correctness of the matches could be verified automatically, and real images, where where it had to be done manually. We wrote a simple GUI, which shows the reference image with a particular feature f, and the target image with matching feature f', and lets a user indicate correctness by pressing a key. We compute and report the percentage of correct matches. No special preprocessing, such as histogram thresholding, is done on the test images before the salient features are extracted.

To evaluate our approaches we compare the percentages they yield to those produced by using corners and edges, which are common ways to extract salient features. We define corners the same way as [9] as local maxima of

$$s_{corner}(\sigma) = \sigma^4 |I_{yy}^2 I_{xx} - 2I_x I_y I_{xy} + I_{xx}^2 I_{yy}|, \qquad (1)$$

where image derivatives are computed by convolving the image I with a Gaussian derivative filter of the appropriate σ. Edges are defined as local maxima of the gradient magnitude. Unlike [9] we compute the local maxima in each scale plane, as opposed to over the entire scale volume. This reduces the amount of computation required and seems to yield greater matching accuracy.

The LOF approach takes into account relative feature space density at a particular feature, so we see no need to use local maxima. Instead we use a threshold .3 times the standard deviation above the mean. This threshold was determined empirically, and further investigation is required to find a more principled way of setting it.

For each saliency definition, we extracted the sets of salient points from the reference and the target images, and sorted them by their saliency. Then, proceding down the reference set in order, we found the first 100 self-consistent matches, and sorted those by the similarity between the matched pairs of features. We took the top 25 of those to be tested for correctness.

7.1 Synthetic Data

To generate synthetic data we used an image of a lab, containing a mobile robot (the target from figure 2), whcih is 320x240 pixels. We cropped out 10 randomly chosen sub-images of size 100x100 pixels from it, and generated a range of scaled images from them by subsampling and interpolating. The scaled images range in size from 50% to 200% of the original sub-image, with the increment of 10%. The matching accuracy is averaged for each scale over the 10 randomly chosen sub-images.

The results of this experiment are summarized in a graph in figure 3. The x-axis represents the scale factor of the sub-image, and the y-axis shows the average matching accuracy as a percentage. The corners performed the worst. Our naive approach was better then the edges when the sub-image was unchanged (scale factor 1), but degraded much less gracefully when the scale changed. The LOF approach performed the best. In fact its accuracy was 50% or higer for the scale factors ranging from .9 to 1.4.

It took 124 seconds to test the corners, on average .8 seconds per image. Edges took approximately the same time, and LOF took 417 s., or 2.6 s. per image. The computation was done on a 2GHz Pentum 4 running Linux. The system can be further optimized, and the computation is naturally parallelizable, since each scale plane can be processed independently.

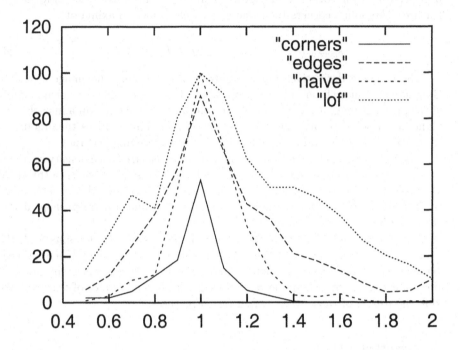

Fig. 2. Accuracy for synthetic data

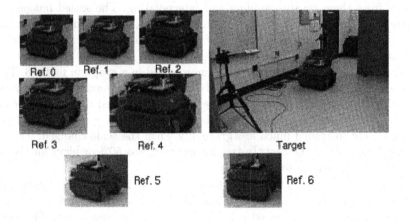

Fig. 3. The reference and target images for task 1.

7.2   Real Data: Task 1

In this series of experiments we matched features from multiple reference images of a mobile robot into a single target, a cluttered scene containing the robot (Figure 2). The reference images 0 - 4 vary in scale with respect to the target. References 5 and 6, while having roughly the same scale, exibit out-of-plane rotation and a background change.

The experimental results for this task are summarized in table 1. It shows that the naive approach performed significantly better then the corner but not as well as the edges. The LOF, however, did as well as the edges in cases 0, 1, and 2, somewhat worse in case 3, and significantly better in cases 4, 5, and 6. Reference 4 has the largest difference in scale from the target, as well as partial occlusion, and references 5 and 6 have out-of-plane rotation, as we mentioned above. Thus the LOF approach appears to be the most robust.

Table 1. Accuracy for task 1.

Ref.	Corners	Edges	Naive	LOF
0	76%	100%	100%	100%
1	52%	96%	92%	96%
2	40%	92%	64%	92%
3	48%	84%	48%	76%
4	0%	28%	8%	44%
5	12%	36%	44%	80%
6	4%	28%	40%	52%

Table 2. Accuracy for task 2.

	Corners	Edges	Naive	LOF
coke	28%	24%	68%	72%
drill	12%	60%	48%	60%
blocks	12%	24%	20%	48%

7.3   Real Data: Task 2

In this task we took three pairs of images produced by cameras mounted on a stereo head and tried to match features from one image to another in each pair. The camera's optical axes are not parallel, so the images in each pair are quite different. No calibration information or any other constraints associated with stereo were used.

The results for the three pairs of images, which we called "coke", "drill", and "blocks" (Figure 4), are summarized in table 2. Here again the LOF approach performed the best.

8   Conclusions and Future Work

In this paper we have presented a novel idea that salient differential features can be viewed as outliers in a high-dimensional space, and therefore outlier detection techniques used in data mining are applicable for their extraction. We have presented two algorithms based on two different outlier detection schemes: the distance-based approach and the LOF. The latter one is a more sophisticated approach, which better fits an intuitive notion of an outlier, and produces more reliable features.

Fig. 4. The image pairs ("coke", "drill", and "blocks") with 25 self-consistent salient features extracted using LOF. The circles' sizes correspond to features' scales.

Further investigation is needed to determine if our concept of saliency can be applied to image features defined by using other means, such as the differential invariants, and using other distance metrics, such as the Mahalanobis distance.

This work is a part of an ongoing effort to build a learning system for object recognition and detection capable of handling an unconstrained environment. The LOF-based salient feature extraction may become an important component of such a system.

References

1. Breunig M. M., Kriegel, H.-P., Ng, R., Sander, J. "LOF: Identifying Density-Based Local Outliers," *Proc. ACM SIGMOD Int. Conf. on Management of Data*, (2000).
2. Delaert, F., Seitz, S. M, Thorpe, C. E., Thrun, S., "Structure from Motion Without Correspondences," *Proc. Computer Vision and Pattern Recognition Conf.*, (2000).

3. Freeman, W. T., and Adelson, E. H. "The design and use of steerable filters," *IEEE Transactions on Pattern Analysis and Machine Intelligence* 13, 9 (1991).

4. Hawkins, D., *Identification of Outliers*, Chapman and Hall, London, (1980).

5. Knorr, E., Ng, R. "Algorithms for Mining Distance-based Outliers in Large Datasets," *Proc. of 24th Int. Conf. On Very Large Data Bases*, (1998).

6. Leclerc, Y.G., Q.T. Luong, et al., "Self-consistency: A novel approach to characterizing the accuracy and reliability of point correspondence algorithms," DARPA Image Understanding Workshop, (1998)

7. Lisin, D., Riseman, E., Hanson, A. "Extracting Salient Image Fetures Using Outlier Detection Techniques," TR UM-CS-2003-002, Dept. of Comp. Sci., UMASS Amherst, (2003)

8. Lindeberg, T. "Feature detection with automatic scale selection," *Intl. Journal of Computer Vision* 30, 2 (1998).

9. Piater, J. *Visual Feature Learning.* Ph.D. dissertation, Dept. of Comp. Sci., UMASS Amherst, (2001).

10. Ravela, S. and A. Hanson, "On Multi-Scale Differential Features for Face Recognition," Vision Interface, Ottawa, (2001).

11. Schultz, H., A. R. Hanson, E. M. Riseman, F. R. Stolle, D. Woo, Z. Zhu, "A Self-consistency Technique for Fusing 3D Information," Invited talk presented at the IEEE 5th Intl. Conf. on Information Fusion, Annapolis, Maryland, (2002).

12. Shokoufandeh, A., Marsic, I., Dickinson, S.J. "View-Based Object Recognition Using Saliency Maps," TR DCS-TR-339, Dept. of Comp. Sci., Rutgers U., (1998).

13. Walker, K. N., Cootes, T. F., Taylor, C. J. "Locating Salient Object Features," Proc. of BMVC, (1998).

14. Zhang, Z., Deriche, R., Faugeras, O., and Luong, Q-T. "A Robust Technique for Matching Two Uncalibrated Images Through the Recovery of the Unknown Epipolar Geometry," *Artificial Intelligence* 78, 1–2, (1995).

Brand Identification Using Gaussian Derivative Histograms

Fabien Pelisson, Daniela Hall, Olivier Riff, and James L. Crowley

Projet PRIMA — Lab. GRAVIR–IMAG
INRIA Rhônes–Alpes
38330 – Montbonnot Saint Martin, France

Abstract. In this article, we describe a module for the identification of brand logos from video data. A model for the visual appearance of each logo is generated from a small number of sample images using multi-dimensional histograms of scale-normalised chromatic Gaussian receptive fields. We compare several state–of–the–art identification techniques, based multi-dimensional histograms. Each of the methods display high recognition rates and can be used for logo identification. Our method for calculating scale normalized Gaussian receptive fields has linear computational complexity, and is thus well adapted to a real time system. However, with the current generation of micro-processors we obtain at best only 2 images per second when processing a full PAL video stream. To accelerate the process, we propose an architecture that applies color based logo detection to initiate a robust tracking process. Tracked logos are then identified off line using receptive field histograms. The resulting real time system is evaluated using video streams from sports Formula-1 races and football.

Keywords: Probabilistic object recognition, histogram matching, invariant feature description

1   Introduction

Advertising is the primary source of revenue for television. During live broadcast of sports events, corporations pay important sums of money to have their logos present in the video production. Because the video stream is edited so as to present the actors and events of the sports match, it is difficult to predict how often and for how long corporate logos will appear. Currently such measures are made by hand after the match, at great cost. There is great demand on the part of both producers and sponsors to have on-line measurement of the frequency and duration of logo appearance in television productions of sporting events.

In this paper we describe a system for real-time detection, identification and tracking of corporate logos in live video of out-door scenes obtained from a bank of cameras that can pan, tilt and zoom. Changing illumination conditions, bad image quality, fast camera motion and significant variations in target size introduce difficult technical problems for our system. Real time detection and

J.L. Crowley et al. (Eds.): ICVS 2003, LNCS 2626, pp. 492–501, 2003.

identification in such a video stream is a particularly challenging problem. We compare different identification strategies with respect to precision and quality of the results. We show how a preprocessing module can be used to overcome limitations in available computing.

Section 2 explains the system architecture and the tasks of the different modules. Section 3 explains the model acquisition step required for identification. In section 4 the different identification algorithms are discussed whose results are given in section 5.

2   System Architecture

In this section we describe the architecture for our real-time logo detection and tracking system. The architecture is shown schematically in figure 1.

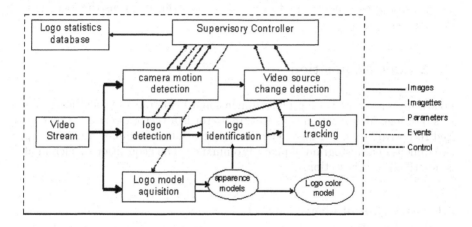

Fig. 1. Architecture of the system

The system is composed of a fast initial detection module based on color histograms and a tracking module using a Kalman filter. The camera motion detection module computes motion the direction and speeds of pan, tilt, and zoom. The module uses results from the other modules such as the motion of targets from the tracking module. A second module detects changes of the camera source. This is an important event, because it requires reinitialization of all other modules. The system contains an off-line process for learning to detect and recognize logos, as described in section 3.

The heart of the system is the logo identification. Reliable detection and recognition can be provided by scale normalized receptive fields [1]. Unfortunately, computing scale normalized receptive fields over 704 x 556 RGB PAL image requires approximately 600 milliseconds using a current generation 1.5

GHz processors. Such a processor can provide receptive fields for a 1/4 PAL scale RGB image. However, in such a case, we loose detection of many logos when the camera is zoomed to wide angle.

The subject of this paper is an architecture in which low-cost color processing is used to detect and track candidate logos. These candidates regions are then recognized using scale normalized receptive fields computed over a limited Region of Interest. This architecture is an example of a reflexive visual process. In such an architecture, a supervisor coordinates the several modules in order to assure robust real-time processing. The supervisor keeps track of targets that have been identified and halts the tracking of a target region when identification fails. The supervisor maintains a description of the system state, and adapts processing in order to maintain video rate under variations in the number and size of targets.

A detection module detects instances of logos as they pass through a detection region, and initiates a tracking process. Once tracking has been established for a logo, it is sent to a detection module. The identification module identifies the regions and passes the results to the supervisor which returns the logo ID and its visibility.

3   Model Acquisition

Logos are represented using multi-dimensional histograms of local feature vectors. For logo identification, this feature vector is a vector of eight scale normalized receptive fields. For logo detection and tracking we employ a much simpler two dimensional histogram of pixel chrominance. The acquisition of such models is described in this section.

3.1   Examples of Logos

Model acquisition requires labeled data. Our experiments are based on the example data displayed in figure 2. The example data must be selected under illumination conditions that are similar to operating conditions. In actual operation, the camera operator will be asked to center a model acquisition region on example of the logos prior to the sporting event. In order to make the acquisition of the training data as simple as possible, we envision a module where a operator marks the corner points of a sample logo. Our experiments have demonstrated that a few such logo observations are sufficient.

3.2   Model Acquisition for Detection Using Chrominance

Publicity displays tend to use color to attract attention. Thus color provides a fast and reliable means to detect potential target regions. The color model for each logo must be acquired from images under actual illumination conditions to eliminate due to the color of the source illumination. We eliminate the effects of illumination intensity (due to clouds or other environmental conditions, by the

Fig. 2. Examples of training data

RGB pixel values to luminance-chrominance space. RGB pixels are transformed to luminance-chrominance space YC_1C_2 according to

$$
\begin{pmatrix} Y \\ C_1 \\ C_2 \end{pmatrix} = \begin{pmatrix} g_r & g_g & g_b \\ \dfrac{3g_g}{2} & -\dfrac{3g_r}{2} & 0 \\ \dfrac{g_b g_r}{g_r^2 + g_g^2} & \dfrac{g_b g_g}{g_r^2 + g_g^2} & -1 \end{pmatrix} \begin{pmatrix} R \\ G \\ B \end{pmatrix} \tag{1}
$$

where g_r, g_b, g_g represent the camera acquisition parameters.

In addition to providing invariance to intensity changes this transformation reduces from 3 to 2 the number of dimensions, thus reducing the number of sample pixels required for training. The number of pixels in the logo samples should have 4 times the number of cells in the chrominance histogram. The optimal number of histogram bins is a trade-off between the number of available sample pixels and the auto-correlation of the probability density function of the chrominance vectors. In our experiments, we have obtained good results with chrominance histograms with 32 bins per axis. Such a histogram has 32 x 32 = 1024 cells and can be reliably constructed using 3 sample imagettes of size 64 x 64 = 4096 pixels.

During model acquisition, two histograms are composed for each logo. The first of these histograms contains only the pixels in the designated logo region. The second contains all of the pixels in the current image. Baye's rule shows that the ratio of these two histograms provides a look-up table that gives the probability of finding a logo pixel given its color.

The detection module uses the ratio of histograms as a look-up table that provides the probability that a pixel is a logo based on its chrominance. These probabilities are thresholded and a simple connected components algorithm is used to remove outliers and provide a region of interest. The first moment (or center of gravity) of the detection probabilities provides an estimate of the position of the logo. The second moment provides an estimate of the spatial extent. These moments are introduced to a robust tracking process that uses the position and size a logo in one frame to specify a region of interest (ROI) for detection in the next image. Tracking maintains the identity of a logo across frames.

3.3   Model Acquisition for Identification

A ratio of color histograms has a low false negative rate and is thus useful for detecting potential candidate regions for logos. However, chrominance results in a significant number of false positives. Thus a more reliable method is required to identify tracked regions.

Gaussian receptive fields [3,5,7,8,9] provide a local feature description that is easily made invariant to scale and orientation [2,4].

In our implementation we use feature vectors composed of 1st and 2nd derivatives in the luminance channel and 0th and 1st derivatives in the chrominance channels. All features are normalized for local orientation and scale. Gaussian derivatives are computed using a fast scale invariant binomial pyramid. We dispose an efficient implementation for filtering using recursive filters [12] and for scale selection using a Laplacian pyramid [1]. The binomial pyramid algorithm allows us to process 43 ROIs per second with an average ROI size of 100×100 pixels.

4   Logo Identification by Histogram Comparison

This section describes alternative techniques that use multi-dimensional receptive field histograms to identify logos. Section 5 provides an experimental comparison of these techniques.

4.1   Identification Based on Distance Measures between Histograms

The first method identifies logos by computing an intersection measure between histograms. We compare a measure similar to the one proposed by Swain and Ballard [11] and by Schwerdt [10]. For a model histogram H and a query histogram Q the intersection measure $d_\cap(H, Q)$ is computed as

$$d_\cap(H, Q) = \frac{\sum_{i \in C} \min(h_i, q_i)}{\sum_{i \in C} q_i} \qquad (2)$$

where h_i and q_i note the number of elements in the histogram cell. C is the subset of non-empty cells of the query histogram Q.

The intersection measure is not symmetric. However, it does enable a comparison of a query histogram with model histograms having different numbers of elements. In our case, this is an important feature, since the model histograms of different logos are based on different number of pixels.

The identification module takes as input a region of interest from the detection module, constructs a query histogram according to the method described in section 3. The intersection is the computed between the query histogram and each of the model histograms in the database. The module returns the identity of the logo model whose intersection measure is a maximum. If the maximum intersection is not above a minimum threshold, then the region is labeled as not containing a logo.

4.2   Identification from Probabilistic Measures

We compared two methods. The first is based on the probabilistic object recognition method used by Schiele in [8]. The second is a variation, which takes into account the distribution of the features in feature space.

Both methods are more general than the intersection measure described above and can be applied to any probability distribution. We have a number of imagettes $O = \{O_1, O_2, \ldots, O_m\}$ of the target logos. From these we compute a sample distribution $p(O, M)$, with M set of all feature vectors. Assuming dependence between the models O_i and the feature vectors m_j, this dependence can be expressed by Bayes rule:

$$p(O_i, m_j) = p(O_i|m_j)p(m_j) = p(m_j|O_i)p(O_i) \tag{3}$$

where $p(O_i)$ is the a priori probability of model O_i, $p(m_j)$ is the a priori probability of the feature vector, and $p(m_j|O_i)$ is the probability of m_j given O_i modeled by the histogram. To enable recognition, we need to compute $p(O_i|m_j)$.

We assume that $p(O_i)$ is uniform and $p(m_k)$ is estimated by the global histogram. Estimating $p(O_i|m_k)$ for a single feature vector is relatively unreliable, because different logos may contain similar regions. The joint probability $p(O_i|\bigwedge_k m_k)$ for a region of feature vectors $m_1, m_2, \ldots, m_n$ provides reliable discrimination. We compute $p(O_i|m_k)$ according to

$$p(O_i|\bigwedge_{k=1}^n m_k) = \frac{\prod_k p(m_k|O_i)p(O_i)}{\prod_k p(m_k)} \tag{4}$$

To solve the identification problem, we calculate for all model objects O_i the probability $p(O_i|\bigwedge_{k=1}^n m_k)$. The identification result is the highest probability above a threshold.

An interesting point is how the feature vectors for identification are selected among the feature vectors in the query region of interest. We compare several strategies. The first strategy corresponds to select feature vectors according to an uniform spatial distribution.

The second strategy, in the following referred to as "distribution", selects the features according to the distribution of the features in feature space. This means that frequent features are selected more often than less frequent features. This has the advantage that features that contribute most to the probability density are represented accordingly. Less frequent features are more sensitive to noise and tend to be unreliable. The disadvantage of this method is that more feature points need to be selected before a reliable response can be returned. On the other hand, an any-time implementation can optimize for either speed or precision.

5   Experimental Evaluation

5.1   The Image Database

Our experiments use logos derived from two mpeg video sequences from formula one races. The logos undergo significant scale changes and we observe rapid camera motion. The images have a resolution of 352 × 288 pixels. The ROIs containing logos have a size from 102 × 31 pixels to 32 × 16 pixels. Connected components smaller than 400 pixels are ignored.

5.2   Performance of the Detection Module

The goal of the detection module is to reduce the surface of the region that is treated by the identification module. The module detects 1 or 2 ROIs per frame. In the case of 2 large ROIs, the speed up is of factor 16 with respect to treating the entire image and in the case of two small ROIs, the speed up reaches factor 99. This justifies the use of a detection module in order to obtain a video-rate logo identification system using available computing power.

Fig. 3. Detection of false positive due to similar color distribution.

On the image database, the detection module detects 85% of the logos in the video sequence. Among the detected ROIs, 28% are false positives. This can be expressed as a precision of 72% and a recall of 85%. Precision and recall are defined as function of correct detections, false positives (insertions) and false negatives (missed targets).

$$\text{precision} = \frac{\text{correct}}{\text{correct} + \text{false positive}} \tag{5}$$

$$\text{recall} = \frac{\text{correct}}{\text{correct} + \text{false negative}} \tag{6}$$

Figure 3 shows a typical case of a false positive detection. The ROI on the right border displays similar color distributions than the "helix" logo. Such outlier regions are very difficult to remove because the module relies only on colour. This problem can not be overcome without losing correct targets. The detection module should run in real time and can therefore not process additional information.

5.3   Performance of the Identification Module

The identification module obtains a list of ROIs from the detection module. For each ROI, the module should return the logo ID, if a logo is present. We have evaluated three methods explained in section 4 (histogram intersection, probabilistic recognition according to uniform and feature space distribution). We observe superior recognition rates for the probabilistic recognition methods (94.7% for the probabilistic methods and 92.6% for the intersection measure).

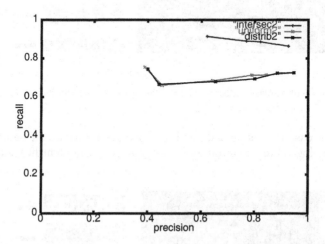

Fig. 4. Precision recall curves for histogram intersection and probabilistic recognition according to uniform distribution and distribution in feature space. All method display high precision. The probabilistic recognition method has lower recall than the histogram intersection measure.

To avoid the selection of a threshold we have generated precision/recall curves (see figure 4) according to equations 5 and 6 and varying over the minimum acceptance threshold. The probabilistic methods miss more targets than the intersection measure. The probabilistic methods select 10% of the points within the ROI. The consideration of 20% or 30% of the points did not improve the performance. This means, that the probabilistic measure has significant advantages concerning computational complexity.

The intersection measure displays high precision and high recall, but requires more computation time. When computation time is crucial, the probabilistic methods should be preferred. The approaches have difficulties in detecting the non-presence of a logo, because the system has not learned a class for "no logo".

Figure 5 shows a typical example of a correct identification. The detection module has found a ROI containing a logo. The probability $p(O_i|ROI)$ is computed for all logos O_i. The highest probability above a threshold is returned as result.

Figure 6 displays a difficult case. Here the gray box is confused with the logo "qantas". A human observer agrees that the box and the logo are similar. This

Fig. 5. Example of a correct identification. The upper foster logo is identified correctly.

is a problem case that is very difficult to solve. A solution can be obtained by learning topological information and use it to verify the identification results.

Fig. 6. Example of a difficult case. The module confuses the gray box marked classification with the qantas logo.

6   Conclusion and Outlook

We have proposed an architecture for a real-time system for the detection and identification logos from video sequences. Precise identification of logos in unconstrained environments is a difficult task and can not be expected to meet real-time constraints. For this reason we have proposed a preprocessing module that detects potential logo candidates and passes them on to identification.

We have evaluated different identification algorithms, using histogram intersection and probabilistic recognition. All methods provide high recognition rates, but return a significant percentage of false positives. The intersection measure performs best out of the tested methods.

We have observed several problems. For every region of interest, the most likely logo is computed. For this reason the system performs badly on ROIs that do not contain a logo that reduces the precision of the identification. Learning a non-logo class can solve this problem. Naturally the non-logo class is much more complex than the logo class. For this reason we propose a bootstrapping approach as in [6], where the classification system is trained on misclassified samples.

Using the same idea, we can implement an incremental learning approach by systematically adding correct samples to the training database online. The histogram approach can easily be adapted for incremental learning.

References

1. J.L. Crowley, O. Riff, and J. Piater. Fast computation of characteristic scale using a half octave pyramid. In *Intern. Workshop on Cognitive Computing*, 2002.
2. W.T. Freeman and E.C. Pasztor. Learning low-level vision. In *ICCV99*, pages 1182–1189, 1999.
3. D. Hall, V. Colin de Verdière, and J.L. Crowley. Object recognition using coloured receptive fields. In *ECCV00*, Dublin, Ireland, June 2000.
4. T. Lindeberg. Feature detection with automatic scale selection. *IJCV*, 30(2):79–116, 1998.
5. D.G. Lowe. Object recognition from local scale-invariant features. In *ICCV99*, pages 1150–1157, 1999.
6. E. Osuna, R. Freund, and F. Girosi. Training support vector machines: an application to face detection. In *CVPR97*, Puerto Rico, June 1997.
7. R.P.N. Rao and D.H. Ballard. An active vision architecture based on iconic representations. *Artificial Intelligence*, 78(1–2):461–505, 1995.
8. B. Schiele and J.L. Crowley. Recognition without correspondence using multidimensional receptive field histograms. *IJCV*, 36(1):31–50, January 2000.
9. C. Schmid and R. Mohr. Local greyvalue invariants for image retrieval. *PAMI*, 1997.
10. K. Schwerdt and J.L. Crowley. Robust face tracking using color. In *Intern. Conf. on Face and Gesture Recognition*, pages 90–95, Grenoble, France, March 2000.
11. M.J. Swain and D.H. Ballard. Color indexing. *IJCV*, 7(1):11–32, 1991.
12. L.J. van Vliet, I.T. Young, and P.W. Verbeek. Recursive gaussian derivative filters. In *ICPR98*, pages 509–514, August 1998.

Context Based Object Detection from Video*

Lucas Paletta and Christian Greindl

Joanneum Research
Institute of Digital Image Processing
Wastiangasse 6, 8010 Graz, Austria
{lucas.paletta,christian.greindl}@joanneum.at

Abstract. The past few years have seen a dramatic request for semantic video analysis. Object based interpretation in real-time imposes increased challenges on resource management to maintain sufficient quality
of service, and requires careful design of the system architecture. This paper focuses on the role of context for system performance in a multi-stage
object detection process. We extract context from simple features to determine regions of interest, provide an innovative method to identify the
object's topology from local object features, and we outline the concept
for a correspondingly structured system architecture. Performance im-
plications are analysed with reference to the application of logo detection
in sport broadcasts and provide evidence for the crucial improvements
achieved from context information.

1 Introduction

Research on video analysis has recently been focussing on object based interpretation, e.g., to refine semantic interpretation for the precise indexing and sparse
representation of immense amounts of image data [11,4,15]. Object detection in
real-time, such as for video annotating and interactive television [1], imposes
increased challenges on resource management to maintain sufficient quality of
service, and requires careful design of the system architecture.

Existing methods for object detection optimize single stage mapping from
local features to object hypotheses [14,20]. This requires either complex classifiers
that suffer from the course of dimensionality and require prohibitive computing
resources, or provides rapid simple classifiers with lack of specificity. In contrast,
cascaded object detection [8,25] has been proposed to decompose the mapping
into a set of classifiers that operate on a specific level of abstraction and focus
on a restricted classification problem.

Context information has been identified to improve video interpretation processes within several tasks of analysis, such as object recognition [5]. Bayesian
networks as the probabilistic representation for the recognition of motion based
surveillance scenarios [10] demonstrated efficient classification for further analysis. Statistical context priming for object detection has been outlined in a

---

* This work is funded by the European Commission's IST project DETECT under
grant number IST-2001-32157.

J.L. Crowley et al. (Eds.): ICVS 2003, LNCS 2626, pp. 502–512, 2003.

Bayesian framework [24] on the basis of global image features, emphasizing the correlation between scene and object events.

The major contribution of this work is to investigate the impact of *spatial context information* to the performance of object detection processes, in particular with reference to objects represented by local image features, such as receptive fields [9,22]. The key innovation lies in providing a Bayesian method to extract *context from local topology* (Section 4.2). The method is understood being embedded within a global framework on integrated evaluation of object and scene specific context (see [24]). The rationale behind this methodology is the development of a generic cognitive detection system that aims at more robust, rapid and accurate event detection from streaming video.

A highly challenging object detection task is the recognition of relevant events in outdoor scenes, such as the detection of company brands (logos) in 'Formula One' broadcasts. Covering all occurrences of outdoor objects at video rate despite all sources of ambiguity still represents an important research task. Experiments using the proposed object detection methods provide evidence that context information in general provides a more rapid and more accurate identification of video events.

2   Context in Object Detection Processes

Context is described in terms of *information that is necessary to be observed* and that can be *used to characterize situation* [7]. We refer to the ontology and the formalization that has been recently defined with reference to perceptual processes for the recognition of activity [6], and a Bayesian framework on context statistics [24], with particular reference to video based object detection processes.

In a probabilistic framework, object detection requires the evaluation of

$$p(\varphi, \sigma, \mathbf{x}, o_i|\mathbf{y}), \tag{1}$$

i.e., the probability density function of object o_i, at spatial location $\mathbf{x}$, with pose φ and size σ given image measurements $\mathbf{y}$. A common methodology is to search the complete video frame for object specific information. In cascaded object detection, search for simple features allows to give an initial partitioning into object relevant regions of interest (ROIs) and a background region.

The *object detection system's context* is composed of a model of the *external context* of the embedding environment, plus a model of the object's *internal context*, i.e., *the object's topology characterized by geometric structure and associated local visual events* (e.g., local appearances) [24] so that local information becomes characterized with respect to the object's model (e.g., Fig. 3b). Observation based discrimination processes are involved in the extraction of the external and internal context of detection events. Thereby, measurements $\mathbf{y}$ are separated into *local* object features representing object information $\mathbf{y}_L$ and the corresponding local visual *environment* represented by context features $\mathbf{y}_E$. Assuming that, given the presence of an object o_i at location $\mathbf{x}$, features $\mathbf{y}_L$ and $\mathbf{y}_E$ are independent, we follow [24] to decompose Eq.1 into

$$p(\mathbf{y}|\varphi, \sigma, \mathbf{x}, o_i) = p(\mathbf{y}_L|\varphi, \sigma, \mathbf{x}, o_i) \cdot p(\mathbf{y}_E|\varphi, \sigma, \mathbf{x}, o_i). \tag{2}$$

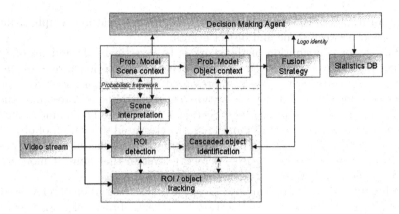

Fig. 1. Discrimination processes and models involved in the extraction of internal and external context of object detection events.

Cascaded object detection leads to an architecture that processes from simple to complex visual information, and derives from global to local object hypotheses (e.g., [8,25]). Reasoning processes and learning might be involved to select the most appropriate information according to an objective function and learn to integrate complex relationships into simple mappings. They are characterized by tasks, goals, states defined with respect to a model of the process, and actions that enable transitions between states.

Examples of discrimination processes are depicted in Figure 1. A process for 'ROI detection' (Section 3) is a simple mapping from complete frames to probabilities on object (logo) hypotheses, or categories of object identities. 'Object identification' is an example for an entity grouping process [6]. A federation of discriminatory processes is controlled by a supervising decision making agent [8, 18].

3   Context from Simple Features

The detection of ROIs is highly relevant to focus more complex processing on restricted image areas. Most commonly is the extraction of *generic* interest operators [13] that are intended to provide ROIs from universally defined image operators. In contrast, the learning of object specific, simple feature operators is described here to provide contextual information.

Detection regions. The context information represented by a region of interest (ROI) is here understood in a Bayesian framework between the observable variable of local features $\mathbf{y}(\mathbf{x})$ and the object information o_i by $p_o(o_i|\mathbf{y})$. For real-time video interpretation, $\mathbf{y}_L$ should be rapidly extracted from local information, e.g., using color analysis $\mathbf{y} = (y_r, y_g, y_b)$. Learning of object specific color filters that represent $p_o(o_i|\mathbf{y})$ is performed on the basis of color histograms [22, 9] or mixture of Gaussians [3,17].

Fig. 2. Context from fusion of simple feature operators. (a) Video frame. (b,c) Confidence maps w.r.t. bluish and white object color (dark=hi confidence), respectively. (d) Segmentation from bluish feature operator. (e) Confidence map from fusion of (b) and (c) information.

A rapid object specific, pixel based color filter is developed using the EM algorithm [3,17]: It computes the unconditional distribution on the basis of a Gaussian mixture model, $p(\mathbf{y}(\mathbf{x})) = \sum_{j=1}^{M} P(j)\varphi_j(\mathbf{y}(\mathbf{x}))$, where model priors $P(j)$ and kernels $\varphi_j(\mathbf{x})$ are parametrized with respect to class specific pixel values, i.e., $p(\mathbf{y}|\Omega_i)$ w.r.t. color class Ω. Ω does not necessarily represent an object identity but might refer to an abstract category, e.g., 'vegetation'. Figure 2(b,c) illustrates how two independent color filters related to the object 'foster' provide information per pixel on $p_o(o_i|\mathbf{y})$.

Fusion of regions. Exploiting the spatial context in the co-location of class specific pixel regions is easily perfomed using decision information with $p_o(o_i|\mathbf{y})$ (see above). In general, integrating the posteriors $P(o_i, c_1|\mathbf{y})$ for a first color c_1 and $P(o_i, c_2|\mathbf{y})$ for a second color, c_2, into a posterior in terms of a probability distribution over object hypotheses is derived from $P(o_i|\mathbf{y}) = \sum_{j=1}^{C} P(o_i, c_j|\mathbf{y})$. We get $P(o_i, c_j|\mathbf{y})$ from Bayesian recursion of $P(\mathbf{y}|o_i, c_j)$ which has been modelled by the mixture described above.

Figure 2(d) demonstrates the segmentation according to the object specific 'bluish' filter in (b), and the fusion of confidences in (b) and (c) into (e). The results demonstrate a highly local focus of attention from pixel based contexual information.

4   Context from Local Object Information

Recently, the requirement to formulate object representations on the basis of local information has been broadly recognized [22,16]. Crucial benefits from decomposing the recognition of an object from global into local information are, increased tolerance to partial occlusion, improved accuracy of recognition (since only relevant - i.e., most discriminative - information is queried for classification) and genericity of local feature extraction that may index into high level object abstractions. In this paper we are using simple brightness information to define local appearances, but the proposed approach is general enough to allow any intermediate, locally generated information to be used as well, such as Gaussian filter banks [12], etc.

Context information can be interpreted from the relation between local object features [22] or within the temporal evolution of an object's appearance [2, 19]. Decomposing the complete object information into local features transforms $p(o_i|\mathbf{y}_L)$ into $p(o_i|\mathbf{y}_{L_1}, ..., \mathbf{y}_{L_N})$, N determines the size of the object specific environment. The *grouping* of conditionally observable variables to an *entity of semantic content*, i.e., a visual object, is an essential perceptual process [6]. Section 4.1 describes aggregations of local evidence, and Section 4.2 evaluates topology information from configurations of local responses.

4.1   Decision Fusion from Local Information

A Bayesian analysis of context is defined on the basis of the local statistics about the visual information. Given the measurement about object o_i under visual parameter φ_j, the likelihood of obtaining feature vector $\mathbf{y}$ is denoted by $p(\mathbf{y}|o_i, \varphi_j)$. The likelihood might be estimated from a set of sample images with fixed o_i and φ_j, capturing the inaccuracies in the parameter φ_j such as moderate light variations or segmentation errors [18]. Via Bayesian inversion one obtains then $P(o_i, \varphi_j|\mathbf{y}) = p(\mathbf{y}|o_i, \varphi_j)P(\varphi_j|o_i)P(o_i)/p(\mathbf{y})$. A posterior estimate with respect to the object hypotheses o_i is given by $P(o_i|\mathbf{y}) = \sum_j P(o_i, \varphi_j|\mathbf{y})$.

The posterior beliefs in object hypotheses $P(o_i|\mathbf{y})$ obtained from each single measurement $\mathbf{y}$ are iteratively updated with new evidence. Context between observable variables can be simplified using Bayesian decision fusion in terms of a naive Bayes classifier [18], i.e, assuming no statistical dependence between the variable (though they are actually correlated due to the underlying physical object) by

$$P(o_i|\mathbf{y}_1, \ldots, \mathbf{y}_N) = \alpha P(o_i) \prod_{n=1}^{N} P(\mathbf{y}_n|o_i), \qquad (3)$$

N is the number of grouped measurements and α a normalizing factor. A fusion scheme based on conditional independence leads therefore to a formalization

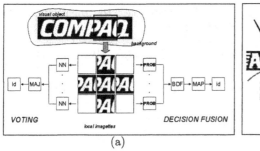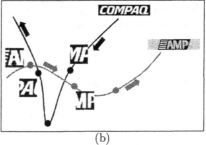

(a)   (b)

Fig. 3. Spatial context from local information. (a) Context from voting or decision fusion. (b) Context from topology: similar features from distinct objects - shifts in different directions.

which is *associative* and *commutative* in time, neglecting any information contained in the temporal order of measurements. Figure 3(a) illustrates voting and fusion schemes.

Experimental results of sport video interpretation (Section 5) demonstrate that fusion extracts a kind of local context representing a simple and rapid update scheme that enables real-time view planning [21,18].

4.2 Spatial Context from Topology

The relevance of structural dependencies in object localization [22,23] has been stressed before, though the existing methodologies merely reflect co-location in the existence of local features. The presented work outlines full integration of topological relations between local features within a framework on Bayesian conditional analysis of *perception-action* sequences as follows.

Topological information is derived from the relation between the stored object model - the set of trajectories in feature space - and the actions (shift of the focus of attention) that are mapped to changes in the model parametrization. Figure 3(b) illustrates the described concept in the reference frame of the local appearance based object model. Introducing the representation of actions a_i into Bayesian fusion [18] leads to

$$P(o_i, \varphi_j | \mathbf{y}_1, a_1, \mathbf{y}_2) = \alpha P(o_i, \varphi_j | \mathbf{y}_1, a_1) p(\mathbf{y}_2 | o_i, \varphi_j, \mathbf{y}_1, a_1). \qquad (4)$$

Spatial context is now exploited using the conditional term $P(o_i, \varphi_j | \mathbf{y}_1, a_1)$: The probability for observing view (o_i, φ_j) as a consequence of deterministic action $a_1 = \Delta\varphi_1$ must be identical to the probability of having measured at the action's starting point before, i.e. at view $(o_i, \varphi_j - \Delta\varphi_1)$, thus $P(o_i, \varphi_j | \mathbf{y}_1, a_1) \equiv P(o_i, \varphi_j - \Delta\varphi_1 | \mathbf{y}_1)$. Note that this obviously does not represent a naive Bayes classifier since it explicitly represents the dependency between the observable variables $\mathbf{y}_i, a_i$.

Furthermore, the probability density of $\mathbf{y}_2$, given the knowledge of view (o_i, φ_j), is conditionally independent on previous observations and actions, and therefore $p(\mathbf{y}_2|o_i, \varphi_j, \mathbf{y}_1, a_1) = p(\mathbf{y}_2|o_i, \varphi_j)$. The recursive update rule for *conditionally dependent* observations accordingly becomes,

$$P(o_i, \varphi_j|\mathbf{y}_1, a_1, \ldots, a_{N-1}, \mathbf{y}_N) = \alpha p(\mathbf{y}_N|o_i, \varphi_j)P(o_i, \varphi_j - \Delta\varphi_{N-1}|\mathbf{y}_1, a_1, \ldots, \mathbf{y}_{N-1})$$
(5)

and the posterior, using $\mathbf{Y}_N^a \equiv \{\mathbf{y}_1, a_1, \ldots, a_{N-1}, \mathbf{y}_N\}$, is then given by

$$P(o_i|\mathbf{Y}_N^a) = \sum_j P(o_i, \varphi_j|\mathbf{Y}_N^a).$$
(6)

The experimental results in Figures 5 and 6 demonstrate that context is crucial for rapid discrimination from local object information. The presented methodology assumes knowledge about (i) the scale of actions and of (ii) the directions with reference to the orientation of the logo, which can be gained by ROI analysis beforehand (Section 3).

5   Experimental Results

The experiments were performed on object detection in 'Formula One' broadcast videos. Outdoor events provide challenging data due to illumination changes, changes in scale and pose, and partial occlusions. The industry is interested in application such as annotation of sport events [1] or automatic detection of company brands (logos) for publicity evaluation.

The proposed object detection system first applies ROI detection based on learned color classifiers (Section 3). Within these detection regions, it extracts spatial context from local features. The following paragraphs illustrate the performance on fusion (i) without and (ii) with topology from local information.

(i) Context from aggregation. Object identification from local context is applied on the extracted ROI (Figure 4(a,b)), assuming that the video frames have been processed by learned color filters (Section 3). Each object is represented by graylevel image parts (i.e., imagettes [9]) the center of which is determined by constant shifts along the horizontal object axis (Figure 4(c)), and projected into eigenspace of dimension 10. Table 1 depicts results from different schemes to aggregate individual, co-located imagette interpretations. Fusion from locally preselected imagettes by majority voting completely outperforms nearest-neighbor (NN) search and majority voting.

(ii) Context from topology. Spatial context from topology can be easily extracted based on a predetermined estimate on scale and orientation of the object of interest. This is computed (i) from the topology of the ROI (Section 3), and from (ii) estimates on $p_\varphi(\varphi|\sigma, \mathbf{x}, o_i, \mathbf{y}_E)$ and $p_s(\sigma|\mathbf{x}, o_i, \mathbf{y}_E)$ from global image features [24]. We present a recognition experiment from spatial context on 3 selected logos (Figure 5(a)) with local appearance representation as described above, and a 3-dimensional eigenspace representation to model highly ambiguous visual information. Table 2 demonstrates how n-step recognition from local

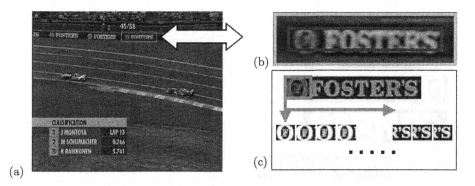

Fig. 4. (a,b) Test image for the comparison of fusion schemes. (c) Imagette representation.

Table 1. Evaluation of different schemes to integrate local object information.

Fusion method	True Pos	False Neg (bgd)	False Neg (logo)
1-NN	53.7 %	26.1 %	19.2 %
Fusion	61.4 %	22.3 %	16.3 %
Voting	84.4 %	5.5 %	10.1 %
Voting/Fusion	89.8 %	3.8 %	6.4 %

Table 2. Evaluation of the accuracy in object recognition for different numbers of fusions and shift steps (actions), and 3 objects (AMP, COM, FOS - see Fig. 5a).

Parameters		1-step recognition				N-step recognition			
Fusions	Shifts	AMP[%]	COM[%]	FOS[%]	avg.[%]	AMP [%]	COM[%]	FOS[%]	avg.[%]
2	2	91,9	71,0	41,1	68,0	96,8	83,9	47,6	76,1
2	20	96,6	76,1	45,6	72,7	98,9	97,7	97,7	98,1
5	5	92,2	75,7	45,6	71,2	99,0	98,1	99,0	98,7
10	2	92,6	76,9	43,5	71,0	99,1	98,2	90,7	96,0
10	20	100,0	82,1	14,3	65,5	96,4	92,9	92,9	94,0

Table 3. Evaluation of the accuracy in pose recognition for $F = 2/S = 2$ and $F = 5/S = 5$ respectively (see Table 2), and different tolerance to pose variations.

Method	Deviation from true pose		
	±0 [%]	±2 [%]	±5 [%]
1-step (2,2)	0,5	1,1	11,9
N-step (5,5)	83,0	98,7	99,0

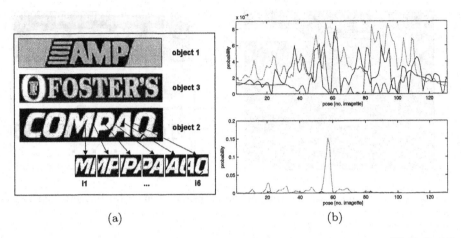

(a)   (b)

Fig. 5. (a) The logo object set and associated imagette test sequence. (b) Probability distribution on pose hypotheses w.r.t. all 3 logo objects from a single imagette interpretation (*top*) and after the 5th fusion of local evidences (*bottom*).

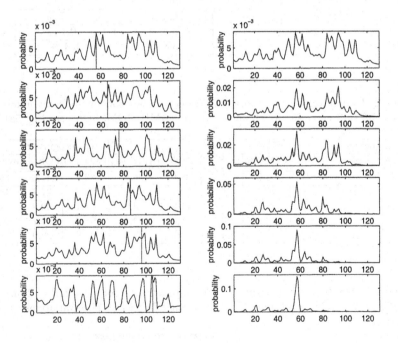

Fig. 6. *Left:* Probability distributions over pose hypotheses (imagette pose no.1-131 within logo) from individual test imagettes no. 1-6, from top to bottom. *Right:* Corresponding fusion results using spatal context from topology illustrating fusion steps no.1-5.

context significantly outperforms single step recognition. While 1-step pose estimation simply breaks down, n-step estimation is highly efficient (Table 3). Figure 6 (right) demonstrates the dramatic decrease of uncertainty in the pose information for object o_2, i.e., $p(o_2, \varphi_j|\mathbf{y})$, from several steps of information fusion according to Eq. 5. Figure 5(b) illustrates the original and final distribution for all objects, $o_1 - o_3$. Note that the entropy in the distribution over pose hypotheses, $p(o_i, \varphi_j|\mathbf{Y}_N^a)$ (Section 4.2) dropped from 8.2 to 5.2 using context from topology, and from 8.2 to 6.8 using evidence aggregations, illustrating much better results for spatial fusion from topology in comparison to fusion aggregation.

6   Conclusions

Context information contributes in several aspects to robust object detection from video. First, object specific context of simple features provides an indexing into regions of interest. Grouping of local features can be rapidly applied and yields improved results. Additional computing derives the *context from the topology of local features* which has been demonstrated to dramatically improve object recognition and to outperform standard fusion methods in sport broadcast videos.

Future work will focus on the extraction of local context from scene information in order to predict the future locations of detection events. In addition, we will investigate how context from topology can be derived without a priori information on scale and object rotation in the image.

References

1. J. Assfalg, M. Bertini, C. Colombo, and A. Del Bimbo. Semantic annotation of sports videos. *IEEE Multimedia*, 9(2):52–60, 2002.
2. S. Becker. Implicit learning in 3D object recognition: The importance of temporal context. *Neural Computation*, 11(2):347–374, 1999.
3. S. Belongie, C. Carson, H. Greenspan, and J. Malik. Color- and texture-based image segmentation using em and its applications to content-based image retrieval. In *Proc. International Conference on Computer Vision*, pages 675–682. Bombay, India, 1998.
4. A. Del Bimbo. *Visual Information Retrieval*. Morgan Kaufmann Publishers, San Francisco, CA, 1999.
5. F. Bremond and M. Thonnat. A context representation for surveillance systems. In *Proc. Workshop on Conceptual Descriptions from Images*, 1996.
6. J. L. Crowley, J. Coutaz, G. Rey, and P. Reignier. Perceptual components for context aware computing. In *Proc. 4th International Conference on Ubiquitous Computing*, 2002.
7. A. K. Dey. Understanding and using context. In *Proc. 3rd International Conference on Ubiquitous Computing*, 2001.
8. B. A. Draper. Learning control strategies for object recognition. In K. Ikeuchi and M. Veloso, editors, *Symbolic Visual Learning*, chapter 3, pages 49–76. Oxford University Press, New York, 1997.

9. D. Hall, C. de Verdiere, and J.L. Crowley. Object recognition using coloured receptive fields. In *Proc. European Conference on Computer Vision*, 2000.
10. S. Hongong, F. Bremond, and R. Nevatia. Bayesian framework for video surveillance application. In *Proc. International Conference onPattern Recognition*, 2000.
11. M. Irani and P. Anandan. Video indexing based on mosaic representation. *IEEE Transactions on Pattern Analysis and Machine Intelligence*, 86(5):905–921, 1998.
12. L. Itti, C. Koch, and E. Niebur. A model of saliency-based visual attention for rapid scene analysis. *IEEE Transactions on Pattern Analysis and Machine Intelligence*, 20(11):1254–1259, November 1998.
13. B. Mel. Seemore: Combining color, shape, and texture histogramming in a neurally-inspired approach to visual object recognition. *Neural Computation*, 9:777–804, 1997.
14. A. Mohan, C. Papageorgiou, and T. Poggio. Example-based object detection in images by components. *IEEE Transactions on Pattern Analysis and Machine Intelligence*, 23(4):349–361, 2001.
15. M.R. Naphade and T.S. Huang. A probabilistic framework for semantic video indexing, filtering, and retrieval. *IEEE Transactions on Multimedia*, 3(1):141–151, 2001.
16. S. Obdrzalek and J. Matas. Object recognition using local affine frames on distinguished regions. In *Proc. British Machine Vision Conference*, 2002.
17. L. Paletta, G. Paar, and A. Wimmer. Mobile visual detection of traffic infrastructure. In *Proc. IEEE International Conference on Intelligent Transportation Systems*, pages 616–621, Oakland, CA, 2001.
18. L. Paletta and A. Pinz. Active object recognition by view integration and reinforcement learning. *Robotics and Autonomous Systems*, 31(1-2):71–86, 2000.
19. L. Paletta, M. Prantl, and A. Pinz. Learning temporal context in active object recognition using Bayesian analysis. In *Proc. International Conference on Pattern Recognition*, pages 695–699, 2000.
20. F. Sadjadi. *Automatic Target Recognition XII*. Proc. of SPIE Vol. 4726, Aerosense 2002, Orlando, FL, 2002.
21. B. Schiele and J. L. Crowley. Transinformation for active object recognition. In *Proc. International Conference on Computer Vision*, pages 249–254, 1998.
22. B. Schiele and J.L. Crowley. Recognition without correspondence using multidimensional receptive field histograms. *International Journal of Computer Vision*, pages 31–50, 2000.
23. C. Schmid. A structured probabilistic model for recognition. In *Proc. IEEE International Conference on Computer Vision*, 1999.
24. A. Torralba and P. Sinha. Statistical context priming for object detection. In *Proc. IEEE International Confernce on Computer Vision*, 2001.
25. P. Viola and M. Jones. Rapid object detection using a bossted cascade of simple features. In *Proc. IEEE Conference on Computer Vision and Pattern Recognition*, 2001.

A Multimedia System Architecture for Automatic Annotation of Sports Videos

William Christmas, Edward Jaser, Kieron Messer, and Josef Kittler

University of Surrey, UK
{w.christmas,e.jaser,k.messer,j.kittler}@ee.surrey.ac.uk

Abstract. ASSAVID is an EU-sponsored project which is concerned with the development of a system for the automatic segmentation and semantic annotation of sports video material. In this paper we describe the architecture for a system that automatically creates high-level textual annotation for this material, to create a fully automatic sports video logging process.

The proposed technique relies upon the concept of "cues" which attach semantic meaning to low-level features computed on the video and audio. Experimental results on sports video provided by the BBC demonstrate that this method is working well. The system merges and synchronises several streams of cues derived from the video and audio sources, where each stream may have a different latency.

1 Introduction

The ever-increasing popularity of sport means that there is a vast amount of sports footage being recorded every day. For example, each year the British Broadcasting Corporation (BBC) provides coverage of the Wimbledon tennis championships. During this event up to fifteen different live feeds are being recorded simultaneously. At the end of the Wimbledon fortnight over one thousand tapes of sports-related footage are brought back to the BBC headquarters. All this video data is generated from just one event. The BBC records hundreds of different sporting events each year.

Ideally, all this sports video should be annotated, and the annotation metadata generated from it should be stored in a database along with the video data. Such a system would allow an operator to retrieve any shot, or important event within a shot, at a later date. Also the level of annotation provided by the system should be adequate to facilitate simple text-based queries. For example a typical query could be: "Retrieve the shot when Alan Shearer scored the winning goal against Germany in Euro 2000". Such a system would have many uses, such as in the production of television sport programmes and documentaries. It would help also ensure our cultural preservation.

Due to the large amount of material being generated, manual annotation is both impractical and very expensive. However, automatic annotation is a very demanding and an extremely challenging computer vision task as it involves high-level scene interpretation - a holy grail of computer vision. It is unlikely

J.L. Crowley et al. (Eds.): ICVS 2003, LNCS 2626, pp. 513–522, 2003.

that an efficient, fully automated video annotation system will be realised in the near future.

Perhaps the most well known automatic video annotation system reported in the literature is Virage [2]. Virage has an open framework which allows for the integration of many audio and video analysis tools in real time, and places the data into an industry-standard database such as Informix or Oracle. However, the number of analysis tools available is limited, although always expanding. The main problem with Virage is that no effort has been made to bridge the gap between the information provided by the low-level analysis tools and the high-level interpretation of the video, which is required for our application.

Other work, specific to some form of sports annotation include [10] in which camera motion is used to help in the automatic annotation of basketball. Mo et al. utilise state transition models, which include both top-down and bottom-up processes, to recognise different objects in sports scenes [6]. In [11] work has been undertaken to distinguish between sports and non-sports MPEG compressed video. Finally, MIT have been working on the analysis of American football video [4].

The ASSAVID [1] project is concerned with the development of a novel system which will provide a semantic annotation of sports video in text form. This annotation segments the sports video into semantic categories (e.g. type of sport) and permits the user to formulate queries to retrieve events that are significant to that particular sport (e.g. goal, foul). ASSAVID will provide the complete system. The engine consists of a set of software tools for the generation of the high-level annotation for incoming sports video. These tools are based on a set of lower-level audio and video analysis tools, which we term cue detectors. All the cue detectors are designed so that their outputs are presented in a consistent way, to facilitate the addition of further tools in the future. A contextual reasoning engine is then used to analyse the output of these cue detectors and attach semantic information to the video being analysed.

In this paper we describe the whole system from an architectural point of view. We also show how the annotation appears when the system is operating, and discuss some experimental results. The rest of this paper is organised as follows. In the next section the architecture of the complete system is described, and includes an example of the annotation produced by the system. The cue generation process is central to the system architecture, and so is described in some detail in Section 3. Section 4 provides some details of the decision-tree classifier that is used to perform the sports recognition, together with some experimental results. We draw some conclusions in Section 5.

2   The ASSAVID System Architecture

One of the novel aspects of the system is the use of "cues", which provide a means of representing intermediate-level information derived from a variety of feature detectors in a common format. Cues are simple features from the real world, such as "grass", "running track", "swimming pool lane". Thus the concepts

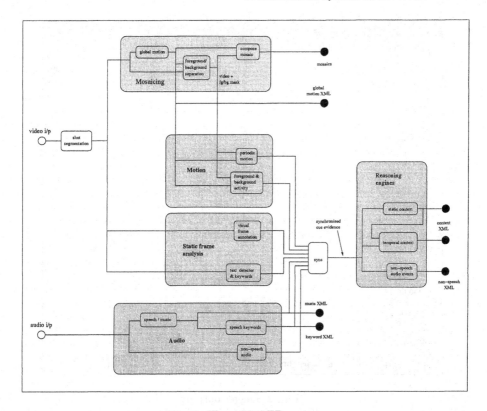

Fig. 1. The ASSAVID system

they represent are at a higher semantic level than those generated by typical feature detectors. This aspect enables new feature detectors to be added without redesigning the whole system. Thus the system can be considered roughly speaking as consisting of the following stages:

feature detection → cue detection → synchronising → reasoning engine

In addition a shot detector segments the video into shots.[1]

The system is represented in Fig. 1. Several feature detectors are used, on both video and audio data, each creating its own sets of feature vectors. There are several cue detectors corresponding to each feature detector, each one trained to recognise its own low-level cue. The entire ensemble of cue evidence is then combined into a single stream. Since the various feature detectors have different latencies, the cue evidence has to be resynchronised at this point. The output of the synchroniser has a latency corresponding to the slowest of its inputs. The cue evidence is grouped corresponding to the video shots at this point.

The entire cue evidence stream is then fed to the reasoning engine, which consists of modules that make various types of inference about the video content.

---

[1] The shot detector was provided by ASSAVID project partner Dipartimento di Sistemi e Informatica, Università degli Studi di Firenze.

Timecode	Shot.Change	Sport	Audio
00:00:00...		tennis	
00:00:06...	1		
00:00:06...	2		
00:00:07...	1		
00:00:07...		(undecided)	
00:00:09...	1		
00:00:09...	2		
00:00:09...		tennis	
00:00:18...	1		
00:00:18...	2		
00:00:19...	1		
00:00:19...		(undecided)	
00:00:20...	1		
00:00:20...	2		
00:00:20...	2		
00:00:20...		(undecided)	
00:00:22...	1		
00:00:22...		swimming	
00:00:23...			Clapping : 0.888544
00:00:24...	1		
00:00:24...		tennis	
00:00:31...	1		
00:00:31...	2		
00:00:31...		(undecided)	
00:00:33...	1		
00:00:33...	2		
00:00:33...		tennis	
00:00:39...	1		

Fig. 2. Logger output

There are currently two components of the reasoning engine: a sports classifier (described in Section 4) and a simple non-speech audio classifier.

The outputs of the reasoning engine components are textual annotation in an XML format, and are submitted to a logger. An example of the annotation from the logger is shown in Fig. 2.[2] The video sequence in this example consisted of alternating shots of the tennis court and close-ups of the players. The items that are correctly identified as tennis correspond to shots of the actual tennis play, while those that were undecided or incorrectly classified correspond to close-ups of the players. The clapping annotation corresponded to a game point.

The current system integrates feature detectors and associated cues for visual frame annotation (actually three separate detectors) and non-speech audio. Within the ASSAVID project as a whole we have also developed detectors for periodic motion analysis, motion activity, text detection and speech keyword detection, which will be integrated in a similar fashion.

---

[2] The logger display is part of a process scheduler provided by ASSAVID project partner Advanced Computer Systems Spa.

3   The ASSAVID "Cue" System

The objective in the automatic annotation of video material is to provide indexing material that describes as usefully as possible the material itself. In much of the previous work in this area (for example [5]), the annotation consisted of the output of various feature detectors. By itself, this information bears no semantic connection to the actual scene content – it is simply the output of some image processing algorithms. The cue concept takes the process a stage further. By means of a set of training processes, we aim to generate an association between the feature detector outputs and the occurrence of actual scene features. We denote this association as a "cue". Thus for example we might train the system to associate the output of a texture feature detector with crowds of people in the scene. We can then use this mechanism to generate confidence values for the presence of a crowd in a scene, based on the scene texture. These cues can then be combined in the contextual reasoning engine to generate higher-level information, e.g. the type of sport being played.

The cue system works as follows. We assume that a feature detector method (feature detector + associated classifier) generates a series of scalar values $\{m\}$. The classifier has been trained separately for each relevant cue C so that an output m discriminates between audio-visual data that does or does not contain the cue. In a further training process, we estimate conditional probability density functions $p(m|C)$ and $p(m|\overline{C})$ (where $\overline{C}$ denotes the absence of the cue), in the form of histograms. Adequate training data for each cue has to be found; for example, for a cue based on features from static images, typically up to about 5 or 10 images are needed that contain the cue (depending on the method), together with 30 or 40 that do not contain the cue.

In the testing mode, the system reads off values for $p(m|C)$ and $p(m|\overline{C})$ from the two p.d.f.s. The posterior probability, $P(C|m)$, is computed as:

$$P(C|m) = \frac{p(m|C)P(C)}{p(m|C)P(C) + p(m|\overline{C})\left(1 - P(C)\right)} \tag{1}$$

The prior probabilities $P(C)$ are set equal to 0.5. To avoid the possibility of a division by zero, when reading off the p.d.f. values we replace the rectangular bins of the histogram with a set of Gaussian-shaped functions that have a peak value of 1 and that preserve the unit area of the density function estimate.

Thus there are three stages to creating cue evidence: two one-off off-line processes, to train the classifier and to create the p.d.f.s, and a "run-time" process to create the actual cue evidence that feeds the contextual reasoning stage.

4   Sports Classifier

In this section we discuss the use of a decision tree [3,7,8] as a tool for classifying shots into sport categories. A decision tree is a supervised classifier, built from training samples, each described by a set of attributes and a class label. A decision tree contains a root node, a set of decision nodes (also called internal nodes) and a set of class nodes (also called terminal nodes or leaf nodes). Classification in decision trees proceeds from top to bottom. Depending on its attributes, the instance being classified navigates through the decision tree till it reaches a class node. The navigation is guided by the rules of the decision nodes visited. The instance is assigned the label attached to the class node at which its navigation terminates.

The input data is cue evidence selected from the cue evidence stream discussed in Sections 2 and 3. The cues chosen for the sports classifier have been chosen such that they are representative of objects occurring within the set of sports being investigated. The cue detectors operate on a set of keyframe images, and for each keyframe the posterior probability of a cue, $P(C|m)$, is computed from eq. (1).

4.1   Constructing the Decision Tree

Let $\mathcal{X} = \{X_1, X2, ..., X_N\}$ be set of N shots. And let $\mathcal{S} = \{S_1, S_2, ..., S_n\}$ be a set of n sports being investigated. The process of constructing a decision tree classifier requires a training set $\mathcal{T} = \{(X_i, S_j) : X_i \in \mathcal{X}, S_j \in \mathcal{S}\}$ of shots, each being assigned a label of the sport it belongs to, a splitting criterion and stopping rules. The splitting criterion is used to recursively partition the training set in a way that increases the homogeneity of its partitions. The most popular splitting criterion is the information impurity (also called entropy impurity)[9]:

$$info(\omega) = entropy(\omega) = -\sum_i P(\omega_i)\, log_2(P(\omega_i)) \qquad (2)$$

where $P(\omega_i)$ is the frequency of patterns in category ω_i. Suppose that $\mathcal{C}$ is a test, testing one of the cue values, that partitions $\mathcal{T}$ into $\mathcal{T}_1, \mathcal{T}_2, ..., \mathcal{T}_r$; then the weighted average information impurity over these partitions is computed by

$$info_C(\mathcal{T}) = \sum_{i=1}^{r} \frac{|\mathcal{T}_i|}{|\mathcal{T}|}\, info(\mathcal{T}_i) \qquad (3)$$

where $|\mathcal{T}_i|$ denotes the size of the set $\mathcal{T}_i$. In order to evaluate the goodness of partitioning using $\mathcal{C}$, the information gain is computed to measure the reduction achieved in information impurity obtained if $\mathcal{C}$ is applied.

$$gain(\mathcal{C}) = info(\mathcal{T}) - info_C(\mathcal{T}) \qquad (4)$$

At each node, all the possible tests are investigated and the test with the highest information gain is selected to define the partition. The partitioning stops when one of the stopping rules is triggered at a node. This node becomes a class node and a label S_j which represent the sport with the largest number of shots is attached to it.

Table 1. Sports investigated

Boxing	S_1
Cycling	S_2
Gymnastics	S_3
Hockey	S_4
Judo	S_5
Shooting	S_6
Swimming	S_7
Taekwondo	S_8
Tennis	S_9
Track Events	S_{10}
Weight-lifting	S_{11}
Yachting	S_{12}

4.2 Experiments

The database used in the following experiments comprises video material from the 1992 Barcelona Olympic games. The material covers twelve Olympic sport disciplines (Table 1). There are 1678 shots in the data base. Two configurations were set up. In the first configuration we split the data into two sets. A training set formed from 20% of the data was used for constructing the decision tree and the remaining 80% was used for testing. The training error of the constructed decision tree was 17.6%. The misclassification rate of the tree on the test set was 44%. Table 2 shows the confusion matrix for the decision tree classifier.

Table 2. Confusion matrix for sports classification(Training set 20%, Test set 80%). Error=0.44

	S_1	S_2	S_3	S_4	S_5	S_6	S_7	S_8	S_9	S_{10}	S_{11}	S_{12}
S_1	**27**	1	6	0	1	2	7	14	1	0	4	1
S_2	0	**11**	2	6	1	2	9	2	4	5	3	4
S_3	1	1	**18**	5	0	8	8	2	4	2	8	2
S_4	0	0	4	**92**	1	13	13	1	15	13	15	2
S_5	8	1	0	2	**35**	6	17	10	0	0	6	3
S_6	3	0	0	8	1	**9**	9	1	10	6	12	0
S_7	3	3	7	5	0	6	**214**	7	2	3	11	5
S_8	6	0	1	1	1	1	5	**43**	3	0	1	0
S_9	0	1	1	7	0	3	4	1	**55**	5	5	0
S_{10}	1	8	4	12	0	19	8	3	5	**167**	24	1
S_{11}	4	1	3	15	1	4	9	4	5	4	**42**	6
S_{12}	1	3	3	11	0	0	22	2	3	2	12	**35**

In the second configuration, the training set was increased to 50% of the data, leaving 50% for testing. The results are shown in Table 3. The error rate on the training set this time was 16.6%, and the misclassification rate 38% on the test set. Hence by increasing the number of samples for training, a useful improvement in the classification performance was obtained.

Table 3. Confusion matrix for sports classification(Training set 50%, Test set 50%). Error=0.38

	S_1	S_2	S_3	S_4	S_5	S_6	S_7	S_8	S_9	S_{10}	S_{11}	S_{12}
S_1	23	0	2	1	3	0	3	6	1	0	0	1
S_2	0	8	2	9	2	0	4	0	0	3	0	2
S_3	1	2	12	6	1	1	2	1	0	11	0	0
S_4	0	1	3	66	1	7	3	1	5	12	2	4
S_5	4	0	1	4	38	1	0	4	0	0	0	3
S_6	3	0	0	4	5	9	2	1	1	8	3	1
S_7	3	2	3	6	0	2	133	1	1	8	0	7
S_8	4	0	0	0	1	0	5	27	0	0	0	2
S_9	0	1	0	2	1	3	6	0	32	3	2	1
S_{10}	1	3	5	4	2	11	5	0	5	117	1	3
S_{11}	4	6	1	9	3	5	7	0	3	7	12	4
S_{12}	0	1	0	2	0	0	11	0	0	0	4	41

From Table 2 and Table 3, we can see that some sports performed well: swimming, taekwondo, tennis and track events all have a classification performance greater than 60%. Also, for these sports, the extra training data in Table 3 made little overall difference. Some sports (shooting, cycling, weight-lifting and gymnastics) had a disappointing performance. For cycling, weight-lifting and gymnastics, this can be explained from the fact that we do not extract any cues that are sufficiently characteristic of them. From the list of cues in Table 4 we can see that weight-lifting and gymnastics are not represented, and cycling is represented with two cues. For shooting, from the shots database we found that, out of 74 shots representing shooting, only 13 contain a view of *Shooting Target*.

4.3   Refining the Ground-Truth

Looking at the shots, it was found that many of them were not really representative of the ground-truth sport. Significant number of the shots were close-ups of the players or were crowd shots. The experiment was repeated after eliminating such shots. As shown in Table 5 and Table 6, the classification rate increased by 7% for the (20-80) configuration and 13% for the (50-50) configuration.

5   Conclusions

In this paper we present a novel architecture for the automatic annotation of sports video material. The system at present is still at a relatively youthful stage, with a limited range of types of output. However the architecture is also

Table 4. Cues

MNS Cues	NeuralNet Cues	TexureCodes Cues
AthleticsTrack	AthleticsTrack	AthleticsTrack
ClayTennisSurface	BoxingRing	BoxingRing
HockeyGround	ClayTennisSurface	ClayTennisSurface
IndoorCrowd	HockeyGround	CloseUp
JudoMat	IndoorCrowd	HockeyGround
Ocean	Net-JudoMat	IndoorCrowd
OutdoorCrowd	Ocean	JudoMat
ShootingTarget	OutdoorCrowd	Ocean
SwimmingPool	ShootingTarget	OutdoorCrowd
TaekwondoMat	SwimmingLanes	ShootingTarget
	SwimmingPool	SwimmingLanes
	TaekwondoMat	SwimmingPool
	WoodCycleTrack	TaekwondoMat
		WoodCycleTrack

Table 5. Confusion matrix for sports classification after refining the ground-truth (Training set 20%, Test set 80%). Error=0.37

	S_1	S_2	S_3	S_4	S_5	S_6	S_7	S_8	S_9	S_{10}	S_{11}	S_{12}
S_1	**15**	0	1	1	1	0	2	9	0	0	2	0
S_2	2	**5**	3	0	2	0	0	1	0	5	5	0
S_3	7	5	**16**	11	0	1	0	3	0	7	8	1
S_4	1	11	5	**63**	0	0	0	6	0	0	7	0
S_5	0	5	10	0	**28**	2	0	9	0	0	1	1
S_6	3	0	1	0	0	**3**	0	0	0	0	1	0
S_7	0	0	2	0	7	0	**124**	6	0	0	2	1
S_8	8	0	0	2	4	0	2	**25**	0	0	0	0
S_9	0	0	0	0	0	0	0	0	**23**	1	0	0
S_{10}	0	3	3	0	0	12	0	0	1	**114**	2	0
S_{11}	5	4	16	12	4	1	1	6	0	0	**48**	1
S_{12}	2	7	1	4	1	0	18	12	0	0	4	**45**

a flexible one, because of the use of the cue generators, each of which generates cue evidence in an identical format. This makes it simple to add new types of feature detector in the future. Through the use of the synchroniser, it is also straightforward to add new types of reasoning engine: a new engine is fed with the synchroniser output, and it selects from the cue evidence stream those cues that it has been trained to use.

Further feature detectors and reasoning engines are planned for the project. Some of these are now ready for integration, including feature detectors for periodic motion analysis, motion activity, text detection and speech keyword detection, and a contextual reasoning engine based on hidden Markov models.

Table 6. Confusion matrix for sports classification after refining the ground-truth (Training set 50%, Test set 50%). Error=0.25

	S_1	S_2	S_3	S_4	S_5	S_6	S_7	S_8	S_9	S_{10}	S_{11}	S_{12}
S_1	12	0	2	1	1	0	3	2	0	0	0	0
S_2	1	2	5	2	0	0	0	0	0	2	1	1
S_3	3	0	22	2	2	0	0	0	0	1	3	4
S_4	0	0	3	43	0	0	0	0	0	0	6	1
S_5	4	0	4	0	28	0	0	0	0	0	1	0
S_6	0	0	0	0	0	1	0	0	0	1	2	1
S_7	0	0	2	0	0	0	87	0	0	0	0	1
S_8	1	0	1	1	6	0	4	21	0	0	1	2
S_9	0	0	1	0	0	0	0	0	20	0	0	0
S_{10}	0	1	3	1	0	0	1	0	0	69	1	0
S_{11}	1	0	6	2	1	0	2	0	0	3	33	4
S_{12}	0	0	1	1	1	0	10	0	0	0	6	40

Acknowledgements. This work was supported by the IST-1999-13082 AS-SAVID and IST-2001-34401 VAMPIRE projects funded by the European IST Programme.

References

1. http://www.bpe-rnd.co.uk/assavid/.
2. http://www.virage.com.
3. L Breiman, J Friedman, R Olshen, and C Stone. *Classification and regression trees.* Wadsworth International Group, 1984.
4. S.S. Intille and A.F. Bobick. A framework for representing multi-agent action from visual evidence. In *Proceedings of the National Conference on Artificial Intelligence (AAAI),* July 1999.
5. B Levienaise-Obadia, W Christmas, J Kittler, K Messer, and Y Yusoff. Ovid: towards object-based video retrieval. In *Proceedings of Storage and Retrieval for Video and Image Databases VIII (part of the SPIE/ITT Symposium: Electronic Imaging'2000),* Jan 2000.
6. H. Mo, S. Satoh, and M. Sakauchi. A study of image recognition using similarity retrieval. In *First International Conference on Visual Information Systems (Visual'96),* pages 136–141, 1996.
7. S K V Murthy. *On Growing Better Decision Trees from Data.* PhD thesis, Johns Hopkins University, Baltimor, Maryland, 1996.
8. J R Quinlan. Induction of decision trees. In *Machine Learning,* volume 1, page 81 106, 1986.
9. J R Quinlan. *C4.5 : Programs for machine learning.* Morgan Kaufmann, 1993.
10. D.D. Saur, Y.-P. Tan, S.R. Kulkarni, and P.j. Ramadge. Automated analysis and annotation of basketball video. In *SPIE Storage and Retrieval for Still Image and Video Databases V, Vol.3022,* pages 176–187, 1997.
11. V.Kobla, D.DeMenthon, and D.Doermann. Identifying sporst video using replay, text and camera motion features. In *SPIE Storage and retrieval for Media Database 2000,* pages 332–342, 2000.

Automatic Video Interpretation: A Recognition Algorithm for Temporal Scenarios Based on Pre-compiled Scenario Models

Van-Thinh Vu, François Brémond, and Monique Thonnat

Project ORION of I.N.R.I.A. Sophia Antipolis,
2004 route des Lucioles, BP93-06902 Sophia Antipolis Cedex, France.
{Thinh.Vu,Francois.Bremond,Monique.Thonnat}@sophia.inria.fr
http://www-sop.inria.fr/orion/orion-eng.html

Abstract. This paper presents a new scenario recognition algorithm for Video Interpretation. We represent a scenario model with the characters involved in the scenario, with its sub-scenarios and with the constraints combining the sub-scenarios. By pre-compiling the scenario models, the recognition algorithm processes temporal constraints by decomposing complex scenarios into intermediate sub-scenarios to reduce the algorithm complexity. We have tested the recognition algorithm on several videos of a bank agency to try to recognize a scenario of "Attack". We conclude by showing experimental results of the efficiency of this algorithm for real time temporal scenario recognition.

Keywords. Automatic Video Interpretation, Scenario Recognition, Chronicle Recognition, Temporal Constraint Resolution, Scenario Representation.

1   Introduction

A problem of current focus in cognitive vision is Automatic Video Interpretation ([1], [2], [3], [4], [8], [11], [12]). The goal is to develop a systematic methodology for the design, implementation and integration of cognitive vision systems for recognizing scenarios involved in a scene depicted by a video sequence. An Automatic Video Interpretation System (AVIS) as described in Fig. 1, takes as input (1) a priori knowledge containing scenario models predefined by experts and the 3D geometric and semantic information of the observed environment and (2) video streams acquired by the camera(s). The output of the system is the set of recognized scenarios at each instant. In this paper, we focus on the module of scenario recognition. The scenario recognition module takes as input the a priori knowledge of the scene and a stream of individuals tracked by a vision module.

To solve scenario recognition issues, we first propose a language to describe scenario models and second a Temporal Constraint Resolution approach to recognize in real time scenario occurrences. Our scenario representation is mainly based on the representation of T. Vu, F. Bremond and M. Thonnat [12] and also based on the one of M. Ghallab and C. Dousson [4]. In this paper, we focus on the optimization of the recognition method presented in [12]. We enhance the processing of temporal operators by pre-compiling scenario models to decompose them into simpler scenario models. By this way, the scenario recognition algorithm uses a linear search compared to an exponential search for similar state of the art algorithms.

J.L. Crowley et al. (Eds.): ICVS 2003, LNCS 2626, pp. 523–533, 2003.
© Springer-Verlag Berlin Heidelberg 2003

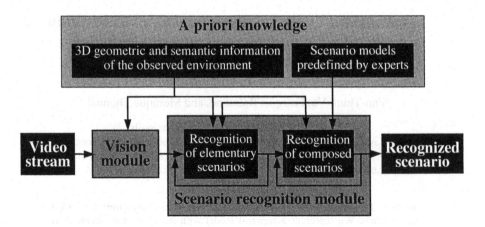

Fig. 1. Overview of an Automatic Video Interpretation System.

We present in section 2 some related works. Our scenario representation is described in section 3. The recognition algorithm is detailed in section 4. We conclude our paper by showing experimental results.

2   Related Works

For 20 years and particularly since the years 90s, a problem of focus in cognitive vision has been Automatic Video Interpretation. There are now several research units and companies defining new approaches to design systems that can understand human activities in dynamic scenes. Three main categories of approaches are used to recognize temporal scenarios based on (1) a *probabilistic/neural network* combining potentially recognized scenarios, (2) a *symbolic network* that Stores Totally Recognized Scenarios (STRS) and (3) a *symbolic network* that Stores Partially Recognized Scenarios (SPRS).

For the computer vision community, a natural approach consists of using a probabilistic/neural network. The nodes of this network correspond usually to scenarios that are recognized at a given instant with a computed probability. For example, in 1996, A. J. Howell, H. Buxton [7] proposed an approach to recognize a scenario based on a neuronal network (time delay Radial Basis Function). Two years later, F. Bremond, S. Hongeng and R. Nevatia [6] proposed a scenario recognition method that uses concurrence Bayesian threads to estimate the likelihood of potential scenarios.

For the artificial intelligent community, a natural way to recognize a scenario is to use a symbolic network which nodes correspond usually to the boolean recognition of scenarios. For example, in 2000, N. Rota and M. Thonnat [11] used a declarative representation of scenarios defined as a set of spatio-temporal and logic constraints. They used a traditional constraint resolution technique to recognize scenarios. To reduce the processing time for the recognition step, they proposed to check the consistency of the constraint network using the AC4 algorithm [9]. More recently, in

2002, R. Gerber, H. Nagel and H. Schreiber [5] defined a method to recognize a scenario based on a fuzzy temporal logic. In the same year, T. Vu, F. Bremond and M. Thonnat [12] present an approach to optimize the temporal constraint resolution by ordering in time the sub-scenarios of the scenario to be recognized. The common characteristic of these approaches is to store all totally recognized scenarios (recognized in the past).

Another approach consists of using symbolic network and to store partially recognized scenarios (to be recognized in the future). For example, in the years 90s, M. Ghallab and C. Dousson [4] have used the terminology *chronicle* to express a *temporal scenario*. A chronicle is represented as a set of temporal constraints on time-stamped events. The recognition algorithm keeps and updates partial recognition of scenarios using the propagation of temporal constraints based on RETE algorithm. Their applications are dedicated to the control of turbines and telephonic networks. Some years later, N. Chleq and M. Thonnat (1996) [3] made an adaptation of temporal constraints propagation for video surveillance. In the same period, C. Pinhanez and A. Bobick [10] have used Allen's interval algebra to represent scenarios and have presented a specific algorithm to reduce its complexity.

All these techniques allow an efficient recognition of scenarios, but there are still some temporal constraints which can not be processed. For example, most of these approaches require that the scenarios are bounded in time [4], or process temporal constraints and atemporal constraints in the same way [11].

We can distinguish two main categories of approaches to recognize a scenario based on a symbolic network: the STRS approaches recognize scenarios based on an analysis of scenarios recognized in the past ([11], [12]), whereas the SPRS approaches recognize scenarios based on an analysis of scenarios that can be recognized in the future [4]. The STRS approaches recognize a scenario by searching in the set of previously recognized scenarios a set of sub-scenarios matching the scenario model to be recognized. Thus, if the system fails to recognize a scenario, it will have to retry the same process (re-verify the same constraints) in the next instant, implying a costly processing time. A second problem is that STRS algorithms have to store and maintain all occurrences of previously recognized scenarios. The SPRS approaches recognize a scenario by predicting the expected scenarios to be recognized in the next instants. Thus, the scenarios have to be bounded in time to avoid the never ending expected scenarios. A second problem is that SPRS algorithms have to store and maintain all occurrences of partially recognized scenarios, implying a costly processing space.

The method presented in this article is a STRS approach taking advantages of the SPRS approaches. The objective is to reduce the processing time when searching in the past (list of previously recognized scenarios) for an occurrence of a given scenario model.

3   Scenario Representation

Our goal is to make explicit all the knowledge necessary for the system to be able to recognize scenarios occurring in the scene. The description of this knowledge has to be declarative and intuitive (in natural terms), so that the experts of the application domain can easily define and modify it. Thus, the recognition process uses only the knowledge represented by experts through scenario models.

Let Φ be the set of scenarios and Ω be the set of scenario models.

For each $\omega \in \Omega$ model of a scenario instance $\rho \in \Phi$, we note $\rho = \rho(\omega)$ and $\omega = \alpha(\rho)$:

a) $\alpha(\rho)$ is the set of actors involved in ρ and $\alpha(\omega)$ is the set of characters (actor variables) corresponding to the actors $\alpha(\rho)$,

b) $\beta(\rho)$ is the set of sub-scenario instances that compose ρ and $\beta(\omega)$ is the set of temporal variables corresponding to sub-scenario models of $\beta(\rho)$. If $\beta(\rho) = \varnothing$, ρ is called *elementary scenario*, if not, ρ is called *composed scenario*. We note $\rho(v)$ a scenario instance corresponding to the value of a temporal variable v. The recognition of a scenario is a boolean value in a time interval,

c) $\gamma(\omega)$ is the set of constraints of ω expressing relations between characters $\alpha(\omega)$ and sub-scenarios $\beta(\omega)$. We note $\gamma^T(\omega)$ the set of *temporal* constraints of ω, and $\gamma^A(\omega) = \gamma(\omega) \setminus \gamma^T(\omega)$ the set of *atemporal* constraints of ω. $c \in \gamma(\omega)$ is called *temporal* constraint if c includes at least one temporal variable.

```
Scenario(Attack,
    Characters((cashier : Person), (robber : Person))
    SubScenarios(
        (cas_at_pos, inside_zone, cashier, "Back_Counter")
        (rob_enters,changes_zone,robber, "Entrance_zone","Infront_Counter")
        (cas_at_safe, inside_zone, cashier, "Safe")
        (rob_at_safe, inside_zone, robber, "Safe") )
    Constraints( (rob_enters during cas_at_pos)
                 (rob_enters before cas_at_safe)
                 (cas_at_pos before cas_at_safe)
                 (rob_enters before rob_at_safe)
                 (rob_at_safe during cas_at_safe) ) )
```

Fig. 2. Representation of a bank scenario "Attack": (1) the cashier is at his/her position behind the counter, (2) the robber enters the bank and moves toward the front of the counter then (3) both of them arrive at the safe door.

An actor can be a person tracked as a *mobile object* by the vision module or a *static object* of the observed environment like a chair. A person is represented by his/her characteristics: his/her position in the observed environment, width, velocity,.... A static object of the environment is defined by a priori knowledge (before processing) and can be either a zone of interest (a plane polygon as the entrance zone) or a piece of equipment (a 3D object such as a desk). A zone is represented by its vertices and a piece of equipment is represented by the vertices of its 3D bounding box. The zones and the equipment constitute the scene context of the observed environment [1]. Static objects and mobile objects are called *scene-objects*.

In our representation, any scenario ρ involves at least one person, and is defined on a time interval called $\delta(\rho)$. An interval is represented by its starting and ending times noted $start(\rho)$ and $end(\rho)$. For a temporal variable v corresponding to $\alpha(\rho)$, we also note that $start(v)$ and $end(v)$ for its starting and ending times. Defining scenario on a time interval is important for the experts to describe scenarios in a natural way.

Fig. 2 represents a model of a bank scenario "Attack". This scenario involves two characters, a cashier and a robber.

This representation is similar to previous representation of scenarios [12]. The difference is that we distinguish the temporal constraints combining sub-scenarios from atemporal constraints.

4   Scenario Recognition

The scenario recognition process has to detect which scenario is happening from a stream of observed persons tracked by a vision module at each instant. The recognition process takes also as input the a priori knowledge of the scene and the scenario models. We suppose that the persons are correctly tracked: their characteristics (their position in the scene, their height,...) are well detected and at two successive instants, two persons having the same name correspond to the same real person.

To recognize the pre-defined scenario models at each instant, we first select a set of scenario templates (called triggers) that indicate which scenarios can be recognized. These templates correspond to an elementary scenario or to a scenario that terminates with a sub-scenario recognized at the current instant. Secondly we find solutions for each of these scenario templates by looking for sub-scenario instances already recognized in the past to complete the scenario template (the resolution of a scenario template is described in section 4.1). A solution of a scenario model ω is a set of actors that are involved in the recognized scenario and the list of corresponding sub-scenario instances satisfying all the constraints of ω.

```
for each elementary scenario model ESM
    create a trigger T of type 1 for ESM
    for each solution ρₑ of T
        if ρₑ is not extensible then
            add ρₑ to the list of recognized scenarios
            add all triggers of type 2 of ρₑ to the list LT
        if ρₑ is extensible with ρ'ₑ recognized at the previous instant then
            merge ρₑ with scenario ρ'ₑ
            add all triggers of type 2 and 3 of ρ'ₑ to LT
while (LT ≠ ∅)
    order LT by the inclusive relation of scenario models
    for each trigger T ∈ LT
        for each solution ρ_c of T
            add ρ_c to the list of recognized scenarios
            add all triggers of type 2 and 3 of ρ_c to LT
```

Fig. 3. Overview of the scenario recognition algorithm.

We define a "trigger" as a scenario template which can be recognized. There are three types of triggers: (1) the elementary scenario models, (2) composed scenarios with specified actors and (3) composed scenarios already recognized at the previous instant. At the current instant, we initiate a list LT of triggers with all triggers of first type (*i.e.* elementary scenario models) as shown on Fig. 3. Once we have recognized an elementary scenario ρ_e, we try to extend ρ_e with a recognized scenario ρ'_e at the previous instant (the extension of a scenario is the extension of its ending time). If ρ_e can not be extended, we add the triggers of type 2 that terminate with ρ_e to the list LT. If ρ_e is extended with ρ'_e, we add the triggers of type 2 and 3 that terminate with ρ'_e. The triggers of type 2 are the templates of a composed scenario instantiated with the actors of ρ'_e and the triggers of type 3 are the templates of a composed scenario ρ_c already recognized at the previous instant and that terminates with ρ'_e. After this step, there is a loop process first to order the list LT by the inclusive relation of scenario model contained in the triggers and second to solve the triggers of LT. If a trigger contains a template of a scenario ρ'_c that can be solved (*i.e.* totally instantiated), we add the triggers of type 2 and 3 that terminate with ρ'_c. Once, a scenario is recognized, we add it to the list of already recognized scenarios indexed by a graph combining the scenario models and the list of actors to speed up the search process.

4.1   Finding Solutions for a Scenario Model

The algorithm for finding a solution for a scenario template (trigger) consists in a loop of selecting a set of actors then of verifying the corresponding constraints until all combinations of actors have been tested. This selection of actors leads the recognition algorithm to an exponential combination in function of the number of actors. However, in practice, there are few actors in scenario models, so the recognition algorithm can still be real time.

For a scenario model ω contained in a trigger, we first check the atemporal constraints $\gamma^a(\omega)$ on actor variables. For this step, we select a set of actors corresponding to $\alpha(\omega)$. If ω is a composed scenario model and has been selected by a second type trigger (*i.e.* a partially instantiated scenario template), some actor variables can already be instantiated. Once the actors have been selected, we check all atemporal constraints. These atemporal constraints are ordered with the occurrence order of the actor variables (in a compilation phase) to speed up the recognition process [12]. If the scenario is an elementary scenario, after the verification of its atemporal constraints, the scenario is said to be recognized. If the scenario is a composed scenario, after the verification of its atemporal constraints, its actors have been instantiated but its temporal constraints still need to be verified.

To verify the temporal constraints of a composed scenario model, we extract from the set of recognized scenario instances a sub-set of recognized sub-scenarios satisfying the constraints defined in the scenario model. To search for sub-scenarios, the STRS algorithms of the state of the art (*i.e.* [12]) process usually the temporal operators by ordering the sub-scenarios in time.

Once we find a solution of a scenario model, we store the recognized scenario instance and we add to the list LT the trigger terminating with this scenario. If the scenario is an elementary scenario, we also try to extend this solution (scenario instance) with a scenario of same type (same model and same actors) recognized at the previous instant. First, if such a scenario does not exist, we just add the solution to the set of recognized scenarios. Second, if it is possible to extend the solution, we merge these two elementary scenario instances (we merge their time interval) to obtain only one elementary scenario which corresponds to a continuously recognized scenario. The extension of one elementary scenario can lead recursively to the extension of all previously recognized scenarios terminated by this scenario (as described in the previous section).

The STRS algorithms of state of the art perform at each instant a complete search process among all possible scenarios and sub-scenarios leading to an exponential algorithm. We propose to analyze temporal constraints of each scenario to order its sub-scenarios. Then the search space is reduced by decomposing the initial model into a set of simple scenarios models easy to recognize.

4.2   Decomposition of a Composed Scenario

A composed scenario is a sequence of sub-scenarios partially ordered in time. Each sub-scenario corresponds to a temporal variable in the corresponding scenario model. The STRS algorithms usually re-search already recognized sub-scenarios and re-verify the temporal constraints contained in any composed scenario until they find a solution for this scenario. For example, if a scenario ω is composed of three sub-scenarios: ω_1 before ω_2 before ω_3 and if ω_3 has been recognized, it make sense to try to recognize the main scenario ω. Therefore, the STRS algorithms will try all combinations of scenario instances $\rho(\omega_1)$, $\rho(\omega_2)$ with $\rho(\omega_3)$ which can lead to a combinatory explosion.

If a scenario is composed of only two sub-scenarios ($\omega = [\omega_1$ before $\omega_2]$) and if the sub-scenario instance $\rho(\omega_2)$ has been recognized, the algorithm has to search only for one sub-scenario instance $\rho(\omega_1)$ in the list of recognized scenarios and this implies just a linear search. Therefore, as soon as the sub-scenario verifies a constraint, then the corresponding scenario is recognized and stored. To obtain a fast method to recognize a scenario model with a linear search algorithm, we propose to decompose any scenarios into scenarios composed at most of two sub-scenarios.

4.3   Compilation of Predefined Scenario Models

In this section, we focus on the compilation of predefined composed scenario models. To do this, we propose an initial phase compiling a composed scenario model ω in the following steps: (1) order in time the temporal variables of ω, (2) generate intermediate scenario models for ω and (3) link the generated intermediate scenario models by using the constraints defined in ω.

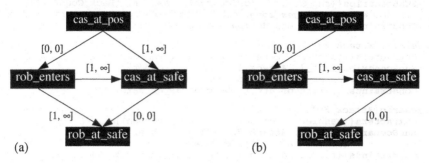

Fig. 4. Ordering in time the temporal variables of a scenario model "Attack": (a) all constraints and (b) the necessary constraints after simplifying the initial graph.

To order in time the temporal variables $\beta(\omega)$, we use a graph based method (based on [4]). The graph nodes are the temporal variables and the arcs are the temporal constraints between two variables. The arcs are oriented and are represented by time interval corresponding to the time delay between the ending times of the two variables. For example, the constraint c_i between v_i, v_j is represented by an interval [a, b] indicating that v_j can end in the interval $[end(v_i)+a, \ end(v_i)+b]$. The constraint *before* is represented by $[1, \infty]$. After building the initial graph with all temporal constraints between temporal variables of ω, we compute the equivalent complete graph (to check the graph consistency) and we simplify the graph by removing unnecessary arcs to obtain the least constrained graph. The variables are ordered by the order of the ending time. The initial and simplified graphs for the scenario "Attack" (Fig. 2) are shown on Fig. 4.

After ordering in time the temporal variables of ω, we generate intermediate scenario models composed at most of two sub-scenarios. For each intermediate scenario model ω, we call *start* (noted $\pi(\omega)$) the first sub-scenario of ω; and we call *termination* (noted $\tau(\omega)$) the second sub-scenario of ω.

Suppose that $\beta(\omega) = (v_1, v_2,..., v_n)$ is a sequence of n (n > 2) partially ordered temporal variables. We generate n-1 intermediate models $\omega^1, \omega^2,..., \omega^{n-1}$ as followed:

$\beta(\omega^1) = (v_1, v_2)$ and

$\beta(\omega^i) = (v^i, v_{i+1})$ for i > 1, where v^i corresponds to the scenario of model ω^{i-1},

$\alpha(\omega^i) = \alpha(\pi(\omega^i)) \cup \alpha(\tau(\omega^i))$,

$\gamma^T(\omega^i)$ is composed of the temporal constraints corresponding to the arcs entering v_{i+1} (i.e. $\tau(\omega^i)$) in the simplified graph. We can notice that several temporal operators of Allen's algebra can be ignored in this step because they are well expressed by order of temporal variables in the graph. Another task consists of modifying the constraints to adapt to the new scenario models.

$\gamma^A(\omega^i)$ is composed of the atemporal constraints involving actor variables belonging to $\alpha(\omega^i)$ for i = 1 and belonging to $\alpha(\omega^i)$ but not to $\alpha(\omega^{i+1})$ for i > 1. To avoid using the same constraint two times in two different intermediate scenarios, the atemporal constraints must involve at least one actor variable which belongs to $\alpha(\omega^i)$ but not to $\alpha(\omega^{i-1})$.

```
Scenario(Attack_1,
    Characters((cashier : Person), (robber : Person))
    SubScenarios((cas_at_pos, inside_zone, cashier, "Back_Counter")
        (rob_enters, changes_zone, robber, "Entrance_zone", "Infront_Counter"))
    Constraints((cas_at_pos during rob_enters) ))

Scenario(Attack_2,
    Characters((cashier : Person), (robber : Person))
    SubScenarios((att_1, Attack_1, cashier, robber)
            (cas_at_safe, inside_zone, cashier, "Safe") )
    Constraints(((start of att_1) before cas_at_safe) ))

Scenario(Attack_3,
    Characters((cashier : Person), (robber : Person))
    SubScenarios((att_2, Attack_2, cashier, robber)
            (rob_at_safe, inside_zone, robber, "Safe") )
    Constraints((rob_at_safe during(termination of att_2)))))
```

Fig. 5. Three intermediate scenario models are generated for the compilation of the scenario model "Attack", and this model is equivalent to "Attack_3".

By using this compilation method, we can obtain all composed scenario models with one or two temporal variables. In this phase, we also check the consistency of scenario models by detecting recurrent definitions (*i.e.* graph cycles) and the utilization of undefined scenario models. The recognition of compiled scenario models is identical to the recognition of not-compiled scenario models. The gain in processing time is due to the search algorithm: we just try to find one scenario instance in the list of previously recognized scenarios instead of trying all combinations of scenario instances.

5   Experiments and Results

To validate our recognition algorithm, we first integrated the algorithm with a vision module to obtain an operational interpretation system and then we have realized three types of tests: (1) on recorded videos taken in a bank branch and in a metro station to verify if the algorithm can correctly recognize the predefined scenario models, (2) on live videos acquired on-line from cameras installed in an office and in a bank branch to verify if the algorithm can work robustly on a long time mode, (3) on recorded videos taken in a bank branch to study how the complexity of the algorithm depends on the scenario models (i.e. number of sub-scenarios).

Table 1. The recognition of temporal scenarios using videos from a bank branch and from a metro station.

	Number of tested sequences	Average number of persons/frame	Recognition rate (%)	Number of false alarms
Bank cam. 1	10	4	80	0
Bank cam. 2	1	2	100	0
Metro cam. 2	3	2	100	0

In the first experiment, we verify on recorded videos that the algorithm correctly recognizes several types of "Bank attack" scenarios and several types of "Vandalism against a ticket machine" scenarios. Table 1 shows that the predefined scenarios were correctly recognized in most of the cases. The interpretation system fails to recognize some scenarios only in the cases when the vision module misses to detect the people in the scene. We have not detected any false alarm during all the experiment. The non-detection of false alarms can be explained by the fact that the scenarios are very constrained and there are unlikely to be recognized by error.

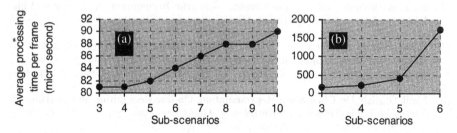

Fig. 6. The processing time (a) of the new algorithm is close to linear time and (b) the processing time of the classical STRS algorithm is exponential in function of the number of sub-scenarios.

In the second experiment, we installed the interpretation system in an office and in a bank and we connected the system to two on-line cameras to acquire directly live videos. In this experiment, we use the bank scenarios and we slightly modified them to use them in the office. We ran the system in the bank for few hours and continuously during 24h in the office. As in the first experiment, the scenarios were most of the time correctly recognized, showing that the recognition algorithm can work reliably and robustly in real-time and in continuous mode.

In the third experiment, we studied the processing time of the algorithm focusing on the resolution of temporal constraints. In this experiment (shown on Fig. 6a), we tested eight configurations of scenario models: the first configuration is made of scenarios containing 3 sub-scenarios and the last configuration is made of scenarios containing 10 sub-scenarios. On the bank videos containing 300 frames, we found that the processing time of the classical STRS algorithm is exponential in the number of sub-scenarios (shown on Fig. 6b), whereas the processing time of our algorithm is closely linear with the number of sub-scenarios.

6   Conclusion

In this paper, we have presented a fast scenario recognition algorithm focusing on temporal constraints resolution. First, we have shown that classical STRS algorithms recognize a scenario by performing an exponential search. Second, we have described how the pre-compilation of scenarios enables the recognition algorithm to check temporal constraints by performing linear search in the list of previously recognized scenarios. Due to this new algorithm, the behavior recognition in bank monitoring becomes real time.

However, the recognition process can get into a combinatory explosion depending on the number of actors defined in the scenario models. Therefore, our current work consists of studying how scenario models can be decomposed in term of actors to limit the combinatory explosion.

References

[1] François Brémond. **Environnement de résolution de problèmes pour l'interprétation de séquences d'images**. *Thèse, INRIA-Université de Nice Sophia Antipolis*, 10/1997.
[2] Francois Bremond and Gerard Medioni. **Scenario Recognition in Airborne Video Imagery**. *Interpretation of Visual Motion Workshop, Computer Vision and Pattern Recognition (CVPR98)*, Santa Barbara, June 1998.
[3] Nicolas Chleq and Monique Thonnat. **Realtime image sequence interpretation for video-surveillance applications**. *International conference on Image Processing (ICIP'96)*. Proceeding IEEE ICIP'96. Vol 2. pp 801-804. Lausanne, Switzerland. September 1996.
[4] Malik Ghallab. **On Chronicles: Representation, On-line Recognition and Learning**. *5th International Conference on Principles of Knowledge Representation and Reasoning (KR'96)*, Cambridge (USA), 5-8 Novembre 1996, pp.597-606.
[5] R. Gerber, H. Nagel and H. Schreiber. **Deriving Textual Descriptions of Road Traffic Queues from Video Sequences**. *The 15-th European Conference on Artificial Intelligence (ECAI'2002)*, Lyon, France, 21-26 July 2002, pp.736-740.

[6]   S. Hongeng, F. Bremond and R. Nevatia. **Representation and Optimal Recognition of Human Activities**. In *IEEE Proceedings of Computer Vision and Pattern Recognition*, South Carolina, USA, 2000.

[7]   A.J. Howell and H. Buxton. **Active vision techniques for visually mediated interaction**. *Image and Vision Computing*, 2002.

[8]   Tony Jebara et Alex Pentland. **On Reversing Jensen's Inequality**. *In Neural Information Processing Systems 13*, NIPS 13, 12/2000.

[9]   Roger Mohr et Thomas C. Henderson. **Arc and Path Consistency Revisited**. *Research Note, Artificial Intelligence*, pp225-233, vol28, 1986.

[10] Claudio Pinhanez et Aaron Bobick. **Human Action Detection Using PNF Propagation of Temporal Constraints**. *M.T.T Media Laboratory Perceptual Section Technical Report No. 423*, 04/1997.

[11] Nathanaël Rota et Monique Thonnat. **Activity Recognition from Video Sequences using Declarative Models**. *14th European Conference on Artificial Intelligence (ECAI 2000)*, Berlin, Proceeding ECAI'00 – W. Horn (ed.) IOS Press, Amsterdam, 20-25/08/2000.

[12] Van-Thinh Vu, François Bremond and Monique Thonnat. **Temporal Constraints for Video Interpretation**. *The 15-th European Conference on Artificial Intelligence (ECAI'2002)*, Lyon, France, 21-26 July 2002.

Trajectory Based Assessment of Coordinated Human Activity*

Marko Jug[1], Janez Perš[1], Branko Dežman[2], and Stanislav Kovačič[1]

[1] Faculty of Electrical Engineering, University of Ljubljana,
Tržaška 25, SI-1000 Ljubljana, Slovenia
marko.jug@krka.si, {janez.pers, stanek}@fe.uni-lj.si
http://vision.fe.uni-lj.si
[2] Faculty of Sport, University of Ljubljana,
Gortanova 22, SI-1000 Ljubljana
brane.dezman@sp.uni-lj.si

Abstract. Most approaches to detection and classification of human activity deal with observing individual persons. However, people often tend to organize into groups to achieve certain goals, and human activity is sometimes more readily defined and observed in the context of whole group, where the activity is coordinated among its members. An excellent example of this are team sports, which can provide valuable test ground for development of methods for analysis of coordinated group activity. We used basketball play in this work and developed a probabilistic model of a team play, which is based on the detection of key events in the team behavior. The model is based on expert coach knowledge and has been used to assess the team performance in three different types of basketball offense, based on trajectories of all players, obtained by whole-body tracker. Results show that our high-level behaviour model may be used both for activity recognition and performance evaluation in certain basketball activities.

Keywords: human motion, group activity, activity analysis, sport analysis

1 Introduction

Observation and analysis of human motion by the means of computer vision strives to answer several questions [6]: *where* (the position), *who* (the identity) and *what is he/she doing* - the activity the observed person is engaged in.

Fair amount of work [1,13,15,16,9,3] has been devoted to human activity recognition in the past years. Nevertheless, most of the related research has been focused on the problem of recognizing the activity of a single isolated subject, with several exceptions, for example [8] and [4].

It is known that people tend to organize into groups to achieve certain goals. The activity of such group, especially the *coordinated activity* is in the center of

* This work was supported by the Ministry of Science and Technology of the Republic of Slovenia (Research program 1538-517)

J.L. Crowley et al. (Eds.): ICVS 2003, LNCS 2626, pp. 534–543, 2003.

our work. Although group consists of individuals, their actions are not isolated. The group activity should be observed in the context of the group and group goals. Moreover, relations between members of the group become important if we want to answer the question "What are *they* doing?"

Team sports are excellent example of coordinated group activity: the teams have clearly defined goals, which need cooperation between individual players. Outcome of the particular group activity (offense and defense, for example) depends both on cooperation of the team and individual skills of team members. Team sports have well defined rules, which form the foundation of the play. Actions of the team members are coordinated in space and time. All this increases complexity of the play, and interference from the opposing team severely impacts its course. This makes the team sports the ideal test ground for developing and testing the algorithms for group activity detection, recognition and evaluation. Our research is based on the game of basketball.

This paper is structured as follows: first, we present the way the data has been obtained for our study. Next, we present the important properties and rules of the basketball play, which have been used to develop the model of the play, which is presented next. The model has been adjusted and tested using the real data. An expert (basketball coach) comments are used to interpret the results.

2   Tracking

During the past several years we have witnessed rapid advancement in video and computer technology. This enabled many ways of acquiring human motion that previously have not been possible. We used the computer-vision based system for tracking players in the sport matches, which is described in detail in [11]. The calibrated system is permanently installed in sports hall and available for experiments. The tracking has been performed automatically using the methods described in [12], under human supervision. Human supervision guarantees that the obtained data is consistent and contains no major errors. The output of the system are smoothed trajectories of all the players on the basketball court, for the whole duration of the experiment. The error of the tracking system has been previously measured by the means of field tests [11] and has been found to be 0.3-0.6 m RMS (court center - boundary) for position and 0.2 m/s for velocity measurements.

Therefore, our approach is based entirely on player trajectories, obtained by tracking of whole body. Position of the player is represented by a pair of coordinates in the 2D coordinate system of the court, and can be seen as an approximation of the 2D position of player gravity center.

3   Basketball

Basketball is the team sport, played by two opposing teams on a court, measuring 28×15 meters and divided into two equal halves, as shown in Fig. 1. Teams score points by throwing a ball in the opponent's basket, and the team with the highest score wins. Baskets of both teams are placed at the opposite ends of the court, and teams play in opposite direction. The ultimate goal of each team is to get a ball, come to a throwing range by outsmarting the opponent's defense and score a point. When the opposing (other) team gets the ball, team goes to defense mode and tries to prevent opponents from achieving the previously described goal.

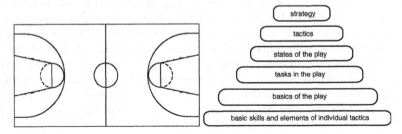

Fig. 1. Left: basketball court. The direction of the play is left to right for one team and right to left for the other. Right: hierarchical structure of the basketball play.

3.1   Basketball Offense and Its Properties

Basketball play consists of two interchanging phases (from the viewpoint of one team): offense and defense. In this work, we focused on basketball offense. Therefore, our model of the play includes only the players from one team, and is, as presented, limited only to offensive play. The structure of a basketball play can be decomposed hierarchically, as shown in Fig. 1. The basic building blocks of team play are *basic skills (technical elements)* and *elements of individual tactics*. We call these elements, defined in Table 1 the *key events*.

Table 1. Key events as manifestation of tactical basketball elements in offensive play.

move	Smooth motion of a player, without rapid direction changes.
getting open	Conclusion of a move; before stopping or before a rapid change in direction and/or velocity.
cutting	Rapid, nearly straight motion towards or over particular court region.
pick, screen	Meeting of two players, where first one sets the block (standing still) and the second one exploits it by running as close as possible to the first one.

These events may be grouped according to certain spatio-temporal relations to describe a particular *type* of offensive play. We focused on three types of basketball offense ("52", "Flex" and "Moving stack"), shown schematically in Figs. 2, 3 and 4.

4   Recognition System and Model of the Play

We mainly followed the approach by Intille and Bobick [8] in development of the recognition system. The system is given a set of trajectories of individual

Player 1 uses the high screen on the ball by 5. Player 2 runs off the staggered triple screen by 4, 3 and 5.

Player 4 then turns and backscreens for 3. Player 3 pops to the ballside wing. 5 ducks into lane. 1 looks for 2, 3, or 5.

Fig. 2. Basic motion of players in the "52" offense. Numbers denote players. Adapted from [5].

players, and its objective is to establish whether they correspond to a particular type of the team play. The type of the play is defined by its model. Our approach has the following stages:

- The position, velocity, acceleration, angle and angular velocity of the players are fed into probability estimation functions, which assign the grades in the interval [0,1] to the predefined scenarios, which describe relations between different players, and players and the playing court, e.g. "player A is on the right side of player B". In this example, the highest grade means that players A and B are *exactly* at the modeled positions, while lower grades indicate certain amount of discrepancy between the predefined and observed positions.
- Graded descriptions are then grouped according to the definition of *key events*, as defined in Table 1. In our case, key events are strongly related to the elements of the basketball tactics and technique, therefore expert (coach) knowledge becomes essential. The output of this stage are numerical grades in interval [0,1] which describe the probability that a certain key event has been observed.
- Since the actions of the players are coordinated, the sequence of observed key events is graded according to their temporal relationship [2] (for example before). Finally, probability that certain type of play has been observed is calculated using NoisyAnd and NoisyOr models [10]. For example, let us model certain action by the set of weights that correspond to the key events A, B and C, weighted as (A, 0.9), (B, 0.5) and (C, 0.4). Invoking NoisyAnd when only B and C (but not A) have been observed will result in probability of 0.1 (1 - 0.9).

Our main contribution is the use of properly defined high-level *key events*, which simplifies the descriptions of the actions and allows for easy formalization of expert (coach) knowledge about *how* does particular action (offense) looks like.

The floor is balanced, with the players filling five positions on the court. There is a basic overload on the ballside before the motion begins. One initiates the offense by passing the ball to 2. 3 uses the 4's screen and cuts to the basket.

1 then screens for 4 who comes up the lane and replaces 1 in his original position. 2 has the option to either pass to 3 cutting to basket or to 4 looking for the jump-shot. If 2 passes to 4 the offense is initiated to the other side of the floor.

The rotation is the same, 5 uses the screen by 3 to cut to the basket. 2 sets the screen for 3 who opens up on the wing. 1 moves away from the basket and the rotation is complete.

Fig. 3. Basic motion of players in the "Flex" offense. Numbers denote players. Adapted from [14].

Player 1 should be the team's top ballhandler because he controls the ball until the inside players in the stack, 4 and 5, pop out of the downscreens set by 2 and 3, and an entry pass can be made.

1 chooses to pass to 5. After the pass, 1 screens down for the offside post player 2, who moves to the point. This motion takes away the offside help's primary helper (X2) and permits 3 to play one-on-one in the ballside post area.

5 may pass the ball to 2, and the basic motion may be repeated.

If 3 doesn't have a shot and 5 is not open the next pass option is to 2 on the high post after which the offense is effectively reset.

Fig. 4. Basic motion of players in the "Moving Stack" offense. Numbers denote players. Adapted from [7].

Figure 5 shows the diagram of temporal relations for the offense "52", defined in Fig. 3. Three different models have been built by translating expert knowledge about basketball offense (provided by one of the authors) into the logical structure. This knowledge includes certain thresholds (for example, the definition of "fast" motion), above mentioned weights in the NoisyAnd and NoisyOr models and the specification of temporal relations (sequence, allowed intervals) between the events. The accuracy of the underlying tracking system was also taken into the account in model design, by choosing the appropriate threshold values.

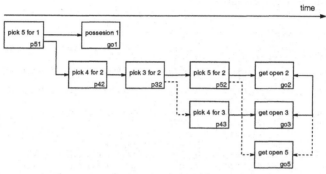

Fig. 5. Diagram of temporal relations for the offense "52".

The procedure to calculate an estimate of probability that the execution of offense "52" was observed can be derived from such diagram. As an illustration, sample algorithm for the offense "52" is provided below. Players are marked s1 through s5 and uppercase labels denote regions of the court. For the purpose of our experiments, all algorithms were implemented in the the C++ code.

```
is_52L(Group S={s1,s2,s3,s4,s5}) {          bgo1p51 = before(go1, p51)
  p51 = is_picking(s5,s1, WING_LB)          bp42p51 = before(or_p42, p51)
  p42_1  = is_picking(s4,s2, POST_LO_L)     bp32p42 = before(or_p32, or_p42)
  p42_2  = is_picking(s4,s2, CORNER_LB)     bgo3p43 = before(or_go3, or_p43)
  p32_1  = is_picking(s3,s2, POST_LO_L)     bp52p32 = before(p52, or_p32)
  p32_2  = is_picking(s3,s2, CORNER_LB)     bgo2p52 = before(go2, p52)
  p43_1  = is_picking(s4,s3, POST_LO_L)
  p43_2  = is_picking(s4,s3, CORNER_LB)     wgo2go3 = within(bgo2p52, bgo3p43, 25)
  p52 = is_picking(s5,s2, WING_LB)          n_and   = NOISYAND(0.0,
                                                      (bgo1p51, 0.9),
  go1 = is_gopen(s1, WING_LT, WING_LB)                (bp42p51, 0.9),
  go2 = is_gopen(s2, POST_HI_L, CORNER_LT)            (bp32p42, 0.7),
  go3 = is_gopen(s3, CORNER_LT, POST_LO_L)            (bp52p32, 0.9),
  go3c   = is_cutting(s3, POST_LO_L)                  (bgo2p52, 0.9),
                                                      (wgo2go3, 0.4))
  or_p42 = OR(p42_1, p42_2)
  or_p32 = OR(p32_1, p32_2)                 is_52L := n_and
  or_p43 = OR(p43_1, p43_2)                 }
  or_go3 = OR(go3, go3c)
```

5   Experiments and Results

The experiments were performed in the sports hall under the guidance of two experienced basketball coaches. Ten students of the basketball class were participating in the experiments. We divided them into two teams, the "green team" (experienced players) and the "yellow team" (less experienced players). The coaches instructed players how to play particular type of offense.

All three types of offense were played with numerous repetitions, both with and without the presence of the defensive team. The number of test video sequences totaled 74, and tracking of players with subsequent analysis was performed on all of them.

Table 2. Results for the green team offense of the type "52". "green" denotes the trials without the defense team, "play" denotes trials with passive defense present. "/" sign means "Comment not necessary".

sequence:	roles:	probability:	remarks:
52-01-green	P1,P5,P3,P4,P2	0,9254	/
52-02-green	P1,P5,P3,P4,P2	0,7482	unclear relation before(p32, p42)
52-03-green	P1,P5,P3,P4,P2	0,9088	/
52-04-green	P1,P5,P3,P4,P2	0,0573	2 does not open at the right place
52-05-green	P1,P5,P3,P4,P2	0,9417	/
52-06-green	P1,P5,P3,P4,P2	0,7392	unclear relation before(p32, p42)
52-07-green	P1,P5,P3,P4,P2	0,8454	/
52-08-green	P1,P5,P3,P4,P2	0,9840	training sequence
52-09-green	P1,P5,P3,P4,P2	0,9079	/

sequence:	roles:	probability:	remarks:
52-01-play	P1,P4,P2,P3,P5	0,4181	p51, 1 too far from screen
52-02-play	P1,P5,P3,P4,P2	0,3135	p43, 3 too far from screen
52-03-play	P1,P5,P3,P4,P2	0,0394	poorly performed screens
52-04-play	P1,P5,P3,P4,P2	0,2472	poorly performed screens
52-05-play	P1,P5,P3,P4,P2	0,1957	poor p51, taken into account several times? different before needed?
52-06-play	P1,P5,P3,P4,P2	0,9368	/
52-07-play	P1,P3,P5,P4,P2	0,2555	poor p51
52-08-play	P1,P5,P3,P4,P2	0,3383	poor p51 and p42
52-09-play	P2,P5,P3,P4,P1	0,8847	/
52-10-play	P1,P5,P3,P4,P2	0,1786	poor p51
52-11-play	P1,P3,P5,P4,P2	0,5903	poor p51
52-12-play	P1,P3,P5,P4,P2	0,1016	poor p51 and p42

Since we built the model with the expert knowledge alone, some model adjustment was needed. In the process of adjustment, we used the trajectories of several flawlessly executed offensive actions (the training set). The structure of the model and several parameters were adjusted, until the model yielded high probability of particular type of offense for the training trajectory set. This way, the model is fitted to the knowledge of a particular expert, which may be desirable in some circumstances and undesirable in others.

In some instances the algorithm was unable to infer the type of offense that is about to be played from the starting formation. In these cases, we manually initialized the algorithm for the particular type of offense. These video sequences are marked by italic text in the remainder of the section.

The results are structured as follows: the offense type, number of particular sequence and team color is specified in the first column. In the second column the roles of the players are specified (e.g. P1, P5, P2 ... means that the person P1 was playing in the role of player 1 from Fig. 3, person P5 was playing in the role of player 2, etc.) The third column shows the probability that particular type of offense was observed by the system, and last column contains expert coach observations and explanations about particular action and explanation

Table 3. Results for the offense of the type "flex". "green" denotes the trials by green team without the defense team, "play" denotes trials by both teams with passive defense present. TOP and BOTTOM denote the two possible directions of the basic motion.

sequence:	roles:	probability:	remarks:
flex-01-green	BOTTOM,P4,P5,P3,P2,P1	0,9928	/
	TOP,P5,P2,P1,P3,P4	0,6817	4 does not open, poor p53
flex-02-green	BOTTOM,P2,P1,P3,P4,P5	0,9000	/
	TOP,P1,P4,P5,P3,P2	0,1187	/
flex-03-green	BOTTOM,P1,P2,P5,P4,P3	0,9697	/
	TOP,P2,P4,P3,P5,P1	0,9488	/
flex-04-green	TOP,P2,P1,P5,P4,P3	0,8842	/
	BOTTOM,P1,P4,P3,P5,P2	0,2795	no p15
flex-05-green	TOP,P1,P2,P5,P4,P3	0,8464	/
	BOTTOM,P2,P4,P3,P5,P1	1,0000	/
flex-06-green	BOTTOM,P1,P2,P5,P4,P3	1,0000	/
	TOP,P2,P4,P3,P5,P1	0,1495	5 does not open, poor p35, p13
	BOTTOM,P4,P5,P1,P3,P2	0,4692	unfinished
flex-07-green	BOTTOM,P2,P1,P3,P4,P5	0,9985	/
	TOP,P1,P4,P5,P3,P2	0,7932	poor p13 (both moving)
flex-08-green	BOTTOM,P2,P1,P3,P4,P5	0,9809	/
	TOP,P1,P4,P5,P3,P2	0,2366	3 opens poorly, poor p35
flex-09-green	BOTTOM,P2,P1,P3,P4,P5	0,9989	/
	TOP,P1,P4,P5,P3,P2	0,5928	2 does not open, poor p13
flex-10-green	BOTTOM,P2,P1,P3,P4,P5	0,9725	/
	TOP,P1,P4,P5,P3,P2	0,9688	/
flex-11-green	TOP,P1,P2,P5,P4,P3	1,0000	/
flex-12-green	BOTTOM,P2,P1,P3,P4,P5	1,0000	/
	TOP,P1,P4,P5,P3,P2	0,5372	poor p13 and opening of 2
	BOTTOM,P4,P3,P2,P5,P1	0,6917	poor screens
sequence:	roles:	probability:	remarks:
flex-01-play	BOTTOM,P2,P3,P1,P5,P4	0,3355	green offense
	TOP,P3,P5,P4,P1,P2	0,9912	/
	BOTTOM,P5,P1,P2,P4,P3	0,1344	/
	TOP,P1,P4,P3,P2,P5	0,1079	/
flex-02-play	TOP,P1,P2,P5,P4,P3	0,9733	green offense
	BOTTOM,P2,P4,P3,P5,P1	0,9434	/
flex-03-play	TOP,P1,P2,P5,P4,P3	0,9293	green offense
	BOTTOM,P2,P4,P3,P5,P1	0,4000	/
flex-04-play	TOP,P1,P2,P5,P4,P3	0,8498	green offense
	BOTTOM,P2,P4,P3,P5,P1	0,1756	/
flex-05-play	TOP,P1,P2,P5,P4,P3	0,8178	green offense
	BOTTOM,P2,P4,P3,P5,P1	0,1565	/
flex-06-play	TOP,P1,P2,P5,P4,P3	0,9928	green offense
	BOTTOM,P2,P4,P3,P5,P1	0,3562	/
flex-10-play	BOTTOM,P1,P2,P5,P4,P3	1,0000	green offense
	TOP,P2,P4,P3,P5,P1	0,2500	/
flex-11-play	*BOTTOM,P2,P1,P3,P4,P5*	1,0000	yellow offense
	TOP,P1,P4,P5,P3,P2	0,8850	/
flex-12-play	*BOTTOM,P1,P2,P3,P4,P5*	0,3600	yellow offense
	TOP,P2,P4,P5,P3,P1	1,0000	/
flex-13-play	TOP,P1,P2,P4,P5,P3	0,3621	yellow offense
flex-14-play	TOP,P1,P2,P3,P4,P5	0,3016	yellow offense
	BOTTOM,P2,P4,P5,P3,P1	0,1419	/
flex-15-play	TOP,P1,P2,P5,P4,P3	0,2471	yellow offense
	BOTTOM,P2,P4,P3,P5,P1	0,5242	/

why particular probability has been assigned. Applying inappropriate descriptions to the test video sequences (confusion analysis) yielded low results (around 0.1). Therefore, those results are not presented here.

Table 4. Results for the offense of the type "moving stack". "green" and "yellow" denote the trials by green and yellow team without the defense team, respectively, "play" denotes trials by both teams with passive defense present.

sequence:	roles:	prob.:	remarks:
motion-01-green	P1,P3,P2,P5,P4	0,9753	/
	P3,P5,P4,P1,P2	0,9834	/
motion-02-green	*P1,P3,P2,P4,P5*	0,9304	/
	P3,P4,P5,P1,P2	0,9564	/
motion-03-green	P1,P3,P2,P4,P5	0,9866	/
	P3,P4,P5,P1,P2	0,9132	/
motion-04-green	P1,P3,P2,P4,P5	0,9750	/
	P3,P4,P5,P1,P2	0,9862	/
motion-05-green	P1,P3,P2,P5,P4	0,9673	/
	P3,P5,P4,P1,P2	0,6648	simultaneous screens p54, p32 absent
motion-06-green	P1,P3,P2,P5,P4	0,9914	/
motion-07-green	P1,P2,P3,P5,P4	0,9770	/
motion-08-green	P1,P3,P2,P4,P5	0,9549	/
	P2,P4,P5,P3,P1	0,6742	p51 on wrong position, out of sync
motion-09-green	P1,P3,P2,P4,P5	0,9968	
	P3,P4,P5,P1,P2	0,8850	/
motion-10-green	P1,P3,P2,P4,P5	0,9351	/
	P2,P4,P5,P3,P1	0,7404	/

sequence:	roles:	prob.:
motion-01-yellow	P1,P3,P2,P4,P5	0,9925
	P3,P4,P5,P1,P2	0,8272
motion-02-yellow	P1,P2,P3,P5,P4	0,6397
	P2,P5,P4,P1,P3	0,6375
motion-03-yellow	P1,P3,P2,P4,P5	0,9115
	P3,P4,P5,P1,P2	0,3612
motion-04-yellow	P1,P3,P2,P4,P5	0,9878
	P3,P4,P5,P1,P2	0,9392
motion-05-yellow	P1,P3,P2,P5,P4	0,9703
	P3,P5,P4,P1,P2	0,5756
motion-06-yellow	P1,P2,P3,P5,P4	0,8073
	P2,P5,P4,P1,P3	0,5554
motion-07-yellow	P1,P2,P3,P5,P4	0,9637
	P2,P5,P4,P1,P3	0,5669

sequence:	roles:	probability:	remarks:
motion-01-play	*P1,P3,P2,P4,P5*	0,7683	green offense
	P3,P4,P5,P1,P2	0,4280	/
motion-02-play	P1,P3,P2,P4,P5	0,4701	green offense
	P3,P4,P5,P1,P2	0,5000	/
motion-03-play	*P1,P2,P3,P5,P4*	0,9834	green offense
motion-04-play	P2,P3,P1,P4,P5	0,8886	green offense
	P3,P4,P5,P2,P1	0,4057	/
motion-05-play	P1,P3,P2,P4,P5	0,2857	green offense
	P2,P4,P5,P3,P1	0,3095	/
motion-06-play	P1,P2,P3,P5,P4	0,6198	green offense
	P3,P5,P4,P2,P1	0,4529	/
motion-07-play	P1,P3,P2,P4,P5	0,9738	green offense
	P3,P4,P5,P1,P2	0,7690	/
motion-08-play	P1,P2,P3,P5,P4	0,9275	green offense
	P3,P5,P4,P2,P1	0,5667	/
motion-09-play	P1,P3,P2,P4,P5	0,6666	green offense
	P3,P4,P5,P1,P2	0,8341	/
motion-12-play	P1,P2,P3,P5,P4	0,8352	yellow offense
	P2,P5,P4,P1,P3	0,6733	/
motion-13-play	P1,P2,P3,P5,P4	0,6883	yellow offense
	P2,P5,P4,P1,P3	0,3803	/
motion-17-play	P1,P2,P5,P3,P4	0,8653	yellow offense
	P2,P3,P4,P1,P5	0,6971	/

6   Conclusion

Results show strong correlation between the quality of the performance of the particular action and the probability that particular action has been observed. This is due to the use of key events, which are closely tied to the key events of the basketball play. Therefore, our system could be used in automated assessment of team performance, monitoring players' progress in the course of training. The concept of key events enables the expert to obtain explanations, why the particular performance received low grades, by inspecting the grades of each individual key event, and thus learning the reasons for the poor performance of the team. This is demonstrated by expert comments on presented results.

It is not surprising that the existence of the defensive team greatly reduces the performance of the team; players are obstructed by the sole presence of the defense players, even with passive defense.

The presented results show adequate sensitivity of our model to improperly executed actions. Additionally, extremely low grades are assigned to the types of the play which do not match the model used.

References

1. A. Ali and J. K. Aggarwal. Segmentation and recognition of continuous human activity. In *IEEE Workshop on Detection and Recognition of Events in Video*, pages 28–35, Vancouver, Canada, July, 8 2001.
2. J. F. Allen. Maintaining knowledge about temporal intervals. *Communications of ACM*, 26(11):832–843, 1983.
3. B. A. Boghossian and S. A. Velastin. Image processing system for pedestrian monitoring using neural classification of normal motion patterns. *Measurement and Control (Special Issue on Intelligent Vision Systems)*, 32(9):261–264, 1999.
4. B. A. Boghossian and S. A. Velastin. Motion-based machine vision techniques for the management of large crowds. In *IEEE 6th International Conference on Electronics, Circuits and Systems ICECS 99*, Cyprus, September 5–8 1999.
5. J. Calipari, editor. *Basketball's Half-Court Offense*. Masters Press, Indianapolis, Indiana, USA, 1996.
6. I. A. Essa. Computers seeing people. *AI Magazine*, 20(1):69–82, 1999.
7. H. L. Harkins and J. Krause, editors. *Motion Game Offenses for Men's and Women's Basketball*. Coaches Choice Books, Champaign, Illinois, ZDA, 1997.
8. S. S. Intille. A framework for recognizing multi-agent action from visual evidence. In *Proceedings of the National Conference on Artificial Intelligence, AAAI '99*, April 1999.
9. E. Koller-Meier and L. Van Gool. Modeling and recognition of human actions using a stochastic approach. In *Proceedings of the 2nd European Workshop on Advanced Video-Based Surveillance Systems 2001 (AVBS'01)*, pages 17–28, September 2001.
10. J. Pearl. *Probabilistic Reasoning in Intelligent Systems: Networks of Plausible Inference*. Morgan Kaufmann, San Mateo, CA, second edition, 1991.
11. J. Perš, M. Bon, S. Kovačič, M. Šibila, and B. Dežman. Observation and analysis of large-scale human motion. *Human Movement Science*, 21(2):295–311, 2002.
12. J. Perš and S. Kovačič. Tracking people in sport: Making the use of partially controlled environment. In Wladyslaw Skarbek, editor, *Lecture notes in computer science: Proceedings of 9th International Conference on Computer Analysis of Images and Patterns CAIP'2001*, pages 384–391. Springer Verlag, 2001.
13. C. Rao and M. Shah. View-invariant representation and learning of human action. In *IEEE Workshop on Detection and Recognition of Events in Video*, pages 55–63, Vancouver, Canada, July, 8 2001.
14. R. Righter, editor. *Flex: The Total Offense*. Championship Books, Ames, Iowa, USA, 1984.
15. R. Rosales and S. Sclaroff. 3d trajectory recovery for tracking multiple objects and trajectory guided recognition of actions. In *CVPR 1999*, Fort Collins, Colorado, June 23–25 1999.
16. L. Zeinik-Manor and M. Irani. Event-based analysis of video. In *CVPR 2001*, pages II:123–130, Kauai, Hawaii, December 9–14 2001.

Author Index

Lecture Notes in Computer Science

For information about Vols. 1–2528

please contact your bookseller or Springer-Verlag

Vol. 2566: T.Æ. Mogensen, D.A. Schmidt, I.H. Sudborough (Eds.), The Essence of Computation. XIV, 473 pages. 2002.

Vol. 2567: Y.G. Desmedt (Ed.), Public Key Cryptography – PKC 2003. Proceedings, 2003. XI, 365 pages. 2002.

Vol. 2568: M. Hagiya, A. Ohuchi (Eds.), DNA Computing. Proceedings, 2002. XI, 338 pages. 2003.

Vol. 2569: D. Gollmann, G. Karjoth, M. Waidner (Eds.), Computer Security – ESORICS 2002. Proceedings, 2002. XIII, 648 pages. 2002. (Subseries LNAI).

Vol. 2570: M. Jünger, G. Reinelt, G. Rinaldi (Eds.), Combinatorial Optimization – Eureka, You Shrink!. Proceedings, 2001. X, 209 pages. 2003.

Vol. 2571: S.K. Das, S. Bhattacharya (Eds.), Distributed Computing. Proceedings, 2002. XIV, 354 pages. 2002.

Vol. 2572: D. Calvanese, M. Lenzerini, R. Motwani (Eds.), Database Theory – ICDT 2003. Proceedings, 2003. XI, 455 pages. 2002.

Vol. 2574: M.-S. Chen, P.K. Chrysanthis, M. Sloman, A. Zaslavsky (Eds.), Mobile Data Management. Proceedings, 2003. XII, 414 pages. 2003.

Vol. 2575: L.D. Zuck, P.C. Attie, A. Cortesi, S. Mukhopadhyay (Eds.), Verification, Model Checking, and Abstract Interpretation. Proceedings, 2003. XI, 325 pages. 2003.

Vol. 2576: S. Cimato, C. Galdi, G. Persiano (Eds.), Security in Communication Networks. Proceedings, 2002. IX, 365 pages. 2003.

Vol. 2578: F.A.P. Petitcolas (Ed.), Information Hiding. Proceedings, 2002. IX, 427 pages. 2003.

Vol. 2580: H. Erdogmus, T. Weng (Eds.), COTS-Based Software Systems. Proceedings, 2003. XVIII, 261 pages. 2003.

Vol. 2581: J.S. Sichman, F. Bousquet, P. Davidsson (Eds.), Multi-Agent-Based Simulation II. Proceedings, 2002. X, 195 pages. 2003. (Subseries LNAI).

Vol. 2583: S. Matwin, C. Sammut (Eds.), Inductive Logic Programming. Proceedings, 2002. X, 351 pages. 2003. (Subseries LNAI).

Vol. 2585: F. Giunchiglia, J. Odell, G. Weiß (Eds.), Agent-Oriented Software Engineering III. Proceedings, 2002. X, 229 pages. 2003.

Vol. 2586: M. Klusch, S. Bergamaschi, P. Edwards, P. Petta (Eds.), Intelligent Information Agents. VI, 275 pages. 2003. (Subseries LNAI).

Vol. 2587: P.J. Lee, C.H. Lim (Eds.), Information Security and Cryptology – ICISC 2002. Proceedings, 2002. XI, 536 pages. 2003.

Vol. 2588: A. Gelbukh (Ed.), Computational Linguistics and Intelligent Text Processing. Proceedings, 2003. XV, 648 pages. 2003.

Vol. 2589: E. Börger, A. Gargantini, E. Riccobene (Eds.), Abstract State Machines 2003. Proceedings, 2003. XI, 427 pages. 2003.

Vol. 2590: S. Bressan, A.B. Chaudhri, M.L. Lee, J.X. Yu, Z. Lacroix (Eds.), Efficiency and Effectiveness of XML Tools and Techniques and Data Integration over the Web. Proceedings, 2002. X, 259 pages. 2003.

Vol. 2591: M. Aksit, M. Mezini, R. Unland (Eds.), Objects, Components, Architectures, Services, and Applications for a Networked World. Proceedings, 2002. XI, 431 pages. 2003.

Vol. 2592: R. Kowalczyk, J.P. Müller, H. Tianfield, R. Unland (Eds.), Agent Technologies, Infrastructures, Tools, and Applications for E-Services. Proceedings, 2002. XVII, 371 pages. 2003. (Subseries LNAI).

Vol. 2593: A.B. Chaudhri, M. Jeckle, E. Rahm, R. Unland (Eds.), Web, Web-Services, and Database Systems. Proceedings, 2002. XI, 311 pages. 2003.

Vol. 2594: A. Asperti, B. Buchberger, J.H. Davenport (Eds.), Mathematical Knowledge Management. Proceedings, 2003. X, 225 pages. 2003.

Vol. 2595: K. Nyberg, H. Heys (Eds.), Selected Areas in Cryptography. Proceedings, 2002. XI, 405 pages. 2003.

Vol. 2597: G. Păun, G. Rozenberg, A. Salomaa, C. Zandron (Eds.), Membrane Computing. Proceedings, 2002. VIII, 423 pages. 2003.

Vol. 2598: R. Klein, H.-W. Six, L. Wegner (Eds.), Computer Science in Perspective. X, 357 pages. 2003.

Vol. 2599: E. Sherratt (Ed.), Telecommunications and beyond: The Broader Applicability of SDL and MSC. Proceedings, 2002. X, 253 pages. 2003.

Vol. 2600: S. Mendelson, A.J. Smola, Advanced Lectures on Machine Learning. Proceedings, 2002. IX, 259 pages. 2003. (Subseries LNAI).

Vol. 2601: M. Ajmone Marsan, G. Corazza, M. Listanti, A. Roveri (Eds.) Quality of Service in Multiservice IP Networks. Proceedings, 2003. XV, 759 pages. 2003.

Vol. 2602: C. Priami (Ed.), Computational Methods in Systems Biology. Proceedings, 2003. IX, 214 pages. 2003.

Vol. 2604: N. Guelfi, E. Astesiano, G. Reggio (Eds.), Scientific Engineering for Distributed Java Applications. Proceedings, 2002. X, 205 pages. 2003.

Vol. 2606: A.M. Tyrrell, P.C. Haddow, J. Torresen (Eds.), Evolvable Systems: From Biology to Hardware. Proceedings, 2003. XIV, 468 pages. 2003.

Vol. 2607: H. Alt, M. Habib (Eds.), STACS 2003. Proceedings, 2003. XVII, 700 pages. 2003.

Vol. 2609: M. Okada, B. Pierce, A. Scedrov, H. Tokuda, A. Yonezawa (Eds.), Software Security – Theories and Systems. Proceedings, 2002. XI, 471 pages. 2003.

Vol. 2612: M. Joye (Ed.), Topics in Cryptology – CT-RSA 2003. Proceedings, 2003. XI, 417 pages. 2003.

Vol. 2614: R. Laddaga, P. Robertson, H. Shrobe (Eds.), Self-Adaptive Software: Applications. Proceedings, 2001. VIII, 291 pages. 2003.

Vol. 2615: N. Carbonell, C. Stephanidis (Eds.), Universal Access. Proceedings, 2002. XIV, 534 pages. 2003.

Vol. 2618: P. Degano (Ed.), Programming Languages and Systems. Proceedings, 2003. XV, 415 pages. 2003.

Vol. 2619: H. Garavel, J. Hatcliff (Eds.), Tools and Algorithms for the Construction and Analysis of Systems. Proceedings, 2003. XVI, 604 pages. 2003.

Vol. 2621: M. Pezzè (Ed.), Fundamental Approaches to Software Engineering. Proceedings, 2003. XIV, 403 pages. 2003.

Vol. 2622: G. Hedin (Ed.), Compiler Construction. Proceedings, 2003. XII, 335 pages. 2003.

Vol. 2626: J.L. Crowley, J.H. Piater, M. Vincze, L. Paletta (Eds.), Computer Vision Systems. Proceedings, 2003. XIII, 546 pages. 2003.